Fritz Kemmler / Iryna Rieker

Medieval English: Literature and Language

5th Edition

Dr. Fritz Kemmler lehrt am Englischen Seminar der Universität Tübingen.
Iryna Rieker, M.A. war Mitarbeiterin am Englischen Seminar der Universität Tübingen.

Bibliografische Information der Deutschen Nationalbibliothek

Die Deutsche Nationalbibliothek verzeichnet diese Publikation in der Deutschen National-
bibliografie; detaillierte bibliografische Daten sind im Internet über http://dnb.dnb.de abrufbar.

5., überarbeitete und erweiterte Auflage 2012
4., vollständig neu bearbeitete Auflage 2008
3., überarbeitete Auflage 2005
2., vollständig neu bearbeitete und erweiterte Auflage 1994
1. Auflage 1980

Die 1.–3. Auflage ist unter dem Titel „Alt- und Mittelenglische Literatur" erschienen.

© 2012 · Narr Francke Attempto Verlag GmbH + Co. KG
Dischingerweg 5 · D-72070 Tübingen

Internet: http://www.narr-studienbuecher.de
E-Mail: info@narr.de

Satzsystem: TUSTEP
Printed in the EU

ISSN 0941-8105
ISBN 978-3-8233-6664-5

Preface

This book continues the new approach in Medieval English Studies adopted for the fourth edition (2008). Unlike most course books on Medieval English, which focus on either Old *or* Middle English, we have sought to show how interconnected Old and Middle English can and must be. This is seen not only at the level of the language, but also in the texts themselves, in the topics and themes important to Medieval culture.

Numerous years of teaching Old and Middle English have convinced us of the importance of looking at both of these languages in their context: Medieval English. We are confident that the interconnectedness of our approach will make learning one or both of these languages considerably easier.

In order to give the reader a direct impression of Medieval literary production, several manuscript pages have been reproduced in this book: Corpus Christi College Cambridge, MS 173, fol. 10^r (p. 93), Bodleian Library, MS Hatton 20, fol. 1^r (p. 111), Bodleian Library, MS Digby 86, fol. 138^r (p. 197) and British Library, MS Harley 2253, fol. 63^v (p. 211). Special thanks to these libraries for their permission to reproduce these manuscript pages.

Naturally, many have helped us extensively with this project. First and foremost, we would like to thank Richard Szydlak, Tübingen's cartographer, for creating two maps especially for this book. Thomas Kemmler contributed the Indo-European languages diagram. Also thanks to Wendy Smith for taking care of the proofreading. We would also like to thank our publisher, Gunter Narr, and his team for their continuing support and encouragement as to a fifth edition. Finally, we wish to thank our families for their generous assistance and for putting up with us, especially during the last weeks.

Candlemas, 2012   *Iryna Rieker, Fritz Kemmler*

Contents

Abbreviations VIII

Introduction 1

1. The Origins of English 2
   Old and Middle English Dialects 4
   Writing Systems 6
   Pronunciation 7

2. Phonology 12
   Vowel Change: Post-vocalic Consonants and Consonant Groups 13
   Old English Vowels: Further Changes 16
   Old English Vowels and their Continuation in Middle English 17
   English Vowels: Quantitative Changes 18
   Late Middle and Early Modern English Developments 20
   Vowels in Unstressed Syllables 21
   Consonants 22
   Loanwords 25

3. Morphology 26
   Introduction 26
   Nouns 26
   Adjectives 35
   Adverbs 39
   Pronouns 40
   Numerals 45
   Verbs 47
   Strong Verbs 49
   Weak Verbs 56
   Preterite-Present Verbs 61
   Irregular Verbs 64

4. Syntax 67
   Introduction 67
   Nominal Forms: Function and Use 68
   Verbal Forms: Function and Use 71
   Negation 76
   Main Clauses 77
   Dependent Clauses 78
   Medieval English Verse 85

5. Old English Texts 87
   Introduction 87
   Text 1: The Old English Heptateuch 88
   Text 2: Selections from the Anglo-Saxon Chronicle 90
   Text 3: The Old English Bede 99
   Text 4: The Old English Orosius 106
   Text 5: King Alfred 109
   Text 6: Ælfric's Life of King Oswold 114
   Text 7: Wulfstan's Sermon to the English 121
   Text 8: The Old English Apollonius 127
   Text 9: The Anglo-Saxon Chronicle – Brunanburh 131
   Text 10: The Battle of Maldon 135
   Text 11: The Dream of the Rood 145

6. Middle English Texts 151
   Introduction 151
   Text 1: The Peterborough Chronicle 152
   Text 2: The Middle English Physiologus 157
   Text 3: Kentish Sermons 160
   Text 4: Ayenbite of Inwit 163
   Text 5: The South English Legendary 167
   Text 6: Sir Gawain and the Green Knight 175
   Text 7: Piers Plowman 185
   Text 8: The Fox and the Wolf 195
   Text 9: King Horn 202
   Text 10: Middle English Lyric Poetry 208
   Text 11: The Northern Homily Cycle 224
   Text 12: York Plays 229
   Text 13: Geoffrey Chaucer 241
   Text 14: Robert Henryson 257

7. Glossaries 265
   Old English Glossary 267
   Middle English Glossary 318

8. Bibliography 392

Abbreviations

The following abbreviations have been used in parts 1–6:

A	accusative	WML	West Midlands
C	consonant	WS	West Saxon
D	dative	M 1/17	Middle English Texts:
eMnE	early Modern English		Text 1, line 17
fem.	feminine	O 1/17	Old English Texts:
G	genitive		Text 1, line 17
l., ll.	line, lines	ă	short vowel
lME	late Middle English	ā	long vowel
masc.	masculine	ā̆	short and long vowel
ME	Middle English	ạ	closed vowel
MnE	Modern English	ą	open vowel
MnG	Modern German	1–7	classes of strong verbs
MS	manuscript	I-III	classes of weak verbs
N	nominative	*	hypothetical
OHG	Old High German	>	becomes
pl.	plural	<	was
RP	Received Pronunciation	< >	graph, grapheme
sg.	singular	[ ]	pronunciation
SW	Southwest	/ /	phoneme
V	vowel	' '	meaning

Introduction

The focus of this book is on *Medieval English* as a whole – neither exclusively on *Old English* nor on *Middle English*. This means that in the chapters which are concerned with grammar, we have placed emphasis on aspects of continuity, not difference. We treat the development of English as a continuum, not as separate periods with three separate languages. Our selection of both Old and Middle English texts also seeks to present some texts with close thematic affinities.

One of these thematic affinities, for example, is supplied by the Norman Conquest of 1066 and its representation in one of the manuscripts of the *Anglo-Saxon Chronicle*. The *Life of Wulfstan* is a Middle English saint's life devoted to the last Anglo-Saxon bishop of the diocese of Worcester – and it presents a rather surprising outlook and 'English' perspective on the theme of the Norman Conquest of 1066.

Continuity is also shown by the maps inside the front and back covers. Many maps in handbooks illustrate the dialects of English, whereas our maps use Modern English place names and show the sites of three battles which were decisive for the history of England. By referring to the maps when studying the texts, readers will be able to contextualise the often abstract geographical information given in a specific text.

Despite the emphasis on aspects of the continuity of English, Old English and Middle English, are *foreign languages*. This means that in order to acquire a basic competence in Medieval English, you should memorise the important inflectional paradigms (especially pronouns) in the Morphology section. You should also be familiar with the most important differences in the area of Syntax. In order to parse verbs, you have to be familiar with the *conjugational endings* and with the so-called 'tense stems' of strong, weak and preterite-present verbs. Finally, the basic paradigms of irregular verbs should be memorised, since they occur with high frequency.

The ability to read Old and Middle English texts in the original is one of the many skills which can be gained by a thorough study of this book. Relying on translations of medieval texts only is a poor substitute for a direct exploration of our cultural past. To facilitate the task of reading and understanding the texts chosen for this book, we provide explanatory and textual notes for every text and detailed glossaries can be found at the back of the book. Students and readers who are prepared to take up this challenge will be able to explore on their own the fascinating world of Medieval English Literature and Language.

1. The Origins of English

English belongs to the family of Germanic languages which is part of the even larger family of Indo-European languages. Because there are so many cognates in most of the modern European languages, Sir William Jones hypothesised in 1786 that all of these languages must have a common origin. As a Sanskrit scholar, he noticed strong similarities between Sanskrit and other European languages, for example English *father*, German *Vater*, Icelandic *faðir* as well as Greek and Latin *pater*, Spanish *padre*, French *père*, Persian *pedar* and Sanskrit *pitar*. These languages and many others are all descendants of a single language which is now called Indo-European (see diagram). It was probably spoken around 5000–3000 BC.

Indo-European underwent an initial split into an eastern and a western family. The *k* sound, for example in the Indo-European word for hundred (**kmtóm*), became an *s* in the eastern languages; thus, the Indo-European languages can be divided into *centum* (western) and *satem* (eastern) languages. The western branch divided again, and Proto-Germanic (the theorised root of all Germanic languages) had developed by around 100 BC. The main characteristics which all Germanic languages share include initial syllable stress, the appearance of weak verbs as well as a strong and weak declension of adjectives, a simplification of the tense and the case system, and the First Sound Shift (Grimm's Law and Verner's Law). The First Sound Shift had three steps:

voiceless stops became fricatives: p, t, k → f, Θ, h

voiced stops became voiceless stops: b, d, g → p, t, k

voiceless aspirates became voiced stops: bh, dh, gh → b, d, g.

As shown above, the Germanic languages all have an initial *f* sound in the word *father*, where the original Indo-European had (and indeed, most surviving descendants still have) a *p*. Similarly, **treyes* becomes *three*, **krn-* becomes *horn* and so on.

An exception to Grimm's Law can also be seen in the development of the word *father*. We would expect the *t* in Indo-European **pətér* to become a Θ in West Germanic. However, in words in which stress had shifted from the second to the first syllable, according to the normal Germanic development, *t* (provided it was not followed by a voiceless sound; see § 30), first became Θ, and then ð. This can still be seen in Icelandic *faðir*, whereas the *d* in Old English *fæder* is a further West Germanic development of ð.

Proto-Germanic was spoken in southern Norway and Sweden, Denmark and the area around the River Elbe. It then split further into West Germanic (English, High and Low German), East Germanic (Gothic) and North Germanic (Scandinavian). After the Romans left Britain in the early 5th century, the West Germanic tribes on the Continent were able to invade and conquer the island. Old English developed out of West Germanic partly due to the subsequent isolation of the Angles and Saxons in Britain. One of the biggest changes was to the vowels, especially lengthening in a nasal context (e. g., **uns* becomes *ūs*, **andar* becomes *ōþer* and **fimf* becomes *fīf*).

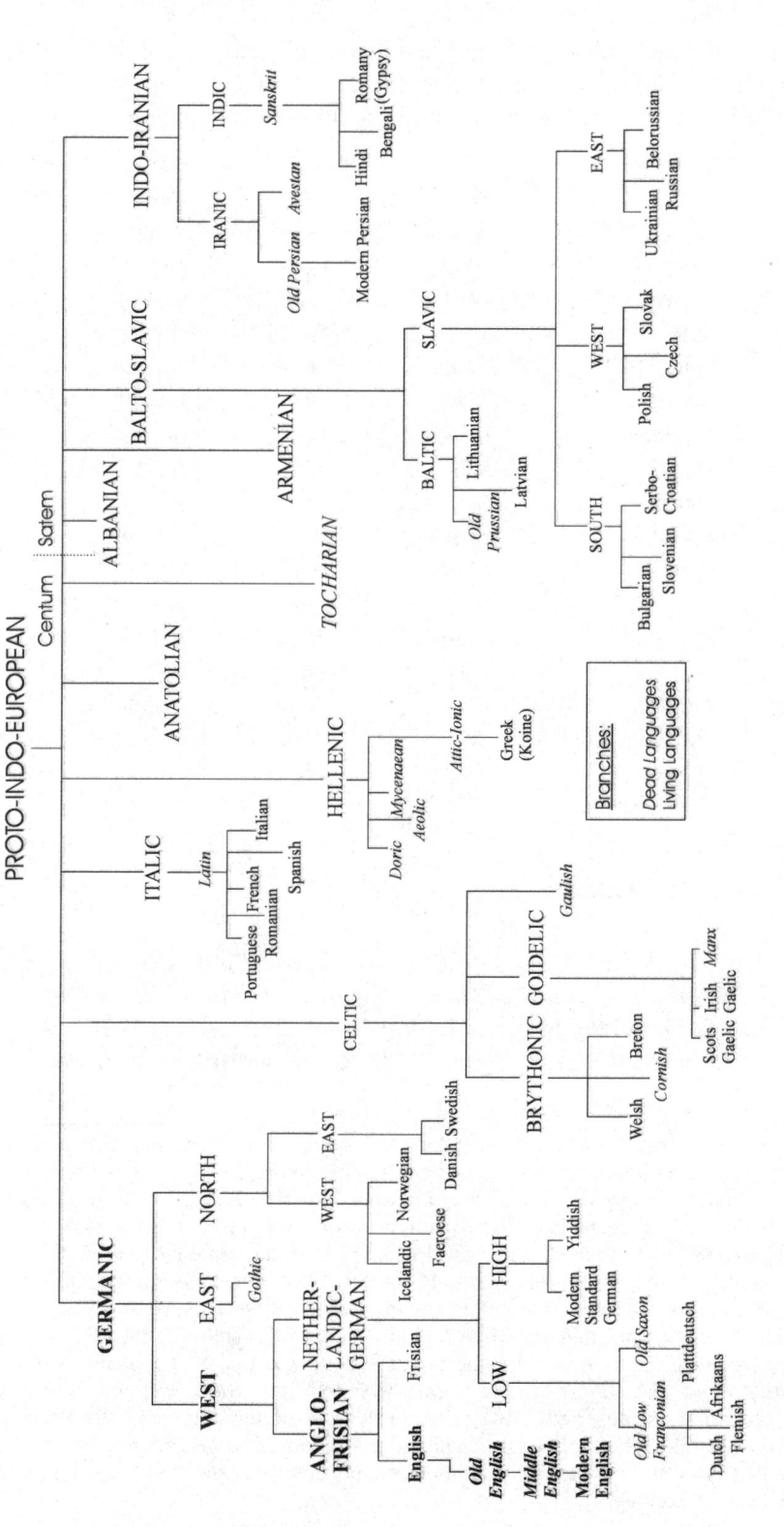

The table below provides examples which indicate both similarities and differences of cognate words. Examples from Latin and the medieval and modern varieties of both German and English are depicted here to show similar vowel qualities to Indo-European.

IE	Latin	OHG	MnG	OE	MnE
a	ager	ackar	Acker	æcer	acre
e	edō	eӡӡan	essen	etan	eat
i	vidua	wituwa	Witwe	widewe	widow
o	octo	ahto	acht	eahta	eight
u	—	sunu	Sohn	sunu	son
ə	pater	fater	Vater	fæder	father
ā	frāter	bruoder	Bruder	brōþor	brother
ē	sēmen	sāt	Saat	sǣd	seed
ī	suīnus	swīn	Schwein	swīn	swine
ō	flōs	bluoma	Blume	blōma	'bloom'
ū	mūs	mūs	Maus	mūs	mouse
ai	haedus	geiӡ	Geiß	gāt	goat
ei	—	stīgan	steigen	stīgan	–
oi	—	ein	ein	ān	one
au	augēre	ouhhōn	—	ēacian	'to eke'
eu	—	cheosan, kiosan	'küren'	cēosan	to choose
ou	rūfus	rōt	rot	rēad	red

Old and Middle English Dialects

Our knowledge of 'early English history' derives to a considerable extent from the Venerable Bede's *Historia Ecclesiastica Gentis Anglorum* (*Church History of the English People* – see O 3), written in the early decades of the 8th century. In book I, chapter xv, a detailed account of the arrival of the Germanic tribes in England is provided:

> The 449th year of the incarnation of our Lord, Marcian having with Valentinian obtained the kingdom, the 46th in succession from Augustus, held it seven years. In whose time the nation of the English or Saxons, being sent for of the said king into Britain, landed there in three long ships ... Now the strangers had come from three of the more mighty nations in Germany, that is, the Saxons, the Angles and the Jutes. Of the Jutes came the people of Kent and the settlers in Wight, that is the folk that hold the Isle of Wight, and they which in the province of the West Saxons are called unto this day the nation of the Jutes, right over against the Isle of Wight. Of the Saxons, that is, of that region which now is called of the Old Saxons [i. e. Holstein], descended the East Saxons, the South Saxons and the West Saxons. Further, of the Angles, that is, of that country which is called Angeln [i. e. Slewsick] and from that time to this is said to stand deserted between the provinces of the Jutes and the Saxons, descendeth the East Angles, the Uplandish Angles, the Mercians and all the progeny of the Northumbrians, that is, of the people that inhabiteth the north side of the flood Humber, and the other nations of the Angles.

In the Old English translation of Bede's *Historia* this account is somewhat more difficult to understand and also shorter:

> Ða wæs ymb feower hund wintra 7 nigon 7 feowertig fram ures Drihtnes menniscnysse, þæt Martianus casere rice onfeng 7 vii gear hæfde. Se wæs syxta eac feowertigum fram Augusto þam casere. Ða Angel þeod 7 Seaxna wæs geladod fram þam foresprecenan cyninge, 7 on Breotone com on þrim myclum scypum ... Comon hi of þrim folcum ðam strangestan Germanie, þæt of Seaxum 7 of Angle 7 of Geatum. Of Geata fruman syndon Cantware, 7 Wihtsætan; þæt is seo ðeod þe Wiht þæt ealond oneardað. Of Seaxum, þæt is of ðam lande þe mon hateð Ealdseaxan, coman Eastseaxan 7 Suðseaxan 7 Westseaxan. And of Engle coman Eastengle 7 Middelengle 7 Myrce 7 eall Norðhembra cynn; is þæt land ðe Angulus is nemned, betwyh Geatum 7 Seaxum; is sæd of þære tide þe hi ðanon gewiton oð to dæge, þæt hit weste wunige.

Since Bede mentions three 'nations' (þrym folcum), it can be assumed that the language now called Old English (or Anglo-Saxon) would have been far from homogeneous. Indeed, the written records of Old English show a considerable amount of variation, especially in the written representation of vowels in stressed syllables (see *Writing Systems* and § 2, 3 and 9).

It has become customary to differentiate between several major dialects in Old English times: Northumbrian, Mercian, West Saxon and Kentish (see map inside the front cover). Since Northumbrian and Mercian have several linguistic features in common, these two dialects are often referred to as Anglian. The majority of the extant Old English texts show marked features of the West Saxon dialect.

Remark: See Bähr (2001), Appendix 2, "Methods in Old English Dialectology", pp. 176–191, on the problems of differentiating Old English dialects.
It should be pointed out that the map for Old English dialects inside the front cover is highly arbitrary as to dialectal borders. Dialectal areas are based on the ancient borders of the former territories of Northumbria, Mercia, Kent and Wessex. Both maps have been supplied with the aim of contextualising and explaining the largely abstract terms for Old and Middle English dialects.

The majority of early Middle English texts originate in a different area of England – in the so-called East Midland region, and are not descended from West Saxon. With reference to the major Old English dialectal areas these early Middle English texts are based on the Mercian dialect. In addition, the East Midland provenance of early Middle English texts is one of the major reasons for a high number of Scandinavian loan-words in these texts – a considerable part of the East Midland region had been granted to the Scandinavian invaders by the 'Treaty of Alfred and Guthrum' of 886. The long-standing use of the West Saxon standard had prevented a large-scale adoption of Scandinavian loan-words even into late West Saxon texts; however, loan-words must have been a regular feature of spoken late Old English.

For Middle English a distinction of six major dialects has become customary: Northern, West Midlands, East Midlands, Southern, Kentish and London (see map inside back cover). Since the corpus of Middle English texts includes texts from all over the country, dialectal variation is a heavily marked feature of Middle English literature.

Remark:

The most important dialectal features of the individual texts will be pointed out at the end of the introductory sections.

While in the past Middle English dialectology was based on the reflexes of Old English vowels and consonants in the five major dialects, the publication of *A Linguistic Atlas of Late Medieval English* (1986) has led to a major change in methodology. The criteria used in the *Atlas* (hereafter referred to as *LALME*) are a list of highly frequent words and their spellings (questionnaire method). On the basis of manuscripts to which a definite area of origin can be attributed, item maps were compiled. These item maps can then be used to determine the origin of other Middle English texts. Since this book contains earlier texts than those considered for the *Atlas* ("The period chosen for the *Atlas* is, in general, to be regarded as the century from 1350 to 1450, but the choice is itself problematic, and it has not been found practicable to keep strictly to those limits."; I.3) and since the *Atlas of Early Medieval English* has not yet been published, some of the traditional methods have been used for determining the provenance of Middle English texts not covered by *LALME*. Information on the provenance of early Middle English texts found in Laing (1993) is also provided.

Writing Systems

Before Christian monks began to use the Latin alphabet from about the 7th century onwards, one of the runic alphabets (the 'futhork', see table below) was used by the Germanic tribes who had settled on the British Isles. A comparison of both writing systems will show that the runic alphabet had more signs than the Latin alphabet with its twenty-three characters. Compared to the alphabet used in Modern English, the Latin alphabet used in Old English times lacked the following characters: *v* (represented by *u*), *j* (represented by *i*) and *w*.

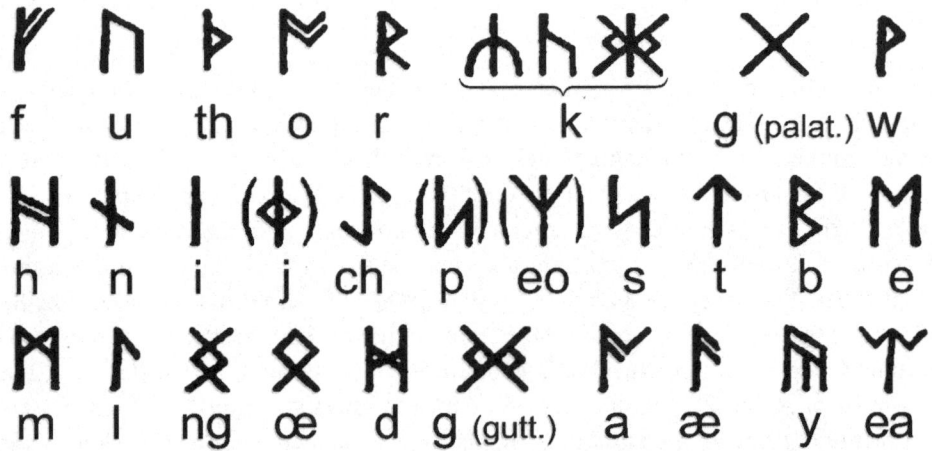

The Anglo-Saxon Runic Alphabet ('futhork')

Since Old English had additional sounds not found in Latin, the Old English scribes added several characters accordingly. Two characters for consonantal sounds were taken over from the runic alphabet: þ, Þ (thorn) and the so-called 'wynn' rune (for *w*). Only one character for a vowel sound had to be taken over from the runic alphabet: æ, Æ (aesh). A further character, ð, Ð (eth), was borrowed from the Irish inventory of characters. Occasionally, *d* and the digraph *th* were used instead of þ and ð, and <w> appeared as <uu>, <vv> or even <vu> or <uv>.

Although Old English, Middle English and Modern English writing is based on the Latin alphabet, the letter shapes in both Old English and Middle English manuscripts are somewhat different if compared to contemporary practice (see pp. 93, 111, 197 and 211). The most conspicuous differences can be seen in the shapes of *e, f, g, r, s* and *w*.

A composite alphabet for both Old English and Middle English includes the following series of characters: a, æ, b, c, d, e, f, g/ʒ, h, i, j, k, l, m, n, o, p, q, r, s, t, th/þ/ð, u/v, v/u, w/uu/vv, x, y and z; occasionally the ligature <œ> was used by Old English scribes. These characters could be used as single characters, double characters or in particular combinations.

In Old English, two identical vowel signs in sequence are not very frequent (cf. O 7/4 *aa* and O 3/127 *booc*); however a fixed set of combinations occurs frequently: *ea, eo, io* and *ie*. It can be said with a high degree of certainty that these combinations represent diphthongs. With the exception of *w*, consonantal signs occur frequently as doublets (geminates). Special combinations of consonantal signs are: *cg* (always in post-vocalic position), *sc* (in pre- and post-vocalic position) and word initial *cw-, hl-, hr-, hw-* and *wl-, wr-*.

In Middle English, two identical vowel signs in sequence are quite frequent and usually indicate a long vowel, e. g. <ee>, whereas the sequence *ea* does not represent, as it did in Old English, a diphthong but a long, open *e*-sound. Since all Old English diphthongs were modified in Middle English times, typical graph-sequences indicating diphthongs in Middle English are: $V+i$ or $V+u/w$, e. g. *ai, au/aw; ei, eu/ew; oi, ou/ow* and *iu/iw*. Special combinations of two different consonantal characters are also a feature of Middle English; however, of the typical Old English word-initial patterns, only *wr-* was retained and *hw-* is now written *wh-*.

Pronunciation

In contrast to Modern English, it can be said that every letter should be pronounced in reading Old English – thus, *-mm-* should be pronounced as a sequence of two m's, *cn-* as k+n, and word-final *-e* following a consonant must also be pronounced – e. g. *swimman*: s+w+i+m+m+a+n; *cniht*: k+n+i+/x/+t; *cume*: k+u+m+e.

Old English Consonants

Most consonants in Old English and Middle English may be pronounced as in Modern English: *b d k l m n p t*. In Old English and in most cases in Middle English *w* is much the same as in Modern English.

c is pronounced /k/ when it occurs in combination with other consonants (except
-*cg*-) or when it is preceded or followed by one of the vowels *a, o, u* or *y*;
is pronounced /tʃ/ in word-initial position when followed by *i* or in medial position
between *æ/i* and *e* and in word-final position when preceded by *i*. In O 1, this
'palatalised' *c* is marked by a superscript dot <ċ>. Examples are: *ċild, ċiriċe, iċ*.

cg is pronounced as its corresponding sequence *dg* /dʒ/ in Modern English. Thus, Old
English *bricge* can be pronounced as Modern English *bridge*; however, the word-
final -*e* has to be pronounced as well.

f, s can be voiced /v/, /z/ and voiceless /f/, /s/. Voiced pronunciation only occurs in
voiced contexts (i. e. between vowels and voiced consonants) and voiceless in all
other positions, especially word-initial and word-final.

g is pronounced as /g/ before *a, o* and *u* and when followed by a consonant;
is pronounced /j/ in word-initial position when followed by *i* or *e*; in medial and
final position when preceded by *æ, e* and *i*. In O 1 this palatalised *g* is indicated by
a superscript dot, *ġ*. Examples are: *ġif, ġēar, dæġ, hīġ*;
in medial position it was pronounced similarly to *ch* as in Scottish *loch* or *g* as in
some varieties of Modern German; e. g. *magan* /maxan/.

h in word-initial position is pronounced just as in Modern English;
is pronounced /ç/ after *i* or *e*;
is pronounced /x/ after other vowels.

r in word-initial position was pronounced probably as a trilled sound;
in other positions it was pronounced as a guttural *r*.

sc in word-initial position is usually pronounced just as *sh* in Modern English;
is pronounced as /sk/ in words like *āscian*, and maybe in *Scottas* (however, the
variant *Sceotta* seems to indicate a pronunciation of *sh-* /ʃ/.

þ, ð have a voiced articulation in voiced contexts; they were pronounced voiceless in
all other positions, especially in word-initial and word-final position.

Old English Vowels: Monophthongs

It is important to be aware of the fact that Old English vowels are contrasted in two
ways: according to their *quality* (just as in Modern English we differentiate between *a,
e, i, o, u* etc.) and according to their *quantity* (i. e. length). In other words, in Old
English, quantity always had phonemic implications, as in the two words *gŏd* (short) =
Modern English *god* and *gōd* (long) = Modern English *good*.

ă resembles the quality of the *u* in Modern English *cut*; *ā* is similar to the quality of
the *a* in Modern English *father*.

ǽ resembles the quality of the *a* in Modern English *cat*; *ǣ* is a 'lengthened'
pronunciation of the same Modern English vowel.

ĕ resembles the quality of the *e* in Modern English *set*; *ē* is a 'lengthened'
pronunciation of the same Modern English vowel.

ĭ resembles the quality of the *i* in Modern English *pit*; *ī* is pronounced as *ee* in
Modern English *meet*.

ŏ resembles the quality of the *o* in Modern English *god*; *ō* is a 'lengthened' and
'closed' pronunciation of the same Modern English vowel.

ŭ resembles the quality of the *u* in Modern English *put*; ū is pronounced as *oo* in Modern English *tooth*.

ў and ȳ have no correspondence in Modern English; the quality of these vowels resembles that of German *ü* or *u* in French, e. g. *tu*.

Old English Vowels: Diphthongs

As noted above, there were four diphthongs in Old English, *ea, eo, io* and *ie*, and these can be long or short.

In all probability, ĕa and ēa were pronounced as the combination of æ̆+a; ĕo and ēo as ĕ+o; ĭe and īe as ĭ+e; ĭo and īo as ĭ+o.

Middle English Consonants

The Middle English consonants *b d h l m n p s t r w* were probably pronounced as they are pronounced in Modern English. However, *w* in post-vocalic position is in many instances the second element of a diphthong (just as in Modern English *know*) or, always in combination with *o*, a digraph representing a 'long' *u* (as in *found*, which was pronounced as the <oo> in *food*). In general, there is a greater variety of spellings in Middle English due to the adoption of French writing practices in the wake of the Norman Conquest of 1066.

It should be noted that after the feature 'consonantal length' (signalled by geminates) had been abolished and word-final *-e* was no longer pronounced, the above consonants can be found as geminates in medial position, i. e. *-VCCe*, as in *wedde* /wed/. However, word-final *-e* could still be pronounced in poetry if required by the metre. The pattern *-VCCe* was used to indicate a short vowel from late Middle English onwards.

The pronunciation of the other Middle English consonants and their representation in writing can be found in the table below.

/tʃ/ as in Modern English *ch*eese is usually written <c> and later increasingly as <ch>, in medial position also <cch>.

/k/ is usually written <c>, <k> (when followed by <i, e, n, l>), <qu>, <kk> and <ck>.

/dʒ/ as in Modern English bri*dge* between vowels is usually written <gg>, in word-initial position <g, j> and <i>; between palatal vowels and followed by *n* it is usually written <ng>, cf. Middle English *senge*, Modern English *singe*; in word-final position from the 15th century onwards it is increasingly written <dg>.

/g/ is written <ʒ, g> and <gu>; after consonantal length had been abolished the digraph <gg> can also be found.

/f/ is usually written <f>, in French loanwords it is occasionally written <ph>; after consonantal length had been abolished the pattern <ff> was also used.

/v/ is usually written <f, u, fu>, later also <v>.

/θ/ as in Modern English *th*anks is usually written <þ, ð, th, thþ>, occasionally <ht>.

/ð/ as in Modern English *th*at is usually written <þ, ð, th>, occasionally <ht>.

/z/ is usually written <s, ʒ, z>.

/ʃ/ as in Modern English *sh*ip is usually written <sc, ss, sh, sch>; later also <ch, schch, ssh, ssch, schs, sshs>.

/x/   as in German 'a*ch*' is usually written <h, ʒ, g, ʒh>, rarely <gh>; later on usually
       <gh>, in the northern areas also <ch>.
/ʍ/   as in Modern English aspirated (i. e. with breath) *wh*ich is usually written <wh,
       w>, in the northern areas also <quh, qu, qw>.
/ŋ/   as in Modern English thi*ng* and always preceding *g* and *k*: <ng> and <nk>.
/w/   in the earliest texts the 'wynn' rune can still be found; later it is written <w, u,
       v>.
/j/   as in Modern English *y*es is usually written <ʒ> and <g>; in late Middle English
       <y>, in the northern areas <yh>.

Middle English Vowels: Monophthongs

The short monophthongs *e, o* are mostly written <e> and <o>. Vowels in unstressed
syllables are usually written <e>.

/i/   is usually written <i>; from the 13th century onwards and in the context of *n, m,*
       v, u, w it is frequently written <y>, occasionally <u>.
/œ/   as in Modern German 'hölzern' retained in the dialect of the WML and the South
       until the late 12th century is written <eo, ue, œ, o> and later <u>.
/a/   <a, æ, e> and <ea> in early texts.
/u/   <u> or <v>, in the context of *m, n, v, w* it is frequently written <o>.
/y/   as in Modern German 'M*ü*tze' is usually written <u> in the areas where it had
       not been unrounded (see § 10).

The word-final pattern –*V+C+e* is increasingly used to indicate words with a long
monophthong.

/i:/   is usually written <i>, occasionally <ii>, <ij> and later, especially in the context
       of *m, n* and *v* also <y>; in addition, the digraphs <ei> and <ey> can be found.
/e:/   is written <e, eo, œ, ue, o, eu, u> in early texts, later usually <e> and <ei>.
/ɛ:/   as in Modern German 'schw*e*r' is written <æ, ea> and <e> until 1300, later
       usually written <e> and <ee>, from the 15th century onwards <ea>.
/a:/   is usually written <a>, sometimes <aa>; in the north <ai, ay> are also used.
/ɔ:/   as in Modern English th*ou*ght up to the 13th century usually written <a, o, oa>,
       later <o> and <oo>; in late Middle English <oa> can be found again; French
       practice can be seen in <oe>.
/o:/   until the 14th century written <o>; later frequently <oo>, still later occasionally
       <ou, oe>.
/u:/   until the 13th century usually written <u, uw, ow>, thereafter <ou, ov, ow>, in
       northern areas <o> can be found.
/ø:/   as in Modern German 'sch*ö*n' only in the dialects of the WML and the SW until
       the 14th century; there it is written <eo, oe, ue, o, eu, u>.
/y:/   as in Modern German 'tr*ü*be' is usually written <y, u, ui, uy> in the areas where
       it had not been unrounded (see § 10).

Middle English Vowels: Diphthongs

As pointed out above, none of the Middle English diphthongs are based on the diphthongs of Old English. Middle English diphthongs are the product of contextually conditioned changes of earlier monophthongs; see § 4 for the origin of Middle English diphthongs.

/ai/ as in Modern English *aye* is usually written <æi, ei, ey, eʒ, æʒ, aʒ>; later, however, written <ai, ay, ei, ey>.

/au/ as in Modern English n*ow* is usually written <au>; when followed by a *v* is usually written <aw>.

/ou/ as in Modern English sh*ow* is usually written <aw, au, ou, ow>; later on exclusively <ou> and <ow>.

/iu/ as in Modern English f*ew* is usually written <iw, eow, uw, ew, eu>; later also written <ew, eu, uw, u, w, iu, iw, yw, ui>.

/eu/ as in Modern German 'F*eu*er' is usually written <eouw, eow, uw, eaw, ew, eu>; later generally <eu> and <ew>.

/oi/ is written <oi> and <oy>.

/ui/ as in Modern English g*ooey* is written <oi> and <oy>; occasionally also <ui>.

For the system of phonemic contrast consult Samuels (1972:135–153). Detailed accounts can be found in Barber (2006), Baugh/Cable (1978), Berndt (1982), Brunner (1960–62), Faiß (1989), Görlach (1994), Lass (1999), Luick (1964), Pinsker (1969), Pyles (1971/2004), Romaine (1998) and Strang (1970).

2. Phonology

§ 1 General Remarks

This section is concerned first of all with those specific phonetic contexts which can be shown to have been decisive in the history of English. Thus, the history of vowels and consonants from West Germanic to Old English will not be traced, as is often the case in introductory handbooks; the focus is rather on the influence of these contexts on the development of vowels and consonants in stressed syllables.

The first of these contexts to be considered is restricted to Old English and affects the development of West Germanic *a (both short and long). According to traditional terminology the context is that of *brightening* and *retraction* and involves the quality of the vowels which follow the accented syllable. As will be seen below, this development is the root of some of the dialectal differences in Middle English.

The second context can be called 'the influence of post-vocalic consonants and consonant groups'; according to the terminology of older accounts these contexts comprise *West Saxon and Kentish breaking* in Old English times; *new diphthongs* in Middle English; and the *early modern changes* due to the influence of tautosyllabic (i. e. belonging to the same syllable) post-vocalic *r*.

The third area concerns differences in vowel quality which cannot be directly attributed to a specific and well definable context. In traditional terminology, this is the process called *i-mutation*.

In a fourth section, the important quantitative changes in the history of English will be considered.

Finally, there is a brief account of one of the most decisive changes in the history of English vowel sounds: the Great Vowel Shift.

A summary of the reflexes of Old English vowels (both monophthongs and diphthongs) in Middle English will also be provided.

§ 2 West Germanic Monophthongs and Diphthongs

West Germanic *ă was regularly raised ('brightened') to ǽ in West Saxon and Northumbrian; however, it was raised even further to ě in the Mercian and Kentish dialects.

West Germanic *ā was regularly raised to ǽ in West Saxon, but to ē in the other dialects of Old English. This difference can be seen in examples like West Saxon *dǽg* versus Kentish and Mercian *deg* 'day'; and West Saxon *lǽdan* and Anglian and Kentish *lēdan* 'to lead'.

This regular process was blocked by a nasal consonant (*m* or *n*) immediately following West Germanic *ǎ. In this phonetic context the short vowel is written both *a* and *o*: *land, lond* 'land'. The long vowel is written *o*: *spōn* 'spoon', *mōna* 'moon'.

The regular development of West Germanic *ǎ was also blocked by a velar vowel (*a, o, u*) in the next syllable. This special development can still be seen in the paradigm of the nouns *dæg* 'day' and *mǽg* 'kinsman':

N sg.	dæg	mæg	N pl.	dagas	māgas
G sg.	dæges	mæges	G pl.	daga	māga
D sg.	dæge	mæge	D pl.	dagum	māgum
A sg.	dæg	mæg	A pl.	dagas	māgas.

In Middle English times, this difference was levelled out. However, in earlier texts it can still be found, written as *dayes* M 11/11 (from the singular, see § 5) versus *dawes* M 5/19 (from the plural, see § 6).

The regular development of West Germanic *ă̄* in West Saxon was also blocked by the processes called 'breaking' (see next section), i-mutation (short *a* only; see § 9), and when the consonant *w* followed directly after the vowel. This can be seen for example in the third tense stem of the strong verb *sāwon* '(they) saw', in contrast to *cwǣdon* '(they) spoke', both belonging to class 5.

Remark: For the process called 'back umlaut' or 'back mutation' and its consequences on *æ* see Brunner (1967: 80–89), Campbell (1974: 85–93), and Hogg (1992: 152–166).

All West Germanic diphthongs were modified in Old English, as a comparison with Modern German will show.

ai > *ā*: *stān, hāt*: 'Stein, heiß'
au > *ēa*: *ēage, ēac*: 'Auge, auch'
eu > *ēo*: *dēop, dēor*: 'tief, Tier'
iu > *īo* > *ēo*: *līode, lēode*: 'Leute'.

Vowel Change: Post-vocalic Consonants and Consonant Groups

§ 3 West Saxon and Kentish Breaking

Evidence of breaking is an important criterion in Old English dialectology; it can be used to differentiate the southern from both the midlands and northern dialects, i. e. 'Anglian' versus West Saxon and Kentish texts.

Primary *short* palatal monophthongs (i. e. original, not palatal as a result of i-mutation, see § 9) followed by r+C or l+C are represented by a sequence of two vowel signs representing a diphthong in West Saxon and Kentish. In the Anglian dialects a monophthong remains; however, in the case of æ+l+C the *æ* is lowered to *a*; cf. WS *eald*, Anglian *ald*.

ă > *ĕa*: *ĕarm* 'arm'; *hĕard* 'hard'
ĕ > *ĕo*: *hĕorte* 'heart'; *ĕorl* 'earl'
ĭ > *ĭo* > *ĕo*: *hĭorde, hĕorde*, WS *hierde* 'shepherd'
ă > *ĕa ĕald* 'old'
ĕ > *ĕo seolh* 'seal'

It should be noted that the combination r+C seems to have had a stronger effect on the preceding vowel than the combination l+C; in West Saxon, breaking occurs regularly only before l+h and l+c, whereas in Kentish l+f also leads to breaking – WS, Anglian *self*, Kentish *seolf*.

Both *short* and *long* primary palatal vowels were subject to breaking when they were
followed by h (which could be followed by a second consonant).

ǣ > ĕa: *nēah* 'near'

ē̆ > ĕo: *fĕohtan* 'to fight' (no forms with *ē have survived)

ῐ > ĭo > ĕo: *mῐox, mĕox* (<x> for /xs/) 'dung'; *lēoht* 'light' (adjective).

Breaking can be seen especially in the first and second tense stems of strong verbs
belonging to classes 3 and 5 (see § 69, 71) where verbs with and without breaking can
be found:

feohtan	*feaht*	breaking throughout (V+h)
sēon	*seah*	breaking throughout (V+h)
ceorfan	*cearf*	breaking throughout (V+r+C)
helpan	*healp*	breaking second stem only (V+l+C)
specan	*spæc*	no breaking context.

§ 4 New Diphthongs in Middle English

New diphthongs in Middle English can be attributed to the context specified above:
V+C. Some of the changes occurred in late Old English times already, in particular in
the sequence palatal vowel+g (where *g* represented the semi-vowel /j/). In Middle
English times, there is an even greater variety of post-vocalic contexts, all of which
led to new diphthongs or, in some instances, long monophthongs.

The new Middle English diphthongs share an important feature: the second element
is *i* in palatal contexts and *u* in velar contexts. Middle English words with the
diphthongs *oi* and *ui* do not fit this pattern, as the first elements are velar vowels. It
can thus be inferred that these words must have a different origin; indeed, they are
loan-words, for example French *noise*; in *boy*, the etymology is far from being clear.

§ 5 Old English Palatal Vowels + <g>

A palatal vowel followed by g (/j/) became a diphthong of which the second vowel
was written either <i> or <y>:

OE ă+g > *æi, ai, ay*: OE *dæg, fæger* > ME *dai, day, fair*

OE ǣ+g > *ei, ey* and later *ai, ay*: OE *lǣgon* > ME *laie(n), laye(n)*

OE ĕ+g > *ei, ey* and later *ai, ay*: OE *plegian* > ME *pleie(n), playe(n)*

OE ē+g > *ei, ey* and later *ai, ay*: Old Kentish *grēg* > ME *grai, gray*.

        When followed by a vowel the usual development is to Middle English
        ī followed by schwa (ə): OE *ēage* > *ye* [iː(j)ə]

OE ῐ+g > *ī* beginning in late Old English: OE *nigon* > ME *nīn(e)*

The development of Old English ȳ+g into Middle English is more complicated
because the dialects have different results:

                 ME *biʒeþ* (North, EML)

OE *he byġeþ* ⟨————→ ME *buʒeþ* > *buieþ* (WML, SW)

                 ME *beʒeþ* (Kentish)

OE *drȳge*

                → ME *drīȝe* > *drīe, drȳe* (North, EML)

                → ME *druȝe* > *druie, druye* (WML, SW)

                → ME *drēȝe* > *drīe* (Kentish)

§ 6 Old English Velar Vowels + <g>

Following a velar vowel, *g* represented a voiced fricative /ɣ/. This fricative was replaced by the velar vowel *u* (written both *u* and *w*) and became thus the second element of a new diphthong.

OE *ă*+*g* > *au, aw*: OE *dagas* > ME *dawes*

OE *ā*+*g* > *ou, ow*: OE *āgen* > ME *owen*

OE *ŏ*+*g* > *ou, ow*: OE *boga, slōgon* > ME *bowe, slowen*

OE *ŭ*+*g* > *u, uu, ou* and *ow*: OE *fugol, būgan* > ME *foul, bouen*

§ 7 Old English Vowels + <w>

In OE, a post-vocalic <w> represented a semi-vowel; in ME times the semi-vowel became a full vowel and combined with the preceding vowel to form a diphthong with *u* as the second element. This process had already begun in late Old English times. In many such instances OE *w* continued to be written <w> in ME times.

OE *ă*+*w* > *au, aw*: OE *awel* > ME *awel, aul*

OE *ā*+*w* > *ou, ow*: OE *blāwan* > ME *blowe(n)*

OE *ō*+*w* > *ou, ow*: OE *flōwan* > ME *flowe(n)*

OE *ǣ*+*w* > *eu, ew*: OE *lǣwed* > ME *lewed*

OE *ēa*+*w* > *eu, ew*: OE *fēawe* > ME *fewe*

OE *ĕo*+*w* > *eu, ew*: OE *speowian, brēowan* > ME *spewe(n), brewe(n)*

OE *ī*+*w* > *iw, ue*: OE *Tīwesdæg* > ME *Tiwesday, Tuesday*

Remark: Post-vocalic *w* in Old English when preceded by *ĕ* or *ĭ* generally caused diphthongs, as can be seen in OE *hweowol* 'wheel' and *ðrĭowa* 'thrice'. Post-vocalic *w* following West Germanic **ă* blocked the usual development to Old English *ǣ* (see § 2).

§ 8 Old English Vowels + <h>

It is important to bear in mind that there are two basic contexts which need to be differentiated: palatal V+h resulting in the new sequence palatal V+i+h/gh and velar V+h resulting in the new sequence velar V+u/w+h/gh. The post-vocalic fricative written <h> ultimately became silent and the new diphthong or long monophthong was a compensation for the loss of a consonant. In some cases, the former fricative *h* developed into a new fricative *f* in which case it is always preceded by either a long or a short vowel, as in *laugh* and *cough*.

It should be noted that the vowel glides in Middle English times and their subsequent developments are very different from West Saxon and Kentish breaking (see § 3), in which the post-vocalic fricative seems to have been retained and in which only palatal vowels followed by *h* were affected.

OE *ĕ*+*h* > *ei* > *ai*: OE *þeh* > ME *þeigh*

OE *ē*+*h* > *ei* > *ī*: OE *nēh* > ME *neih*

OE *ă*+*h* > *au*: OE *naht* > ME *naught*

OE *ā+h* > *ou*: OE *nāht* > ME *nought*
OE *ŏ+h* > *ou*: OE *gefohten* > ME *foughte(n)*
OE *ō+h* > *ou* > *ū*: OE *genōh* > ME *ynough*

Old English Vowels: Further Changes

Even today, different vowels qualities can be found in etymologically related words, such as *tooth* versus *teeth*, *brother* vs. *brethren* and so on. In Old and Middle English these differences were even more numerous. They can be traced back to the influence of the vowel *i* or the semi-vowel *j* in the next syllable. This syllable was either syncopated (see § 21) or the *i* or *j* was weakened to *e*. This process is called i-mutation and can also be found in other Germanic languages, for example German.

§ 9   Old English i-mutation

Except for *e* and *ǣ* (from West Germanic **ā*, see § 2) Old English vowels were subject to i-mutation, as can be seen in the following table:

ŭ   > y̆, later ĭ – as in *mūs* (singular) and *mȳs* (plural)
ŏ   > œ̆ > ĕ – as in *long* (positive) and *lengra* (comparative)
ă, æ̆ > æ > e – as in *lang* (positive) and *lengra* (comparative)
ā   > ǣ (from West Germanic **ai*) – as in *stān* (noun) and *stǣnen* (adjective)
ĭo   > ĭe > ĭ, y̆ – as in *wulle* (noun) and *wyllen* (adjective)
ĕa   > ĭe > ĭ, y̆ in West Saxon, otherwise ĕ – as in *gelēafa* (noun) and *gelīefan* (verb)
ēo   > īe – *sēon* (infinitive) and *siehþ* (3rd singular present indicative)

The results of i-mutation are therefore a *raising* of palatal vowels and a *fronting* of velar vowels. While it is difficult to point out the factors responsible for these changes, it would appear that the results of i-mutation (raising and fronting) contributed to a kind of vocalic harmony, avoiding extreme qualitative contrast between two adjoining syllables.

The effects of i-mutation in Old English can easily be seen in the following contexts:
1. In the 2nd and 3rd person singular present of strong verbs (abolished in early Middle English)
2. In the dative singular and nominative and accusative plural (occasionally also in the genitive singular) of athematic nouns (i-mutation in the dative singular was abolished in early Middle English; it was retained and indeed generalised throughout the plural)
3. In the dative singular of three of the five nouns expressing family relationship: *brōþor*, *mōdor* and *dohtor* (abolished in early Middle English)
4. In the comparative and superlative of certain adjectives and adverbs (abolished in early Middle English except for *elder, eldest*)
5. In the present stem of the weak verbs belonging to class Ib (as for example *tell* versus *told*)

In the following areas i-mutation was a regular feature, even though there are no longer any non-mutated forms:

6. In class I weak verbs derived from nouns (*dēman* 'deem' and *dōm* 'doom')
7. In nouns belonging to the i-stems (*cyme* 'arrival' and *cuman* 'come')
8. In adjectives derived from nouns using the suffix *-iþ-* (*lengþu* 'length' and *lang, long* 'long')
9. In adjectives derived from nouns using the suffix *-īna* (*gylden* 'golden' and *gold*)
10. In feminine nouns derived from masculine nouns (*wylf* 'she-wolf' and *wulf* 'he-wolf').

Old English Vowels and their Continuation in Middle English

§ 10 Monophthongs

Old English *short* monophthongs remained much the same in Middle English times, except for /æ/ which was lowered to /a/ and /y/ which was either unrounded or remained the same (see below).

Old English *long* monophthongs also remained much the same in Middle English, except for *ā* which was raised to a long open *o* /ɔː/ in the areas south of the River Humber; in the north, Old English *ā* remained unchanged. Old English *ǣ* was slightly raised to a long, open *e*-sound /ɛː/ and West Saxon *ǣ*, derived from West Germanic *ā*, was also raised to /ɛː/.

The development of Old English *y̆* in the various dialects of Middle English can be summarised thus:

OE *y̆* > ME
- /i/, /iː/ North and EML
- /y/, /yː/ WML and Southwest
- /e/, /eː/ Kent and Southeast

§ 11 Diphthongs

All Old English diphthongs became monophthongs in Middle English; these changes had already started in late Old English times, with transitional stages in the 11th century.

OE *ĕa* > ME *æ* > *a*
OE *ĕo* > ME /ø/ > *e*
OE *ēa* > ME /æː/ > *ę̄*, approximately MnE /ɛː/
OE *ēo* > ME /øː/ > *ę̄*, approximately MnE /eː/

English Vowels: Quantitative Changes

§ 12 Old English Lengthening

Lengthening took place either very early, i. e. before our first written records, or in late Old English times. *Early* lengthening results from the loss of a consonant in certain contexts: the consonants involved are *h*, *w* and *g*.

Loss of *h* occurred regularly when the consonant was preceded and followed by a vowel. Thus, the infinitive *sēon* has a long diphthong, whereas the preterite *seah* has a short diphthong, because the *h* was retained. There are quite a number of verbs in Old English showing quantitative differences in the present tense forms on the one hand and the preterite on the other; these verbs are called 'contracted verbs'. A similar quantitative contrast sometimes occurs in the inflection of nouns ending in *-h*: the consonant is lost when the inflectional syllable begins with a vowel. This is the case in OE *feoh* (nominative) and *fēos* (genitive): the inflectional syllable for the genitive is *-es*, therefore *-h-*, now in intervocalic position, was dropped and compensatory lengthening occurred. A similar loss of *h* occurred in the combination *-rhV-* and *-lhV-*, see for example OE *fēolan* (infinitive) and *fealh* (preterite).

Word-final *w* after vowels was also dropped, with compensatory lengthening; see for example, OE *cnēo* (nominative) and *cneowes* (genitive).

Especially in late West Saxon, palatal *g* was dropped when it was followed by either *d* or *n*; see for example *sægde* and *sǣde* as well as *frignan* and *frīnan*.

In *late* Old English times, lengthening occurred before consonant groups consisting of either a liquid (l, r) or nasal (m, n) followed by a homorganic voiced plosive (b) or any other homorganic voiced consonant. The consonant groups which triggered lengthening are *mb, nd, ng, ld, rd* as well as *rl, rn* and *rð, rs* when followed by a vowel. As a rule, vowel length remained stable for *i* and *u* when followed by *ld, mb, nd* and for *a* when followed by *ld*. Modern English examples which were subject to late Old English lengthening are: *child, climb, bind* and *bound* as well as *old*.

Lengthening, however, did not occur when a third consonant followed. This can be seen in Modern English *child*, based on lengthened /i:/, and Modern English *children* where lengthening was blocked by the third consonant. As a rule, lengthening also did not occur when a word was used in an unstressed position, such as auxiliaries (*scolde, wolde*), prepositions (*under*) and conjunctions (*and*).

§ 13 Old English Shortening

Originally long vowels were shortened before three consonants (*gōdspell* > *gŏdspell*) and also before two consonants, if at least two unstressed syllables followed (*hlāfmæsse* > *hlamæsse*). Shortening also occurred in words which were used in unstressed positions (*þēah* > *þeah*).

In the period of transition from Old to Middle English, shortening also took place when a long vowel was followed by two consonants (except for homorganic groups) which require great articulatory effort. This condition is fulfilled for example in OE *brōhte* with its sequence long vowel followed by a fricative followed by a voiceless dental stop.

§ 14 Middle English Lengthening

This process can be assigned to the 12th and 13th centuries. Lengthening only took place in words consisting of two syllables of which the first ended in a vowel (an 'open syllable') and the second had a vowel other than *i*. Lengthening in this context occurred regularly with *a, e, o* in the first syllable. Examples are:

OE *nă-ma* > ME *nā-me*

OE *bĕ-ran* > ME *bē-re*

OE *nŏ-su* > ME *nō-se*

As a rule, lengthening did not occur when a word was used in an unstressed position, as for example *have*, versus Modern English *behave*. Lengthening also did not occur when the vowel of the second syllable was *i*: see OE *ma-nig* 'many', *he-fig* 'heavy', *pe-nig* 'penny' which have a short vowel in Modern English.

With *i* or *u* in the first syllable, lengthening also involved a lowering of the initial quality of the vowel and occurred mainly in the northern areas. Some northern lengthened forms were taken over by the standard language. Examples are:

OE *wŭ-du* > ME *wō-de* 'wood'

OE *wĭ-cu* > ME *wē-ke* 'week'

Middle English lengthening probably occurred as compensatory lengthening in order to avoid too great a number of monosyllabic words with a short syllable. It should also be seen in the context of the loss of word-final *e* (see § 22).

§ 15 Middle English Shortening

Shortening took place in later Middle English when a long vowel was followed by two (or more) consonants, occasionally even before two homorganic consonants (see § 12). Shortening also took place when two unstressed syllables followed, as for example ME *hŏliday* versus the adjective *holy* /hɔːli/.

§ 16 Early Modern English Quantitative Changes

Long monophthongs could be shortened in the 16th or 17th century when either a dental consonant or the consonant /k/ followed immediately. This shortening has occurred in *book, foot, good* with underlying late Middle English *ō*, raised to [uː] by the Great Vowel Shift (see § 18) and thereafter shortened to /ʊ/. Shortening of late Middle English *ō* has also taken place in *blood*; however, the Modern English pronunciation is /ʌ/. These differences clearly indicate that the present distribution of /uː/, /ʌ/ and /ʊ/ must have evolved gradually and over a longer period of time.

Late Middle English short *a* was lengthened before voiceless fricatives and became [æː], such as in *staff, glass* and *path*. This lengthened vowel [æː] is still a feature of American English, while in British English it was lowered to [ɑː].

Late Middle and Early Modern English Developments

§ 17 Post-vocalic *r* and *l*

In Modern British English, a post-vocalic *r* belonging to the same syllable is not pronounced. As a rule, the vowel preceding the *r* is either pronounced as a long monophthong, a diphthong or a triphthong, as for example in *bird*, *moor* and *fire*.

The silencing of *r* in post-vocalic position started in late Middle English times and its effects can readily be seen in the lowering of earlier *e+r* to *a+r*, as for example in ME *fer, ferre* > late ME *far*; see M 6/13 *fer* and M 14/40 *far*.

In late Middle English *u*-glides developed where short *a, o, u* is immediately followed by *l*, see for example *tauld* (M 14/140). The diphthong resulting from this change meant in many instances that further changes occurred during the Great Vowel Shift (see next section). In some words, the *u*-glide may have been responsible for the silencing of the post-vocalic *l* when it was followed by a further consonant, as for example in *half*.

§ 18 The Great Vowel Shift

This change is perhaps the most important in the history of English vowel sounds. It began in the late 15th century and extended over several centuries, affecting late Middle English long monophthongs and diphthongs. The changes can be summarised thus: long vowels were raised and *i* as well as *u* became diphthongs; all diphthongs were monophthongised. So far no convincing hypotheses have been advanced as to the reasons for this change. The following table shows the major developments.

lME	eMnE	MnE	RP	(as in)
[aː]	[æː]	[ɛː] [eː]	[eɪ]	name
[eː]	[iː]	[iː]	[iː]	meet
[ɛː]	[eː]	[eː]	[eɪ]	great
[iː]	[əi]	[aɪ]	[aɪ]	ride
[oː]	[uː]	[uː]	[uː]	boot
[ɔː]	[oː]	[oː]	[əʊ]	boat
[uː]	[əʊ]	[əʊ]	[aʊ]	house
[aʊ]	[ɔː]	[ɔː]	[ɔː]	law
[ɔʊ]	[oː]	[oː]	[əʊ]	snow
[ai]	[æː]	[ɛː] [eː]	[eɪ]	day
[əʊ] [iʊ]	[yu]	[yu]	[juː]	few
[ɔi]	[ɔɪ]	[ɔɪ]	[ɔɪ]	boy
[ʊɪ]	[əɪ]	[əɪ] [ɔɪ]	[ɔɪ]	join

§ 19 Early Modern English Short Vowels

In general, most short vowels have remained much the same since late Middle English, unless they are followed by *r* or *l* (see § 17). Only late Middle English *a* and *u* show considerable changes:

lME	eMnE	MnE	RP	(as in)
[a]	[æ]	[æ]	[æ]	that
[ʊ]	[ə] [ʌ]	[ʌ]	[ʌ]	but

Vowels in Unstressed Syllables

§ 20 Qualitative Changes

In Old English, the most important qualitative change is certainly the increasingly indistinct quality of the vowels of inflectional syllables. Originally, these vowels had the function of marking grammatical categories. Thus, in the case of nouns belonging to the *a-stems*, the ending *-as* marked both nominative and accusative plural, as for example *stan-as*; the ending *-es* marked genitive singular, as for example *stan-es*. Since in unstressed syllables *a* lost its former quality and tended towards schwa /ə/, written <e>, the inflectional syllable for the nominative/accusative plural and for the genitive singular was no longer distinct. Therefore the different functions once signalled by the inflectional endings had to be inferred more and more from the context. The 'new' construction *of+noun*, expressing the concept *possession*, one of the chief functions of the inflected genitive, was increasingly adopted to distinguish the inflectional genitive from the plural, since both were marked by the same inflectional syllable.

A similar development can be seen in the area of conjugational endings. In Old English, the ending *-on* indicates the category 'preterite plural indicative', whereas *-en* indicates 'present and preterite plural subjunctive', and *-an* 'present infinitive'. A similarly poorly marked differentiation can be seen in the form of the third person present singular indicative, ending in many cases in *-eþ*, and the present plural indicative, ending mainly in *-aþ*. When the original quality of the vowel of these inflectional endings tended towards schwa /ə/ and was increasingly written <e>, new means had to be found to differentiate the vitally important category *mood*, i. e. *indicative* versus *subjunctive*.

§ 21 Syncope

The term 'syncope' denotes the loss of the medial syllables when inflectional syllables are added: *hālig* (nominative) plus dative ending (-um) would have led to **hāl-ig-um*, but actually resulted in *hāl-gum*. Syncope after *long syllables* had already occurred before the first written records. This is the explanation for apparent irregularities in the paradigms of nouns and adjectives with a long vowel, as for example in *brōðres* (genitive) and *brōðor* (nominative); similarly *hālgan* (genitive singular) and *hālig* (nominative singular).

In late Old, English syncope occurred also after a short vowel, in particular when the new sequence was *C+l/r*, as can be seen in *fingres* (genitive) and *finger* (nominative) as well as *micle* and *micele*.

§ 22 Apocope

The term 'apocope' denotes the loss of final vowels and consonants. Apocope is a marked feature especially of Middle English and should be seen together with Middle English Lengthening (see above, § 14).

Apocope had already begun in late Old English, particularly in the northern dialect, where word-final -n in inflectional syllables disappeared. This process gained considerable momentum in Middle English and increasingly began to affect the vowel preceding the word-final -n. Ultimately, apocope led to the loss of almost all conjugational endings of verbs, including the infinitive. With reference to nouns, apocope resulted in the almost total abolition of the once highly frequent plural morphs -an, -en which survive only in Modern English oxen.

It should be noted that even though word-final -n in inflectional syllables disappeared almost completely, it has been retained in the past participle of strong verbs in those cases where the contrast between present tense and non-finite preterite had originally been a quantitative one, as for example in Middle English wrīte(n) (infinitive) and wrĭtten (past participle).

It should also be noted that even though the final -n in inflectional syllables disappeared almost completely, the now word-final vowel, which gradually became silent, was retained in writing. Retaining the mute word-final -e in writing was an efficient means of indicating that the preceding vowel was long. In Modern English, the structure (C)+V+C+e is a reliable indication that the vowel is either pronounced as a diphthong or a long monophthong, as for example ate, write and rude.

§ 23 Parasitic Vowels

Parasitic vowels may occur in unstressed syllables, especially when the stressed syllable ends in r or l and a further consonant follows. The parasitic vowel u is inserted after a velar vowel, i after a palatal vowel, in order to facilitate pronunciation. A parasitic vowel can be found in the genitive heriges (O 9/31; nominative here) and in the dative byrig (O 2/22 etc.; nominative burh).

Consonants

§ 24 Fronting and Assibilation

These two changes are very complex and affect the pronunciation of the original velar consonants g and k (written <c>), as well as the consonant group sk (written <sc>). It can be said with certainty that in a palatal context, the velar consonant g was either fronted to the semi-vowel j or became the affricate /ʤ/; original velar k was fronted to /ʧ/ and the consonant group sk became /ʃ/. These changes occurred before the earliest written records.

Word initial k became /ʧ/ and g became /j/ when followed by primary palatal vowels: see for example ceorl /ʧeorl/ ('churl') as opposed to the German cognate 'Kerl' and giefan /jevan/ ('give') as opposed to German 'geben'.

Medially in palatal contexts, *g* became /j/ and /ʤ/ and /k/ became /ʧ/ as in *dæges* /dæjes/ ('day'), *sengan* /senʤan/ ('singe') and *sēcan* /se:ʧan/ ('seek') as well as *þencan* /θenʧan/ ('think').

Word-final /k/ preceded by *i* became /ʧ/ as in *pic* /piʧ/ ('pitch'); geminated *g* became /ʤ/ when it followed a palatal vowel, as in *secg* /seʤ/ ('man'), and /j/ as in *dæg* /dæj/ ('day').

§ 25 Initial Palatal Consonants

Palatal consonants in word-initial position are frequently followed by vocalic digraphs; it is difficult to say whether these digraphs represent diphthongs proper or are simply an indication of the palatal quality of the preceding word-initial consonant or consonant group. The consonants involved are Germanic **j* (<g>, <i>), and the fronted consonants *k*, *c* and *g*, as well as the consonant group *sk* (see § 24).

Germanic **j* in word-initial position followed by the velar vowel *u* is written as <iu->, <gio-> and <geo->, as for example in *iung, giong, geong* 'young'; followed by *ŏ* the written forms are *io* and *eo* and when *ā* followed the form was *ēa*: as for example *geoc, gioc* 'yoke' and *gēara* 'yore'. It can be shown by the later development of *yoke* and *yore* that the pattern is different from the ordinary Old English diphthongs which show a falling stress from the first to the second element; here, however, the second element was stressed.

Word-initial palatal *sc-* followed by a velar vowel frequently triggers digraphs, as for example in *sceolde* compared to *scolde* 'should' or *sceacan* 'shake'.

Word-initial palatal *sc-*, *g* and *c* /ʧ/ followed by a palatal vowel in West Saxon produced the following changes: *ĕ* > *ĭe*; *ǣ* > *ĕa*. Compare for example *giefan* 'give' and *gīet* 'yet'; *sceaft* 'shaft', *ceaster* 'city', *geat* 'gate'.

§ 26 Assimilation and Dissimilation

Both assimilation and dissimilation should be seen as strategies to facilitate the pronunciation of unwieldy consonant clusters.

Assimilation is mainly a feature of word formation (composition and derivation) which often produces a direct sequence of two difficult consonants. Thus, *-fm-* is usually assimilated to *-mm-*, as for example in *Lammasse* (M 1/1; < OE *hlāfmæsse*); it also occurs with *-pf-*, as for example in *chaffare* (M 7/33 < OE *cēap+faru*); *-vd-* usually becomes *-dd-*, as in ME *hadde, hadden* based on OE *hæfde, hæfdon* (see Old English Glossary under *habban* and Middle English Glossary under *have*). Old English *blētsunge* (O 1/32) appears as Middle English *blessyng* (M 10.1/8) and Middle English *lossum* is based on OE *lēofsum*. Assimilation also affects the dental consonants *þ* and *d* when followed by either a liquid (*l, r*) or a nasal (*m, n*). Examples are OE *fæder* and Modern English *father*. Sequences of two words are also subject to assimilation when the first ends in and the second begins with a dental, as for example in *atte* on the basis of *at+þe*.

Dissimilation took place in awkward consonant clusters, especially *h* or *s* preceding *f* or *þ*. This is the case in Modern English *nostrils* on the basis of Middle English *nosethirles* and Middle English *is tat* (M 2/30) based on *is þat*.

§ 27 Parasitic Consonants

Parasitic consonants were added to facilitate the pronunciation of unwieldy consonant clusters: *b, d* in a voiced context and *p, t* in a voiceless context. In Middle English, parasitic consonants appear in the context of *mr, nr, ml, nl, lr, mn* as well as *mt, ms, sn.*

A parasitic *b* appears in *thromblede* (M 3/38; 'stumbled'); a parasitic *d* appears in Modern English *thunder* (< OE *þunres* (genitive) from *þunor* (nominative)). The voiceless parasitic *p* appears in *nempnede* (M 7/178) versus *nemne* (M 10.8/9).

§ 28 Metathesis

Metathesis (i. e. transposition of two letters or sounds) most frequently occurs in the sequence *–Vrh(t)* in Old English which appears as *–rV(g)h(t)* in Middle English. Examples are ME *wrohte, wroht, ywroght* based on OE *worhte, geworht* (see glossaries under 'wyrcan' and 'work') and OE *þurh* versus Modern English *through.*

A further context is Old English *–rV+dental* which appears later as *–Vr+dental*: OE *þrittig* (O 6/94) becomes Modern English *thirty.*

§ 29 Simplification of Consonant Groups

This process affects mainly the consonants *l, w, v, þ,* as can be seen in the following examples. Old English *-lc-* /ltʃ/ becomes Middle English /tʃ/ as in *suilce* and *swiche,* Modern English *such.* Old English *eal swā* is simplified to Middle and Modern English *also.* The voiced fricative *v* frequently disappears when followed by *n* or *d,* as for example in Middle English *han,* based on *hav(e)n,* or *hed, heed,* based on Old English *hēafod.*

§ 30 Verner's Law

An exception to Grimm's Law (see chapter 1) seems to be evident in the various qualities of stem-final consonants in the tense stems of some strong verbs. Verner's Law provides an explanation for these differences. This variation can be seen in the first and second tense stems of strong verbs on the one hand, and the third and fourth stems on the other. The different consonants which result are a consequence of the shifting accent in Indo-European and its effects on fricatives. Verner's Law states that fricatives become voiced when they occur in a voiced context, provided the accent does not fall on the preceding syllable. Since in Indo-European the position of the word accent depended on the number of syllables, whereas in Germanic it fell on the first syllable, the variation between voiced and voiceless fricatives was a regular phenomenon.

Verner's Law accounts for the regular variation between these pairs of voiced and voiceless fricatives:

  -́f and v-́; -́θ and ð-́; -́x and ɣ-́ and -́s and z-́

  (-́ indicates the position of the accent).

In Old English, the first and second tense stems can be traced back to Indo-European forms in which the accent preceded the stem-final consonant; fricatives in this position therefore remained voiceless. The third and fourth stems, however, are based on forms in which the accent in Indo-European shifted to a syllable following the stem-final consonant; fricatives in this position therefore became voiced. Subsequent changes in the system of consonants and the peculiarities of the Old English writing system (no differentiation between voiceless /f/ and voiced /v/) have obscured this regular variation. Further, voiced /z/ became /r/; /ɣ/ in certain contexts became /w/ and /ð/ became /d/. As a result, the manifestation of Verner's Law in Old English can be summarised as the variation between þ/d, s/r and h/w – as in:

weorþan, wearþ wurdon, worden
cēosan, cēas   curon, coren
sēon, seah   sawon, sewen.

Old English strong verbs like *rīsan – rās – rĭson – risen* show that Verner's Law was gradually abandoned. In Modern English, Verner's Law can still be seen in *was – were* and *seethe – sodden*.

The operation of Verner's Law will be pointed out in the section concerning strong verbs in Old English (see § 66 ff.).

Loanwords

§ 31 Scandinavian Loanwords

Most Scandinavian loanwords could be easily assimilated in Old English, with only slight changes, as both are Germanic languages. For most Scandinavian vowels Middle English had corresponding qualities, except for *au* which can be found with a wide variety of spellings; thus *vindauga* 'window' is written both *windoʒe* and *windowe*.

Scandinavian *iū* usually appears as long close *e* in Middle English: *miūkr – meke* (M 11/2).

As far as word-initial consonants followed by a palatal vowel are concerned, Middle English shows a mixture of forms involving the consonants *g*, *k* and *sk*. Words inherited from Old English show a palatal word-initial consonant (see § 24), Scandinavian loanwords, however, guttural *g*, *k* and *sk-*: /jive/ versus /give/ 'give'; /tʃirtʃe/ versus /kirk/ 'church' and the characteristic word-initial /sk-/ as in *skill*, *skies*, etc.

§ 32 French Loanwords

Since Old French was not a Germanic language, more efforts and a number of compromises had to be made in accommodating Old French loanwords within the phonetic system of Middle English.

Whereas the Old French diphthongs *ai*, *ei*, *au*, *eu*, *öu* and *ue* could be easily adapted, *oi* had no correspondence in Middle English and was therefore adopted probably without any changes.

Apart from in the West Midlands and the Southwest, there were no corresponding vowels for French /y/; it was in most cases taken over as /u/.

In Old French the sequence *a+nasal+b/f/g/ch* was quite frequent, whereas in Middle English this pattern was not available. To accommodate the original pattern as closely as possible, diphthongs in *au* appear frequently: *chaumber, sauf, aungell, braunch*.

3. Morphology

Introduction

This chapter will cover the following areas for both Old and Middle English: nouns, adjectives, adverbs, pronouns, numerals and verbs. An introduction to every part of speech summarises their pertinent properties, usually in contrast to Modern English, with occasional reference to Latin. An additional section is devoted to the discussion of the most important diachronic changes. Paradigms, supplemented with notes, show the most important inflectional forms.

Nouns

§ 33 General Remarks

For a better understanding of the several declensional classes of nouns and their development from Old to Middle English, some general remarks on the morphological properties of nouns and their grammatical categories are appropriate.

In Indo-European, nouns consisted of a *stem* (root and suffixes, if any), a so-called *thematic element* indicating the declensional class, and an ending for *case and number*. For the nominative and accusative singular, the ending could be ∅. The few nouns without a thematic element are usually called *athematic nouns*.

These early characteristics of nouns can be illustrated by a few examples taken from Latin. Latin *piscis* 'fish' can be divided into stem – thematic element – inflectional ending: *pisc-i-s*; since the thematic element is *i*, *piscis* belongs to the so-called *i-stems*. Latin *homo* 'man' can be assigned to the so-called *n-stems* on the basis of the declensional form for the dative singular: *hom-in-i*. Latin *genus* 'gender', i. e. *gen-us-∅* in combination with its inflectional form for the dative singular *gen-er-i* can be assigned to the so-called *s-stems*. Finally, Latin *urb-s* 'town' shows that there is no thematic element between the stem and the declension ending; it therefore belongs to the *athematic nouns*.

In Proto-Germanic and to an even greater extent in Old English, final syllables indicating both thematic element and inflection became indistinct when the word accent shifted to the preceding root syllable. This means there are hardly any characteristics left that indicate to which inflectional class a certain noun belongs. Nevertheless, there are some characteristics which help to determine the original final syllables through their influence on the vowel of the stressed syllable. Thus, the *y* in the Old English noun *hyge* 'thought' is a secondary palatal vowel caused by i-mutation of *u* (cf. Odin's raven called 'Huginn') and therefore must have had the ending *-iz*, thus **hug-iz*.

In Old English, just as in Latin and Modern German, nouns had the following grammatical categories or parameters:

1. *gender:* feminine, masculine and neuter; starting in late Old English times, this category gradually became unimportant, and was practically abolished in Middle English;
2. *case:* nominative (vocative), genitive, dative (which could have instrumental function) and accusative; this category began to lose its importance from late Old English times onwards and was almost totally abolished in Middle English;
3. *number:* singular and plural.

Most of these categories were poorly marked. *Gender* is unmarked and can only be determined for the singular in combination with demonstrative pronouns because their inflections express gender. Most endings can indicate several different cases and/or numbers. The only ending which definitively marks the categories *case* and *number* is the sequence V+s. This is only found in the a-stems, as for example *dæg-es* (genitive singular) and *dag-as* (nominative or accusative plural). Since vowels in unstressed syllables (and inflectional syllables are never stressed) began to lose their once distinctive quality and were increasingly pronounced with the quality of a schwa /ə/, the word-final sequence *V+s* in late Old English can be assumed to have expressed the basic oppositions *singular* versus *plural* and *common case* versus *possessive case*. Retaining the original graph in these contexts (-es and -as) was the result of the stable writing system in West Saxon which was used until the 13th century. Diachronically, the word-final sequence *V+s* is the only stable inflectional element.

In Middle English times, the category *gender* with its poor inflectional marking was abandoned quite early. The only indicator of gender in Middle English was the personal pronoun for the third person singular, since it retained the category gender. Under the influence of Norman, some Old English nouns took on a new gender, as for example *love, sun, and moon*; the first two were feminine in Old English and became masculine in Middle English, whereas the third was masculine in Old English and became feminine in Middle English.

In Middle English writings *feminine* gender is sometimes associated with small birds, such as the nightingale. In M 8/6–7 reference to the fox is made by means of the personal pronoun *he*. Gender can also be expressed in allegorical poetry, when personifications like *justice, love* or *truth* are referred to by pronouns; see M 7/241–242: *Til Abstinence myn aunte haue ʒeue me leue – / And ʒut haue y hated here al my lyf-tyme.* In many of these instances, gender is taken over from the source language, usually either Latin or French.

The category *case* was retained in early Middle English, especially in the (linguistically) more conservative southern areas. Nevertheless, it was gradually replaced – except for the inflected genitive – by analytical means, such as prepositions and word order, differentiating direct and indirect objects, as well as marking adverbials. In late Old English, constructions can be found which express the idea *origin*, one of the major functions of the genitive, by the preposition *of*. Under the influence of *de*, which in French marks origin and expresses a possessive relation, the prepositional phrase *of+noun* gradually took over all the other functions of the old inflected genitive (see § 98).

Of the former grammatical categories, *number* has remained fairly stable. There were some changes; however, these led to a more reliable distinction between singular and plural. The phonologically stable word-final pattern *V+s* from the a-stems to show *plural* gradually replaced the other inflectional endings which had also expressed plural. The significance of the almost universal plural marker is underlined by the fact that in a few instances, a new singular without *-s* was introduced for nouns inherited from Old English or borrowed from Norman which ended in *-s*; as for example Old English *piose, peose* and the Modern English singular *pea*, and Old French *cherise* and the Modern English singular *cherry*.

Even though the number of Old English nouns which express plural by the ending *-an* was very high, only Modern English *oxen* has retained this marking.

Athematic nouns (see § 44) had different vowel qualities in the nominative and accusative plural, cf. *mūs* (singular) and *mȳs* (plural). This characteristic was also retained to a small extent.

In general, it can be said that the major changes in the system of English nouns had been effected by late Middle English times.

§ 34 Inflection of Nouns

In Old English, three basic types of inflection have to be considered: nouns with a vocalic thematic element, nouns with a consonantal thematic element and the so-called athematic nouns (radical consonant declension). As a rule, it is very difficult to infer the inflectional class to which a noun belongs on the basis of the data available. This is due to the reduction of unstressed syllables which once conveyed this information (see § 21 and 22).

With reference to the older Indo-European languages, ten declensions or stems can be reconstructed: four vocalic declensions (also called 'strong' declension), five consonantal declensions (also called 'weak' declension) and the so-called athematic declension.

1. a-stems (Indo-European *o*-stems)	6. r-stems
2. ō-stems (Indo-European *ā*-stems)	7. nt-stems
3. i-stems	8. s-stems
4. u-stems	9. t-stems
5. n-stems	10. athematic stems.

Despite this great diversity and a general lack of clearly marked categories, there are three rules for determining both case and number, though not gender, for all stems:
– the nominative and accusative plural have the same ending;
– the genitive plural of all nouns ends in *-a*;
– the dative plural of all nouns ends in *-um* (late West Saxon in *-an*).

§ 35 The a-stems

Nouns belonging to this class are either masculine or neuter. The declension of masculine nouns is illustrated by *dæg* 'day', *stān* 'stone' and *finger*. The declension of neuter nouns is illustrated by *lim* 'limb', *word* and *hēafod* 'head'.

	short-		long-		polysyllabic	
N sg.	dæg	lim	stān	word	finger	hēafod
G	dæges	limes	stānes	wordes	fingres	hēafdes
D	dæge	lime	stāne	worde	fingre	hēafde
A	dæg	lim	stān	word	finger	hēafod
N pl.	dagas	limu	stānas	word	fingras	hēaf(o)du
G	daga	lima	stāna	worda	fingra	hēafda
D	dagum	limum	stānum	wordum	fingrum	hēafdum
A	dagas	limu	stānas	word	fingras	hēaf(o)du

Remark: Neuter nouns with a short stem have *-u* in the nominative and accusative plural (see *lim*), those with a long stem do not have an ending at all (see *word*). The Modern English noun *sheep* was a neuter noun with a long stem in Old English; this explains why there is no *s* marking the plural in Modern English.

The a-stems have two subgroups: the so-called *ja-stems* and the *wa-stems*. Nouns belonging to the first subgroup show i-mutation and gemination when the stem syllable is short; those belonging to the second subgroup have either *-u* or *-w* following the stem-final consonant.

The paradigm for the ja-stems is for *here* 'army' and *secg* 'man', both masculine, and *cynn* 'race' and *wīte* 'punishment', both neuter. The paradigm for the wa-stems is for *bearu* 'grove' (masc.) and *searu* 'device' (neuter).

	here	secg	cynn	wīte
N sg.	here	secg	cynn	wīte
G	herges	secges	cynnes	wītes
D	herge	secge	cynne	wīte
A	here	secg	cynn	wīte
N pl.	hergas	secgas	cynn	wītu
G	herga	secga	cynna	wīta
D	hergum	secgum	cynnum	wītum
A	hergas	secgas	cynn	wītu

	bearu	searu		bearwas	searu
N sg.	bearu	searu	N pl.	bearwas	searu
G	bearwes	searwes	G	bearwa	searwa
D	bearwe	searwe	D	bearwum	searwum
A	bearu	searu	A	bearwas	searu

§ 36 The ō-stems

All nouns in this class are feminine. The paradigm is for *talu* 'tale', *wund* 'wound', and *sāwol* 'soul'.

	short-	long-	polysyllabic
N sg.	talu, -o	wund	sāwol
G	tale	wunde	sāwle
D	tale	wunde	sāwle
A	tale	wunde	sāwle
N pl.	tala, -e	wunda, -e	sāwla, -e
G	tala, -ena	wunda, -ena	sāwla
D	talum	wundum	sāwlum
A	tala, -e	wunda, -e	sāwla, -e

The ō-stems also have two subgroups; the so-called *jō-stems* and the *wō-stems*. The paradigm for the first subgroup is for *synn* 'sin' and *gierd* 'rod'. The paradigm for the second subgroup is for *sinu* 'sinew' and *lǣs* 'pasture'.

	synn	gierd	sinu	lǣs
N sg.	synn	gierd	sinu	lǣs
G	synne	gierde	sinwe	lǣswe
D	synne	gierde	sinwe	lǣswe
A	synne	gierde	sinwe	lǣswe
N pl.	synna, -e	gierda, -e	sinwa, -e	lǣswa, -e
G	synna	gierda	sinwa	lǣswa
D	synnum	gierdum	sinwum	lǣswum
A	synna, -e	gierda, -e	sinwa, -e	lǣswa, -e

§ 37 The i-stems

Nouns in this class can be any gender. In late Old English, the masculine and neuter nouns joined the a-stems; the feminine nouns joined the ō-stems. The paradigm is for *stice* 'stitch' and *giest* 'guest' (masc.), *spere* 'spear' (neuter) and *dǣd* 'deed' (fem.).

	stice	g(i)est	spere	dǣd
N sg.	stice	g(i)est	spere	dǣd
G	stices	g(i)estes	speres	dǣde
D	stice	g(i)este	spere	dǣde
A	stice	g(i)est	spere	dǣd
N pl.	stice, -as	g(i)estas	speru, -o	dǣde, -a
G	stica	g(i)esta	spera	dǣda
D	sticum	g(i)estum	sperum	dǣdum
A	stice, -as	g(i)estas	speru, -o	dǣde, -a

Remark: Abstract nouns ending in -*scipe* are declined like masculine nouns with a short syllable.

§ 38 The u-stems

Nouns beloning to this class are either feminine or masculine. In late Old English, feminine nouns join the ō-stems, masculine nouns the a-stems. The paradigm is for *sunu* 'son' and *feld* 'field' (masc.) as well as *duru* 'door' and *hand* (fem.).

	short	long	short	long
N sg.	sunu, -o, -a	feld	duru	hand
G	suna	felda, -es	dura	handa
D	suna, -u, -o	felda, -e	dura	handa
A	sunu, -o, -a	feld	dura	hand
N pl.	suna, -u, -o	felda, -as	dura	handa
G	suna	felda	dura	handa
D	sunum	feldum	durum	handum
A	suna, -u, -o	felda, -as	dura	handa

§ 39 The n-stems

Nouns belonging to this group are either feminine or masculine; there are only two neuter nouns, *ēage* and *ēare*. The paradigm is for *hunta* (masc.) 'hunter', *flēa* (masc.) 'flea', *ēage* (neuter) 'eye', *tunge* (fem.) 'tongue' and *bēo* (fem.) 'bee'.

		contracted			contracted
N sg.	hunta	flēa	ēage	tunge	bēo
G	huntan	flēan	ēagan	tungan	bēon
D	huntan	flēan	ēagan	tungan	bēon
A	huntan	flēan	ēage	tungan	bēon
N pl.	huntan	flēan	ēagan	tungan	bēon
G	huntena	flēana	ēagena	tungena	bēona
D	huntum	flēa(u)m	ēagum	tungum	bēom
A	huntan	flēan	ēagan	tungan	bēon

Remark: Many feminine nouns with a short vowel end in -*u* in the nominative singular (similar to nouns with short vowels belonging to the ō-stems).

§ 40 The r-stems

Only five nouns belong to this class, all expressing family relationship: brother, daughter, sister, father and mother. Brother, mother and daughter show i-mutation in the dative singular: *brēþer, mēder, dehter.*

	masculine		feminine		
N sg.	fæder	brōþor	mōdor	dohtor	sweostor
G	fæder, -eres	brōþor	mōdor	dohtor	sweostor
D	fæder	brēþer	mēder	dehter	sweostor
A	fæder	brōþor	mōdor	dohtor	sweostor
N pl.	fæderas	brōþor, brōþru	mōdor, mōdru, -dra	dohtor	sweostor
G	fædera	brōþra	mōdra	dohtra	sweostra
D	fæderum	brōþrum	mōdrum	dohtrum	sweostrum
A	fæderas	brōþor, brōþru	mōdor, mōdru, -dra	dohtor	sweostor

§ 41 The nt-stems

Nouns belonging to this group are masculine as a rule; feminine nouns are extremely rare. Originally, these nouns were present participles used as nouns. The paradigm illustrates the declension of *frēond* 'friend' (the verbal basis is *frēogan* 'to love').

N sg.	frēond	N pl.	frīend, frēond, -as
G	frēondes	G	frēonda
D	frīend, frēonde	D	frēondum
A	frēond	A	frīend, frēond, -as

§ 42 The s-stems

Only a few neuter nouns belong to this class. The paradigm illustrates the declension of *lamb* and *cild* 'child'.

N sg.	lamb	cīld	N pl.	lambru	cīld, cīldru
G	lambes	cīldes	G	lambra	cīldra
D	lambe	cīlde	D	lambrum	cīldrum
A	lamb	cīld	A	lambru	cīld, cīldru

Remark: The variation between long and short *i* is due to late Old English lengthening (see § 12). – The *s* of the 's-stems' appears as *r* in Old English (see § 30).

§ 43 The t-stems

Only a very few nouns from this class have been preserved. The most important are:
hæle 'hero', masculine:

N sg.	hæle, hæleþ	N pl.	hæleþ (later also hæleþas)
G	hæleþes	G	hæleþa
D	hæleþe	D	hæleþum
A	hæleþ	A	hæleþ (later also hæleþas)

The masculine noun *mōnað* 'month' is conjugated similarly to *hæle*; however, syncope (see § 21) occurs when the declensional suffix is syllabic: *mōnðes, mōnðe* etc. The paradigm for *mæg(e)þ* 'maiden', feminine and *ealu* 'ale', neuter, is:

NA sg.	mægeþ, mægþ	NA pl.	mæg(e)þ	NA sg.	ealu
GD	mægeþ	G	mægþa	GD	ealoþ
		D	mægþum	G pl.	ealeþa

§ 44 Athematic Nouns

Athematic nouns can be feminine or masculine. The paradigm is for *fōt* (masc.) 'foot', *hnutu* (fem.) 'nut' and *mūs* (fem.) 'mouse'. Athematic nouns regularly show i-mutation in the dative singular and nominative and accusative plural. This class is also called *radical consonant declension*.

N sg.	fōt	hnutu	mūs
G	fōtes	hnute	mūse
D	fēt	hnyte	mȳs
A	fōt	hnutu	mūs
N pl.	fēt	hnyte	mȳs
G	fōta	hnuta	mūsa
D	fōtum	hnutum	mūsum
A	fēt	hnyte	mȳs

Commentary:

1. The genitive singular of some feminine nouns with a long vowel ends either in -*e* or follows the dative, as for example in *bōc* 'book', genitive singular either *bēc* or *bōce*; similarly *burg, byr(i)g, burge* 'town, castle'.
2. There is only one neuter noun: *scrūd* 'garment, shroud' which usually shows i-mutation in the dative singular: *scrȳd* (however, *scrūde* is also recorded). The nominative and accusative plural do not show i-mutation: *scrūd*; the genitive plural is *scrūda*.

§ 45 Classes of Nouns in Middle English

As has already been pointed out in § 33, the system of nouns was considerably simplified in Middle English. Nonetheless, nouns in early Middle English can be traced back to the major inflectional classes in Old English:
- nouns originally belonging to the vocalic stems usually have a plural ending in -*s*;
- nouns originally belonging to the n-stems have a plural ending in -*n*, the singular usually occurs without -*n*;
- nouns originally belonging to the athematic declension have a plural indicated by a mutated vowel; i-mutation in the singular has been levelled.

§ 46 Early Middle English Paradigms

The paradigm below indicates the major types; the properties of the individual groups are explained in the commentary.

	group I	group Ia	group Ib	group II	group III
	a-stem	ja-stem	ō-stem	n-stem	athematic
N sg.	stoon	ende	soule	name	foot
G	stoones	endes	soules	name(n)	footes
(D)	stoone	ende	soule	name(n)	foote
(A)	stoon	ende	soule	name(n)	foot
N pl.	stoones	endes	soules	namen	feet
G	stoones	endes	soules	namen, -ene	feet, -es
(D)	stoones	endes	soules	namen	feet
(A)	stoones	endes	soules	namen	feet

Commentary:
1. The monosyllabic noun *stoon* was an a-stem whereas the bisyllabic noun *ende* was a ja-stem. Later, *ende* was subject to apocope (see § 22) and became monosyllabic.
2. The noun *soule* was an ō-stem. Originally this noun ended in the consonant -*l*; however, the vocalic ending of the accusative singular has been carried over to the nominative.
3. The noun *name* belonged to the n-stems in Old English. As a consequence of apocope (see § 22), practically all nouns joined the group with plurals in -*s*; Modern English *oxen* is the only exception.
4. In group III, *foot* was an athematic noun. Since the crucial difference between singular and plural was signalled by the mutated vowel, the mutated vowel was abolished in the singular. Beginning in early Middle English, some athematic nouns joined the group with plurals in -*s*, as for example *book* and *nut*. Why this unusual marking of the plural has been retained in some nouns while it was abolished in others may be explained by differences in frequency in everyday language. In the predominantly rural communities, the plural forms *feet, geese, lice, mice, men* and *women* were certainly used with higher frequency than the 'learned' word *book*.
5. Beginning in late Old English, word-final *n* disappears in the northern dialects. In Middle English times, nouns in northern texts chiefly show the features of group I and III.
6. Nouns following group II are rarely found in texts which originated in the Midlands.
7. In the conservative dialects of the southern areas, all inflectional groups can be encountered as late as the 14th century.

§ 47 Late Middle English and Modern English Paradigms

In addition to groups I and III, not counting the single noun in group II (oxen), late Middle and early Modern English nouns show the following features:

– plurals in -r going back to the Old English s-stems, as for example *child – childer*, later *children* with -en added from the n-stems;

– zero-plurals as in Modern English *deer* and *folk*, and *horse* in Early Modern English; these can be traced back to neuter nouns with long vowels, as illustrated above in the paradigm for *word* (see § 35);

– 'mixed' plurals, as in 'children' (above) or as in Modern English *brother* and *brethren* (with i-mutation and -en). The potential of two available plurals can be used for the purposes of semantic differentiation: *brothers* versus *brethren;*

– 'pluralia tantum', such as *breeches, spectacles, hosen* often result from technological development, although the precursor of 'breeches' is Old English *brōc* 'covering for the leg', plural *brēc*.

Adjectives

§ 48 Introduction

Indo-European languages have different declensions for adjectives. In Latin, for example, adjectives are declined like nouns, following either the vocalic or consonantal declension. In Old English, the *strong declension* of adjectives comes from the original vocalic declension of nouns, but a few endings from the pronominal system have been added. An innovation in all Germanic languages is the creation of a *weak declension*. The use of these two declensions depended on the syntactic and semantic context in which adjectives appeared. The *weak declension* was used after a definite article, demonstrative or possessive pronoun; in all other cases the *strong declension* is used. Note that *ōþer* is always declined strong in Old English and comparatives are always declined weak; superlatives can be both. This differentiation survived into early Middle English but only for monosyllabic adjectives ending with a consonant, and only in so far as the categories case, gender, and number were still in use.

Adjectives are declined according to *case, number* and *gender* of the noun they describe. They can be used attributively (*the green house*) and as complement (*the house is green*). In Old English, adjectives used as complement were declined strong, if at all.

Apart from the four irregular adjectives, *comparison* in Old English was shown by means of suffixes. Occasionally, adjectives show i-mutation in the comparative and superlative, as for example *eald – ieldra – ieldesta* (old – older/elder – oldest/eldest). In Middle English, a third means of comparison entered the language, probably due to French influence: the use of *more – most* for comparatives and superlatives (cf. French *plus – le plus*).

§ 49 The Strong Declension

The endings of the strong declension are derived from a mixture of the *a*- and *ō-stems* and the endings of demonstrative pronouns (italicised in the paradigm below). The paradigm shows declensions for all three genders. The three examples *gōd* 'good', *glæd* 'glad' and *hālig* 'holy' have been chosen because they show different phenomena which can occur in the declension of adjectives (see below).

	masc.	neuter	fem.
N sg.	gōd	glæd	hālig-u, -o
G	gōd-es	glad-es	hālig-*re*
D	gōd-*um*	glad-*um*	hālig-*re*
A	gōd-*ne*	glæd	hālg-e
I	gōd-e	glad-e	
N pl.	gōd-*e*	glad-u, -o	hālg-a, -e
G	gōd-*ra*	glæd-*ra*	hālig-*ra*
D	gōd-um	glad-um	hālg-um
A	gōd-e	glad-u, -o	hālg-a, -e

The following exceptions should be observed:
– Polysyllabic adjectives with a long root vowel show syncope (see § 21); see the paradigm for *hāligu*.
– For more information on the different vowel qualities in *glæd* see § 2.
– -*wa*-/-*wō-stem* adjectives have -*w*- when the declension ending begins with a vowel (i. e. nominative *geolu* but genitive *geolwes* and accusative feminine *geolwe* 'yellow').
– Adjectives with word-final -*h* may lose their *h* and contract (see for example nominative *hēah* 'high' and dative plural *hēam*, accusative singular masculine *hēan*, *hēanne* (O 11/40), comparative *hīerran* (O 5/52) in contrast to *hēahne* (O 6/143)).

In Middle English, some traces of the strong declension of adjectives can be found in early southern texts, for example -*es* for genitive singular masculine and neuter as well as -*re* for genitive and dative singular feminine and genitive plural, -*ne* for accusative singular masculine. However, these endings disappeared in late Middle English.

   In the eastern and northern dialects, monosyllabic adjectives ending in a consonant usually do not have an ending in the singular, whereas the plural often ends in -*e*, as for example in *go(o)d* (singular) and *go(o)de* (plural). However, with the loss of word-final -*e* in late Middle English (see apocope, § 22) number was no longer marked for adjectives.

§ 50 The Weak Declension

The inflectional endings of the weak declension are those of the nouns belonging to the n-stems. The use of the weak declension has been indicated above (see § 48) and will be discussed in more detail in § 102.

	sg. mask.	sg. neuter	sg. fem.	plural
N	gōd-a	gōd-e	gōd-e	gōd-an
G	gōd-an	gōd-an	gōd-an	gōd-ra, -ena
D	gōd-an	gōd-an	gōd-an	gōd-um
A	gōd-an	gōd-e	gōd-an	gōd-an

Remark: The genitive plural usually has the ending *-ra* just as in the strong declension. However, occasionally the ending *-ena* can be found, as for example in A 5/33: *gōdena wiotena*.

Only a few traces of the weak declension can be found in Middle English. Monosyllabic adjectives ending in a consonant may show word-final *-e* in the singular as well as in the plural: *go(o)de* (singular and plural). In late Middle English the loss of word-final *-e* (apocope, see § 22) levelled the differences between strong and weak declension.

Remark: Occasionally adjectives in post-position may show a marking for the plural; this is probably due to the influence of French, as for example in M 4/36: *uayre and likerouses* (the Middle English text is based on a French original).

§ 51 Comparison of Adjectives

As pointed out in § 48, there are three modes of comparison in English. Old English had two of these, comparison by suffixes and comparison by means of other roots. In Middle English, the so-called 'analytic comparison' gained ground, probably a result of French influence.

Comparison by suffixes

The suffix for the *comparative* in Old English, *-ra*, is based on two earlier suffixes: *-ōza-* and *-iza-*. The second suffix causes i-mutation with certain adjectives, as can be seen in the table below. The comparative is declined according to the weak declension.

In Middle English, the suffix for the comparative is *-re*, later *-er*. In early Middle English texts, i-mutation can still be found, as for example in M 11/35: *elder*.

The suffixes for the *superlative* in Old English are *-est-* and *-ost-* and are based on two earlier suffixes: *-ist-* and *-ōst-*. Under the influence of *-ist-*, the superlative of certain adjectives shows i-mutation (see table). The superlative can be declined according to the strong or the weak declension (see § 49–50).

In Middle English, the ending for the superlative is *-est* and early texts still have superlatives showing i-mutation. Except for Modern English *elder, eldest*, i-mutation in the comparison of adjectives has been levelled.

Paradigm for Old English

positive	comparative	superlative	
blind	blindra	blindost(a)	'blind'
hālig	hāligra	hāl(i)gost(a)	'holy'
blīþe	blīþra	blīþost(a)	'joyful'
gearu	gearora	gearwost(a)	'ready'

with i-mutation:

eald	ieldra	ieldest(a)	'old'
geong	gingra, geongra	gingest(a)	'young'
hēah	hīer(r)a	hīehst(a)	'high'
lang	lengra	lengest(a)	'long'
sceort	scyrtra	scyrtest(a)	'short'

Some adjectives, derived from adverbs and prepositions, have the infix *-m-* in the superlative instead of *-est, -ost*, as for example *forma* 'the first, foremost', *meduma* 'the middlemost', *hindema* 'the hindmost'. However, frequently the suffix *-est* is added so that *-mest* became the typical suffix for the superlative.

Irregular Comparison

Only four adjectives derive their comparative and superlative from a different root. These are the two adjectives involving moral judgement: *good* and *evil* and the two adjectives expressing degree: *much* and *little*. It should be noted that in many other Indo-European languages these four adjectives also show this 'irregularity' in comparison, as for example in Latin: *bonus – melior – optimus*; *malus – peior – pessimus*; *magnus – maior – maximus*; and *parvus – minor – minimus*.

The paradigms for Old and Middle English are:

positive	comparative	superlative
gōd	bet(e)ra, bettra; sĕlra, sĕlla	bet(e)st, betsta; sēlest(a), sēlost(a)
yfel	wi(e)rsa, wyrsa	wi(e)rrest(a), wyrresta, wi(e)rst(a), wyrst(a)
micel	māra	mǣst(a)
lȳtel	lǣssa	lǣst(a)
good	bet(t)re, better, bet	best
evel	werse, wyrse, wurse	werst, wyrst, wurst
muchel, mochel	mare, more, ma, mo	mast, most
littel	lesse, lasse	leste.

Analytic Comparison

This mode of comparison, with *more* marking the comparative and *most* the superlative, was not a regular feature of Old English. Occasionally, however, periphrastic comparisons can be found in late Old English, marking the comparative by *swiþor* or *bet* and the superlative by *swiþost* or *betst*. From the 14th century onwards, mono- and polysyllabic adjectives, irrespective of their provenance, increasingly showed comparatives with *ma, mo, mare, more* and superlatives with *mast, most*. In many instances, particularly in poetry, metrical and stylistic issues will have guided the choice between suffix comparison and analytic comparison. The tendency of avoiding polysyllabic words also favoured analytic comparison.

Adverbs

§ 52 General Remarks

Adverbs in English are either *primary* or *secondary* adverbs. Primary adverbs are either derived from pronouns, as for example *þā* 'then, there', or from prepositions, as for example *inne* 'inside'. Secondary adverbs are either derived from adjectives or from nouns. Apart from the derivational suffix for secondary adverbs, no major changes have taken place in the history of this word class.

§ 53 Primary Adverbs

Primary adverbs refer to time and place. The system for Old English was very elaborate, as can be seen in the table below. Moreover, primary adverbs can be used to introduce relative clauses: Old English *ðær*, Middle English *where* (see § 123).

In Old English, adverbs of place are differentiated according to the basic perspectives relating to place, a feature which has survived into Modern English, where it is usually associated with formal style.

	place where	place to which	place from which
'there'	ðǣr	ðider	ðonan
'where?'	hwǣr	hwider	hwonan
'here'	hēr	hider	heonan
'after'	æfter		æftan
'inside'	inne	inn	innan
'outside'	ūte	ūt	ūtan
'above'	uppe	upp	uppan, ufan
'northward'	norð		norðan
'southward'	sūð		sūðan
'eastward'	ēast		ēastan
'westward'	west		westan

In Middle English, *there* and *where* occur with high frequency. In addition, many new relative adverbs were derived on the basis *where* followed by a preposition: *wheremid* 'with which', *whereof* 'from / of which', *wheron* 'upon which', and so on (see Middle English Glossary under 'where').

§ 54 Secondary Adverbs

In Old English, adverbs were usually derived from adjectives by adding the suffix *-e*, as for example *heard, lang* (adjectives) and *hearde, lange* (adverbs). When the adjective already ends in *-e* the adverb has the same form, as in *clǣne* 'clean'. Adverbs could be derived from adjectives ending in *-lic* by adding *-e*; gradually *-līce* became regarded as an adverbial suffix. Thus, two adverbs could be derived from the same base: *hearde* and *heardlīce*. This became the basis for the Modern English semantic differentiation between *hard* and *hardly*: 'Working hard or hardly working?'

Some adverbs were derived from adjectives by adding the endings *-unga, -inga* and *-enga*, as for example *dearnunga* 'secretly', A 3/11: *eallinga* 'entirely', A 8/14: *fǣringa* 'suddenly'.

Adverbs could also be derived from inflected forms of adjectives, especially from the genitive singular, as for example *ealles* 'entirely', *micles* 'much', or from the dative, as for example *miclum* 'much' and *lȳtlum* 'little'.

Alternatively, adverbs could be derived from the inflected forms of nouns, especially from the genitive singular, as for example *dæges* 'by day' and *nihtes* 'by night', *(un)ðonces* '(un)willingly'. Derivation from the dative plural is also frequent, as for example *hwīlum* 'at times' and also from compounds ending in -*mǣlum*, such as *dropmǣlum* 'in drops', *stæpmǣlum* 'gradually'. Occasionally, adverbs were derived from the accusative singular of an adjective in combination with a noun, as for example *ealneg* 'always' (< 'ealne weg' as in O 4/2, 8 and O 5/56).

In Middle English, secondary adverbs were mainly derived from adjectives by adding -*ly*, which might be a shortened form of Old English -*līce* or may derive from the Scandinavian -*ligr*. Some of the adverbs derived from nouns can still be found in Middle English, such as *whilom* 'formerly' (M 13/279), *nihtes* 'at night' (M 10.1/11).

§ 55 Comparison of Adverbs

Only adverbs derived from adjectives by adding the suffix -*e* can be compared. The suffix for the comparative is -*or* and for the superlative it is -*ost* and occasionally -*est*: for example *hearde* – *heardor* – *heardost* and *longe* – *leng* – *lengest*, showing the influence of i-mutation in the comparative and superlative. Some traces of the comparative with the influence of i-mutation can be found in early Middle English texts, see for example *leng* (M 5/15).

The comparative of some adverbs had been derived by the suffix *-iz* which, before it disappeared, caused i-mutation. Examples are: *well* – *bet* 'well – better', *yfele* – *wi(e)rs, wyrs* 'evil – worse', *longe* – *leng* 'long – longer', *ēaþe* – *īeð, ȳð* 'easily – more easily'.

In Middle English, the comparative usually ends in -*er* and the superlative in -*est*, for example *longer, longest*. In Modern English -*er* and -*est* can only be used with monosyllabic adverbs; otherwise *more* and *most* are used.

Pronouns

§ 56 Introduction

In comparison to Modern English, the system of pronouns in Old and Middle English shows a much higher level of complexity, especially as regards feminine singular and third person plural personal pronouns and demonstratives. Old English has a fairly regular system of pronouns; this system, however, developed in different directions in the various Middle English dialects. As a result, there is a great variety of forms in Middle English which can have different meanings in different dialects. The personal pronoun for the third person nominative singular feminine in Old English was *hēo*; the diphthong developed into *ē* in Middle English and the form became therefore identical with the pronoun for the third person nominative singular masculine *hē*. Since it is absolutely necessary to differentiate genders in the third person singular (see for example M 9/107, where confusion can arise) it was necessary to find the distinct forms which became *he* and *she*. As can be seen in the tables, many different paths were taken in the various dialects until *she* became the leading form. How exactly *she* developed remains a mystery.

The plural forms present fewer difficulties. The forms beginning with a dental, predominant in the North and the East Midlands dialects as a result of Scandinavian influence, eventually replaced the Old English forms beginning with *h-* since they show a stronger contrast to the singular.

The dual forms (first and second person – primarily used in poetry) survived into the 13th century until they finally disappeared. An innovation in Middle English was the differentiation between familiar *thee, thou* and polite *you, ye*, which probably resulted from French and Norman influence.

Old and Middle English did not have standard forms for the reflexive pronouns; the modern forms developed only gradually. Ordinary dative and accusative forms were used with reflexive meaning, as for example *hine werede* 'he defended himself' (O 2/11–12); *tilen him so ðe sowles fode* 'provide himself with food for the soul' (M 2/34). Reflexivity, however, could also be expressed by an inflected form of *self* following the pronoun, as for example '*hine sylfne underþeodde*' (no one) subjected himself' (O 3/13); *Nu loke euerich man toward himseluen* 'now consider yourself' (M 3/39–40).

§ 57 Personal Pronouns

First person pronouns: singular

	Old English	Middle English	Modern English
N	ĭc	ich, I	I
G	mīn	min, mi	my, mine
D	mĕ̄	mĕ̄	(to) me
A	mĕ̄	mĕ̄	me

Remark: In Middle English times, northern texts may also have *ih* and *ik*, developed from Scandinavian *ek*.

First person pronouns: plural

	Old English	Middle English	Modern English
N	wĕ̄	wē	we
G	ūre	ūr(e), our(e)	our
D	ūs	ŭs, ous	(to) us
A	ūs	ŭs, ous	us

Second person pronouns: singular

	Old English	Middle English	Modern English
N	þŭ̄	þŭ̄, þou	you (thou)
G	þĭn	þĭ(n), thi(n)	your (thine)
D	þĕ̄	þĕ̄, thee, the	(to) you
A	þĕ̄	þĕ̄, thee, the	you

Second person pronouns: plural

	Old English	Middle English	Modern English
N	gĕ̄	ʒĕ̄, yee, ye	you
G	īower, ēower	ēower, ʒūre, your(e)	your
D	īow, ēow	eow, eu, iu	(to) you
A	īow, ēow	eow, eu, iu	you

Remark: Consult the Middle English glossary under *you* for further variants of the second person plural.

First and second person dual: 'we two; you two'

N	wit	git
G	uncer	incer
D	unc	inc
A	unc(it)	inc(it)

Third person pronouns: masculine singular

	Old English	Middle English	Modern English
N	hĕ̄	hĕ̄, ha, a	he
G	his	his	his
D	him	him	(to) him
A	hine, hiene	him, hine	him

Remark: In Middle English, the nominative singular forms *ha, a* appear in unstressed position only; see Middle English glossary. The accusative singular *hine* can be found only in early southern texts; see Middle English glossary.

Third person pronouns: neuter singular

	Old English	Middle English	Modern English
N	hit	hit, it	it
G	his	his	its
D	him	him	(to) it
A	hit	hit, it	it

Third person pronouns: feminine singular

	Old English	Modern English
N	hīo, hēo	she
G	hi(e)re, hyre	her
D	hi(e)re, hyre	(to) her
A	hī(e)	her

Third person feminine in Middle English

	North	EML	WML, South
N	ȝho, cho, scho	sche, she	heo, hue, ho, he, ha, hi
G		hire, here, hir, her	
D		hir, hire, hure	
A		hir, hire, hure	

Remark: The form *sche* appears in London and in the West from the 14th century onwards. A form typical of western texts of the 14th and 15th centuries is *here*. A feature of early southern texts is *heo*.

Third person pronouns: plural

	Old English	Modern English
N	hī, hīe, hȳ	they
G	hi(e)ra, hiora, heora, hyra	their
D	him, heom	(to) them
A	hīe, hī, hȳ	them

Third person pronouns: plural in Middle English

	North	Midlands	South
N	þai, þay, thai	þei, þeȝ	hy, heo, ho, he, ha, a
G	þayr, thair, thar	heore, her(e), hor, hure, hyr, hire; þeir	hore, hare, heore, hor, here, hure, hire
D	þaim, thaim, thame	heom, hem	hi, his(e), hys, ys, heom, hem, hom, ham
A	þaim, thaim, thame	heom, hem	hi, his(e), hys, ys, heom, hem, hom, ham

Remark: The forms *ha* and *ham* appear in unstressed position only. Starting in the 14th century, *þei* can also be found in the Northwest Midlands and in London.

§ 58 Demonstrative Pronouns

In Old English, there were two types of demonstrative pronouns: one had the function of the definite article, the other was the demonstrative pronoun proper. This system was radically modified in Middle English times: *þe/the* became the definite article. As gender and case were gradually given up, the concept of proximity and distance we have in Modern English *this* and *that* was introduced using the building blocks of the Old English definite article and demonstrative pronoun.

Definite article (the forms in brackets are primarily found in later texts)

	sg. masc.	sg. neuter	sg. fem.	plural
N	sē̆	þæt	sīo, sēo	þā
G	þæs	þæs	þǣre	þāra (þǣra)
D	þǣm (þām)	þǣm (þām)	þǣre	þǣm (þām)
A	þone	þæt	þā	þā
I	þȳ, þon	þȳ, þon		

Demonstrative pronoun (*i* and *y* are interchangeable in later texts)

	sg. masc.	sg. neuter	sg. fem.	plural
N	þĕs	þis	þīos, þēos	þās
G	þis(s)es	þis(s)es	þisse	þissa
D	þis(s)um	þis(s)um	þisse	þis(s)um, þios(s)um
A	þisne	þis	þās	þās
I	þȳs, þīs	þȳs, þīs		

During Middle English times, this highly complex system of demonstrative pronouns was simplified considerably. In early Middle English texts there is still a variety of forms left over from Old English, especially in the generally more conservative southern texts. However, by late Middle English times practically all forms had been reduced to *this, these* (expressing proximity) and *that, those* (expressing distance). For more information about the demonstrative pronouns in the Middle English texts, consult *þa, þane, that, thes, this* and *þos* in the glossary.

§ 59 Interrogative Pronouns

As can be seen in the paradigms below, the forms of the interrogative pronouns *who* and *what* remain largely the same from Old to Middle English.

Old English

N	hwă̄	hwæt
G	hwæs	hwæs
D	hwǣm (hwām)	hwǣm (hwām)
A	hwone	hwæt
I		hwȳ, hwī

Commentary:

1. In addition to the above interrogatives, Old English also had the following pronouns, which could be used both as noun and adjective: *hwæþer* 'which of the two', *hwelc/hwilc* 'which' and *swelc* 'such (a)'. They were declined as strong adjectives.
2. It should be noted that *hwæt* followed by a genitive means 'what a' (*hwæt monna* 'what a man').
3. Additional instrumental forms include *hū* 'how' (adverb) and *hwon, hwan* (in adverbial phrases): *tō hwon, for hwon* 'why' (O 3/147).

Middle English

N	whō, wō, huo; whā, quā, quhā	N	hwat, what, wat; quat, quhat; hwet
G	whōs(e); quās	G	whōs(e), quās, whes
D	whōm, wōm; whām,	D	whōm; quām; what,
A	whōm, wōm; whām,	A	hwat, what, wat; quat, quhat; hwet

Commentary:

1. As in Old English, the additional forms *wheþer, whilche, whiche, wulche, whuche, whilk* and *quilk* were used.
2. The interrogative adverb in Middle English is *why* from Old English *hwī, hwȳ*.

§ 60 Possessive Pronouns

The genitive forms of the personal pronouns were used as possessive pronouns. First and second person forms were declined as strong adjectives. Third person forms were not declined at all. Starting in the 15th century, the northern forms *hers, theirs, ours* and *yours* were used in the south as well.

§ 61 Indefinite Pronouns

Indefinite pronouns can be used as both noun and adjective. In Old English, they were declined as strong adjectives.
The major Old English forms are:

āhwā, āhwelc, āhwæt 'someone, something'
(e)all 'all'
ǣlc 'each'
ǣnig 'any'; *nǣnig* 'no'
(n)āwuht, (n)ōwuht, (n)āwiht, (n)ōwiht, (n)auht, (n)āht, (n)ōht 'no, none; some(thing)'
gehwæþer, ǣghwæþer, ǣgþer 'both'
nāthwā, nāthwelc, samhwelc 'someone, anyone'
(n)ōhwæþer, (n)āwþer, (n)ōwþer, (n)auþer, (n)āþer 'neither; either (one)'
se ilca, se sylfa 'the same'
sum 'some, a'
swelc, swilc, swylc 'such (a)'

The major Middle English forms are:

al 'all'   *everychon* 'each one, everyone'
ani, any 'any'   *many, mony* 'many, many a one'
auȝt, oght 'anything'   *on, an* 'someone'
both(e), baþe 'both'   *non(e), no, nan(e), na* 'none'
ech, ich, alc 'each'   *other* 'other'
echon 'each one'   *som(e), sum* 'some'
eyþer 'either'   *swich, swilk, such* 'such'
everych 'each, each one, every'   *þelli, þulli* 'such'

Numerals

§ 62 Introduction

Numerals include nouns, adjectives and adverbs. Like all nouns and adjectives some numerals were inflected in Old English and early Middle English as well.

In addition to cardinals and ordinals, there were multiplicatives (built with the Old English suffix *-feald*, Middle English *-fold*), which were used as adjectives: *ānfeald, twīefeald* and so on.

Numerals used as adverbs include Old English *ǣne, tuwa/twie, þriwa* 'once, twice, thrice' or the periphrastic forms on the basis of *sīþ* 'time': *ǣne sīþa, -e, twǣm, þrim, fīf, twentigum sīðum* etc. In Middle English, adverbial numerals ended in *-es*: *ones, anes, twies* etc.

§ 63 Cardinals

In Old and early Middle English, the cardinals 1–3 were inflected, whereas 4–19 were only inflected when used as nouns. Cardinals used as nouns are followed by a genitive, see for example *xxxi wintra* 'thirty-one years' (O 2/6).

	Old English	Middle English
1	ān	an, on, oo
2	twā	twa, twei, tway, two
3	þrī	þri, þrie, þreo, þro, þree
4	fēower	feower, feor, fower, four, foure
5	fīf	fif; infl. five
6	siex, syx	sex, six; infl. sixe, sexe
7	seofon	seouen, seuen; infl. seouene, seuene
8	eahta	ehte, eight(e); acht, aght, aught
9	nigon	niȝen, niȝe, nin(e), nēȝen, neen
10	tīen, tȳn	teon, teen, ten; infl. teene, tene
11	en(d)le(o)fan	endleue(ne), enleue(ne), elleue(ne)
12	twelf	twelf; infl. twelue, tweolf, tweolue
13	þrēotȳne, -tēne	þreoten(e), þretten(e), þritten(e)
14	fēowertāne, -tēne	fourtene
20	twĕntig	twenti
30	þrītig	þritti, þretti; thirti
40	fēowertig	feowerti, fowerti, feorti, fourti
50	fīftig	fifti
60	siextig, syxtig	sexti, sixti, three score
70	(hund)seofontig	seoventi, seventi, hundseventi
80	(hund)eahtatig	eiȝteti, eiȝti; also fourscore
90	(hund)nigontig	niȝenti, ninti
100	hundtēontig, hundred	hundred, hundrid, hondred, hundreþ
110	hundendlyftig	hundred and ten
120	hundtwelftig, hundtwentig	hundred and twenti
200	tū hund	two hondred
300	þrīo hund	þre hondred
1000	þūsend	þousend, þousind, þousand, þousond

Old English *ān* is declined as a strong adjective; the accusative usually appears as *ænne*.

Paradigm for *twā* and *þrīo*:

	masc.	neuter	fem.	masc.	neuter	fem.
N/A	twēgen	tū, twā	twā	þrī(e)	þrīo, þrēo	þrīo, þrēo
G		twēg(e)a, twēgra			þrīora, þrēora	
D		twǣm, twām			þrim (þrīm, þēom)	

Declined forms of 1–3 may also occur in Middle English, especially in southern texts. Old English *bā* ('both') becomes Middle English *ba*, *bō* (M 10.6/22), *beie*, *baþe*, *boþe*.

§ 64 Ordinals

Ordinals are declined as weak adjectives, except for *ōðer*, which is strong. In Middle English, the declensional endings were reduced to *-e*.

	Old English	Middle English
1st	forma, formesta, fyrmest(a)	furste, firste, uerste, ferste
2nd	ōðer, æfterra	oþer, secounde
3rd	þridda	þrid(d)e, þrede, þirde, þerd
4th	fēorþa	feorþe, ferþe; fourþe; ferde, firde, furde, uerþe
5th	fīfta	fifte, fifthe
6th	siexta, syxta, sixta	sexte, sixte
7th	seofoða	se(o)ve(n)þe, sefþe, sefte, sevende, sevente
8th	eahtoða	ehtuþe, eiʒtiþe, eiʒt, aʒtþe
9th	nigoða	niʒeþe, niʒhende, neʒende, ni(e)nd, nin(e)þe
10th	tēoða	teoþe, teþe, tenþe, tēnde
11th	endlifta	endlefte, ellefte, ellevende, enlevenþ
12th	twelfta	tweolfte, twelfte
13th	þrēotēoða	þreteoþe, -teþe, -tenþe, -tende
20th	twentigoða	twentiʒeþe, -tiʒþe, -tiþe, -ties

In manuscripts, higher ordinals appear in Roman numerals. Starting in the 15th century, Arabic numerals were also used.

Verbs

§ 65 General Remarks

A descriptive model for Modern English verbs is a highly complex undertaking if the historical perspective is not taken into account. However, when considering the historical perspective, most, if not all, problems can be solved quite easily.

Verbs can be inflected ('conjugated'); therefore, a detailed description of the parameters pertaining to conjugation is necessary. Since these parameters (*grammatical categories*) have changed considerably in the history of English, a concise discussion of their origins and development will also be provided.

The grammatical categories pertaining to verbs in English are:

1. *tense:* present and preterite; this category was considerably modified from Old to Modern English;
2. *mood:* indicative, imperative and subjunctive; as verb endings began to disappear in late Old English, the subjunctive mood became indistinguishable from the indicative; modal verbs were increasingly used to express the subjunctive;
3. *number:* singular and plural; originally signalled by means of different conjugational endings, number was increasingly by the subject;
4. *person:* 1st, 2nd and 3rd singular present indicative were differentiated in Old and Middle English; there was only one form for the plural;

5. *voice:* active; the passive was expressed by periphrastic constructions;
6. *non-finite forms:* two infinitives and both the present and past participles.

From Old to Modern English, verbs can be divided into *strong verbs*, *weak verbs*, *preterite-present verbs*, and *irregular verbs*. This division is based on the way in which the important category *tense* is marked. This system can best be understood by looking at the way the preterite is marked in contrast to the present:

1. In *strong verbs* the category tense is marked by different vowel qualities and quantities, as in *write–wrote–written*; these regular differences are called *ablaut*. Strong verbs can be divided into *seven classes*.
2. In *weak verbs* the category tense is marked by adding a *dental suffix* (-(e)d, -t is appended to the stem) in the preterite, as in *kiss–kissed–kissed*. Weak verbs are an innovation in Germanic and can be divided into *three classes*.
3. In *preterite-present verbs* the category tense is marked by both ablaut and dental suffix; past tense forms can also convey the concept 'modality', as for example in *may–might*.
4. In *irregular verbs* the category tense is marked in various ways. There are only four irregular verbs in English: *to be, to do, to go* and *(to) will*. With the exception of *to do*, an innovation in Germanic, the other irregular verbs were inherited (together with their 'irregularities') from Indo-European, see for example the verbs *esse, ire* and *velle* in Latin.

With reference to *strong verbs*, it is necessary to differentiate *four tense stems*. These are marked by different vowel qualities and quantities. All finite and non-finite forms can be derived from these four stems.

With reference to *weak verbs*, it is necessary to differentiate *three tense stems*. The second and third of these is marked by a dental suffix which originally could be syllabic, as originally in 'kiss-ed', or non-syllabic, as in 'kep-t'.

While it is quite easy to differentiate the individual classes of both strong and weak verbs in Old English, differentiation is a decidedly more difficult undertaking in both Middle and Modern English. Some of these difficulties result from the changes in vowel quality and quantity from Old to Modern English. Qualitative and quantitative change as well as the loss of inflectional endings have also obscured the once clearly marked differentiation between present and preterite in relation to *strong verbs*. It was therefore necessary to adopt new means to convey the crucial difference between present and preterite (see below).

The dental suffix used to differentiate between present and preterite in *weak verbs* was not subject to many significant changes in the history of English. The changes which took place only led to a less clear differentiation of the original three classes of weak verbs.

The four *irregular verbs* are a stable system in the history of English. *Preterite-present verbs* can also be considered as a relatively stable system, even though there have been a few losses and modifications (e. g. *witan* 'to know').

The history of *strong verbs* is very different. Originally there were some 300 strong verbs (not counting forms with prefixes); only about half that number can now be found in Modern English. Many originally strong verbs were increasingly conjugated weak; even highly frequent verbs like *help* have adopted weak preterite forms. In general, *weak verbs* can be said to be the only productive verbal system in English. Most loan verbs, whether borrowed from Scandinavian or Norman, follow the pattern of weak verbs. Today, the pattern of weak verbs is used for all new creations.

Strong Verbs

§ 66 The System

In Old English, strong verbs had four *tense stems* from which a complete conjugational paradigm can be derived. These stems are:

1. the present stem, from which all finite and non-finite present tense forms are derived;
2. a first preterite stem for the 1st and 3rd person singular preterite indicative;
3. a second preterite stem from which all other finite preterite forms are derived;
4. a fourth stem for the past participle which could be used with or without the prefix *ge-*, provided the verb itself did not have a prefix.

On the basis of the inherited ablaut patterns, strong verbs in Old English can be differentiated into 6 classes. Originally reduplicating verbs (doubling of the first syllable; cf. Latin: *tang-ere – te-ti-gi*) are listed under 'class' 7.

The second and third person present indicative show i-mutation if the vowel is subject to i-mutation. This can be seen in the following examples: *sēon* (infinitive) 'to see', *sēo* (1st singular present indicative) and *siehst, siehþ* (2nd and 3rd singular present indicative).

The quality of the post-vocalic consonant or consonant group can decisively influence both quality and quantity of the preceding accented vowel. Furthermore, certain word-initial consonants can also result in a change of the following vowel. Understanding the system of strong verbs in Old English requires a great familiarity with some of the phonological changes and developments illustrated in the first part of this book. The most important of these are *breaking* (see § 3), *contraction* (see § 12), *i-mutation* (see § 9), and *Verner's Law* (see § 30) as can be seen in the description of the individual classes of strong verbs below. Most of these seeming irregularities were abolished in Middle English times.

In the development from Old to Middle English the following modifications and simplifications are of special importance:

1. Due to the phonological changes in vowel quality and quantity, the originally well-marked contrast between present and preterite became less marked; in some cases, new distinctive patterns were introduced to ensure that this semantically crucial contrast could be maintained.
2. The effects of i-mutation in the 2nd and 3rd person singular present indicative were levelled out.
3. The second singular past indicative was no longer derived from the third tense stem, but from the second.

4. The number of tense stems was later reduced to three, in some instances to two stems. It can be said that a decisive factor in this reduction process was to retain a strong (i. e. qualitative) contrast between present and preterite.
5. The effects of Verner's Law were abolished and Modern English only retains a few instances of Verner's Law in adjectives derived from past participles, such as *forlorn* and *sodden* and in the forms *was – were*.
6. The loss of inflectional endings necessitated the use of an explicit subject so that the distinction *singular* versus *plural*, which was no longer marked by inflectional endings of the predicate, could be taken over by the subject.
7. In Middle English, the prefix *ge-* for past participles was retained at first and then became either *i-* or *y-*. The potential of the prefix could be used by poets if the metre required an extra syllable.

§ 67 Class 1

The basic ablaut pattern for class 1 is

OE	ī–ā–ĭ–ĭ	wrītan – wrāt – writon – (ge)writen
ME	ī–ǭ–ĭ–ĭ	wrīte(n) – wrǭt – wrĭten – (i/y)wrĭten
MnE	i–o–i	write – wrote – written

and originally involved both qualitative and quantitative differentiation.

Commentary:

1. Many class 1 verbs have survived in Middle and Modern English; write, rise, smite and so on.
2. Some verbs show Verner's Law in Old English, for example *snīðan – snāð – snidon – sniden* 'to cut'. The paradigm for Old English *rīsan* is an exception in that the third and fourth tense stems never show Verner's Law.
3. There are also some contracted verbs in this class, for example *þīon/þēon – þāh – þigon – þigen* 'to prosper'.
4. In Middle English, the infinitive and past participle may occur with a long *e*, due to Middle English lengthening.
5. In Modern Standard English the past participle retains word-final *n* for better contrast.
6. Modern English *shrive* shows both strong and weak past tense forms; only the weak preterite is used for example in *glide* and *slide*.
7. The loanwords *rive(n)* 'to split' (Scandinavian) and *strive* (Norman) are rather exceptional because they are conjugated strong.

§ 68 Class 2

The basic ablaut pattern for class 2 is

OE	ēo–ēa–ŭ–ŏ	cēosan – cēas – cŭron – (ge)cŏren
ME	ē–ę̄–ŭ–ǭ	chēse(n) – chę̄s – cŭren/chǭsen – (i/y)cǭren/chǭsen
MnE		choose – chose – chosen

Commentary:

1. Most strong verbs belonging to class 2 have disappeared; others have adopted the dental suffix of the weak verbs for the formation of the preterite; see for example *creep*, Old English *crēopan*: M 13/450, 484 strong preterite; 417 weak preterite. In general, the surviving Modern English forms are not based on the Old English pattern.
2. In Old English, some verbs had *ū* instead of *ēo* in the present stem, as for example *lūcan* 'to lock' and *brūcan* 'to use'.

3. Some verbs show Verner's Law, as for example *cēosan* (as above) and *tēon – tēah – tugon – (ge)togen* and also *sēoðan* 'to seethe'; the past participle can still be found in Modern English: *sodden*.
4. After word-initial palatal /tʃ/ the usual falling diphthong could change to a rising diphthong, as in Old English *cēosan* 'to choose' and Middle English *chēse(n), chōse(n)*.
5. The past participle shows *ō* under the influence of Middle English lengthening.
6. Modern English 'to fly' also belongs to class 2; in Old English, the stems are *flēogan – flēah – flugon – flogen*; the Modern English forms have been influenced by Old English *flēon* 'to flee', also class 2.

§ 69 Class 3

The basic pattern for strong verbs belonging to class 3 is quite simple: *e–æ–u–o*. However, the two consonants which follow the vowel have led to many changes in the later history of these verbs.

When the post-vocalic consonant group starts with a nasal (*m, n*), the pattern is

OE	i–a/o–u-u	bindan – band/bond – bundon – (ge)bunden
ME	ĭ–ă/ŏ–ŭ–ŭ	binde(n) – bǫnd – bounden – (i/y)bounden
MnE	i–ou–ou	bind – bound – bound

with a certain amount of variation in both Middle and Modern English. The differences can be traced back to the second consonant in the group – late Old English lengthening (see § 12) was stable when the consonant group was *-nd* (and originally *-mb*). In contrast, short vowels will be found in Middle and Modern English when the consonant group is *-ng, -nk* and *-mp*, as in *sing – sang – sung* and *drink – drank – drunk*.

The basic pattern is different when the consonant group starts with a liquid (*l, r*):

OE	e/eo/ie–ea–u–o	helpan – healp – hulpon – holpen
ME	e–a–u/o–o	helpe(n) – halp – hulpen – (i/y)holpen
MnE	(e–e–e)	help – helped – helped

and the different vowel qualities in Old English can be explained by breaking (*eo* and *ea*; see § 3) and the influence of word-initial palatal consonants (*ie*; see § 25).

There is a third pattern which involves yet another post-vocalic consonant group:

OE	eo–ea–u–o	feohtan – feaht – fuhton – (ge)fohten
ME	i–au–ou–ou	fighte – faught – foughten – (i/y)foughten
MnE	i–ou–ou	fight – fought – fought

and involves both breaking (see § 3) and the rise of new diphthongs in Middle English (see § 4).

Commentary:
1. Modern English still has a considerable number of verbs from class 3. However, verbs like *climb* and *help* show that, in some cases, the preterite has become weak.
2. In Old English, some verbs show a group of three consonants following the vowel, as for example *bersten* 'to burst'. The group of three consonants was the result of metathesis (see § 28).
3. In Old English, some verbs have the vowel *u* in the present stem; for example *murnan* 'to mourn'.

§ 70 Class 4

The pattern is similar to that in class 3; however, there is only *one* post-vocalic consonant which is either a liquid or a nasal. When followed by a liquid, the patterns are:

OE	e–æ–ǣ–o	beran – bær – bǣron – (ge)boren
ME	ę̄–a–ē–ǭ	bēre(n) – bar – bēren – (i/y)bǭren
MnE	ea–o–o	bear – bore – born

When followed by a nasal, the patterns are irregular:

OE	u–ō–ō–u	cuman – c(w)ōm – c(w)ōmon – cumen
	i–ō–ō/ā–u	niman – nōm – nōmon – numen
ME	o/u–a/ō–ō–o/u	comen/cumen – cam/cōm – cōmen – (i/y)comen/cumen
	i–a/o–ō/ā–u	nimen – na/om – nā/ōmen – nomen
MnE	o–a–o	come – came – come

Commentary:

1. The verb *brecan* also belongs to class 4, although the post-vocalic consonant is *neither* a liquid nor a nasal: brecan – bræc – brǣcon – brocen 'to break'. Modern English *broke, broken* shows that the vowel of the fourth tense stem was chosen for the entire preterite.
2. Modern English has very few verbs belonging to this class; apart from the above forms, *steal – stole – stolen* is an example of the traditional paradigm.

§ 71 Class 5

The pattern is similar to that of classes 3 and 4; in contrast to class 4, the post-vocalic consonant is neither a liquid nor a nasal.

OE	e–æ–ǣ–e	specan – spæc – spǣcon – specen
ME	ę̄–a–ē–ę̄/ǭ	spę̄ken – spak – spę̄ken – (i/y)spę̄ken/spǭken
MnE	e–o–o	speak – spoke – spoken

Commentary:

1. In Old English, some verbs in class 5 show Verner's Law, for example *cweðan – cwæð – cwǣdon – (ge)cweden* 'to speak'.
2. The influence of word-initial palatal consonants can be seen in *giefan – geaf – gēafon – giefen/gefen* 'to give'.
3. Breaking, contraction as well as Verner's Law can be found in *sēon – seah – sāwon – (ge)sewen* 'to see'.
4. In Old English, three verbs show gemination and i-mutation in the present stem: *biddan* 'to bid, ask', *sittan* 'to sit' and *licgan* 'to lie'. While *licgan* and *sittan* are still in use (probably due to their high frequency in everyday language), *biddan* has almost completely been replaced by *pray*.
5. As *speak – spoke – spoken* clearly show, new vowel qualities were introduced for the preterite stems in late Middle or Early Modern English.

§ 72 Class 6

While the basic pattern is quite simple, there are some verbs with special characteristics.

OE	a–ō–ō–a	sc(e)acan – scōc – scōcon – (ge)scacen
ME	ā–ō–ō–ā	shāke(n) – shōk – shōken – (i/y)shāken
MnE	a–oo–a	shake – shook – shaken

Commentary:

1. In Old English, some contracted verbs belong to this class, such as *slēan – slōg – slōgon – slagen/slægen* 'to slay'. The Modern English preterite *slew* was adopted from class 7.
2. Some verbs show i-mutation and gemination in the present stem, for example *hebben- hōf – hōfon – hafen/hæfen* 'to heave'; Old English *swerian* also shows i-mutation.
3. Old English *standan – stōd – stōdon – standen* has a post-vocalic *n* in the present and past participle stems.

§ 73 Class 7

Originally, the verbs belonging to this class showed the feature *reduplication* (cf. Latin *pungere – pupugi*) in the (finite) preterite stems. Due to later developments the finite preterite was shortened to one syllable and differences in vowel quality were levelled out.

OE	V–ē/ēo–ē/ēo–V	feallan – fēoll – fēollon – feallen
ME	V–ē–ē–V	falle – fēl – fēllen – (i/y)fallen
MnE	V–e–V	fall – fell – fallen

Commentary:

1. In Old English, some contracted verbs can be found in this class, for example *fōn – fēng – fēngon – fangen* 'to catch'.
2. Modern English has retained quite a few verbs from class 7, such as *hold, know, grow, let*. Old English *wēpan* 'to weep' became weak.

§ 74 Conjugation of Strong Verbs in Old English

The conjugation of strong verbs is illustrated by *beran*, class 5; *helpan*, class 3 and *tēon* ('to draw'), class 2.

present indicative

1st sg.	bere	helpe	tēo
2nd sg.	birest	hilpst	tīehst
3rd sg.	bireþ	hilpþ	tīehþ
pl.	beraþ	helpaþ	tēoþ

present subjunctive

sg.	bere	helpe	tēo
pl.	beren	helpen	tēon

imperative

sg.	ber	help	tēoh
2nd pl.	beraþ	helpaþ	tēoþ

present participle

	berende	helpende	tēonde

preterite indicative

1st sg.	bær	healp	tēah
2nd sg.	bǣre	hulpe	tuge
3rd sg.	bær	healp	tēah
pl.	bǣron	hulpon	tugon

preterite subjunctive

sg.	bǣre	hulpe	tuge
pl.	bǣren	hulpen	tugen

past participle

	boren	holpen	togen

Commentary:

1. The conjugational suffixes for the 2nd and 3rd singular present indicative were originally *-is*, *-iþ*, leading to i-mutation.
2. The suffix for the imperative of the 1st plural occurs sometimes as *-an*; however, the usual form is that of the subjunctive plural: *-en*.
3. Syncope usually shows in the 2nd and 3rd singular present indicative, irrespective of whether the vowel is long or short. Syncope is very rare when the stem-final consonant is *-r, -l, -m*, or *-n*.
4. Following syncope, complex word-final consonant clusters are modified: geminated consonants preceding the ending for the 2nd and 3rd singular present indicative are simplified: winn-an – win-st; bidd-an – bit-st; find-an – fint; stīgan – stīhst; cēosan – cīest.

§ 75 Conjugation of Strong Verbs in Middle English

As the detailed presentation of the several classes of strong verbs in the preceding sections clearly shows, it is hardly possible to devise full inflectional paradigms for strong verbs in Middle English. The tables below therefore concentrate on the endings only, with a differentiation between *early* and *late* Middle English.

As a rule, early Middle English texts show the traditional Old English conjugational suffixes. However, the vowels of these suffixes are usually written *e*.

Early Middle English conjugational suffixes

present

indicative		imperative		subjunctive	
1st sg.	-e	sg.	-∅	sg.	-e
2nd sg.	-est	1st pl.	-en	pl.	-en
3rd sg.	-eþ/-eth	2nd pl.	-eþ/-eth		
pl.	-eth				

infinitive: -e(n)   present participle: -ende

preterite

indicative		subjunctive	
1st sg.	-∅	sg.	-e
2nd sg.	-e	pl.	-en
3rd sg.	-∅		
pl.	-e(n)		

past participle: (y-/i-). . .-en

Late Middle English conjugational suffixes (present tense)

	South	WML	EML	North
indicative				
1st sg.	-e	-e	-e	-e(s)
2nd sg.	-(e)st	-(e)st	-(e)s(t)	-(e)s
3rd sg.	-(e)þ/th, -t	-(e)þ/th, -t	-(e)þ/th/s	-(e)s
pl.	-(e)þ/th	-(e)n	-(e)n/s	-es
subjunctive				
sg.	-e	-e	-e	-e
pl.	-en	-en	-e(n)	-e
imperative				
sg.	-∅, -e	-∅, -e	-∅, -e	-∅, -e
pl.	-(e)þ/th	-(e)þ/th	-(e)þ/th/s	-(e)s
infinitive	-en	-en	-e(n)	-e
present participle	-inge	-ende	-ende, -ande	-ande

Commentary:
1. The table indicates the most important differences in the dialects of Middle English.
2. The effect of i-mutation in the 2nd and 3rd person singular present indicative is retained in early southern texts.
3. The traditional ending for indicative present plural (*-eth*) was replaced early in Middle English times by *-en*. The reason may have been that the 3rd singular present indicative (*-eþ*) and the plural present indicative (*-aþ*) had become identical.
3. In the course of the 14th century, word-final *-n* begins to disappear, even in the more conservative southern dialects. As a result, the infinitive and the plural no longer had endings.
4. Word-final *-e* gradually became silent in the course of the 14th century. However, it continued to be written and could be used as an indication of a long vowel in the preceding stressed syllable. Word-final *-e* could be pronounced if the metre required an additional syllable.
5. Starting in the 14th century, the traditional ending *-end* for the present participle was replaced by *-ing*; the present participle and the verbal noun ending in *-ing* had become identical.

Weak Verbs

§ 76 The System

In Old English, weak verbs can be divided into three classes: class I, also called *-ja-*verbs, class II, also called *-ōja-* verbs, and class III, also called *-ai-* verbs. As has already been pointed out, the preterite of weak verbs is marked by a dental suffix, which is syllabic after short stem vowels (e. g. *frĕm-ed-e*) and non-syllabic after long stem vowels (e. g. *dēm-de*).

Weak verbs in class I are mostly derived from nouns, adjectives and strong verbs, as for example *dēm-an* which is derived from the noun *dōm*. There are two subdivisions in class I:

– Class Ia verbs have the same vowel (derived from i-mutation) in both the present and the preterite; verbs with short stems have a syllabic dental suffix, those with long stems have a non-syllabic dental suffix.
– Class Ib verbs always have a non-syllabic dental suffix and in most verbs the stem vowel shows i-mutation in the present tense forms, whereas i-mutation did not take place in the preterite.

Weak verbs of class II are mostly derived from nouns and strong verbs, as for example *fisc-ian* which is derived from the noun *fisc*. A derivation from the strong verb *findan* is *fand-ian* 'to test'.

Class III comprises only four verbs.

In Middle English times, the differentiation into three classes cannot be retained any longer. A more powerful model for the description of weak verbs in Middle English is one which is based on (1) the quality of the dental suffix (syllabic versus non-syllabic) and (2) the quality of the vowel of the stem syllable.

§ 77 Class Ia

Weak verbs belonging to this class always show i-mutation; in addition, those with a short stem show gemination – except in the 2nd and 3rd present indicative, in the imperative singular, and when the word-final consonant is *-r*. Verbs with short stems have a syllabic dental suffix, those with long stems, however, have a non-syllabic dental suffix. The past participle can be used either with or without the prefix *ge-*. Examples are:

fremman	fremede	fremed	'to accomplish'
nerian	nerede	nered	'to save'
dēman	dēmde	dēmed	'to judge' ('deem')
cēpan	cēpte	cēped	'to keep'
cyssan	cyste	cyssed	'to kiss'
drencan	drenhte	drenced	'to drench'

Commentary:
1. When the post-vocalic consonant is voiceless, the dental suffix is *-t*, as in *cēpan*.
2. When a dental is the second of two post-vocalic consonants, the suffix is usually assimilated, as in *send-an* (infinitive) and *send-e* (preterite).
3. Verbs ending in *-nc-* show the cluster *-nht-* in the preterite, as in *drenc-an* and *drenh-t-e*.

§ 78 Class Ib

As has been pointed out above, weak verbs belonging to class Ib show i-mutation (see § 9) in the present stem only. The vowel in the preterite represents the original quality, but may be subject to change, in particular breaking (see § 3) and the influence of post-vocalic nasal consonants (see § 2).

The dental suffix is always non-syllabic and is either -*d*, following voiced consonants, or -*t* after voiceless consonants and -*g*. Examples are:

cwellan	cwealde	cweald	'to kill'
tellan	tealde	teald	'to tell'
settan	sette	set(t)	'to set'
lecgean	legde	legd	'to lay'
bycgean	bohte	boht	'to buy'
reccean	reahte	reaht	'to narrate'
tǣcean	tǣhte, tāhte	tǣht, tāht	'to teach'
þencean	þōhte	þōht	'to think'
bringan	brōhte	brōht	'to bring'

Most of the weak verbs in class Ib can be found in Modern English; as a rule, the different vowel qualities marking the present and the preterite have been preserved.

§ 79 Class II

As the historical derivational suffix was -*ōja*-, the vast number of verbs belonging to this class show neither i-mutation nor gemination. The infinitive always ends in -*ian* and the conjugated forms for the present tense, except for the 2nd and 3rd singular and the imperative singular, have an -*i*- preceding the conjugational syllable. The dental suffix is always syllabic and originally it was -*od*-, -*ud*-; later it was also written -*ad*- and -*ed*-. Examples are:

andswarian	andswarode	andswarod	'to answer'
āscian	āscode	āscod	'to ask'
bodian	bodode	bodod	'to preach'
lōcian	lōcode	lōcod	'to look'

§ 80 Class III

Only four verbs, all of which occur frequently, can be assigned to this class. These verbs are *habban* 'to have', *libban* 'to live', *secg(e)an* 'to say' and *hycg(e)an* 'to think'. Class III weak verbs show great variation as to their inflected forms, especially in the preterite (see paradigm, § 86).

§ 81 Weak Verbs in Middle English

The descriptive model for weak verbs in Old English cannot be retained for Middle English. Since the number of weak verbs increased considerably in Middle English times due to the large-scale borrowing from both Scandinavian and Norman, a new descriptive model is necessary. A simple, but at the same time flexible model is proposed here, which can accommodate the great variety of weak verbs: weak verbs with a *syllabic* dental suffix, weak verbs with a *non-syllabic* dental suffix, and weak verbs with *non-syllabic* dental suffix and *different vowels*.

§ 82 Weak Verbs with Syllabic Dental Suffix

Weak verbs from class Ia in Old English had a syllabic dental suffix, provided the stem was short and did not end in -d, -t, -s or -g. Weak verbs from class II in Old English and most weak verbs borrowed from Norman also joined this group, provided they end in a consonant. The verb *live(n)*, which in Old English belonged to class III, also meets the criteria syllabic dental suffix, one vowel quality. Examples are:

present	preterite	past participle	
her(i)en	herede	(y/i-)hered	'to praise'
loven	lovede	(y/i-)loved	'to love'
serven	servede	(y/i-)served	'to serve'
liven	livede	(y/i-)lived	'to live'

§ 83 Weak Verbs with Non-syllabic Dental Suffix

Old English weak verbs from class Ia with long stems belong to this group. In addition, weak verbs ending in -d, -t, -s, -g can be assigned to this group, as well as verbs borrowed from Norman which end in a vowel. The former class III verbs *habban* 'to have' and *secg(e)an* 'to say' also have non-syllabic dental suffixes. Examples are:

present	preterite	past participle	
keepen	kepte	(y/i-)kept	'to keep'
senden	sente	(y/i-)sent	'to send'
setten	sette	(y/i-)set	'to set'
leyen	leide	(y/i-)leid	'to lay'
kissen	kiste	(y/i-)kist	'to kiss'
heren	herde	(y/i-)herd	'to hear'
preien	preide	(y/i-)preid	'to pray'
haven	hafde,	(y/i-)hafd,	'to have'
	hadde	(y/i-)had	

Remark: Middle English 'have' shows a great variety of forms in the several dialects; see Middle English Glossary under 'have'.

§ 84 Weak Verbs with Non-syllabic Dental Suffix and Different Vowels

This group comprises the weak verbs from class Ib in Old English as well as a few verbs borrowed from Norman. Examples are:

present	preterite	past participle	
techen	taughte, taʒte	(y/i-)taught	'to teach'
tellen	tolde, talde	(y/i-)told	'to tell'
cac(c)hen	caughte	(y/i-)caught	'to catch'

§ 85 Old English Paradigms for Weak Verbs Class I and II

Examples for class I are *nerian* 'to save', *fremman* 'to perform', and *dēman* 'to judge'; class II is illustrated by *bodian* 'to preach'.

present indicative

1st sg.	nerie	fremme	dēme	bodi(g)e
2nd sg.	nerest	fremest	dēm(e)st	bodast
3rd sg.	nereþ	fremeþ	dēm(e)þ	bodaþ
pl.	neriaþ	fremmaþ	dēmaþ	bodiaþ

present subjunctive

sg.	nerie	fremme	dēme	bodie
pl.	nerien	fremmen	dēmen	bodien

imperative

sg.	nere	freme	dēm	boda
2nd pl.	neriaþ	fremmaþ	dēmaþ	bodiaþ

present participle

	neriende	fremmende	dēmende	bodiende

preterite indicative

1st sg.	nerede	fremede	dēmde	bodode
2nd sg.	neredest	fremedest	dēmdest	bododest
3rd sg.	nerede	fremede	dēmde	bodode
pl.	neredon	fremedon	dēmdon	bododon

preterite subjunctive

sg.	nerede	fremede	dēmde	bodode
pl.	nereden	fremeden	dēmden	bododen

past participle

	nered	fremed	dēmed	bodod

§ 86 Old English Paradigm for Weak Verbs Class III

present indicative

1st sg.	hæbbe	libbe	secge	hycge
2nd sg.	hæfst, hafast	liofast	sægst	hogast, hyg(e)st
3rd sg.	hæfþ, hafaþ	liofaþ	sægþ	hogaþ, hyg(e)þ
pl.	habbaþ	libbaþ	secg(e)aþ	hycg(e)aþ

present subjunctive

sg.	hæbbe	libbe	secge	hycge
pl.	hæbben	libben	secgen	hycgen

imperative

sg.	hafa	liofa	sæge	hoga, hyge
pl.	habbaþ	libbaþ	secg(e)aþ	hycg(e)aþ

present participle

	habbende	libbende	secgende	hycgende

preterite indicative

1st sg.	hæfde	lifde	sæ(g)de	hog(o)de
2nd sg.	hæfdest	lifdest	sæ(g)dest	hog(o)dest
3rd sg.	hæfde	lifde	sæ(g)de	hog(o)de
pl.	hæfdon	lifdon	sæ(g)don	hog(o)don

preterite subjunctive

sg.	hæfde	lifde	sæ(g)de	hog(o)de
pl.	hæfden	lifden	sæ(g)den	hog(o)den

past participle

	hæf(e)d	lifd	sæ(g)d	hog(o)d

Commentary:

1. The preterite forms in -od- pertaining to *hycgan* were modelled on the conjugation of class II verbs.
2. The imperative for the first person plural is sometimes -an; usually the ending is -en taken from the subjunctive plural.

§ 87 Middle English Endings of Weak Verbs: Present Tense

The table lists the characteristic endings of the major Middle English dialects.

	North	Midlands	South
infinitive	-Ø	-(i)en	-(i)en
indicative			
1st sg.	-(e)	-e	-e
2nd sg.	-es, -is	-es(t), -st	-est, -st
3rd sg.	-es, -is	-es, -eþ/-th	-eþ/-th
pl.	-es, -is	-es, -en	-eþ/-th
subjunctive			
sg.	-(e)	-e	-e
pl.	-(en)	-e(n)	-en
imperative			
sg.	-Ø	-Ø, -e	-Ø, -e
pl.	-es	-eþ/-th	-eþ/-th
participle	-and(e)	-and, -ende, -inde, -ing(e)	-ing(e)

§ 88 Middle English Endings of Weak Verbs: Past Tense

The table differentiates the three classes discussed above (see § 76)

	group I	group II		group III	
indicative					
1st sg.	loved(e)	kept(e)	herd(e)	taught(e)	told(e)
2nd sg.	lovedest	keptest	herdest	taughtest	toldest
3rd sg.	loved(e)	kept(e)	herd(e)	taught(e)	told(e)
pl.	loved(en)	kept(en)	herd(en)	taught(en)	told(en)
subjunctive					
sg.	loved(e)	kept(e)	herd(e)	taught(e)	told(e)
pl.	loved(en)	kept(en)	herd(en)	taught(en)	told(en)
participle					
	loved	kept	herd	taught	told

Preterite-Present Verbs

§ 89 The System

Preterite-present verbs were originally strong verbs whose past tense had taken on present meaning, as in Latin *nōvi* (perfect tense) 'I have learned=I know'. Since *ablaut* could not be used to mark the preterite, new forms for the preterite were created by using the dental suffix of weak verbs.

From a formal point of view, preterite-present verbs therefore show both *ablaut* and have a *dental suffix*; however, in contrast to strong verbs, the second singular present indicative of preterite-present verbs is not derived from the third tense stem, but from the second, and is marked off from the first and third person singular by the conjugational suffix *-st*. A third characteristic of almost all preterite-present verbs is that not all conjugational forms have been preserved. On the semantic level, most preterite-present verbs express modality. They can therefore be considered as the precursors of the Modern English *modal auxiliaries*.

§ 90 Class 1

There two preterite-present verbs which can be assigned to this class: *witan* 'to know' and *agan* 'to possess'. The paradigms are:

	Old English	Middle English
infinitive	witan	wite(n)
1st/3rd sg.	wāt	wāt, wōt
2nd sg.	wāst	wāst, wōst
pl.	witon	wite(n)
subjunctive sg.	wite	wite(n)
imperative sg.	wite	wite
imperative pl.	witað	wite
present participle	witende	
past tense:		
sg./pl.	wisse, wiste; wiston	wiste
past participle	gewiten	
infinitive	agan	owe(n), oȝe(n); aghe, awe
1st/3rd sg.	āg, āh	ough, ogh; agh, augh
2nd sg.	āhst	owest; aghte
pl.	āgon, ǣgen	owe(n); aȝe, awe, agh
subjunctive sg.	āge	
imperative sg.	āge	
past tense:		
sg./pl.	āhte; āhton	oughte, oghte; aghte, aughte
past participle	ǣgen	

Remark: The negated forms are *nāt, nāst, nyton, nyte, nysse, nyste* and *nāh, nāgon, nāhte*. In Middle English they are *not, nute, niste*.

§ 91 Class 2

There are very few recorded forms for *dugan* 'to avail' in Old English; the evidence is even more scarce in Middle English.

	Old English	Middle English
infinitive	duʒan	duʒen, dowe(n)
1st/3rd sg.	dēag, dēah	deigh, dow
pl.	duʒon	
subjunctive	duge, dyge	
present participle	·duʒende	
past tense:		
sg./pl.	dohte; dohton	do(u)ghte

§ 92 Class 3

Four verbs can be assigned to this class: *unnan* 'to grant', *cunnan* 'to know, can', *þurfan* 'to need' and *dear* 'to dare'.

	Old English	Middle English
infinitive	unnan	
1st/3rd sg.	an(n), on(n)	an, on
pl.	unnon	
imperative	unne	
past tense	ūðe	ūþe
past participle	unnen	
infinitive	cunnan	cunnen, connen
1st/3rd sg.	can(n), con(n)	can, con
2nd sg.	const, canst	canst, const
pl.	cunnon	cunneþ, conneþ
subjunctive	cunne	
present participle		cunninde, cunnand, cunnyng
past tense:		
sg./pl.	cūðe; cūðon	couþe, coude
past participle	cūð (adjective)	
infinitive	þurfan	
1st/3rd sg.	þearf	þar(f)
2nd sg.	þearft	þarft, þerft
pl.	þurfon	þurve(n)
subjunctive	þurfe	þurve
present participle	þearfende	
past tense:		
sg./pl.	þorfte; þorfton	þurfte, þorfte
infinitive		durren
1st/3rd sg.	dear(r)	dar, der
2nd sg.	dearst	darst, derst

pl.	durron	durre(n), dor(en)
subjunctive	durre, dyrre	durre
past tense:		
sg./pl.	dorste; dorston	durst, dorste

§ 93 Class 4

Three verbs can be assigned to this class: *sculan, sceolan* 'shall' *munan* 'to remember' and *geneah* 'be enough'.

	Old English	Middle English
infinitive	sculan, sceolan	
1st/3rd sg.	sceal	schal, schel
2nd sg.	scealt	schalt, schult
pl.	sculon, sceolon	schule(n), schollen
subjunctive	scyle, scule, sceole	schulle
past tense:		
sg./pt.	sc(e)olde; sc(e)oldon	scholde, schulde
infinitive	munan	munen, monen
1st/3rd sg.	mon, man	mun, mon
2nd sg.	monst, manst	
pl.	munon	mune(n), mon
subjunctive	mune	mune
imperative	gemyne, gemune	
present participle	munende	
past tense	munde	munde
past participle	munen	
sg.	be-/geneah	
pl.	genugon	
subjunctive	genuge	
past participle	benohte	

§ 94 Class 6

An infinitive for 'must' is not recorded. Starting in the 15th century, *moste* was also used for the present tense.

	Old English	Middle English
1st/3rd sg.	mōt	mo(o)t
2nd sg.	mōst	most
pl.	mōton	mote(n)
subjunctive	mōte	mo(o)te
past tense	mōste	moste, muste

§ 95 Uncertain Class

The forms for *mæg* 'may' are:

	Old English	Middle English
infinitive		muʒen, mowen
1st/3rd sg.	mæg	mai, mei
2nd sg.	meaht, miht	might
pl.	magon	maʒe, mawe, mai, muʒe, mowe
subjunctive	mæge	maʒe, mawe, mowe
present participle	magende	
past tense	meahte, mihte	mighte, moughte, moghte, mughte

Remark: The forms for the present singular increased in Middle English times. In the North, forms for the 2nd singular were *maght, maught*, later *maist, mai*.

Irregular Verbs

§ 96 The System

Only four verbs belong to this group: *bēon* 'to be', *gān* 'to go', *dōn* 'to do', and *willan* '(to) will'. Three of these were inherited from Indo-European; 'dōn' is an innovation of Germanic.

The following paradigm for *bēon* applies to the West Saxon dialect and lists only the more frequent forms in Middle English.

	Old English	Middle English	Modern English
infinitive	bēon	beon, ben	to be
present indicative			
1st sg.	eom, bēo	am, eom, em	am
2nd sg.	eart, bist	art, ert	are
3rd sg.	is, biþ		
pl.	sint, sindon	are(n)	are
	bīoþ, bēoþ		
subjunctive			
sg.	sī(e), sȳ	beo, be	be
	bīo, bēo		
pl.	sī(e)n, sȳn	beon, ben	be
	bīoþ, bēoþ		
imperative			
sg.	bīo, bēo; wes	beo, be	be
pl.	bīoþ, bēoþ,	beoþ, beþ, ben	be
	wesaþ		
present participle	bēonde, wesende	beyng, beande	being
preterite indicative			
1st sg.	wæs	was, wes	was
2nd sg.	wǣre	were	were

3rd sg.	wæs	was, wes	was
pl.	wæron	were(n)	were
subjunctive			
sg.	wære	were, ware, wore	was, were
pl.	wæren	weren, ware, wore	were
past participle	bēon	(i/y)be(n), bee(n)	been

Remark: Middle English *are(n)* is based on the Old English Mercian forms *(e)arun*. A selection of negated forms can be found in the glossaries following the main entry (bēon; be).

The chief forms for *dōn, gān* and *willan* in Old English are:

present indicative			
1st sg.	dō	gā	wille
2nd sg.	dēst	gǣst	wilt
3rd sg.	dēþ	gǣþ	wil(l)e
pl.	dōþ	gāþ	willaþ
subjunctive			
sg.	dō	gā	wil(l)e
pl.	dōn	gān	willen
imperative			
sg.	dō	gā	
pl.	dōþ	gāþ	
present participle	dōnde	gānde	willende
preterite indicative			
1st sg.	dyde	ēode	wolde
2nd sg.	dydest	ēodest	woldest
3rd sg.	dyde	ēode	wolde
pl.	dydon	ēodon	woldon
subjunctive			
sg.	dyde	ēode	wolde
pl.	dyden	ēoden	wolden
past participle	dōn	gegān	

The chief Middle English forms:

1. *do*

infinitive	do(n)
1st sg.	do
2nd sg.	dost; dos (North); dest (early southern texts)
3rd sg.	doþ, doth; dos (North); deþ (early southern texts)
pl.	doþ, doth; do(n) (Midlands); dos (North)
subjunctive sg.	do
pl.	do(n)
present participle	doinde; doing (later, South); doende (Midlands); doande (North)
preterite	dude (Southwest and WML); dede (Kent); dide, dede (North and Midlands)
past participle	i/y-do, don

2. *go*

infinitive	go(n) (North: ga)
1st sg.	go; ga (North)
2nd sg.	gost; gest (in early southern texts); gas, gast (North)
3rd sg.	goþ, goth, geþ (early southern texts); gas (North)
pl.	goþ (South); go(n) gan (Midlands); gas, gos (North)
subjunctive sg.	go, ga
pl.	go(n), ga
present participle	goinde, goende; goande, gangande (North)
preterite	eode, ode, ede, ȝeode (early texts); ȝede, ȝode (later); went (from the 15th century onwards)
past participle	(i/y-)go(n), go(n); gan, gain (North)

3. *will*

infinitive	willen, will
1st/3rd sg.	wille, wil; welle (Midlands); wule, wole (South)
2nd sg.	wilt, wult, wolt
pl.	willeþ, woleþ (South); wille(n), wol(l)en, wolle (Midlands); will, welyn, wol(l)e(n) (North)
subjunctive sg.	wille, wulle, wole
pl.	wille(n), wulle(n), wole(n)
preterite	wolde, wulde; walde (North and West)
past participle	wold

Remarks

1. Forms for the present in *wol-* are new forms and were derived from the preterite *wold-*.
2. For negated forms, see the glossary.

4. Syntax

Introduction

Looking at Modern English syntax from a historical perspective, the differences are not as radical as they are in the area of phonology or morphology. The major differences can be assigned to a few areas. One of these is the elaborate system of tense forms in Modern English. A second major difference concerns the highly restricted possibilities of inversion in Modern English, resulting chiefly from the loss of inflection, as pointed out in the previous chapter.

One of the constant features of English syntax is the basic pattern of most main clauses from the time of the first written records until today: subject – predicate – object(s). In Old English, however, the subject need not be expressed explicitly since it could be inferred from the (conjugated) predicate. Also, Old English texts usually have quite simple predicates – the inflection is either for the present tense (excluding the progressive) or past tense (so-called 'simple past'). As regards objects, Old English usually distinguishes the indirect from the direct object by inflection: the indirect object was marked by the dative, the direct by the accusative. Further, certain verbs took neither the dative nor the accusative but rather the genitive.

Especially in Old English, constructions can be found which involve impersonal verbs, such as *mislīcian* 'to displease', *misðyncan* 'to err' and *þyncan* 'to seem, appear'. These imply a neuter subject, i. e. *it*, and the person involved is usually indicated by a dative inflection. Examples (involving *þyncan*) can be found in O 3/8, 147; O 10/66 and O 11/4; O 8/113 provides an example involving *mislīcian* and a further instance can be found in O 7/103, involving *mislimpan* 'to be unsuccessful'. O 5/7 provides an example involving *spōwan*, 'to be successful'. Impersonal verbs can also be found in (early) Middle English texts: M 6/135: 'For me þink hit not semly'; M 8/47: 'him þoute' as well as M 7/9 and 137: 'me mette' and 'mette me' – 'I dreamed'; M 7/34: 'it semeþ'; M 5/218: 'heom luste slepe'; M 12/68: 'Me liste' and M 13/90–91: 'me liste', 'me list'.

Of course, there are some more differences in the field of syntax. However, these are not major differences, but differences in detail. In the following sections the emphasis has been placed on the use of *nominal forms*, the use of both *finite* and *non-finite forms of verbs*, and the methods of *co-ordination* and *subordination*.

Remark: Detailed models involving a different terminology can be found in Hogg (1992: 168–289) and Blake (1992: 207–408). A detailed account of Old English syntax can be found in Mitchell (1985). A comprehensive treatment of Middle English Syntax is yet to be written.

Nominal Forms: Function and Use

The grammatical categories of nouns in Indo-European are: *case, number, gender* and *declensional class.* These categories were expressed by a complex system of in-flectional suffixes. Grammatical suffixes expressing case and number indicate whether nouns or pronouns are used as subject (suffixes or lack thereof for the nominative), direct object (suffixes for the accusative), indirect object (suffixes for the dative) or adverbial (suffixes for the ablative). Not all cases have a distinct suffix – in Latin, dative and ablative plural usually have the same suffix – so it is necessary that other means be used in order to convey the full information of an utterance to the recipient. Since the process of decoding information is performed on a sequential-linear level, it can reasonably be assumed that other means (signals) are used by which the recipient will be able to establish a dynamic hierarchy of information. A very likely method for this is the use of fixed syntactic structures, especially at the beginning of an utterance. Starting an utterance with certain parts of speech can be interpreted by the recipient that the basic information is either given at the beginning, in the middle or at the end.

In view of the fact that English has lost most grammatical suffixes, fixed structural patterns became more and more important. Some of these structural patterns replacing the former category *case* will be discussed in the following sections.

§ 97 Nominative

The nominative is used in Old and Middle English just as it is used in Modern English – to mark both the subject (and its constituents) and the person addressed directly (vocative). In some Old English texts which are based on a Latin original, the Latin vocative can be found, provided it differs from the nominative. See for example O 8/36, 44, 49, 66 and 113.

§ 98 Genitive

The basic function of the genitive is specification (delimiting, describing etc.). In Old English, the genitive is used
1. to express a possessive relation (possessive genitive);
2. as subjective genitive, as in O 2/14: *on þæs wīfes gebǣrum* 'upon the woman's behaviour'; the noun inflected for the genitive noun is the active role (i. e. the woman was crying);
3. as objective genitive, as in O 1/27: *mīn eġe* 'fear of me'; the genitive is the passive role;
4. with a defining and describing function, as in O 2/24 *dōm fēos ond londes* 'judgement (amount) of money and land';
5. as partitive genitive, as in O 2/16 *hiera ... gehwelcum* and *hiera nǣnig* 'every one of them' and 'none of them';
6. to mark an adverbial; see § 54 and the examples listed there;
7. after certain verbs and adjectives, as in O 2/1, 24–25: *benam ... his rīces* 'deprived him of his kingdom'; *him þæs rīces ūðon* 'granted him the rule'; the glossary indicates which verbs and adjectives take the genitive.

In early Middle English texts most of the above functions of the genitive can still be found. One of the main functions of the genitive, the marking of possessive relations, could also be expressed by means of the prepositional *of-periphrasis* which, in Old English, was used to denote origin. In light of the French influence with the prepositional possessive construction *de+noun/pronoun*, the *of-periphrasis* was used more and more often.

The inflected genitive is used in Middle English
1. to mark a possessive relationship, as in M 9/111 *Hornes herte*; and,
2. to express an adverbial relation; see § 54 and the examples listed there.

Increasingly, other functions of the genitive were taken over by the *of-periphrasis*. From about the late 13th century onwards, the so-called *absolute genitive* can be found, as in *And ran to Londoun unto Seinte Poules* 'and hurried to London, to St Paul's [cathedral]'.

§ 99 Dative

The main function of the dative is to mark the indirect object, usually a person. In Old English, the dative is used
1. to mark the indirect object;
2. to indicate possession, as in the entry for the year 797 of the *Anglo-Saxon Chronicle*: *Hēr Rōmane Leone þǣm pāpan his tungon forcurfon* 'In this year the Romans cut off the tongue of Pope Leo';
3. with the function of an adverbial, as in O 2/5: *miclum gefeohtum* 'in great battles' and O 10/210: *wiga wintrum geong, wordum mǣlde* 'A warrior young in years spoke with these words' (see also § 54 and the examples cited there);
4. in translations from Latin to render the ablative absolute (dative absolute);
5. after certain adjectives and verbs, as in O 6/101: *God, gemiltsa ūrum sāwlum!* 'Lord, have mercy on our souls', and O 6/131: *wōdum gelīcost* 'resembling madmen'; adjectives and verbs followed by a dative are marked in the glossary.

As long as there were inflections for the demonstrative pronoun in Middle English, it was possible to distinguish a dative in its function as indirect object. After inflection had been abolished, the indirect object was marked either by the preposition *to* or by its fixed position in the sentence.

§ 100 Accusative

In Old English, the accusative marks the goal of the verbal action. It is used
1. to mark the direct object;
2. with adverbial function; see § 54 and the examples cited there.

As long as there were inflections for the demonstrative pronoun in Middle English, it was possible to distinguish an accusative in its function as the direct object. After inflection had been abolished, the direct object was marked by a fixed position in the sentence.

§ 101 Instrumental

Inflectional endings for the instrumental in Old English only exist in the strong
declension of adjectives (singular, masculine and neuter; see § 49) and in the
declension of both demonstrative pronouns (singular, masculine and neuter, see § 58).
The instrumental was used

1. to mark the circumstances of the verbal action, as in O 2/8 *lȳtle werode* 'with a
   small army';
2. to indicate a certain point in time, as in O 3/65 *þȳ endlyftan gēare his rīces* 'in the
   eleventh year of his rule'.

§ 102 Adjectives and Verbal Nouns

As pointed out in § 48, attributive adjectives in Old and early Middle English could be
inflected either strong or weak. In Old English prose texts, adjectives are declined
weak when preceded by an article, a demonstrative pronoun or a possessive pronoun
(just as in Modern German). Ordinals above three, comparatives and usually
superlatives also follow the weak declension. Adjectives used predicatively, however,
follow the strong declension in most instances. These rules also apply to participles
used as adjectives; however, it should be remembered that participles can be used
without inflection.

In marked contrast to Modern English, adjectives could be used as nouns in both
Old and (early) Middle English since they were subject to inflection. In later Middle
English, adjectives used as non-generic nouns (i. e. 'the poor') are marked, just as they
are in Modern English, by *one* ('the poor one').

§ 103 Infinitive

In Old and Middle English, the *unmarked infinitive* (i. e. marked only by the
derivational ending) is used following modal verbs, such as *cunnan, willan* and *sceal*.
Modals in combination with adverbs expressing motion, however, can be used without
an infinitive, as in O 1/6 *þǣr þǣr hīe tō scoldon* 'where they should go to'. The
unmarked infinitive is used in Old English after verbs expressing a commandment, as
in O 5/1: *Ælfred kyning hāteð grētan Wǣrferð biscep* – literally: 'King Alfred
commands to greet Bishop Wǣrferð'.

Old English also has an *inflected infinitive* (also called *gerundium*). This infinitive
is marked by the inflectional syllable *-ne* and is always preceded by the preposition *tō*.
The inflected infinitive is used

1. to express purpose, as in O 1/6–7 *tō ofslēanne Īsaac* 'in order to kill Isaac';
2. to mark an obligation or duty; as a rule, it follows a finite form of *bēon* 'to be' and
   may express a consecutive relation, as in O 5/45–46 *ðā ðe nīedbeðearfosta sīen
   eallum monnum tō wiotonne* '(those books) which are the most important to be
   known by everybody'.
3. as complement of a verb expressing an incipient action, as in O 6/28 *Ōswold
   ongann embe Godes willan tō smēagenne* 'Oswald began to think about the will of
   God';
4. as complement of an adjective or noun (sometimes in imitation of a Latin genitival
   gerundium, such as 'ars recte dicendi'). See O 3/124–125: *swā wynsumu tō
   gehȳranne* 'so delightful to listen to';

5. as subject or object, as in *tō sittanne on mīne swȳðran healfe . . . nys mē inc tō syllanne* 'it is not in my power to grant to you (the gift of) sitting to my right'.

In Middle English, the unmarked infinitive is used after modals. Following the loss of the derivational syllable *-(i)an* (see § 22), the infinitive marked by the preceding preposition *to* is increasingly used; the emphatic marking is *for to*, and *for till* in northern texts. This form of the infinitive functions in Middle English as the inflected infinitive had in Old English (see above). A Middle English innovation is the *perfect infinitive*; however, it is not used very often. Its function is to express unreality, as in M 7/220 *Then gan he wake wel wanne and wolde* haue ydronke 'Then he woke up all pale and would have liked to have a drink' and M 13/483 *He wende have cropen by his felawe John* 'He thought to have crept (in) by his fellow John'.

While rare in Old English, the *passive infinitive* can be found frequently in Middle English, as in M 6/239–240 *disserued þou habbez / To be ȝederly ȝolden* 'you have disserved to be repaid promptly'.

Verbal Forms: Function and Use

The conjugational paradigms in § 74 and 75 clearly demonstrate that there were only two conjugations in Old and Middle English: the first for the *present tense*, the second for the *past tense*. Nevertheless, it is possible to express the three complex categories of temporal relationship (anteriority – simultaneity – posteriority) by means of two conjugational tense forms only. The complex system of tense forms in Modern English is a comparatively recent achievement (18th century) and is based on the tense forms and their use in Latin. The structures signalling, for example, *present perfect* and *past perfect* in Modern English, can already be found in Old English; however, these structures had not yet been functionalised and were not subject to specific grammatical rules.

§ 104 Present Tense

The *indicative present* is used to
1. mark the current present;
2. state a fact, as in O 4/15: *Þæt Estland is swȳðe mycel* 'This eastern country is very large';
3. mark an ongoing action in the present, as in O 10/45: *Gehȳrst þū, sǣlida, hwæt þis folc segeð?* 'Sailor, can you hear what this army *is saying*';
4. mark a future action (future I), as in O 1/12: *God forescēawað* 'God will provide';
5. mark an action which will be complete in the future (future in the past) as in '*Sē mon, se þe nū dēmeþ þǣm earmum būton mildheortnesse, þonne biþ þām eft heard dōm getēod.*' 'He who has (will have) judged the poor without mercy will receive a stern judgement himself'.

The *present subjunctive* was used to
1. express future II, as in *gif hwa gefeohte on cyninges huse, sie he scyldig ealles his ierfes* 'anybody fighting (having fought) in the king's house will lose his entire inheritance';

2. to express a wish or request, as in O 5/16: *Gode ælmihtegum sīe ðonc* 'Thanks to the Almighty'.

Remark: Only *bēon* has forms conjugated for the present indicative which in most instances have a future meaning; these are those with word-initial *b-* (see the paradigm, § 96).

§ 105 Past Tense

The *preterite indicative* is used in Old English
1. to indicate a single completed action;
2. to indicate a continuing action in the past, as in *þa ða men slepon, þa com his feonda sum* 'while the men were sleeping, one of his enemies arrived';
3. to convey the meaning of the present perfect in Modern English, as in *ic mid ealre heorte þe gewilnode* 'I have been longing for you with all my heart';
4. to express anteriority in the past, i. e. 'past perfect' as in O 1/13: *þe him gesweotolode God* 'which God had pointed out to him'. Anteriority in the past (past perfect) is also frequently marked by the temporal adverb *ǣr* 'earlier, before', as in O 6/120: *þone þe hī ǣr forsōcon* 'whom they had rejected earlier/before'.
The *preterite subjunctive* is used
1. in main clauses to express a wish that will not come true (irrealis);
2. in dependent clauses, when the main clause is in the preterite (see below, mood).

In Middle English, the use of the preterite shows hardly any differences. An innovation in Middle English is the *historic present*, as in M 8/84–85: *Þe wolf* haueþ *hounger swiþe gret, / For he nedde ʒare i-ete* 'The wolf is very hungry now / Since he has not eaten anything for a long time'; it seems probable that the historic present was adopted from Old French.

§ 106 Periphrastic Tense Forms

Apart from the simple (synthetic) conjugated forms listed above, the periphrastic (analytic) forms need to be considered in both Old and Middle English. The latter consist of a participle (either the present or the past participle), an infinitive and a finite form of *bēon* or *habban* or a modal. It is important to differentiate between
1. constructions simply marking tense;
2. passive constructions (see § 108, *voice*);
3. constructions similar to the progressive in Modern English (see § 109, *aspect*);
4. constructions expressing modality (see § 110, *mood*).
In Old and Middle English, complex predicates can be found which strongly resemble the *present perfect* and the *past perfect* of Modern English. These constructions consist of a finite form of *habban* or *bēon* plus a past participle. Examples are O 3/11: *Ic þē sōðlīce andette þæt ic cūðlīce geleornad hæbbe* 'I tell you truly that I have indeed learned' (similarity with the present perfect) and O 2/13–14: *oþ þæt hīe hine ofslægenne hæfdon* 'until they had killed him'.

In contrast to Modern English, the participle can be inflected and used like an adjective (as in the second example) and the word order is different. Nonetheless, there are constructions in which the participle is not inflected, as in O 5/34: *ond ðā bēc ealla be fullan geliornod hæfdon* 'and had learned all the books completely'. Some of these constructions show a bracket-structure: finite auxiliary – object(s) – past participle. However, constructions identical to those in Modern English can also be found, as in O 8/33: *þū hafast nū geednīwod his ealde sār* 'you have now renewed his old grief'.

While constructions involving *habban* only occur with the past participle, constructions with *bēon* occur with both the present and the past participle. An example is O 2/13: *Ond hīe alle on þone cyning wǣrun feohtende* 'and they were all fighting against the king'. While the example just quoted is indeed very close to the progressive form in Modern English, the second example, found in O 3/7–8, is not: *Þā hæfde hē gesprec and geþeaht mid his witum and syndriglīce wæs fram him eallum frignende* 'Then he had a conversation and a council with his advisers and asked every one of them'. A third example, found in O 5/11, involves a finite form of *bēon* together with a past participle: *swæ clǣne hio wæs oðfeallenu on Angelcynne* 'so completely had it (teaching) declined in England'.

In Middle English, periphrastic constructions are more frequent than in Old English. However, they are not (yet) subject to rules as they are in Modern English. Examples involving a finite form of *have* can be found in M 1/23–24: *Micel hadde Henri king gadered gold and syluer* 'King Henry had collected a large amount of gold and silver'; M 6/50: *as I haf herd carp* 'as I have heard (related)'; and M 7/198: *Til Glotoun hadde yglobbed a galoun and a gylle* 'until Glotoun had drunk a glass too much'. Examples involving a finite form of *to be* can be found in M 8/14: *Hennen weren þerinne icrope* 'hens had crept into (it)'; and M 11/36: *Was ane of þa seuyn wonand* 'one of these seven resided'.

In addition to constructions involving *to be* and *to have*, Middle English has special constructions for both present and past tense. One of these is a finite form of *ginne(n)*, used as an auxiliary and followed by an infinitive. The auxiliary is not to be translated since it only serves to signal either present or past tense. See for example M 11/56: *Downe of his palfray gan he liht* 'he dismounted from his horse'. Northern texts not only have *gan*, but also *can, con* as well as *couth*. Examples are M 6/127 *To þe kyng he can enclyne* 'he inclined towards the king'; M 13/288: *And whan the hors was laus, he gynneth gon* 'And when the horse was free, it starts running' (see Middle English Glossary under *gynneth*). Although constructions involving *gan* can have the function of marking an inchoative (i. e. beginning) action, in most instances they are special past tense forms only. They are frequently found in poetry because *gan* has the potential of an extra stressed syllable – if required by the metre.

§ 107 Future

In Old English, constructions involving *sceal* plus infinitive can hardly be considered as periphrastic future because *sceal* expresses obligation. This is different in constructions involving *willan* plus infinitive; however, the basic meaning of *willan* (volition) is still present.

In Middle English, future is increasingly signalled by *shall* plus infinitive, but also *wille(n)* plus infinitive. The original meaning of *shall* soon receded into the background, whereas *wille(n)* still retained the semantic element volition. A further future construction can be found in Middle English: *worþe*, supplying a future for *be(n)*. An example is M 8/96: *Ich wot, toniȝt Ich worþe ded* 'I know that I will be dead by tonight'.

§ 108 Voice

Old English has only one verb with an inflectional passive: *hātte* 'is called, was called'. Otherwise, the passive is expressed by a periphrastic (analytic) construction involving either *bēon* or *weorðan* followed by a past participle. The use of *bēon* or *weorðan* makes no difference; they are interchangeable. The agent of a passive construction is indicated by several prepositions, not exclusively by the precursor of Modern English *by*. The most frequent prepositions are: *æt, fram, wiþ, mid, of, be*.

Compared to Modern English with its high number of passive constructions, especially those without an agent (i. e. *It is/was/has been + past participle*, sometimes called *impersonal passive*), Old English, and to a certain extent Middle English, has fewer passive constructions. Old and Middle English tended to use an impersonal active construction based on the subject *man, mon* 'one' which conveys the same quality of information as the impersonal passive. 'One does something' is also possible in Modern English, although one tends to avoid it. Beginning in the 16th century, the *man, mon* construction started to disappear.

In Old English, passive constructions were originally only possible with verbs which took a direct object marked by the accusative, e. g. *he ofslōh þone cyning* (*þone cyning* is clearly accusative); the passive version would be *sē cyning wæs ofslægen (æt him)*. With the levelling of cases, passive constructions involving the dative object in the active became possible.

In Middle English, the passive requires a finite form of *be(n)* and occasionally *worþe* 'to become', followed by a past participle. Especially in southern texts, *worþe* can still be found in the 16th century. The impersonal active construction involving *man, mon, me, men* is also available in Middle English and is used quite frequently.

Passive constructions in general are more frequent in Middle English, since the difference between dative and accusative had been levelled. Thus, passive constructions with verbs originally taking a dative object became possible in Middle English, as can be seen in the following examples from Chaucer's *Canterbury Tales*: *How that I may been holpen and in what wyse* 'How I can be assisted and in what way' (v, 1044). Similarly, passive constructions involving verbs with a prepositional object are also possible as a result of the abolishment of the category *case*. An example is *I was sent for*.

From the late 15th century onwards, the passive construction involving *become* followed by a past participle can be found. This construction can be found more frequently in early Modern English. For the passive infinitive see § 103.

§ 109 Aspect

As has already been mentioned above (see § 106), constructions consisting of a finite form of *bēon* followed by a present participle can be found in Old English. Some of these constructions are very close to the Modern English progressive. It would appear, therefore, that English writers favoured a special form of the predicate to accommodate the progressive aspect instead of using adverbs. A predicate marked for aspect can also frequently be found in Middle English. In addition to the progressive aspect, further types of aspect have to be considered:

1. the *inchoative* aspect, in Middle English expressed by an inflected form of *gin(ne)* followed by an infinitive; later, this construction functioned as special preterite (see § 106);
2. the *frequentative* or *habitual* aspect, expressed by *wil . . ., wold . . .* followed by an infinitive; an example can be found in O 6/72: *Hē wolde æfter ūhtsange oftost hine gebiddan* 'He would pray after matins as frequently as possible';
3. the *causative* aspect, expressed by a finite form of *do, make* (*ger* in northern texts) and followed by an infinitive; M 8/126: *Þi soule-cnul Ich wile do ringe* 'I will have a death-knell rung for you'; M 12/199: *Garre Satan helpe þat we wer wroken* 'Get Satan to help us so that we can be avenged'.

§ 110 Mood

The use of the subjunctive in dependent clauses will be discussed in the sections on these clauses. The present section discusses the use of the subjunctive in main clauses.

In Old English, the subjunctive is marked in both the present and preterite tense by conjugational endings: *-e* in the singular and *-en* in the plural, as in *find-e* (present subjunctive singular), *find-en* (present subjunctive plural), *fund-e* (preterite subjunctive singular) and *fund-en* (preterite subjunctive plural). Due to apocope (see § 22), it became more and more difficult to differentiate indicative and subjunctive starting in late Old English. A differentiation between indicative and subjunctive is crucial for understanding the modality of an utterance (i. e. factual, assumed, projected); as a result, modal verbs (i. e. most preterite-present verbs) were increasingly used to replace the former inflectional subjunctive. As a consequence, those modal verbs as well as the irregular verb *willan* lost their original meaning.

In Old English, the *present subjunctive* is used in main clauses to express either a wish that can be fulfilled or an order. The subjunctive can also be found in main clauses when the speaker or author wishes to express his personal attitude towards the subject-matter. Subjunctive is also used in clauses which contain a demand, a wish or an opinion. An example can be found in O 5/16: *Gode ælmihtegum sīe ðonc* 'thanks be to God Almighty'.

The *preterite subjunctive* is used in main clauses with unfulfillable wishes, as in *eala gif he wǣre hund!* 'If only he were a dog!'

In Middle English, the *present subjunctive* is used in main clauses expressing a wish, as for example in *God beo iþoncked* 'thanks to God'. In main clauses which express an (apparently) unfulfillable wish, the preterite subjunctive is used, as in M 8/4: *Him were leuere meten one hen* 'He would have preferred to meet a hen'.

Negation

§ 111 Negation

Two basic types of negation will be discussed in this section: predicate negation (when the verb is negated) and constituent negation (when other parts of the sentence are negated: nouns, adjectives, and adverbs). Whereas in Modern Standard English, predicate negation and constituent negation cannot be combined (e. g. 'I didn't see nobody'), a combination of both types was possible in Old and Middle English and in early Modern English as well. In Modern Standard English, constituent negation can only be combined to express a positive, such as 'not unlikely', 'not impossible' and so on. Such constructions can be used as a stylistic means.

In Old and Middle English, a combination of both predicate and constituent negation is quite common; this is nonetheless not necessarily the same as simple negation, but often gives the negation extra force. For example O 4/18–19: *And* ne *bið ðǣr* nǣnig *ealo gebrowen mid Estum* 'and the Estonians do not brew ale (at all)' – the negative particle *ne* negates the predicate *bið* and the object *ealo* is negated by the pronominal ajective *nǣnig*. A sentence with three negated elements can be found in M 1/37–38: ne *uuæren* næure nan *martyrs swa pined* 'it has never been the case that any martyrs have been tortured in such a way' – the predicate *uuæren* is negated by the negative particle *ne*, the negated predicate is further negated by the adverb *næure* and the subject *martyrs* is negated by the pronominal adjective *nan*.

In Old and Middle English, the predicate is negated by the particle *ne* immediately preceding the verb. For purposes of emphasis, *ne* may be moved into front position leading to inversion, as in O 9/65b–67a: *Ne wearð wæl māre . . . gefylled* 'Never had so many been killed'. Inversion can also be found in Middle English, as the example in M 8/77 clearly shows: *Ne beþ nout ȝet þre daies ago* 'Less than three days ago'. In Modern English, inversion is only possible with negative adverbs or negative adverb clauses in head position ('Hardly had I begun . . .'; 'So little has been said . . .').

In Old and Middle English, the concept *neither . . . nor* is expressed by the corresponding conjunctions *ne . . . ne* as for example in O 7/48–50: *Ne bearh nū foroft gesib gesibban þē mā þe fremdan, ne fæder his bearne, ne hwīlum bearn his āgenum fæder, ne brōþor ōþrum; ne ūre ǣnig his līf fadode swā swā hē scolde, ne gehādode regollīce, ne lǣwede lahlīce*; as well as in M 1/47–48: *ðat he ne myhte nowiderwardes, ne sitten ne lien ne slepen.*

In Old and Middle English, the negative particle may combine with certain verbs which are used frequently. These include the finite forms *bēon* 'to be' (see glossaries under *bēon* and *be*) and both finite and non finite forms of *habban* (see glossaries under *habban* and *have*), *willan* (see glossaries under *willan* (2) and *wille* (2)), and *witan* 'to know' (see glossaries under *witan* and *wit* (2)).

Emphatic negation can also be expressed by reinforcing the negative particle by *nā*, *nō*, either preceding *ne* or following the verb, as for example in O 7/63: *swā man nā ne scolde,* 'as indeed one should not' and O 7/124: *hȳ ne scamað nā* 'they are not at all ashamed', or even, in complex predicates, *ne* preceding the finite verb and *nā* preceding the past participle, as in O 8/47: *ac hēo næfð hine nā wel geleornod* 'she has not learned this art well (at all)'. Emphatic negation is also expressed by the collocation *næs nā* (with *næs* probably a shortened form of *n(e)alles*), as in *Næs nā mid golde...* 'not with gold by any means'. The adverb *nǣfre* 'never' can be combined with a negated predicate, as in O 2/26–27: *ond hīe nǣfre his banan folgian noldon* 'and that they would never (ever) accept his murderer' and as in M 9/7: *Þat y neuere ne þoȝte* '(that) which I never (ever) intended'.

Constituent negation in Old and Middle English is expressed by either pronominal adjectives like *nān, nōn* in Old English, Middle English *none* 'no one', or by affixes. Originally, only two prefixes expressed the idea of negation: Old English *un-* and *mis-*. The suffix expressing negation is Old English *-lēas*, Middle and Modern English *-less*.

The most important changes relating to negation in Middle English are the replacement of the negative particle *ne* (which precedes the verb) by the adverb *not* (which follows the verb), as in M 6/147: *And if I carp not comlyly* 'and if I do not speak in a courtly manner'.

Due to the influence of Norman French, the number of prefixes expressing negation increased: *des-, dis-* could be used side by side with the traditional prefixes *mis-* and *un-*.

Main Clauses

§ 112 General Remarks

This section concentrates on Old English prose. Due to the fact that Old English still had both nominal and verbal inflection, variation (inversion) from the standard pattern of *subject – predicate – object* is often found, especially in Old English poetry.

Apart from the basic structure subject–predicate, Old English frequently shows the patterns subject–...–predicate and predicate–subject. Variation is also possible as to the objects. If something is moved towards the beginning of the sentence, it is usually being emphasised, as for example in the relative clause in O 1/13: *þe him gesweotolode God* 'which God had pointed out to *him*' or in the main clause O 6/9: *Ōswold him cōm tō* 'Oswald came to *him*'. In both instances, the pronominal object is emphasised, whereas in its usual position following the predicate it would be in a comparatively unstressed position.

§ 113 Concord

As long as inflectional endings for both nouns and verbs are an active and distinctive category in the texts, concord in Old and early Middle English offers little difficulty. However, there are a few areas which may present some difficulties and will therefore be discussed below.

1. Indefinite pronouns and collective subjects may correspond with a predicate inflected either for the plural or the singular, depending on the perspective of the speaker/author, as in O 4/36 and 44: *þonne rīdeð ǣlc... and hyt mōtan habban eall* 'then everyone rides off ... and they may retain it completely'; *ān mǣgð, þæt hī magon cyle gewyrcan* 'a tribe (and these people) can produce cold'. In early Middle

English, conditions are still similar, as M 1/62 shows: *al þe tunscipe flugæn for heom* 'the entire population of the place fled because of them'.

2. When there are two subjects, the first preceding and the second following the predicate, the predicate usually takes the number from the subject preceding it, as in O 2/1: *Hēr Cynewulf benam Sigebryht his rīces and Westseaxna wiotan* 'In this year Cynewulf and the council of the West Saxons deprived Sigebryht of his rule'.

3. Relative clauses introduced by *þāra þe* may have predicates inflected either for the singular or the plural, as in O 5/49: *ðāra ðe ðā spēda hæbben* 'those who have the means'.

§ 114 Complex Nominal Structures

In Old and Middle English, complex nominal structures are usually split – one portion preceding the predicate, the other following it. These structures may be encountered in the context of the subject, the object, or with genitives, adjectives and adverbials.

1. Subject: *eower mod is awend and eower andwlita* 'your mind has changed and your appearance (as well)'.

2. Object: *þa he þone cniht agef and þæt wif* 'when he returned the young man and the woman'.

3. Genitive: *Inwæres broþur and Healfdenes* 'the brother of Inwære and Healfdene (Inwære's brother and Healfdene's)'.

4. Adverbials: *þa þe in Norþhymbrum bugeað and on East Englum* 'those living in Northumbria and East Anglia'.

5. Adjectives: *þæt hi næfre ær swa clæne gold, ne swa read ne gesawon* 'that they had never seen gold which was so pure and so red'.

Dependent Clauses

The following sections deal with the various types of dependent clauses. A division will be made between dependent noun clauses (subject and object clauses), adverbial clauses introduced by conjunctions, and relative clauses.

Just as in Modern English, the conjunction *that* can be used for different types of subordinate clauses. In Old and Middle English, the function of *that* can be differentiated by a preceding adverb like *swā* or *so*. This sequence can be found in consecutive clauses, even in Modern English ('so that . . .').

Conjunctions in Old English often consist of several words in sequence. The prepositions *for* and *mid* followed by a dative or instrumental demonstrative pronoun are very frequent (see Old English Glossary under *for* and *mid*).

In Middle English, complex conjunctions with *for* can still be found (see Middle English Glossary under *for*), while *mid* had been replaced by *with*. Compounds frequently found in Middle English begin with either *there* or *where* (see Middle English Glossary).

Another important aspect in dependent clauses is *mood*. In most dependent clauses, either indicative or subjunctive can be used, but the subjunctive would express a different meaning. When an author chooses to use the subjunctive, he wants to express doubt, or uncertainty, or scepticism about what he is saying (or reporting).

§ 115 Object Clauses

Object clauses, including indirect speech, are introduced by the conjunction *þæt* or *þætte*, as can be seen in O 4/1: *Wulfstān sǣde þæt hē gefōre* 'Wulfstan said that he started from' (indirect speech). Object clauses can also be introduced by verbs expressing a thought or a feeling, as in O 5/13–14: *ond ic wēne ðætte nōht monige begiondan Humbre nǣren* 'and I think that there were not many beyond the River Humber'. In this example, the subjunctive is used rather for rhetorical effect than to express doubt or uncertainty. However, object clauses may take both indicative and subjunctive.

In Middle English, object clauses are also introduced by *that*, as can be seen in M 6/160–161: *redly I trowe / Þat þou schal byden þe bur* 'I am confident that you will stand this stroke'. A further example is M 5/177: *And seiden, þat þere nas non oþur þat so wuyrþe were þare-to.* 'And said that there was no other as worthy for it'. As in Old English, both indicative and subjunctive can be found in object clauses.

§ 116 Indirect Questions

Indirect questions are usually introduced by interrogative adverbs or interrogative pronouns. Examples are O 1/11: *Fæder mīn, iċ āscie hwǣr sēo offrung sīe* 'My father, I ask you where the offering is' (adverb), and O 3/7–8: *wæs [he] fram him eallum frignende hwylc him þūhte and gesawen wǣre* 'he asked everyone what their opinions were' (pronoun).

§ 117 Temporal Clauses

The relation of a temporal clause to the main clause is either that of *anteriority*, *simultaneity* or *posteriority*. Temporal clauses may also indicate a particular point of time in relation to two actions. Specific conjunctions introducing temporal clauses signal the nature of the relation. In Old English in particular, the specific temporal relationship governs the use of indicative and subjunctive.

In Old English, the following conjunctions are used for temporal clauses:
1. simultaneity ('while, as long as') is indicated by *þā (þā)*, *þonne*, *mid þām (þe)*, *þā hwīle (þe)*, *swā lange swā*;
2. posteriority ('after') is indicated by *siððan* and *þæs þe*;
3. anteriority ('before') is indicated by *ǣr*, *ǣr þǣm (þe)*, *ǣr þan (þe)*;
4. a point of time is indicated by: *oð*, *oð þe*, *oð þæt* and *hwonne*.

Temporal clauses usually take the indicative; however, the subjunctive is used in temporal clauses introduced by *ǣr* 'before' and *hwanne, hwonne, hwænne* 'when'. The conjunction then expresses the relation 'posteriority' and that the action in the dependent clause has not yet started. An example is O 2/9: *ǣr hine þā men onfunden* 'before the men discovered him'. An example for 'when' is provided by O 11/135b–138: *and ic wēne mē . . . hwænne mē Dryhtnes rōd . . . gefetige* 'and I imagine . . . when the cross of the lord fetches (will fetch) me'. The subjunctive can also be used in connection with other conjunctions when it is required by the context (i. e. events which have not yet taken place). An example is O 1/15: *syððan hē ofslægen wurde* 'after he was (would be) killed' (the action is yet to be performed).

In Middle English, the following conjunctions are used in temporal clauses:

1. simultaneity is indicated by *þo, þat time þat* as well as by *hwile, whil(e) (þat)*;
2. posteriority is indicated by *to time, til þat*;
3. anteriority is indicated by *ar, er, or*;
4. a point of time is indicated by *when, whanne*.

In temporal clauses introduced by *ar, er, or*, the subjunctive can be found frequently; the subjunctive is also found when required by the context. Otherwise, temporal clauses take the indicative. An example of a temporal clauses showing subjunctive is provided by M 6/165: *er we fyrre passe* 'before we (may) go on'.

§ 118 Causal Clauses

Causal clauses in Old and Middle English are introduced by the conjunction *for*. In Old English, *for* is usually followed by a dative or instrumental demonstrative pronoun, with *þe* as an optional component (see Old English Glossary under *for*). In addition, causal causes can be introduced by *þæs þe*, as in O 4/40: *and þæs þe hȳ be þǣm wegum ālecgað* 'and because they distribute (his possessions) in this way'. A further possibility is the instrumental *þȳ* and *þȳ þe*, as in O 4/44–45: *and þȳ þǣr licgað þā dēadan men . . . þæt hȳ . . .* 'and this is why the dead are lying there . . . because they . . .'. The adverb *nū* may also introduce a causal clause; when it does so, a correspondung *nū* will be found in the main clause, as in O 1/19–20: *Nū iċ oncnēow sōðlīċe þæt þū swīðe ondrǣtst God, nū þū þīnne āncennedan sunu ofslēan woldest for him*. 'Now I know for certain that you fear God very much, because you wanted to kill your only born son for him'.

Causal clauses in Old English may take either the indicative or the subjunctive. As a rule, the subjunctive is used when the cause was considered to be a pretext.

The conjunction *for* usually introduced causal clauses in Middle English. More complex conjunctions include *therefore*, not infrequently in corresponding use, as in M 4/78–80: *And þeruore þet zuyche zennes arizeþ . . . þeruore ich wylle . . .* 'And because such sins are committed . . . therefore I will . . .'.

Despite being very common in Modern English, the causal conjunction *because* appears relatively late in Middle English; not infrequently it is written as two words, as in M 13/85: *By cause he was of carpenteris craft* 'Because he was a carpenter'. Causal clauses can also be introduced by *since*, which was originally a purely temporal conjunction in Old English (see Middle English Glossary under *since*). An example can be found in M 6/145: *And syþen þis note is so nys* 'And since this affair is so silly'. Occasionally, *now* is also used as a conjunction for causal clauses, just as in Old English (see above).

§ 119 Clauses of Purpose and Result

Even though the quality of the information conveyed by these two types of clauses is different, they will be considered together here because of their structural similarity. Both types of clauses express the temporal relation *posteriority* with reference to the main clause. Clauses of purpose indicate an intention, whereas clauses of result indicate a necessary or hypothetical consequence resulting from the statement contained in the main clause.

In Old English, clauses of purpose and result are introduced by the conjunctions *þæt(te), swā þæt* '(so) that'. An example is O 1/16: *þæt hē hine ġeoffrode* '(so) that he could sacrifice him' and O 3/110–111: *þæt ealra heora dōme gecoren wǣre* '(so) that all their opinion could be ascertained'. Because clauses of purpose are hypothetical, they often take the subjunctive. A clause of result can be found in O 3/4–5: *þæt hī ealle ætsomne on līfes willan Crīste gehālgade wǣran* 'so that all of them could be consecrated together to Christ at the fountain of life'; the preceding if-clause suggests that *wǣran* is subjunctive. Negated clauses of purpose and result are introduced by *þȳ (þē) lǣs þe* 'lest', as can be seen in O 6/170: *þē lǣs þe hē sylf losige* 'so that he will not perish / lest he perish'. The subjunctive is often used in negated clauses.

In Middle English, the conjunction for clauses of purpose and result also is *þat, so þat*. In early texts, the subjunctive can still be found.

§ 120 Clauses of Concession

In Old English, clauses of concession are introduced by the conjunction *þēah (þe)*. Usually the subjunctive is used in these clauses, as can be seen in O 7/40 *þēah man swā ne wēne* 'although we may not think so'. Concession can also be shown by the adverb *þēah* in both main and subordinate clauses, as in O 8/23–24: *Ðēah ðū stilli sȳ and unrōt, þēah ic þīne æðelborennesse on ðē gesēo.* 'Although you are quiet and unhappy, I nevertheless recognise noble origin in you'. Concessive clauses can also be expressed by corresponding *sam ... sam*, as in O 4/47: *sam hit sȳ sumor sam winter* 'be it summer or winter'.

In Middle English, concessive clauses are introduced by the conjunctions *þah, þoh, (al)though*. In early texts, the inflectional subjunctive can still be found, as in M 10.3/24: *þah he hire oþes swere* 'even if he were to swear her an oath'. Chaucer also uses the subjunctive in concessive clauses: *And though that he were worthy, he was wys* 'and even though he was brave he was also wise'.

§ 121 Conditional Clauses

In Latin, conditional clauses are differentiated according to the degree of reality, probability or unreality. Clearly defined rules governed the use of either indicative or subjunctive (present or past). Although present and preterite subjunctive could be expressed by conjugational means in Old English, there were no clear rules defining their usage.

In Old English, conditional clauses are introduced by the conjunction *gif*. As a rule, the indicative is used for conditions which are considered to be real. An example is provided by O 6/161–162: *gif þū ǣnig þincg hæfst of þæs hālgan reliquium, syle mē* 'if you have any relics from this saint, give them to me'. Present subjunctive is used when the speaker is in doubt about the degree of condition, as in O 3/17–19: *For þon mē þynceð wīslic, gif þū gesēo þā þing beteran ... þæt wē þām onfōn* 'Therefore I think it suitable, if you consider these things to be better ... that we accept them'. When the condition is considered to be unfulfillable, the preterite subjunctive is used, as in O 3/16–17: *gif ūre godo ǣnige mihte hæfdon, þonne woldan hīe mē mā fultumian* 'if our gods had any power, they would give me greater help'. For exceptions, as in

Modern English *if not, unless*, the conjunction *būtan* is used in Old English, as in O 5/65–67: *Forðȳ ic wolde, ðætte hīe ealneg æt ðǣre stōwe wǣren, būton se biscep hīe mid him habban wille* 'Therefore I want them (the books) to be in that place all the time unless the bishop wishes to have them with him'.

In Middle English, conditional clauses are introduced by the conjunctions *ȝif, yef* (see Middle English Glossary under *if*). As in Old English, the use of indicative or subjunctive depends on the reality of the condition. Conditional clauses can also be introduced by the conjunction *and*, as can be seen in M 14/88: *Ȝit wald my self fane help the, and I mocht* 'Yet I would help you willingly if I could', as well as in M 10.8/9–10: *Y wolde nemne hyre to-day / ant y dorste hire munne* 'I would reveal her name today / if I dared mention her'.

§ 122 Comparative Clauses

In Old English, comparative clauses are introduced by the conjunction *þonne* when different aspects are compared. In such comparisons, the main clause contains a comparative, as in O 10/31b–33: *and ēow betere is / þæt gē þisne gārrǣs mid gafole forgyldon, / þonne wē swā hearde hilde dǣlon* 'and it would be better if you bought off this attack with tribute than if we engaged in fierce battle'. If no difference is involved, comparative clauses are introduced by *swā (swā)*, as in O 3/5: *Þā dyde se cyning, swā swā hē cwæð* 'Then the king did as he had said'. Hypothetical comparisons are introduced by both *swā* and *swilce*, as in O 3/22–23: *swylc swā þū æt swǣsendum sitte* 'just as if you were sitting at a banquet'. The subjunctive is frequently found in hypothetical comparisons.

The instrumental forms of the demonstrative pronoun (*þȳ, þē*) are also used in comparative clauses when an incremental-consecutive meaning is intended, as in O 5/38–39: *ond woldon, ðæt hēr ðȳ māra wīsdōm on londe wǣre, ðȳ wē mā geðēoda cūðon* 'and wanted more wisdom to be in this country with the more languages we understood'.

In Middle English, *þanne* introduces comparative clauses involving difference, as in M 4/99: *oþer red hi wolden do þer to, þanne hi doþ* 'they would adopt measures different from those which they practice now'. When similarity is involved, *so* and *as* can be found frequently, as in M 7/232: *And as an hound þat eet gras so gan y to brake* 'and, as a dog that has eaten grass, I began to vomit'. Early texts frequently show corresponding *alswa, also . . . also* (from OE *eal(l) swā*). These constructions often imply consecutive meaning, especially when the conjunction *for* is used. An example can be found in M 4/46–48: *Vor ase hit ne is no zenne uor to habbe richesses . . . alsuo hit ne is no zenne uor to ethe þe guode metes* 'For just as it is not a sin to possess wealth, it is also not a sin to enjoy good meals'. Comparative clauses involving an incremental-consecutive meaning usually show the corresponding conjunctions *þe . . . þe*, as in M 4/46: *And þe more þet is þe ilke uerlichhede, þe more is þe zenne* 'And the greater the haste, the graver the sin'.

§ 123 Relative Clauses

Relative clauses may refer to any nominal constituent of a preceding clause, irrespective of whether this is a main clause or a subordinate clause. Relative clauses can therefore refer to subject, object(s) or adverbials. Depending on the quality of the information conveyed in a relative clause, a distinction is made between *defining* or *restrictive* (essential information) and *non-defining* or *non-restrictive* (additional information) relative clauses. This distinction applies not only to Modern English, but also to Old and Middle English and indeed to many other languages.

In Old English, the standard *relativum*, or headword of the relative clause, is the particle *þe*. Since particles (in contrast to 'relative pronouns') are not inflected, it is occasionally quite difficult to determine whether the relativum is the subject, object or adverbial of the relative clause. This difficulty can be illustrated in the following relative clause: *oð ðone dæg, þe hī hine forbærnað* (O 4/25) 'until the day when (on which) they burn him' – *þe* is thus an adverbial of time in the relative clause. Since the particle *þe* used as relativum is ambiguous, it is used most often in relative clauses when it is either the subject or the direct object, as in O 3/107 (subject): *Þā cōm hē on morgenne tō þǣm tūngerēfan þe his ealdormon wæs* 'Then in the morning he came to the reeve who was his superior'; or in O 1/2 (direct object): *Nim þīnne āncennedan sunu Īsaac, þe þū lufast* 'Take your only born son Isaac, whom you love'.

In order to avoid ambiguity in relative clauses, the relativum *þe* is frequently preceded or followed by an inflected demonstrative pronoun. It is therefore easy to determine whether the relativum is the indirect object of the relative clause, expresses a genitive (possessive) relation, or functions as an adverbial. An example is provided in O 3/33–34: *cwæð, þæt hē wolde Paulīnus þone bisceop geornlīcor gehȳran be þǣm Gode sprecende,* þǣm þe hē bodade 'he said that he would like to listen more attentively to Bishop Paulinus speaking about the God for whom he was preaching'.

Remark: In O 3 the relativum *þe* can frequently be found in those sentences in which the Latin text of the *Historia Ecclesiastica* has a relativum declined for the ablative: *tīd þe hē inne bið*: 'ipso quidem tempore, quo intus est' (l. 26); *mid heora hegum þe hēo ymbsette wǣron*: 'cum septis, quibus erant circumdata' (l. 46).

When the relativum is preceded by a demonstrative pronoun, the pronoun may refer to a corresponding pronoun in the main clause, as in O 6/119–120: *and bǣdon þæs on mergen þæt hī mōston þone sanct mid ārwurðnysse underfōn* þone þe hī ǣr forsōcon 'and in the morning they requested that they might receive the saint whom they had rejected earlier' – since the subject *hī* immediately follows *þe*, there is no ambiguity in respect of *þe*.

When the relativum marks an adverbial, the preposition either precedes or follows the predicate, as in O 4/30: *nȳhst þǣm tūne ðe se dēada man on līð* 'closest to the house in which the dead man is lying'; see also O 6/146–147 *būton þām ānum poste, þe þæt hālige dūst on āhangen wæs* 'except for that single post on which the holy earth had been hung'.

The function of the relative particle *þe* can also be expressed explicitly by an inflected personal pronoun, as in O 11/86: *ǣghwylcne ānra þāra þe him bið egesa tō mē* 'all of those who fear me' where *him* is dative.

Relative clauses can also be introduced by a relative adverbs, such as *þǣr* 'where' or *swā hwǣr swā* 'wherever', as in O 1/6: *þā hīe þā dūne ġesāwon, þǣr þǣr hīe tō scoldon* 'when they could see the mountain (where) they should go to'.

A further relativum available in Old English is the multi-functional *ðæt*, as in O 3/38: *on þysse lāre þæt sylfe sōð scīneð þæt ūs mæg þā gyfe syllan ēcre ēadignesse* 'in this doctrine the very truth which can give us the gift of eternal happiness is apparent'.

Relative clauses without a relativum (contact clauses) can already be found in Old English, though not as frequently as in Modern English. Usually the predicate of such contact-clauses is either a conjugated form of *bēon* 'to be', *habben* 'to have' or *hātte, hāten* 'is, was called', as in O 3/9–10: *Him þā andswarode his ealdorbisceop, Cēfi wæs hāten* 'He was then given an answer by his high-priest, called Coefi'.

In Old English, relative clauses can be found which do not refer to a preceding clause; rather, their reference is right bound. The relativum is usually *sē ðe* as in O 7/65–66 *gelȳfe sē þe wille* 'he who wants to believe this should believe it'. The relativum can also be *swā hwā swā* or *swā hwelc swā* 'whoever' as in O 2/15: *swā hwelc swā þonne gearo wearþ* 'whoever was ready (then)'. In indefinite adverbial relative clauses the relativum is *and swā hwǣr swā* as in O 6/74: *swā hwǣr swā hē wæs, hē wurðode ǣfre God* 'and wherever he was he always honoured God'.

In Middle English, the relative particle was soon replaced by *þat* since *þe* was used for the definite article. In early Middle English texts, *þe* can still be found at the head of relative clauses; see Middle English Glossary under *þe*. Like *þe*, *þat* is indeclinable and is just as ambiguous – even more so, considering the other functions of *that* (conjunction and demonstrative pronoun).

In contrast to Modern English, *that* could be used with reference to both people and things in Middle English. Probably in order to differentiate the many functions of *that*, in later Middle English it is often preceded by *which*, as in M 13/470: *Which that I heelp my sire for to stele.* 'Which I helped my father to steal' shortest [stick] shall begin'.

The oblique forms (*whose* and *whom*) of the interrogative pronoun *who* acquired relative function in later Middle English, as in M 12/81–82: *'This is my sone', he saide, / 'In whome me paies full wele'.* 'This is my beloved Son, in whom I am well pleased' (King James Bible).

Indefinite relative clauses in Middle English are usually introduced by *whoso*; frequently the predicate is conjugated for the subjunctive or is a modal auxiliary, as can be seen in *Whoso be rebel to my juggement* 'he who rebels against my decree' (subjunctive); *whoso kan hym rede* 'everyone who can read him (Plato)' (modal); versus M 10.8/35: *Whose loueþ vntrewe* 'he who loves unfaithfully' (indicative).

Adverbial relative clauses usually start with *there, where* or even *þer huer*, see M 4/82.

Just as in Old English, contact clauses are not as frequent in Middle English as they are in Modern English. M 13/382 contains a contact clause: *And whan that dronken al was in the crowke* 'And when all that was in the crock was drunken'.

Medieval English Verse

Old English Poetry

Old English poetry uses a completely different style from that which modern readers
will be familiar with. Old English poetry did not rhyme, nor did it have metrical feet;
rather, being Germanic, it used the *alliterative long-line*. A long-line is composed of
two *half-lines*, each with two stressed syllables and between two and seven unstressed
syllables (the second half-line does not always have two stressed syllables), and these
two half-lines are separated by a *caesura*. The two half-lines (*a* and *b*) are connected
to each other through a system of *alliteration* – words beginning with the same sound.
The alliterative long line is a complicated system with many rules. First of all, only
stressed syllables can alliterate with each other. Secondly, the first stress of the second
half-line must alliterate with one (or both) of the stressed syllables in the first half-
line. All vowels alliterate with each other, even with diphthongs, and some consonant
clusters can only alliterate with the same consonant cluster (*sc*, *sp*, *st* cannot alliterate
with *s* alone or with *s* and another consonant).
If we take a look at the opening of the *Battle of Brunanburh*:

> Her Æþelstan cyn*ing*,   eor*la* dryh*ten*,
> beor*na* beah*gifa*,   *and his* bro*þor* eac,
> Ead*mund* æþe*ling*,   eald*orlangne* tir
> ge*slogon æt* sæ*cce*   sweor*da* ecg*um*

The stressed syllables are not italicised. As can be seen, Æ and *eo* alliterate in the first
line, *b* alliterates three times in the second, vowels (including a diphthong) again in the
third line, and *s* and *s*-compounds (but not *sc*, *sp* or *st*) in the fourth line.

In order to compose in this exacting system, an Old English poet, or *scop*, had
several tools to help him.

Variation – a *scop* had a large *word-hoard*; synonyms that could be interchanged as
necessary for the alliteration and metre. For example, God could be *God* and *dryhten*,
but also *heahfæder*, *heofonrices weard* (O 11, ll. 91 and 134), and a variety of others.

Kennings – "Kenning" is the Old Norse term for a kind of metaphor used in
Germanic poetry. A Kenning is either a compound noun or two nouns (one in the
genitive), which metaphorically describe something; they are pictorial, and can be
very difficult to decode. For example, *hildewulf*, 'battle-wolf' and *garbeam*, 'spear-
tree' both mean *warrior*.

Formulas – there are many stock formulas or phrases which occur frequently in
poetry. These could be used to satisfy metrical and alliterative demands as necessary.
A very common formula was the *maþelode* formula which introduced a direct speech:
Byrhtnoð maþelode, Beowulf maþelode, etc. Also certain imagery or scenes were
formulaic, and included in many poems, such as the *beasts of battle* (see O 9/60–65)
or the *arming of the hero* and so on.

Poetic vocabulary – Old English poets used a vocabulary different to that employed
by prose writers. Not only unusual or uncommon words were chosen, but also unusual
compounds. This includes, unfortunately for the translator, many *hapax legomena*:
words which only appear once (or in only one text) in the whole Old English corpus.

Middle English Poetry

When English regained its status as a literary language after the Norman Conquest, not only the sounds and structures of the language had been completely changed: Norman-French influence had also left its mark on the way English was written. This can especially be seen in poetry. The alliterative long line had almost completely disappeared, and the French model of rhymed verse had established itself as the new English model. Such verse is generally iambic, and though there are a few instances of trochaic feet or inversion, the regular variation of stressed and unstressed syllables had replaced the Germanic system of two stresses with several unstressed syllables. In order to maintain this rigid structure, Middle English poets often used word-final *e* as a full syllable, although this had vanished from normal speech. For example, in M 10/5, l. 2: *by grene wode to seche play* the *-e* in *grene* and *seche* are pronounced in order to satisfy the tetrametre, but not in *wode*. Stanza form varies immensely, but it is usually also based on the French, occasionally on the Latin model. Alliteration is often used in these poems as a stylistic device, but the alliterative line, as we know it from Old English, does not play a role until later.

In the mid-fourteenth century, the *alliterative revival* began; Middle English poets began to revive the alliterative poetic tradition. The *Gawain-poet* is perhaps the best example of this (see M 6), remaining truest to the original Old English form, although several other poets, such as Langland (M 7), also used the Old English alliterative long-line, if not quite according to the rules. Most Middle English alliterative poets use some sort of stanza form, occasionally adding rhymes. *Sir Gawain and the Green Knight*, for example, employs a bob-and-tail at the end of each stanza. Middle English alliterative verse can also be said to have too many alliterations. Old English poetry always had two or three alliterations, whereas in Middle English, many more (or fewer) can be used (O 6/2: Þe borȝ britt*ened and* brent *to* bron*dez and askez*). Over the next century, Middle English alliterative poetry increasingly incorporated more and more stanzaic and rhyming tendencies, until the alliterative aspect had receded into the background.

5. Old English Texts

Introduction

The eleven Old English texts have been chosen to represent a wide range of Old English culture and literary genres. All of the main themes in the development of Anglo-Saxon England, including the progression of the church and learning, as well as the formation of a national English state, are shown in the texts. Many of the texts were a part of King Alfred's learning reform or later attempts to educate the people; this includes original works of instruction, translations, as well as personal statements. The selections of poetry and *Apollonius* show us a different side of Anglo-Saxon life.

The texts chosen were all composed between the 9th and the 11th centuries. The literary genres include biblical translation (text 1), historiographical writing (texts 2, 3, 4 and 9), utilitarian prose (text 5), homiletic prose (texts 6 and 7) and secular entertainment (text 8). The three poems printed here belong to secular poetry (texts 9 and 10) and religious poetry (text 11). All of the texts are of West-Saxon provenance, except Apollonius, which is East-Saxon.

All texts are preceded by an introduction which focuses on the specific features of the individual text. In addition, information on the manuscript is provided and references to editions are given. The introductory section also points out the most important linguistic features of the text.

The texts are accompanied by footnotes at the bottom of the page; line numbers are used as references.

Anthologies providing a larger selection of texts are: Bright (1971), Kaiser (1961), Marsden (2004), Sweet (1967), Treharne (2004). – Literary histories for Old English are Anderson (1949), Baugh (1967), Göller (1971), Greenfield/Calder (1986), Schirmer (1983), Wrenn (1967).

Text 1: The Old English Heptateuch: Genesis 22:1–19

In the 10th century, the West Saxon nobleman Æðelweard asked Ælfric, later Abbot of Eynsham, if he would be willing to translate the book of Genesis into Old English, so that parts of the Bible would be available in the vernacular. As Ælfric says in his preface to the translation of Genesis, translating the Bible is not an unproblematic issue. First of all, Ælfric was concerned about the challenge inherent in translating the Bible, for translating the word of God is a dangerous undertaking; if God himself dictated the books of the Heptateuch (the five books of Moses, Joshua and Judges), then meddling with his choice of words could be sacrilegious. A direct translation is in any case not possible because of the differences between English and Latin grammar. Further, if Ælfric were to try to retain only the literal meaning, the figurative meaning of many sentences could be lost in translation, for "seo boc is swiþe deop gastlice to understandenne" (it is difficult to understand the meaning of this very profound book). This problem aside, Ælfric's second main concern remains – the validity of such a task at all: does the untrained lay person have the competence to deal with the word of God? A lay reader could, by reading the text literally without the help of a clergyman, assume he should live as in the times of Abraham and Jacob, marrying his sister(s), however "ne byð se man na Cristen" (that man is not a Christian at all). Symbolism and meaning in the text could be lost on the ordinary reader, Ælfric argued, and the common people could assume that the literal meaning of the Bible should be followed in all cases.

Although Ælfric claims that he will translate the text as literally as possible, this is not what he actually does. In the end, Ælfric has chosen to translate the meaning as best as possible, translating entire sentences so that the meaning comes across, sacrificing subordinate clauses and descriptive terms as necessary. In many cases, the Old English Genesis deviates substantially from the original, as glossed in the footnotes.

Sources: Bodleian Library, Oxford, MS Laud Misc. 509. – Marsden (2008); Mitchell/Robinson (1992); Crawford (1922).

God wolde þā fandian Abrahames ġehīersumnesse and clipode his naman and cwæð him þus tō: 'Nim þīnne āncennedan sunu Īsaac, þe þū lufast, and far tō þām lande *Visionis* hraðe and ġeoffra hine þǣr uppan ānre dūne.' Abraham þā ārās on þǣre ilcan nihte and fērde mid twām cnapum tō þām fierlenan lande, and Īsaac
5   samod, on assum rīdende.

---

1 *wolde*] the auxiliary is the translator's addition.

1 *Abrahames ġehīersumnesse*] In the Vulgate the direct object of 'fandian' is Abraham, not 'gehīersumnesse'.

3 *hraðe*] the adverb was added by the translator.

3 *ānre dūne*] The relative clause ('super unum montium quem monstravero tibi' – 'upon one of the mountains which I will tell thee of') has been left out.

4 *nihte*] The preparations for the journey ('and saddled his ass . . . and clave the wood') have been omitted.

4 *fierlenan lande*] The adjective 'fierlenan' (far) has been introduced by the translator and the relative clause 'quem praeceperat ei Deus' ('which God had told him') has been left out.

Þā on þām þriddan dæġe, þā hīe þā dūne ġesāwon þǣr þǣr hīe tō scoldon tō ofslēanne Īsaac, þā cwæð Abraham tō þām twām cnapum þus: 'Anbīdiað ēow hēr mid þām assum sume hwīle. Iċ and þæt ċild gāð unc tō ġebiddenne, and wē siððan cumað sōna eft tō ēow.' Abraham þā hēt Īsaac beran þone wudu tō þǣre

10   stōwe, and hē self bær his sweord and fȳr. Īsaac þā āscode Abraham his fæder: 'Fæder mīn, iċ āscie hwǣr sēo offrung sīe. Hēr is wudu and fȳr.' Him andwyrde sē fæder: 'God foresċēawað, mīn, sunu, him self þā offrunge.'

Hīe cōmon þā tō þǣre stōwe þe him ġesweotolode God and hē þǣr wēofod ārǣrde on þā ealdan wīsan and þone wudu ġelōgode, swā swā hē hit wolde

15   habban tō his suna bærnette, syððan hē ofslæġen wurde. Hē ġeband þā his sunu and his sweord ātēah, þæt hē hine ġeoffrode on þā ealdan wīsan. Mid þām þe hē wolde þæt weorc beġinnan, þā clipode Godes engel arodlīċe of heofonum: 'Abraham!' Hē andwyrde sōna. Sē engel him cwæð þā tō: 'Ne ācwele þū þæt ċild, ne þīne hand ne āstreċe ofer his swēoran! Nū iċ oncnēow sōðlīċe þæt þū swīðe

20   ondrǣtst God, nū þū þīnne āncennedan sunu ofslēan woldest for him.'

Þā beseah Abraham sōna underbæc and ġeseah þǣr ānne ramm betweox þām brēmelum be þām hornum ġehæft. And hē āhefde þone ramm tō þǣre offrunge and hine þǣr ofsnāð Gode tō lāce for his sunu Īsaac. Hē hēt þā þā stōwe *Dominus videt,* þæt is 'God ġesiehð', and ġīet is ġesæġd swā, *In monte Dominus videbit,*

25   þæt is 'God ġesiehð on dūne.' Eft clipode se engel Abraham and cwæð: 'Iċ swerie þurh mē selfne, sæġde se Ælmihtiga, nū þū noldest ārian þīnum āncennedan suna, ac þē wæs mīn eġe māre þonne his līf, iċ þē nū blētsie and þīnne ofspring ġemaniġfealde swā swā steorran on heofonum and swā swā sandċēosol on sǣ. Þīn ofspring sceal āgan hira fēonda gatu, and on þīnum sǣde bēoð ealle

30   þēoda ġeblētsode, for þām þe þū ġehīersumodest mīnre hǣse þus.' Abraham þā ġeċierde sōna tō his cnapum and fērdon him hām swā mid heofonliċre blētsunge.

---

6 *þǣr . . . tō scoldon*] 'sculan' in combination with adverbs of place imply the infinitive – 'to which they should (go)'.

7 *ēow*] 'ēow' is used reflexively.

8 *unc*] 1st person dual, used reflexively

11 *sīe*] The present subjunctive expresses doubt.

12 *foresċēawað*] present indicative with future meaning

13 *ġesweotolode*] must be understood as past perfect.

15 *ofslæġen wurde*] Past subjunctive is used to indicate an event that is yet to occur. The temporal clause is an addition.

19–20 *Nū . . . nū*] The second 'nū' brings in an additional element of causality.

25 *ġesiehð*] present indicative with future meaning

31 *mid heofonliċre blētsunge*] has been added by the translator.

Text 2: Selections from the Anglo-Saxon Chronicle

The *Anglo-Saxon Chronicle* is the single most important work of history for early England. The seven manuscripts (and single fragment) which we have of the *Anglo-Saxon Chronicle* all stem from an original compiled during the reign of King Alfred, shortly after 891.

After his successful military campaigns against the Vikings, Alfred the Great initiated a program of learning, as he thought the level of knowledge had dropped to such a point that many priests could "not even read" the Latin Vulgate (see Alfred's preface to his translation of Gregory's *Cura Pastoralis*: 'very few English on this side of the Humber were able to understand their mass book in English or even translate a letter from Latin into English, and I think there were not many beyond the Humber either' – see text 5, lines 12–14).

The Chronicle of the history of the Anglo-Saxon people seems to have been begun as a part of this ambitious project. Up to the year 891, the chronicle was compiled using various older sources, including Bede's and Isidore's church histories (*Historia Ecclesiastica Gentis Anglorum* and *Historia de regibus Gothorum, Vandalorum et Suevorum*), as well as West Saxon annals, Easter Tables, and regional histories and genealogies. The continuations of the *Chronicle* were sometimes done on a year-to-year basis or in batches (as is the case for the years 978–1016 in versions CDE). These continuations were in turn copied or used in other compilations.

The quality (and quantity – see facsimile) of the entries varies immensely depending upon the year. Until 891, most entries are very short, summarising any major occurrences, if there had been any events worthy of note. These entries briefly relate events of great importance: deaths of kings, martyrdoms, occasionally events taking place on the continent, and natural disasters or events (especially comets). As the later chroniclers were able to describe events within living memory, the entries become more detailed. Local touches were also added, so that we find regional histories or details about specific monasteries. Some entries or groups of entries are composed such that an authorial voice seems to be trying to persuade us to believe 'his' version of events.

The year 755 is an exception among the entries preceding the time of King Alfred. Its length alone is out of the ordinary, but also many aspects of how the text is written deviate from the habitual (early) style. The feud between Cynewulf and Cyneheard takes on an almost dramatic aspect in comparison to the entries surrounding it. Here we see a depiction of loyalty, its conflict with the bonds of kinship, and the tragedy this produces. To further dramatise these events, the author employs dialogue in the decisive moments of the story. Although the author has some stylistic difficulties (an extensive and perhaps even excessive use of pronouns, especially lines 24–33), the entry for 755 is the first successful 'story' in the Chronicle.

The second section from the *Anglo-Saxon Chronicle* printed here provides information about the first phase of the Viking invasion in the course of the 9th century. The events presented in these entries should be seen in connection with text 9, *The Battle of Brunanburh*, commemorating a decisive victory over the Vikings.

The entries for the years 867–873 show an interesting development in Viking military activities. Whereas earlier on, the Vikings had raided Britain with highly mobile and comparatively small naval units returning home for the winter months, the entry for 868 mentions that the Vikings had again decided to spend the winter months in England – see line 46 'wintersetl' (the first instance of winter-quarters is recorded under the year 855). This is also pointed out in the entry for 870, with winter quarters moving from Nottingham to Thetford (see lines 53–54). The compiler's account tells a grim story: the country was conquered by the Vikings after they had killed King Edmund.

The entry for 871 tells a quite different story: in this year, the English army was victorious on one occasion, even though the second battle ended in a defeat. Starting with the year 871, considerable attention is paid to the future king, Alfred the Great. The new military leader, to be sure, was defeated in several battles. However, as line 80 clearly shows, he is presented as a courageous fighter opposing a large army with only a small band of warriors, 'lȳtle werede'. This phrase takes on the quality of a 'leitmotif' in later entries, such as for the year 878 where it occurs twice. This portrayal would seem to suggest that the chronicle entries were intended as a monument to a couragous, motivated and victorious king who succeeded in arranging a peace treaty with the Vikings. This treaty is mentioned with a considerable amount of detail in the entry for the year 878.

By the year 1066, we see a development not only in storytelling, but also in the level of English which is used. The ambiguous use of pronouns in the entry for 755 has all but disappeared, with the author using appositions to clearly define which king is currently in action. Unlike several of the other versions of the Chronicle, the author of MS D seems to clearly position himself on the side of Harold Godwinson (line 110, *Harold ure cyng*); the other chroniclers call Harold's legitimacy into question (MS E) or avoid mentioning the issue altogether (MS A and C).

Several aspects of the text remain unclear; as Harold goes into battle against William *mid ðam mannum, þe him gelæstan wolden* (lines 126–127), we are given the impression that Harold no longer has the full support of his thanes and subjects (compare to text 5 in the Middle English section, lines 58–94). Nonetheless, we have a 'heroic' representation of Harold, who despite William's 'treachery' (in line 125 *Wyllelm him com ongean on unwær*) is able to lead a noble attack (line 126, *Ac se kyng þeah him swiðe heardlice wið feaht*). The Chronicler goes so far as to express criticism of the new king, William, an aspect which we do not see in the other manuscripts. By positioning William's promise (lines 148–149) among adverbs of concession, the author questions the veracity of such statements (lines 144–150: *and þeah, Swaþeah*).

Despite its West Saxon provenance, the first portion of the text shows certain non-WS features: for example, breaking (see § 3) does not occur in *aldormon* (ll. 3, 5, 20, 32, 58, 61 and 84) and *alle* (ll. 13, 17, 32 and 55). West Germanic *ā remains <æ>, even when there is a velar vowel in the next syllable: *mǣgas, mǣgum* (ll. 25 and 27), which could be a feature of late WS usage. Spelling variants for *-od-* in the preterite of class II weak verbs occur regularly: *-ad-* and *-ud-* in *wunade* (l. 4) and *-ud-* in *lōcude* (l. 12). In the third portion of the text, we can see some features typical of late OE. The ending for the dsg. m. and n. *-um* for adjectives occurs as both *-an* and *-on*: *mid micclan his here* (l. 111) and *tō ūran kyninge* (l. 118). The regular ending *-um* for the dpl. of nouns occurs once as *-on*: *synnon* (l. 130). Word-initial *hw-* appears as *w-* in *wīle* (l. 102); *hytte* (l. 110) is a Scandinavian loanword.

Sources: Corpus Christi College, Cambridge, MS 173 (for the year 755 as well as for the years 867–873); BL MS Cotton Tiberius B.iv. (for the year 1066). – Marsden (2004); Mitchell/Robinson (1992); Thorpe (1861), Plummer/Earle (1892), Garmonsway (1954), Swanton (1996). – Secondary literature: Towers (1963); Kemmler (2002). – Facsimile: Flower (1941).

755.   Hēr Cynewulf benam Sigebryht his rīces and Westseaxna wiotan for unryhtum dǣdum, būton Hamtūnscīre; ond hē hæfde þā oþ hē ofslōg þone aldormon þe him lengest wunode. And hiene þā Cynewulf on Andred ādrǣfde; ond hē þǣr wunade oþ þæt hiene ān swān ofstang æt Pryfetes flōdan – ond hē
5   wrǣc þone aldormon Cumbran. Ond se Cynewulf oft miclum gefeohtum feaht uuiþ Bretwālum. Ond ymb .xxxi. wintra þæs þe hē rīce hæfde, hē wolde ādrǣfan ānne æþeling se was Cyneheard hāten; ond se Cyneheard wæs þæs Sigebryhtes brōþur. Ond þā geāscode hē þone cyning lȳtle werode on wīfcȳþþe on Merantūne ond hine þǣr berād ond þone būr ūtan beēode, ǣr hine þā men onfunden þe mid
10   þām kyninge wǣrun.

Ond þā ongeat se cyning þæt, ond hē on þā duru ēode ond þā unhēanlīce hine werede oþ hē on þone æþeling lōcude; ond þā ūt rǣsde on hine ond hine miclum gewundode. Ond hīe alle on þone cyning wǣrun feohtende oþ þæt hīe hine ofslægenne hæfdon. Ond þā on þæs wīfes gebǣrum onfundon þæs cyninges
15   þegnas þā unstilnesse ond þā þider urnon, swā hwelc swā þonne gearo wearþ and radost. Ond hiera se æþeling gehwelcum feoh and feorh gebēad, ond hiera nǣnig hit geþicgean nolde; ac hīe simle feohtende wǣran oþ hīe alle lǣgon, būtan ānum Bryttiscum gīsle, and sē swīþe gewundad wæs.

---

1 *Cynewulf . . . Sigebryht*] Cynewulf, a relative of West Saxon King Sigebryht; see MS Laud 636: 'Her Cynewulf benam Sigebrihte his mæge his rice'.
1 *Westseaxna wiotan*] 'the West Saxon Council' is the second subject; the predicate in Old English usually refers to the subject immediately preceding it, in this case Cynewulf.
2 *þā*] i. e. Hampshire (feminine)
3 *þe . . . wunode*] 'who had been loyal to him the longest'.
3 *Andred*] a big forest which stretched from the county of Kent to the county of Hampshire.
4 *Pryfetes flōdan*] a river near Privett (in Hampshire)
5 *Cumbran*] *Cumbra* is the loyal *aldormon* of line 3.
6 *Bretwālum*] the British; referring to the (Celtic) British in the county of Cornwall
6 *ymb xxxi wintra . . . hæfde*] in the 31st year of his reign.
8 *hē*] Cyneheard
8 *on . . . Merantūne*] 'when visiting a woman in Merton (Surrey)'
9 *būr*] refers to a separate chamber within the building (Modern English *bower*).
15–16 *urnon . . . radost*] 'they hurried (there) as soon as they were armed and as fast as they could get armed (to help the king)'.
18 *Bryttiscum gīsle*] The British hostage was a safety against surprise attacks.

Þā on morgenne gehīerdun þæt þæs cyninges þegnas þe him beæftan wǣrun
20 þæt se cyning ofslǣgen wæs. Þā ridon hīe þider; ond his aldormon Ōsrīc ond
Wīferþ his þegn ond þā men þe hē beæftan him lǣfde ǣr, ond þone æþeling on
þǣre byrig mētton þǣr se cyning ofslǣgen læg. Ond þā gatu him tō belocen
hæfdon ond þā þǣrtō ēodon.

Ond þā gebēad hē him hiera āgenne dōm fēos ond londes, gif hīe him þæs rīces
25 ūþon, ond him cȳþde þæt hiera mǣgas him mid wǣron, þā þe him from noldon.
Ond þā cuǣdon hīe þæt him nǣnig mǣg lēofra nǣre þonne hiera hlāford ond hīe
nǣfre his banan folgian noldon. Ond þā budon hīe hiera mǣgum þæt hīe gesunde
from ēodon. Ond hīe cuǣdon þæt tæt ilce hiera gefērum geboden wǣre þe ǣr mid
þām cyninge wǣrun. Þā cuǣdon hīe þæt hīe hīe þæs ne onmunden, 'þon mā þe
30 ēowre gefēran þe mid þām cyninge ofslǣgene wǣrun.' Ond hīe þā ymb þā gatu
feohtende wǣron oþ þæt hīe þǣrinne fulgon; ond þone æþeling ofslōgon ond þā
men þe him mid wǣrun, alle būtan ānum, se wæs þæs aldormonnes godsunu; ond
hē his feorh generede, ond þēah hē wæs oft gewundad.

Ond sē Cynewulf rīcsode .xxxi. wintra, and his līc līþ æt Wintanceastre ond
35 þæs æþelinges æt Ascanmynster; ond hiera ryhtfæderencyn gǣþ tō Cerdice.

867.   Hēr fōr se here of Ēast Englum ofer Humbre mūþan tō Eoforwicceastre on
Norþhymbre, and þǣr wæs micel ungeþuǣrnes þǣre þēode betweox him selfum,
and hīe hæfdun hiera cyning āworpenne Ōsbryht, and ungecyndne cyning
underfēngon Ællan. And hīe late on gēare tō þām gecirdon þæt hīe wiþ þone here
40 winnende wǣrun, and hīe þēah micle fierd gegadrodon, and þone here sōhton æt
Eoforwicceastre, and on þā ceastre brǣcon, and hīe sume inne wurdon, and þǣr

22–23 *þā gatu . . . hæfdon*] 'Cyneheard's retainers had locked the gates'. However, *him* could
also refer to Cynewulf's men, who wished to prevent Cyneheard and his men from fleeing by
locking the doors.

24 *hē*] Cyneheard

24 *hiera āgenne dōm*] They were free to fix the amount themselves (literally: 'their own
judgement').

26 *cuǣdon hīe:*] Cynewulf's retainers

27 *budon hīe*] Cynewulf's retainers

28 *ēodon*] subjunctive: 'could go'

28 *Ond hīe*] Cyneheard's retainers

28 *hiera gefērum*] the relatives of Cynewulf's retainers

29 *cuǣdon hie*] Cyneheard's retainers

30 *ēowre gefēran*] Cynewulf's fallen retainers. Note the abrupt change to direct speech, see
ēowre 'your'.

31 *hīe*] Cynewulf's retainers

32 *aldormonnes*] refers to Ōsrīc, l. 20.

35 *Cerdice*] the legendary founder of the West Saxon royal line

36 *here*] always refers to the Viking army, while the *fierd* or *fyrd* is the home army.

36 *Humbre*] the River Humber

36 *Eoforwicceastre*] York

37 *Norþhymbre*] Northumbria

38–39 *Ōsbryht . . . Ællan*] Nothing is known about these two kings. It is probably significant
that the people deposed their (weak) king in these times of war and chose a more promising
successor who had no claim to the throne. However, both kings were killed in action later in
the same year.

was ungemetlic wæl geslægen Norþanhymbra, sume binnan, sume būtan; and þā cyningas bēgen ofslægene, and sīo lāf wiþ þone here friþ nam. And þȳ ilcan gēare gefōr Ealchstān bisceop, and hē hæfde þæt bisceoprīce .l. wintra æt
45 Scīreburnan, and his līc līþ þǣr on tūne.

868. Hēr fōr se ilca here innan Mierce tō Snotengahām, and þǣr wintersetl nāmon; and Burgræd Miercna cyning and his wiotan bǣdon Æþered Westseaxna cyning and Ælfred his brōþur þæt hīe him gefultumadon, þæt hīe wiþ þone here gefuhton. And þā fērdon hīe mid Wesseaxna fierde innan Mierce oþ Sno-
50 tengahām, and þone here þǣr mētton on þām geweorce, and þǣr nān hefelic gefeoht ne wearþ, and Mierce friþ nāmon wiþ þone here.

869. Hēr fōr se here eft tō Eoforwīcceastre, and þǣr sæt .i. gēar.

870. Hēr rād se here ofer Mierce innan Eastengle and wintersetl nāmon æt Þēodforda, and þȳ wintre Ēadmund cyning him wiþ feaht, and þā Deniscan sige
55 nāmon, and þone cyning ofslōgon, and þæt lond all geēodon. And þȳ gēare gefōr Ceolnoþ ærcebiscep.

871. Hēr cuōm se here tō Rēadingum on Westseaxe, and þæs ymb .iii. niht ridon .ii. eorlas ūp. Þā gemētte hīe Æþelwulf aldorman on Englafelda, and him þǣr wiþ gefeaht and sige nam. Þæs ymb .iiii. niht Æþered cyning and Ælfred his brōþur
60 þǣr micle fierd tō Rēadingum gelǣddon, and wiþ þone here gefuhton, and þǣr wæs micel wæl geslægen on gehwæþre hond, and Æþelwulf aldormon wearþ ofslægen, and þā Deniscan āhton wælstōwe gewald. And þæs ymb .iiii. niht gefeaht Æþered cyning and Ælfred his brōþur wiþ alne þone here on Æscesdune, and hīe wǣrun on twǣm gefylcum: on ōþrum wæs Bachsecg and
65 Halfdene þā hǣþnan cyningas, and on ōþrum wǣron þā eorlas. And þā gefeaht se cyning Æþered wiþ þāra cyninga getruman, and þǣr wearþ se cyning Bagsecg ofslægen; and Ælfred his brōþur wiþ þāra eorla getruman, and þǣr wearþ Sīdroc eorl ofslægen se alda, and Sīdroc eorl se gioncga, and Ōsbearn eorl, and Fræna eorl, and Hareld eorl, and þā hergas bēgen geflīemde, and fela þūsenda
70 ofslægenra, and onfeohtende wǣron oþ niht. And þæs ymb .xiiii. niht gefeaht Æþered cyning and Ælfred his brōður wiþ þone here æt Basengum, and þǣr þā Deniscan sige nāmon. And þæs ymb .ii. mōnaþ gefeaht Æþered cyning and

45 *Scīreburnan*] Sherborne, Dorset
46 *Mierce*] the former kingdom of Mercia
46 *Snotengahām*] Nottingham
47 *Burgræd Miercna cyning*] Burgræd was king of Mercia.
53 *Eastengle*] East Anglia
54 *Ēadmund*] King Edmund of East Anglia was venerated as a saint after his death as a martyr.
56 *Ceolnoþ*] Ceolnoth, archbishop of Canterbury, 833–870
57 *Rēadingum*] Reading
58 *Englafelda*] Englefield, Barkshire
64 *Æscesdune*] Ashdown, Berkshire
65 *Halfdene*] Halfdan, king of the Danes, was in command of the Danish army since its arrival in 865.
71 *Basengum*] Basing, Hampshire

Ælfred his brōþur wiþ þone here æt Meretune, and hīe wærun on tuæm gefylcium, and hīe būtū geflīemdon, and longe on dæg sige āhton; and þær wearþ
75 micel wælsliht on gehwæþere hond, and þā Deniscan āhton wælstōwe gewald. And þær wearþ Hēahmund biscep ofslægen, and fela gōdra monna; and æfter þissum gefeohte cuōm micel sumorlida; and þæs ofer Ēastron gefōr Æþered cyning, and hē rīcsode .v. gēar, and his līc līþ æt Winburnan.

Þā fēng Ælfred Æþelwulfing his brōþur tō Wesseaxna rīce; and þæs ymb ānne
80 mōnaþ gefeaht Ælfred cyning wiþ alne þone here lȳtle werede æt Wiltūne, and hine longe on dæg geflīemde, and þā Deniscan āhton wælstōwe gewald. And þæs gēares wurdon .viiii. folcgefeoht gefohten wiþ þone here on þȳ cynerīce be sūþan Temese, and būtan þām þe him Ælfred þæs cyninges brōþur, and ānlipig aldormon, and cyninges þegnas oft rāde onridon þe mon nā ne rīmde, and þæs
85 gēares wærun ofslægene .viiii. eorlas and ān cyning; and þȳ gēare nāmon Westseaxe friþ wiþ þone here.

872. Hēr fōr se here tō Lundenbyrig from Rēadingum, and þær wintersetl nam, and þā nāmon Mierce friþ wiþ þone here.

873. Hēr fōr se here on Norþhymbre, and hē nam wintersetl on Lindesse æt
90 Tureces iege, and þā nāmon Mierce friþ wiþ þone here.

1066. On þissum gēare cōm Harold cyng of Eoforwīc tō Westmynstre tō þām Ēastran, þe wæron æfter þām middanwintre þe se cyng forðfērde; and wæron þā Ēastran on þone dæg .xvi. kalendas Mai. Þā wearð geond eall Englaland swylc tācen on heofenum gesewen, swylce nān man ær ne geseah. Sume men cwēdon
95 þæt hit cometa se steorra wære þone sume men hātað þone fæxedon steorran; and hē ætēowde ærest on þone æfen Letania Maior .viii. kalendas Mai, and swā scān ealle þā seofon niht. And sōna þēræfter cōm Tostig eorl in fram begeonde sæ intō Wiht mid swā miclum liðe swā hē begitan mihte; and him man geald þær ægþær ge feoh ge metsunge. And Harold cyng, his brōþor, gegædrade swā micelne
100 sciphere and ēac landhere swā nān cyng hēr on lande ær ne dyde, for þām þe him

---

73 *Meretune*] probably Merton, Oxfordshire
76 *Hēahmund*] Hēahmund was bishop of Sherborne.
77 *sumorlida*] a great summer army, probably under the command of Guthrum, which whom Alfred will eventually sign a treaty.
78 *Winburnan*] Wimborne, Dorstet
80 *Wiltūne*] Wilton, Wiltshire
83 *Temese*] the River Thames
87 *Lundenbyrig*] London
89 *Lindesse*] Lindsey, today Lincolnshire
90 *Tureces iege*] Torksey, Lincolnshire
92 *Ēastran*] Holy Week up to and including Easter Sunday
92 *se cyng*] Edward the Confessor, who died on the 5th of January 1066.
93 *.xvi. kalendas Mai*] 16th of April
96 *Letania Maior .viii. kalendas Mai*] The date of this feast day is the 25th of April; 'æfen (eve) viii kalendas' is thus the 24th of April.
97 *Tostig eorl*] Harold's brother, earl of Northumbria from 1055–1056
100 *sciphere and ēac landhere*] 'here' usually refers to the enemy forces in the Chronicle.

wæs gecȳðd þæt Wyllelm Bastard wolde hider and ðis land gewinnen: eallswā hit
syððan āēode. And þā wīle cōm Tostig eorl intō Humbran mid sixtigum scipum,
and Ēadwine eorl cōm mid lanferde and ādrāf hine ūt, and þā butsacarlas hine
forsōcan. And hē fōr tō Scotlande mid .xii. snaccum, and hine gemētte þǣr
105   Harold cyng of Norwegon mid þrēom hund scypum, and Tostig him tō bēah and
his man wearð. And hī fōron þā bēgen intō Humbran oð þæt hī cōmon tō
Eoforwīc; and heom þǣr wið fuhton Ēadwine eorl and Morkere eorl, his brōðor,
ac þā Normen āhton sige. Man cȳðde þā Harolde, Engla cynge, þæt þis wæs þus
gefaren, and þis gefeoht wæs on Uigilia Sancti Mathei.
110   Ðā cōm Harold ūre cyng on unwær on þā Normenn and hytte hī begeondan
Eoforwīc æt Stemfordbrygge mid micclan here englisces folces, and þǣr wearð
on dæg swīðe stranglic gefeoht on bā halfe. Þār wearð ofslægen Harold Harfagera
and Tosti eorl, and þā Normen þe þǣr tō lāfe wǣron wurdon on flēame, and þā
engliscan hī hindan hetelīce slōgon oð þæt hīg sume tō scype cōman, sume
115   ādruncen, sume ēac forbærnde, and swā mislīce forfarene þæt þǣr wæs lȳt tō
lāfe; and Engle āhton wælstōwe geweald. Se kyng þā geaf gryð Ōlāfe, þæs Norna
cynges suna, and heora biscoppe, and þān eorle of Orcanēge, and eallon þān þe
on þām scypum tō lāfe wǣron. And hī fōron þā ūpp tō ūran kyninge, and swōron
āðas þæt hī æfre woldon fryð and frēondscype intō þisan lande haldan; and se
120   cyng hī lēt hām faran mid .xxiiii. scypum. Þās twā folcgefeoht wǣron gefremmede binnan fīf nihtan.
        Ðā cōm Wyllelm eorl of Normandīge intō Pefnesēa on Sancte Michæles
mæsseǣfen, and sōna þæs hī fēre wǣron, worhton castel æt Hæstingaport. Þis
wearð þā Harolde cynge gecȳdd, and hē gaderade þā mycelne here and cōm him
125   tōgēnes æt þǣre hāran apuldran. And Wyllelm him cōm ongēan on unwær, ǣr his
folc gefylced wǣre. Ac se kyng þēah him swīðe heardlīce wið feaht mid þām
mannum þe him gelǣstan woldon; and þǣr wearð micel wæl geslægen on ǣgðre
healfe. Ðǣr wearð ofslægen Harold kyng, and Lēofwine eorl his brōðor, and
Gyrð eorl his brōðor, and fela gōdra manna; and þā Frencyscan āhton wælstōwe
130   geweald: eallswā heom God ūðe for folces synnon.

---

101 *Wyllelm Bastard*] William the Conqueror is often called 'bastard' in English sources (see
M 5/65, 93 and 206).
101–102 *eallswā . . . āēode*] The subordinate clause clearly shows that this entry was
composed *after* the Battle of Hastings (see also 'lengtene', line 150).
103 *Ēadwine*] earl of Mercia
103 *hine*] Tostig
105 *Harold cyng of Norwegon*] King Harald Sigurdsson of Norway (1046–1066)
107 *Morkere*] earl of Northumbria
109 *Uigilia Sancti Mathei*] September 20th
111 *Stemfordbrygge*] Stamford Bridge (northeast of York) where the Norwegian invading army
was decisively repelled.
112 *Harold Harfagera*] The chronicler here confuses King Harald's actual epithet 'harðráði'
(the hard) with 'hárfagri' (the fair-haired).
116 *Ōlāfe*] Olaf, King Harald of Norway's son
122 *Pefnesēa*] Pevensey (Sussex), an ancient Roman fortress west of Hastings
122–123 *Sancte Michæles mæsseǣfen*] September 28th
129 *Frencyscan*] 'the French' (probably derogatory)
129–130 *wælstōwe geweald*] see line 116: 'Engle āhton wælstōwe geweald'

Aldred arcebiscop and sēo burhwaru on Lundene woldon habban þā Ēadgār cild tō kynge, eallswā him wel gecynde wæs. And Ēadwine and Morkere him behēton þæt hī mid him feohtan woldon; ac swā hit æfre forðlīcor bēon sceolde, swā wearð hit fram dæge tō dæge lætre and wyrre, eallswā hit æt þām ende eall
135 gefērde. Þis gefeoht wæs gedōn on þone dæg Calesti pāpe. And Wyllelm eorl fōr eft ongēan tō Hæstingan, and geanbīdode þǣr hwæðer man him tō būgan wolde. Ac þā hē ongeat þæt man him tō cuman nolde, hē fōr ūpp mid eallon his here þe him tō lāfe wæs and him syððan fram ofer sǣ cōm, and hergade ealne þone ende þe hē oferfērde oð þæt hē cōm tō Beorhhāmstede. And þǣr him cōm ongēan
140 Ealdred arcebiscop, and Ēadgār cild, and Ēadwine eorl, and Morkere eorl, and ealle þā betstan men of Lundene, and bugon þā for nēode þā mǣst wæs tō hearme gedōn. And þæt wæs micel unrǣd þæt man ǣror swā ne dyde, þā hit God bētan nolde for ūrum synnum; and gȳsledan and swōron him āðas, and hē heom behēt þæt hē wolde heom hold hlāford bēon. And þēah onmang þisan hī hergedan eall
145 þæt hī oferfōron.

Ðā on midwintres dæg hine hālgode tō kynge Ealdred arcebiscop on West-mynstre, and hē sealde him on hand mid Crīstes bēc and ēac swōr, ǣr þan þe hē wolde þā corōna him on hēafode settan, þæt hē wolde þisne þēodscype swā wel haldan swā ǣnig kyncg ætforan him betst dyde, gif hī him holde bēon woldon.
150 Swāþēah leide gyld on mannum swīðe stīð, and fōr þā on þām lengtene ofer sǣ tō Normandīge and nam mid him Stīgand arcebiscop, and Ægelnāð abbod on Glæstingabiri, and Ēadgār cild, and Ēadwine eorl and Morkere eorl and Wælþēof eorl, and manege ōðre gōde men of Englalande. And Ōda biscop and Wyllelm eorl belifen hēr æfter and worhton castelas wīde geond þās þēode, and earm folc
155 swencte – and ā syððan hit yflade swīðe. Wurðe gōd se ende, þonne God wylle.

---

131 *Aldred arcebiscop*] Ealdred, Archbishop of York
131–132 *Ēadgār cild*] great-grandchild of King Æthelred and descendant of the West Saxon royal line
135 *þone dæg Calesti pāpe*] the feast day of Pope Callixtus I, i. e. Saturday, October 14th, 1066
147 *hē sealde*] 'William promised'
147 *Crīstes bēc*] the New Testament
147–148 *hē wolde*] Ealdred
150 *lengtene*] spring of 1067
151 *Stīgand arcebiscop*] Stīgand was Archbishop of Canterbury.
153 *Wælþēof eorl*] powerful earl who ruled Huntingdon, Northampton, Bedford, and Cambridge
153 *Oda biscop*] William's half-brother, Bishop of Bayeux
153–154 *Wyllelm eorl*] William fitz Osbern, seneschal of King William

Text 3: The Old English Bede

Bede's *Historia Ecclesiastica Gentis Anglorum* is the most important historical source for the early history of Anglo-Saxon England. Bede writes a history of the English people in five books beginning with the conquest of England by Caesar and continuing up to 731. The original is in Latin and was translated into Old English about one hundred and fifty years later. Obviously, this work fits perfectly into the educational program began by King Alfred (see introductions O 2 and 5), but the problem of the identity of the translator has not been solved to date.

Much in the style of Orosius' *Historiae adversum paganos* and Eusebius' *Historia Ecclesiastica* (available to him in Latin translation), Bede shows the development and (moral) progression of Christianity in England, and of England under the influence of Christianity. The historicity of his own text is, however, extremely important to Bede, who indeed shows an ongoing conscientiousness regarding the events he describes. Similar to a modern historian, Bede relies primarily on primary sources, which he had sent to him from monasteries throughout England. As he emphasises in his prologue, *Ut autem in his quae scripsi, vel tibi, vel ceteris auditoribus sive lectoribus huius Historiae occasionem dubitandi subtraham, quibus haec maxime auctoribus didicerim breviter intimare curabo* – 'And to the intent that I may put both you and all others that shall hear or read the said History out of all doubt of the verity in those things I have written, I will be careful briefly to show you what authors I have chiefly followed in the making thereof'. In this respect he was successful; modern historians (albeit working with fewer sources than Bede was able to use) have not been able to find many inaccuracies in his account. At the same time, what we could anachronistically call a 'modern' approach is tempered by the medieval desire to 'tell a good tale', whence come the details that a modern reader would not expect in a history: miracles and marvels. As Bede was convinced that the Christianisation of England was part of God's divine plan, the manifestation of God's power at times of great importance was made evident in the form of comets, plagues or other inexplicable events. As a natural progression, the conflict of the Irish-Celtic Church versus the Roman Church is perhaps somewhat exaggerated; the Council of Whitby and the succeeding triumph of Roman Christianity is portrayed as a central event in the history of England.

The conversion of King Edwin in 627 (ii. 13) is described both as a historical event as well as a dramatic step towards the Christianisation of all England. The narrative style allows the reader a feeling of actually witnessing the events which Bede describes, and much action has been added to the narrative to achieve this effect. On the other hand, we have the development of Old English Christian poetry: Cædmon the poet and one of his poems feature in the beginning of this development (iv. 24). Cædmon's biography and the dream in which he receives his poetic abilities are described similarly to Edwin's conversion; with the addition of dialogue, the reader is drawn further into the story. Cædmon's poetic skills are a direct gift from God, so it is clear that his poetry must serve the will of God, praising him and helping others to come to his service (see ll. 71–73, 134–136). The closing of the Cædmon episode is very moving – Cædmon speaks about his coming death and emphasises how unimportant worldly fame is to him, and that he has only worked to please God (see ll. 161, 168).

Cædmon's Hymn shows how the use of the poetic diction and alliterative verse from Germanic heroic poetry can be transported from a pagan setting to a Christian one. It is foremost among Old English Christian poetry, the first of an impressive genre that spawned *Andreas, Exodus, Judith,* and *The Dream of the Rood* (O 11).

The text shows some non-WS features: breaking does not occur in *aldormen* (l. 31); however it does occur in *ealdormann, ealdormannum, ealdormon* (ll. 20, 23, 107). Forms like *wytum* (l. 3), but *witum* (l. 7); *syndon* (ll. 14, 18); *clypode* (l. 35), *clyppan* (l. 118) demonstrate that earlier *i* tended to be written as *y* (i. e. it appears that *y* under the influence of i-mutation was in the process of being unrounded to *i*. Other features of the text include vocalic digraphs after the word-initial palatal consonant group *sc-*: *bisceop, ealdorbisceop* (ll. 6, 9, 33); *biscop, biscope* (ll. 42, 44, 52, 62); *sceolde, sceoldon* (ll. 2, 82 144); *scolde, scolden* (ll. 47, 162). OE *ā* under the influence of i-mutation occurs as *e*, an Anglian feature, versus WS *æ*: *nēalēhte, nēalēcan* (ll. 61, 83). Occasionally, vocalic length is indicated by a digraph: *booc* (l. 127) and *wiites* (l. 132).

Sources: Corpus Christi College, Oxford, MS 279 und Bodleian Library, Oxford, MS Tanner 10. – Marsden (2004); Mitchell/Robinson (1992); Miller (1890), Schipper (1899). – Secondary literature: Whitelock (1963).

Þā se cyning þā þās word gehȳrde, þā andswarode hē him and cwæð þæt hē æghwæþer ge wolde ge sceolde þām gelēafan onfōn þe hē lærde; cwæð hwæþere þæt hē wolde mid his frēondum and mid his wytum gesprec and geþeaht habban, þæt gif hī mid hine þæt geþafian woldan þæt hī ealle ætsomne on līfes willan
5 Crīste gehālgade wǣran. Þā dyde se cyning swā swā hē cwæð, and se bisceop þæt geþafade.

Þā hæfde hē gesprec and geþeaht mid his witum, and syndriglīce wæs fram him eallum frignende hwylc him þūhte and gesawen wǣre þēos nīwe lār and þǣre godcundnesse bīgong þe þǣr lǣred wæs. Him þā andswarode his eal-
10 dorbisceop, Cēfi wæs hāten: "Geseoh þū, cyning, hwelc þēos lār sīe þe ūs nū bodad is. Ic þē sōðlīce andette þæt ic cūðlīce geleornad hæbbe þæt eallinga nāwiht mægenes ne nyttnesse hafað sīo æfæstnes þe wē oð ðis hæfdon and beēodon. For ðon nænig þīnra þegna nēodlīcor ne gelustfullīcor hine sylfne underþēodde tō ūra goda bīgange þonne ic, and nōht þon lǣs monige syndon þā
15 þe māran gefe and fremsumnesse æt þē onfēngon þonne ic, and in eallum þingum māran gesynto hæfdon. Hwæt, ic wāt, gif ūre godo ǣnige mihte hæfdon, þonne woldan hīe mē mā fultumian, for þon ic him geornlīcor þēodde ond hȳrde. For þon mē þynceð wīslic, gif þū gesēo þā þing beteran and strangran þe ūs nīwan bodad syndon, þæt wē þām onfōn."

_____

1 *him*] Bishop Paulinus
4 *līfes willan*] literally: 'the fountain of life'; here a reference to the baptismal font
19 *onfōn*] 'should accept' (plural present subjunctive)

20 Þæs wordum ōþer cyninges wita and ealdormann geþafunge sealde, and tō
þǣre sprǣce fēng and þus cwæð: "Þyslic mē is gesewen, þū cyning, þis andwearde līf manna on eorðan tō wiðmetenesse þǣre tīde þe ūs uncūð is; swylc swā
þū æt swǣsendum sitte mid þīnum ealdormannum and þegnum on wintertīde, and
sīe fȳr onǣled and þīn heall gewyrmed, and hit rīne and snīwe and styrme ūte;
25 cume ān spearwa and hrædlīce þæt hūs þurhflēo, cume þurh ōþre duru in, þurh
ōþre ūt gewīte. Hwæt, hē on þā tīd þe hē inne bið, ne bið hrinen mid þȳ storme
þæs wintres; ac þæt bið ān ēagan bryhtm and þæt lǣsste fæc, ac hē sōna of wintra
on þone winter eft cymeð. Swā þonne þis monna līf tō medmiclum fæce ætȳweð:
hwæt þǣr foregange, oððe hwæt þǣr æfterfylige, wē ne cunnon. For ðon gif þēos
30 nīwe lār ōwiht cūðlicre ond gerisenlicre brenge, þæs weorþe is þæt wē þǣre
fylgen." Þeossum wordum gelīcum ōðre aldormen and ðæs cyninges geþeahteras
sprǣcan.
    Þā gēn tōætȳhte Cēfi and cwæð þæt hē wolde Paulīnus þone bisceop geornlīcor
gehȳran be þām Gode sprecende þām þe hē bodade. Þā hēt se cyning swā dōn. Þā
35 hē þā his word gehȳrde, þā clypode hē and þus cwæð: "Geare ic þæt ongeat þæt
ðæt nōwiht wæs þæt wē beēodan; for þon swā micle swā ic geornlīcor on þām
bīgange þæt sylfe sōð sōhte, swā ic hit lǣs mētte. Nū þonne ic openlīce ondette
þæt on þysse lāre þæt sylfe sōð scīneð þæt ūs mæg þā gyfe syllan ēcre ēadignesse
and ēces līfes hǣlo. For þon ic þonne nū lǣre, cyning, þæt þæt templ and þā
40 wīgbedo þā ðe wē būton wæstmum ǣnigre nytnisse hālgodon, þæt wē þā hraþe
forlēosen ond fȳre forbærnen." Ono hwæt, hē þā se cyning openlīce ondette þām
biscope ond him eallum þæt hē wolde fæstlīce þām dēofolgildum wiðsacan ond
Crīstes gelēafan onfōn.
    Mid þȳ þe hē þā se cyning from þǣm foresprecenan biscope sōhte ond āhsode
45 heora hālignesse þe hēo ǣr biēodon, hwā ðā wīgbed ond þā hergas þāra
dēofolgilda mid heora hegum þe hēo ymbsette wǣron, hēo ǣrest āīdligan ond
tōweorpan scolde, þā ondswerede hē: "Efne ic. Hwā mæg þā nū, þā þe ic longe
mid dysignesse beēode, tō bysene ōðerra monna gerisenlecor tōweorpan þonne ic
seolfa þurh þā snytro þe ic from þǣm sōðan Gode onfēng?" Ond hē ðā sōna from
50 him āwearp þā īdlan dysignesse þe hē ǣr beēode, ond þone cyning bæd þæt hē
him wǣpen sealde ond stōdhors, þæt hē meahte on cuman ond dēofolgyld
tōweorpan; for þon þām biscope heora hālignesse ne wæs ālȳfed þæt hē mōste
wǣpen wegan ne elcor būton on mȳran rīdan. Þā sealde se cyning him sweord,
þæt hē hine mid gyrde, ond nom his spere on hond ond hlēop on þæs cyninges
55 stēdan ond tō þǣm dēofulgeldum fērde. Þā ðæt folc hine þā geseah swā
gescyrpedne, þā wēndon hēo þæt hē teola ne wiste, ac þæt hē wēdde. Sōna þæs
þe hē nēalēhte tō þǣm herige, þā scēat hē mid þȳ spere þæt hit sticode fæste on
þǣm herige, ond wæs swīðe gefēonde þǣre ongytenesse þæs sōðan Godes

---

20 *Þæs*] 'whose' (genitive singular masculine) referring to Coefi, l. 10
27 *ēagan bryhtm*] blink of an eye
31 *Þeossum wordum gelīcum*] 'with similar words'
45 *heora hālignesse*] gsg. referring to 'biscope': 'the priest of their religion'
56 *teola ne wiste*] 'that he had lost his wits'.
56–57 *Sōna . . . hē*] 'as soon as he'

bīgonges. Ond hē ðā hēht his gefēran tōweorpan ealne þone herig ond þā
60 getimbro ond forbærnan. Is sēo stōw gȳt ætēawed gū þāra dēofulgilda, nōht feor
ēast from Eoforwīcceastre, begeondan Deorwentan þǣre ēa; ond gēn tō dæge is
nemned Gōdmundingahām þǣr se biscop, þurh ðæs sōðan Godes inbryrdnesse,
tōwearp ond fordyde þā wīgbed þe hē seolfa ǣr gehālgode.

Ðā onfēng Ēadwine cyning mid eallum þǣm æðelingum his þēode ond mid
65 micle folce Crīstes gelēafan ond fulwihte bæðe, þȳ endlyftan gēare his rīces.

In ðeosse abbudissan mynstre wæs sum brōðor syndriglīce mid godcundre gife
gemǣred ond geweorðad. For þon hē gewunade gerisenlice lēoð wyrcan, þā ðe tō
æfæstnisse ond tō ārfæstnisse belumpen, swā ðætte swā hwæt swā hē of
godcundum stafum þurh bōceras geleornode, þæt hē æfter medmiclum fæce in
70 scopgereorde mid þā mǣstan swētnisse ond inbryrdnisse geglǣngde, ond in
Engliscgereorde wel geworht forþbrōhte. Ond for his lēoþsongum monigra
monna mōd oft tō worulde forhogdnisse ond tō geþēodnisse þæs heofonlican līfes
onbærnde wǣron. Ond ēac swelce monige ōðre æfter him in Ongelþēode
ongunnon æfæste lēoð wyrcan, ac nǣnig hwæðre him þæt gelīce dōn meahte. For
75 þon hē nales from monnum ne þurh mon gelǣred wæs, þæt hē þone lēoðcræft
leornade, ac hē wæs godcundlīce gefultumed, ond þurh Godes gife þone songcræft onfēng. Ond hē for ðon nǣfre nōht lēasunge, ne īdles lēoþes wyrcan
meahte, ac efne þā ān þā ðe tō æfestnesse belumpon, ond his þā æfestan tungan
gedafenade singan.
80 Wæs hē se mon in weoruldhāde geseted oð þā tīde þe hē wæs gelȳfdre ylde,
ond hē nǣfre nǣnig lēoð geleornade. Ond hē for þon oft in gebēorscipe, þonne
þǣr wæs blisse intinga gedēmed, þæt hēo ealle sceoldon þurh endebyrdnesse be
hearpan singan, þonne hē geseah þā hearpan him nēalēcan, þonne ārās hē for
scome from þǣm symble, ond hām ēode tō his hūse. Þā hē þæt þā sumre tīde
85 dyde þæt hē forlēt þæt hūs þæs gebēorscipes, ond ūt wæs gongende tō nēata
scipene, þāra heord him wæs þǣre neahte beboden, þā hē ðā þǣr in gelimplice
tīde his leomu on reste gesette ond onslēpte, þā stōd him sum mon æt þurh swefn,
ond hine hālette ond grētte, ond hine be his noman nemnde: 'Cedmon, sing mē
hwæthwugu.' Þā ondswarede hē ond cwæð: 'Ne con ic nōht singan. Ond ic for
90 þon of þeossum gebēorscipe ūt ēode, ond hider gewāt for þon ic nāht singan ne

60 *Is . . . dēofulgilda*] 'this place, formerly dedicated to the idols, can still be seen today'.
61 *Eoforwīcceastre*] York
61 *Deorwentan*] the River Derwent
62 *Gōdmundingahām*] Goddmanham, Yorkshire
66 *ðeosse abbudissan mynstre*] refers to Abbess Hild and the monastery of Whitby in
Yorkshire.
72 *mōd*] Nominative plural, not singular, is suggested by the predicate 'onbærnde wǣron'
(l. 73); in Bede's Latin, we find *animi* (plural).
75 *nales . . . mon*] see Gal 1:1: 'Paul, an apostle, not of men, neither by man, but by Jesus
Christ, and God the Father'.
79 *gedafenade*] impersonal use: 'and (which it) befitted his pious tongue to sing'.

cūðe.' Eft hē cwæð, sē ðe wið hine sprecende wæs: 'Hwæðre þū mē āht singan.'
Þā cwæð hē: 'Hwæt sceal ic singan?' Cwæð hē: 'Sing mē frumsceaft.' Þā hē ðā
þās andsware onfēng, þā ongon hē sōna singan in herenesse Godes Scyppendes
þā fers ond þā word, þe hē næfre gehȳrde, þǣre endebyrdnesse þis is:

95 Nū sculon herigean heofonrīces Weard,
  Meotodes meahte ond his mōdgeþanc,
  weorc Wuldorfæder, swā hē wundra gehwæs,
  ēce Drihten, ōr onstealde.
  Hē ærest sceōp eorðan bearnum
100 heofon tō hrōfe, hālig Scyppend.
  Þā middangeard monncynnes Weard,
  ēce Drihten, æfter tēode
  fīrum foldan, Frēa ælmihtig.

Þā ārās hē from þǣm slǣpe, ond eal þā þe hē slǣpende song fæste in gemynde
105 hæfde, ond þǣm wordum sōna monig word in þæt ilce gemet Gode wyrðes
songes tō geþēodde.

 Þā cōm hē on morgenne tō þǣm tūngerēfan þe his ealdormon wæs, sægde him
hwylce gife hē onfēng. Ond hē hine sōna tō þǣre abbudissan gelǣdde, ond hire
þā cȳðde ond sægde. Þā hēht hēo gesomnian ealle þā gelǣredestan men ond þā
110 leorneras, ond him ondweardum, hēt secgan þæt swefn ond þæt lēoð singan, þæt
ealra heora dōme gecoren wǣre, hwæt oððe hwonon þæt cuman wǣre. Þā wæs
him eallum gesegen, swā swā hit wæs, þæt him wǣre from Drihtne sylfum
heofonlic gifu forgifen. Þā rehton hēo him ond sægdon sum hālig spell ond
godcundre lāre word; bebudon him þā, gif hē meahte, þæt hē in swinsunge
115 lēoþsonges þæt gehwyrfde. Þā hē ðā hæfde þā wīsan onfongne, þā ēode hē hām
tō his hūse and cwōm eft on morgenne, ond þȳ betstan lēoðe geglenged him
āsong ond āgeaf þæt him beboden wæs.

 Ðā ongan sēo abbudisse clyppan ond lufigean þā Godes gife in þǣm men; ond
hēo hine þā monade ond lǣrde þæt hē woruldhād ānforlēte ond munuchād
120 onfēnge: ond hē þæt wel þafode. Ond hēo hine in þæt mynster onfēng mid his
gōdum, ond hine geþēodde tō gesomnunge þāra Godes þēowa, ond hēht hine
lǣran þæt getæl þæs hālgan stæres ond spelles. Ond hē eal þā hē in gehȳrnesse
geleornian meahte, mid hine gemyndgade, ond swā swā clǣne nēten eodorcende
in þæt swēteste lēoð gehwerfde. Ond his song ond his lēoð wǣron swā wynsumu
125 tō gehȳranne þætte seolfan þā his lārēowas æt his mūðe wreoton ond leornodon.

---

108 *abbudissan*] the reference is to Hild.
110 *him ondweardum*] 'in their presence' (instrumental dative)
111 *gecoren wǣre*] 'could be ascertained'; the subjunctive is quite frequent in clauses of
purpose.
111 *cuman wǣre*] the subjunctive expresses uncertainty.
112 *gesegen*] the subject 'it' has to be supplied: 'Then it was shown to all of them'.
118 *abbudisse*] i. e. Hild
120 *mynster*] the monastery of Whitby
121 *gōdum*] ambiguous; Bede's Latin 'cum omnibus suis' suggests the meaning '(Hild) and
her entire community'.
123 *clǣne nēten eodorcende*] see Lev 11:3

Song hē ǣrest be middangeardes gesceape ond bī fruman moncynnes ond eal
þæt stǣr Genesis (þæt is sēo ǣreste Moyses booc); ond eft bī ūtgonge Israhēla
folces of Ǣgypta londe ond bī ingonge þæs gehātlandes, ond bī ōðrum monegum
spellum þæs hālgan gewrites canōnes bōca, ond bī Crīstes menniscnesse ond bī
130 his þrōwunge ond bī his ūpāstīgnesse in heofonas, ond bī þæs Hālgan Gāstes
cyme ond þāra apostola lāre; ond eft bī þǣm ege þæs tōweardan dōmes ond bī
fyrhtu þæs tintreglican wiites ond bī swētnesse þæs heofonlecan rīces hē monig
lēoð geworhte. Ond swelce ēac ōðer monig be þǣm godcundan fremsumnessum
ond dōmum hē geworhte. In eallum þǣm hē geornlīce gēmde þæt hē men ātuge
135 from synna lufan ond māndǣda ond tō lufan ond tō geornfulnesse āwehte gōdra
dǣda; for þon hē wæs se mon swīþe ǣfæst ond regollecum þēodscipum
ēaðmōdlīce underþēoded. Ond wið ðǣm þā ðe in ōðre wīsan dōn woldon, hē wæs
mid welme micelre ellenwōdnisse onbærned; ond hē for ðon fægre ænde his līf
betȳnde ond geendade.
140   For þon þā ðǣre tīde nēalǣcte his gewitenesse ond forðfōre, þā wæs hē
fēowertȳnum dagum ǣr þæt hē wæs līchomlicre untrymnesse þrycced ond
hefgad, hwæðre tō þon gemetlīce þæt hē ealle þā tīd meahte ge sprecan ge
gongan. Wæs þǣr in nēaweste untrumra monna hūs, in þǣm heora þēaw wæs þæt
hēo þā untrumran ond þā ðe æt forðfōre wǣron inlǣdan sceoldon, ond him þǣr
145 ætsomne þegnian. Þā bæd hē his þegn on ǣfenne þǣre neahte þe hē of worulde
gongende wæs, þæt hē in þǣm hūse him stōwe gegearwode, þæt hē gerestan
meahte. Þā wundrode se þegn for hwon hē þæs bæde, for þon him þūhte þæt his
forðfōr swā nēah ne wǣre; dyde hwæðre swā swā hē cwæð ond bibēad. Ond mid
þȳ hē ðā þǣr on reste ēode, ond hē gefēonde mōde sumu þing mid him sprecende
150 ætgædere, ond glēowiende wæs þe þǣr ǣr inne wǣron, þā wæs ofer middeneaht
þæt hē frægn hwæðer hēo ǣnig hūsl inne hæfdon. Þā ondswarodon hēo ond
cwǣdon: 'Hwylc þearf is ðē hūsles? Ne þīnre forþfōre swā nēah is, nū þū þus
rōtlīce ond þus glædlīce tō ūs sprecende eart.' Cwæð hē eft: 'Berað mē hūsl tō.'
Þā hē hit þā on honda hæfde, þā frægn hē hwæþer hēo ealle smolt mōd ond būton
155 eallum incan blīðe tō him hæfdon. Þā ondswaredon hȳ ealle ond cwǣdon þæt hēo
nǣnigne incan tō him wiston, ac hēo ealle him swīðe blīðemōde wǣron. Ond hēo
wrixendlīce hine bǣdon þæt hē him eallum blīðe wǣre. Þā ondswarade hē ond
cwæð: 'Mīne brōðor, mīne þā lēofan, ic eom swīðe blīðemōd tō ēow ond tō
eallum Godes monnum.' Ond swā wæs hine getrymmende mid þȳ heofonlecan
160 wegneste, ond him ōðres līfes ingong gegearwode. Þā gȳt hē frægn hū nēah þǣre
tīde wǣre þætte þā brōðor ārīsan scolden ond Godes lof rǣran ond heora ūhtsong
singan. Þā ondswaredon hēo: 'Nis hit feor tō þon.' Cwæð hē: 'Teala; wuton wē

---

136 *regollecum*] dative plural referring to the monastic rule

140 *nēalǣcte*] impersonal use of the verb: 'it drew near'

141 *þæt . . . wæs*] the clause 'þæt he wæs' need not be translated. Bede's Latin (bk. iv, ch.
xxiv) reads: 'Nam propinquante hora sui decessus, quatuordecim diebus, praeveniente
corporea infirmitate, pressus est'.

143 *untrumra monna hūs*] the infirmatory of a monastery

152 *Ne . . . nēah is,*] here and at l. 160, *nēah* 'near, close' is specified by a dative: 'þīnre
forþfōre' and 'þǣre tīde'; the subject 'it' has to be supplied.

wel þǣre tīde bīdan.' Ond þā him gebæd ond hine gesegnode mid Crīstes
rōdetācne, ond his hēafod onhylde tō þām bolstre, ond medmicel fæc onslēpte;
165   ond swā mid stilnesse his līf geendade. Ond swā wæs geworden þætte, swā swā
hē hlūttre mōde ond bilwitre ond smyltre wilsumnesse Drihtne þēode, þæt hē ēac
swylce swā smylte dēaðe middangeard wæs forlǣtende, ond tō his gesihðe
becwōm. Ond sēo tunge þe swā monig hālwende word in þæs Scyppendes lof
gesette, hē ðā swelce ēac þā ȳtmǣstan word in his herenisse, hine seolfne
170   segniende ond his gāst in his honda bebēodende, betȳnde. Ēac swelce þæt is
gesegen þæt hē wǣre gewis his seolfes forðfōre, of þǣm wē nū secgan hȳrdon.

163 *him gebæd ond hine gesegnode*] *him* and *hine* are used with reflexive function.
168 *sēo tunge*] The translator construes the ablative of the original Latin ('illaque lingua') as
 nominative: 'and with his tongue'.
170–171 *is gesegen*] literally: 'that can be seen', i. e. 'it is evident'

Text 4: The Old English Orosius

The *Historiae Adversum Paganos*, written by Orosius in the early 5th century, was translated into Old English in the early 9th century: also a part King Alfred's educational reform. Orosius wrote a seven-volume universal history of the world just after Rome had been sacked by the Visigoths. In the face of pagan criticism, Orosius felt it necessary to defend Christianity and to prove that the disasters of the preceding years were not caused by Christianity, but by paganism. Indeed, he seeks to prove how much better the world has become since the advent of Christianity; the wars, epidemics, droughts, natural catastrophes and crimes (especially those on a mass scale, or those committed by a ruler) which occurred before his times are shown to be the natural result of a pagan society, whereas the recent disasters result rather from the continued practice of paganism than from the conversion to Christianity.

   Orosius was not the first Christian apologetic writer, but his history is the first Christian apologetic history. As such, his work fits perfectly into Alfred's program: the *Historiae* is both an encyclopaedic history of the world as well as a Christian treatise (see O 5/43–45). Like most of the Alfredian translations, this translation shows the typical traits – it is relatively free, translating the meaning rather than the exact wording (see also introduction to O 1). Additionally, the translator has reduced Orosius' polemic and added two eyewitness reports to enhance the geographic part of the history, which was lacking in its treatment of northern Europe and Scandinavia. These reports seem to have been made directly to Alfred, (*Ohthere sæde his hlaforde, Ælfrede cyninge* – 'Ohthere told his lord, King Alfred'), which led scholars to believe that Alfred himself had translated the history, an assumption which has since been abandoned. Ohthere, a Norwegian, reports to Alfred of his homeland and the trips he has made throughout Norway and Finland, describing also the customs of the Finns. Wulfstan, whose name could be either Viking or Anglo-Saxon, reports about his journey to what is now Estonia, and the customs of the people living there.

The text shows several late WS features: original *sel-* appears as <syl-> *sylf* (l. 5). Diphthongs under the influence of i-mutation appear as <y> versus earlier <ie>: *hȳrað* (ll. 4, 7). Loss of *g* when followed by *d* occurs (with compensatory lengthening) in *sæde* (l. 1). Occasionally the dative plural ends in *n*: *Swēon* (l. 7) versus regular *m*.

Sources: British Library, London, MS Cotton Tiberius B.i. – Bately (1980); Sweet (1883). – Secondary literature: Ekblom (1960), Bately (1970), Liggins (1970).

Wulfstān sæde þæt hē gefōre of Hæðum, þæt hē wǣre on Trūsō on syfan dagum and nihtum, þæt þæt scip wæs ealne weg yrnende under segle. Weonoðland him wæs on stēorbord, and on bæcbord him wæs Langaland and Lǣland and Falster and Scōnēg; and þās land eall hȳrað tō Denemearcan. And þonne Burgenda
5 land wæs ūs on bæcbord, and þā habbað him sylf cyning. Þonne æfter Burgenda

1 *Trūsō*] probably Truso, Poland
3–4 *Langaland, Lǣland, Falster; Scōnēcg*] the islands of Langeland, Lolland and Falster; Skåne (Sweden)
4 *hȳrað tō Denemearcan*] 'are governed by Denmark'
5 *Burgenda land*] the island of Bornholm

lande wǣron ūs þās land þā synd hātene ǣrest Blēcingaēg and Mēore and
Ēowland and Gotland on bǣcbord; and þās land hȳrað tō Swēon. And Weonodland wæs ūs ealne weg on stēorbord oð Wīslemūðan. Sēo Wīsle is swȳðe
mycel ēa, and hīo tōlīð Wītland and Weonodland; and þæt Wītland belimpeð tō
Estum. And sēo Wīsle līð ūt of Weonodlande and līð in Estmere; and se Estmere
is hūru fīftēne mīla brād. Þonne cymeð Ilfing ēastan in Estmere of ðǣm mere ðe
Trūsō standeð in staðe, and cumað ūt samod in Estmere, Ilfing ēastan of Estlande
and Wīsle sūðan of Winodlande. And þonne benimð Wīsle Ilfing hire naman, and
ligeð of þǣm mere west and norð on sǣ: for ðȳ hit man hǣt Wīslemūða.

Þæt Estland is swȳðe mycel, and þǣr bið swȳðe manig burh, and on ǣlcere
byrig bið cyningc. And þǣr bið swȳðe mycel hunig and fiscað; and se cyning and
þā rīcostan men drincað mȳran meolc, and þā unspēdigan and þā þēowan drincað
medo. Þǣr bið swȳðe mycel gewinn betwēonan him. And ne bið ðǣr nǣnig ealo
gebrowen mid Estum, ac þǣr bið medo genōh.

And þǣr is mid Estum ðēaw, þonne þǣr bið man dēad, þæt hē līð inne unforbǣrned mid his māgum and frēondum mōnað, ge hwīlum twēgen; and þā
kyningas and þā ōðre hēahðungene men swā micle lencg swā hī māran spēda
habbað, hwīlum healf gēar þæt hī bēoð unforbǣrned and licgað bufan eorðan on
hyra hūsum. And ealle þā hwīle þe þæt līc bið inne, þǣr sceal bēon gedrync and
plega, oð ðone dæg þe hī hine forbǣrnað. Þonne þȳ ylcan dæg þe hī hine tō þǣm
āde beran wyllað, þonne tōdǣlað hī his feoh þæt þǣr tō lāfe bið æfter þǣm
gedrynce and þǣm plegan, on fīf oððe syx, hwȳlum on mā, swā swā þæs fēos
andefn bið. Ālecgað hit ðonne forhwǣga on ānre mīle þone mǣstan dǣl fram
þǣm tūne, þonne ōðerne, ðonne þǣne þriddan, oþ þe hyt eall ālēd bið on þǣre
ānre mīle; and sceall bēon se lǣsta dǣl nȳhst þǣm tūne ðe se dēada man on līð.
Ðonne sceolon bēon gesamnode ealle ðā menn ðe swyftoste hors habbað on þǣm
lande, forhwǣga on fīf mīlum oððe on syx mīlum fram þǣm fēo. Þonne ærnað hȳ
ealle tōweard þǣm fēo; ðonne cymeð sē man se þæt swiftoste hors hafað tō þǣm
ǣrestan dǣle and tō þǣm mǣstan, and swā ǣlc æfter ōðrum, oþ hit bið eall
genumen. And sē nimð þone lǣstan dǣl se nȳhst þǣm tūne þæt feoh geǣrneð.
And þonne rīdeð ǣlc hys weges mid ðān fēo, and hyt mōtan habban eall; and for
ðȳ þǣr bēoð þā swiftan hors ungefōge dȳre. And þonne hys gestrēon bēoð þus
eall āspended, þonne byrð man hine ūt, and forbǣrneð mid his wǣpnum and
hrægle. And swīðost ealle hys spēda hȳ forspendað mid þān langan legere þæs

---

6–7 *Blēcingaēg . . . Gotland*] Blekinge (Sweden); Möre (Sweden); the islands of Öland and
Gotland

7 *hȳrað tō Swēon*] 'are governed by Sweden'

8 *Wīslemūðan*] the mouth of the Vistula – the passage between Frisches Haff and the Bay of
Danzig

9 *Wītland*] region east of the Vistula

10 *Estum*] the 'Easterners', probably the Baltic Prussians

16 *hunig*] Before the introduction of sugar, honey was used as a sweetener and as such was an
important export of this area.

25 *þe*] 'the day on which'

25 *þȳ ylcan dæg*] 'on the very same day' (*dæg* is not inflected)

36 *mōtan*] plural present: 'and they may'

40 dēadan mannes inne, and þæs þe hȳ be þǣm wegum ālecgað þe þā fremdan tō
  ærnað and nimað. And þæt is mid Estum þēaw þæt þǣr sceal ælces geðēodes
  man bēon forbærned; and gyf þār man ān bān findeð unforbærned, hī hit sceolan
  miclum gebētan.

     And þǣr is mid Estum ān mǣgð þæt hī magon cyle gewyrcan; and þȳ þǣr
45 licgað þā dēadan men swā lange and ne fūliað, þæt hȳ wyrcað þone cyle hine on.
  And þēah man āsette twēgen fætels full ealað oððe wæteres, hȳ gedōð þæt ōðer
  bið oferfroren, sam hit sȳ sumor sam winter.

---

40 *and þæs þe hȳ*] 'and because they' (distribute his possessions)
44 *mǣgð, þæt hī*] 'a tribe which'
44 *cyle gewyrcan*] How this was possible still remains a mystery.
45 *þæt*] 'because'
46 *ealað*] see lines 18–19, where it is claimed that the Estonians don't brew beer.
46 *ōðer*] 'one of the two'; the pronominal adjective 'ægþer: both (of the two)' would seem to
  make more sense.

Text 5: King Alfred

King Alfred the Great's legacy is a combination of military and educational triumph. This can be seen in some of the statues erected in his memory, for example at his birthplace, Wantage, where he is depicted holding a sword as well as a scroll. During his reign from 871–899, Alfred was not only able to limit the Viking expansion in England, signing the Treaty of Alfred and Guthrum in 886, but also instituted a period of learning, know as the "Alfredian Renaissance" (see also introduction to O 2). Because Latin competence had so strongly declined (ll. 11–16), Alfred felt it necessary to translate all important Christian works into English. Alfred began this project himself by translating Gregory the Great's *Cura Pastoralis* – the "Hierdeboc", which was then to be copied for every bishopric in his realm. Also a part of his project are Boethius' *Consolatio Philosophiae*, Orosius' *Historiae Adversum Paganos* (see O 4), and Augustinus' *Soliloquies* and Bede's *Historia Ecclesiastica Gentis Anglorum* (see O 3). Though Alfred was once held to be responsible for most of these translations, the *Cura Pastoralis* and *Consolatio Philosophiae* are the only works that are now attributed to him.

In the Preface to *Cura Pastoralis*, Alfred explains to the bishops he wishes to enlist in his project (in this manuscript, to Bishop Wærferð) why he feels it necessary to begin such a project, and also attempts to justify his own translation attempt. He emphasises the problems involved in translation, typifying medieval methods of translation: "hwilum word be worde, hwilum andgit of andgiete" (sometimes word for word, sometimes thought for thought). Indeed, as he continues, he has translated "as well as I have understood and as far as I can bring across in the most meaningful way" (l. 66). Here we see definite parallels to Ælfric (see O 1), who originally did not want to translate the Bible at all for fear of losing or misconstruing meaning, and thereby confusing the public.

Not only the text itself, but also the freely composed Preface have extremely cumbersome sentence structure, which shows the practice of relying upon Latin grammatical structure, even when composing original Old English works. In this we can see how seldom Old English was used for prose before this time. Alfred's works of translation are therefore not only the impulse upon which the educational system of the next two centuries was based, but also for the development of an Old English prose style.

The text shows several inconsistencies, such as the occasional lack of breaking before *ld*, as in *onwald* (l. 4) (versus *onweald*, l. 6). Instead of regular West Saxon *ǣ*, *ē* occurs occasionally, as in *lēfdon* (l. 21). Different graphs are used for the vowels in unstressed medial and final syllables, as in *hīersumedon* (l. 5), *wundrade* (l. 33) for earlier -*od*-.

Sources: Bodleian Library, Oxford, MS Hatton 20. – Marsden (2004);
Mitchell/Robinson (1992); Sweet (1871). – Secondary literature: Klaeber (1923),
Duckett (1956). – Facsimile: Ker (1956).

Ælfred kyning hāteð grētan Wærferð biscep his wordum luflīce ond frēondlīce.
Ond ðē cȳðan hāte ðæt mē cōm swīðe oft on gemynd hwelce wiotan iū wǣron
giond Angelcynn, ǣgþer ge godcundra hāda ge woruldcundra; ond hū gesǣliglica
tīda ðā wǣron giond Angelcynn; ond hū ðā kyningas ðe ðone onwald hæfdon
5 ðæs folces Gode ond his ǣrendwrecum hīersumedon; ond hīe ǣgðer ge hiora
sibbe ge hiora siodu ge hiora onweald innanbordes gehīoldon, ond ēac ūt hiora
ēðel rȳmdon; ond hū him ðā spēow ǣgðer ge mid wīge ge mid wīsdōme; ond ēac
ðā godcundan hādas, hū giorne hīe wǣron ǣgðer ge ymb lāre ge ymb liornunga,
ge ymb ealle ðā ðīowotdōmas ðe hīe Gode dōn scoldon; ond hū man ūtanbordes
10 wīsdōm ond lāre hieder on lond sōhte; ond hū wē hīe nū sceoldon ūte begietan,
gif wē hīe habban sceoldon. Swǣ clǣne hīo wæs oðfeallenu on Angelcynne ðæt
swīðe fēawa wǣron behionan Humbre ðe hiora ðēninga cūðen understondan on
Englisc, oððe furðum ān ǣrendgewrit of Lǣdene on Englisc āreccean; ond ic
wēne ðætte nōht monige begiondan Humbre nǣren. Swǣ fēawa hiora wǣron ðæt
15 ic furðum ānne ānlēpne ne mæg geðencean be sūðan Temese, ðā ðā ic tō rīce
fēng. Gode ælmihtegum sīe ðonc ðætte wē nū ǣnigne onstal habbað lārēowa.
Ond for ðon ic ðē bebīode ðæt ðū dō, swǣ ic gelīefe ðæt ðū wille, ðæt ðū ðē ðissa
woruldðinga tō ðǣm geǣmetige, swǣ ðū oftost mæge, ðæt ðū ðone wīsdōm ðe ðē
God sealde, ðǣr ðǣr ðū hiene befæstan mæge, befæste. Geðenc hwelc wītu ūs ðā
20 becōmon for ðisse worulde, ðā ðā wē hit nōhwæðer ne selfe ne lufodon ne ēac
ōðrum monnum ne lēfdon; ðone naman ǣnne wē lufodon ðætte wē Crīstne
wǣren, ond swīðe fēawa ðā ðēawas.

---

1 *Wærferð*] Bishop Wǣrferð of Worcester, 873–915; he translated Gregory's *Dialogues* into
Old English.

1 *wordum*] dative plural with instrumental force: 'with his words'.

2 *hāte*] By switching from the third person singular (i. e. 'Ælfred kyning hāteð' to the first
person, Alfred uses a more personal style than is usual in official letters.

7 *hū . . . spēow*] 'and how successful they were then'

10 *hīe*] refers to 'lāre'

13 *of Lǣdene*] 'from the Latin'

14 *begiondan Humbre*] 'beyond the Humber' refers to the former centre of learning in
Northumbria.

15 *be sūðan Temese*] 'south of the Thames'; the Thames was the northern border of the West
Saxon kingdom (see map inside the front cover).

15–16 *tō rīce fēng*] 'when I succeeded to the throne'.

20 *hit*] refers to 'wīsdōm' (masculine); natural gender has replaced grammatical gender in this
case.

21 *lēfdon*] This is a spelling variant of West Saxon *lǣfdon* (inf. *lǣfan*, to leave behind, to pass
on)

22 *ond . . . ðēawas*] 'but only a few of us (loved) the duties'.

Ðā ic ðā ðis eall gemunde, ðā gemunde ic ēac hū ic geseah, ǣr ðǣm ðe hit eall
forhergod wǣre ond forbærned, hū ðā ciricean giond eall Angelcynn stōdon
25   māðma ond bōca gefylda, ond ēac micel mengeo Godes ðīowa; ond ðā swīðe
lȳtle fiorme ðāra bōca wiston, for ðǣm ðe hīe hiora nānwuht ongietan ne meahton, for ðǣm ðe hīe nǣron on hiora āgen geðīode āwritene. Swelce hīe cwǣden:
'Ūre ieldran, ðā ðe ðās stōwa ǣr hīoldon, hīe lufodon wīsdōm ond ðurh ðone hīe
begēaton welan ond ūs lǣfdon. Hēr mon mæg gīet gesīon hiora swæð, ac wē him
30   ne cunnon æfter spyrigean. Ond for ðǣm wē habbað nū ǣgðer forlǣten ge ðone
welan ge ðone wīsdōm, for ðǣm ðe wē noldon tō ðǣm spore mid ūre mōde
onlūtan.'
Ðā ic ðā ðis eall gemunde, ðā wundrade ic swīðe swīðe ðāra gōdena wiotena
ðe giū wǣron giond Angelcynn, ond ðā bēc ealla be fullan geliornod hæfdon, ðæt
35   hīe hiora ðā nǣnne dǣl noldon on hiora āgen geðīode wendan. Ac ic ðā sōna eft
mē selfum andwyrde ond cwæð: 'Hīe ne wēndon ðætte ǣfre menn sceolden swǣ
reccelēase weorðan, ond sīo lār swǣ oðfeallan – for ðǣre wilnunga hīe hit
forlēton, ond woldon ðæt hēr ðȳ māra wīsdōm on londe wǣre, ðȳ wē mā geðēoda
cūðon.'
40   Ðā gemunde ic hū sīo ǣ wæs ǣrest on Ebriscgeðīode funden, ond eft, ðā hīe
Crēacas geliornodon, ðā wendon hīe hīe on heora āgen geðīode ealle, ond ēac
ealle ōðre bēc. Ond eft Lǣdenware swǣ same; siððan hīe hīe geliornodon, hīe hīe
wendon ealla ðurh wīse wealhstodas on hiora āgen geðīode. Ond ēac ealla ōðra
Crīstna ðīoda sumne dǣl hiora on hiora āgen geðīode wendon. Forðȳ mē ðyncð
45   betre, gif īow swǣ ðyncð, ðæt wē ēac sume bēc, ðā ðe nīedbeðearfosta sīen
eallum monnum tō wiotonne, ðæt wē ðā on ðæt geðīode wenden ðe wē ealle
gecnāwan mægen; ond gedōn swǣ wē swīðe ēaðe magon mid Godes fultume, gif
wē ðā stilnesse habbað, ðætte eall sīo gioguð ðe nū is on Angelcynne frīora
monna, ðāra ðe ðā spēda hæbben, ðæt hīe ðǣm befēolan mægen, sīen tō
50   liornunga oðfæste, ðā hwīle ðe hīe tō nānre ōðerre note ne mægen, oð ðone first
ðe hīe wel cunnen Englisc gewrit ārǣdan. Lǣre mon siððan furður on Lǣdengeðīode ðā ðe mon furður lǣran wille, ond tō hīerran hāde dōn wille.
Ðā ic ðā gemunde hū sīo lār Lǣdengeðīodes ǣr ðissum āfeallen wæs giond
Angelcynn, ond ðēah monige cūðon Englisc gewrit ārǣdan, ðā ongan ic
55   ongemang ōðrum mislicum ond manigfealdum bisgum ðisses kynerīces ðā bōc
wendan on Englisc ðe is genemned on Lǣden *Pastoralis* ond on Englisc
'Hierdebōc', hwīlum word be worde, hwīlum andgit of andgiete, swǣ swǣ ic
hīe geliornode æt Plegmunde mīnum ǣrcebiscepe ond æt Assere mīnum biscepe

---

24 *forhergod . . . forbærned*] refers to the pillaging (especially monasteries) by the Vikings.
40 *sīo ǣ*] i. e. the Old Testament, in particular the Mosaic law ('ǣ')
40 *on Ebriscgeðīode*] in Hebrew
41 *Crēacas*] 'the Greeks' (nominative plural)
42 *Lǣdenware*] 'the Romans'
50 *ðā hwīle . . . mægen*] 'for as long as they are unable to take on any other duty'
51 *on Lǣdengeðīode*] 'in Latin'
52 *tō hīerran hāde*] probably refers to ordination ('to a higher office').
53 *lār Lǣdengeðīodes*] 'instruction in Latin'

ond æt Grimbolde mīnum mæsseprīoste ond æt Iōhanne mīnum mæsseprēoste.
60 Siððan ic hīe ðā geliornod hæfde, swæ swæ ic hīe forstōd ond swæ ic hīe
andgitfullīcost āreccean meahte, ic hīe on Englisc āwende; ond tō ælcum biscepstōle on mīnum rīce wille āne onsendan; ond on ælcre bið ān æstel se bið on
fīftegum mancessa. Ond ic bebīode on Godes naman ðæt nān mon ðone æstel
from ðǣre bēc ne dō ne ðā bōc from ðǣm mynstre – uncūð hū longe ðǣr swæ
65 gelǣrede biscepas sīen swæ swæ nū, Gode ðonc, welhwǣr siendon. Forðȳ ic
wolde ðætte hīe ealneg æt ðǣre stōwe wǣren, būton se biscep hīe mid him
habban wille, oððe hīo hwǣr tō lǣne sīe, oððe hwā ōðre bī wrīte.

---

58 *hīe*] refers to 'Hierdebōc'.
58–59 *Plegmunde . . . Iōhanne*] scholars whom Alfred had brought to Wessex. Plegmund came
from Mercia and was consecrated Archbishop of Canterbury in 890. Asser, a Welshman, was
Alfred's biographer and was later consecrated Bishop of Sherborne. Grimbold was a Frank and
Johannes came from Saxony.
63 *mancessa*] (genitive plural) gold coin to the value of 30 silver pence
64 *uncūð*] 'although we cannot know'
67 *oððe . . . bī wrīte*] 'or someone copies it'.

Text 6: Ælfric's Life of King Oswold

Ælfric of Eynsham, who lived from around 950–1010, was the most prolific writer in Old English besides Wulfstan (see O 7). He was educated in the Old Minster at Winchester under Æþelwold, and around 987 he moved to Cerne Abbas. In 1005 he became Abbot of Eynsham. Ælfric thought of himself mainly as a teacher, writing saints' lives and homilies, grammatical works and biblical commentaries. One of his greatest (and undoubtedly most popular) works was the *Homiliae Catholicae*; three volumes, the first two of which contain 40 items each, including sermons, saints' lives and other homiletic works. Many of these are intended to be read at specific feast days, and thus are arranged chronologically. The third volume, the *Lives of the Saints*, was also written to strengthen people's faith. Almost a quarter of the saints in the third volume are Anglo-Saxon (including the kings Edmund and Oswald, but also the virgin Æþelthryth and the confessor Swithin). The first two volumes were written in the early 990s, and the third volume, from which this text, the Life of King Oswald, is taken, was written around 996 or 997.

The details for the *Life of King Oswald* have mostly been adapted from Bede's *Historia Ecclesiastica Gentis Anglorum* (iii. 1–3, 5–6, 9–13). While Bede had explained Oswald's life chronologically, Ælfric has altered the details somewhat so as to achieve a traditional structure of a saint's life: first the life itself is described, then his passion, and finally the miracles. Oswald's piety is contrasted with the immorality of the heathens against whom he fights, and each battle is built into the didactics of the story. Oswald's victory over Ceadwalla is a result of his piety, whereas his defeat at the hands of Penda is merely the instrument of his martyrdom. The various miracles which occur after his death show his final triumph, and the triumph of Christianity.

As Bede describes his own reasons for writing, namely to help the students at the monastery (see OE 3), so too does Ælfric seem to have had the same concerns. He wrote the *Colloquy* in Latin (which was later translated into Old English by someone else), the *Excerpationes de arte grammatica anglice* and a glossary specifically to help students learn (*forðan ðe stæfcræft is seo cæg ðe ðære boca andgit unlicð* – 'because grammar is the key to unlocking the meaning of these books'). Similarly, in the Latin introductions to his *Homiliae Catholicae*, Ælfric emphasises that he is writing the homilies in order to educate those not able to study themselves, so as to help them save their souls. For Ælfric, this includes the traditional dogma of the Church; he has not involved himself in controversial matters whatsoever, not even the Immaculate Conception, which was an issue of heated debate at the time.

Ælfric states in his prologue that he has translated into plain speech as best as he could, so that his texts may be of help to the less-educated. Indeed, they are much easier to read than, for example, Wulfstan's sermons; at the same time they have a rhythmic style, which led many scholars to believe they were works of poetry. This has since been abandoned.

A close look at the opening lines of the *Life of King Oswold* will show that the text indeed has highly rhythmical elements, supported by alliteration:

> Æfter ðan ðe Áugustinus to Éngla lànde becóm,
> wæs sum ǽðele cýning, Óswold geháten,
> on Norðhýmbra lánde, gelýfed swỳðe on Gód,

se férde on his iúgoðe fram fréondum and mágum
to Scótlande on sǽ, and þær sóna wearð gefúllod,
and his geféran sámod þe him míd síþedon.

While they are very rhythmic, Ælfric's texts do not fulfil the demands of alliterative poetry. A new approach to Ælfric's use of metrical devices and the development of late Old English verse in general can be found in Bredehoft (2005).

One of the prominent features of late West Saxon is the sequence *syl-* for earlier *sel-*: *sylf* (l. 13, 47 etc.), *sylfne* (l. 100) and *syllan* (l. 61, 174). This agrees with *y* for earlier *ie*, as in *gelȳfed* (l. 2, 5); *gelȳfan* (l. 163); *fylle* (l. 8, 101), *ylde* (l. 94) etc. The loss of palatal *g* when followed by *d* (with compensatory lengthening) is also a regular late West Saxon feature: *foresǣdan, sǣde, foresǣdon* (l. 22, 58, 107 etc.), *mǣden* (l. 135, 136), *ālēdon* (l. 17) and *gelēd* (l. 109). The *eo*-diphthong caused by breaking has been monophthongised to *u* under the influence of a preceding *w*: *wurðmynte* (l. 11, 19 etc.); *ārwurðne* (l. 33). The ending for the dative singular of adjectives when declined weak is *-um*: *lǣwedum* (l. 51; instead of earlier *-an*); *sylfrenan* following *ān* shows that the adjective is no longer following the strong declension.

Sources: British Library, London, MS Cotton Julius E.vii. – Needham (1976); Skeat (1881). – Secondary literature: Bethurum (1932), Wolpers (1964), Lipp (1969), Kuhn (1973).

Æfter ðan ðe Augustīnus tō Engla lande becōm, wæs sum æðele cyning, Ōswold gehāten, on Norðhymbra lande, gelȳfed swȳþe on God. Sē fērde on his iugoðe fram frēondum and māgum tō Scotlande on sæ, and þær sōna wearð gefullod and his gefēran samod þe him mid sīþedon. Betwux þām wearð ofslagen
5   Ēadwine his ēam, Norðhymbra cynincg, on Crīst gelȳfed, fram Brytta cyninge, Cedwalla gecīged, and twēgen his æftergengan binnan twām gēarum. And sē Cedwalla slōh and tō sceame tūcode þā Norðhymbran lēode æfter heora hlāfordes fylle, oð þæt Ōswold se ēadiga his yfelnysse ādwæscte.
    Ōswold him cōm tō and him cēnlīce wiðfeaht mid lȳtlum werode, ac his
10 gelēafa hine getrymde and Crīst him gefylste tō his fēonda slege. Ōswold þā ārǣrde āne rōde sōna Gode tō wurðmynte, ǣr þan þe hē tō ðām gewinne cōme, and clypode tō his gefērum: "Uton feallan tō ðǣre rōde, and þone Ælmihtigan biddan þæt hē ūs āhredde wið þone mōdigan fēond þe ūs āfyllan wile. God sylf wāt geare þæt wē winnað rihtlīce wið þysne rēðan cyning, tō āhreddene ūre
15 lēode." Hī fēollon þā ealle mid Ōswolde on gebedum, and syþþan on ærne mergen ēodon tō þām gefeohte, and gewunnon þær sige swā swā se Wealdend

---

1 *Augustīnus*] missionary sent by Pope Gregory the Great; he arrived in England (*Engla lande*) in 597.
2 *Ōswold*] King of Northumbria, 633–641
3 *Scotlande on sæ*] the former kingdom of Dalriada north of the Firth of Clyde was Oswald's place of exile.
5 *Ēadwine*] King Eadwine of Northumbria, defeated by Cedwalla in 632
6 *Cedwalla*] king of the British (*Brytta*) of Gwynnedd (North Wales)
6 *æftergengan*] refers to Osric und Eanfrith, the Kings of Deira and Bernicia.

him ūðe for Ōswoldes gelēafan, and ālēdon heora fȳnd, þone mōdigan Cedwallan
mid his micclan werode, þe wēnde þæt him ne mihte nān werod wiðstandan.

Sēo ylce rōd siððan, þe Ōswold þǣr ārǣrde, on wurðmynte þǣr stōd; and
20 wurdon fela gehǣlde untrumra manna and ēac swilce nȳtena þurh ðā ylcan rōde,
swā swā ūs rehte Bēda. Sum man fēoll on īse þæt his earm tōbærst, and læg þā on
bedde gebrocod forðearle, oð þæt man him fette of ðǣre foresǣdan rōde sumne
dæl þæs mēoses þe hēo mid beweaxen wæs; and se ādliga sōna on slǣpe wearð
gehǣled on ðǣre ylcan nihte þurh Ōswoldes geearnunga. Sēo stōw is gehāten
25 Heofonfeld on Englisc, wið þone langan weall þe þā Rōmaniscan worhtan, þǣr
þǣr Ōswold oferwan þone wælhrēowan cynincg. And þǣr wearð siþþan ārǣred
swīðe mǣre cyrce Gode tō wurðmynte þe wunað ā on ēcnysse.

Hwæt ðā, Ōswold ongann embe Godes willan tō smēagenne sōna swā hē rīces
gewēold, and wolde gebīgan his lēoda tō gelēafan and tō þām lifigendan Gode;
30 sende ðā tō Scotlande þǣr se gelēafa wæs ðā, and bæd ðā hēafodmenn þæt hī his
bēnum getīþodon, and him sumne lārēow sendon þe his lēoda mihte tō Gode
gewēman – and him wearð þæs getīþod. Hī sendon þā sōna þām gesǣligan
cyninge sumne ārwurðne bisceop, Aidan gehāten. Sē wæs mǣres līfes man on
munuclicre drohtnunga, and hē ealle woruldcara āwearp fram his heortan, nānes
35 þinges wilnigende būtan Godes willan. Swā hwæt swā him becōm of þæs
cyninges gifum oððe rīcra manna, þæt hē hraðe dǣlde þearfum and wǣdlum mid
welwillendum mōde.

Hwæt ðā, Ōswold cyning his cymes fægnode, and hine ārwurðlīce underfēng
his folce tō ðearfe, þæt heora gelēafa wurde āwend eft tō Gode fram þām
40 wiþersæce þe hī tō gewende wǣron. Hit gelamp þā swā þæt se gelēaffulla cyning
gerehte his witan on heora āgenum gereorde þæs bisceopes bodunge mid blīþum
mōde, and wæs his wealhstod, for þan þe hē wel cūþe Scyttysc and se bisceop
Aidan ne mihte gebīgan his sprǣce tō Norðhymbriscum gereorde swā hraþe
þāgīt.

45 Se biscop þā fērde bodigende geond eall Norhymbra land gelēafan and fulluht,
and þā lēode gebīgde tō Godes gelēafan, and him wel gebysnode mid weorcum
symle and sylf swā leofode swā swā hē lǣrde ōðrum. Hē lufode forhæfednysse
and hālige rǣdinge, and iunge men tēah georne mid lāre, swā þæt ealle his
gefēran þe him mid ēodon, sceoldon sealmas leornian oððe sume rǣdinge, swā
50 hwider swā hī fērdon þām folce bodigende. Seldon hē wolde rīdan, ac sīðode on
his fōtum, and munuclīce leofode betwux ðām lǣwedum folce mid mycelre
gescēadwīsnysse and sōþum mægnum.

---

21 *Bēda*] see *Historia Ecclesiastica*, iii.2. Bede's account is more detailed.

21 *Sum . . . īse*] Bede's account of this miracle (see *Historia Ecclesiastica*, iii.2) refers to
Bothelm, one of the brethren of the church at Hexham.

25 *Heofonfeld*] Bede uses the name 'Hefenfelth' (probably Heavenfield close to Hadrian's
Wall, northwest of Hexham) for the location of the decisive battle of 635.

25 *langan weall*] Hadrian's Wall

27 *mǣre cyrce*] Bede explicitly refers to the Church of Hexham ('fratres Hagustaldensis
ecclesiae, quae non longe abest', *Historia Ecclesiastica*, iii.2).

33 *Aidan*] Scottish missionary who brought Irish Christianity from Iona to Northumbria.

42 *cūþe Scyttysc*] see line 3, 'Scotlonde on sǣ'. Bede is much more precise: 'quia nimirum tam
longo exilii sui tempore linguam Scottorum iam plene didicerat', *Historia Ecclesiastica*, iii.4.

Þā wearð se cynincg Ōswold swīðe ælmesgeorn and ēadmōd on þēawum and
on eallum þingum cystig. And man āhrǣrde cyrcan on his rīce geond eall and
55 mynsterlice gesetnysse mid micelre geornfulnysse. Hit gelamp on sumne sǣl þæt
hī sǣton ætgædere, Ōswold and Aidan, on þām hālgan Ēasterdæge. Þā bǣr man
þām cyninge cynelice þēnunga on ānum sylfrenan disce, and sōna þā inn ēode ān
þæs cyninges þegna þe his ælmyssan bewiste, and sǣde þæt fela þearfan sǣtan
geond þā strǣt, gehwanon cumene tō þæs cyninges ælmyssan. Þā sende se cyning
60 sōna þām þearfum þone sylfrenan disc mid sandum mid ealle, and hēt tōceorfan
þone disc and syllan þām þearfum heora ǣlcum his dǣl: and man dyde ðā swā.
Þā genam Aidanus se æðela bisceop þæs cyninges swȳþran hand mid swīðlicre
blysse, and clypode mid gelēafan þus cwæðende him tō: "Ne forrotige on
brosnunge þēos geblētsode swȳðra!" And him ēac swā geēode swā swā Aidanus
65 him bæd, þæt his swīðre hand is gesundful oð þis.

Ōswoldes cynerīce wearð gerȳmed þā swȳðe, swā þæt fēower þēoda hine
underfēngon tō hlāforde: Peohtas and Bryttas, Scottas and Angle, swā swā se
ælmihtiga God hī geānlǣhte tō ðām for Ōswoldes geearnungum þe hine ǣfre
wurðode. Hē fulworhte on Eferwīc þæt ǣnlice mynster þe his mǣg Ēadwine ǣr
70 begunnon hæfde; and hē swanc for heofonan rīce mid singālum gebedum –
swīþor þonne hē hogode hū hē gehēolde on worulde þā hwīlwendlican geþincðu
þe hē hwōnlīce lufode. Hē wolde æfter ūhtsange oftost hine gebiddan, and on
cyrcan standan on syndrigum gebedum of sunnan ūpgange mid swȳðlicre
onbryrdnysse; and swā hwǣr swā hē wæs, hē wurðode ǣfre God ūp āwendum
75 handbredum wiþ heofones Weard.

On þām ylcan tīman cōm ēac sum bisceop fram Rōmebyrig, Birinus gehāten,
tō Westsexena kyninge, Cynegyls gehāten; sē wæs ðāgīt hǣðen and eall
Westsexena land. Birinus witodlīce gewende fram Rōme be ðæs pāpan rǣde þe
ðā on Rōme wæs, and behēt þæt hē wolde Godes willan gefremman and bodian
80 þām hǣþenum þæs Hǣlendes naman and þone sōðan gelēafan on fyrlenum
landum. Þā becōm hē tō Westseaxan þe wæs ðāgȳt hǣþen, and gebīgde þone
cynincg Kynegyls tō Gode and ealle his lēode tō gelēafan mid him. Hit gelamp þā
swā þæt se gelēaffulla Ōswold, Norðhymbra cyning, wæs cumen tō Cynegylse,
and hine tō fulluhte nam, fægen his gecyrrednysse. Þā gēafon þā cynegas,
85 Cynegyls and Ōswold, þām hālgan Birine, him tō bisceopstōle, þā burh
Dorcanceaster. And hē þǣrbinnan wunode, Godes lof ārǣrende, and gerihtlǣcende þæt folc mid lāre tō gelēafan tō langum fyrste oð þæt hē gesǣlig sīþode
tō Crīste. And his līc wearþ bebyrged on ðǣre ylcan byrig oð þæt Hædde
bisceop eft his bān ferode tō Wintanceastre, and mid wurðmynte gelōgode binnan
90 Ealdan Mynstre, þǣr man hine wurðað gȳt.

56 *hālgan Ēasterdæge*] Easter Sunday, the most important Christian feast day
67 *Peohtas . . . Angle*] the Celtic tribes, Picts, British and Scottish as well as the Germanic
  Angles, who had come from the Continent.
76 *Birinus*] The *Anglo-Saxon Chronicle* records the mission of Birinus in the year 634.
77 *Cynegyls*] According to the *Anglo-Saxon Chronicle*, he reigned from 611 to 641/642.
78 *pāpan*] Pope Honorius I (625–638)
84 *hine . . . nam*] 'was his godfather'. In some manuscripts of the *Anglo-Saxon Chronicle* this
  baptism doesn't occur until 635.
89 *Hædde bisceop*] Hæddi, bishop of Wessex, 676–705

Hwæt þā, Ōswold cyning his cynedōm gehēold hlīsfullīce for worulde, and mid micclum gelēafan and on eallum dǣdum his Drihten ārwurðode oð þæt hē ofslagen wearð for his folces ware on ðām nigoðan gēare þe hē rīces gewēold, þā þā hē sylf wæs on ylde eahta and þrittig gēare. Hit gewearð swā be þām þæt him 95 wann on Penda, Myrcena cyning, þe æt his mǣges slege ǣr, Ēadwines cyninges, Cedwallan fylste; and sē Penda ne cūðe be Crīste nān þincg, and eall Myrcena folc wæs ungefullod þā gīt. Hī cōmon þā tō gefeohte tō Maserfelda bēgen, and fēngon tōgædere oð þæt þǣr fēollon þā Crīstenan, and þā hǣðenan genēalǣhton tō þām hālgan Ōswolde. Þā geseah hē genēalēcan his līfes geendunge, and gebæd 100 for his folc þe þǣr feallende sweolt, and betǣhte heora sāwla and hine sylfne Gode, and þus clypode on his fylle: "God, gemiltsa ūrum sāwlum!" Þā hēt se hǣþena cynincg his hēafod of āslēan and his swīðran earm, and settan hī tō myrcelse.

Þā, æfter Ōswoldes slege, fēng Ōswīg his brōðor tō Norðhymbra rīce, and rād 105 mid werode tō þǣr his brōðor hēafod stōd on stacan gefæstnod, and genam þæt hēafod and his swīðran hand, and mid ārwurðnysse ferode tō Lindisfarnēa cyrcan. Þā wearð gefylled, swā wē hēr foresǣdon, þæt his swīðre hand wunað hāl mid þām flǣsce būtan ǣlcere brosnunge, swā se bisceop gecwæð. Se earm wearð gelēd ārwurðlīce on scrīne, of seolfre āsmiþod, on Sancte Pētres mynstre binnan 110 Bebbanbyrig be þǣre sǣ strande, and līð þǣr swā andsund swā hē of āslagen wæs.

His brōþor dohtor eft siððan on Myrcan wearð cwēn, and geāxode his bān, and gebrōhte hī tō Lindesīge tō Bardanīge mynstre, þe hēo micclum lufode. Ac þā mynstermenn noldon for menniscum gedwylde þone sanct underfōn, ac man slōh 115 ān geteld ofer þā hālgan bān binnan þǣre līcreste.

Hwæt þā, God geswutelode þæt hē hālig sanct wæs, swā þæt heofonlic lēoht ofer þæt geteld āstreht stōd ūp tō heofonum swilce hēalic sunnbēam ofer ealle ðā niht, and þā lēoda behēoldon geond ealle þā scīre, swīðe wundrigende. Þā wurdon

---

90 *Ealdan Mynstre*] the Old Minster (i. e. Anglo-Saxon cathedral) at Winchester

91 *hlīsfullīce for worulde*] 'glorious in worldly respect'

93 *ofslagen wearð*] The death of Oswald is dated at 641 or 642, depending on the manuscript of the *Anglo-Saxon Chronicle*.

93 *nigoðan gēare . . . gewēold*] 'in the ninth year of his reign'

95 *Penda*] King of Mercia (632–654)

96 *Cedwallan*] see ll. 6–7

97 *Maserfelda*] probably Oswestry (Shropshire); according to Bede the battle was fought on August 5th.

104 *Ōswīg*] Oswiu was King of Bernicia from 641 to 654; after his victory over Penda he was king of all Northumbria (654–670).

105 *tō þǣr*] 'to the place where'

112 *brōþor dohtor*] The reference is to the wife of Ethelred, king of Mercia.

113 *Lindesīge*] a former kingdom in the northern area of what is today Lincolnshire.

114 *menniscum gedwylde*] Here Ælfric is vague (probably on purpose); Bede on the other hand tells us explicitly that the monks didn't think Oswald was their lawful king; see *Historia Ecclesiastica*, iii.11.

116 *sanct*] Oswald was venerated as a saint immediately after his death; his feast day is the 5th of August.

þā mynstermen micclum āfyrhte, and bǣdon þæs on mergen þæt hī mōston þone
120 sanct mid ārwurðnysse underfōn þone þe hī ǣr forsōcon. Þā ðwōh man þā hālgan
bān, and bær intō þǣre cyrcan ārwurðlīce on scrīne, and gelōgodon hī ūpp. And
þǣr wurdon gehǣlde þurh his hālgan geearnunge fela mettrume menn fram mislicum coþum. Þæt wæter þe man þā bān mid āþwōh binnan þǣre cyrcan wearð
āgoten swā on ānre hyrnan; and sēo eorðe siþþan þe þæt wæter underfēng wearð
125 manegum tō bōte. Mid þām dūste wurdon āflīgde dēofla fram mannum þā þe on
wōdnysse ǣr wǣron gedrehte.

Ēac swilce þǣr hē fēol on þām gefeohte ofslagen, men nāmon þā eorðan tō
ādligum mannum, and dydon on wæter wanhālum tō þicgenne: and hī wurdon
gehǣlede þurh þone hālgan wer. Sum wegfarende man fērde wið þone feld; þā
130 wearð his hors gesīcclod, and sōna þǣr fēol, wealwigende geond ðā eorðan
wōdum gelīcost. Mid þām þe hit swā wealweode geond þone wīdgillan feld, þā
becōm hit embe lang þǣr se cynincg Ōswold on þām gefeohte fēoll, swā swā wē
ǣr foresǣdan. And hit sōna ārās swā hit hrepode þā stōwe, hāl eallum limum, and
se hlāford þæs fægnode. Se ridda þā fērde forð on his weg, þider hē gemynt
135 hæfde. Þā wæs þǣr ān mǣden licgende on paralisyn lange gebrocod. Hē began þā
tō reccenne hū him on rāde getīmode, and mann ferode þæt mǣden tō þǣre
foresǣdan stōwe. Hēo wearð þā on slǣpe, and sōna eft āwōc, ansund eallum
limum fram þām egeslican broce; band þā hire hēafod, and blīðe hām fērde,
gangænde on fōtum swā hēo gefyrn ǣr ne dyde.

140 Eft siððan fērde ēac sum ǣrendfæst ridda be ðǣre ylcan stōwe, and geband on
ānum clāþe of þām hālgan dūste þǣre dēorwurðan stōwe, and lǣdde forð mid
him þǣr hē fundode tō. Þā gemētte hē gebēoras blīðe æt þām hūse; hē āhēng þā
þæt dūst on ǣnne hēahne post, and sæt mid þām gebēorum blissigende samod.
Man worhte þā micel fȳr tōmiddes ðām gebēorum; and þā spearcan wundon wið
145 þæs rōfes swȳðe oð þæt þæt hūs fǣrlīce eall on fȳre wearð; and þā gebēoras
flugon āfyrhte āweg. Þæt hūs wearþ ðā forburnon, būton þām ānum poste, þe þæt
hālige dūst on āhangen wæs: sē post āna ætstōd ansund mid þām dūste, and hī
swȳðe wundroden þæs hālgan weres geearnunga, þæt þæt fȳr ne mihte þā moldan
forbǣrnan. And manega menn siððan gesōhton þone stede, heora hǣle feccende
150 and heora frēonda gehwilcum.

Þā āsprang his hlīsa geond þæt land wīde, and ēac swilce tō Īrlande, and ēac
sūþ tō Franclande, swā swā sum mæsseprēost be ānum men sǣde. Se prēost
cwæð þæt ān wer wǣre on Īrlande gelǣred sē ne gȳmde his lāre, and hē līthwōn
hogode embe his sāwle þearfa oððe his Scyppendes beboda, ac ādrēah his līf on
155 dyslicum weorcum oð ðæt hē wearð geuntrumod and tō ende gebrōht. Þā clypode
hē þone prēost, þe hit cȳdde eft þus, and cwæð him tō sōna mid sārlicre stemne:
"Nū ic sceall geendian earmlicum dēaþe and tō helle faran for fracodum dǣdum;
nū wolde ic gebētan, gif ic ābīdan mōste, and tō Gode gecyrran and tō gōdum
þēawum, and mīn līf āwendan eall tō Godes willan; and ic wāt þæt ic ne eom

---

138 *band . . . hēafod*] 'put on a kerchief' (see Bede: 'caput linteo cooperuit').
152 *Franclande*] the Frankish kingdom; Oswald was venerated in the south of Germany and in
the north of Italy (see introduction to M 11).

160 wyrðe þæs fyrstes, būton sum hālga mē þingie tō þām Hǣlende Crīste. Nū is ūs
gesǣd þæt sum hālig cyning is on ēowrum earde, Ōswold gehāten; nū, gif þū
ǣnig þincg hæfst of þæs hālgan reliquium, syle mē, ic þē bidde." Ðā sǣde se
prēost him: "Ic hæbbe of þām stocce þe his hēafod on stōd; and gif þū gelȳfan
wylt, þū wurþest hāl sōna."

165 Hwæt þā, se mæsseprēost þæs mannes ofhrēow, and scōf on hālig wæter of
þām hālgan trēowe, sealde þām ādligan of tō sūpenne, and hē sōna gewyrpte and
syððan leofode lange on worulde, and gewende tō Gode mid eallra heortan and
mid hālgum weorcum; and swā hwider swā hē cōm, hē cȳdde þās wundra. For þȳ
ne sceall nān mann āwǣgan þæt hē sylfwylles behǣt þām ælmihtigan Gode,
170 þonne hē ādlig bið, þē lǣs þe hē sylf losige, gif hē ālīhð Gode þæt.

Nū cwæð se hālga Bēda, þe ðās bōc gedihte, þæt hit nān wundor nys þæt se
hālga cynincg untrumnysse gehǣle, nū hē on heofonum leofað, for ðan þe hē
wolde gehelpan þā þā hē hēr on līfe wæs þearfum and wannhālum, and him
bigwiste syllan. Nū hæfð hē þone wurðmynt on þǣre ēcan worulde mid þām
175 ælmihtigan Gode for his gōdnysse. Eft se hālga Cūðberht, þā þā hē gīt cnapa
wæs, geseah hū Godes ænglas feredon Aidanes sāwle, þæs hālgan bisceopes,
blīðe tō heofonum, tō þām ēcan wuldre þe hē on worulde geearnode.

Þæs hālgan Ōswoldes bān wurdon eft gebrōht æfter manegum gēarum tō
Myrcena lande, intō Glēawceastre, and God þǣr geswutelode oft fela wundra
180 þurh þone hālgan wer. Sȳ þæs wuldor þām Ælmihtigan ā tō worulde. *Amen.*

169 *þæt*] 'that which'

171 *Bēda . . . gedihte*] see Bede, *Historia Ecclesiastica*, iii.9–13

175 *Cūðberht*] St. Cuthbert spent his life as a hermit, until he was appointed Bishop of
Lindisfarne by King Egfrid in 685.

Text 7: Wulfstan's Sermon to the English

Wulfstan became Bishop of London in 996, and Archbishop of York and Bishop of Worcester in 1002. These two offices were often held in plurality, and Wulfstan held both until 1016, retaining York until his death in 1023. Though little is known of him before 996, we can assume that he either belonged to the upper class or had connections, for his rise both in politics as well as in the Church was rapid. He helped draft the law codes both under the reign of King Æþelred and his Danish successor Cnut (the ability to work effectively under kings of two different nationalities was also possessed by his successor, St. Wulfstan of Worcester; see M 5), reformed the codes of the Church (*Institutes of Policy* and *Canons of Edgar*), and composed many didactic sermons.

Wulfstan's sermons often have an eschatological focus, as is the case in *The Sermon of the Wolf*. This can be seen as a direct result of the times Wulfstan lived in; the Danish raids in England had been on the increase since 980 (see O 10), and the payments of tribute were likewise on the increase. After Æþelred was forced into exile for a year in 1013 (the death of the Danish king and conqueror, Svein Forkbeard, in 1014 allowed Æþelred's return), two years of increased hostilities followed, culminating in the Danish leadership of England under Cnut the Great and his sons, which lasted from 1016 to 1042. *The Sermon of the Wolf* was written in 1014, directly after Æþelred's return from exile.

In a time of extreme political upheaval, Wulfstan sought the cause of their woes much in the same way as Gildas in his *De Excidio et Conquestu Britanniae*: God is punishing the English (or British, in Gildas' case) for their sins. While Gildas focuses on the corruption among the clergy as the cause of the invasion of the Angles and Saxons, Wulfstan has a much wider bed of sin to draw from; the English clergy is the least of England's problems. England's whole society is *aa swa leng swa wyrse*: God's laws are not obeyed, the ties of kinship in general are collapsing, leading to various crimes, betrayals, and slavery, and the very hierarchy of society threatens to collapse. This strongly moralising work focuses on the evils in English society; it is a far cry from *The Battle of Brunanburh* (O 8), which triumphs in English unity, or even *The Battle of Maldon* (O 10), which celebrates English values in the face of defeat. *The Sermon of the Wolf* ends with a series of *utan*-clauses, exhorting the people to improve themselves in order to end the current misery.

The topic of slavery, particularly of the English being sold into foreign hands, is a main point in Wulfstan *cristenes folces to fela man gesealde ut of þysan earde nu ealle hwile; and eal þæt is Gode lað, gelyfe se þe wille* – 'too many Christian people have been sold from our country for a long time now, and this is loath to God, believe it if you will' (ll. 64–65; the topic is continued in the lines that follow). Slavery seems to have been a pressing point of these times, just as it seems to have been in St. Wulfstan's time (see M 5) if we accept the evidence in William of Malmesbury's *Life of St. Wulfstan*, chapter 20.

Though *The Sermon of the Wolf* is a prose work, Wulfstan emphasises, for example, the crimes and sins of society using alliteration (ll. 109–121 and 134–139), adding alliterative stressed phrases throughout the text for emphasis. His use of rhetoric figures is extensive.

The *Sermo Lupi* contains many features typical of late West Saxon. These include the levelling of vowel quality in unstressed syllables, as in *lehtreð* for earlier *lehtrað* (l. 120). The ending of plural preterite indicative (*-on*) frequently appears as *-an*, as in *spǣcan* and *wǣran* (both l. 8). Earlier *ðone* is written *þæne* (l. 82, 83, 93 and 98), whereas *ðonne* appears as *þænne* (l. 6). The text also shows a few loans from Scandinavian, such as *grið* (l. 64 and 35), *griðian* (l. 28), and *griðlēase* (l. 31). Instead of Old English *riht*, the text uses the Scandinavian loanword *lagu* (l. 19, 27 etc.; see Old English Glossary).

Sources: British Library MS Cotton Nero A.i. – Bethurum (1957), Whitelock (1976). – Secondary literature: Wilcox (2000). – Facsimile: Loyn (1971).

Sermo Lupi ad Anglos quando Dani maxime persecuti sunt eos, quod fuit anno millesimo XIIII ab incarnatione domini nostri Iesu Cristi

    Lēofan men, gecnāwað þæt sōð is: ðēos worold is on ofste, and hit nēalǣcð þām ende, and þȳ hit is on worolde aa swā leng swā wyrse, and swā hit sceal

5 nȳde for folces synnan ǣr Antecrīstes tōcyme yfelian swȳþe, and hūru hit wyrð þænne egeslic and grimlic wīde on worolde.

    Understandað ēac georne þæt dēofol þās þeode nū fela gēara dwelode tō swȳþe, and þæt lȳtle getrēowþa wǣran mid mannum, þēah hȳ wel spǣcan, and unrihta tō fela rīcsode on lande; and næs ā fela manna þe smēade ymbe þā bōte

10 swā georne swā man scolde, ac dæghwāmlīce man īhte yfel æfter ōðrum and unriht rǣrde and unlaga manege ealles tō wīde gynd ealle þās þeode. And wē ēac for þām habbað fela byrsta and bysmara gebiden, and, gif wē ǣnige bōte gebīdan scylan, þonne mōte wē þæs tō Gode ernian bet þonne wē ǣr þysan dydan. For þām mid miclan earnungan wē geearnedan þā yrmða þe ūs on sittað, and mid

15 swȳþe micelan earnungan wē þā bōte mōtan æt Gode gerǣcan, gif hit sceal heonanforð gōdiende weorðan.

    Lā hwæt, wē witan ful georne þæt tō miclan bryce sceal micel bōt nȳde, and tō miclan bryne wæter unlȳtel, gif man þæt fȳr sceal tō āhte ācwencan; and micel is nȳdþearf manna gehwilcum þæt hē Godes lage gȳme heonanforð georne and

20 Godes gerihta mid rihte gelǣste. On hǣþenum þēodum ne dear man forhealdan lȳtel ne micel þæs þe gelagod is tō gedwolgoda weorðunge; and wē forhealdað ǣghwǣr Godes gerihta ealles tō gelōme. And ne dear man gewanian on hǣþenum þēodum inne ne ūte ǣnig þǣra þinga þe gedwolgodan brōht bið and tō lācum betǣht bið; and wē habbað Godes hūs inne and ūte clǣne berȳpte. And

25 Godes þēowas syndan mǣþe and munde gewelhwǣr bedǣlde; and gedwolgoda þēnan ne dear man misbēodan on ǣnige wīsan mid hǣþenum lēodum, swā swā man Godes þēowum nū dēð tō wīde, þǣr crīstene scoldan Godes lage healdan and Godes þēowas griðian.

1–2 *Sermo . . . Cristi*] 'The sermon of the Wolf to the English, when the Danes were most severely persecuting them, which was in the thousand and fourteenth year from the incarnation of our Lord Jesus Christ'.

4 *aa . . . wyrse*] 'the longer it goes on the worse it is getting'

5 *Antecrīstes tōcyme*] see 1 John 2:18

20 *Godes gerihta*] God's dues, i. e. tithes

Ac sōð is þæt ic secge, þearf is þǣre bōte, for þām Godes gerihta wanedan tō
30　lange innan þysse þēode on ǣghwylcan ænde, and folclaga wyrsedan ealles tō
swȳþe, and hālignessa syndan tō griðlēase wīde, and Godes hūs syndan tō clǣne
berȳpte ealdra gerihta and innan bestrȳpte ǣlcra gerisena; and wydewan syndan
fornȳdde on unriht tō ceorle, and tō mænege foryrmde and gehȳnede swȳþe; and
earme men syndan sāre beswicene and hrēowlīce besyrwde and ūt of þysan earde
35　wīde gesealde swȳþe unforworhte fremdum tō gewealde; and cradolcild
geþēowede þurh wælhrēowe unlaga for lȳtelre þȳfþe wīde gynd þās þēode; and
frēoriht fornumene and þrǣlriht genyrwde and ælmæsriht gewanode; and hrædest
is tō cweþenne, Godes laga lāðe and lāra forsawene; and þæs wē habbað ealle
þurh Godes yrre bysmor gelōme, gecnāwe sē þe cunne; and se byrst wyrð
40　gemǣne, þēh man swā ne wēne, eallre þysse þēode, būtan God beorge.

For þām hit is on ūs eallum swutol and gesēne þæt wē ǣr þysan oftor brǣcan
þonne wē bēttan, and þȳ is þysse þēode fela onsǣge. Ne dohte hit nū lange inne
ne ūte, ac wæs here and hunger, bryne and blōdgyte on gewelhwylcan ende oft
and gelōme; and ūs stalu and cwalu, strīc and steorfa, orfcwealm and uncoþu, hōl
45　and hete and rȳpera rēaflāc derede swȳþe þearle, and ungylda swȳðe gedrehtan,
and ūs unwedera foroft wēoldan unwǣstma; for þām on þysan earde wæs, swā hit
þincan mæg, nū fela gēara unrihta fela and tealte getrȳwða ǣghwǣr mid
mannum. Ne bearh nū foroft gesib gesibban þē mā þe fremdan, ne fæder his
bearne, ne hwīlum bearn his āgenum fæder, ne brōþor ōþrum; ne ūre ǣnig his līf
50　fadode swā swā hē scolde, ne gehādode regollīce, ne lǣwede lahlīce. Ac worhtan
lust ūs tō lage ealles tō gelōme, and nāþor ne hēoldan ne lāre ne lage Godes ne
manna swā swā wē scoldan. Ne ǣnig wið ōþerne getrȳwlīce þōhte swā rihte swā
hē scolde, ac mǣst ǣlc swicode and ōþrum derede wordes and dǣde; and hūru
unrihtlīce mǣst ǣlc ōþerne æftan hēaweþ mid sceandlican onscytan, dō māre, gif
55　hē mǣge. For þām hēr sȳn on lande ungetrȳwþa micle for Gode and for worolde,
and ēac hēr sȳn on earde on mistlice wīsan hlāfordswican manege. And ealra
mǣst hlāfordswice sē bið on worolde þæt man his hlāfordes sāule beswīce; and
ful micel hlāfordswice ēac bið on worolde þæt man his hlāford of līfe forrǣde,
oððon of lande lifiendne drīfe; and ǣgþer is geworden on þysan earde;
60　Ēadweard man forrǣdde and syððan ācwealde and æfter þām forbærnde and
Æþelred man drǣfde ūt of his earde. And godsibbas and godbearn tō fela man
forspilde wīde gynd þās þēode; and ealles tō mænege hālige stōwa wīde

---

32–33 *wydewan . . . ceorle*] 'widows are forced to (re)marry (against all custom)' – usually
widows were encouraged not to marry again.
35 *wīde gesealde*] This is a clear reference to slave trading.
36 *geþēowede*] The current Anglo-Saxon practice of selling babies into slavery was later
repealed by King Cnut (1016–1035).
45 *ungylda*] This could refer to the Danegeld, i. e. tribute paid to the Vikings to pay off attacks;
see O 10, introduction and ll. 29–41.
58 *of līfe forrǣde*] 'plot against (his lord's) life'
60 *Ēadweard*] King Edward the Martyr (975–979) was killed by the men of his half-brother,
Æþelred, who succeeded him.
61 *Æþelred*] King Æþelred fled to Normandy in 1013 to evade the Danish king Swein; he
regained the throne in 1014.

forwurdan þurh þæt þe man sume men ǣr þām gelōgode, swā man nā ne scolde,
gif man on Godes griðe mǣþe witan wolde; and crīstenes folces tō fela man
65 gesealde ūt of þysan earde nū ealle hwīle; and eal þæt is Gode lāð, gelȳfe sē þe
wille.

And scandlic is tō specenne þæt geworden is tō wīde, and egeslic is tō witanne
þæt oft dōð tō manege, þe drēogað þā yrmþe, þæt scēotað tōgædere and āne
cwenan gemǣnum cēape bicgað gemǣne, and wið þā āne fȳlþe ādrēogað, ān
70 æfter ānum, and ǣlc æfter ōðrum, hundum gelīccast, þe for fȳlþe ne scrīfað, and
syððan wið weorðe syllað of lande fēondum tō gewealde Godes gesceafte and his
āgenne cēap, þe hē dēore gebōhte. Ēac wē witan georne hwǣr sēo yrmð gewearð
þæt fæder gesealde bearn wið weorþe, and bearn his mōdor, and brōþor sealde
ōþerne fremdum tō gewealde; and eal þæt syndan micle and egeslice dǣda,
75 understande sē þe wille. And gȳt hit is māre and ēac mǣnigfealdre þæt dereð
þysse þēode: mænige synd forsworene and swȳþe forlogene, and wed synd
tōbrocene oft and gelōme; and þæt is gesȳne on þysse þēode þæt ūs Godes yrre
hetelīce on sit, gecnāwe sē þe cunne.

And lā, hū mæg māre scamu þurh Godes yrre mannum gelimpan þonne ūs dēð
80 gelōme for āgenum gewyrhtum? Ðēh þrǣla hwylc hlāforde æthlēape and of
crīstendōme tō wīcinge weorþe, and hit æfter þām eft geweorþe þæt wǣpngewrixl weorðe gemǣne þegene and þrǣle, gif þrǣl þæne þegen fullīce āfylle,
licge ǣgylde ealre his mǣgðe; and, gif se þegen þæne þrǣl þe hē ǣr āhte fullīce
āfylle, gylde þegengylde. Ful earhlice laga and scandlice nȳdgyld þurh Godes
85 yrre ūs sȳn gemǣne, understande sē þe cunne; and fela ungelimpa gelimpð þysse
þēode oft and gelōme. Ne dohte hit nū lange inne ne ūte, ac wæs here and hete on
gewelhwilcan ende oft and gelōme, and Engle nū lange eal sigelēase and tō
swȳþe geyrigde þurh Godes yrre; and flotmen swā strange þurh Godes þafunge
þæt oft on gefeohte ān fēseð tȳne, and hwīlum lǣs, hwīlum mā, eal for ūrum
90 synnum. And oft tȳne oððe twelfe, ǣlc æfter ōþrum, scendað tō bysmore þæs
þegenes cwenan, and hwīlum his dohtor oððe nȳdmāgan, þǣr hē on lōcað, þe lǣt
hine sylfne rancne and rīcne and genōh gōdne ǣr þæt gewurde. And oft þrǣl
þæne þegen þe ǣr wæs his hlāford cnyt swȳþe fæste and wyrcð him tō þrǣle þurh
Godes yrre.

95 Wālā þǣre yrmðe and wālā þǣre woroldscame þe nū habbað Engle, eal þurh
Godes yrre! Oft twēgen sǣmen, oððe þrȳ hwīlum, drīfað þā drāfe crīstenra
manna fram sǣ tō sǣ, ūt þurh þās þēode, gewelede tōgædere, ūs eallum tō
woroldscame, gif wē on eornost ǣnige cūþon āriht understandan; ac ealne þæne
bysmor þe wē oft þoliað wē gyldað mid weorðscipe þām þe ūs scendað; wē him
100 gyldað singāllīce, and hȳ ūs hȳnað dæghwāmlīce; hȳ hergiað and hȳ bærnað,
rȳpaþ and rēafiað and tō scipe lǣdað; and lā, hwæt is ǣnig ōðer on eallum þām
gelimpum būtan Godes yrre ofer þās þēode swutol and gesǣne?

---

69 *gemǣnum cēape*] 'as a joint purchase'
81–82 *wǣpngewrixl . . . þrǣle*] Ordinarily servants were not allowed to take up weapons at all,
  much less use them against their lords, as is implied here.
84 *þegengylde*] This refers to the *wergeld*, the price to be paid for murder or maiming; the
  exact price differed depending on the social status of the victim.

Nis ēac nān wundor þēah ūs mislimpe, for þām wē witan ful georne þæt nū fela gēara mænn nā ne rōhtan foroft hwæt hȳ worhtan wordes oððe dǣde: ac wearð
105 þes þēodscipe, swā hit þincan mæg, swȳþe forsyngod þurh mænigfealde synna and þurh fela misdǣda: þurh morðdǣda and þurh māndǣda, þurh gītsunga and þurh gīfernessa, þurh stala and þurh strūdunga, þurh mannsylena and þurh hǣþene unsida, þurh swicdōmas and þurh searacræftas, þurh lahbrycas and þurh ǣswicas, þurh mǣgrǣsas and þurh manslyhtas, þurh hādbrycas and þurh
110 ǣwbrycas, þurh siblegeru and þurh mistlice forligru. And ēac syndan wīde, swā wē ǣr cwǣdan, þurh āðbricas and þurh wedbrycas and þurh mistlice lēasunga forloren and forlogen mā þonne scolde; and frēolsbricas and fæstenbrycas wīde geworhte oft and gelōme. And ēac hēr sȳn on earde apostatan ābroþene and cyrichatan hetole and lēodhatan grimme ealles tō manege, and oferhogan wīde
115 godcundra rihtlaga and crīstenra þēawa, and hōcorwyrde dysige ǣghwǣr on þēode oftost on þā þing þe Godes bodan bēodaþ, and swȳþost on þā þing þe ǣfre tō Godes lage gebyriað mid rihte.

And þȳ is nū geworden wīde and sīde tō ful yfelan gewunan þæt menn swȳþor scamað nū for gōddǣdan þonne for misdǣdan, for þām tō oft man mid hōcere
120 gōddǣda hyrweð and godfyrhte lehtreð ealles tō swȳþe, and swȳþost man tǣleð and mid olle gegrēteð ealles tō gelōme þā þe riht lufiað and Godes ege habbað be ǣnigum dǣle. And þurh þæt þe man swā dēð þæt man eal hyrweð þæt man scolde heregian and tō forð lāðet þæt man scolde lufian, þurh þæt man gebringeð ealles tō manege on yfelan geþance and on undǣde, swā þæt hȳ ne scamað nā,
125 þēh hȳ syngian swȳðe and wið God sylfne forwyrcan hȳ mid ealle, ac for īdelan onscytan hȳ scamað þæt hȳ bētan heora misdǣda swā swā bēc tǣcan, gelīce þām dwǣsan þe for heora prȳtan lēwe nellað beorgan ǣr hȳ nā ne magan, þēh hȳ eal willan.

Hēr syndan þurh synlēawa, swā hit þincan mæg, sāre gelēwede tō manege on
130 earde. Hēr syndan mannslagan and mǣgslagan and mæsserbanan and mynster-hatan, and hēr syndan mānsworan and morþorwyrhtan, and hēr syndan myltestran and bearnmyrðran and fūle forlegene hōringas manege, and hēr syndan wiccan and wælcyrian, and hēr syndan rȳperas and rēaferas and worolstrūderas, and, hrǣdest is tō cweþenne, māna and misdǣda ungerīm ealra. And þæs ūs ne
135 scamað nā, ac ūs scamað swȳþe þæt wē bōte āginnan swā swā bēc tǣcan, and þæt is gesȳne on þysse earman forsyngodan þēode.

Ēalā, micel magan manege gȳt hērtōēacan ēaþe beþencan þæs þe ān man ne mehte on hrǣdinge āsmēagan, hū earmlīce hit gefaren is nū ealle hwīle wīde gynd þās þēode. And smēage hūru georne gehwā hine sylfne and þæs nā ne latige
140 ealles tō lange. Ac lā, on Godes naman, utan dōn swā ūs nēod is, beorgan ūs sylfum swā wē geornost magan, þē lǣs wē ætgædere ealle forweorðan.

Ān þēodwita wæs on Brytta tīdum, Gildas hātte, sē āwrāt be heora misdǣdum, hū hȳ mid heora synnum swā oferlīce swȳþe God gegrǣmedan þæt hē lēt æt

---

126 *bēc*] This refers to the penitential books used in the Anglo-Saxon Church with precise regulations as to sins and penalties.
142 *Gildas*] a 6th century British monk, author of *De Excidio Britanniae*, a historical account lamenting the downfall of the British, which he attributed to the sins of both clergy and laity.

nȳhstan Engla here heora eard gewinnan and Brytta dugeþe fordōn mid ealle.
145 And þæt wæs geworden, þæs þe hē sǣde, þurh rīcra rēaflāc and þurh gītsunge
wōhgestrēona, ðurh lēode unlaga and þurh wōhdōmas, ðurh biscopa āsolcennesse
and þurh lȳðre yrhðe Godes bydela, þe sōþes geswugedan ealles tō gelōme and
clumedan mid ceaflum þǣr hȳ scoldan clypian. Þurh fūlne ēac folces gǣlsan and
þurh oferfylla and mænigfealde synna heora eard hȳ forworhtan and selfe hȳ
150 forwurdan.

Ac wutan dōn swā ūs þearf is, warnian ūs be swilcan; and sōþ is þæt ic secge,
wyrsan dǣda wē witan mid Englum þonne wē mid Bryttan āhwār gehȳrdan; and
þȳ ūs is þearf micel þæt wē ūs beþencan and wið God sylfne þingian georne. And
utan dōn swā ūs þearf is, gebūgan tō rihte, and be suman dǣle unriht forlǣtan,
155 and bētan swȳþe georne þæt wē ǣr brǣcan; and utan God lufian and Godes
lagum fylgean, and gelǣstan swȳþe georne þæt þæt wē behētan þā wē fulluht
underfēngan, oððon þā þe æt fulluhte ūre forespecan wǣran; and utan word and
weorc rihtlīce fadian, and ūre ingeþanc clǣnsian georne, and āð and wed wǣrlīce
healdan, and sume getrȳwða habban ūs betwēonan būtan uncræftan; and utan
160 gelōme understandan þone miclan dōm þe wē ealle tō sculon, and beorgan ūs
georne wið þone weallendan bryne helle wītes, and geearnian ūs þā mærþa and
þā myrhða þe God hæfð gegearwod þām þe his willan on worolde gewyrcað.
God ūre helpe. Amen.

---

159 *sume getrȳwða*] 'a certain amount of loyalty'
163 *God ūre helpe*] 'God help us!'

Text 8: The Old English Apollonius

The *Apollonius* story was one of the most popular fictional stories in the Middle Ages. Probably coming from a now lost Greek source, Latin versions of the story served as the base for many other medieval translations and adaptations. John Gower, Chaucer's contemporary, made use of the story in Book 8 of his *Confessio Amantis*. We find the story of Apollonius in the extremely popular collection of narratives called *Gesta Romanorum* and Shakespeare based his play *Pericles, Prince of Tyre* on the *Historia Apollonii Regis Tyri*. The tale of Apollonius was very popular through the entire Middle Ages and its popularity continued into the Early Modern period; the 11th century translation into Old English was, however, the first translation into a living language.

Unfortunately, only the beginning and the end of the Old English translation have survived. Apollonius, Lord of Tyre, uncovers the incestuous relationship between the King of Antioch, Antiochus, and his daughter. Antiochus seeks to have Apollonius killed as a result, and Apollonius is forced to flee, beginning a series of adventures. He shipwrecks on the coast of Pentapolis, where he is taken into King Arcestrates' court. The following chapters, in which he becomes tutor to the king's daughter, Arcestrate, who then falls in love with him, are reproduced here. After the king's daughter rejects her other suitors and chooses Apollonius, the king gives Apollonius permission to marry his daughter. The manuscript breaks off here, but from the Latin versions we know what takes place in the missing parts: the couple marry, and Antiochus dies for his sins, after which Apollonius seeks to return to Antioch with his new wife. She falls into a coma while giving birth to their daughter Thasia, and because Apollonius believes she has died, she is put in a watertight coffin. This coffin washes up on the shores of Ephesus, where Arcestrate is awakened and given to the service of the Goddess Diana. Apollonius gives his daughter Thasia to a friend to raise, Stranguillio, whose wife later tries to kill the girl. Captured by pirates before she can be murdered, Thasia is then sold to a brothel in Mytilene. By telling her sad story to the king, she is able to preserve her virginity until Apollonius finally saves her. Apollonius weds her to the king and, after a prophetic dream, sails with the newlyweds to Ephesus. The rest of the story has been preserved in the Old English translation: Apollonius' wife hears his story and then recognises him. They all return, Strangiullio and his wife are punished, and they live happily ever after.

Along with only a few other texts, *Wonders of the East* and *The Letter of Alexander to Aristotle*, *Apollonius* shows a different side of Old English literature from that to which we are normally accustomed: a love of the exotic and the unusual. *Apollonius*, however, is the only one of the three which presents the exotic in the frame of an adventure story, and can be seen as the first English novel.

The most conspicuous feature of the text is the graph-sequence *-ænC* in words which are subject to i-mutation, as for example *gewænde, gewændon* (l. 16, 74), *bewænde* (l. 31), *gemængde* (l. 42, 56), *stæfne* (l. 57), *geswænctest* (l. 105) and *āsænde* (l. 110). West Saxon usually has *e* in this context; *hearpe-strengas* (l. 55) and *geendode* (l. 73) agree with West Saxon practice. Forms like *misðingð* (l. 9), *gesingodest* (l. 32), *dide, didon* (l. 83, 111) and *scrīdde* (l. 50) suggest that the unrounding of *y* is well on its way; however, *cyning* and its inflected forms retain *y*. The later history of diphthongs in *eo* as a result of breaking can be seen in forms like *dēorwurðan* (l. 4, 68), *wurðlicum* (l. 18), *wurðlīcost* (l. 83) and *wurðscipes* (l. 85); under the influence of *w* the diphthong has been smoothed to *u*. The dative singular of *dohtor*, a noun belonging to the r-stems (see § 40), does not show i-mutation: *tō ðāre dohtor* (l. 31); *mīnre dohtor* (l. 110). Finally, the text shows the new definite article *þe* (l. 73) for earlier *se*.

Sources: Corpus Christi College, Cambridge, MS 201. – Marsden (2004); Goolden (1958); Raith (1956).

Ðā ēode Apollonius in and gesæt þār him getǣht wæs, ongēan ðone cyngc. Ðār wearð ðā sēo þēnung in geboren and æfter þām cynelic gebēorscipe; and Apollonius nān ðingc ne ǣt, ðēahðe ealle ōðre men ǣton and blīðe wǣron. Ac hē behēold þæt gold and þæt seolfor and ðā dēorwurðan rēaf and þā bēodas and þā
5   cynelican þēnunga. Ðāðā hē þis eal mid sārnesse behēold, ðā sæt sum eald and sum æfestig ealdorman be þām cynge. Midþīþe hē geseah þæt Apollonius swā sārlīce sæt, and ealle þingc behēold, and nān ðingc ne ǣt, ðā cwæð hē tō ðām cynge: "Ðū gōda cyngc, efne þes man þe þū swā wel wið gedēst, hē is swīðe æfestful for ðīnum gōde." Ðā cwæð se cyngc: "Ðē misðingð; sōðlīce, þes iunga
10   man ne æfestigað on nānum ðingum ðe hē hēr gesihð; ac hē cȳð þæt hē hæfð fela forloren." Ðā beseah Arcestrates se cyngc blīðum andwlitan tō Apollonio and cwæð: "Ðū iunga man, bēo blīðe mid ūs, and gehiht on God þæt þū mōte silf tō ðām sēlran becuman."

[c. 15] Midþīðe se cyning þās word gecwæð, ðā fǣringa þār ēode in ðæs
15   cynges iunge dohtor, and cyste hyre fæder and ðā ymbsittendan. Þā hēo becōm tō Apollonio, þā gewǣnde hēo ongēan tō hire fæder and cwæð: "Ðū gōda cyningc and mīn se lēofesta fæder, hwæt is þes iunga man þe ongēan ðē on swā wurðlicum setle sit mid sārlicum andwlitan? Nāt ic hwæt hē besorgað." Ðā cwæð se cyningc: "Lēofe dohtor, þes iunga man is forliden, and hē gecwēmde mē
20   manna betst on ðām plegan; forðām ic hine geladode tō ðysum ūrum gebēorscipe. Nāt ic hwæt hē is, ne hwanon hē is; ac gif ðū wille witan hwæt hē sȳ, āxsa hine, forðām þē gedafenað ðæt þū wite." Ðā ēode þæt mǣden tō Apollonio and mid forwandigendre sprǣce cwæð: "Ðēah ðū stilli sȳ and unrōt, þēah ic þīne æðelborennesse on ðē gesēo. Nū þonne, gif ðē tō hefig ne þince, sege mē þīnne
25   naman, and þīn gelymp ārece mē." Ðā cwæð Apollonius: "Gif ðū for nēode āxsast æfter mīnum naman, ic secge þē: ic hine forlēas on sǣ. Gif ðū wilt mīne æðelborennesse witan, wite ðū þæt ic hīg forlēt on Tharsum." Ðæt mǣden cwæð: "Sege mē gewislīcor þæt ic hit mǣge understandan." Apollonius ðā sōðlīce hyre ārehte ealle his gelymp, and æt þāre sprǣcan ende him fēollon tēaras of ðām
30   ēagum.

[c. 16] Midþȳþe se cyngc þæt geseah, hē bewǣnde hine ðā tō ðāre dohtor and cwæð: "Lēofe dohtor, þū gesingodest; midþȳþe þū woldest witan his naman and his gelimp, þū hafast nū geednīwod his ealde sār. Ac ic bidde þē þæt þū gife him swā hwæt swā ðū wille." Ðā ðā þæt mǣden gehīrde þæt hire wæs ālȳfed fram

─────────

20 *plegan*] refers to a game played earlier, in which Apollonius had shown his dexterity.

35 hire fæder þæt hēo ǣr hyre silf gedōn wolde, ðā cwæð hēo tō Apollonio: "Apolloni, sōðlīce þū eart ūre; forlǣt þīne murcnunge, and nū ic mīnes fæder lēafe habbe, ic gedō ðē weligne." Apollonius hire þæs þancode, and se cyngc blissode on his dohtor welwillendnesse, and hyre tō cwæð: "Lēofe dohtor, hāt feccan þīne hearpan and gecīg þē tō þīne frȳnd, and āfirsa fram þām iungan his
40 sārnesse."

Ðā ēode hēo ūt, and hēt feccan hire hearpan; and sōna swā hēo hearpian ongan, hēo mid winsumum sange gemǣngde þāre hearpan swēg. Ðā ongunnon ealle þā men hī herian on hyre swēgcræfte, and Apollonius āna swīgode. Ðā cwæð se cyningc: "Apolloni, nū ðū dēst yfele, forðāmþe ealle men heriað mīne dohtor on
45 hyre swēgcræfte, and þū āna hī swīgende tǣlst." Apollonius cwæð: "Ēalā, ðū gōda cyngc, gif ðū mē gelīfst, ic secge þæt ic ongite þæt sōðlīce þīn dohtor gefēol on swēgcræft, ac hēo næfð hine nā wel geleornod. Ac hāt mē nū sillan þā hearpan, þonne wāst þū þæt þū nū gīt nāst." Arcestrates se cyning cwæð: "Apolloni, ic oncnāwe sōðlīce þæt þū eart on eallum þingum wel gelǣred." Ðā
50 hēt se cyng sillan Apollonige þā hearpan. Apollonius þā ūt ēode, and hine scrīdde and sette ǣnne cynehelm uppon his hēafod, and nam þā hearpan on his hand, and in ēode and swā stōd þæt se cyngc and ealle þā ymbsittendan wēndon þæt hē nǣre Apollonius, ac þæt hē wǣre Apollines, ðāra hǣþenra god. Ðā wearð stilnes and swīge geworden innon ðāre healle. And Apollonius his hearpenægl genam,
55 and hē þā hearpe-strengas mid cræfte āstirian ongan, and þāre hearpan swēg mid winsumum sange gemǣngde. And se cyngc silf and ealle þe þār andwearde wǣron, micelre stæfne cliopodon and hine heredon. Æfter þisum forlēt Apollonius þā hearpan and plegode, and fela fægera þinga þār forð tēah þe þām folce ungecnāwe wæs and ungewunelic; and heom eallum þearle līcode ǣlc þāra þinga
60 ðe hē forð tēah.

[c. 17] Sōðlīce, midþȳþe þæs cynges dohtor geseah þæt Apollonius on eallum gōdum cræftum swā wel wæs getogen, þā gefēol hyre mōd on his lufe. Ðā æfter þæs bēorscipes geendunge cwæð þæt mǣden tō ðām cynge: "Lēofa fæder, þū lȳfdest mē lītle ǣr þæt ic mōste gifan Apollonio swā hwæt swā ic wolde of þīnum
65 goldhorde." Arcestrates se cyng cwæð tō hyre: "Gif him swā hwæt swā ðū wille." Hēo ðā swīðe blīðe ūt ēode and cwæð: "Lārēow Apolloni, ic gife þē be mīnes fæder lēafe twā hund punda goldes and fēower hund punda gewihte seolfres and þone mǣstan dǣl dēorwurðan rēafes and twēntig ðēowa manna." And hēo þā þus cwæð tō ðām þēowum mannum: "Berað þās þingc mid ēow þe ic behēt Apol-
70 lonio mīnum lārēowe, and lecgað innon būre beforan mīnum frēondum." Þis wearð þā þus gedōn æfter þāre cwēne hǣse; and ealle þā men hire gife heredon ðe hīg gesāwon.

Ðā sōðlīce geendode þe gebēorscipe; and þā men ealle ārison and grētton þone cyngc and ðā cwēne, and bǣdon hīg gesunde bēon, and hām gewǣndon. Ēac
75 swilce Apollonius cwæð: "Ðū gōda cyngc and earmra gemiltsigend, and þū cwēn

---

47 *gefēol*] 'has only begun'
53 *Apollines*] Apollo
73–74 *grētton . . . bēon*] words of parting – a translation of the Latin 'uale dicentes regi et reginae'

lāre lufigend, bēon gē gesunde." Hē beseah ēac tō ðām þēowum mannum þe þæt
mǣden him forgifen hæfde, and heom cwæð tō: "Nimað þās þing mid ēow þe mē
sēo cwēn forgeaf, and gān wē sēcan ūre gesthūs þæt wē magon ūs gerestan."

Ðā ādrēd þæt mǣden þæt hēo nǣfre eft Apollonium ne gesāwe swā raðe swā
80 hēo wolde, and ēode þā tō hire fæder and cwæð: "Ðū gōda cyningc, līcað ðē wel
þæt Apollonius, þe þurh ūs tōdæg gegōdod is, þus heonon fare, and cuman yfele
men and berēafian hine?" Se cyngc cwæð: "Wel þū cwǣde. Hāt him findan hwǣr
hē hine mæge wurðlīcost gerestan." Ðā dide þæt mǣden swā hyre beboden wæs;
and Apollonius onfēng þāre wununge ðe hym getǣht wæs, and ðār in ēode Gode
85 þancigende ðe him ne forwyrnde cynelices wurðscipes and frōfres.

[c. 18] Ac þæt mǣden hæfde unstille niht, mid þāre lufe onǣled þāra worda
and sanga þe hēo gehȳrde æt Apollonige; and nā leng hēo ne gebād ðonne hit
dæg wæs, ac ēode sōna swā hit lēoht wæs, and gesæt beforan hire fæder bedde.
Ðā cwæð se cyngc: "Lēofe dohtor, for hwī eart ðū þus ǣrwacol?" Ðæt mǣden
90 cwæð: "Mē āwehton þā gecneordnessan þe ic girstandæg gehȳrde. Nū bidde ic ðē
forðām þæt þū befǣste mē ūrum cuman Apollonige tō lāre." Ðā wearð se cyningc
þearle geblissod, and hēt feccan Apollonium and him tō cwæð: "Mīn dohtor
girnð þæt hēo mōte leornian æt ðē ðā gesǣligan lāre ðe þū canst; and gif ðū wilt
þisum þingum gehȳrsum bēon, ic swerige ðē þurh mīnes rīces mægna þæt swā
95 hwæt swā ðū on sǣ forlure, ic ðē þæt on lande gestaðelige." Ðāðā Apollonius þæt
gehȳrde, hē onfēngc þām mǣdene tō lāre, and hire tǣhte swā wel swā hē silf
geleornede.

[c. 19] Hyt gelamp ðā æfter þisum binnon fēawum tīdum þæt Arcestrates se
cyngc hēold Apollonius hand on handa, ond ēodon swā ūt on ðāre ceastre strǣte.
100 Þā æt nȳhstan cōmon ðār gān ongēan hȳ þrȳ gelǣrede weras and æþelborene þā
lange ǣr girndon þæs cyninges dohtor. Hī ðā ealle þrȳ tōgædere ānre stefne
grētton þone cyngc. Ðā smercode se cyng ond heom tō beseah ond þus cwæð:
"Hwæt is þæt, þæt gē mē ānre stefne grētton?" Ðā andswerode heora ān ond
cwæð: "Wē bǣdon gefirn þȳnre dohtor, ond þū ūs oftrǣdlīce mid elcunge
105 geswænctest; forðām wē cōmon hider tōdæg þus tōgædere. Wē syndon þȳne
ceastergewaran of æðelum gebyrdum geborene. Nū bidde wē þē þæt þū gecēose
þē ǣnne of ūs þrȳm, hwilcne þū wille þē tō āðume habban." Ðā cwæð se cyningc:
"Nabbe gē nā gōdne tīman ārēdodne; mīn dohtor is nū swīðe bisy ymbe hyre
leornunga. Ac þēlǣsþe ic ēow ā leng slǣce, āwrītað ēowre naman on gewrite ond
110 hire morgengife; þonne āsǣnde ic þā gewrita mīnre dohtor, þæt hēo sylf gecēose
hwilcne ēower hēo wille." Ðā didon ðā cnihtas swā, ond se cyngc nam ðā gewrita
ond geinseglode hī mid his ringe ond sealde Apollonio þus cweðende: "Nim nū,
lārēow Apolloni, swā hit þē ne mislīcyge, ond bryng þīnum lǣringcmǣdene."

_____

79 _nǣfre . . . raðe_] 'that she wouldn't see Apollonius again' [as soon as she wished]

Text 9: The Anglo-Saxon Chronicle – Brunanburh

The transmission of *The Battle of Brunanburh* is unusual, for it is a poem in MS ABCD of the *Anglo-Saxon Chronicle*. According to manuscript F, "in this year Athelstan (and Edmund, his brother) led levies to Brunanburh, and there fought against Anlaf: with the help of Christ, they had the victory (and there slew five knights and eight jarls)" (Garmonsway, 1954). The battle at Brunanburh (the exact location remains unknown) was one of many battles fought by Æþelstan and his brothers, Eadmund and Eadred (924–939; 939–946; 946–955 respectively), who through these victories were able to reduce Viking influence and pave the way to a united country of England. The years 924 to 955 are written in one hand, which suggests one author composed all of the entries, including the two poems contained among them.

In 937, Olafr Guðfriðarson, the Norse King of Dublin, had allied with Constantinus, the Celtic King of Scotland. They met somewhere in Scotland or northern England, and marched south on Æþelstan. Æþelstan took his West Saxon army north to meet them, picking up Mercians (see l. 24b) along the way. After a decisive English victory in which both Constantinus and Olafr were killed, the Norse returned to Dublin by way of the *Dinges mere*, 54b – possibly the River Dee.

Much emphasis is placed on the ruling family and their relations to one another (*gebroþor* ll. 2b, 57a), as well as to their noble heritage (*afaran Eadweardes* – descendants of Edward the Elder and Alfred the Great, l. 7a, 52; *æþeling, geæþele*, ll. 3a, 7b, 58a). At the same time, the unity of the Angles and the Saxons is proclaimed (l. 70a) against all other enemies, British, Welsh and Norse. The poem ends with a reference to the "beasts and birds of battle", portending further victory for the English, and proceeds to link these developments to English historical ascendency (*þe us secgað bec, ealde uðwitan*, ll. 68b–69a). All of these aspects show a very partial poet, seeking to justify Æþelstan's claim to a united English throne, and a rise of English nationalism at the time. Indeed, the poet glorifies the pride which the Anglo-Saxons must feel, thematising the shame of their enemies (for example, the Norse *hreman ne þorfte* – dared not boast, ll. 39b; see also 44b, 47b, 56, 59).

The style of the poem reflects a poet well versed in heroic diction and style. He employs the traditional alliterative verse, applying many rhetorical devices, for example understatement and metaphor (both kennings and heitis).

This text has the usual spelling variants: instead of the regular ending *-on* for preterite plural, we find *-an* and *-un*: *clufan* (l. 5), *crugun* (l. 10) etc. The dative plural occasionally ends in *-an*: *mylenscearpan* (l. 24), *hamora lāfan* (l. 6) etc. Non-WS features include mutated *ē*, cf. *geflēmed* (l. 32) and *nēde* (l. 33) for WS *ie, y*.

Sources: Corpus Christi College, Cambridge, MS 173. – Dobbie (1942); Marsden (2004). – Secondary literature: Johnson (1968), Lawler (1973), Frese (1986).

937. Hēr Æþelstān cyning,   eorla dryhten,
beorna bēahgifa,   and his brōþor ēac,
Ēadmund æþeling,   ealdorlangne tīr
geslōgon æt sæcce   sweorda ecgum
5   ymbe Brunanburh.   Bordweal clufan,
hēowan heaþolinde   hamora lāfan,
afaran Ēadweardes,   swā him geæþele wæs
from cnēomǣgum,   þæt hī æt campe oft
wiþ lāþra gehwæne   land ealgodon,
10   hord and hāmas.   Hettend crungun,
Sceotta lēoda   and scipflotan
fǣge fēollan,   feld dænnede
secga swāte,   siðþan sunne ūp
on morgentīd,   mǣre tungol,
15   glād ofer grundas,   Godes condel beorht,
ēces Drihtnes,   oð sīo æþele gesceaft
sāh tō setle.   Þǣr læg secg mænig,
gārum āgēted,   guma norþerna
ofer scild scoten,   swilce Scittisc ēac,
20   wērig, wīges sæd.   Wesseaxe forð
ondlongne dæg   ēorodcistum
on lāst legdun   lāþum þēodum,
hēowan hereflēman   hindan þearle
mēcum mylenscearpan.   Myrce ne wyrndon
25   heardes hondplegan   hæleþa nānum,
þǣra þe mid Anlāfe   ofer ǣra gebland
on lides bōsme   land gesōhtun,
fǣge tō gefeohte.   Fīfe lægun
on þām campstede   cyningas giunge,
30   sweordum āswefede,   swilce seofene ēac
eorlas Anlāfes,   unrīm heriges,

---

1 *Æþelstān*] West Saxon king, 925–939
2 *bēahgifa*] Kings gave rings to their retainers in return for services rendered.
3 *Ēadmund*] Æþelstan's halfbrother, followed him as king from 939–946
3 *ealdorlangne tīr*] 'eternal glory'
6 *hamora lāfan*] 'with their swords' – the product of hammers
11 *scipflotan*] in this case pirates or Vikings
12 *dænnede*] The meaning is uncertain: 'flowed'.
19 *Scittisc*] the Scots
20 *Wesseaxe*] the West Saxon army
21 *ondlongne dæg*] all day long
22 *on . . . legdun*] 'on the heels of'
24 *mylenscearpan*] 'very sharp'
24 *Myrce*] the Mercians
26 *Anlāfe*] King of Dublin
26 *ǣra gebland*] 'rolling waves' (the turbulence of the ocean)
27 *on lides bōsme*] 'in the bosom of the ship'

flotan and Sceotta. Þǣr geflēmed wearð
Norðmanna bregu,   nēde gebēded,
tō lides stefne   lītle weorode;
35 crēad cnear on flot,   cyning ūt gewāt
on fealene flōd,   feorh generede.
Swilce þǣr ēac se frōda   mid flēame cōm
on his cȳþþe norð,   Costontīnus,
hār hilderinc,   hrēman ne þorfte
40 mǣca gemānan;   hē wæs his mǣga sceard,
frēonda gefylled   on folcstede,
beslagen æt sæcce,   and his sunu forlēt
on wælstōwe   wundun forgrunden,
giungne æt gūðe.   Gelpan ne þorfte
45 beorn blandenfeax   bilgeslehtes,
eald inwidda,   ne Anlāf þȳ mā;
mid heora herelāfum   hlehhan ne þorftun,
þæt hī beaduweorca   beteran wurdun
on campstede   cumbolgehnāstes,
50 gārmittinge,   gumena gemōtes,
wǣpengewrixles,   þæs hī on wælfelda
wiþ Ēadweardes   afaran plegodan.
Gewitan him þā Norþmen   nægledcnearrum,
drēorig daraða lāf,   on Dinges mere
55 ofer dēop wæter   Difelin sēcan,
eft Īraland,   ǣwiscmōde.
Swilce þā gebrōþer   bēgen ætsamne,
cyning and æþeling,   cȳþþe sōhton,
Wesseaxena land,   wīges hrēmige.
60 Lētan him behindan   hrǣw bryttian
saluwigpādan,   þone sweartan hræfn,
hyrnednebban,   and þane hasewanpādan,
earn æftan hwīt,   ǣses brūcan,
grǣdigne gūðhafoc   and þæt grǣge dēor,
65 wulf on wealde.   Ne wearð wæl māre
on þis ēiglande   ǣfre gīeta

---

33 *Norðmanna bregu*] 'King of the Norse', i. e. Anlāf
34 *tō lides stefne*] 'prow of the ship'
38 *Costontīnus*] King of Picts and Scots
47 *herelāfum*] 'survivors (of the army)'
49 *cumbolgehnāstes*] 'clash of standards', battle
54 *daraða lāf*] those who had survived the spears.
54 *Dinges mere*] The location is unknown.
61 *saluwigpādan*] 'the dark-feathered one'
62 *hyrnednebban*] 'the horny-beaked one'
62 *hasewanpādan*] 'the grey-feathered one'
64 *gūðhafoc*] 'war-hawk'

folces gefylled   beforan þissum
sweordes ecgum,   þæs þe ūs secgað bēc,
ealde ūðwitan,   siþþan ēastan hider
70 Engle and Seaxe   ūp becōman,
ofer brād brimu   Brytene sōhtan,
wlance wīgsmiþas,   Wēalas ofercōman,
eorlas ārhwate   eard begēatan.

Text 10: The Battle of Maldon

According to the Peterborough Chronicle (MS C of the *Anglo-Saxon Chronicle*), a battle was fought in the year 991: *Her wæs Gypeswic gehergod, and æfter þam swiðe raðe wæs Brihtnoð ealdorman ofslægen æt Mældune. And on þam geare man gerædde þæt man geald ærest gafol Deniscan mannum for þam mycclan brogan þe hi worhton be þam særiman, þæt wæs ærest X þusend punda.* – 'Here Ipswich was raided, and very soon after that Ealdorman Byrhtnoð was killed at Maldon; and in that year it was first decided that tax be paid to the Danish men because of the great terror which they wrought along the sea coast. That was at first 10 thousand pounds'.

The battle at Maldon (see first map) would probably have been quickly forgotten, had not a poem been written to celebrate the defeat of the English at the hands of the Vikings.

During the reign of Æþelred the Unready (978–1016), Viking attacks in England were once again on the increase, and the king was increasingly unable to repel them. Æþelred is accused of allowing a large amount of cowardice and disloyalty, a concern which seems to be reflected in Byrhtnoð's army as described in this poem (see ll. 6–10; 185–188; 238–239). A common practice during his reign, perhaps resulting from his weakness as a military leader, was to pay the Vikings tribute (*gafol*) instead of engaging in open battle with them. *The Battle of Maldon* thematises one of what were many English defeats in the context of the second wave of Viking attacks in the closing decades of the 10th century.

Cast from the position of the losing side, this poem has completely different goals from those of the *Battle of Brunanburh*, for example. Brunanburh is a celebration of an English victory and the ensuing unity, whereas Maldon, while commemorating the sacrifice which Byrhtnoð and his army make, seems rather to be a statement on current English politics. Beginning on a dark note, the poem foreshadows the inevitable defeat which will occur (see the formulaic *þa hwile þe*, ll. 14, 83, 235, 272). The practice of paying the Vikings tribute is criticised in the speeches between the Viking messenger and Byrhtnoð.

The theme of cowardice and loyalty is one of the main topics of the poem, from the first lines describing the young nobleman who decides not to be a coward (l. 5), the retreat of the cowards after Byrhtnoð's death (ll. 185–201), and finally the condemnation by Offa in his death speech (ll. 231–242). The topic of Byrhtnoð's *ofermode*, seen as the turning point of the poem by much of the critical literature, is at most a secondary issue: upon Byrhtnoð's death, most of the rest of the poem is taken up by speeches of his loyal retainers, proclaiming their willingness to fight to the death. The Vikings, on the other hand, are hardly characterised: they are battle-wolves (*wælwulfas*, l. 96a), warriors and heathens (*hæðene scealcas*, l. 181b) at most. Their role in the poem is of the adversary, and their exact names or attributes are unimportant to the author's purposes.

The single transmitted manuscript was burned in a fire in 1731, but a transcription from 1726 has been preserved. Both the beginning and the end of the poem are missing; however, the structure of the poem suggests that only a small part has been lost.

The language of the poem uses the traditional heroic vocabulary (cf. the formulaic *maþelode*, ll. 42, 309) and various words for shield (cf. *bord, lind, rand, scyld*), spear (cf. *æsc, daroð, gar, spere*) and warrior (cf. *beorn, cempa, hæleð, hyse*), as one would expect. In the absence of an original manuscript, it is difficult to comment further on the linguistic features of the text.

Sources: Bodleian Library, Oxford, MS Rawlinson B. 203. – Scragg (1991). – Secondary literature: Clark (1968), Gneuss (1976), Scragg (1991).

                     * * * brocen wurde.
     Hēt þā hyssa hwæne   hors forlǣtan,
     feor āfӯsan,   and forð gangan,
     hicgan tō handum,   and tō hige gōdum.
5   Þā þæt Offan mǣg   ǣrest onfunde,
     þæt se eorl nolde   yrhðo geþolian,
     hē lēt him þā of handon   lēofne flēogan
     hafoc wið þæs holtes,   and tō þǣre hilde stōp;
     be þām man mihte oncnāwan   þæt se cniht nolde
10 wācian æt þām wigge,   þā hē tō wǣpnum fēng.
     Ēac him wolde Ēadric   his ealdre gelǣstan,
     frēan tō gefeohte;   ongan þā forð beran
     gār tō gūþe.   Hē hæfde gōd geþanc,
     þā hwīle þe hē mid handum   healdan mihte
15 bord and brād swurd;   bēot hē gelǣste,
     þā hē ætforan his frēan   feohtan sceolde.
       Ðā þǣr Byrhtnōð ongan   beornas trymian,
     rād and rǣdde,   rincum tǣhte
     hū hī sceoldon standan,   and þone stede healdan,
20 and bæd þæt hyra randas   rihte hēoldon
     fæste mid folman,   and ne forhtedon nā.
     Þā hē hæfde þæt folc   fægere getrymmed,
     hē līhte þā mid lēodon,   þǣr him lēofost wæs,
     þǣr hē his heorðwerod   holdost wiste.
25   Þā stōd on stæðe,   stīðlīce clypode
     wīcinga ār,   wordum mælde,
     sē on bēot ābēad   brimlīþendra
     ǣrænde tō þām eorle,   þǣr hē on ōfre stōd:
     "Mē sendon tō þē   sǣmen snelle,
30 hēton ðē secgan,   þæt þū mōst sendan raðe
     bēagas wið gebeorge;   and ēow betere is

---

2 *Hēt*] The subject is Byrhtnoð.

7–8 *lēofne … hafoc*] The adjective 'lēofne' refers to 'hafoc'. Offa's relative doesn't seem to have expected that he would be participating in a fierce battle. He sends his hawk away when he realises that this will be a more serious affair than a hunting party with hawks.

þæt gē þisne gārræs   mid gafole forgyldon,
þonne wē swā hearde   hilde dǣlon.
Ne þurfe wē ūs spillan,   gif gē spēdaþ tō þām;
35   wē willað wið þām golde   grið fæstnian.
Gyf þū þæt gerǣdest   þe hēr rīcost eart,
þæt þū þīne lēoda   lȳsan wille,
syllan sǣmannum   on hyra sylfra dōm
feoh wið frēode,   and niman frið æt ūs,
40   wē willaþ mid þām sceattum   ūs tō scype gangan,
on flot fēran,   and ēow friþes healdan."
     Byrhtnōð maþelode,   bord hafenode,
wand wācne æsc,   wordum mǣlde,
yrre and ānrǣd   āgeaf him andsware:
45   "Gehȳrst þū, sǣlida,   hwæt þis folc segeð?
Hī willað ēow tō gafole   gāras syllan,
ǣttrenne ord   and ealde swurd,
þā heregeatu þe ēow   æt hilde ne dēah.
Brimmanna boda,   ābēod eft ongēan,
50   sege þīnum lēodum   miccle lāþre spell,
þæt hēr stynt unforcūð   eorl mid his werode,
þe wile gealgian   ēþel þysne,
Æþelredes eard,   ealdres mīnes
folc and foldan;   feallan sceolon
55   hæþene æt hilde.   Tō hēanlic mē þinceð
þæt gē mid ūrum sceattum   tō scype gangon
unbefohtene,   nū gē þus feor hider
on ūrne eard   in becōmon.
Ne sceole gē swā sōfte   sinc gegangan;
60   ūs sceal ord and ecg   ǣr gesēman,
grim gūðplega,   ǣr wē gofol syllon."
     Hēt þā bord beran,   beornas gangan,
þæt hī on þām ēasteðe   ealle stōdon.
Ne mihte þǣr for wætere   werod tō þām ōðrum;
65   þǣr cōm flōwende   flōd æfter ebban,

---

32 *forgyldon*] The imagery of payment, money and trade (see 'forgyldon (l. 32), dǣlon (l. 33), spēdaþ (l 34), golde (l. 35)' and 'syllan (l. 38)') in the messenger's speech emphasises the current practice between the Vikings and the English of paying Danegeld in order to evade actual battle.

45 *Gehȳrst . . . segeð?*] Byrhtnoð asks the Viking messenger if he can hear the English army, who are in an uproar because of his demands. Both Byrhtnoð and his army are determined to engage the Vikings in battle.

46 *gafole gāras*] The alliteration highlights the irony in Byrhtnoð's answer; the only thing the English are willing to 'trade' is battle.

55–61 *hēanlic . . . syllon*] Byhrtnoð continues in an ironic vein, mirroring and even mocking the Viking's speech. Both on a lexical and stylistic level the messenger's words are twisted ('gārræs mid gafole' (l. 32) becomes 'grim gūðplege . . . gofol' (l. 61)).

lucon lagustrēamas.   Tō lang hit him þūhte,
hwænne hī tōgædere   gāras bēron.
Hī þǣr Pantan strēam   mid prasse bestōdon,
Ēastseaxena ord   and se æschere.
70 Ne mihte hyra ǣnig   ōðrum derian,
būton hwā þurh flānes flyht   fyl genāme.
Se flōd ūt gewāt;   þā flotan stōdon gearowe,
wīcinga fela,   wīges georne.
Hēt þā hæleða hlēo   healdan þā bricge
75 wigan wīgheardne,   sē wæs hāten Wulfstān,
cāfne mid his cynne,   – þæt wæs Cēolan sunu –
þe ðone forman man   mid his francan ofscēat,
þe þǣr baldlīcost   on þā bricge stōp.
Þǣr stōdon mid Wulfstāne   wigan unforhte,
80 Ælfere and Maccus,   mōdige twēgen,
þā noldon æt þām forda   flēam gewyrcan,
ac hī fæstlīce   wið ðā fȳnd weredon,
þā hwīle þe hī wǣpna   wealdan mōston.
Þā hī þæt ongēaton,   and georne gesāwon
85 þæt hī þǣr bricgweardas   bitere fundon,
ongunnon lytegian þā   lāðe gystas:
bǣdon þæt hī ūpgangan   āgan mōston,
ofer þone ford faran,   fēþan lǣdan.
Ðā se eorl ongan   for his ofermōde
90 ālȳfan landes tō fela   lāþere ðēode.
Ongan ceallian þā   ofer cald wæter
Byrhtelmes bearn   (beornas gehlyston):
"Nū ēow is gerȳmed,   gāð ricene tō ūs,
guman tō gūþe;   God āna wāt
95 hwā þǣre wælstōwe   wealdan mōte."
    Wōdon þā wælwulfas,   for wætere ne murnon,
wīcinga werod,   west ofer Pantan,
ofer scīr wæter   scyldas wēgon,
lidmen tō lande   linde bǣron.
100 Þǣr ongēan gramum   gearowe stōdon
Byrhtnōð mid beornum;   hē mid bordum hēt
wyrcan þone wīhagan,   and þæt werod healdan
fæste wið fēondum.   Þā wæs feohte nēh,
tīr æt getohte;   wæs sēo tīd cumen

68 *Pantan strēam*] the River Blackwater
81 *flēam gewyrcan*] A central issue of this poem, the theme of flight, is first introduced here.
   However unsuitable its position here appears to be – the English are in a very secure position –
   the combination with the doom formula in l. 83 'þā hwīle þe' portends ill: see ll. 185–201.
102 *wīhagan*] Byrhtnōð has ordered his men to form a shield wall as a line of defence. 'Haga'
   (hedge, enclosure) conveys a sense of impenetrability.

105 þæt þǣr fǣge men   feallan sceoldon.
Þǣr wearð hrēam āhafen,   hremmas wundon,
earn ǣses georn;   wæs on eorþan cyrm.
Hī lēton þā of folman   fēolhearde speru,
[grimme] gegrundene   gāras flēogan;
110 bogan wǣron bysige,   bord ord onfēng,
biter wæs se beadurǣs,   beornas fēollon
on gehwæðere hand,   hyssas lāgon.
Wund wearð Wulfmǣr,   wælrǣste gecēas,
Byrhtnōðes mǣg;   hē mid billum wearð,
115 his swustersunu,   swīðe forhēawen.
Þǣr wearð wīcingum   wiþerlēan āgyfen:
gehȳrde ic þæt Ēadweard   ānne slōge
swīðe mid his swurde,   swenges ne wyrnde,
þæt him æt fōtum fēoll   fǣge cempa;
120 þæs him his ðēoden   þanc gesǣde,
þām būrþēne,   þā hē byre hæfde.
Swā stemnetton   stīðhicgende
hysas æt hilde,   hogodon georne
hwā þǣr mid orde   ǣrost mihte
125 on fǣgean men   feorh gewinnan,
wigan mid wǣpnum;   wæl fēol on eorðan.
Stōdon stædefæste;   stihte hī Byrhtnōð,
bæd þæt hyssa gehwylc   hogode tō wīge,
þe on Denon wolde   dōm gefeohtan.
130   Wōd þā wīges heard,   wǣpen ūp āhōf,
bord tō gebeorge,   and wið þæs beornes stōp.
Ēode swā ānrǣd   eorl tō þām ceorle:
ǣgþer hyra ōðrum   yfeles hogode.
Sende ðā sē sǣrinc   sūþerne gār,
135 þæt gewundod wearð   wigena hlāford;
hē scēaf þā mid ðām scylde,   þæt se sceaft tōbærst,
and þæt spere sprengde,   þæt hit sprang ongēan.
Gegremod wearð se gūðrinc: hē mid gāre stang
wlancne wīcing,   þe him þā wunde forgeaf.
140 Frōd wæs se fyrdrinc;   hē lēt his francan wadan
þurh ðæs hysses hals,   hand wīsode
þæt hē on þām fǣrsceaðan   feorh gerǣhte.

_____

105 *fǣge men*] The poet does not specify the nationality of the 'doomed men'. This doom formula is therefore portentious for both sides.
117 *gehȳrde ic*] Here the narrator speaks in the first person. This would seem to imply that the poem is based on an oral report (from one of the cowards?). However, 'gehȳrde ic' is also a common poetic formula.
129 *Denon*] The Viking invaders in Eastgern England were usually Danes; as a result, *Dene* became a synonym for Viking. *Denon* is used here so as to alliterate with *dōm*.

Ðā hē ōþerne   ofstlīce scēat,
þæt sēo byrne tōbærst;   hē wæs on brēostum wund
145 þurh ðā hringlocan,   him æt heortan stōd
ætterne ord.   Se eorl wæs þē blīþra,
hlōh þā, mōdi man,   sǣde Metode þanc
ðæs dægweorces   þe him Drihten forgeaf.
Forlēt þā drenga sum   daroð of handa,
150 flēogan of folman,   þæt sē tō forð gewāt
þurh ðone æþelan   Æþelredes þegen.
Him be healfe stōd   hyse unweaxen,
cniht on gecampe,   sē full cāflīce
brǣd of þām beorne   blōdigne gār,
155 Wulfstānes bearn,   Wulfmǣr se geonga;
forlēt forheardne   faran eft ongēan;
ord in gewōd,   þæt sē on eorþan læg
þe his þēoden ǣr   þearle gerǣhte.
Ēode þā gesyrwed   secg tō þām eorle;
160 hē wolde þæs beornes   bēagas gefeccan,
rēaf and hringas   and gerēnod swurd.
Ðā Byrhtnōð brǣd   bill of scēðe,
brād and brūnecg,   and on þā byrnan slōh.
Tō raþe hine gelette   lidmanna sum,
165 þā hē þæs eorles   earm āmyrde.
Fēoll þā tō foldan   fealohilte swurd:
ne mihte hē gehealdan   heardne mēce,
wǣpnes wealdan.   Þā gȳt þæt word gecwæð
hār hilderinc,   hyssas bylde,
170 bæd gangan forð   gōde gefēran.
Ne mihte þā on fōtum leng   fæste gestandan;
hē tō heofenum wlāt   * * *
"Ic þancie þē,   ðēoda Waldend,
ealra þǣra wynna   þe ic on worulde gebād.
175 Nū ic āh, milde Metod,   mǣste þearfe
þæt þū mīnum gāste   gōdes geunne,
þæt mīn sāwul tō ðē   sīðian mōte,
on þīn geweald,   þēoden engla,
mid friþe ferian;   ic eom frymdi tō þē
180 þæt hī helsceaðan   hȳnan ne mōton."
Ðā hine hēowon   hǣðene scealcas,
and bēgen þā beornas   þe him big stōdon,
Ælfnōð and Wulmǣr   bēgen lāgon,
ðā onemn hyra frēan   feorh gesealdon.

147 *mōdi man*] If 'mōdi' is taken as a positive attribute, then Byrhtnōð's 'ofermōde' (l. 89)
should be seen in the same light.
149 *drenga*] here used pejoratively

185   Hī bugon þā fram beaduwe   þe þǣr bēon noldon:
         þǣr wurdon Oddan bearn   ǣrest on flēame,
         Godrīc fram gūþe,   and þone gōdan forlēt,
         þe him mǣnigne oft   mearh gesealde;
         hē gehlēop þone eoh   þe āhte his hlāford,
190   on þām gerǣdum   þēh hit riht ne wæs,
         and his brōðru mid him   bēgen ǣrndon,
         Godwine and Godwīg,   gūþe ne gȳmdon,
         ac wendon fram þām wīge   and þone wudu sōhton,
         flugon on þæt fæsten,   and hyra fēore burgon,
195   and manna mā   þonne hit ǣnig mǣð wǣre,
         gyf hī þā geearnunga   ealle gemundon
         þe hē him tō duguþe   gedōn hæfde.
         Swā him Offa on dæg   ǣr āsǣde,
         on þām meþelstede,   þā hē gemōt hæfde,
200   þæt þǣr mōdiglīce   manega sprǣcon,
         þe eft æt þearfe   þolian noldon.
             Þā wearð āfeallen   þæs folces ealdor,
         Æþelredes eorl;   ealle gesāwon
         heorðgenēatas   þæt hyra hearra læg.
205   Þā ðǣr wendon forð   wlance þegenas,
         unearge men   efston georne:
         hī woldon þā ealle   ōðer twēga,
         līf forlǣtan   oððe lēofne gewrecan.
         Swā hī bylde forð   bearn Ælfrīces,
210   wiga wintrum geong,   wordum mǣlde,
         Ælfwine þā cwæð   (hē on ellen sprǣc):
         "Gemunað þāra mǣla   þe wē oft æt meodo sprǣcon,
         þonne wē on bence   bēot āhōfon,
         hæleð on healle,   ymbe heard gewinn:
215   nū mæg cunnian   hwā cēne sȳ.
         Ic wylle mīne æþelo   eallum gecȳþan,
         þæt ic wæs on Myrcon   miccles cynnes;
         wæs mīn ealda fæder   Ealhelm hāten,
         wīs ealdorman,   woruldgesǣlig.

---

188 *mænigne oft mearh gesealde*] According to the poet, Godrīc's flight is especially shameful in view of the many gifts he had received from his lord.

198–201 *Swā . . . noldon*] This could be implicit criticism of Byrhtnoð: he should have reckoned with deserters. However, Byrhtnoð's determination before and during the battle shows his great courage.

213–215 *bēot āhōfon . . . cēne sȳ*] Ælfwine's speech echoes Offa's warning of the day before (l. 198–201). The danger posed by deserters is something many of them were aware of. Nevertheless, Byrhtnoð could rely on a number of 'mōdige' (l. 80) 'heorðgenēatas' (l. 204) in his 'heorðwerod' (l. 24). The series of speeches which now follows takes up and develops the theme of courage and determination in the face of death.

217 *Myrcon*] Mercians

220 Ne sceolon mē on þǣre þēode   þegenas ætwītan
     þæt ic of ðisse fyrde   fēran wille,
     eard gesēcan,   nū mīn ealdor ligeð
     forhēawen æt hilde.   Mē is þæt hearma mǣst:
     hē wæs ǣgðer mīn mǣg   and mīn hlāford.”

225 Þā hē forð ēode,   fǣhðe gemunde,
     þæt hē mid orde   ānne gerǣhte
     flotan on þām folce,   þæt sē on foldan læg
     forwegen mid his wǣpne.   Ongan þā winas manian,
     frȳnd and gefēran,   þæt hī forð ēodon.

230 Offa gemǣlde,   æscholt āsceōc:
     “Hwæt þū, Ælfwine, hafast   ealle gemanode,
     þegenas tō þearfe.   Nū ūre þēoden līð,
     eorl on eorðan,   ūs is eallum þearf
     þæt ūre ǣghwylc   ōþerne bylde

235 wigan tō wīge,   þā hwīle þe hē wǣpen mæge
     habban and healdan,   heardne mēce,
     gār and gōd swurd.   Ūs Godrīc hæfð,
     earh Oddan bearn,   ealle beswicene:
     wēnde þæs formoni man,   þā hē on mēare rād,

240 on wlancan þām wicge,   þæt wǣre hit ūre hlāford;
     forþan wearð hēr on felda   folc tōtwǣmed,
     scyldburh tōbrocen.   Ābrēoðe his angin,
     þæt hē hēr swā manigne   man āflȳmde!”
     Lēofsunu gemǣlde,   and his linde āhōf,

245 bord tō gebeorge;   hē þām beorne oncwæð:
     “Ic þæt gehāte,   þæt ic heonon nelle
     flēon fōtes trym,   ac wille furðor gān,
     wrecan on gewinne   mīnne winedrihten.
     Ne þurfon mē embe Stūrmere   stedefæste hæleð

250 wordum ætwītan,   nū mīn wine gecranc,
     þæt ic hlāfordlēas   hām sīðie,
     wende fram wīge;   ac mē sceal wǣpen niman,
     ord and īren.”   Hē ful yrre wōd,
     feaht fæstlīce,   flēam hē forhogode.

255 Dunnere þā cwæð,   daroð ācwehte,
     unorne ceorl,   ofer eall clypode,
     bæd þæt beorna gehwylc   Byrhtnōð wrǣce:
     “Ne mæg nā wandian   sē þe wrecan þenceð
     frēan on folce,   ne for fēore murnan.”

260 Þā hī forð ēodon,   fēores hī ne rōhton;

_____

242 *scyldburh tōbrocen*] Offa suggests that the reason the battle has turned against the English
   is because the traitors broke the line of defence (‘wīhagan’, l. 102; ‘scyldburh’) when they ran
   away. However, the line of defence has been reformed by l. 277 (‘bordweall’).

ongunnon þā hīredmen   heardlīce feohtan,
grame gārberend,   and God bǣdon
þæt hī mōston gewrecan   hyra winedrihten,
and on hyra fēondum   fyl gewyrcan.
265   Him se gȳsel ongan   geornlīce fylstan;
hē wæs on Norðhymbron   heardes cynnes,
Ecglāfes bearn,   him wæs Æscferð nama.
Hē ne wandode nā   æt þām wīgplegan,
ac hē fȳsde forð   flān geneahhe;
270   hwīlon hē on bord scēat,   hwīlon beorn tǣsde,
ǣfre embe stunde   hē sealde sume wunde,
þā hwīle ðe hē wǣpna   wealdan mōste.
        Þā gȳt on orde stōd   Ēadweard se langa,
gearo and geornful,   gylpwordum spræc
275   þæt hē nolde flēogan   fōtmǣl landes,
ofer bæc būgan,   þā his betera leg.
Hē bræc þone bordweall,   and wið ðā beornas feaht,
oðþæt hē his sincgyfan   on þām sǣmannum
wurðlīce wrec   ǣr hē on wæle lǣge.
280   Swā dyde Æþerīc,   æþele gefēra,
fūs and forðgeorn,   feaht eornoste,
Sībyrhtes brōðor,   and swīðe mænig ōþer
clufon cellod bord,   cēne hī weredon;
bærst bordes lærig,   and sēo byrne sang
285   gryrelēoða sum.   Þā æt gūðe slōh
Offa þone sǣlidan,   þæt hē on eorðan fēoll,
and ðǣr Gaddes mǣg   grund gesōhte:
raðe wearð æt hilde   Offa forhēawen.
Hē hæfde ðēah geforþod   þæt hē his frēan gehēt,
290   swā hē bēotode ǣr.   wið his bēahgifan
þæt hī sceoldon bēgen   on burh rīdan,
hāle tō hāme,   oððe on here crincgan,
on wælstōwe   wundum sweltan.
Hē læg ðegenlīce   ðēodne gehende.
295   Ðā wearð borda gebræc;   brimmen wōdon,
gūðe gegremode;   gār oft þurhwōd
fǣges feorhhūs.   Forð þā ēode Wīstān,
Þurstānes sunu,   wið þās secgas feaht;

266 *Norðhymbron*] the Northumbrians
269 *flān geneahhe*] 'plenty of arrows'
271 *ǣfre ... wunde*] In this line rhyme replaces alliteration; see Bredehoft (2005).
277 *Hē bræc þone bordweall*] The topic of the line of defence is taken up again; however in
this case the breaking of the line has a positive connotation. First Ēadweard (l. 273), then
Æþerīc (l. 280) and 'swīðe mænig ōþer' (l. 282) break the line intentionally in order to kill as
many Vikings as possible before they fall themselves.

hē wæs on geþrange   hyra þrēora bana,
300   ǣr him Wīgelmes bearn   on þām wæle lǣge.
Þǣr wæs stīð gemōt;   stōdon fæste
wigan on gewinne;   wīgend cruncon,
wundum wērige;   wæl fēol on eorþan.
Ōswold and Ealdwold   ealle hwīle,
305   bēgen þā gebrōþru,   beornas trymedon,
hyra winemāgas   wordon bǣdon
þæt hī þǣr æt ðearfe   þolian sceoldon,
unwāclīce   wǣpna nēotan.
    Byrhtwold maþelode,   bord hafenode,
310   sē wæs eald genēat,   æsc ācwehte;
hē ful baldlīce   beornas lǣrde:
"Hige sceal þē heardra,   heorte þē cēnre,
mōd sceal þē māre,   þē ūre mægen lȳtlað.
Hēr līð ūre ealdor   eall forhēawen,
315   gōd on grēote;   ā mæg gnornian
sē ðe nū fram þīs wīgplegan   wendan þenceð.
Ic eom frōd fēores;   fram ic ne wille,
ac ic mē be healfe   mīnum hlāforde,
be swā lēofan men,   licgan þence."
320   Swā hī Æþelgāres bearn   ealle bylde,
Godrīc tō gūþe.   Oft hē gār forlēt,
wælspere windan   on þā wīcingas,
swā hē on þām folce   fyrmest ēode,
hēow and hȳnde,   oð þæt hē on hilde gecranc.
325   Næs þæt nā se Godrīc   þe ðā gūðe forbēah.
                    * * * * *

309–310 *Byrhtwold maþelode . . . æsc ācwehte*] The repetition of the maþelode-formula, accompanied by the action of shield-raising and spear-shaking, is an indication of the importance of what is to be said. Both Byrhtnoð and Byrhtwold hold decisive speeches at different points in the battle – Byrhtnoð to intimidate the Vikings, Byrhtwold to encourage the few remaining English.

Text 11: The Dream of the Rood

The Dream of the Rood is perhaps the most artistic religious poem written in Old English. Originally an oral work, our text was written down in the late 10th century; however, the poem itself must be much older. Several of the lines of this poem have been inscribed on the Ruthwell Cross in runes (ll. 39–42, 44–49, 56–59, and 62–64). As the Ruthwell Cross dates to the late 7th to early 8th century, *The Dream of the Rood* must have been composed sometime before that, likely with Anglian authorship (see below).

The poem itself presents a much different view of the Passion from that which readers will be familiar with from its representation in the High Middle Ages and onward. The Early Middle Ages often used the symbol of the cross for the suffering of Christ, without depicting Christ himself at all. This poem includes Christ; however, the typical scene of Christ suffering, as we know it, for example, from various paintings, does not at all come to force here. Christ is not represented as a suffering victim, nor is he the confused son of God: "My God, why have you forsaken me?" does not appear, nor anything which could express a similar sentiment (see Matthew 27:46 and Mark 15:34). Christ is a valiant hero marching to battle, and his emotions and thoughts are hidden from us. His Godly nature is shown by his superiority and willingness to suffer; his human nature is shown in that he bleeds and dies – but this depiction fails to arouse compassion and pity in us; it rather produces admiration for the hero.

Indeed, this poem seeks to impress the reader (or listener) with the severity of the Crucifixion in another way: through the use of *prosopopoeia*, the author gives us a view of the Crucifixion from the point of view of the cross. The cross is the opposite of Christ – the cross is weak, unsure of himself, afraid, and suffers immensely. He is only able to withstand the torments of crucifixion because his lord Christ will not allow him to do otherwise. The cross has been torn from his forest, misused by the Romans to bear their criminals, and finally forced to kill his own lord. Many times the cross repeats how weak he feels, and that he would like to disobey Christ's will and let him down or crush his enemies, but he *ne dorste* (ll. 35, 42, 45, 47). The cross feels the pain, is wounded and covered with blood. After Christ has died, the cross is felled, and buried ignominiously (l. 75). Like Christ, however, the cross is found and reborn. Adorned with jewels (l. 77), he is able to experience the same sort of resurrection as Christ, which the cross himself cannot witness.

The frame for the experiences of the cross, and thereby Christ, is a dream vision. The dreamer, a poor sinner, sees the glory of the cross, witnesses the Passion through the eyes of the cross, and afterwards the cross explains to him the significance of what he has seen. The cross, an instrument of torture, has been honoured above all others (ll. 90 ff), just as Mary now presides over humanity after Eve (a woman) plunged humanity into dishonour. Parallel to this, Christ will come to redeem all mankind on the last day (ll. 103–109). The dreamer is able to learn from the cross: only aware of his own sins at the beginning of the poem (ll. 13, 20), the dreamer is filled with hope and happiness for the future and the promises of heaven (ll. 122, 124–126).

The text shows several non-WS features: West Germanic *$\bar{a}$ is written <e> in *blēdum* (l. 149), the regular WS form being *blǣdum* (see § 2). The influence of word-initial palatal is absent in *sceððan* (l. 47) versus WS *sceaððan*. Breaking (see § 3) before r+C does not occur in *wergas* (l. 31). Under the influence of i-mutation (see § 9) *ēa* is written <e> (versus WS *īe, ȳ*) in *bestēmed* (ll. 22, 48). The 3sg. present indicative of *magan* appears as both *meahte* (early form; l. 18) and *mihte* (l. 37).

Sources: Vercelli, Biblioteca Capitolare CXVII. – Marsden (2004); Mitchell/Robinson (1992); Swanton (1970). – Secondary literature: Woolf (1958, 1970), Lee (1972), Orton (1980). – Facsimile: Sisam (1976).

    Hwæt, ic swefna cyst   secgan wylle,
    hwæt mē gemǣtte   tō midre nihte,
    syðþan reordberend   reste wunedon.
    Þūhte mē, þæt ic gesāwe   syllicre trēow
5   on lyft lǣdan,   lēohte bewunden,
    bēama beorhtost.   Eall þæt bēacen wæs
    begoten mid golde;   gimmas stōdon
    fægere æt foldan scēatum,   swylce þǣr fīfe wǣron
    uppe on þām eaxlgespanne.   Behēoldon þǣr engel Dryhtnes ealle
10   fægere þurh forðgesceaft;   ne wæs ðǣr hūru fracodes gealga,
    ac hine þǣr behēoldon   hālige gāstas,
    men ofer moldan   and eall þēos mǣre gesceaft.
        Syllic wæs se sigebēam –   and ic synnum fāh,
    forwundod mid wommum.   Geseah ic wuldres trēow
15   wǣdum geweorðod,   wynnum scīnan,
    gegyred mid golde;   gimmas hæfdon
    bewrigen weorðlīce   Wealdendes trēow.
    Hwæðre ic þurh þæt gold   ongytan meahte
    earmra ǣrgewin,   þæt hit ǣrest ongan
20   swǣtan on þā swīðran healfe.   Eall ic wæs mid sorgum gedrēfed;
    forht ic wæs for þǣre fægran gesyhðe;   geseah ic þæt fūse bēacen
    wendan wǣdum and blēom: hwīlum hit wæs mid wǣtan bestēmed,
    beswyled mid swātes gange,   hwīlum mid since gegyrwed.
        Hwæðre ic þǣr licgende   lange hwīle
25   behēold hrēowcearig   Hǣlendes trēow,
    oð ðæt ic gehȳrde,   þæt hit hlēoðrode;
    ongan þā word sprecan   wudu sēlesta:

----

4 *syllicre*] elative: 'very strange'
5 *on lyft lǣdan*] passive meaning – 'lifted into the air'
8 *foldan scēatum*] 'at the surface of the earth' or 'at the corners of the earth' – this would mean that the four points of the cross symbolise the four points of the compass.
10 *fægere . . . forðgesceaft*] refers to the 'hālige gāstas' of line 11 – the angels who remained faithful to God during Lucifer's revolt.
13 *sigebēam*] literally 'the tree of victory' – a metaphor for the Cross
19 *earmra ǣrgewin*] 'the ancient struggle of the wretched' – the wretched being Christ and the Cross.

'Þæt wæs gēara iū   – ic þæt gȳta geman –
þæt ic wæs āhēawen   holtes on ende,
30   āstyred of stefne mīnum.   Genāman mē ðǣr strange fēondas,
geworhton him þǣr tō wǣfersȳne,   hēton mē heora wergas hebban;
bǣron mē þǣr beornas on eaxlum,   oð ðæt hīe mē on beorg āsetton;
gefæstnodon mē þǣr fēondas genōge.   Geseah ic þā Frēan mancynnes
efstan elne micle,   þæt hē mē wolde on gestīgan.
35   Þǣr ic þā ne dorste   ofer Dryhtnes word
būgan oððe berstan,   þā ic bifian geseah
eorðan scēatas.   Ealle ic mihte
fēondas gefyllan,   hwæðre ic fæste stōd.
Ongyrede hine þā geong hæleð   – þæt wæs God ælmihtig! –
40   strang and stīðmōd;   gestāh hē on gealgan hēanne,
mōdig on manigra gesyhðe,   þā hē wolde mancyn lȳsan.
Bifode ic, þā mē se beorn ymbclypte;   ne dorste ic hwæðre būgan tō eorðan,
feallan tō foldan scēatum,   ac ic sceolde fæste standan.
Rōd wæs ic ārǣred;   āhōf ic rīcne Cyning,
45   heofona Hlāford;   hyldan mē ne dorste.
Þurhdrifan hī mē mid deorcan næglum;   on mē syndon þā dolg gesīene,
opene inwidhlemmas;   ne dorste ic hira ǣnigum sceððan.
Bysmeredon hīe unc būtū ætgædere;   eall ic wæs mid blōde bestēmed,
begoten of þæs guman sīdan,   siððan hē hæfde his gāst onsended.
50   Feala ic on þām beorge   gebiden hæbbe
wrāðra wyrda: geseah ic weruda God
þearle þenian.   Þȳstro hæfdon
bewrigen mid wolcnum   Wealdendes hrǣw;
scīrne scīman   sceadu forðēode,
55   wann under wolcnum.   Wēop eal gesceaft,
cwīðdon Cyninges fyll: Crīst wæs on rōde.
Hwæðere þǣr fūse   feorran cwōman
tō þām Æþelinge;   ic þæt eall behēold.
Sāre ic wæs mid sorgum gedrēfed,   hnāg ic hwæðre þām secgum tō handa
60   ēaðmōd, elne mycle.   Genāmon hīe þǣr ælmihtigne God,
āhōfon hine of ðām hefian wīte;   forlēton mē þā hilderincas
standan, stēame bedrifenne;   eall ic wæs mid strǣlum forwundod.
Ālēdon hīe ðǣr limwērigne;   gestōdon him æt his līces hēafdum;
behēoldon hīe ðǣr heofenes Dryhten,   and hē hine ðǣr hwīle reste,

---

31 *him*] reflexive
37 *ic mihte*] 'I could have'
52 *þenian*] passive
57 *fuse*] 'the eager ones' – this seems to refer to Joseph of Arimathea and Nicodemus, who took Jesus' body from the cross.
62 *strǣlum*] 'with arrows', metaphor for the nails of l. 46
63 *hēafdum*] The dative plural with singular meaning is an Old English idiom; see also 'brēostum', line 118.

65 mēðe æfter ðām miclan gewinne.   Ongunnon him þā moldern wyrcan
beornas on banan gesyhðe,   curfon hīe ðæt of beorhtan stāne;
gesetton hīe ðæron sigora Wealdend.   Ongunnon him þā sorhlēoð galan
earme on þā æfentīde,   þā hīe woldon eft sīðian,
mēðe fram þām mǣran Þēodne;   reste hē ðǣr mǣte weorode.

70 Hwæðere wē ðǣr grēotende   gōde hwīle
stōdon on staðole;   stefn ūp gewāt
hilderinca;   hrǣw cōlode,
fæger feorgbold.   Þā ūs man fyllan ongan
ealle tō eorðan;   þæt wæs egeslic wyrd!

75 Bedealf ūs man on dēopan sēaþe;   hwæðre mē þǣr Dryhtnes þegnas,
frēondas gefrūnon,
gyredon mē   golde and seolfre.
    Nū ðū miht gehȳran,   hæleð mīn se lēofa,
þæt ic bealuwara weorc   gebiden hæbbe,

80 sārra sorga   Is nū sǣl cumen,
þæt mē weorðiað   wīde and sīde
menn ofer moldan   and eall þēos mǣre gesceaft,
gebiddaþ him tō þyssum bēacne.   On mē Bearn Godes
þrōwode hwīle;   for þan ic þrymfæst nū

85 hlīfige under heofenum   and ic hǣlan mæg
ǣghwylcne ānra   þāra þe him bið egesa tō mē.
Iū ic wæs geworden   wīta heardost,
lēodum lāðost,   ǣr þan ic him līfes weg
rihtne gerȳmde,   reordberendum.

90 Hwæt, mē þā geweorþode   wuldres Ealdor
ofer holtwudu,   heofonrīces Weard,
swylce swā hē his mōdor ēac,   Marīan sylfe,
ælmihtig God,   for ealle menn
geweorðode   ofer eall wīfa cynn.

95   Nū ic þē hāte,   hæleð mīn se lēofa,
þæt ðū þās gesyhðe   secge mannum;
onwrēoh wordum,   þæt hit is wuldres bēam,
se ðe ælmihtig God   on þrōwode
for mancynnes   manegum synnum

100 and Adomes   ealdgewyrhtum.
Dēað hē þǣr byrigde;   hwæðere eft Dryhten ārās
mid his miclan mihte,   mannum tō helpe.

---

69 *mǣte weorode*] 'with little company' – understatement for 'alone'
70 *wē*] the three crosses on Mount Golgatha
75 *þegnas*] could refer to St. Helena, who discovered the cross and adorned it with gold and
    silver.
76 the second half-line is missing.
79–80 *þæt . . . sorga*] 'that I have suffered at the hands of the guilty and heavy sorrow'.
86 *þāra . . . mē*] 'those who fear me'

Hē ðā on heofenas āstāg.   Hider eft fundaþ
on þysne middangeard,   mancynn sēcan
105 on dōmdæge,   Dryhten sylfa,
ælmihtig God,   and his englas mid,
þæt hē þonne wile dēman,   se āh dōmes geweald,
ānra gehwylcum,   swā hē him ǣrur hēr
on þyssum lǣnan   līfe geearnaþ
110 Ne mæg þǣr ǣnig   unforht wesan
for þām worde,   þe se Wealdend cwyð:
frīneð hē for þǣre mænige,   hwǣr se man sīe,
se ðe for Dryhtnes naman   dēaðes wolde
biteres onbyrigan,   swā hē ǣr on ðām bēame dyde.
115 Ac hīe þonne forhtiað,   and fēa þencaþ,
hwæt hīe tō Crīste   cweðan onginnen.
Ne þearf ðǣr þonne ǣnig   anforht wesan,
þe him ǣr on brēostum bereð   bēacna sēlest;
ac ðurh ðā rōde sceal   rīce gesēcan
120 of eorðwege   ǣghwylc sāwl,
sēo þe mid Wealdende   wunian þenceð.'
    Gebæd ic mē þā tō þām bēame   blīðe mōde,
elne mycle,   þǣr ic āna wæs
mǣte werede.   Wæs mōdsefa
125 āfȳsed on forðwege,   feala ealra gebād
langunghwīla.   Is mē nū līfes hyht,
þæt ic þone sigebēam   sēcan mōte
āna, oftor   þonne ealle men,
well weorþian.   Mē is willa tō ðām
130 mycel on mōde,   and mīn mundbyrd is
geriht tō þǣre rōde.   Nāh ic rīcra feala
frēonda on foldan,   ac hīe forð heonon
gewiton of worulde drēamum,   sōhton him wuldres Cyning;
lifiaþ nū on heofenum   mid Hēahfædere,
135 wuniaþ on wuldre;   and ic wēne mē
daga gehwylce,   hwænne mē Dryhtnes rōd,
þe ic hēr on eorðan   ǣr scēawode,
on þysson lǣnan   līfe gefetige,
and mē þonne gebringe,   þǣr is blis mycel,
140 drēam on heofonum,   þǣr is Dryhtnes folc
geseted tō symle,   þǣr is singāl blis;
and mē þonne āsette,   þǣr ic syþþan mōt
wunian on wuldre,   well mid þām hālgum

107–109 *þæt . . . geearnaþ*] 'in order to pass judgement – He in whom judgement lies – on
everyone as they have earned in this transitory life'.
133 *him*] reflexive
135 *ic . . . mē*] 'I long for'

drēames brūcan.   Sī mē Dryhten frēond,
145 se ðe hēr on eorðan   ǣr þrōwode
on þām gealgtrēowe   for guman synnum;
hē ūs onlȳsde   and ūs līf forgeaf,
heofonlicne hām.   Hiht wæs genīwad
mid blēdum and mid blisse,   þām þe þǣr bryne þolodan.
150 Se Sunu wæs sigorfæst   on þām sīðfate,
mihtig and spēdig,   þā hē mid manigeo cōm,
gāsta weorode,   on Godes rīce,
Anwealda ælmihtig,   englum tō blisse
and eallum ðām hālgum,   þām þe in heofonum ǣr
155 wunedon on wuldre,   þā heora Wealdend cwōm,
ælmihtig God,   þǣr his ēðel wæs.

---

149 *bryne*] an allusion to the harrowing of hell and the redemption of the righteous from the
fires of hell
150 These lines allude to Christ's triumph in hell, releasing the souls held captive there.

6. Middle English Texts

Introduction

The fourteen Middle English texts have been chosen to represent a wide range of Middle English culture, literary genres, and dialects. Important developments in Middle English times, such as the English recovery after the Norman Conquest, the wave of religious instruction literature and developments in literature in general, can all be seen in the progression of the texts. Some of these works can be considered 'medieval bestsellers', such as Chaucer, Langland and *The Prick of Conscience*, whereas other texts were known only regionally (*York Plays, Kentish Sermons*).

The texts chosen were composed between the 11th and the 15th centuries. The literary genres include historiographical writing (text 1), animal literature (texts 2, 8 and 14), homiletic literature (texts 3 and 11), religious instruction (text 4), saint's life (text 5), romances (texts 6 and 9), vision and allegory (text 7), lyrics (text 10), drama (text 12) and frame narrative (text 13).

The texts also show the wide variety of dialects present in Middle English. There are two texts from the East Midlands (texts 1 and 2), two Kentish works (texts 3 and 4), the West Midlands are represented by texts 5–7, and texts 8–10 represent the South, the Southwest and East Anglia. The North is represented by texts 11 and 12, text 13 represents the London area, and text 14 is Middle Scots.

All texts are preceded by an introduction which focuses on the specific features of the individual text. In addition, information on the manuscript is provided and references to editions are given. The introductory section also points out the most important linguistic features of the text.

The texts are accompanied by footnotes at the bottom of the page; line numbers are used as references.

Anthologies of Middle English texts are: Bennett/Smithers (1968), Dunn/Byrnes (1973), Garbáty (1984), Kaiser (1961), Mossé (1969), Owen/Owen (1971), Robertson (1970), Trapp (1973), Treharne (2004). – Literary histories are Baugh (1967), Bolton (1970), Schirmer (1983), Standop/Mertner (1967).

Text 1: The Peterborough Chronicle

The *Peterborough Chronicle* is the continuation of the version of the *Anglo-Saxon Chronicle* (see O 2) which was kept in Peterborough (see maps). Unlike the other chronicles, which either break off in 1066 with the Norman Conquest or shortly thereafter, the *Peterborough Chronicle* was continued until 1154. From the years 1080 to 1154, this chronicle is the only original text written in the English language; all other writing in English ceased, and was replaced by Latin or Norman. This means that the *Peterborough Chronicle* is not only an important historical source, but is also of enormous importance for scholars and students of the English language. The changes which begin in late Old English and to a great extent are already complete in early Middle English can be seen as they develop through the *Peterborough Chronicle*.

The following passage shows the political turbulence after the relatively stable reign of Henry I. After William the Conqueror and all of his direct male heirs had died, his granddaughter Matilda (daughter of Henry I) and his grandson Stephen (the son of William's daughter Adela) contended for the throne. The Anarchy resulted – a time of instability, in which Stephen and Matilda constantly fought against each other, and the needs of the country were neglected. The entries for 1135 and 1137 are a (somewhat exaggerated) list of the injustices and corruption which occurred during Stephen's reign. Indeed, the author overtly expresses a preference for the previous King Henry, criticising Stephen as much as possible. For example, despite King Henry's efforts to collect a large amount of gold and silver, Stephen wasted it, and did not use any of it to buy indulgences for the dead king, a common practice of the time (ll. 24–25).

The author of these passages not only comments on events of national significance, but also local events, such as the acts of the Abbot Martin. He also adds what is one of the first pieces of anti-Semitic diatribe, and describes what was to become almost a traditional topos in Christian literature: the Jewish murder of a Christian child.

The so-called 'Final Continuation' of the *Peterborough Chronicle* shows a number of difficult written forms which resulted from the influence of both Norman and Latin scribal practice. The most important of these will be pointed out in the following table. No attempt is made to equate the written evidence with a largely hypothetical early Middle English pronunciation.

1. OE *ā* appears as <a> in: *sua* (l. 5); *wua sua* (l. 10); *nan, na* (l. 9, 10, 24, 30, 31, 37, 55, 65); *athes* (l. 31); *bathe* (l. 35); *mare* (l. 57, 66); *stanes* (l. 43). However, *nammore* (l. 52) indicates that the change from Old English *ā* to Middle English *ǭ* had already begun. The evidence of *onne* (l. 45) is doubtful. It may either represent the preposition *on* or the (inflected) Old English *ānne*. The context suggests the preposition rather than the numeral.
2. The evidence of *sæden* (l. 4, 65) suggests that *g* had been dropped when immediately followed by *d*.
3. OE and late WS *ȳ* appears as both <i> and <y>: *sinnes* (l. 67); *yfel, yuele* (l. 15, 35, 68); *circe, circewican* (l. 58, 70, 76).
4. West Saxon breaking is absent in *ald* (l. 3).
5. OE *ēa* is usually represented by single vowel graphs <æ, e>; as in *ræuede(n)* (l. 7, 53, 60), *ded* (l. 5), *hefed* (l. 39), *hæued* (l. 40); *beom* (l. 46) is an exception.

6. OE *ēo* is written <e, æ> and <eo>: *frend* (l. 7), *heold, heolden* (l. 31, 32, 68 etc.); *undep* (l. 43); *ben* (l. 22, 86); *dær, dære* (l. 10, 54).

7. OE *æ+ʒ* is written <æi> or <ai> and only once <ei>: *dei* (l. 2), *dæi, dæies, dæis* (l. 2, 5, 36, 53, 69), *mai* (l. 49).

8. OE *ǣ* (derived from West Germanic **ai* under the influence of i-mutation) is written <æ> and <e>: *sæ* (l. 1, 21); *hethen* (l. 57); *del* (l. 83); *todeld* (l. 23); *flesc* (l. 55).

9. OE *ǣ* (derived from West Germanic **ā*) is written <æ> and <a>: *uuare, uuaren* (l. 3, 34), *wæron, uuæren* (l. 16, 31, 37 etc.).

10. Apocope seems to have taken place in the infinitive of *sei* (l. 10).

11. The conjugational ending for plural present is usually *-eð* (< OE *-aþ*); however, *lien* (l. 76) foreshadows the later ending *-en*.

12. The ending of the accusative plural of the personal pronoun for the third person is *-m*: *heom* (l. 36, 37, 38 etc.). This indicates that dative and accusative had already been levelled.

13. Adjectives are no longer marked for number: *nan martyrs* (l. 37); *cnotted strenges* (l. 40).

14. The noun *sunne* (l. 3) takes both the neuter and masculine personal pronoun: 'it' and 'him' (l. 3).

According to Laing this is "Peterborough language."

Sources: Bodleian Library, Oxford, MS Laud Misc. 636. – Clark (1970); Plummer/Earle (1892). – Secondary literature: Garmonsway (1954), Shores (1971).

Millesimo cxxxv. On þis gære for se king Henri ouer sæ æt te Lammasse. And ðat oþer dei, þa he lai an slep in scip, þa þestrede þe dæi ouer al landes, and uuard þe sunne suilc als it uuare thre niht ald mone, an sterres abuten him at middæi. Wurþen men suiðe ofuundred and ofdred and sæden ðat micel þing sculde cumen
5 herefter: sua dide, for þat ilc gær warth þe king ded ðat oþer dæi efter Sancte Andreas massedæi on Normandi. Þa þestreden sona þas landes, for æuric man sone ræuede oþer þe mihte. Þa namen his sune and his frend and brohten his lic to Engleland and bebirieden in Redinge. God man he wes, and micel æie wes of him; durste nan man misdon wið oðer on his time. Pais he makede men and
10 dær. Wua sua bare his byrthen gold and sylure, durste nan man sei to him naht bute god.

   Enmang þis was his nefe cumen to Engleland, Stephne de Blais; and com to Lundene, and te lundenisce folc him underfeng, and senden ęfter þe ærcebiscop

---

1 *þis gære*] Henry I left England in 1133; he died in 1135.

1 *Lammasse*] Lammas (Day): 1st of August

5–6 *Sancte Andreas massedæi*] 30th of November – King Henry died on the 1st of December.

6–7 *for . . . mihte*] 'for immediately everyone started to rob as much as he could' – 'þe' refers to *æuric man*.

7 *sune*] Robert of Gloucester, an illegitimate son of Henry I

8 *Redinge*] Reading; Henry I was buried at Reading Abbey, which he had founded in 1121.

10 *dær*] refers to the animals in the Royal Forests, which were well protected against poachers.

12 *Stephne*] Stephen, Count of Blois, crowned King of England in 1135

Willelm Curbuil; and halechede him to kinge on Midewintre Dæi. On þis kinges
15　time wes al unfrið and yfel and ræflac, for agenes him risen sona þa rice men þe
wæron swikes, alre fyrst Balduin de Reduers; and held Execestre agenes him, and
te king it besæt, and siððan Balduin acordede. Þa tocan þa oðre and helden her
castles agenes him. And Dauid king of Scotland toc to uuerrien him. Þa,
þohuuethere þat, here sandes feorden betwyx heom, and hi togædere comen and
20　wurðe sæhte, þoþ it litel forstode.

Millesimo cxxxvii. Ðis gære for þe king Stephne ofer sæ to Normandi; and
ther wes underfangen, forþi ðat hi uuenden ðat he sculde ben alsuic alse the eom
wes, and for he hadde get his tresor; ac he todeld it and scatered sotlice. Micel
hadde Henri king gadered gold and syluer, and na god ne dide me for his saule
25　tharof.

Þa þe king Stephne to Englaland com, þa macod he his gadering æt Oxeneford.
And þar he nam þe biscop Roger of Serebyri and Alexander biscop of Lincol and
te canceler Roger, hise neues, and dide ælle in prisun til hi iafen up here castles.
Þa the suikes undergæton ðat he milde man was and softe and god and na iustise
30　ne dide, þa diden hi alle wunder. Hi hadden him manred maked and athes suoren,
ac hi nan treuthe ne heolden. Alle he wæron forsworen and here treothes forloren,
for æuric rice man his castles makede and agænes him heolden, and fylden the
land ful of castles. Hi suencten suyðe þe uurecce men of þe land mid
castelweorces. Þa þe castles uuaren maked, tha fylden hi mid deoules and yuele
35　men. Þa namen hi þa men, þe hi wenden, ðat ani god hefden, bathe be nihtes and
be dæies, carlmen and wimmen, and diden heom in prisun and pined heom efter
gold and siluer untellendlice pining: for ne uuæren næure nan martyrs swa pined
alse hi wæron. Me henged up bi the fet and smoked heom mid ful smoke. Me
henged bi the þumbes other bi the hefed and hengen bryniges on her fet. Me dide
40　cnotted strenges abuton here hæued and uurythen it ðat it gæde to þe hærnes. Hi
diden heom in quarterne þar nadres and snakes and pades wæron inne, and
drapen heom swa. Sume hi diden in crucethur – ðat is, in an cęste þat was scort
and nareu and undep – and dide scærpe stanes þerinne and þrengde þe man
þærinne ðat him bræcon alle þe limes. In mani of þe castles wæron lof and grin:

---

14 *Willelm Curbuil*] William de Corbeil, Archbishop of Canterbury, 1123–1136
14 *Midewintre Dæi*] Christmas Day
16 *Balduin de Reduers*] Balduin de Reviers led a revolt against King Stephen.
18 *Dauid*] King David of Scotland had sworn fealty to Matilda, daughter of Henry I, and not to
King Stephen.
27 *Roger . . . Serebyri*] Roger, Bishop of Salisbury, one of the most powerful and influential
men of the time
27 *Alexander biscop of Lincol*] Alexander, Bishop of Lincoln, a nephew of Bishop Roger
28 *hise neues*] 'nephews' – a euphemism. Chancellor Roger was actually the son of Bishop
Roger.
29–30 *na iustise ne dide*] 'inflicted no (serious) punishment'
30 *alle wunder*] 'every possible atrocity'
34 *castelweorces*] 'compulsory labour in the erection of castles'
34 *fylden hi*] 'they filled them with'
44 *lof and grin*] 'fetters and chains'

45 ðat wæron rachenteges ðat twa oþer thre men hadden onoh to bæron onne. Þat
was sua maced, ðat is, fæstned to an beom – and diden an scærp iren abuton þa
mannes throte and his hals ðat he ne myhte nowiderwardes, ne sitten ne lien ne
slepen, oc bæron al ðat iren. Mani þusen hi drapen mid hungær.

I ne can ne I ne mai tellen alle þe wunder ne alle þe pines ðat hi diden wrecce
50 men on þis land; and ðat lastede þa xix wintre, wile Stephne was king, and æure
it was uuerse and uuerse. Hi læiden gældes on the tunes æure um wile and
clepeden it "tenserie". Þa þe uurecce men ne hadden nammore to gyuen, þa
ræueden hi and brendon alle the tunes ðat wel þu myhtes faren al a dæis fare,
sculdest thu neure finden man in tune sittende ne land tiled. Þa was corn dære and
55 flesc and cæse and butere, for nan ne wæs o the land. Wrecce men sturuen of
hungær. Sume ieden on ælmes þe waren sum wile rice men. Sume flugen ut of
lande. Wes næure gæt mare wreccehed on land, ne næure hethen men werse ne
diden þan hi diden. For ouer sithon ne forbaren hi nouther circe ne cyrceiærd, oc
namen al þe god ðat þarinne was, and brenden sythen þe cyrce and al tegædere.
60 Ne hi ne forbaren biscopes land ne abbotes ne preostes, ac ræueden munekes and
clerekes, and æuric man other þe ouermyhte. Gif twa men oþer iii coman ridend
to an tun, al þe tunscipe flugæn for heom: wenden ðat hi wæron ræueres. Þe
biscopes and lered men heom cursede æure, oc was heom naht þarof, for hi
uueron al forcursæd and forsuoren and forloren. War sæ me tilede, þe erthe ne bar
65 nan corn, for þe land was al fordon mid suilce dædes. And hi sæden openlice ðat
Crist slep and his halechen. Suilc, and mare þanne we cunnen sæin, we þoleden
xix wintre for ure sinnes.

On al þis yuele time heold Martin abbot his abbotrice .xx. wintre and half gær
and .viii. dæis mid micel suinc, and fand þe munekes and te gestes al þat heom
70 behoued, and heold mycel carited in the hus. And þoþwethere wrohte on þe circe
and sette þarto landes and rentes, and goded it suythe and læt it refen, and brohte
heom into þe neuuæ mynstre on Sancte Petres mæssedæi mid micel wurtscipe:
ðat was anno ab Incarnatione Domini Millesimo cxl, a combustione loci .xxiii.
And he for to Rome and þær wæs wæl underfangen fram þe Pape Eugenie; and
75 begæt thare priuilegies, an of alle þe landes of þabbotrice and an oþer of þe

---

50 *xix wintre*] i. e. nineteen years
52 *tenserie*] 'protection money'
57 *hethen men*] 'heathens' – this probably refers to the Viking attacks of the 9th to 11th
  centuries during which much ravaging and pillaging occurred.
58 *ouer sithon*] either 'against all custom' or 'frequently'
61 *æuric . . . ouermyhte*] 'the stronger robbed the weaker'.
68 *xx wintre*] i. e. twenty years
69 *gestes*] Travellers could take lodging and replenish their provisions at monasteries.
70 *carited*] the giving of alms on feast days
71 *læt it refen*] 'had a new roof erected'
72 *heom*] i. e. the monks
72 *Sancte Petres mæssedæi*] 29th of June
73 *a . . . xxiii*] 23 years after the old church had burned down, which took place in 1116.
74 *Pape Eugenie*] Pope Eugene III (1145–1163)
75 *priuilegies*] 'letters of protection' intended to secure the estates of the monastery against
  their appropriation by the king or his barons.

landes þe lien to þe circewican, and, gif he leng moste liuen, alse he mint to don
of þe horderwycan. And he begæt in landes, þat rice men hefden mid strengthe:
of Willelm Malduit, þe heold Rogingham þæ castel, he wan Cotingham and
Estun; and of Hugo of Walteruile he uuan Hyrtlingbyri and Stanewig and lx
80 solidos of Aldewingle ælc gær. And he makede manie munekes, and plantede
winiærd and makede mani weorkes, and wende þe tun betere þan it ær wæs; and
wæs god munec and god man, and forþi him luueden God and gode men.

     Nu we willen sægen sume del wat belamp on Stephnes kinges time. On his
time þe Iudeus of Noruuic bohton an Cristen cild beforen Estren and pineden him
85 alle þe ilce pining ðat ure Drihten was pined; and on Lang Fridæi him on rode
hengen for ure Drihtines luue, and sythen byrieden him; wenden ðat it sculde ben
forholen. Oc ure Dryhtin atywede ðat he was hali martyr. And te munekes him
namen and bebyried him heglice in þe mynstre. And he maket þurh ure Drihtin
wunderlice and manifældlice miracles; and hatte he Sanct Willelm.

---

76 *circewican*] office of the sacrist; the sacrist was mainly responsible for the sacred vessels.
76 *gif . . . liuen*] 'had he been granted a longer life'
77 *horderwycan*] office of the steward; the steward was responsible for both wardrobe and
cellar.
78 *Willelm . . . castel*] William Malduit was the commander of Rockingham Castle in Northamptonshire.
78 *Cotingham*] Cottingham in Northamptonshire
79 *Estun*] Great Easton in Leicestershire
79 *Hugo of Walteruile*] one of the tenants of the estates of the monastery
79–80 *Hyrtlingbyri . . . Aldewingle*] Irthlingborough, Stanwick, and Aldwinkle in Northamptonshire – *lx solidos*: sixty shillings
80–81 *plantede winiærd*] 'had a vineyard made'
83 The events which follow are the first example of a steadily growing number of stories about
Jews who ritually murdered Christian children. Anti-Semitism was on the rise during the High
Middle Ages; see for example also Chaucer's "Prioress's Tale".
84 *Iudeus of Noruuic*] The Jews came to England in the wake of the Norman Conquest;
Norwich was one of their early settlements.
85 *Lang Fridæi*] Good Friday
89 *Sanct Willelm*] His feast day is the 26th of March. William was never formally canonised;
he was, however, one of the popular saints of East Anglia.

Text 2: The Middle English Physiologus

The *Physiologus* is a collection of stories about animals, their characteristics, and what the characteristics mean. There are several late antique versions of the *Physiologus*, the first probably Greek, which was then translated into Latin and other languages. The analysis of the animals in the *Physiologus* is obviously based upon the Christian tradition of scriptural exegesis, as the animals and their behaviour are explained in a moralising way, as can also be seen in M 3, the *Kentish Sermon*. This technique presents a strong contrast to the Aristotelian tradition, which, beginning with the *Historia animalium*, focuses rather on aspects of animals. Aristotle's goal was to present animals systematically in order to compile a scientific work on the topic, rather than to educate, which is the case in the *Physiologus*. By reading and listening to the *Physiologus*, Christians are supposed to understand God and Christ's omnipresence in nature, and the actions of animals reflect this and show, or even confirm, Christian moral teachings.

The various Physiologus translations have several common elements as to their composition. Characteristics and behaviour of carefully selected animals are first described, then these aspects are allegorised. For the most part, however, the characteristics and behaviour depicted are based rather on fantasy than on actual observations. This also applies to the animals presented: the first animal chosen is often the lion, and many real animals and even stones are described and allegorised, the phoenix and unicorn, for example, often feature in the catalogue. The tradition of bestiaries, which arose in the 12th century, seems to be based on the Physiologus tradition, but there are several decisive differences. Although bestiaries are also catalogues of animals (including fictional animals) with an accompanying moral tale, an important part of a bestiary are the elaborate illustrations, which are not as prevalent in the Physiologus literature. The allegory in bestiaries also tended to be reduced to a moral story or simply left out.

Our Middle English metrical *Physiologus* is an adaptation of the Latin *Physiologus Theobaldi*, a work about which we know little more than the name of the author. The earliest manuscript dates from the late 11th or early 12th century. The anonymous Middle English translator often translates the Latin original directly, but just as often translates extremely freely, to the extent of adding his own material. This is especially the case in the chapter about the eagle, printed here; likewise, the whale and its art of deception is expanded considerably.

Old English *ā* is usually written <o>, as in *ston* (l. 16, 53); *lore* (l. 25, 61); however it is written <a> in *gast* (l. 60). This is an indication that the text does have some northern characteristics. Since OE *y̆* is written <i>, as in *listen* (l. 19) and *fir* (l. 54), the South and the West Midlands can be excluded. Both word-initial and word-final <-sc> is written <s>, /s/, as in *fis(ses)* (l. 35, 38, 40 etc.) and *sal* (l. 24, 32 etc.), *sipes* (l. 96, 102). The area of origin is the more northerly parts of the East Midlands. – According to Laing this is "language of W Norfolk."

Sources: British Library, London, MS Arundel 292. – Wirtjes (1991); Morris (1872), Hall (1920). – Secondary literature: White (1954), Diekstra (1985).

Natura aquile

Kiðen I wille ðe ernes kinde   [27]
Also Ic it o boke rede; / Wu he neweð his ȝuðhede,
Hu he cumeð ut of elde, / Siðen hise limes arn unwelde,
Siðen his bec is alto wrong, / Siðen his fliȝt is al unstrong,
5 And his egen dimme. / Hereð wu he neweð him;
A welle he sekeð ðat springeð ai, / Boðe bi nigt and bi dai;
Ðerouer he fleȝeð and up he teð / Til ðat he ðe heuene seð, /
Ðurȝ skies sexe and seuene / Til he cumeð to heuene.
So riȝt so he cunne, / He houeð in ðe sunne.
10 Ðe sunne swiðeð al his fliȝt / And oc it makeð his egen briȝt;
Hise feðres fallen for ðe hete / And he dun mide to ðe wete,
Falleð in ðat welle grund, / Ðer he wurðeð heil and sund
And cumeð ut al newe, / Ne were his bec untrewe.
His bec is ȝet biforn wrong, / Ðoȝ hise limes senden strong.
15 Ne maiȝ he tilen him non fode / Himself to none gode.
Ðanne goð he to a ston, / And he billeð ðeron;
Billeð til his bec biforn / Haueð ðe wrengðe forloren.
Siðen wið his riȝte bile / Takeð mete ðat he wile.

Significacio

Al is man, so is tis ern – / Wulde ȝe nu listen –
20 Old in hise sinnes dern, / Or he bicumeð Cristen.
And tus he neweð him, ðis man, / Ðanne he nimeð to kirke;
Or he it biðenken can, / His eȝen weren mirke.
Forsaket ðore Satanas / And ilk sinful dede;
Takeð him to Iesu Crist, / For he sal ben his mede.
25 Leueð on ure Louerd Crist / And lereð prestes lore.
Of his eȝen wereð ðe mist, / Wiles he dreccheð ðore.
His hope is al to Gode ward, / And of his luue he lereð,
Ðat is te sunne sikerlike; / Ðus his siȝte he beteð.
Naked falleð in ðe funt-fat, / And cumeð ut al newe,
30 Buten a litel – wat is tat? / His muð is ȝet untrewe.
His muð is ȝet wel unkuð / Wið pater noster and crede.
Fare he norð er fare he suð, / Leren he sal his nede:
Bidden bone to Gode / And tus his muð riȝten,
Tilen him so ðe sowles fode / Ðurȝ grace off ure Driȝtin.

---

8 *skies . . . seuene*] 'regardless of the clouds'
10 *Ðe sunne . . . briȝt*] 'The sun causes both his wings and eyes to shine brightly.'
15 *Himself . . . gode*] 'for his own use'
20 *sinnes dern*] 'the original sin'
25 *prestes lore*] the Pater Noster and the Creed (see line 31) which, according to the decrees of
the Fourth Lateran Council, every Christian should know.
30 *wat is tat*] 'trifle'

Natura cetegrandie

35 Cethegrande is a fis, / Ðe moste ðat in water is, [335]
Ðat tu wuldes seien ȝet, / Ȝef ðu it soȝe, wan it flet,
Ðat it were a neilond / Ðat sete one ðe se-sond.
Ðis fis, ðat is vnride, / Ðanne him hungreð, he gapeð wide.
Vt of his ðrote it smit an onde, / Ðe swetteste ðing ðat is o londe.
40 Ðerfore oðre fisses to him draȝen. / Wan he it felen, he aren faȝen;
He cumen and houen in his muð: / Of his swike he arn uncuð.
Ðis cete ðanne his chaueles luketh, / Ðise fisses alle in sukeð.
Ðe smale he wile ðus biswiken, / Ðe grete maiȝ he noȝt bigripen.
Ðis fis wuneð wið ðe se-grund / And liueð ðer eure heil and sund
45 Til it cumeð ðe time / Ðat storm stireð al ðe se,
Ðanne sumer and winter winnen, / Ne mai it wunen ðerinne,
So droui is te sees grund, / Ne mai he wunen ðer ðat stund,
Oc stireð up and houeð stille, / Wiles ðat weder is so ille.
Ðe sipes ðat arn on se fordriuen / Loð hem is ded and lef to liuen;
50 Biloken hem and sen ðis fis: / A neilond, he wenen, it is.
Ðerof he aren swiðe faȝen, / And mid here migt ðarto he draȝen.
Sipes on festen / And alle up gangen
Of ston mid stel in ðe tunder / Bel to brennen one ðis wunder,
Warmen hem wel and heten and drinken. / Ðe fir he feleð and doð hem sinken,
55 For sone he diueð dun to grunde: / He drepeð hem alle wiðuten wunde.

Significacio

Ðis deuel is mikel wið wil and maȝt, / So wicches hauen in here craft.
He doð men hungren and hauen ðrist / And mani oðer sinful list.
Tolleð men to him wið his onde, / Wo so him folegeð, he findeð sonde.
Ðo arn ðe little, in leue laȝe; / Ðe mikle ne maiȝ he to him draȝen –
60 Ðe mikle, I mene ðe stedefast, / In riȝte leue mid fles and gast.
Wo so listneð deueles lore, / On lengðe it sal him rewen sore:
Wo so festeð hope on him, He sal him folȝen to helle dim.

---

49 *sipes*] ship's crew
49 *fordriuen*] 'that have lost their way'
50 *Biloken hem*] 'look about' (reflexive)
54 *and . . . sinken*] 'and sinks them'
57 *He doð*] 'He causes'
59 *little . . . laȝe*] 'those of little faith'
61 *On lengðe*] 'in the long run'

Text 3: Kentish Sermons

Maurice de Sully, Bishop of Paris from 1160 until his death in 1196, wrote a cycle of 67 homilies sometime between 1168 and 1175. Five of these homilies were translated in the 13th century from French into Middle English Kentish dialect. This gives us a picture of this dialect in its early stages (compare to M 4 – also Kentish, but written 100 years later).

The sermons themselves are not of high literary value; the standard allegorical scriptural exegesis is used to explain the Bible passages. According to the fourfold scriptural exegesis, a given text has four levels of meaning. The first is the *literal* level, which is simply the level of the story told. The second level is the *allegorical* level, which strives to show the meaning of the characters and events – the allegory. The third level, the *tropological* or *moral* level, applies the interpretation of the text thus far to how a Christian should act and behave. This is a combination of specifically Christian moral conduct and also the ethical norms of society.

The following text has these first three levels of interpretation: the first two paragraphs are the retelling of the story of the Wedding at Cana, the third paragraph explains what the water and wine symbolise, and the last paragraph applies these characteristics to our actions – that good Christians should look to themselves, considering whether their blood is like water or wine, and reform themselves, if necessary. The fourth level of interpretation, the *anagogical*, is missing in this text. The anagogical level applies to the soul and its ascent to heaven, or its proximity to God.

This sermon, taken from John 2,1 ff, was composed for the third Sunday after Epiphany.

The text shows a number of features typical of the Kentish dialect. The most important of these are:
1. OE (WS) $\breve{y}$ (Old Kentish $\breve{e}$) is written <e>: *bredale* (l. 2, 4 etc.), *bregume* (l. 19), *fer* (l. 31), *euel, euele* (l. 27, 28 etc.).
2. WS *æ* (Old Kentish *e*) is written <e>: *hest* (l. 21), *þet* (l. 2, 5 etc.); however, it is also frequently written <a> as in *faten* (l. 12, 14), *þat* (l. 3, 4 etc.), *water, watere* (l. 12, 15, 18 etc.), *spac* (l. 9).
3. OE *æ+g* (Old Kentish *e+g*) is written <ei>, <ey> and <e>: *seide, seyde* (l. 6, 9, 11, 16 etc.), *sede* (l. 7; the spelling also suggests loss of *g* when immediately followed by *d*).

LALME on MS Laud Misc. 471: Linguistic Profile 6050, Kent.

Sources: Bodleian Library, Oxford, MS Laud Misc. 471. – Bennett/Smithers (1968); Morris (1872). – Secondary literature: Robson (1952).

Nuptie facte sunt in Chana Galilee, et erat mater Iesu ibi; vocatus est autem Iesus ad nuptias et discipuli eius. Þet holi godspel of today us telþ þet a bredale was imaked ine þo londe of Ierusalem, in ane cite þat was icleped Cane, in þa time þat Godes sune yede in erþe flesliche. To þa bredale was ure Leuedi Seinte
5 Marie and ure Louerd Iesus Crist and hise deciples. So iuel auenture þet wyn failede at þise bredale; þo seide ure Leuedi Seinte Marie to here sune: "Hi ne habbet no wyn." And ure Louerd answerde and sede to hire: "Wat belongeth hit to me oþer to þe, wyman?" Nu ne dorste hi namore sigge, ure Lauedi; hac hye spac to þo serganz þet seruede of þo wyne, and hem seyde: "Al þet he hot yu do,
10 so doþ."

And ure Louerd clepede þe serganz and seyde to hem: "Folvellet," ha seyde, "þos ydres [þet is to sigge þos croos oþer þos faten] of watere." For þer were vi ydres of stone, þet ware iclepede baþieres, wer þo Gius hem wesse for clenesse and for religiun, ase þe custome was ine þo time. Þo serganz uuluelden þo faten
15 of watere, and hasteliche was iwent into wyne bie þo wille of ure Louerde. Þo seide ure Lord to þo serganz: "Moveth togidere and bereth to Architriclin" [þat was se þet ferst was iserued]. And also hedde idrunke of þise wyne þet ure Louerd hedde imaked of þe watere (ha niste nocht þe miracle, ac þo serganz wel hit wiste þet hedde þet water ibrocht), þo seide Architriclin to þo bredgume:
20 "Oþer men," seyde he, "doþ forþ þet beste wyn þet hi habbeþ, ferst at here bredale; and þu hest ido þe contrarie, þet þu hest ihialde þet beste wyn wath nu!" Þis was þe commencement of þo miracles of ure Louerde, þet he made flesliche in erþe; and þo beleuede on him his deciples. I ne sigge nacht þet hi ne hedden þerbefore ine him beliaue; ac fore þe miracle þet hi seghe, was here beliaue þe
25 more istrengþed.

1–2 *Nuptie*] cf. *King James Bible*: "And the third day there was a marriage in Cana of Galilee; and the mother of Jesus was there: And both Jesus was called, and his disciples."
3 *Cane*] the city of Cana in Galilee
8 *wyman*] The phrase 'mine hour is not yet come' has been omitted. The following sentence ('Nu . . . Lauedi') is an addition.
9 *of þo wyne*] partitive genitive based on the French phrase *del vin* in the original. The whole relative clause is an addition.
12 *ydres*] is a rendering of 'hydriae' from the Vulgate; the meaning is explained in the next sentence.
12–13 *vi ydres of stone*] The original participial construction is missing: 'six water-pots . . . containing two or three firkins apiece'.
13 *þet . . . baþieres*] The relative clause is an addition.
14 *ase . . . time*] another addition
15 *and hasteliche . . . Louerde*] another addition
16 *Moveth togidere*] 'pour a cup'
17–18 *þet . . . watere*] The relative clause has been added.
20–21 *ferst . . . bredale*] The preacher leaves out Architriclin's recommendation to serve the good wine first; the bad wine should be served later, 'cum inebriati fuerint – and when men have well drunk'.
22 *commencement . . . Louerde*] While the following relative clause 'þet . . . erþe' has been added, the original 'et manifestavit gloriam suam – and manifested forth his glory' of the Vulgate has been omitted.

Nu ye habbeþ iherd þe miracle; nu ihereþ þe signefiance. Þet water bitockned
se euele Cristeneman. For also þet water is natureliche schald and akelþ alle þo
þet hit drinkeþ, so is se euele Cristeman chald of þo luue of Gode, for þo euele
werkes þet hi doþ; ase so is lecherie, spusbreche, roberie, manslechtes,
30   husberners, bakbiteres, and alle oþre euele deden, þurch wyche þinkes man
ofserueth þet fer of helle, ase Godes oghe mudh hit seid. And alle þo signefied
þet water þet þurch yemere werkes oþer þurch yemer iwil liesed þo blisce of
heuene. Þet wyn, þat is naturelliche hot ine himselue, and anhet alle þo þet hit
drinked, betokned alle þo þet bied anheet of þe luue of ure Lorde.

35   Nu, lordinges, ure Lord God Almichti, þat hwylem in one stede and ine one
time flesliche makede of watere wyn, yet ha deþ mani time: maked of watere wyn
gostliche wanne þurch his grace maked of þo euele manne good man, of þe
orgeilus umble, of þe lechur chaste, of þe niþinge large; and of alle oþre folies, so
ha maket of þo watere wyn. Þis his si signefiance of þe miracle. Nu loke euerich
40   man toward himseluen, yef he is win, þet is to siggen, yef he is anheet of þo luue
of Gode, oþer yef he is water, þet is, yef þu art chold of Godes luue. Yef þu art
euel man, besech ure Lorde þet he do ine þe his uertu, þet ha þe wende of euele
into gode, and þet he do þe do swiche werkes þet þu mote habbe þo blisce of
heuene. *Quod uobis prestare dignetur.*

---

26 *signefiance*] At this point the second level of meaning (allegorical) comes into play; this is
shown in the use of the present tense.

35 *Nu*] At this point the third level of meaning (moral) comes into play; this is also shown in
the use of the present tense.

36 *yet . . . maked*] 'which he continues to do often: he makes'

38–39 *and of . . . watere wyn*] 'and the same goes for the other vices: in this way he turns water
into wine'

44 *Quod . . . dignetur*] 'May you be offered this [by Jesus Christ]'.

Text 4: Ayenbite of Inwit

Ayenbite of Inwit, or the *Prick of Conscience*, is a translation of the French *Somme le roi*, written by Philipp the Bold's confessor (late 13th century) and intended to be a work of religious instruction. After the 4th Lateran Council of 1215, literature for religious instruction increased significantly, as it was necessary to implement the new decrees promulgated by the council. The council was summoned by Pope Innocent III for several reasons, among others a plan for a new crusade. One of the main focuses, however, was essentially a reformation of the church canons and of the clergy itself: better education for priests, as well as the laity, was deemed necessary. According to canon 21, *omnius utriusque sexus*, every Christian was required to confess at least once a year. Further, the sacrament of the Eucharist at Easter was also required to be taken by every Christian yearly. Any person refusing to carry out these tasks could be denied church access or Christian burial. The priests in turn were given substantially more power over the lives of their parishioners.

This Middle English translation of the French *Somme le roi* was completed on the 27th of October 1340: we know this from an inscription by the translator, Dan Michel, *Þis boc is dan Michelis of Northgate / y-write an englis of his oȝene hand. þet hatte: Ayenbyte of inwyt. And is of þe bochouse of saynt Austines of Canterberi* – 'this book was written by Dan Michel of Northgate and is called *Remorse of Conscience*. It is from Saint Augustine's Library in Canterbury'.

Dan Michel emphasises the intentions of the Lateran Council with this translation: *þis boc is ywrite / uor englisse men, þet hi wyte / hou hi ssolle ham-zelue ssriue, / and maki ham klene / ine þise liue* – 'this book has been written/translated for the English, so that they can know how to confess and to make themselves clean in this life'. As with most other handbooks on the topic of confession, the main topics include the Ten Commandments and the vices and virtues (especially the seven deadly sins). The sacraments, which are usually described, are mostly left out in *Ayenbite of Inwit*; only the sacrament of confession is dealt with under the virtue fortitude. Additionally, *Ayenbite of Inwit* contains an *ars moriendi*, and various thoughts regarding the nature of knowledge and good and evil.

The vices and virtues are dealt with allegorically, as can be seen in this selection from the chapter about gluttony: the tongue, Lady Swallow, for example, desperately desires more, and tries to convince her owner to continue eating even if he has already had enough (ll. 70–74). The tavern is depicted as the school of the devil (l. 53), a place in which many vices can arise, especially gluttony. This view of taverns can also be seen in the Morality Plays of the 15th and 16th centuries, in which the protagonist often begins his path into sin in a tavern.

In general, it can be said that Dan Michel was not a very competent translator. A more valuable aspect of the text lies in the fact that Dan Michel consistently reproduced the Kentish dialect, giving us a representative picture of Kentish English in the 14th century.

A Kentish provenance of the text is clearly suggested by the following features:
1. OE (WS) *æ* (Old Kentish *e*) is written <e>: *þet* (l. 3 etc.), *eppel* (l. 35), *efter, efterward* (l. 25, 58, 59 etc.).
2. OE *y* (Old Kentish *e*) is written <e>: *zenne* (l. 2, 4, 5 etc.), *cherche* (l. 23, 82).

3. OE *ēa* is written <ea>, <ya>, <ye>, <yea> and (when shortening has taken place) <a> *heaued* (l. 1, 2, 29), *greate* (l. 58, 64); *sseaweþ, sseawy* (l. 34, 82), *hyalde* (l. 38), *hyealde* (l. 37), *grat* (l. 8, 19, 58 etc.).

LALME on MS Arundel 57: Linguistic Profile 5890, Kent.

Sources: British Library, London, MS Arundel 57. – Morris (1965). – Secondary literature: Pfander (1936), Pantin (1955).

Þe zeuende heaued of þe beste.
Þe zeuende heaued of þe kueade beste, zuo is þe zenne of þe mouþe. And þeruore þet þe mouþ heþ tuo offices, huerof þe on belongeþ to þe zuelȝ, ase to þe mete an to þe drinke; þe oþer zuo is in speche, þeruore him to-delþ þe ilke zenne in tuo
5 deles principalliche. Þet is to wytene: in zenne of glotounye, þet is ine mete and in drinke; and ine zenne of kueade tonge, þet is ine fole spekinge.
    And uerst zigge we of þe zenne of glotounye. Þet is a vice þet þe dyeuel is moche myde ypayd and moche onpayþ God. Be zuych zenne heþ þe dyeuel wel grat miȝte in manne. Huer-of we redeþ ine þe godspelle þet God yaf yleaue þe
10 dyeulen to guo in to þe zuyn. And þo hi weren ine ham, hise adreynten ine þe ze, ine tokninge, þet þe glotouns ledeþ lif of zuyn and þe dyeuel heþ yleaue to guo in ham, and hise adrenche ine þe ze of helle; and ham to do ete zuo moche, þet hi to-cleue; and zuo moche drinke, þet hy ham adrencheþ.
    Huanne þe kempe heþ his uelaȝe yueld and him halt be þe þrote wel onneaþe
15 he arist. Alsuo hit is of þan þet þe dyeuel halt be þa zenne. And þeruore bleþeliche he yernþ to þe þrote, ase þe wolf to þe ssepe him uor to astrangli ase he dede to Euen and to Adam in paradys terestre. Þet is þe vissere of helle, þet nymþ þane viss bi þe þrote and by þe chinne. Þis zenne moche mis-payþ God. Vor þe glotoun makeþ to grat ssame huanne he makeþ his god of ane zeche uol of
20 dong, þet is of his wombe, þet he loueþ more þanne God and ine him ylefth and him serueþ. God him hat ueste, þe wombe zayþ 'Þou ne sselt, ac et longe and a-trayt.' God him hat be þe morȝen arise, þe wombe zayþ, 'Þo ne sselt, ich am to uol, me behoueþ to slepe. Þe cherche nys non hare, hy abyt me wel.' And huanne he arist, he begynþ his matyns and his benes and his oreysones and zayþ, 'A God,
25 huet ssolle we ete to day? Huader me ssolle eny þing uynde, þet by worþ?' Efter þise matynes comeþ þe laudes and he zayþ, 'A God, huet we hedde guod wyn yesteneuen and guode metes.' And efterþan he beweþ his zennes and zayþ, 'Allas', he zayþ, 'ich habbe y-by nyeȝ dyad to niȝt. To strang wes þet wyn teue. Þet heaued me akþ. Ich ne ssel by an eyse, al-huet ich habbe ydronke.'

---

9 *godspelle*] see Matthew 8:30–32, Mark 5:11–13, Luke 8:32–33
12 *and hise adrenche*] 'and drown his captives'
17 *paradys terestre*] This refers to the Garden of Eden, see Genesis 3.
24 *matyns*] matins (morning service)
26 *laudes*] lauds (prayer before noon)

30   Þous to þe kueade zayþ. Þis zenne let man to ssame. Vor alþeruerst he becomþ
tauernyer. Þanne he playþ ate des. Þanne he zelþ his oȝen. Þanne he becomþ
ribaud, holyer and þyef. And þanne me hine anhongeþ. Þis is þet scot, þet me ofte
payþ. [. . .]
      Nou miȝt þou ysi, uor þet we habbeþ hyer yzed, þet uele ginnes heþ þe dyeuel
35   uor to nime þet uolk be þe þrote. Uor uerst he sseaweþ ham þe wynes and þe
metes þet byeþ uayre and likerouses, ase he dede to Euen þane eppel. And þet yef
hit him ne is naȝt worþ, he him zayþ: 'Eth an drink ase þe ilke and þe ilke;
uelaȝrede þe behoueþ hyealde, yef þe wylt þet me ne scorne þe naȝt and þet me
þe ne hyalde uor papelard.' Oþer he him zayþ: 'Þe helþe of þine bodye þou sselt
40   loki, uor huo þet ne heþ helþe, he ne heþ naȝt. Ne by naȝt manslaȝþe of þe selue;
þou sselt to þine bodye þe sostinonce.' Oþer he him zayþ: 'Nim yeme of þe
guodes þet þou dest oþer miȝt do. Þou ne est naȝt uor þe lost of þine bodye, ac to
serui God. Þou sselt þine strengþe loki to God, ase zayþ Dauiþ.' Þise sceles byeþ
zuo cleuiinde þet þe wyseste and þe holyiste man byeþ oþerhuyl becaȝt.
45   Þe þridde boȝ of þise zenne is to uerliche yerne to þe mete, ase deþ þe hond to
þe hes. And þe more þet is þe ilke uerlichhede, þe more is þe zenne. Vor ase hit
ne is no zenne uor to habbe richesses, ac his to moche louye, alsuo hit ne is no
zenne uor to ethe þe guode metes, ak ethe his to uerliche oþer disordeneliche.
Ethe metes byeþ guode to guode and to ham þet be scele and be mesure his vseþ
50   and hise nimeþ mid þe sause of þe drede of oure lhorde. Vor me ssel euremo
habbe drede þet me ne mys-nyme be ouerdede, and me ssel herye God and yelde
hym þonkes of his yefþes. And be þe zuetnesse of þe mete, þet wyþ-oute ne may
by, me ssel þenche Godes zuetnesse and to þe ilke mete þet uelþ þe herte. Þeruore
me ret ine hous of religion ate mete, uor þet huanne þet bodi nymþ his mete of
55   one half, þet þe herte nyme his of oþer half.
      Þe uerþe boȝ of þise zenne of þan, þet to nobleliche wylleþ libbe, þet
despendeþ and wasteþ uor to uelle hare glotonye, hwer-of an hondred poure
miȝten libbe and ynoȝliche by ueld. Zuich uolk zeneȝeþ ine uele maneres. Verst
in greate despenses þet hi makeþ. Efterward ine þan þet hi hit vseþ ine to grat
60   hete and ine to grat lost. And efterward ine þe ydele blisse þet hi habbeþ. Vor hit
ne is naȝt onlepiliche lecherie of zuelȝ, ac hit is wel ofte uor bost þet hi zecheþ
zuo riche metes and makeþ zuo uele mes: huer-of ofte comeþ uele kueades.

---

31 *oȝen*] 'possessions'
34 *uor . . . yzed*] 'as we have said here'
36 *And þet yef*] 'and if'
41 *þou . . . sostinonce*] 'you are obliged to give your body sustenance'
43 *Dauiþ*] Psalms 58:10
43–44 *Þise . . . cleuiinde*] 'these arguments are so tempting'
49 *Ethe metes*] The source text reads: *toutes uiandes* – 'all foods'.
52–53 *And . . . me*] 'and when tasting the sweetness of the food, which cannot be sufficient,
   you . . .'
56 *of þise . . . of þan*] 'is the sin of those'
57 *uor . . . glotonye*] 'to satisfy their gluttony'

Þe vifte boȝ is þe bysihede of glotuns þet ne zecheþ bote to þe delit of hare
zuelȝ. Þise byeþ propreliche lechurs þet ne zecheþ bote þe lost of hare zuelȝ. Ine
65 þri þinges nameliche liþ þe zenne of zuyche uolke. Verst ine þe greate bysihede
þet hy habbeþ, to porchaci and to agraiþi. Efterward mid grat lost þet hy habbeþ
ine þe us. Efterward ine þe blisse þet hi habbeþ ine þe recordinge. And huo þet
miȝte telle huyche bysinesse hi doþ to þan þet hare metes by wel agrayþed –
and ech to his oȝene smac! And hou hy moȝe maki of one mete uele mes
70 desgysed uor hare uoule lost! And huanne þe mes byeþ y-come, on efter þe oþer,
þanne byeþ þe burdes and þe trufles uor entremes! And ine þise manere geþ þe
tyme: þe wreche him uoryet, þe scele slepþ, þe maȝe gret and zayþ: 'Dame Zuelȝ,
þo me ssast, ich am zuo uol þet ich to-cleue.' Ac þe tonge, þe lyckestre, him
ansuereþ and zayþ: 'Þaȝ þou ssoldest to-cleue, ich nelle naȝt lete askapie þis
75 mes.' Efter þe lecherie þet is ine etinge, comþ þe blisse þet is ine þe recorder.
Efterward hi wesseþ þet hi hedden nykken of crane and wombe of cou, uor þet þe
mosseles blefte lenger ine þe þrote and more miȝten uorzuelȝe.

Nou þou hest y-hyerd þe zennes þet comeþ of glotounye and of lecherie. And
þeruore þet zuyche zennes arizeþ communliche ine tauerne, þet is welle of zenne,
80 þeruore ich wylle a lite take of þe zennes þet byeþ y-do ine þe tauerne.

Þe tauerne ys þe scole of þe dyeule huere his deciples studieþ, and his oȝene
chapele þer huer me deþ his seruese and þer huer he makeþ his miracles, zuiche
ase behoueþ to þe dyeule. At cherche kan God his uirtues sseawy and do his
miracles: þe blynde to liȝte; þe crokede to riȝte; yelde þe wyttes of þe wode; þe
85 speche to þe dombe; þe hierþe to þe dyaue. Ac þe dyeuel deþ al ayenward ine þe
tauerne. Vor huanne þe glotoun geþ in to þe tauerne, ha geþ opriȝt. Huanne he
comþ a-yen, he ne heþ uot þet him moȝe sostyeni ne bere. Huanne he þerin geþ,
he y-zycþ and y-herþ and specþ wel and onderstant. Huan he comþ ayen, he heþ
al þis uorlore ase þe ilke þet ne heþ wyt ne scele ne onderstondinge. Zuyche byeþ
90 þe miracles þet þe dyeuel makeþ. And huet lessouns þer he ret? Alle uelþe he
tekþ þer: glotounye, lecherie, zuerie, uorzuerie, lyeȝe, miszigge, reneye God,
euele telle, contacky and to uele oþre manyeres of zennes. Þer ariseþ þe cheastes,
þe strifs, þe manslaȝþes; þer me tekþ to stele and to hongi.

Þe tauerne is a dich to þieues and þe dyeules castel uor to werri God and his
95 halȝen. And þo þet þe tauernes sustyeneþ, byeþ uelaȝes of alle þe zennen þet
byeþ y-do ine hare tauernes. And uor zoþe, yef me ham zede oþer dede asemoche
ssame to hire uader oþer to hare moder oþer to hare gromes, ase me deþ to hire
uader of heuene and to oure lheuedy and to þe halȝen of paradis, mochel hi
wolden ham wreþi and oþer red hi wolden do þer to, þanne hi doþ.

---

63 *to*] 'to' is unnecessary
66 *mid grat lost*] 'in the great pleasure'
67–68 *And . . . telle*] rhetorical question: 'and who could describe'
69 *and . . . smac*] 'and each according to his own tastes'
73 *ssast*] i. e. *sslast* – 'you are killing me'
92 *euele telle*] literally: 'to count badly', i. e. to cheat
98–99 *mochel . . . doþ*] 'they would become very angry and would act differently from how
they do (now)'.

Text 5: The South English Legendary

The *South English Legendary* is a series of saints' lives written for different Christian holidays. Both the *temporale* and the *sanctorale* (holidays dedicated to Christ, including Sundays, as opposed to those dedicated to particular saints) were included in the register of 92 saints' lives. There are 51 manuscripts of the *South English Legendary*, which attests that the *Legendary* was extremely popular in the Middle Ages; only the *Canterbury Tales*, *Prick of Conscience* and *Piers Plowman* have been transmitted more extensively. The various manuscripts have been reworked over the centuries, so that we have several from as late as the 15th century, although the date of composition is postulated to be in the late 13th century.

An especially interesting aspect of the *South English Legendary* is that, as in Ælfric's *Lives of the Saints* (see introduction to O 6), many English saints are included. In addition to Thomas of Canterbury, the *Legendary* includes the Anglo-Saxon saintly Kings Eadmund, Eadweard and Oswald (see O 6 and M 11), as well as the Archbishop Dunstan and Bishop Cuthbert. Kenelm and Wulfstan, who can be seen as local saints of the West Midlands, where this text originates, are also included.

Wulfstan of Worcester, whose *Life* is printed here, lived through several very tumultuous decades in Anglo-Saxon England. Born in the beginning of the 11th century, Wulfstan experienced the conquering of England first by Cnut, and eventually by William of Normandy. At a young age, Wulfstan began to be promoted to important church offices as a result both of his piety as well as of his powerful friends and relatives. After studying at Benedictine monasteries, he was promoted to Prior of Worcester, and eventually to bishop of the diocese. These events are treated briefly in his *Life*, but the biography of the saint only begins to unfold with the proof of his holiness: his first miracle (ll. 31ff). Wulfstan's promotion to Bishop of Worcester in 1062 is the beginning of a historical episode in his *Life*: England's transition from an Anglo-Saxon to a Norman monarchy and the effects. Wulfstan was the only bishop allowed to keep his office by William the Conqueror. In this episode, the author transcends the realm of hagiography and allows himself to comment on the political situation during Wulfstan's times, as well as during the author's own life. The Conquest of 1066 is depicted as a result of treachery, the Normans only being able to win England because so many of King Harold's nobles turned against him. This possibility is left open in the *Anglo-Saxon Chronicle* (see O 2/126 ff.), but is not directly articulated as in Wulfstan's *Life* (see ll. 64; 75–94). At this point, the *Life* takes a political turn. Wulfstan's worthiness as a saint is still a main topic; however, not only his piety and dedication are emphasised, but also his political efforts as a lone but determined Anglo-Saxon cleric in a world dominated by Normans.

William tries to remove Wulfstan from his office, criticising him for being too ignorant (ll. 120–122) for such a position, which Wulfstan humbly accepts. As a condition for his resignation, however, Wulfstan demands that Edward the Confessor, who invested him in this office, should also be the one to take it away. By thrusting his staff into Edward's grave, which then nobody is capable of removing except Wulfstan himself, Wulfstan stages a divine judgement, similar to the sword in the stone motif found in several of the King Arthur stories. As a result of this divine evidence, Wulfstan's enemies must beg him to keep his office. The relevance of these events for contemporary life is emphasised by the use of the present tense in lines 90: *ʒeot huy beothþ ore kingues echone* – 'they are still our kings'.

A West Midland provenance is strongly suggested by the following features:
1. OE ȳ is written <u> und <uy>: *luyte, luytel* (l. 21, 22, 108, 121); *sturien* (l. 4), *nullen* (l. 21), *muche, muchele* (l. 24, 42, 77, 80 185 und 227), *i-chulle* (l. 132). However, *nelle* (l. 133, 135) appears twice.
2. The form of the personal pronoun for the third person plural is *huy* throughout.

According to the *LALME* on MS Laud Misc. 108, "[t]he language is mixed, and suggests a western (probably Gloucs [Gloucestershire]) original, with an East Anglian overlay".

Sources: Bodleian Library, Oxford, MS Laud Misc. 108. Horstmann (1887). – Secondary literature: Jankofsky (1992); Booth (2002); Kemmler (2002).

> Seint Wolston, bischop of Wyrecestre   was here of Engelonde,
> Swiþe holi man he was al is lif,   ase ich me vnder-stonde.
> Þe ȝwile he was a ȝong child,   clene lif he ladde i-novȝ:
> Ȝwane oþur children ornen to pleiȝe,   toward churche he drouȝ.
> 5   Seint Edward was kyng þo,   þat nouþe in heouene is,
> And þe bischop of Wyricestre   Briȝttey heiȝte, i-wis.
> Of þis bischop Briȝtei   Seint Wolston is ordre nam,
> Ech aftur oþur, ase it fel,   so þat he preost bi-cam.
> Þe bischop vnder-feng him sethþe   and monek him makede i-wis
> 10   In þe priorie of Wiricestre,   þat noble hous and gret is.
> Swyþe wel is ordre he heold   in þat priorie
> And al is wille was for-to payȝe   God and Seinte Marie.
> In none bedde he nolde come,   ake ȝwane oþere ȝeoden þar-to,
> Bi-fore an auter he wolde go   his oresones for-to do;
> 15   Ȝwane þe dede slep him ouer-eode   þat he ne miȝte no leng gon,
> His heued he wolde legge a-doun   opon þe harde ston,
> Ope one grece bifore þe auter   oþur is bok þare-vnder do,
> And liggen ane stounde in dweole miengyngue –   al is slep scholde beon so.
> He nolde þreo dawes in þe wyke   no-þing eten with-alle,
> 20   Ne no word speken bote his beden   for nouȝt þat miȝte bi-falle;
> Þe oþur dawes wel luytel he spak   and wel luytel he eat al-so,
> Bote it were a luyte potage: holde he wolde him þer-to.
> So longue he leouede at Wirecestre   in þat holie lijf wel stille,
> Þat he was imaked prior of þat hous   muche a-ȝein is wille.
> 25   His couent he wuste swyþe wel   and to alle guodnesse hem drouȝ,
> Of God and alle guode men   loue he hadde i-nouȝ.
> Þe priorie of Wyricestre   Seint Oswold bi-gan er,

5 *Seint Edward*] Edward the Confessor, King of England, 1042–1066
6 *Briȝttey*] Brihtheah, Wulfstan's half-brother, Bishop of Worcester from 1033 until his death in 1038
18 *dweole miengyngue*] a type of half-sleep or trance in which monks are especially susceptible to temptation.
27 *Seint Oswold*] Oswald, Bishop of Worcester 961–992 and Archbishop of York 971–992

Þat was bi-fore Seint Wolston   neiȝ ane hondred ȝer;
And þat he hadde er bi-gonne,   þe oþur fulfulde, i-wis,
30 So þat þoruȝ heore beire dede   strong weork and heiȝ þare is.
      Ase þis holie man Seint Wolston   in a tyme liet a-rere
A bel-hous of swiþe strong weork   bellen to hanguy þere,
And machouns a-boue and bi-neþe   þare a-boute were,
Bi laddren cloumben up and doun   and þat weork bi-twene al bere,
35 A man þare clemb up bi one laddre   an þo he was up on heiȝ,
Fram eorþe mo þane fourti fet,   ase al þat folk i-seiȝ,
Dounward he ful, ase he mis-stap –   men weren sore a-gaste,
Seint Wolston stod and bi-heold   hou he was a-dounward faste;
He made þe signe of þe croyz   ase he feol to-ward þe grounde:
40 Harmles he feol and hol man i-novȝ,   his limes weren hole and sounde;
And a-ros up and dude is weork,   ase him no-þing nere:
Louerd, muche is þi miȝte   and þat þou cuddest wel þere,
Þat he so harde fram so heiȝe feol   and of eche harme was sker –
Þou art a Louerd, þat wonderes dest   ase seith þe sauter.
45   Hit bi-feol so þat Briȝtey   þe bischop of Wyricestre was ded;
A clerk was bischop after him   þat men cleopeden Aldred,
Þat Seint Wolston louede wel   and he louede him al-so:
For ech guod man wole louien oþur –   it were elles vuele i-do.
Sethþe it bi-fel þat þe erchebischop   of Euerwicke was ded:
50 Erchebischop huy maden þar   þene bischop Aldred.
And þe bischopriche of Wiricestre   vacaunt was and lere,
Seint Wolston was sone i-chose   and bischop i-maked þere.
Bischop him made þe holie man   Seint Edward þe king,
And a-feng him in his dignete   and tok him is staf and ring.
55 His bischopriche he wuste wel   and also is priorie,
And a-forcede him to serui wel   God and Seint Marie.
Four ȝer he hadde bischop i-beo   and nouȝt fulliche fiue,
Þo Seint Edward þe holie kyng   wende out of þis liue:
Gret reuþe it was to al Engelond   so weilawei þe stounde!
60 For straunge men þere comen sethþe   and brouȝten Enguelond to grounde.
      Harold was þo riȝhtest eyr   for non oþur þere nas;
Þe croune he bar of Enguelonde   ȝwuche ȝwile so it was.

---

29 *he*] i. e. Bishop Oswald
46 *Aldred*] Ealdred, Bishop of Worcester 1046–1061 and Archbishop of York 1061–1069
47 *he louede him al-so*] No mention is made of the difficult relationship between Wulfstan and
   Ealdread. As Archbishop of York, Ealdread still claimed revenues from the diocese of
   Worcester, which led to many years of legal action.
58 *wende . . . liue*] Edward died on January 5th, 1066.
60 *straunge men*] This text shows national prejudice against or even resentment of the Norman
   rulers. 'Straunge men' reappears in l. 75 and l. 102; see also the adjective 'vnecouþe' in l. 88
   and the adverbial phrase 'of oþere londe', l. 93.
61 *Harold*] Harold II, King of England, January–October 1066

For Willame Bastard þat was þo   eorl in Noremaundie,
Þouȝte to winne Enguelond   þoruȝ strencþe and tricherie.
65 He let him greiþi folk i-nouȝ   and gret poer with him nam
And with gret strencþe in-to þe se he him dude   and to Enguelonde he cam.
He liet ordeinie is fierd wel   and is banere up arerde
And destruyde and nam al þat he fond   and þat folk sore a-ferde.
   Harold heorde herof telle,   þe king of Enguelonde,
70 He liet greiþie faste is ost   a-ȝein him for-to stonde.
Þe baronie of Enguelonde   redi was wel sone
Þe king to helpe and heom-sulue   ase riȝt was for-to done.
Þe weorre was þo in Enguelonde   deolful and strong i-novȝ,
And eyþur of oþeres men   al-to grounde a-slouȝ.
75   No strencþe ne hadden þis straunge men,   þat were i-come so newe,
Aȝeinest heom of Enguelonde   þe ȝwyle huy wolden beo trewe.
Ake alas þe muchele tricherie   þat þo was and ȝeot is:
Þat brouȝte þo Enguelond   al-to grounde i-wis!
For þe Englische barones bi-comen some   on-treowe and false also,
80 To bi-traiȝe heom-seolf and heore kyng   þat so muche heom truste to.
   Þis Noremauns and þis Englische men   ane dai of bataile huy nome,
Þare ase þe abbeie of þe bataille is   ate daye to-gadere huy come;
To grounde huy smiten and slowen al-so: ake alas þulke stounde,
Þat Enguelond was þoruȝ tresoun   þare i-brouȝt to grounde!
85 For þulke þat þe king truste to   failleden him wel faste,
So þat he was bi-neoþe i-brouȝt   and ouer-come atþe laste;
And to grounde i-brouȝt and alle his   and al Enguelond also,
In-to vnecouþe mannes honde   þat no riȝht ne hadden þar-to;
And neuer-eft it ne cam a-ȝein   to riȝhte eyres none –
90 Vnkuynde eyres ȝeot huy beothþ   ore kingues echone,
And neiȝh-ȝwat alle þis heiȝe men   and of þe loȝwe al-so!
For Willam liet him crouni king,   þo þe bataile was al i-do,
And bi-sette al Enguelond   with men of oþere londe:
Neuereft to is cuynde heritage   ne cam it, ich onder-stonde.

---

63 *Willame Bastard*] Duke William of Normandy (William the Conqueror) was born out of
wedlock; he was crowned King of England after the Battle of Hastings. He ruled over England
from 1066 to 1087; see O 2/92.

68 *destruyde . . . a-ferde*] see also O 2/138–140.

77 *þe muchele tricherie*] In this text the defeat of the English at Hastings is attributed to the
treason of part of the nobility (see l. 84, 'tresoun'). The cryptic phrase 'with those men who
wanted to help him' from OE 2/126–127 could be a similar viewpoint.

82 *abbeie of þe bataille*] a reference to Battle Abbey, which was founded by William and was
one of the richest abbeys in England; see also l. 95–99.

90 *vnkuynde eyres . . . echone*] This line and l. 91 clearly show that the author sides with King
Harold II; in l. 61 Harold is called 'riȝhtest eyr' and thus propagates the English line of
succession.

95   Þis Willam Bastard, þat was king   sethþe him onder-stod,
        Þat he mid vnriȝhte hadde i-sched   mani ane mannes blod;
        And þare as þe bataille was   ane abbeiȝe he liet a-rere,
        Þat 'þe abbeie of þe bataille' is i-cleoped   þat wel noble stand ȝeot þere.
        For heore soulene he as liet a-rere   þat he with vnriȝhte þare a-slouȝ –
100   Ake euere he heold forth þe kynedom   of Enguelonde with wouȝ.
            Ake sone so he was king i-mad   and al Enguelond bi-sette,
        Ase he wolde, with straunge men   and no man ne miȝhte him lette.
        Þis holie bischop Seint Wolston   wel ofte him withseide
        Þat he with on-riȝhte hadde i-do   a swuch luþer dede;
105   And spac a-ȝein him baldeliche   and ne sparede for no drede,
        For he was þo þe cuyndeste Englische man   þat was of enie manhede;
        And for alle oþure weren deseritede neiȝh   þe king was with heom wrothþ,
        Þat he was so luyte a-drad of him   and swor a-non is othþ,
        To pulte him out of is bischopriche   he liet him somoune al-so
110   To Westmunstre, to answerien him   of þat he him hadde mis-do.
            Nou nas nouȝt Seint Wulston   wel gret clerk in lore –
        For þo he scholde to scole gon   to churche he ȝeode wel more.
        To Westmunstre he cam to is day   ase he was i-somoned er.
        Þe king was in grete wrathþe   wel prest to kepe him þer,
115   And þe bischop of Caunterburi   Lanfranc was is name,
        And þe bischop Gondolf of Roucestre   alle to don him schame.
        Seint Wolston bi-fore heom cam   þat a-ȝein him weren so strongue,
        Ase a þeof bi-fore iustise   his dom to vnder-fongue.
            Þe king and þe Erchebischop al-so   speken to him wordes grete,
120   Þat he scholde, ase he wuyrþe was,   is bischop-riche lete;
        For-to holden swuch dignete   to luyte he couþe of lore,
        And huy him hadden to longue i-þoled   and þo nolden huy nonmore;
        And grete foles huy weren þat swuch a fol   formest brouȝte in swch miȝhte,
        And ȝif he was folliche onder-fongue   huy wolden don him out with riȝhte.
125   Seint Wolston stod wel mildeliche   and herknede al þat huy sede –
        Nadde he noman bote God   to his answere him rede.

---

100 *with wouȝ*] The author strengthens his argument of William's unrightful claim on England.
103 *him withseide*] Wulfstan is here portrayed as the great and courageous (see l. 106: 'was of enie manhede') 'English' antagonist of the new Norman rulers. The fact that Wulfstan was one of the most important councillors to William the Conqueror and greatly respected by him is simply left out.
104 *with on-riȝhte*] i. e. as an unjust act
106 *For . . . manhede*] freely: 'He was then the only Englishman who acted like a man'.
107 *heom*] probably an error for 'him'
115 *Lanfranc*] Lanfranc, friend and councillor to William the Conqueror, Archbishop of Canterbury 1070–1089
116 *Gondolf of Roucestre*] Gundulf, a friend of Lanfranc, was consecrated Bishop of Rochester in 1077.
121 *to luyte . . . of lore*] English prelates were often accused of ignorance by their Norman successors.

"Sires," he seide, "riȝht it is   þat ich eoure heste do,
For, sire king, þou art mi souerein   and þe erchebischop al-so.
Þe croce ich habbe ȝare i-bore   þat ȝe i-seothþ here, lo,
130 A-knowe ich am and wel ich wot   þat i-nam nouȝt wuyrþe þer-to.
Ȝwane ȝe wollez þat ich as bi-leue   ase man þat vnwurþe is,
Wel fain i-chulle eouwer heste do   ase mine souereines, i-wis.
Vn-bouȝhsome to holie churche   i-wis, i-nelle be nouȝt:
To ȝelden hire up, ase ȝe me hotez   ich habbe as here i-brouȝt.
135 Ake, for ȝe ne token as me nouȝt   I nelle eou take non,
Ake him þat as me bi-tok   bi-fore eov euerech-on;
Þe guode man þat as me bi-tok   ȝeonde he lijthþ wel stille,
Ich as wulle him taken up   and þanne ich do eoure wille."
    To Seint Edwardes toumbe he wende   þat was of marbre-ston,
140 A nam up is croiz wel mildeliche   and smot þe point þar-on.
Þe staf wende into þe marbre-ston   ase it were in nesche sonde,
And þo heo was inne deope i-nouȝ   þe guode man hine liet stonde.
"Nou," he seide, "ich him habbe bi-take,   him þat as tok me,
And bi-fore eov here   i-ȝolden op þe dignete.
145 Takez as nouþe ȝwam ȝe wollez,   som þat bet beo in lore,
And habbez guod dai nouþe euerech-one –   ȝe ne mouwen esche me non-more."
    Þis holie man wende forth   a-mong heom alle wel softe.
Þat folk stod ase it were i-nome   and bi-heolden þe croce wel ofte,
Hou heo stod in þe marbre-ston   so deope and so faste:
150 Of þe miracle heom wondrede alle   and some weren sore a-gaste.
Some wenden þar-to sone   þe croce up for-to drawe,
Þare nas non so strong of heom   þat miȝhte hire enes wawe.
Huy porueiden er sire Gondolf   bischop of Roucestre,
Þat he scholde aftur Seint Wolston   beon bischop of Wirecestre.
155   Þe erchebischop aros him up   to saisi þe croiz a-non,
Þe bischop of Roucestre wel baldeliche   þudere-ward gan gon,
Þe croiz he nam and faste he drouȝ   in þe marbre-ston:
He ne miȝhte hire nouȝt enes wawien   þat folk wondrede ech-on,
And þare-a-boute wel þicke ornen   þat wonder for-to seo.
160 Þo þe king and þe erchebischop i-seiȝen   þat non oþur it ne miȝhte beo,
Heom of-þouȝte heore dede   and after Seint Wolstan sende,
And þat huy wolden in faire manere   heore trespas a-mende.
    Þe Messagers i-redie weren   and aftur him sone wenden;
Ȝeot þis holie man, for al þe gult   is heorte to heom bende,

---

139 *Edwardes toumbe*] Edward the Confessor was buried in Westminster Abbey, founded by
him.
140 *smot . . . þar-on*] The events related in l. 125–186 would have been interpreted by a
medieval audience as an act of divine intervention. The motif that only the 'chosen' will be
able to wield the symbol of his office has a long tradition: only Arthur could pull Excalibur
from the stone.
153 *Huy*] i. e. the king and the archbishop

165 And seide, "Ich mot nede do   mine souereines wille."
To court he wende a-ȝein to heom   wel mildeliche and stille.
Þo he was to court i-come   huy a-risen a-ȝein him þere,
Þe king and þe erchebischop al-so   and oþere þat þare were.
With gret honur huy cleopeden him forthþ   and for-ȝiuenesse him bede,
170 And boden a-mendi a-ȝein him   al heore grete misdede;
And beden him nime a-ȝein is croce   and don bi heore rede,
For he was bet wuyrþe þare-to   þane ani oþur, huy seide.
        "Nai certes, sires," quath Seint Wolston,   "þat nere me nouȝt to do:
Ich wot wel, þat ȝe seiden soth   þat i-nam nouȝt wuyrþe þare-to;
175 Ake nimeth ȝwam eower wille be   an oþur, þat conne more."
Þe kyng and þe erchebischop also   beden him milce and ore
And seiden, þat þere nas non oþur   þat so wuyrþe were þare-to.
Longue it was are þis holie man   wolde heore wille do,
Ake, for-to obeien is souereins   he wende forth atþe laste
180 And nam þe croce wel mildeliche   þare he stikede hire er so faste.
Also liȝhtliche ase ani-þing   þe croce he gan up drawe,
Þat so mani men fondeden er   and ne miȝhten hire enes wawe.
Þicke orn þat folk a-bouten him   and no wonder it nas!
Þe miracle was sone wide i-kud   þat so apert was.
185 Men anoureden þis holie man   al-so muche ase huy miȝhte:
His power þat him was er bi-nome   he tok aȝein with riȝhte.
A-ȝein to is bischopriche   with gret honour he him drouȝ,
His couent vnder-feng him faire   with grete nobleiȝe i-nouȝ.
        Þis holie man ladde al is lif   swyþe faire and clene.
190 Sijknesses þare weren wel fewe   þat man wolde him offe mene,
Þat he ne brouȝte to hele a-non   þoruȝ ore Louerdes grace.
Sike men wel þicke comen   to him in eche place;
Deue and doumbe and blinde al-so   he helde þoruȝ Godes grace,
Ȝwane huy comen to him   ouȝwere in eche place.
195 So longue he leouede on eorþe here   þat he was of grete elde:
His bodi bi-gan to heuegy swiþe   grete feblesse he fielde.
        A slouȝ feuere him cam on   þat ne nam him nouȝt ful strongue,
Ac heo made is bodi to melte a-wei   þat laste swiþe longue.
Seue niȝht bi-fore þat he deide   his breþren he liet fette alle,
200 And liet him alle his riȝhtes do   and seide, ȝwat heom scholde bi-falle.
Out of þis world to heouene he wende   þare he schal ay bi-leue,
In þe monþe of Ieneuer   a Seint Fabianes eue,
A þousend ȝer and nie hundret   and foure þare-bi-fore,
It was þat ore swete Louerd   on vrþe was i-bore;
205 In þe teoþe ȝere also   of þe kinedom

---

190 *Sijknesses*] From this point on, Wulfstan has the typical attributes of a saint. He effects
   miraculous cures and is the benevolent father (abbot) of his monks.
200 *riȝhtes do*] a reference to the last rites
202 *Seint Fabianes eue*] i. e. January 19th

Of Willam þe rede king þat aftur Willam Bastard cam.
He hadde, are he heonne i-wende foure and þritti ȝer
And four monþes and four dawes i-beo in worlde her.
Four-score ȝer he was old and seuene al-so neiȝh,
210 Are he wende out of þis lijf to þe ioye of heuene an heiȝ.
Þo þis holie man was ded þe monekes comen sone
In þe priorie of Wirecestre and duden þat was to done:
Wuschen þat bodi, ase it was riȝht and to churche it bere,
Þe monekes alle with gret honour þat is breþerne were.
215 Þe seruise a-bouten him huy duden ase it was wel riȝht,
And to seggen heore sauteres al-so þare-bi huy woken a-niȝt.
Þo it was wel with-inne niȝt ase huy seiden in heore boke,
Heom luste slepe swiþe wel þat vnneþes huy miȝten loke;
And some ne miȝhten nouȝt fur-bere ake leiȝen and slepen faste,
220 Some ase it were in dweolkningue heore eiȝene to-gadere huy caste.
Þat holie bodi þat lai þare ded a-mong heom in þe bere
A-ros up wel mildeliche, ase þei it a-liue were,
And a-weiȝhte heom euer-ech-on and bi-gan atþon ende
And al along þe rewe þoruȝ þe queor he gan i-wiende;
225 And euere ase he a-weiȝhte heom sumdel he gan heom chide,
Þat huy nolden with heore slep heore riȝhte tyme a-bide.
So muche was is holi heorte þe ordre for-to wite,
Þat he nolde, þei he were ded his breþerne fur-ȝite!
Þis miracle was sone i-kud ase riȝht was þat it were.
230 At Wirecestre he was i-bured and ȝuyt he liht þere.
Þare man may for is holie bodi mani fair miracle i-seo.
Nou God graunti, þat we mote with him in þe ioye of heouene beo.

206 *Willam þe rede king*] William II, also called Rufus ('rede'), son of William the Conqueror and King of England 1087–1100
207 *foure and þritti ȝer*] Wulfstan was Bishop of Worcester for thirty-four years (1062–1195).
216 *sauteres*] i. e. the singing of psalms

Text 6: Sir Gawain and the Green Knight

Sir Gawain and the Green Knight was written in the late 14th century in the northwest Midlands and is, at first glance, a typical Arthurian romance. The hero, Sir Gawain, is not only the most famous Knight of the Round Table and the best lover, he is also the most prominent hero of all Middle English romances (twelve different romances of Gawain's exploits have been preserved). The frame of this romance undoubtedly meets all the requirements of romance literature; however, this work has many aspects which deviate from the tradition, both in form and content. *Sir Gawain* is one of few romances to directly explore the intricacies of the court, appealing rather to an elite audience than the usual lower aristocracy and middle class. Using courtly language to explore courtly ideals, the conflict inherent in the knightly virtue of *courtaysye* in Gawain is developed throughout this romance.

The anonymous author was, perhaps, more likely a cleric than a nobleman; although his knowledge of both diction and customs of the court is extensive, the moral structure of the poem shows a very well-defined system of beliefs. *Sir Gawain and the Green Knight* is found in only one manuscript, *Cotton Nero A.x.*, and the three other texts accompanying it and written in the same hand are all texts of a strongly religious nature. Homiletic tendencies in *Sir Gawain* appear frequently.

The ambiguity inherent in this romance leads to a number of provocative questions, which take *Sir Gawain* above and beyond the usual dimensions of a romance. Not only the nature of Gawain himself is called into question, but the whole of chivalry and the Arthurian court. At the same time, the author experiments with the structure of the romance, manipulating the usual romance structure. Normally, a romance has five main actions: (1) arrival of a mysterious guest at court with some sort of task or challenge for a worthy knight; (2) the first quest, followed by winning a bride; (3) an inner conflict in the hero, having won the bride; (4) the second quest; (5) return of the now mature hero to Arthur's court. The action of *Sir Gawain* begins at the Christmas banquet with the arrival of the Green Knight and his challenge, which, of course, Sir Gawain accepts. However, already at this point, the author offers critical remarks about this tradition. Gawain's first quest, to seek the Green Knight, is summarily treated in 50 lines, and the author tells us that it would be *to tore to telle of þe tenþe dole* (l. 719, 'too difficult to tell the tenth part'). When Gawain arrives at the court of Bertilak (the Green Knight in disguise), he is confronted with a different court, a perfect and more elegant court than Arthur's. The search for a bride has also been reversed, and Gawain must rather fend off the advances of Bertilak's wife than win a bride himself. Again, the contradictions inherent in chivalry are presented, as Gawain must be loyal to his host and turn down the lady without offending her or infringing on the rules of chivalry. Bertilak makes a deal with Gawain, that they should give each other the spoils of their day, which in Gawain's case are kisses, and a belt from the lady. As the belt seems to Gawain the only possibility of saving himself from impending death at the hands of the Green Knight, and Gawain has promised the lady not to tell her husband about the belt, Gawain breaks his oath to Bertilak and keeps the belt. The climax of *Sir Gawain* is his defeat: though the Green Knight does not kill him, it is made clear to Gawain that he has failed in the virtue of chivalry; a personal crisis results, which we would have expected to occur between the first and second quests. Nor can Gawain overcome this crisis; though both the Green Knight and later Arthur and his court exonerate Gawain of misdoings, he himself is left with a feeling of failure. Self-fulfilment is therefore not possible for Gawain, and the reader is left wondering what can be learned from this.

The selection printed below includes the opening scenes, in which the poet traces the history of England from Troy to the court of Arthur. The arrival of the Green Knight and his challenge as well as the reaction of Arthur's court follows. The dramatic dialogue scenes show the author's talent in constructing the tale, and how this is supported by his extremely diverse vocabulary.

The poem, with its total of 2530 lines, is divided into stanzas varying in length between 12 and 38 alliterative long lines. Every stanza ends with a so-called "bob and wheel," five short lines rhyming *ababa*.

> Síþen þe ség and þe assáut / watz sésed at Tróye,
> Þe bórʒ bríttened and brént / to bróndeʒ and áskez,
> Þe túlk þat þe trámmes / of trésoun þer wróʒt
> Watz tríed for his trícherie, / þe tréwest on érþe.

The alliterative long line used in the poems belonging to the tradition of the *alliterative revival* is not as rigid as the alliterative long line of Old English poetry. A detailed study of the properties of the alliterative patterns in *Sir Gawain and the Green Knight* can be found in Boroff (1962) und Turville-Petre (1976).

The writing used in *Sir Gawain and the Green Knight* presents a number of difficulties which are discussed in the table below.

1. <ʒ> can be used for word-initial /j/: *ʒe, ʒer*; it can also be used for the voiceless palatal fricative when preceded by a palatal vowel and followed by <t> (representing the Old English sequence <-ht->): *wyʒtest, myʒt* etc. Similarly, it can be used for the voiceless velar fricative preceded by a velar vowel and followed by <t> (representing the Old English sequence <-ht->) as in *-aʒt*.
2. The graph <z> represents both /s/ and /z/: *berdlez* (Modern English -less) in contrast to *byholdez, laykez, wedez* etc.
3. The sequence <tz> represents /s/: *hatz* etc.
4. The word-initial Old English sequence <hw->, which in Middle English usually becomes <wh->, is frequently written <qu->, a typically northern feature.

The most important linguistic features indicating a northern provenance are:
1. OE *ā* is written <o> but also <a>: *more* (l. 84 etc.), *hat* (l. 4), *home* (l. 19, 159), *no* (l. 17 etc.), *so* (l. 9 etc.), *wot* (l. 105, 150).
2. OE *ŏ+g* is written <aw> (instead of <ou> or <ow>): *stelbawe* (l. 186).
3. The third person singular present indicative ends in *-es, -ez* and *-z*: *byholdez* (l. 1), *syttes* (l. 7), *hatz* (l. 15 etc.).
4. The present participle ends in *-ande*: *schinande* (l. 20), *blycande* (l. 56), *herande* (l. 201).

LALME on MS Cotton Nero A.x.: Linguistic Profile 26, Cheshire.

Sources: British Library, London, MS Cotton Nero A.x. – Tolkien/Gordon (1967); Waldron (1970), Markus (1974). – Secondary literature: Benson (1965), Burrow (1965), Spearing (1970), Davenport (1978). – Facsimile: Gollancz (1923).

Siþen þe sege and þe assaut watz sesed at Troye,
Þe borȝ brittened and brent to brondeȝ and askez,
Þe tulk þat þe trammes of tresoun þer wroȝt
Watz tried for his tricherie, þe trewest on erþe.
5　Hit watz Ennias þe athel, and his highe kynde,
Þat siþen depreced prouinces, and patrounes bicome
Welneȝe of al þe wele in þe west iles.
Fro riche Romulus to Rome ricchis hym swyþe,
With gret bobbaunce þat burȝe he biges vpon fyrst,
10　And neuenes hit his aune nome, as hit now hat;
Ticius to Tuskan and teldes bigynnes,
Langaberde in Lumbardie lyftes vp homes,
And fer ouer þe French flod Felix Brutus
On mony bonkkes ful brode Bretayn he settez
15　　　wyth wynne,
　　　Where werre and wrake and wonder
　　　Bi syþez hatz wont þerinne,
　　　And oft boþe blysse and blunder
　　　Ful skete hatz skyfted synne.

20　Ande quen þis Bretayn watz bigged bi þis burn rych,
Bolde bredden þerinne, baret þat lofden,
In mony turned tyme tene þat wroȝten.
Mo ferlyes on þis folde han fallen here oft
Þen in any oþer þat I wot, syn þat ilk tyme.
25　Bot of alle þat here bult, of Bretaygne kynges,
Ay watz Arthur þe hendest, as I haf herde telle.
Forþi an aunter in erde I attle to schawe,
Þat a selly in siȝt summe men hit holden,
And an outtrage awenture of Arthurez wonderez.
30　If ȝe wyl lysten þis laye bot on littel quile,

---

1 *Troye*] This 'English' version of the concept *translatio imperii* links the line of British kings to Aeneas of Troy.

3 *tulk ... wroȝt*] a reference to the traitor Antenor, who made a deal with the Greeks and betrayed Troy.

5 *Ennias ... kynde,*] Aeneas and his kin ('kynde') – in this text Romulus, Ticius, Langaberde and Felix Brutus – are the traditional founders of the empires which claim Trojan descent.

7 *west iles*] 'in the west'

8 *ricchis*] Here the author switches to historical present.

11 *Ticius to Tuskan*] The predicate is 'ricchis', l. 8: 'Ticius departs for Tuscany'.

22 *In ... tyme*] 'frequently'

27 *in erde*] literally 'on earth', i. e. an 'earthly' story, not a fairy tale or 'selly' and far from 'outtrage' (exceedingly strange) as some people ('summe men') might be inclined to assume (ll. 28–29).

I schal telle hit as-tit, as I in toun herde,
    With tonge,
   As hit is stad and stoken
   In stori stif and stronge,
35   With lel letteres loken,
   In londe so hatz ben longe.
    [. . .]

Þenn Arthour bifore þe hiȝ dece þat auenture byholdez,   [250]
And rekenly hym reuerenced, for rad was he neuer,
And sayde, 'Wyȝe, welcum iwys to þis place,
40 Þe hede of þis ostel Arthour I hat;
Liȝt luflych adoun and lenge, I þe praye,
And quat-so þy wylle is we schal wyt after.'
'Nay, as help me,' quoþ þe haþel, 'he þat on hyȝe syttes,
To wone any quyle in þis won, hit watz not myn ernde;
45 Bot for þe los of þe, lede, is lyft vp so hyȝe,
And þy burȝ and þy burnes best ar holden,
Stifest vnder stel-gere on stedes to ryde,
Þe wyȝtest and þe worthyest of þe worldes kynde,
Preue for to play wyþ in oþer pure laykez,
50 And here is kydde cortaysye, as I haf herd carp,
And þat hatz wayned me hider, iwyis, at þis tyme.
Ȝe may be seker bi þis braunch þat I bere here
Þat I passe as in pes, and no plyȝt seche;
For had I founded in fere in feȝtyng wyse,
55 I haue a hauberghe at home and a helme boþe,
A schelde and a scharp spere, schinande bryȝt,
Ande oþer weppenes to welde, I wene wel, als;
Bot for I wolde no were, my wedez ar softer.
Bot if þou be so bold as alle burnez tellen,
60 Þou wyl grant me godly þe gomen þat I ask
    by ryȝt.'
   Arþour con onsware,
   And sayd, 'Sir cortays knyȝt,
   If þou craue batayl bare,
65   Here faylez þou not to fyȝt.'

'Nay, frayst I no fyȝt, in fayþ I þe telle,
Hit arn aboute on þis bench bot berdlez chylder.
If I were hasped in armes on a heȝe stede,
Here is no mon me to mach, for myȝtez so wayke.

31–35 *herde . . . loken*] A mere story ('herde') gains a higher truth factor through the process
of being written down ('lel letteres').
54 *in fere . . . wyse*] 'fully armed for battle'
64 *bare*] 'without armour'

70   Forþy I craue in þis court a Crystemas gomen,
     For hit is Ʒol and Nwe Ʒer, and here ar Ʒep mony:
     If any so hardy in þis hous holdez hymseluen,
     Be so bolde in his blod, brayn in hys hede,
     Þat dar stifly strike a strok for an oþer,
75   I schal gif hym of my gyft þis giserne ryche,
     Þis ax, þat is heué innogh, to hondele as hym lykes,
     And I schal bide þe fyrst bur as bare as I sitte.
     If any freke be so felle to fonde þat I telle,
     Lepe lyƷtly me to, and lach þis weppen,
80   I quit-clayme hit for euer, kepe hit as his auen,
     And I schal stonde hym a strok, stif on þis flet,
     Ellez þou wyl diƷt me þe dom to dele hym an other
                       barlay,
         And Ʒet gif hym respite,
85   A twelmonyþ and a day;
         Now hyƷe, and let se tite
         Dar any herinne oƷt say.'

     If he hem stowned vpon fyrst, stiller were þanne
     Alle þe heredmen in halle, þe hyƷ and the loƷe.
90   Þe renk on his rouncé hym ruched in his sadel,
     And runischly his rede yƷen he reled aboute,
     Bende his bresed broƷez, blycande grene,
     Wayued his berde for to wayte quo-so wolde ryse.
     When non wolde kepe hym with carp he coƷed ful hyƷe,
95   Ande rimed hym ful richely, and ryƷt hym to speke:
     'What, is þis Arþures hous,' quoþ þe haþel þenne,
     'Þat al þe rous rennes of þurƷ ryalmes so mony?
     Where is now your sourquydrye and your conquestes,
     Your gryndellayk and your greme, and your grete wordes?
100 Now is þe reuel and þe renoun of þe Rounde Table
     Ouerwalt wyþ a worde of on wyƷes speche,
     For al dares for drede withoute dynt schewed!'
     Wyth þis he laƷes so loude þat þe lorde greued;
     Þe blod schot for scham into his schyre face
105   and lere;
         He wex as wroth as wynde,
         So did alle þat þer were.
         Þe kyng as kene bi kynde
         Þen stod þat stif mon nere,

---

75 *giserne*] a battle-axe, originally similar to a halberd, with a long shaft and a spear point (see also l. 162 and l. 113, 'geserne').

82–83 *Ellez . . . barlay*] 'provided you grant me the right to give him a return stroke'

85 *A . . . day*] formulaic expression for one year

94 *coƷed . . . hyƷe*] 'he screamed out loud'

110 And sayde, 'Haþel, by heuen, þyn askyng is nys,
And as þou foly hatz frayst, fynde þe behoues.
I know no gome þat is gast of þy grete wordes;
Gif me now þy geserne, vpon Godez halue,
And I schal bayþen þy bone þat þou boden habbes.'
115 Lyȝtly lepez he hym to, and laȝt at his honde.
Þen feersly þat oþer freke vpon fote lyȝtis.
Now hatz Arthure his axe, and þe halme grypez,
And sturnely sturez hit aboute, þat stryke wyth hit þoȝt.
Þe stif mon hym bifore stod vpon hyȝt,
120 Herre þen ani in þe hous by þe hede and more.
Wyth sturne schere þer he stod he stroked his berde,
And wyth a countenaunce dryȝe he droȝ doun his cote,
No more mate ne dismayd for hys mayn dintez
Þen any burne vpon bench hade broȝt hym to drynk
125   of wyne.
         Gawan, þat sate bi þe quene,
         To þe kyng he can enclyne:
         'I beseche now with saȝez sene
         Þis melly mot be myne.

130 'Wolde ȝe, worþilych lorde,' quoþ Wawan to þe kyng,
'Bid me boȝe fro þis benche, and stonde by yow þere,
Þat I wythoute vylanye myȝt voyde þis table,
And þat my legge lady lyked not ille,
I wolde com to your counseyl bifore your cort ryche.
135 For me þink hit not semly, as hit is soþ knawen,
Þer such an askyng is heuened so hyȝe in your sale,
Þaȝ ȝe ȝourself by talenttyf, to take hit to yourseluen,
Whil mony so bolde yow aboute vpon bench sytten,
Þat vnder heuen I hope non haȝerer of wylle,
140 Ne better bodyes on bent þer baret is rered.
I am þe wakkest, I wot, and of wyt feblest,
And lest lur of my lyf, quo laytes þe soþe –
Bot for as much as ȝe ar myn em I am only to prayse,
No bounté bot your blod I in my bodé knowe;
145 And syþen þis note is so nys þat noȝt hit yow falles,

---

118 *þat*] refers to Arthur
123 *hys*] also refers to Arthur
128 *saȝez sene*] 'simple words'
130 *Wawan*] i. e. Gawain
133 *legge lady*] 'liege lady', i. e. the queen
142 *And . . . lyf*] 'losing my life would be nothing'
143 *Bot . . . prayse*] 'I only deserve praise in so far as you are my uncle'.

And I haue frayned hit at yow fyrst, foldez hit to me;
And if I carp not comlyly, let alle þis cort rych
      bout blame.'
    Ryche togeder con roun,
150   And syþen þay redden alle same
    To ryd þe kyng wyth croun,
    And gif Gawan the game.

Then comaunded þe kyng þe knyȝt for to ryse;
And he ful radly vpros, and ruchched hym fayre,
155 Kneled doun bifore þe kyng, and cachez þat weppen;
And he luflyly hit hym laft, and lyfte vp his honde,
And gef hym Goddez blessyng, and gladly hym biddes
Þat his hert and his honde schulde hardi be boþe.
'Kepe þe, cosyn,' quoþ þe kyng, 'þat þou on kyrf sette,
160 And if þou redez hym ryȝt, redly I trowe
Þat þou schal byden þe bur þat he schal bede after.'
Gawan gotz to þe gome with giserne in honde,
And he baldly hym bydez, he bayst neuer þe helder.
Þen carppez to Sir Gawan þe knyȝt in þe grene,
165 'Refourme we oure forwardes, er we fyrre passe.
Fyrst I eþe þe, haþel, how þat þou hattes
Þat þou me telle truly, as I tryst may.'
'In god fayth,' quoþ þe goode knyȝt, 'Gawan I hatte,
Þat bede þe þis buffet, quat-so bifallez after,
170 And at þis tyme twelmonyth take at þe an oþer
Wyth what weppen so þou wylt, and wyth no wyȝ ellez
      on lyue.'
    Þat oþer onswarez agayn,
    'Sir Gawan, so mot I þryue
175   As I am ferly fayn
    Þis dint þat þou schal dryue.

'Bigog,' quoþ the grene knyȝt, 'Sir Gawan, me lykes
Þat I schal fange at þy fust þat I haf frayst here.
And þou hatz redily rehersed, bi resoun ful trwe,
180 Clanly al the couenaunt þat I þe kynge asked,
Saf þat þou schal siker me, segge, bi þi trawþe,
Þat þou schal seche me þiself, where-so þou hopes
I may be funde vpon folde, and foch þe such wages
As þou deles me to-day bifore this douþe ryche.'

147–148 *And ... blame*] 'And if I speak improperly, this noble court is not to be blamed'.
159 *þat ... sette*] 'that you can only strike once'
171–172 *and wyth ... on lyue*] 'and at no one else'.
174 *so ... þryue*] 'by my life'
177 *Bigog*] 'by God!'

185 'Where schulde I wale þe,' quoþ Gauan, 'where is þy place?
    I wot neuer where þou wonyes, bi hym þat me wroȝt,
    Ne I know not þe, knyȝt, þy cort ne þi name.
    Bot teche me truly þerto, and telle me how þou hattes,
    And I schal ware alle my wyt to wynne me þeder,
190 And þat I swere þe for soþe, and by my seker traweþ.'
    'Þat is innogh in Nwe Ȝer, hit nedes no more,'
    Quoþ þe gome in þe grene to Gawan þe hende;
    'Ȝif I þe telle trwly, quen I þe tape haue
    And þou me smoþely hatz smyten, smartly I þe teche
195 Of my hous and my home and myn owen nome,
    Þen may thou frayst my fare and forwardez holde;
    And if I spende no speche, þenne spedez þou þe better,
    For þou may leng in þy londe and layt no fyrre –
                bot slokes!
200   Ta now þy grymme tole to þe,
            And let se how þou cnokez.'
            'Gladly, sir, for soþe,'
            Quoþ Gawan; his ax he strokes.

    The grene knyȝt vpon grounde grayþely hym dresses,
205 A littel lut with þe hede, þe lere he discouerez,
    His longe louelych lokkez he layd ouer his croun,
    Let the naked nec to þe note schewe.
    Gauan gripped to his ax, and gederes hit on hyȝt,
    Þe kay fot on þe folde he before sette,
210 Let hit doun lyȝtly lyȝt on þe naked,
    Þat þe scharp of þe schalk schyndered þe bones,
    And schrank þurȝ þe schyire grece, and schade hit in twynne,
    Þat þe bit of þe broun stel bot on þe grounde.
    Þe fayre hede fro þe halce hit to þe erþe,
215 Þat fele hit foyned with her fete, þere hit forth roled;
    Þe blod brayd fro þe body, þat blykked on þe grene;
    And nawþer faltered ne fel þe freke neuer þe helder,
    Bot styþly he start forth vpon styf schonkes,
    And runyschly he raȝt out, þere as renkkez stoden,
220 Laȝt to his lufly hed, and lyft hit vp sone;
    And syþen boȝez to his blonk, þe brydel he cachchez,
    Steppez into stelbawe and strydez alofte,
    And his hede by þe here in his honde haldez;

---

196 *frayst . . . fare*] 'then you will see what I can do'
199 *bot slokes*] 'but enough' (talking)
208 *gederes . . . hyȝt*] 'and lifts it up high': note the use of the historical present.

And as sadly þe segge hym in his sadel sette
225   As non vnhap had hym ayled, þaȝ hedlez he were
        in stedde.
      He brayde his bulk aboute,
      Þat vgly bodi þat bledde;
      Moni on of him had doute,
230   Bi þat his resounz were redde.

For þe hede in his honde he haldez vp euen,
Toward þe derrest on þe dece he dressez þe face,
And hit lyfte vp the yȝe-lyddez and loked ful brode,
And meled þus much with his muthe, as ȝe may now here:
235   'Loke, Gawan, þou be grayþe to go as þou hettez,
And layte as lelly til þou me, lude, fynde,
As þou hatz hette in þis halle, herande þise knyȝtes;
To þe grene chapel þou chose, I charge þe, to fotte
Such a dunt as þou hatz dalt – disserued þou habbez
240   To be ȝederly ȝolden on Nw ȝeres morn.
Þe knyȝt of þe grene chapel men knowen me mony;
Forþi me for to fynde if þou fraystez, faylez þou neuer.
Þerfore com, oþer recreaunt be calde þe behoues.'
With a runisch rout þe raynez he tornez,
245   Halled out at þe hal dor, his hed in his hande,
Þat þe fyr of þe flynt flaȝe fro fole houes.
To quat kyth he becom knwe non þere,
Neuer more þen þay wyste from queþen he watz wonnen.
        What þenne?
250   Þe kyng and Gawan þare
      At þat grene þay laȝe and grenne,
      ȝet breued watz hit ful bare
      A meruayl among tho menne.

Þaȝ Arþer þe hende kyng at hert hade wonder,
255   He let no semblaunt be sene, bot sayde ful hyȝe
To þe comlych quene with cortays speche,
'Dere dame, to-day demay yow neuer;
Wel bycommes such craft vpon Cristmasse,
Laykyng of enterludez, to laȝe and to syng,
260   Among þise kynde caroles of knyȝtez and ladyez.
Neuer þe lece to my mete I may me wel dres,
For I haf sen a selly, I may not forsake.'
He glent vpon Sir Gawen, and gaynly he sayde,
'Now sir, heng vp þyn ax, þat hatz innogh hewen';

---

230 *Bi . . . redde*] 'even before he started talking'.
238 *chose*] 'to go'

265   And hit watz don abof þe dece on doser to henge,
      Þer alle men for meruayl myȝt on hit loke,
      And bi trwe tytel þerof to telle þe wonder.
      Þenne þay boȝed to a borde þise burnes togeder,
      Þe kyng and þe gode knyȝt, and kene men hem serued
270   Of alle dayntyez double, as derrest myȝt falle;
      Wyth alle maner of mete and mynstralcie boþe,
      Wyth wele walt þay þat day, til worþed an ende
            in londe.
         Now þenk wel, Sir Gawan,
275   For woþe þat þou ne wonde
         Þis auenture for to frayn
         Þat þou hatz tan on honde.

---

267 *bi trwe tytel þerof*] 'using it (i. e. the axe) as evidence'
270 *as . . . falle*] either 'as good as could be' or 'just as this noble company deserved'

Text 7: Piers Plowman

Piers Plowman is one of the most important works in Middle English. Over 50 manuscripts have survived, which derive from three common texts (A, B and C). The first version, A, seems to have been written in the early 1360s, was then revised into B in the late 1370s, and the final draft, C, was not yet complete when the author, William Langland, died in 1385.

Piers Plowman enjoyed great success for centuries after it had been written, and remains one of the most complex works of the time. Langland makes use of the popular tradition of *dream poetry*, placing the main action and message of the story within the frame of a dream vision. The poet-narrator falls asleep and has an allegorical dream (in *Piers Plowman* there are several visions), whose significance is explained to him by a guide whom he encounters within the dream. In the case of *Piers Plowman*, the narrator Will finds himself in a strange and corrupt world, which reflects the state of the Church in England in the 14th century. Will, as the visionary is called by his guide (II, 5), meets with corruption, misuse of power, hypocrisy and simony. Some few try to lead a good life, but the poor folk, for example, are blinded by the words of the sinful clergy (see lines 66–80). Indeed, most of the characters in the dream are indifferent about living a good or holy life before the eyes of God. It is in this corrupt world that the dreamer seeks some sort of orientation, which develops into his search for the "shrine of holy truth". On his quest, as he is led through the social, political and moral dimensions of contemporary England, he is shown the various vices present throughout (Passus I-IX constitutes the first vision in the C-Text, used here). The first *visio* culminates in Piers Plowman, Will's guide, attempting to lead the people to plough a half-acre together. This simple effort is, however, too selfless for the characters, and they are sabotaged by their own selfishness and stubbornness; not only does their attempt fail, but chaos breaks out to such an extreme that the dreamer (and the reader with him) feel as if they were back at the beginning.

After this failure, the dreamer begins the second part of his quest, which now has a more spiritual character (Passus X-XVII). The concluding Passus (XVIII-XX) describe the final battle of good against evil, in which Christ saves humanity through his Crucifixion and the Harrowing of Hell, and the succeeding foundation of the Christian Church.

Most of the prologue is printed here, which describes first of all Will's entry into his dream, and the initial situation: the errors of present society. The second part is from Passus VI, the confession scene after Reason has held a sermon. Glotoun goes into a tavern, which was known to be the spawning place of vice. The motif of the tavern appears often in literature of religious instruction (see also M 4/78-end), as it is here that Satan has the most power. In the tavern, most of Seven Deadly Sins (as well as many minor sins) appear in one form or another: Gluttony – eating and drinking; Sloth – sitting around talking, dicing and gaming; Pride – telling stories (often lies); and of course, Lechery – the bar wenches were known to provide more than drinks. Langland also avails himself of the various literary techniques common in sermons and religious handbooks of his time, also including elements of drama in short scenes.

Piers Plowman is written in alliterative long lines. Langland tries to use two alliterations in the first, and one alliteration in the second half-line as much as possible, but resorts to fewer or more alliterations as need be. The caesura falls between the second and third alliteration:

In a śomur śesoun   whan śofte was þe sonne
Y śhope me into śhroudes   as y a śhep were
In ábite as an heremite,   vnholy of werkes,
Wente forth in þe world   wondres to here,
And śay many śellies   and śelkouthe thynges.

The most important linguistic feature of the text is the reflex of Old English *ā* (see § 10), written <o>, as in *vnholy* (l. 3), *wo, bothe* (l. 10, 76) and so on. Old English *a* followed by a nasal is written <o>, as in *mony* (l. 27), *conneth* (l. 35); but it is also written <a>, as in *many, chapman* (l. 5, 62). Late West Saxon *ĕa* followed by <h> is written <ei>, as for example in *seih* (l. 17) and *sey* (l. 109); this is indicative of the changes affecting diphthongs in late West Saxon (see § 4). Old English *y* can be written <u>, /y:/, as in *hulles* (l. 6, 135), *furste* (l. 239), but also <uy> as in *pruyde* (l. 25) and *luyther* (l. 238). In general, the text shows features typical of a Southwest Midlands origin.

Sources: Huntington Library, MS HM 143. – Pearsall (1978); Skeat (1886). – Secondary literature: Robertson/Huppé (1951), Frank (1957), Lawlor (1962), Bloomfield (1963), Vasta (1965), Aers (1975), Griffiths (1985), Samuels (1985, 1988), Du Boulay (1991).

In a somur sesoun whan softe was þe sonne
Y shope me into shroudes as y a shep were;
In abite as an heremite, vnholy of werkes,
Wente forth in þe world wondres to here,
5 And say many sellies and selkouthe thynges.
Ac on a May mornyng on Maluerne hulles
Me biful for to slepe, for werynesse of-walked;
And in a launde as y lay, lened y and slepte,
And merueylousliche me mette, as y may telle.
10 Al þe welthe of the world and þe wo bothe
Wynkyng, as hit were, witterliche y sigh hit;
Of treuthe and tricherye, tresoun and gyle,
Al y say slepynge, as y shal telle.
    Estward y beheld aftir þe sonne
15 And say a tour – as y trowed, Treuthe was there-ynne.
Westward y waytede in a while aftir
And seigh a depe dale – Deth, as y leue,
Woned in tho wones, and wikkede spiritus.

-----

2 *shep*] could refer to an article of clothing, perhaps a cloak of coarse wool; also an allusion to the motif of a wolf in sheep's clothing.
6 *Maluerne hulles*] the Malvern Hills in Worcestershire
7 *for werynesse of-walked*] 'because I was wearied from walking'
9 *me mette*] Langland still uses 'mette' (dream) as an impersonal verb (cf. O 11/2: 'mē gemǣtte').

A fair feld ful of folk fond y þer bytwene
20 Of alle manere men, þe mene and þe pore,
Worchyng and wandryng as þis world ascuth.
    Somme potte hem to þe plogh, playde ful selde,
In settynge and in sowynge swonken ful harde
And wonne þat þis wastors with glotony destrueth.
25 And summe putte hem to pruyde and parayled hem þer-aftir
In continance of clothyng in many kyne gyse.
In preiers and penaunces potten hem mony,
Al for loue of oure lord lyueden swythe harde
In hope to haue a good ende and heuenriche blisse;
30 As ankeres and eremites þat holdeth hem in here selles,
Coueyten noȝt in contreys to cayren aboute
For no likerous liflode here lycame to plese.
    And summe chesen chaffare – þei cheueth þe bettre,
As it semeþ to oure sighte that suche men ythryueth;
35 And summe murthes to make as mynstrels conneth,
Wolleth neyther swynke ne swete, bote sweren grete othes,
Fyndeth out foule fantasyes and foles hem maketh
And hath wytt at wille to worche yf þei wolde.
That Poule prechede of hem preue hit y myhte;
40 *Qui turpiloquium loquitur* is Luciferes knaue.
    Bidders and beggers fast aboute ȝede
Til here bagge and here bely was bretful ycrammed,
Fayteden for here fode and foughten at þe ale.
In glotonye þo gomus goth þei to bedde
45 And ryseþ with rybaudrye þo Robardus knaues;
Slep and also slewthe sueth suche euer.
    Pilgrymes and palmers plighten hem togyderes
To seke seynt Iame and seyntes of Rome,

---

19 *A fair feld*] see Matthew 13:38, 'the field is the world . . .'.
22 *hem*] is in most instances used as a reflexive pronoun: 'some applied themselves to the plough'.
25–26 *And . . . gyse*] 'And some gave themselves over to pride and dressed in various fashions'.
31–32 *Coueyten . . . plese*] 'do not desire to roam the country or indulge their bodies with delicious food'.
35 *mynstrels*] Langland's general condemnation of minstrels here is not typical of the tradition of moral theology, which differentiates between 'good' and 'bad' minstrels.
38 *And . . . wille*] 'and have enough intelligence'
39 *Poule prechede*] perhaps a reference to 2 Thess. 3:10
40 *Qui . . . loquitur*] 'He who speaks foolish words'; see Eph. 5:4
43 *fayteden . . . fode*] 'begged falsely for their food'
45 *Robardus knaues*] i. e. robbers
47 *palmers*] Pilgrims returning from the Holy Land wore a palm-leaf as a sign of their pilgrimage. *Palmers* in this case refers to 'professional pilgrims' who could be hired.
48 *seynt Iame*] the famous shrine of Santiago at Compostela in Galicia

Wenten forth on here way with many wyse tales
50 And hadde leue to lye aftir, al here lyf-tyme.
Eremites on an hep with hokede staues
Wenten to Walsyngham, and here wenches aftir;
Grete lobies and longe þat loth were to swynke
Clothed hem in copis to be knowe fram othere
55 And made hemself heremites, here ese to haue.
    I fonde þer of freris alle þe foure ordres,
Prechyng þe peple for profyt of þe wombe,
And glosede þe gospel as hem good likede;
For coueytise of copis contraryed somme doctours.
60 Mony of þise maistres of mendenant freres
Here moneye and marchandise marchen togyderes.
Ac sith charite hath be chapman and chief to shryue lordes
Mony ferlyes han falle in a fewe ʒeres,
And but holi chirche and charite choppe adoun suche shryuars
65 The moste meschief on molde mounteth vp faste.
    Ther prechede a pardoner as he a prest were
And brouth forth a bulle with bischopis selys,
Sayde þat hymself myhte assoylen hem alle
Of falsnesses of fastynges, of vowes ybrokene.
70 Lewed men leued hym wel and lykede his wordes
And comen and knelede to kyssen his bulles;
A bounchede hem with his bulles and blered here yes
And raughte with his rageman rynges and broches.
Thus ʒe gyue ʒoure gold glotons to helpe
75 And leneth hit lorelles þat lecherye haunten.
Were þe bischop yblessed and worth bothe his eres
His seel sholde nouʒt be ysent in deseyte of þe people.

---

52 *Walsyngham*] The shrine devoted to the Virgin Mary at Walsingham (Norfolk) was the second most popular place of pilgrimage after Canterbury.

56 *foure ordres*] the four religious orders of the Franciscans, Dominicans, Augustinians and Carmelites

58 *And . . . likede*] 'and interpreted the Gospels according to their own purposes' – a frequent complaint

59 *doctours*] 'church fathers'

60 *mendenant freres*] mendicant friars

61 *Here . . . togyderes*] 'they trade souls (only) for money'.

62 *Ac . . . lordes*] 'And since charity (i. e. the friars) has turned merchant and main confessor of lords'

66 *prechede a pardoner*] Pardoners were not allowed to preach – unless they had a special licence from the bishop.

72 *A . . . yes*] 'he tapped them on the head (in forgiveness) and blurred their eyes', i. e. deceived them.

73 *rageman*] contemptuous name for a document (see l. 67: 'bulle') with many seals

76 *yblessed . . . eres*] This refers to the consecration of a bishop: 'If the bishop had (God's) blessing and was worth anything at all'.

77 *seel*] the seal on the document (*rageman*) mentioned in l. 73

Ac it is nouȝt by þe bischop, y leue, þat þe boy precheþ, –
For þe parsche prest and þe pardoner parten þe seluer
80 That þe peple in parsches sholde haue, yf þei ne were.
    Persones and parsche prestis pleyned to þe bischop
That here parsches were pore sithe þis pestelence tyme,
To haue a licence and a leue in Londoun to dwelle
And synge þer for symonye while seluer is so swete.
85   Bischopes and bachelers, bothe maystres and doctours,
That han cure vnder Crist and crownyng in tokene
And ben charged with holy chirche charite to tylie,
That is lele loue and lyfe among lered and lewed,
Leyen in Londoun in lenton and elles.
90 Summe seruen þe kynge and his siluer tellen,
In þe cheker and in þe chancerye chalengen his dettes
Of wardus and of wardemotis, wayues and strayues;
And summe aren as seneschalles and seruen oþer lordes
And ben in stede of stewardus and sitten and demen.
95   Consience cam and cused hem – and þe comune herde hit –
And seide, 'Ydolatrie ȝe soffren in sondrye places manye
And boxes ben yset forth ybounde with yren
To vndertake þe tol of vntrewe sacrefice.
In menynge of myracles muche wex hangeth there:
100 Al þe world wot wel hit myghte nouȝt be trewe,
And for it profiteþ ȝou into pursward ȝe prelates soffren
That lewed men in mysbileue lyuen and dyen.
I leue by oure lord for loue of ȝoure coueytise
That al þe world be the wors, as holy writ telleth

---

78 *boy*]: a derisive term for 'pardoner'
79 *parten þe seluer*] i. e. keep the money for themselves
81 *Persones . . . prestis*] Often a parson held the benefice as an absentee and hired a (poorly) paid priest to carry out the duties of his office.
82 *pestelence tyme*] This refers to the waves of the Black Death in 1348, 1361, 1369 und 1375. The drop in population led to a lower income for the priest.
83 *licence . . . leue*] The priest needed the bishop's permission if he wanted to live outside of his parish.
84 *synge . . . symonye*] meaning: 'and celebrate mass there in order to earn money for the purchase of a better office'.
89 *lenton*] Lent refers to the period preceding Easter, devoted to fasting and meditation.
91 *cheker . . . chancerye*] the offices of the royal exchequer (responsible for revenues ('dettes') and accounts) and the chancellor's court
92 *wardus . . . strayues*] refers to various royal revenues: *wardus* income from the estates of underage orphan nobles; *wardemotis* tax on city assemblies; *wayues* lost property; *strayues* stray animals.
97 *boxes . . . yren*] iron-bound boxes for offerings
99 *In menynge . . . wex*] This is a reference to candles ('wex') lit by the devout in expectation of (further) miracles.
101 *And . . . pursward*] 'and because it fills your purse'

105 What cheste and meschaunce to þe children of Israel
     Ful on hem þat fre were thorwe two fals prestis.
     For Offnies synne and Fines his brother
     Thei were discomfited in batayle and losten *Archa domini*.
     And for here syre sey hem synne and suffred hem do ille
110 And chastisid hem noght þerof and nolde noght rebuken hem,
     Anon as it was tolde hym that þe children of Israel
     Were disconfit in batayle and *Archa domini* lorn
     And his sones slawe ther, anon he ful for sorwe
     Fro his chayere þer he sat and brake his nekke atwene;
115 And al was for vengeance he bet noght his children.
     And for þei were prestis and men of holy chirche
     God was wel þe wrother and took þe raþer vengeance.
          [. . .]
     Thenne cam ther a kyng, knyghthede hym ladde,   [139]
     Myght of tho men made hym to regne.
120 And thenne cam Kynde Wytt and clerkus he made
     And Conscience and Kynde Wit and knyghthed togedres
     Caste þat þe comunes sholde here comunes fynde.
     Kynde Wytt and þe comune contreued alle craftes
     And for most profitable a plogh gonne þei make,
125 With lele labour to lyue while lif on londe lasteth.
          Thenne Kynde Witt to þe kynge and to þe comune saide,
     'Crist kepe þe, kynge, and thy kyneriche
     And leue the lede so þy londe þat Lewte þe louye
     And for thy rightful ruylynge be rewardid in heuene.'
          [. . .]
130 Consience and þe kynge in to court wente   [158]
     Where houed an hundrid in houes of selke,
     Seriantz it semede that serueth at þe barre,
     Pleden for penyes and poundes þe lawe
     And nat for loue of oure lord vnlose here lyppes ones.

107–108 *For Offnies . . . domini*] see 1 Sam. 4:11; 'Offnies' and 'Fines' are genitives.
108 *Archa domini*] Ark of the Covenant
111–113 *Anon . . . anon he*] 'As soon as . . . he'
114 *Fro . . . atwene*] see 1 Sam. 4:18
115 *bet noght his children*] Beating your children is a standard theme in medieval sermons; see
  Prov. 13:24: 'qui parcit virgae suae odit filium suum – he that spareth his rod hateth his son'.
120 *Kynde Wytt*] natural intelligence
122 *Caste . . . fynde*] (Together they) 'decided that the lower estate be responsible for providing
  food for the whole community'.
124 *And . . . make*] 'And made the most useful instrument (for everybody): a plough'.
128 *Lewte*] is a personification of the moral concepts of truth and justice.
133 *for penyes and poundes*] corrupt and avaricious lawyers – a familiar complaint

135 Thow myghtest betre meten myst on Maluerne hulles
Than gete a mum of here mouth ar moneye were hem shewed.
       [. . .]
        ʒut mette me more of mene and of riche,   [219]
As barones and burgeys and bondemen of thorpes,
Al y say slepynge as ʒe shal here heraftur:
140 Bothe bakeres and breweres, bochers and other,
Webbesteres and walkeres and wynners with handes,
As taylers and tanners and tulyers of þe erthe,
As dykers and deluers þat doth here dedis ylle
And dryueth forth here days with '*Dew vous saue, dame Emme.*'
145 Cokes and here knaues cryede, 'hote pyes, hote!
Goode gees and grys! ga we dyne, ga we!'
Tauerners til hem tolde þe same:
'Whit wyn of Oseye and wyn of Gascoyne,
Of þe Reule and of þe Rochele the roost to defye!'
150 Al þis y say sleping and seuyn sythes more.
       [. . .]

        Now bygynneth Glotoun for to go to shryfte   [VI, 350]
And kayres hym to kyrke-ward, his cowpe to shewe.
Fastyng on a Friday forth gan he wende
By Betene hous the brewestere, þat bad hym good morwen,
155 And whodeward he wolde the breuh-wyf hym askede.
    'To holy churche,' quod he, 'for to here masse,
And sennes sitte and be shryue and synege no more.'
        'Y haue good ale, gossip Glotoun, woltow assaye?'
        'Hastow,' quod he, 'eny hote spyces?'
160   'Y haue pepur and pyonie and a pound of garlek,
A ferthyng-worth fenkelsedes, for fastyng-dayes y bouhte hit.'
        Thenne goth Glotoun in and grete othes aftur.
Sesse þe souhteres saet on þe benche,

---

135 *Thow . . . meten*] 'you will rather encounter'
144 *Dew . . . Emme*] 'God save you, Dame Emma'; this refers probably to the bawd Emma of
  Shoreditch, celebrated in many a popular ballad.
147 *Tauerners . . . same*] 'innkeepers praised their wares in similar terms'
148 *Oseye . . . Gascoyne*] Alsace and Gascony
149 *Reule . . . Rochele*] La Reole and La Rochelle
152 *And . . . shewe*] 'and proceeds to church to confess his sins'
154 *Betene*] genitive singular, i. e. 'Betty's'
159 *hote spyces*] 'hot spices' were sometimes associated with heavy drinking.
160 *pyonie*] peony seed; the peony is still used in homeopathy.
161 *ferthyng-worth*] amounting to the value of a farthing
161 *fenkelsedes*] Fennel seeds were used to suppress appetite during fasting.
162 *grete othes*] Swearing along with drinking and gaming are the typical sins committed in
  the tavern (see also M 4/78 ff.).

Watte þe wernare and his wyf dronke,
165 Tymme þe tynekare and tweyne of his knaues,
Hicke þe hackenayman and Hewe þe nedlare,
Claryce of Cockes-lane and the clerc of þe churche,
Syre Peres of Prydie and Purnele of Flaundres,
An hayward, an heremyte, the hangeman of Tybourne,
170 Dawe þe dikere, with a dosoyne harlotes
Of portours and of pikeporses and of pilede toth-draweres,
A rybibour and a ratoner, a rakeare and his knaue,
A ropere and a redyngkynge and Rose þe disshere,
Godefray þe garlek-monger and Gryffyth þe Walshe,
175 And of vphalderes an heep, herly by þe morwe
Geuen Glotoun with glad chere good ale to hansull.
      Clement þe coblere cast of his cloke
And to þe newe fayre nempnede hit forth to sull.
Hicke þe hackenayman hit his hod aftur
180 And bade Bitte þe bochere ben on his syde.
There were chapmen ychose this chaffare to preyse,
That ho-so hadde the hood sholde nat haue þe cloke,
And that the bettere thyng, be arbitreres, bote sholde þe worse.
Tho rysen vp rape and rounned togyderes
185 And preisede this peniworths apart by hemsulue,
And there were othes an heep, for on sholde haue þe worse.
They couthe nat by here consience acorden for treuthe
Til Robyn þe ropere aryse they besouhte
And nempned hym for a noumper, þat no debat were.
190   Hicke þe hostiler hadde þe cloke,
In couenaunt þat Clement sholde the coppe fulle,
And haue Hickes hood þe hostiler and holde hym yserued;
And ho-so repentede hym rathest sholde aryse aftur
And grete syre Glotoun with a galon of ale.
195   There was leyhing and louryng and 'lat go the coppe!'
Bargaynes and beuereges bygan tho to awake,
And seten so til euensong, and songen vmbywhile,

---

167 *Cockes-lane*] a London street, north of the Thames, known for its brothels
168 *Syre Peres of Prydie*] ironic term for a neglectful priest
168 *Purnele of Flaundres*] Flemish women were reputed to be prostitutes.
169 *Tybourne*] The London gallows were in Tyburn.
172 *rybibour*] musician playing the rubible, a small string instrument
173 *redyngkynge*] probably a thatcher
173 *disshere*] a woman who sells food
175 *vphalderes*] second-hand clothes dealers
176 *to hansull*] 'as a welcome drink'
178 *newe fayre*] game in which objects were traded; judges (*arbitreres*, l. 183) decided what to
  do in case traded objects were not of equal value (*bote sholde þe worse*, l. 183).
179 *hit . . . aftur*] 'bet his hat thereupon'

Til Glotoun hadde yglobbed a galoun and a gylle.

His gottes gan to gothly as two grydy sowes;

200 A pissede a potel in a *pater-noster* whyle,

A blew his rownd ruet at his rygebones ende,

That alle þat herde þe horne helde here nose aftur

And wesched hit hadde be wasche with a weps of breres.

He myhte noþer steppe ne stande til he a staf hadde,

205 And thenne gan he go lyke a glemans byche,

Sum tyme asyde and sum tyme arere,

As ho-so layth lynes for to lacche foules.

And when he drow to the dore, thenne dymmede his yes,

And thromblede at the thresfold and threw to þe erthe,

210 And Clement þe coblere cauhte hym by þe myddel

And for to lyfte hym aloft leyde hym on his knees.

Ac Gloton was a greet cherl and greued in þe luftynge

And cowed vp a caudel in Clementis lappe;

Ys none so hungry hound in Hertfordshyre

215 Durste lape of þat lyuynge, so vnlouely hit smauhte.

With alle þe wo of this world his wyf and his wenche

Baren hym to his bed and brouhten hym þer-ynne,

And aftur al this exces he hadde an accidie aftur;

A sleep Saturday and Sonenday til þe sonne ȝede to reste.

220 Then gan he wake wel wanne and wolde haue ydronke;

The furste word that he spake was 'Who halt þe bolle?'

His wif and his inwit edwitede hym of his synne;

A wax ashamed, þat shrewe, and shrofe hym as swythe

To Repentaunce ryht thus: 'Haue reuthe on me,' he saide,

225 'Thow lord that aloft art and alle lyues shope!

To the, God, y, Glotoun, gulty me ȝelde

Of þat y haue trespased with tonge, y can nat telle how ofte,

Sworn "Godes soule and his sides!" and "So helpe me, God almyhty!"

There no nede ne was, many sythe falsly;

230 And ouer-sopped at my soper and som tyme at nones

More then my kynde myhte deffye,

And as an hound þat eet gras so gan y to brake

---

198 *a galoun . . . gylle*] literally: 'a gallon and a gill', i. e. too much

200 *potel . . . whyle*] A *potel* is 4 pints (about 2.5 litres); *pater-noster whyle* – as long as it takes to say this prayer in a hurry.

201 *blew . . . ende*] This refers to flatulence.

205 *glemans byche*] Jesters often had dogs trained to perform tricks.

212 *greued . . . luftynge*] He was difficult to lift (because of his weight).

213 *cowed . . . caudel*] 'threw up a mess'

215 *lyuynge*] i. e. the vomit

218 *accidie*] Sloth is one of the Seven Deadly Sins; here it is used to refer to Glotoun's drunken slumber.

221 *Who . . . bolle*] 'Who's got the cup?'

And spilde þat y aspele myhte – y kan nat speke for shame
The vilony of my foule mouthe and of my foule mawe –
235 On fastyng-dayes bifore noen fedde me with ale
Out of resoun, among rybaudes, here rybaudrye to here.
   Herof, gode God, graunte me forȝeuenesse
Of all my luyther lyf in al my lyf-tyme
For y vowe to verray God, for eny hungur or furste,
240 Shal neuere fysch in þe Fryday defyen in my wombe
Til Abstinence myn aunte haue ȝeue me leue –
And ȝut haue y hated here al my lyf-tyme.'

---

235 *On fastyng-dayes . . . noen*] Only one meal was allowed when fasting, and not before noon.
236 *here rybaudrye to here*] 'in order to hear their jokes'

Text 8: The Fox and the Wolf

The Fox and the Wolf is one of the two examples in Middle English of a secular "beast epic", the other being Chaucer's *Nun's Priest's Tale*. Medieval England seems to have preferred the genre "fable" to "beast epic", even though the beast epic tradition was prevalent on the European continent: the French *Roman de Renart* cycle (from around 1175) spawned a tradition which spread into most other languages, like the Middle High German *Reinhart Fuchs* (from around 1180) and the Middle Dutch *Van den vos Reinaerde* (from around 1250). In England, however, this genre was reserved more for religious purposes, and we find animal lore more often in sermons or in literature for religious instruction as an *exemplum*.

When *The Fox and the Wolf* is compared to similar works from the Continent, it is difficult to find a direct source or sources. It is preserved in only one manuscript, MS Digby 86 (dating *The Fox and the Wolf* to some time before 1300), alongside an Old French version of the *Disciplina Clericalis* by Petrus Alphonsi (1109–1114), of which the 23rd story is 'the Fox and the Wolf in the Well'. Although the plot proceeds differently from the Middle English *The Fox and the Wolf*, it may have nonetheless had an influence on the composition. On the other hand, the *Roman de Renart* also includes the names *Reneuard* and *Sigrim* as we find them in this Fox and Wolf story (see ll. 128 and 133). However, the Middle English tale uses the names only in these two lines, otherwise referring to the 'fox' and the 'wolf'. Indeed, *The Fox and the Wolf* has scenes not found in the *Roman de Renart*, such as the discussion between the fox and the cock, while the *Roman de Renart* has scenes which are missing in this story. The hens, for example, which the fox devours, do not appear in our story – although this scene has obviously been left out after l. 15 as the cock says in l. 28 that the fox has already eaten the others; on the other hand, the scenes in which Reneuard's adultery is discussed are almost entirely left out, which leads to a more effective satire of the sacrament confession (see lines 88–113).

The Fox and the Wolf is in general shorter and more concise than the 4th branch of the *Roman de Renart*, which uses the full dimensions of a beast epic. The Middle English tale, on the other hand, is so compact that it might better be compared to the genre *fabliau* with the main plot of tricking a simpleton (if possible, twice).

The linguistic evidence suggests a Southwest Midland provenance of the text. Old English *ā* is written <o> throughout and rhymes with *ō*. Old English *ǣ* is written <e> and <ee>. Old English *ў* is written <u> in *putte* (l. 121) and could be pronounced /e/ and /i/, as the rhymes show. Word-initial etymological <h-> is missing sometimes as in *oundred* (l. 4). The <h-> can be added when it is not required etymologically, as in *heddre* (l. 22), *houre* (l. 18, 30), *hounderstod* (l. 39) etc.

LALME on MS Digby 86: Linguistic Profile 7790, Gloucestershire.

Sources: Bodleian Library, Oxford, MS Digby 86. – Bennett/Smithers (1968); McKnight (1913). – Secondary literature: Bercovitch (1966), von Kreisler (1970), Bergner (1973). – Facsimile: Tschann (1996).

A vox gon out of þe wode go, / Afingret so þat him wes wo –
He nes neuere in none wise / Afingret erour half so swiþe.
He ne hoeld nouþer wey ne strete, / For him wes loþ men to mete;
Him were leuere meten one hen / Þen half an oundred wimmen!
5   He strok swiþe oueral / So þat he ofsei ane wal.
Wiþinne þe walle wes on hous: / Þe wox wes þider swiþe wous,
For he þohute his hounger aquenche, / Oþer mid mete oþer mid drunche.
Abouten he biheld wel ȝerne. / Þo eroust bigon þe vox to erne
Al fort he come to one walle; / And som þerof wes afalle,
10   And wes þe wal oueral tobroke, / And on ȝat þer wes iloke.
At þe furmest bruche þat he fond / He lep in, and ouer he wond.
Þo he wes inne, smere he lou / And þerof he hadde gome inou
(For he com in wiþouten leue / Boþen of haiward and of reue!)
     On hous þer wes: þe dore wes ope. / Hennen weren þerinne icrope
15   Fiue (þat makeþ anne flok); / And mid hem sat on kok.
Þe kok him wes flowen on hey, / And two hennen him seten ney.
'Wox!' quad þe kok, 'wat dest þou þare? / Go hom! Crist þe ȝeue kare:
Houre hennen þou dest ofte shome.' / 'Be stille, Ich hote, a Godes nome!'
Quaþ þe wox, 'Sire Chauntecler, / Þou fle adoun and com me ner.
20   I nabbe don her nout bote goed – / I have leten þine hennen blod.
Hy weren seke ounder þe ribe, / Þat hy ne miȝtte non lengour libe
Bote here heddre were itake. / Þat I do for almes sake –
Ich haue hem leten eddre-blod. / And þe, Chauntecler, hit wolde don goed
(Þou hauest þat ilke ounder þe splen – / Þou nestes neuere daies ten);
25   For þine lif-dayes beþ al ago / Bote þou bi mine rede do.
I do þe lete blod ounder þe brest, / Oþer sone axe after þe prest.'
'Go wei!' quod þe kok, 'wo þe bigo! / Þou hauest don oure kunne wo –
Go mid þan þat þou hauest nouþe. / Acoursed be þou of Godes mouþe!
For were I adoun, bi Godes nome / Ich miȝte ben siker of oþre shome.
30   Ac weste hit houre cellerer / Þat þou were icomen her,
He wolde sone after þe ȝonge / Mid pikes and stones and staues stronge.
Alle þine bones he wolde tobreke – / Þene we weren wel awreke!'

---

4 *half . . . wimmen*] The fox was often depicted as a lustful creature.
6 *wes . . . wous*] 'was in a hurry to get there'
13 *haiward*] a parish officer in charge of enclosures and fences
16 *him*] need not be translated
16 *two hennen*] Apparently, the fox has already eaten three of the five hens mentioned in l. 15.
20 *leten blod*] The fox is often depicted as a doctor.
22 *heddre*] 'blood in the veins'
22 *Þat . . . sake*] 'I do this out of the goodness of my heart'
23 *eddre-blod*] 'blood in the veins'
24 *splen*] According to medieval medicine, the spleen was the seat of evil passions.
24 *nestes*] 'survive' (in your nest)
26 *I do . . . prest*] 'Either I bleed you (under the breast) or you had better send for the priest'.
30 *cellerer*] The cellarer was responsible for running the farm.

þe mede shal ben lene
Mone on houndret ne bey fiue
Onyer of maidnes ne of wiue
At holdey hem al clene
At hine worche þy to m londe
þer bringey men to shonde
And þat is wel I seene
And þey we sitten þerfor etostlien
Loue of maidnes and of wiue
Or ne sost you ene
O faþel yimony þe haiuey I shend
þorn wham þat alþis worlt I wend
Of swuchde meke and milde
Of hire sprong þat holi bern
At boren wes in bedlehem
And temey al þat is wilde
Oene westte of sunne neof shame
Swie wes sre rihte name
Crist hire I shilde
Oswel for yt false coue
Or beddi ye þis wode shaue
Ou fare into þe filde
Ayeinsate I wes wod
Ouer I come tolutel good
Hiy þe for to sriue
I suere þat ich am ouer come
Or u hire þat lesy þat holi sone
At soffrede wounder fiue
I suerie bi his holi name
Ne shal I neuere suetten shame
Ne maidnes ne bi wiue
Ne out of þis londe wille te
Ne recht neuere weder I fle

A þat ich wille driue
Of þe vox and of þe wolf

A vox gon out of þe wode go
Afingret so þat him wes wo
He nes neuere in none wise
Afingret erour half so swiþe
He ne hoeld nouþer wey ne strete
For him wes loþ men to mete
Him were leuere meten one hen
En half anoundred wimmen
He strok swiþe ouer al
So þat he ofser ane wal
Wiyinne þe walle wes on hous
þe vox wes þider swiþe wous
Vor he yohute his hounger aqnche
þer mid mete oyer mid drunche
Bouten he biheld wel zerne
Vyo þat com biron þe vox to erne
A l fort he come to one wille
And som þer of wes afalle
And wes þe wal ouer al to broke
And on þat þer wes I loke
At þe furmeste bruche þat he fond
He lep in and ouer he wond
þo he wes inne smere he lou
And þer of he hedde dome I nou
For he com in wiyouten leue
Boþen of haiward and of reue
On hous þer wes þe dore wes ope
Hennen weren þerinne I crope
Fiue þat makey anne flok
And mid hem sat on kok
þe kok him wes flowen on hey

He wes stille ne spak namore, / Ac he werþ aþurst wel sore:
Þe þurst him dede more wo / Þen heuede raþer his hounger do.
35 Oueral he ede and sohvte: / On auenture, his wiit him brohute
To one putte wes water inne, / Þat wes imaked mid grete ginne.
Tuo boketes þer he founde: / Þat oþer wende to þe grounde,
Þat wen me shulde þat on opwinde / Þat oþer wolde adoun winde.
He ne hounderstod nout of þe ginne: / He nom þat boket and lop þerinne,
40 For he hopede inou to drinke. / Þis boket biginneþ to sinke:
To late þe vox wes biþout / Þo he wes in þe ginne ibrout.
Inou he gon him biþenche, / Ac hit ne halp mid none wrenche:
Adoun he moste, he wes þerinne – / Ikaut he wes mid swikele ginne.
Hit miȝte han iben wel his wille / To lete þat boket hongi stille.
45 Wat mid serewe and mid drede, / Al his þurst him ouer-hede.
Al þus he com to þe grounde, / And water inou þer he founde.
Þo he fond water, ȝerne he dronk / (Him þoute þat water þere stonk,
For hit wes toȝeines his wille!) / 'Wo worþe,' quaþ þe vox, 'lust and wille,
Þat ne con meþ to his mete! / Ȝef Ich neuede to muchel i-ete,
50 Þis ilke shome neddi nouþe, / Nedde lust iben of mine mouþe.
Him is wo, in euche londe, / Þat is þef mid his honde.
Ich am ikaut mid swikele ginne / Oþer soum deuel me broute herinne.
I was woned to ben wiis, / Ac nou of me idon hit hiis!'
Þe vox wep and reuliche bigan. / Þer com a wolf gon, after þan,
55 Out of þe depe wode bliue, / For he wes afingret swiþe.
Noþing he ne founde, in al þe niȝte, / Wermide his honger aquenche miȝtte.
He com to þe putte, þene vox iherde: / He him kneu wel bi his rerde,
For hit wes his neiȝebore / And his gossip, of children bore.
Adoun bi þe putte he sat. / Quod þe wolf: 'Wat may ben þat
60 Þat Ich in þe putte ihere? / Hertou Cristine oþer mi fere?
Say me soþ – ne gabbe þou me nout: / Wo haueþ þe in þe putte ibrout?'
Þe vox hine ikneu wel for his kun, / And þo eroust kom wiit to him;
For he þoute, mid sommne ginne, / Himself houpbringe, þene wolf þerinne.
Quod þe vox: 'Wo is nou þere? / Ich wene hit is Sigrim þat Ich here.'
65 'Þat is soþ,' þe wolf sede, / 'Ac wat art þou, so God þe rede?'
'A!' quod þe vox, 'Ich wille þe telle – / On alpi word Ich lie nelle.
Ich am Reneuard, þi frend; / And ȝif Ich þine come heuede iwend,
Ich hedde so ibede for þe / Þat þou sholdest comen to me.'
'Mid þe?' quod þe wolf, 'warto? / Wat shulde Ich ine þe putte do?'

----

33 *He*] the fox
40 *biginneþ*] historical present
41 *wes biþout*] 'figured it out'
49 *Þat*] 'for him who'
53 *Ac ... hiis!*] 'but now I'm done for'.
54 *reuliche bigan*] 'pitied himself'
58 *gossip ... bore*] The fox is the godfather of the wolf's children.
67 *And ... iwend*] 'and had I known you were coming'

70 Quod þe vox: 'Þou art ounwiis! / Her is þe blisse of Paradiis –
Her Ich mai euere wel fare, / Wiþouten pine, wiþouten kare.
Her is mete, her is drinke; / Her is blisse wiþouten swinke.
Her nis hounger neuermo, / Ne non oþer kunnes wo –
Of alle gode her is inou!' / Mid þilke wordes þe volf lou.

75 'Art þou ded, so God þe rede, / Oþer of þe worlde?' þe wolf sede.
Quod þe wolf: 'Wenne storue þou, / And wat dest þou þere nou?
Ne beþ nout ʒet þre daies ago / Þat þou, and þi wif also,
And þine children, smale and grete, / Alle togedere mid me hete!'
'Þat is soþ,' quod þe vox, / 'Gode þonk, nou hit is þus

80 Þat Ihc am to Criste vend! / Not hit non of mine frend;
I nolde, for al þe worldes goed, / Ben ine þe worlde, þer Ich hem fond.
Wat shuld Ich ine þe worlde go / Þer nis bote kare and wo,
And liuie in fulþe and in sunne? / Ac her beþ ioies fele cunne –
Her beþ boþe shep and get.' / Þe wolf haueþ hounger swiþe gret,

85 For he nedde ʒare i-ete; / And þo he herde speken of mete,
He wolde bleþeliche ben þare. / 'A!' quod þe wolf, 'gode ifere,
Moni goed mel þou hauest me binome! / Let me adoun to þe kome,
And al Ich wole þe forʒeue.' / 'Ʒe!' quod þe vox, 'were þou isriue,
And sunnen heuedest al forsake, / And to klene lif itake,

90 Ich wolde so bidde for þe / Þat þou sholdest comen to me.'
'To wom shuld Ich,' þe wolf seide, / 'Ben iknowe of mine misdede?
Her nis noþing aliue / Þat me kouþe her nou sriue.
Þou hauest ben ofte min ifere – / Woltou nou mi srift ihere,
And al mi liif I shal þe telle?' / 'Nay!' quod þe vox, 'I nelle.'

95 'Neltou?' quod þe wolf, 'þin ore! / Ich am afingret swiþe sore –
Ich wot, toniʒt Ich worþe ded, / Bote þou do me somne reed.
For Cristes loue, be mi prest!' / Þe wolf bey adoun his brest
And gon to siken harde and stronge. / 'Woltou', quod þe vox, 'srift ounderfonge?
Tel þine sunnen, on and on, / Þat þer beleue neuer on.'

100   'Sone,' quad þe wolf, 'wel ifaie! / Ich habbe ben qued al mi lif-daie:
Ich habbe widewene kors – / Þerfore Ich fare þe wors.
A þousent shep Ich habbe abiten / And mo, ʒef hy weren iwriten;
Ac hit me ofþinkeþ sore. / Maister, shal I tellen more?'
'Ʒe!' quad þe vox, 'al þou most sugge, / Oþer elleswer þou most abugge.'

105 'Gossip!' quod þe wolf, '(forʒef hit me) / Ich habbe ofte sehid qued bi þe.
Men seide þat þou on þine liue / Misferdest mid mine wiue.
Ich þe aperseiuede one stounde, / And in bedde togedere ou founde:
Ich wes ofte ou ful ney / And in bedde togedere ou sey.

---

81 The rhyme is defective; this could imply that the text is corrupt.
81 *hem*] *hem* could refer to *frend* (l. 80) or *goed* (l. 81)
84 *haueþ*] historical present again
100 *wel ifaie*] 'gladly'
101 *widewene kors*] In the Bible, widows and orphans had a privileged status; cf. Ex 22:22,
  James 1:27.

Ich wende, also oþre doþ, / Þat Ich iseie were soþ,
110　And þerfore þou were me loþ – / Gode gossip, ne be þou nohut wroþ!'
'Vuolf!' quad þe vox him þo, / 'Al þat þou hauest herbifore ido,
In þohut, in speche, and in dede, / In euch oþeres kunnes quede,
Ich þe forȝeue at þisse nede.' / 'Crist þe forȝelde!' þe wolf seide,
'Nou Ich am in clene liue, / Ne recche Ich of childe ne of wiue!
115　Ac sei me wat I shal do / And ou Ich may comen þe to.'
Ðo quod þe vox: 'Ich wille þe lere. / Isiist þou a boket hongi þere?
Þer is a bruche of heuene blisse! / Lep þerinne, mid iwisse,
And þou shalt comen to me sone.' / Quod þe wolf: 'Þat is liȝt to done!'
He lep in and way sumdel / (Þat weste þe vox ful wel!)
120　Þe wolf gon sinke, þe vox arise – / Þo gon þe wolf sore agrise!
Þo he com amidde þe putte, / Þe wolf þene vox opward mette.
'Gossip,' quod þe wolf, 'wat nou! / Wat hauest þou imunt – weder wolt þou?'
'Weder Ich wille?' þe vox sede, / 'Ich wille oup, so God me rede!
And nou go doun wiþ þi meel - / Þi beȝete worþ wel smal!
125　Ac Ich am þerof glad and bliþe / Þat þou art nomen in clene liue.
Þi soule-cnul Ich wile do ringe, / And masse for þine soule singe!'
Þe wrecche bineþe noþing ne vind, / Bote cold water and hounger him bind.
To colde gistninge he wes ibede – / Wroggen haueþ his dou iknede!
　　Þe wolf in þe putte stod, / Afingret so þat he ves wod.
130　Inou he cursede þat þider him broute! / Þe vox þerof luitel route.
Þe put him wes þe house ney / Þer freren woneden, swiþe sley.
Þo þat hit com to þe time / Þat hoe shulden arisen ine,
Forto suggen here houssong, / O frere þer wes among
Of here slep hem shulde awecche. / Wen hoe shulden þidere recche,
135　He seide: 'Ariseþ, on and on, / And komeþ to houssong, heuereuchon!'
Þis ilke frere heyte Ailmer – / He wes hoere maister curtiler.
He wes hofþurst swiþe stronge: / Riȝt amidward here houssonge
Al hone to þe putte he hede, / For he wende bete his nede.
He com to þe putte and drou, / And þe wolf wes heui inou.
140　Þe frere mid al his maine tey, / So longe þat he þene wolf isey.
For he sei þene wolf þer sitte, / He gradde: 'Þe deuel is in þe putte!'

---

109 *Þat Ich iseie*] 'That what I saw'
112 *þohut . . . dede*] The reference to 'thought, mouth and deed' can be found in many
medieval confessional manuals: "homo tripliciter peccat, scilicet corde, ore, et opere".
124 *wiþ þi meel*] 'to your meal'
126 *Þi . . . ringe*] 'I'll have the death knell rung for you'.
127 *Þe wrecche . . . bind*] 'the wretch won't find anything down there except for cold water,
and his hunger will continue'.
130 *þat*] 'the one who'
131 *Þe put him*] 'Now the well'
135 *on and on*] 'one after the other'
136 *maister curtiler*] 'head gardener'
138 *Al hone*] 'all alone'

    To þe putte hy gonnen gon, / Alle mid pikes and staues and ston –
Euch mon mid þat he hedde / (Wo wes him þat wepne nedde!)
Hy comen to þe putte, þene wolf opdrowe: / Þo hede þe wreche fomen inowe
145   Þat weren egre him to slete / Mid grete houndes, and to bete!
Wel and wroþe he wes iswonge – / Mid staues and speres he wes istounge.
Þe wox bicharde him, mid iwisse, / For he ne fond nones kunnes blisse
Ne hof dintes forȝeuenesse.   *Explicit*

---

143 *mid þat*] 'with what'
148 *Ne . . . forȝeuenesse*] 'nor an end to the blows'

Text 9: King Horn

King Horn is one of the oldest remaining Middle English romances, composed
sometime in the late 13th or early 14th century in the London area. Obviously based
upon the Anglo-Norman romance *Horn et Rimenild* by Mestre Thomas, composed
between 1170–1180, the Middle English story has been compressed to less than a third
of its source text. The anonymous author has chosen to concentrate almost entirely on
the plot, removing 'unnecessary' details, and also omitting any character development
on the part of Horn. The typical elements of a romance, however, do appear in *King
Horn*: for example, we have the magic ring, prophetic dreams, and of course, the
typical motif of the lost son, who must first prove his worth and then return to reclaim
his heritage.

    King Horn belongs to the series of romances dealing with the 'Matter of England',
alongside *Havelock the Dane* and *Athelston*. The location of the action in *King Horn* is
not based on truth, nor does it claim to be, as is often the case in Arthurian Romances
(see for example, M 6/1–36, where Arthur and his court are put into the historical and
geographical situation of England). Except for Ireland, attempts to locate the
kingdoms mentioned in *King Horn* have been fruitless, and the poet even confuses the
directions in which one must travel in order to reach the different kingdoms.

    The story of *King Horn* begins with pagan pirates, who land in the Kingdom of
Suddene, kill Horn's father King Murri, and put Horn and his friends out to sea in a
rudderless boat. He and his companions land in Westernesse, where King Almair
accepts them into his household. There, Horn receives a knightly education, and the
daughter of the king, Rymenhild, falls desperately in love with him. Unbeknownst to
him, the hero has a traitor in his midst: Fikenhild, one of Horn's companions,
conspires against him, and tells the king that Horn is Rymenhild's lover. This leads to
Horn's second banishment; however, before he goes, the princess gives him a magic
ring which will protect him when he thinks of her. Horn sails to Ireland and serves
King Thurston there, who would like him to marry his daughter; however, Horn
cannot accept this offer, for he has already promised to marry Rymenhild. During an
adventure in Ireland, Horn meets some of the pirates who had killed his father, and is
able to kill their leader. He then receives a message from Rymenhild that she has been
engaged to marry King Modi, and returns disguised as a pilgrim to save her in the last
minute. Before he can marry Rymenhild, Horn says he must return to Suddene and
reclaim his throne, to which end he must take his loyal companion Athulf with him.
The closing scenes of *King Horn* are printed here: Rymenhild's rescue, Horn's
revenge, and the happy end as king and queen of Suddene.

The most prominent linguistic features of the text suggest a provenance close to
London.
1. Old English $\bar{æ}$ (derived from West Germanic $*\bar{a}$) is written <a>: *slape* (l. 79), *þare*
   (l. 117).
2. Old English $\bar{æ}$ (derived from West Germanic $*ai$ under the influence of i-mutation)
   is written <e>: *lede* (l. 67, 132), *swete* (l. 74).
3. Old English $\breve{y}$ is written <e> and <u>: *pelte* (l. 78), *dude* (l. 30, 65, 67 etc.).
4. Grammatical gender is expressed in l. 68: *castel . . . / . . . him biflette* as well as in
   l. 91: *castel . . . / For he . . .* This may be due to the influence of French.
LALME on MS Gg. 4. 27. 2.: Linguistic Profile 6800, Berkshire.

Sources: University Library, Cambridge, MS Gg. 4. 27. 2. – McKnight (1901); Sands (1966), Allen (1984). – Secondary literature: Hill (1957), Arens (1973), Ziegler (1980), Barron (1987).

    Horn sat on chaere, / And bad hem alle ihere.   [1353]
    "King," he sede, "þu luste / A tale mid þe beste.
    I ne seie hit for no blame, / Horn is mi name.
    Þu me to kniȝt houe, / And kniȝthod haue proued.
5 To þe, king, men seide / Þat i þe bitraide;
    Þu makedest me fleme, / And þi lond to reme.
    Þu wendest þat i wroȝte / Þat y neuere ne þoȝte,
    Bi Rymenhild for to ligge, / And þat i wiþsegge.
    Ne schal ihc hit biginne, / Til i Suddene winne.
10 Þu kep hure a stunde, / Þe while þat i funde
    In to min heritage / And to mi baronage.
    Þat lond i schal ofreche, / And do mi fader wreche.
    I schal beo king of tune, / And bere kinges crune.
    Þanne schal Rymenhilde / Ligge bi þe kinge."
15   Horn gan to schupe draȝe, / Wiþ his Yrisse felaȝes.
    Aþulf wiþ him his broþer, / Nolde he non oþer.
    Þat schup bigan to crude, / Þe wind him bleu lude.
    Wiþinne daies fiue / Þat schup gan ariue,
    Abute middelniȝte. / Horn him ȝede wel riȝte.
20 He tok Aþulf bi honde, / And vp he ȝede to londe.
    Hi founde vnder schelde, / A kniȝt hende in felde.
    Þe kniȝt him aslepe lay / Al biside þe way.
    Horn him gan to take, / And sede, "Kniȝt, awake.
    Seie what þu kepest, / And whi þu her slepest.
25 Me þinke, biþine crois liȝte, / Þat þu longest to vre Driȝte.
    Bute þu wule me schewe, / I schal þe tohewe."
    Þe gode kniȝt vp aros; / Of þe wordes him gros.
    He sede, "Ihc haue, aȝenes my wille, / Payns ful ylle.
    Ihc was cristene a while, / Þo i com to þis ille
30 Sarazins blake, / Þat dude me forsake.
    On Crist ihc wolde bileue; / On him hi makede me reue,
    To kepe þis passage / From Horn þat is of age,

---

2 *A tale mid þe beste*] Horn has just returned from his exile in order to claim his bride Rymenhild. He has arrived disguised as a pilgrim and the tale, 'one of the best', is about his adventures in Ireland.
4 *And . . . proued*] 'And I have proved that I am a (true) knight', the subject has to be supplied.
5 *men seide . . . bitraide*] Horn is referring to Fikenhild who had betrayed him by telling the king that he had seduced his daughter.
11 *baronage*] i. e. 'my kingdom'
30 *Sarazins*] 'Sarazins' also meant 'pirates'.

Þat wunieþ bieste, / Kniȝt wiþ þe beste.

Hi sloȝe wiþ here honde, / Þe king of þis londe,

35 And wiþ him fele hundred. / And þerof is wunder

Þat he ne comeþ to fiȝte: / God sende him þe riȝte,

And wind him hider driue, / To bringe hem of liue.

Hi sloȝen kyng Murry, / Hornes fader, king hendy,

Horn hi vt of londe sente; / Tuelf felaȝes wiþ him wente,

40 Among hem Aþulf þe gode, / Min oȝene child, my leue fode.

If Horn child is hol and sund, / And Aþulf wiþute wund,

He luueþ him so dere, / And is him so stere,

Miȝte iseon hem tueie, / For ioie i schulde deie."

    "Kniȝt, beo þanne bliþe, / Mest of alle siþe,

45 Horn and Aþulf his fere, / Boþe hi ben here."

To Horn he gan gon, / And grette him anon.

Muche ioie hi makede þere, / Þe while hi togadere were.

"Childre," he sede, "hu habbe ȝe fare? / Þat ihc ȝou seȝ hit is ful ȝare.

Wulle ȝe þis londe winne, / And sle þat þer is inne?"

50 He sede, "Leue Horn child, / Ȝutt lyueþ þi moder Godhild.

Of ioie he miste, / If heo þe aliue wiste."

    Horn sede on his rime, / "Iblessed beo þe time

I com to Suddene, / Wiþ mine Irisse menne.

We schulle þe hundes teche / To speken vre speche.

55 Alle we hem schulle sle, / And al quic hem fle."

Horn gan his horn to blowe; / His folk hit gan iknowe.

Hi comen vt of stere, / Fram Hornes banere.

Hi sloȝen and fuȝten, / Þe niȝt and þe vȝten.

Þe Sarazins cunde, / Ne lefde þer non in þende.

60 ˙ Horn let wurche / Chapeles and chirche;

He let belles ringe, / And masses let singe.

He com to his moder halle, / In a roche walle.

Corn he let serie, / And makede feste merie.

Murie lif he wroȝte; / Rymenhild hit dere boȝte.

65   Fikenhild was prut on herte, / And þat him dude smerte.

Ȝonge he ȝaf and elde, / Mid him for to helde.

Ston he dude lede, / Þer he hopede spede.

---

44 *Mest . . . siþe*] 'more than ever before'

48 *Þat ic . . . ful ȝare.*] 'I haven't seen you for a very long time'.

51 *Of . . . miste*] 'How happy would she be'

57 *stere . . . Hornes banere*] 'They came to the battlefield upon Horn's signal'.

59 *in þende*] 'in the end'

60–61 *wurche . . . singe*] Horn does this in order to consolidate his power and to restore the Christian faith.

63 *Corn . . . merie*] 'he allowed the corn to become dry (i. e. ripen) and then made a merry feast' (i. e. in celebration of the harvest).

64 *Murie . . . boȝte*] By remaining in his home country and celebrating his victory too long, Horn endangers Rymenhild.

67 *Ston . . . Þer*] 'he had stone brought to where'

Strong castel he let sette, / Mid see him biflette.

Þer ne miȝte liȝte / Bute foȝel wiþ fliȝte;

70 Bute whanne þe see wiþdroȝe, / Miȝte come men ynoȝe.

Fikenhild gan wende / Rymenhild to schende.

To woȝe he gan hure ȝerne; / Þe kyng ne dorste him werne.

Rymenhild was ful of mode; / He wep teres of blode.

Þat niȝt Horn gan swete, / And heuie for to mete

75 Of Rymenhild his make, / Into schupe was itake.

Þe schup bigan to blenche; / His lemman scholde adrenche.

Rymenhild wiþ hire honde / Wolde vp to londe.

Fikenhild aȝen hire pelte / Wiþ his swerdes hilte.

     Horn him wok of slape / So a man þat hadde rape.

80 "Aþulf," he sede, "felaȝe, / To schupe we mote draȝe.

Fikenhild me haþ idon vnder, / And Rymenhild to do wunder.

Crist, for his wundes fiue, / To niȝt me þuder driue."

Horn gan to schupe ride, / His feren him biside.

     Fikenhild, or þe dai gan springe, / Al riȝt he ferde to þe kinge,

85 After Rymenhild þe briȝte, / To wedden hire biniȝte.

He ladde hure bi þe derke, / Into his nywe werke.

Þe fest hi bigunne, / Er þat ros þe sunne.

Er þane Horn hit wiste, / To fore þe sunne vpriste.

His schup stod vnder ture, / At Rymenhilde bure.

90 Rymenhild, litel weneþ heo / Þat Horn þanne aliue beo.

Þe castel þei ne knewe, / For he was so nywe.

Horn fond sittinde Arnoldin, / Þat was Aþulfes cosin,

Þat þer was in þat tide, / Horn for tabide.

"Horn kniȝt," he sede, "kinges sone, / Wel beo þu to londe icome.

95 Today haþ ywedde Fikenhild, / Þi swete lemman, Rymenhild.

Ne schal i þe lie; / He haþ giled þe twie.

Þis tur he let make / Al for þine sake.

Ne mai þer come inne / Noman wiþ none ginne.

Horn, nu Crist þe wisse, / Of Rymenhild þat þu ne misse."

100   Horn cuþe al þe liste / Þat eni man of wiste.

Harpe he gan schewe, / And tok felaȝes fewe,

Of kniȝtes suiþe snelle, / Þat schrudde hem at wille.

Hi ȝeden bi þe grauel, / Toward þe castel.

Hi gunne murie singe, / And makede here gleowinge.

---

68 *Mid . . . biflette*] 'water would surround it'

69 *Þer . . . fliȝte*] 'Nothing could reach it, but a bird by flying.'

71 *gan wende*] 'began to'

73 *Rymenhild . . . mode*] 'Rymenhild was very angry'

74 *mete*] Horn's dream is parallel to a dream Rymenhild had, predicting Horn's separation from her, when Horn was staying at her father's court.

81 *And . . . wunder*] 'and wants to maltreat Rymenhild'

82 *for . . . fiue*] 'by his five wounds'

93 *Horn . . . tabide*] 'to wait for Horn'

102 *Þat . . . wille*] 'who dressed up as musicians according to Horn's wish.'

105   Rymenhild hit gan ihere, / And axede what hi were.
He sede hi weren harpurs, / And sume were gigours.
He dude Horn in late, / Riȝt at halle gate.
He sette him on þe benche, / His harpe for to clenche.
He makede Rymenhilde lay, / And heo makede walaway.
110 Rymenhild feol yswoȝe; / Ne was þer non þat louȝe.
Hit smot to Hornes herte / So bitere þat hit smerte.
He lokede on þe ringe, / And þoȝte on Rymenhilde.
He ȝede vp to borde, / Wiþ gode suerdes orde.
Fikenhildes crune / Þer ifulde adune,
115 And al his men arowe / Hi dude adun þrowe!
Whanne hi weren aslaȝe, / Fikenhild hi dude to-draȝe.
Horn makede Arnoldin þare / King, after king Aylmare,
Of al Westernesse, / For his meoknesse.
Þe king and his homage / Ȝeuen Arnoldin trewage.
120 Horn tok Rymenhild bi þe honde, / And ladde hure to þe stronde,
And ladde wiþ him Aþelbrus, / Þe gode stuard of his hus.
Þe se bigan to flowe, / And Horn gan to rowe.
Hi gunne for ariue / Þer king Modi was sire.
Aþelbrus he makede þer king, / For his gode teching.
125 He ȝaf alle þe kniȝtes ore, / For Horn kniȝtes lore.
Horn gan for to ride; / Þe wind him bleu wel wide.
He ariuede in Yrlonde, / Þer he wo fondede.
Þer he dude Aþulf child, / Wedden maide Reynild.
Horn com to Suddene, / Among al his kenne.
130 Rymenhild he makede his quene, / So hit miȝte wel beon;

---

104 *And . . . gleowinge*] 'and made their merriment'
106 *harpurs . . . gigours*] Minstrels were always welcome at court. Horn and his companions
  are able to play an instrument since musical training was part of a courtly education.
109 *And . . . walaway*] 'and she sang a song of woe.'
110 *feol yswoȝe*] 'fell into a swoon'
112 *ringe*] Rymenhild had given Horn a magic ring to protect him as well as remind him of
  her.
113 *Wiþ . . . orde*] 'with the point of a good sword'
114 *crune*] This could also be an ironic reference to line 13.
116 *Fikenhild . . . to-draȝe*] 'he had Fikenhild drawn and quartered'.
117 *after king Aylmare*] i. e. King Almaire's successor
119 *Þe king . . . trewage*] 'King Aylmar and his retinue swore loyalty to Arnoldin'.
121 *Aþelbrus*] actually Almair's steward and Horn's teacher
123 *king Modi*] While Horn was in Ireland, King Modi had asked for Rymenhild's hand in
  marriage; Horn arrived just in time to prevent the marriage.
125 *He . . . lore*] 'He (Aþelbrus) honoured all knights on account of Horn'.
127 *Þer . . . fondede*] 'where he had found woe'. This probably refers to Horn's battle against
  the Saracen general who had killed his father. In the same battle both of the Irish king's sons
  were killed. While in Ireland, Horn also learned about King Modi's suit for Rymenhild.
128 *maide Reynild*] the King of Ireland's daughter
130 *So . . . beon*] 'so all might be well'

Al folk hem miȝte rewe, / Þat loueden hem so trewe.
Nu ben hi boþe dede; / Crist to heuene hem lede.
Her endeþ þe tale of Horn / Þat fair was and noȝt vnorn.
Make we vs glade eure among, / For þus him endeþ Hornes song.

135 Jesus þat is of heuene king, / Ȝeue vs alle his suete blessing.
Explicit.   Amen.

---

131 *Al folk . . . trewe*] 'They could devote their attention to the people who truly loved them'.
134 *him*] 'him' should not be translated.

Text 10: Middle English Lyric Poetry

The development of 'lyrical poetry' in England came somewhat later than on the Continent. Because the court and upper echelons of the clergy in England were Norman or French up into the 14th century, the French poetic tradition was used exclusively for this audience. Under King Henry II (1154–1189) and his wife Queen Eleonore of Aquitaine, the Anglo-Angevin court was even considered to be a hub of Old French and Old Provençal literary culture. It was not until the Hundred Years' War (1337–1453) and the Black Death pandemic (the first waves beginning in the 1340s) that the English language began to be used for courtly literary composition. The Hundred Years' War led to a national division between the 'English' and the 'French'; at the same time, with the plague decimating the lower classes, the need for workers, who spoke primarily English, rose. Although English had already begun to rise again as the official language in England, these two events hurried the process, and English began to be seen as a language fit for all classes.

Although religious poetry had begun to develop earlier, England only began to develop a courtly lyric tradition beginning in the 14th century, and the secular or courtly tradition never quite equalled the religious tradition. Middle English Lyrics are mostly anonymous, and we have no large collections dedicated entirely to poetry, as is the case on the Continent. A notable exception is MS Harley 2253 of the British Library, in which over half of the lyrics we still have today are preserved.

The *Harley manuscript* (named so after its owner, Robert Harley of Oxford) is a miscellany, containing not only lyrics, but also whatever else was of interest to the compiler, including Latin and Anglo-Norman works, saints' lives, a version of *King Horn* (see M 9) some fabliaux, and even a few recipes. The manuscript can be assigned to the early 14th century and many of the lyrics contributed by one scribe, show the major characteristics of the West Midlands dialect. However, evidence of other dialects can sometimes be seen in the rhyme schemes.

The Harley lyrics are mostly iambic, with two to seven stresses per line. They have a wide variety of rhyme schemes, including mono-rhymed stanzas and tail and end-rhymes, but there are also some cases of alliteration. Alliteration was either used occasionally as a stylistic device (in *The Way of Woman's Love*, alliteration is used in hendiadys, ll. 24 and 26: "wyþ *h*aþeles and wyþ *h*eowes . . . wiþ *g*omenes ant wiþ *g*leowes") or consistently throughout the whole poem (for example, in *The Lover's Complaint*: "Wiþ *l*ongyng y am *l*ad / on *m*olde y waxe *m*ad . . ."), though not following the Old English alliterative system.

An attempt to differentiate between more than two genres of Middle English Lyrics, namely secular and religious, is almost impossible; the terminology used for the various genres in Middle High German, Old French or Old Provençal is based on medieval genre descriptions from these countries, which we hardly have in Middle English. A better model for Middle English consists of a thematic division.

Religious Lyrics are dedicated to four main themes: Christ, Mary, life and death, and the transience of earthly matters, which includes the typical *contemptus mundi* (contempt for the world), *memento mori* ('remember you will have to die') and *ubi sunt* ('where are our forefathers') motifs. A further theme is the adoration of saints and angels. Within these groups, one can further differentiate between *spiritual* and *emotional* tones in which the lyrics are written. This can include praise, love, thanks, instruction, complaint, pity, regret, repentance, pleas, invocation, exhortation, instruction or compassion. The lyrics can also be analysed based upon the social background of the author or the theological or historical conventions.

Secular Lyrics can be divided into love lyrics, political lyrics and lyrics for special occasions. Love lyrics can be further divided into praise, joy, complaint, melancholy, mourning and admonition. Political lyrics can be divided into historical lyrics (celebrating war or battles), as well as political or social tendencies, including debates, grievances or criticism of institutions.

The following ten lyrics are a selection from both categories. The first two poems can be classified as love complaints, the third as a love admonition or warning. Most of the remaining lyrics are religious; the fourth is dedicated to Christ, the fifth to Mary. The sixth poem is a meditative or exhorting lyric in view of Christ's Passion. The seventh and the eighth lyric are both examples of *contrafactum*, or parody. Which of these poems was composed first, unfortunately, cannot be determined.

The last two lyrics (carols) clearly show that obscenity can be found in the Middle Ages just as well as in modern times. The use of metaphors in both poems is very intricate and its main purpose is to mask the high degree of obscenity. While the ninth poem points out the lot of foolish women, i. e. pregnancy, and can thus be seen as a warning against folly, the tenth poem is written in a very different spirit. Sexual activities are the major theme of the poem, as well as the (stereotypical) young maiden, apparently enjoying the 'game' and unable to say no.

The reflex of Old English *ā* is written <o> in all poems. Old English *ȳ* is written <u>, as in *lutel* (1.2, 7.1, 8.1), *sunne* (4.45; 7.33; 8.13 etc.), as is also Old English *y̆*, as in *murgeþ* (3.1), *vmbe* (3.33). All these features are characteristic of the (south) West Midlands. – *LALME* on MS Harley 2253: Linguistic Profile 9260, Herefordshire; St. John's College Cambridge 259: Linguistic Profile 8680, Norfolk

Sources: British Library, London, MS Harley 2253. – St. John's College, Cambridge MS 259. – Huntington Library MS EL. 1160. – Brook (1968); Böddeker (1878), Luria/Hoffman (1974); Robbins (1964), Stemmler (1970), Green (1977). – Secondary literature: Moore (1951), Woolf (1968), Reiss (1972), Bergner (1983), Wenzel (1986), Bayless (2009). – Facsimile: Ker (1965).

1   *Alysoun*

Bytuene Mersh ant Aueril / when spray biginneþ to springe,
þe lutel foul haþ hire wyl / on hyre lud to synge.
Ich libbe in loue-longinge / for semlokest of alle þynge;
he may me blisse bringe; / icham in hire baundoun.

5   An hendy hap ichabbe yhent, / ichot from heuene it is me sent;
from alle wymmen mi loue is lent, / ant lyht on Alysoun.

---

1 *Mersh ant Aueril*] The poem starts out with a typical spring setting; see also M 13.
5–6 *An hendy . . . Alysoun*] These lines are a refrain. Refrains are fairly common in medieval lyrics. All subsequent refrains have been shortened.

On heu hire her is fayr ynoh, / hire browe broune, hire eʒe blake;
wiþ lossum chere he on me loh, / wiþ middel smal ant wel ymake.
Bote he me wolle to hire take / forte buen hire owen make
10   longe to lyuen ichulle forsake / ant feye fallen adoun.   An hendy hap, &c.

Nihtes when y wende ant wake, / forþi myn wonges waxeþ won;
leuedi, al for þine sake / longinge is ylent me on.
In world is non so wyter mon / þat al hire bounte telle con;
hire swyre is whittore þen þe swon, / ant feyrest may in toune.   An hendi, &c.

15   Icham for wowyng al forwake, / wery so water in wore,
lest eny reue me my make / ychabbe yʒyrned ʒore.
Betere is þolien whyle sore / þen mournen euermore.
Geynest vnder gore, / herkne to my roun.   An hendi, &c.

2   *The Lover's Complaint*

Wiþ longyng y am lad, / on molde y waxe mad, / a maide marreþ me;
y grede, y grone, vnglad, / for selden y am sad / þat semly forte se. Leuedi,
þou rewe me! / To rouþe þou hauest me rad. / Be bote of þat y bad; / my
lyf is long on þe. / Leuedy of alle londe, / les me out of bonde; / broht
5   icham in wo. / Haue resting on honde, / ant sent þou me þi sonde / sone, er
þou me slo; / my reste is wiþ þe ro. / Þah men to me han onde, / to loue
nuly noht wonde, / ne lete for non of þo. / Leuedi, wiþ al my miht / my
loue is on þe liht, / to menske when y may; / þou rew ant red me ryht,
to deþe þou hauest me diht, / y deʒe longe er my day; / þou leue vpon
10   my lay; / treuþe ichaue þe plyht / to don þat ich haue hyht / whil
mi lif leste may. / Lylie-whyt hue is, / hire rode so rose on rys, / þat
reueþ me mi rest; / wymmon war ant wys, / of prude hue bereþ þe pris,
burde on of þe best. / Þis wommon woneþ by west, / brihtest
vnder bys; / heuene y tolde al his / þat o nyht were hire gest.

7–8 *On heu . . . ymake*] A typical 'descriptio pulchritudinis': hair, eyes, eyebrows, smile, waist
   and neck are described.
9 *forte . . . make*] 'so that I can be her lover'
11 *wende*] ambiguous: 'I roll around in bed' or 'I walk about (sleepless)'
14 *ant*] read: 'ant she is'
18 *Geynest . . . gore*] 'nicest of all women' literally: 'nicest in a skirt'

2 *for . . . se*] 'I can't get enough of seeing her'.
3 *Be bote . . . bad*] 'be the fulfillment of my longings'
4 *is . . . þe*] 'my life is in your hands'
6 *my reste . . . ro*] 'I'm as restless as a roe deer'.
6 *Þah . . . onde*] 'even when someone hates me'
8 *menske*] read: 'to love you'
13–14 *brihtest . . . bys*] 'most beautiful woman'
14 *heuene . . . gest*] 'Whoever may spend a night with her, would possess heaven completely, I
   think'.

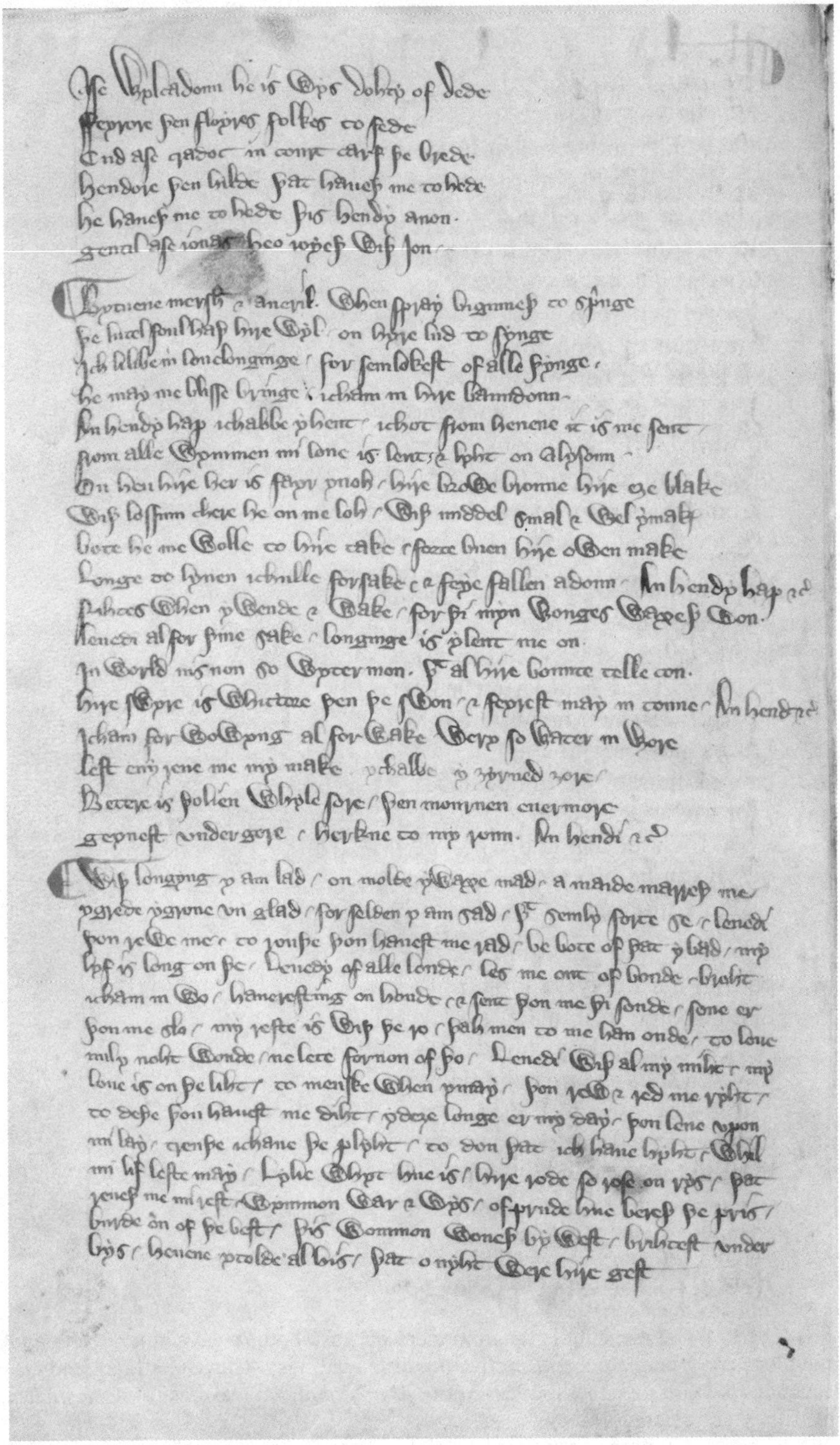

Ase Wyrseldom he is wys dohty of dede
Feyrore þen floyres folkes to fede
Ant ase Gadorn in court carf þe brede.
Hendore þen Hilde þat haueþ me to hede
He haueþ me to hede þis hendy anon.
Gentil ase Ionas heo ioyeþ wiþ Jon.

Bytuene mersh ant aueril. when spray biginneþ to springe
þe lutel foul haþ hire wyl on hyre lud to synge
Ich libbe in louelonginge for semlokest of alle þynge.
he may me blisse bringe. icham in hire baundoun.
An hendy hap ichabbe yhent ichot from heuene it is me sent
from alle wymmen mi loue is lent ant lyht on alysoun
On heu hire her is fayr ynoh hire browe broune hire eȝe blake
wiþ lossum chere he on me loh wiþ middel smal ant wel ymake
bote he me wolle to hire take for te buen hire owen make
longe to lyuen ichulle forsake ant feye fallen adoun. An hendy hap etc.
Nihtes when y wende ant wake for þi myn wonges waxeþ won.
leuedi al for þine sake longinge is ylent me on.
In world nis non so wyter mon. þat al hire bounte telle con.
hire swyre is whittore þen þe swon ant feyrest may in toune. An hendi etc.
Icham for wowyng al forwake wery so water in wore
lest eny reue me my make ychabbe y ȝyrned ȝore
Betere is þolien whyle sore þen mournen euermore
geynest vnder gore herkne to my roun. An hendi etc.

Wiþ longyng y am lad on molde y waxe mad a maide marreþ me
y grede y grone vnglad for selden y am sad þat semly forte se. leuedi
þou rewe me. to rouþe þou hauest me rad be bote of þat y bad my
lyf is long on þe. leuedy of alle londe les me out of bonde broht
icham in wo haue reste on honde ant sent þou me þi sonde sone er
þou me slo my reste is wiþ þe ro þah men to me han onde to loue
nuly noht wonde ne lete for non of þo. Leuedi wiþ al my miht my
loue is on þe liht to menske when y may þou rew ant red me ryht
to deþe þou hauest me diht y deye longe er my day þou leue vpon
mi lay treuþe ichaue þe plyht to don þat ich haue hyht whil
mi lif leste may. Lylie whyt hue is hire rode so rose on rys þat
reueþ me mi rest wymmon war ant wys of prude hue bereþ þe pris
burde on of þe best þis wommon woneþ by west brihtest vnder
bys heuene y tolde al his þat o nyht were hire gest

3 *Advice to Women*

In May hit murgeþ when hit dawes
in dounes wiþ þis dueres plawes,
   ant lef is lyht on lynde;
blosmes bredeþ on þe bowes,
5   al þis wylde wyhtes wowes,
   so wel ych vnderfynde.
Y not non so freoli flour
ase ledies þat beþ bryht in bour,
   wiþ loue who mihte hem bynde;
10   so worly wymmen are by west;
one of hem ich herie best
   from Irlond into Ynde.

Wymmen were þe beste þing
þat shup oure heȝe heuene kyng,
15   ȝef feole false nere;
heo beoþ to rad vpon huere red
to loue þer me hem lastes bed
   when heo shule fenge fere.
Lut in londe are to leue,
20   þah me hem trewe trouþe ȝeue,
   for tricherie to ȝere,
when trichour haþ is trouþe yplyht,
byswyken he haþ þat suete wyht,
   þah he hire oþes swere.

25   Wymmon, war þe wiþ þe swyke,
þat feir ant freoly ys to fyke;
   ys fare is o to founde;
so wyde in world ys huere won
in vch a toune vntrewe is on
30   from Leycestre to Lounde.
Of treuþe nis þe trichour noht,
bote he habbe is wille ywroht
   at steuenyng vmbe stounde;
ah, feyre leuedis, be on war,

---

2 *þis dueres plawes*] i. e. mating rituals among animals
15 *feole*] i. e. 'many men'
16–18 *heo . . . fere*] The meaning is far from clear because both *fenge* and *fere* can be taken as
either noun or verb. There are therefore two possible readings: 'They are all too ready (by their
own account ('red')) to give themselves over to love's (sinful) pleasures (a) if they can catch a
man (b) if they are offered money'.
19–21 *Lut . . . ȝere*] 'There are few (men in this country) you can believe, even if you trust
them completely, for they only think of betrayal'.
25 *war þe wiþ*] 'beware of'
33 *at . . . stounde*] 'at every lover's tryst'

35 to late comeþ þe ȝeynchar
   when loue ou haþ ybounde.

  Wymmen bueþ so feyr on hewe
  ne trowy none þat nere trewe,
   ȝef trichour hem ne tahte;
40 ah, feyre þinges, freoly bore,
  when me ou woweþ, beþ war bifore
   whuch is worldes ahte.
  Al to late is send aȝeyn
  when þe ledy liht byleyn
45   ant lyueþ by þat he lahte;
  ah wolde lylie-leor in lyn
  yhere leuely lores myn,
   wiþ selþe we weren sahte.

---

43 *send aȝeyn*] 'to go back'
44 *when ... byleyn*] 'when she has already given herself to him'
45 *ant ... lahte*] *he* could be masculine or feminine; meaning: 'and lives on prostitution'
48 *we*] 'we' applies to both genders: 'then we (men and women) could live happily and in peace'.

4 *A Spring Song on the Passion*

When y se blosmes springe
  ant here foules song,
a suete loue-longynge
  myn herte þourhout stong,
al for a loue newe,
þat is so suete ant trewe,
  þat gladieþ al my song;
ich wot al myd iwisse
my ioie ant eke my blisse
  on him is al ylong.

When y miselue stonde
  ant wiþ myn eȝen seo
þurled fot ant honde
  wiþ grete nayles threo –
blody wes ys heued,
on him nes nout bileued
  þat wes of peynes freo –
wel wel ohte myn herte
for his loue to smerte
  ant sike ant sory beo.

Iesu, milde ant softe,
  ȝef me streynþe ant myht
longen sore ant ofte
  to louye þe aryht,
pyne to þolie ant dreȝe
for þe, swete Marye;
  þou art so fre and bryht,
mayden ant moder mylde,
for loue of þine childe,
  ernde vs heuene lyht.

Alas, þat y ne con
  turne to him my þoht
ant cheosen him to lemmon;
  so duere he vs haþ yboht,
wiþ woundes deope ant stronge,
wiþ peynes sore ant longe;
  of loue ne conne we noht.
His blod þat feol to grounde

1–2 *blosmes springe... foules song*] The spring setting and the awakening of love are a convention adopted from secular love poetry.
10 *on him... ylong*] 'depends entirely on him'
16–17 *on... freo*] 'there was no part left on his body that was free of pain'.

of his suete wounde
40   of peyne vs haþ yboht.

Iesu, milde ant suete,
    y synge þe mi song;
ofte y þe grete
    ant preye þe among;
45 let me sunnes lete,
ant in þis lyue bete
    þat ich haue do wrong;
at oure lyues ende,
when we shule wende,
50   Iesu, vs vndefong!
            Amen.

---

39 *suete wounde*] 'sweet (i. e. precious) wound' is a traditional oxymoron.

5   *The Five Joys of the Virgin*

Ase y me rod þis ender day
by grene wode to seche play,
mid herte y þohte al on a may,
   suetest of alle þinge.
5   Lyþe, ant ich ou telle may
   al of þat suete thinge.

Þis maiden is suete ant fre of blod,
briht and feyr, of milde mod,
alle heo mai don vs god
10   þurh hire bysechynge;
of hire he tok fleysh ant blod,
   Iesus heuene kynge.

Wiþ al mi lif y loue þat may,
he is mi solas nyht ant day,
15   my ioie ant eke my beste play,
   ant eke my louelongynge;
al þe betere me is þat day
   þat ich of hire synge.

Of alle þinge y loue hire mest,
20   my dayes blis, my nyhtes rest,
heo counseileþ ant helpeþ best
   boþe elde ant ȝynge;
nou y may ȝef y wole
   þe fif ioyes mynge.

25   Þe furst ioie of þat wymman
when Gabriel from heuene cam
ant seide God shulde bicome man
   ant of hire be bore,
ant bringe vp of helle pyn
30   monkyn þat wes forlore.

Þat oþer ioie of þat may
wes o Cristesmasse day,
when God wes bore on þoro lay
   ant brohte vs lyhtnesse;

---

1 *þis ender day*] 'recently'
2 *by grene wode*] the topos 'locus amoenus' is adopted from secular love poetry.
7 *fre of blod*] 'of noble blood'
26 *Gabriel*] see Luke 1:26–31
33 *on þoro lay*] 'in blinding light'

35   þe ster wes seie byfore day,
       þis hirdes bereþ wytnesse.

     Þe þridde ioie of þat leuedy,
     þat men clepeþ þe Epyphany,
     when þe kynges come wery
40   to presente hyre sone
     wiþ myrre, gold, ant encenȝ,
       þat wes mon bicome.

     Þe furþe ioie we telle mawen
     on Estermorewe when hit gon dawen,
45   hyre sone, þat wes slawen,
       aros in fleysh ant bon;
     more ioie ne mai me hauen,
       wyf ne mayden non.

     Þe fifte ioie of þat wymman
50   when hire body to heuene cam,
     þe soule to þe body nam,
       ase hit wes woned to bene.
     Crist, leue vs alle wiþ þat wymman
       þat ioie al forte sene.

55   Preye we alle to oure leuedy,
     ant to þe sontes þat woneþ hire by,
     þat heo of vs hauen merci,
       ant þat we ne misse
     in þis world to ben holy
60   ant wynne heuene blysse.
         Amen.

---

38 *Epyphany*] the feast of Epiphany (January 6th)
41 *myrre . . . encenȝ*] see Matthew 2:11

6 *I Syke When Y Singe*

I syke when y singe
   for sorewe þat y se
when y wiþ wypinge
   biholde vpon þe tre
5 ant se Iesu þe suete
is herte blod forlete
   for þe loue of me;
ys woundes waxen wete,
þei wepen stille ant mete.
10   Marie, reweþ þe.

Heȝe vpon a doune,
   þer al folk hit se may,
a mile from vch toune,
   aboute þe midday,
15 þe rode is vp arered,
his frendes aren afered,
   ant clyngeþ so þe clay.
Þe rode stond in stone;
Marie stont hire one,
20   and seiþ 'Weylaway!'

When y þe biholde
   wiþ euȝen bryhte bo
ant þi bodi colde –
   þi ble waxeþ blo,
25 þou hengest al of blode
so heȝe vpon þe rode,
   bituene þeues tuo –
who may syke more?
Marie wepeþ sore
30   and siht al þis wo.

Þe naylles beþ to stronge,
   þe smyþes are to sleye,
þou bledest al to longe,
   þe tre is al to heyȝe,
35 þe stones beoþ al wete.
Alas! Iesu, þe suete,
   for nou frend hast þou non

---

17 *clyngeþ so þe clay*] literally 'are shrinking as clay', i. e. the number of friends decreases.
19 *hire one*] 'alone'
27 *þeues tuo*] see Matthew 27:38 and Mark 15:27

bote seint Iohan mournynde
ant Marie wepynde
40   for pyne þat þe ys on.

Ofte when y sike
   ant makie my mon,
wel ille þah me like
   wonder is hit non,
45 when y se honge heʒe
ant bittre pynes dreʒe
   Iesu, me lemmon,
his wondes sore smerte,
þe spere al to is herte
50   ant þourh is sydes gon.

Ofte when y syke,
   wiþ care y am þourhsoht;
when y wake, y wyke,
   of serewe is al mi þoht.
55 Alas! Men beþ wode
þat suereþ by þe rode
   ant selleþ him for noht
þat bohte vs out of synne.
He bring vs to wynne
60   þat haþ vs duere boht.

38–39 *seint Iohan . . . Marie*] see John 19:24–27
59 *wynne*] i. e. the joys of paradise

7 *The Way of Christ's Love*

Lvtel wot hit any mon
  hou loue hym haueþ ybounde
þat for vs o þe rode ron
  ant bohte vs wiþ is wounde.
5   Þe loue of him vs haueþ ymaked sounde,
  ant ycast þe grimly gost to grounde.
Euer ant oo, nyht ant day, he haueþ vs in is þohte;
he nul nout leose þat he so deore bohte.

He bohte vs wiþ is holy blod;
  what shulde he don vs more?
10 He is so meoke, milde, ant good,
  he nagulte nout þerfore.
  Þat we han ydon, y rede we reowen sore
  ant crien euer to Iesu, 'Crist, þyn ore!'
15 Euer ant oo, niht ant day, &c.

He seh his fader so wonder wroht
  wiþ mon þat wes yfalle,
wiþ herte sor he seide is oht
  we shulde abuggen alle.
20 His suete sone to hym gon clepe ant calle,
  ant preiede he moste deye for vs alle.
Euer ant oo, &c.

He brohte vs alle from þe deþ
  and dude vs frendes dede.
25 Suete Iesu of Naȝareth,
  þou do vs heuene mede.
  Vpon þe rode why nulle we taken hede?
  His grene wounde so grimly conne blede.
Euer ant oo, &c.

30 His deope wounden bledeþ fast;
  of hem we ohte munne.
He haþ ous out of helle ycast,
  ybroht vs out of sunne.
  ffor loue of vs his wonges waxeþ þunne;
35 his herte blod he ȝef for al monkunne.
Euer ant oo, &c.

---

3 *þat . . . ron*] 'who bled for us on the cross'
16 *so . . . wroht*] 'was so wrathful'
18 *he . . . oht*] 'he swore his oath'.
28 *grene wounde*] 'fresh wound'

8 *The Way of Woman's Love*

Lutel wot hit any mon
 hou derne loue may stonde,
bote hit were a fre wymmon
 þat muche of loue had fonde.
5   Þe loue of hire ne lesteþ nowyht longe;
heo haueþ me plyht ant wyteþ me wyþ wronge.
Euer ant oo for my leof icham in grete þohte;
y þenche on hire þat y ne seo nout ofte.

Y wolde nemne hyre to-day
10   ant y dorste hire munne;
heo is þat feireste may
 of vch ende of hire kunne;
 bote heo me loue, of me heo haues sunne.
Wo is him þat loueþ þe loue þat he ne may ner ywynne.
15 Euer ant oo, &c.

Adoun y fel to hire anon
 ant crie, 'Ledy, þyn ore!
Ledy, ha mercy of þy mon!
 Lef þou no false lore!
20   Ʒef þou dost, hit wol me reowe sore.
 Loue dreccheþ me þat y ne may lyue namore.'
Euer ant oo, &c.

Mury hit ys in hyre tour
 wyþ haþeles and wyþ heowes.
25 So hit is in hyre bour,
 wiþ gomenes ant wiþ gleowes.
 Bote heo me louye, sore hit wol me rewe.
 Wo is him þat loueþ þe loue þat ner nul be trewe.
Euer ant oo, &c.

30 ffayrest fode vpo loft,
 my gode luef, y þe grééte
ase fele syþe ant oft
 as dewes dropes beþ wééte,
 as sterres beþ in welkne ant grases sour ant suete.
35   Whose loueþ vntrewe, his herte is selde sééte.
Euer ant oo, &c.

11–12 *heo . . . kunne*] 'her beauty surpasses all others'.
30 *ffayrest . . . loft*] 'most beautiful of all women'

9 *A, dere God*

A, dere God, qwat I am fayn,
For I am madyn now gane.

Þis enþer day I mete a clerke,
And he was wylly in his werke;
5   He prayd me with hym to herke;
   And hys cownsell all for to layne.

I trow he cowd of gramery,
I xall now telle a good skyll wy;
For qwat I hade siccurly,
10   To warne hys wyll had I no mayn.

Qwan he and me browt un us þe schete,
Of all hys wyll I hym lete;
Now wyll not my gyrdyll met –
   A, dere God, quat xal I sayn?

15   I xall sey to man and page
Þat I haue bene of pylgrymage;
Now wyll I not lete for no rage
   With me a clerk for to pley.

---

7 *gramery*] the reference is to 'grammar'; however, the meaning is probably 'magic'.
11 *browt un us the schete*] 'when we were between the sheets'
13 *Now ... gyrdyll met*] 'Now my belt is too short', i. e. 'I am pregnant'.
16 *pylgrymage*] see M 7/52 where 'pilgrimage' and 'whoring' go hand in hand.

10 *Sir John*

Hey, noyney!
I wyll loue our Ser John and I loue eny.

O Lord, so swett Ser John dothe kys
  At euery tyme when he wolde pley;
Off hym-selfe so plesant he ys:
  I haue no powre to say hym nay.

Ser John loues me, and I loue hym:
  The more I loue hym the more I maye;
He says, 'Swett hart, cum kys me trym':
  I haue no powre to say him nay.

Ser John to me is proferyng
  For hys plesure ryght well to pay,
And in my box he puttes hys offryng:
  I haue no powre to say hym nay.

Ser John ys taken in my mouse-trappe;
  Fayne wold I haue hem bothe nyght and day;
He gropith so nyslye abought my lape,
  I haue no powre to say hym nay.

Ser John geuyth me reluys rynges,
  With praty plesure for to assay,
Furres off the fynest with othyr thynges:
  I haue no powre to say hym nay.

---

13 *in my box . . . hys offryng;*] The literal meaning of 'box' is 'offertory box'; the contextual
  meaning, however, is probably both 'savings box' and 'vagina'.
15 *mouse-trappe*] the rhyme on 'lape' suggests a euphemistic reference: 'vagina'.

Text 11: The Northern Homily Cycle

The Northern Homily Cycle is a series of sermons, intended to be delivered on
Sundays and feast days. Three different versions remain: the 'Original or Unexpanded
Northern Homily Collection', dating from around 1320. A second expanded version in
the West Midlands dialect dates from the 14th century, and the final 'Expanded
Northern Homily Collection' from the late 14th century.

According to the prologue of the first version, the anonymous editor's intentions
were to create instructive Sunday sermons for a laity that could understand neither
Latin nor French. The sermons in *The Northern Homily Cycle* are quite varied and
range from Sunday sermon to feast day sermons, and can be a short exposition of a
biblical text or a well-developed 'story'. In any case, this can be followed by a further
story, which is intended to help illustrate the message of the first part of the text. This
can in turn include many genres, including exemplum, saint's life or even fable.

The following text begins with an exposition, taken from Luke 18:9–14, about the
sin of pride and the importance of humility. This is followed by a 'Life of King
Oswald', an exemplum. The 'Life of Oswald' in this sermon, intended to be read on
the 11th Sunday after Trinity, differs substantially from the Old English *Oswald* (O 6)
or the historian Bede's account of Oswald. King Oswald's chaste marriage is not
mentioned in the Old English sources, which focus rather on his martyrdom and the
miracles which occurred thereafter. The first reference to Oswald's chaste marriage
comes in 1165, in the Oswald-Vita by the monk Reginald. The Middle High German
Münchener Oswald (late 12th century) mentions the tub of water used to ensure that
Oswald and his wife remain chaste, which also bears certain similarities to the
practices of the Cistercian monks. The closest source for our Middle English *Oswald*
is an exemplum from the *Breslau Manuscript* (the manuscript is from the 14th
century, but the exempla probably date from the 12th century). In this edition, the
hermit is not tested by Oswald's wife, and instead of a tub of water, the bed is filled
with nettles. Exactly how these motifs were able to reach England from the Continent
is not clear.

The sermon printed here, beginning at line 17212 of the cycle, is almost complete;
only the short closing section has been omitted.

The reflex of Old English *ā* in rhyming words is written <a> and, in non-rhyming
position, occasionally <o>, as in *more* (l. 12, 27, 45 etc.), *none* (l. 43, 86, 113 etc.).
Since the present participle ends in *-and*, as in *sighand* (l. 18), *wonand* (l. 37, 39),
gapeand (l. 46), *swimand* (l. 48), *wakeand* (l. 93), this is clearly a northern text. –
According to *LALME* on MS Harley 4196, it is "NME" (Northern Middle English).

Sources: British Library, London, MS Harley 4196. – Nevanlinna (1972). – Secondary
literature: Gerould (1905).

Dominica xj estatis secundum Lucam

Dixit Jesus ad quosdam.

In oure godspel Saint Luke vs leres / No man be prowd vntill his peres,
Bot meke and bowsum to all men, / Als Crist will be ensaumple ken
How twa men into þe temple ȝede / At pray to God for þaire misdede.
A phariseu þan was þat ane, / And þat oþer a puplicane.
5 Þe phariseu made his prayere / To God of heuin on this manere:
Deus, gracias ago tibi quia non sum &c. /
"I thank þe, God of heuyn-rike, / Þat I am noght till other like,
Þat lifes in sin of litchery / And vses oþer sere foly, /
To rob and reue and men to sla; / I loue þe, I am nane of þa,
10 Ne I am noght so sinful man / Als es þis sinfull puplican.
I fast twa dayes in ilk a woke; / To gif my tithes lely I luke
Of all my mobils more and les / And of all catell, þat mine es."
   Þe puplicane, bihind he stode / With meke hert and drery mode,
And sarily himself gan mene / Þat he so sinful man had bene.
15 His eghen vp wald he noght lift, / For to ask of God no gift,
So held he himself foul and ill. / On breste he knokked with gude will
Sighand sare with simpill chere / And praied to God on þis manere:
Deus, propicius esto michi peccatori.
He said: "Lord, of me haue mercy, / For a ful sinful man am I."
20 Þus praied he both with hert and hend / Mekely his mis to amend;
Þarfore sais Crist, þat in þat stede / God herd ful wele his bowsum bede.
And vnto his hows went he þan, / Resaiued of God als rightwis man,
Bot so was noght herd his felaws, / Þat rosed and praied so with prowd saus,
For he þat makes himseluen highe / In word or werk or sight of eghe
25 And hethely think of ilk felaw, / I sai ȝow, he sall be made law;
And he þat mekes himself with will / He sall be heghind, als it es skill.
On þis word endis oure godspell, / Bot what it menes, more will I tell.

Exposicio super eundem

Þis phariseu, als sais Saint Bede, / Es man þat here dose haly dede
And kastes out al þat he dose / With pride in hert and euil rose,
30 And makes him better þan he es, / For þat in him es no mekenes.
In his praier he may noght spede; / With grete wordes he gettes no mede.
Þarfore þis haly man vs redes / Þat men be bowsum in þaire bedes
And hald noght here þamseluen slike / Þat nane oþer may be þam like,
For so ane hermite sumtyme wend, / Als by a tale here may be kend.

---

6 *Deus. . . sum*] see Luke 18:11
18 *Deus . . . peccatori*] see Luke 18:13
26 *mekes . . . heghind*] see Luke 18:14
28 *Saint Bede*] the Venerable Bede; see O 3 (introduction)

De vita Sancti Oswaldi regis

35 In Ingland in elder dawse / War seuyn kinges, als clerkes knaws;
In Bamburn in Northhumberland / Was ane of þa seuyn wonand,
Þat Saint Oswalde named es now, / And worthi wele, als we sall trow.
In his land was wonand þan / Ane ermit, halden a haly man.
When he had wond þare threty ȝere, / He wend no man might be his pere
40 Þat in so haly life war stad; / Þarfore in hert sum pride he had.
Prowd bigan he so to be, / Þat no man was so haly als he.
He thankid God, for he was slike, / Þat none in þe land was him like.
For he himself þus haly held, / God ordand, that his pride was feld.
    A day he sat biside a brim, / Twa fissches saw he swithly swim.
45 Þe more folowd þe less to gete, / Gapeand, als he wald him ette;
And als God wald miracle mak, / Right als two men þe fissches spak.
Þe les said swimand to þe mare: / "Frende, I prai þe, me to spare
For þis haly hermites lufe / Þat syttes here on þe bank oboue."
Þe more answerd and said in hy: / "For his luf noght spare will I,
50 Bot to my mete I will þe mak." / And þan þe les eft to him spak:
"For king Oswald luf," said he, / "I pray þe now, thou will spare me."
When þis was said, he lete him pas; / Þe hermit þan awonderd was,
How any king with realte / Might be in better life þan he,
Sen king had will of welth and wife, / And he in pouert led his life.
55   In þe way hamward als he was sett / With þe king Oswald he mett;
And when þe king of him had sight, / Downe of his palfray gan he light
·And hailsed him with louting doune, / And asked of him his benissowne,
For haliest man þe folk him held, / Þat þan in all þat cuntre dweld.
Þe king asked, if he oght walde, / And sone þe hermit to him talde,
60 How he herd of þe fissches strife, / And seþin he frayned of his life.
Þe king kid, he was meke of mode. / "In me," he said, "es nothing gude.
I lede my life in iolite, / With solace sere, als þou may se.
Al welth I haue of werldes win. / And in myself es noght bot syn."
Þe hermit said: "Þat may noght be; / And for his luf, þat died on tre,
65 Lat me þi life all halely wit, / To tak me ensaumpill of it,
For, sertes, I wate ful weterly, / Þat þou ert halier man þan I;
And þat es meruaile vnto me, / Þarfore þi life þou lat me se."
Þe king, to wit, what he wald mene, / Bad, he suld wend to þe quene,
And said: "Haue here my gold ring / And bere with þe vnto tokining,
70 And bid hir wirk right so with þe, / Als scho es wont to wirk with me."
    Þan went þe hermit to þe quene / And talde his takin þam bitwene.
Scho welkumd him with gude entent / And to a chaumber with him scho went.

---

48 *For . . . lufe*] 'for the sake of the holy hermit'
57 *And . . . doune*]'and welcomed him by kneeling down'
61 *Þe king . . . of mode*] freely: 'the king said meekly'
71 *takin þam bitwene*] 'the well-known token'
72 *Scho . . . entent*] 'she received him in a friendly way'.

In kinges wede sune was he cledd, / And to þe hall þe quene him led.
Knightes, squiers obout him drogh; / Ladis and maydens faire inogh.

75 He wessche and was sett sone on dese, / And serued with many mainsum mese.
Gude wane þare was of brede and wine, / And riche seruis of þe kitchine.
Bot when it was doune onane, / Als tit it was to almus tane.
Þe hermit loked and was ful wo, / Þat þai bare his mete him fro.
Þe quene spird at him tiþandes, / Fro brede so for to hald his handes,

80 And with talking scho held him ay, / Till all was broght and born oway.
He thoght, it was done by sum skill / And oþer mete suld cum him till.
And hastily on bord was broght / A mese, þat þe hermit liked noght:
A lafe, al samin made of ry, / Was schorn bifor him curtaisly,
Þarby a pese with water clere: / And þe quene bad him mak gude chere.

85 Scho made him sembland gude and glad, / Bot oþer mete right none he had.
For schame þarof he might ett nane, / And sone þe burdes oway was tane.
    Vnto chamber þai went in hy / Þare had þai mirth of minstralsy.
Knightes and ladis daunced samin; / Þe hermit thoght, it was no gamin,
For ful nobilly fed þai ware, / And him hungerd wonder sare.

90   At euyn he was to chamber led / Euyn vnto the quenes bed.
Þe quene lay right euyn him to, / Als scho with þe king was wont to do.
Faire scho gan him hals and kys / And held him wakeand maugre his.
All-if þe hermit was hungery / ʒit feled he hete of hir body.
He lay in clothes white als milk / And feled þe lady soft als silk.

95 And sone he bourded to þe quene, / Right als he at hame had bene.
Þe quene þan cald foure swiers, / Þat ordand war for swilk affers.
Out of þe bed sune was he drawin / And in a fatt with water thrawin
And halden was he in þat water, / Vntill his teth gan samyn clater.
Þan was he tane and laid ogayne / Right by þe quene, and scho was baine

100 To dri þe water of his hide, / And for to temp him in þat tide
And mak him abill in all-thing, / For to fulfill his fless liking.
And sone it ferd, als I of mene, / And efter help þan cald the quene.
Þan out of þe bed sone was he tane / And dipped eft in flum Jordane;
And þarin hard þai gan him hald, / Vntill he was al clumsed for calde,

105 And by þe quene þan was he laid – / "Allas, allas!" oftsithes he said.
Him had wele leuer at hame haue bene, / Þan so be gestend with þe quene,
For in þat ilk night was he thrise / Serued with þe same seruise;
And by þan it dawed day, / Þe quene rase vp and went hir way;
And þan þai lappid him in a haire / And couerd all ouer-clothes faire;

110 And on the morn þe quene him cald / And asked him, if he oght wald.
He said: "For him, þat last sall ay, / Giues me leue to wend my way.
I aske of þe none oþer thing, / For lang inogh haue I bene king."

---

79 *Þe quene . . . tiþandes*] 'the queen asked him for the latest news'.
92 *And . . . his*] 'and kept him awake against his will'.
108 *And . . . day*] 'at dawn'
109 *haire*] 'a hair shirt'
111 *For him . . . ay*] freely: 'By God'

Þe quene said: "Now hastou sene / My lordes lifing albidene;
And I trow, þou may wit þarby, / Þat þou lifes more esely,
115   For lang tyme haue we samin bene, / And ȝit we err both maidins clene.
If þou haue nede of anything, / Send vnto me or to þe king,
And full frely we will þe giff / Mete and drink, whils þou may liff."
Þe hermit in his gere him graid / And vnto þe quene þus he said:
"I ask nothing bot leue to gang, / For kinges life haue I led ful lang."
120   Þan furth he went and was ful faine / And mendid his life with all his maine.
      Bi þis ensaumple may we se, / Þat no man here suld think þat he
Es so haly in saul and lim, / Þat no man es like vntill him.
Þe man þat wenes so more or les, / Bigilid with preue pride he es.

Text 12: York Plays

The *Mystery Plays* or *Corpus Christi Cycles* are a tradition that developed entirely in the Middle Ages, and is not descended from classical drama. The *Corpus Christi Cycles*, of which four English cycles remain, were performed on the Corpus Christi feast day, which is held on the first Thursday after Trinity Sunday. The feast day was proclaimed by Pope Urban IV (around 1264) in order to celebrate the presence of Christ in the Eucharist. A series of plays, all productions of biblical events, ran throughout the whole day, dramatising creation through to doomsday. Each of the plays was performed by a certain guild in the city, which could sometimes cast an ironic touch on the play itself: the butchers presented the Slaughtering of the Innocents, the bakers the Last Supper, and so on. Each of the guilds had their own pageant-wagon, which they would draw through the town, performing at several different locations one after another. The *Corpus Christi Cycles* aimed to instruct the laity on the proximity of doomsday, how they should behave as Christians, and to present God (and Christ) as he has shown himself to humanity. The *Corpus Christi Cycles* eventually replaced Latin liturgical drama: as medieval society became more secularised, the vernacular was used rather than Latin; the laity could perform as actors and the guilds organise the plays themselves rather than this being maintained by the clergy. In addition, the plays were no longer presented in the church, but on the streets. Each individual play could also draw on other sources than the Bible, including liturgy, legends, apocrypha and the church fathers.

The *York Cycle* is the longest of all the English cycles, but does have some plays identical to the *Towneley Cycle*. It was presented every year. Viewed as one of the best cycles, York includes human insight and character analyses which surpass the other cycles. The language is pithy, colloquial, and often very graphic (as are the plays themselves). The entire demonstration of the 48 plays, each of which stopped at 12 different stations in York, must have lasted around 20 hours, beginning around 4:30 am and ending around midnight.

The Harrowing of Hell (written between 1463 and 1477), was presented by the saddlers. Most of the action is taken from the *Gospel of Nicodemus*. As this gospel is full of dialogue scenes, it could easily be used for the construction of a play. The play begins with a long monologue in which Jesus explains the importance of the actions he is about to commit to the audience – he is in hell before his resurrection, and therefore not in his fleshly nature. The climax, the overcoming of hell and death, is dramatised via a long debate between Jesus and Satan (ll. 213 ff).

The actors' roles are abbreviated as follows: Johannes Baptista – Joh. Bapt.; I, II Diabolus – I, II Diab.

The reflex of Old English $\bar{a}$ is written <o> and <oo>, as for example in *goo* (l. 120, 212, 341 usw.), *sore* (l. 204, 205), *soo* (l. 99 etc.), *moo* (l. 208, 328) and only once is written <a> in *waa* (l. 406) in order to rhyme with *gloria*; this means the text shows northern features. This is confirmed by the reflex of Old English *-āg-* written <aw>, as in *awne* (l. 237) and also *-āw-* which is written <au> and <aw>, as in *saule, saules, saulis* (l. 376, 272 etc.), *knawe(s)* (l. 283, 315); see, however, *knowe* (l. 159). A further northern feature is the form of the present participle ending in *-and*, as in *walkand* (l. 53), *leuand* (l. 55, 127), *lastand* (l. 66). The word-initial *th-* in the 3rd person plural pronouns is a further northern feature, as in *þame* (l. 9), *thare* (l. 18), *þei* (l. 21 etc.). In addition, the third person singular present indicative ends in *-s*, as in *bidis* (l. 23), *menys* (l. 46), *comes* (l. 57) etc., as does the plural: *affies* (l. 29), *liffis* (l. 70), *musteres* (l. 104). – According to *LALME* on MS Additional 35290, the text is probably from northern Lancashire.

Sources: British Library, London, MS Additional 35290. – Beadle (1982; 2009); Smith (1885). – Secondary literature: Woolf (1972), Davidson (1977), Collier (1978).

Jesus	Manne on molde, be meke to me,
	And haue thy maker in þi mynde,
	And thynke howe I haue tholid for þe
	With pereles paynes for to be pyned.
5	The forward of my fadir free
	Haue I fulfillid, as folke may fynde,
	Þerfore aboute nowe woll I bee
	Þat I haue bought for to vnbynde.
	Þe feende þame wanne with trayne
10	Þurgh frewte of erthely foode;
	I haue þame getyn agayne
	Thurgh bying with my bloode.

And so I schall þat steede restore
　　For whilke þe feende fell for synne,
15　Þare schalle mankynde wonne euermore
　　In blisse that schall neuere blynne.
All þat in werke my werkemen were,
　　Owte of thare woo I wol þame wynne,
And some signe schall I sende before
20　　Of grace, to garre þer gamys begynne.
　　　A light I woll þei haue
　　　　To schewe thame I schall come sone.
　　　My bodie bidis in graue
　　　　Tille alle thes dedis be done.

25　My fadir ordand on þis wise
　　Aftir his will þat I schulde wende,
For to fulfille þe prophicyes,
　　And als I spake my solace to spende.
My frendis þat in me faith affies,
30　　Nowe fro ther fois I schall þame fende,
And on the thirde day ryght vprise,
　　And so tille heuen I schall assende.
　　　Sithen schall I come agayne
　　　　To deme bothe goode and ill

14 *For . . . synne*] refers to Lucifer's fall, see Isaiah 14:12.

35		Tille endles joie or peyne;
		Þus is my fadris will.

Tunc cantent.

	Adame	Mi bretheren, harkens to me here,
		Swilke hope of heele neuere are we hadde;
		Foure thowsande and sex hundereth ȝere
40		Haue we bene heere in þis stedde.
		Nowe see I signe of solace seere,
		A glorious gleme to make vs gladde,
		Wherfore I hope oure helpe is nere
		And sone schall sesse oure sorowes sadde.
45	*Eua*	Adame, my husband hende,
		Þis menys solas certayne.
		Such light gune on vs lende
		In paradise full playne.

	Isaiah	Adame, we schall wele vndirstande –
50		I, Ysaias, as God me kende,
		I prechid in Neptalym, þat lande,
		And Zabulon, even vntill ende.
		I spake of folke in mirke walkand
		And saide a light schulde on þame lende.
55		This lered I whils I was leuand,
		Nowe se I God þis same hath sende.
		Þis light comes all of Criste,
		Þat seede to saue vs nowe.
		Þus is my poynte puplisshid –
60		But Symeon, what sais þou?

	Symeon	Þhis, my tale of farleis feele,
		For in þe temple his frendis me fande.
		I hadde delite with hym to dele
		And halsed homely with my hande.
65		I saide, 'Lorde, late thy seruaunt lele
		Passe nowe in pesse to liffe lastand,
		For nowe myselfe has sene thy hele
		Me liste no lengar to liffe in lande'.
		Þis light þou hast purueyed
70		To folkes þat liffis in leede,

51–54 *I prechid . . . lande*] see Isaiah 9:1 ff. and the Gospel of Nicodemus, 18; the reference is to Nephthalim.
60 *Symeon*] see Luke 2:25–35
65–68 *Lorde . . . lande*] see Luke 2:29–32
70 *in leede*] metrical tag (see also l. 135)

Þe same þat I þame saide
I see fulfillid in dede.

| *Joh. Bapt.* | Als voyce criand to folke I kende |

Joh. Bapt.   Als voyce criand to folke I kende
    Þe weyes of Criste als I wele kanne.
75   I baptiste hym with bothe my hende
    Euen in þe floode of flume Jordanne.
   Þe holy goste fro heuene discende
    Als a white dowue doune on hym þanne;
   The fadir voice, my mirthe to mende,
80   Was made to me euen als manne:
    'This is my sone,' he saide,
     'In whome me paies full wele.'
   His light is on vs laide,
    He comes oure cares to kele.

85 *Moyses* Of that same light lernyng haue I:
    To me, Moyses, he mustered his myght,
   And also vnto anodir, Hely,
    Wher we were on an hille on hight.
   Whyte as snowe was his body,
90   And his face like to þe sonne to sight;
   No man on molde was so myghty
    Grathely to loke agaynste þat light.
    Þat same light se I nowe
     Shynyng on vs sarteyne,
95   Wherfore trewly I trowe
     We schalle sone passe fro payne.

 I Diab. Helpe, Belsabub, to bynde þer boyes –
    Such harrowe was neuer are herde in helle.
 II Diab. Why rooris þou soo, Rebalde? Þou royis –
100   What is betidde, canne þou ought telle?
 I Diab. What, heris þou noȝt þis vggely noyse?
    Þes lurdans þat in Lymbo dwelle,
   Þei make menyng of many joies
    And musteres grete mirthe þame emell.
105 *II Diab.* Mirthe? Nay, nay, þat poynte is paste,
    More hele schall þei neuer haue.

---

76 *flume Jordanne*] the River Jordan
82 *'In whome . . . wele'*] 'in whom I am well pleased', Matthew 3:17
87 *Hely*] the prophet Elijah, see 1 Kings 17 ff
97 *Belsabub*] see 2 Kings 1:2
102 *lurdans þat in Lymbo dwelle*] this refers to the concept of the patriarchs of the Old Testament dwelling in Limbo, 'the edge of hell'.

I Diab.		Þei crie on Criste full faste
		And sais he schal þame saue.
Belsabub		ȝa, if he saue þame noght, we schall,
110		For they are sperde in speciall space.
		Whils I am prince and principall
		Schall þei neuer passe oute of þis place.
		Calle vppe Astrotte and Anaball
		To giffe þer counsaille in þis case,
115		Bele-Berit and Belial,
		To marre þame þat swilke maistries mase.
		Say to Satan oure sire,
		And bidde þame bringe also
		Lucifer, louely of lyre.
120	*I Diab.*	Al redy, lorde, I goo.
	Jesus	*Attollite portas, principes,*
		Oppen vppe, ȝe princes of paynes sere,
		Et eleuamini eternales,
		Youre yendles ȝatis þat ȝe haue here.
125	*Sattan*	What page is þere þat makes prees
		And callis hym kyng of vs in fere?
	Dauid	I lered leuand, withouten lees,
		He is a kyng of vertues clere,
		A lorde mekill of myght
130		And stronge in ilke a stoure,
		In batailes ferse to fight
		And worthy to wynne honnoure.
	Sattan	Honnoure? In þe deuel way! For what dede?
		All erthely men to me are thrall.
135		Þe lady þat calles hym lorde in leede
		Hadde neuer ȝitt herberowe, house, ne halle.
	I Diab.	Harke Belsabub, I haue grete drede,
		For hydously I herde hym calle.
	Belliall	We, spere oure ȝates, all ill mot þou spede,
140		And sette furthe watches on þe wall –
		And if he calle or crie
		To make vs more debate,
		Lay on hym þan hardely
		And garre hym gange his gate.

---

113 *Astrotte and Anaball*] name of devils, see Judges 2:13, 3:7, 10:6
115 *Bele-Berit and Belial*] Bele-Berit is probably Baalberith, see Judges 8:33; for Belial see 2 Corinthians 6:15.
121 *Attollite . . . principes*] see Psalms 24:7, 9

145	*Sattan*	Telle me what boyes dare be so bolde
		For drede to make so mekill draye.
	I Diab.	Itt is þe Jewe þat Judas solde
		For to be dede þis othir daye.
	Sattan	Owe, þis tale in tyme is tolde,
150		Þis traytoure traueses vs alway.
		He schall be here full harde in holde,
		Loke þat he passe noght, I þe praye.
	II Diab.	Nay, nay, he will noȝt wende
		Away or I be ware,
155		He shappis hym for to schende
		Alle helle or he go ferre.
	Sattan	Nay faitour, þerof schall he faile,
		For alle his fare I hym deffie.
		I knowe his trantis fro toppe to taile,
160		He leuys with gaudis and with gilery.
		Þerby he brought oute of oure bale
		Nowe late Lazar of Betannye;
		Þerfore I gaffe to þe Jewes counsaille
		Þat þei schulde alway garre hym dye.
165		I entered in Judas
		Þat forwarde to fulfille,
		Þerfore his hire he has
		Allway to wonne here stille.
	Belsabub	Sir Sattanne, sen we here þe saie
170		Þat þou and þe Jewes wer same assente,
		And wotte he wanne Lazar awaye
		Þat tille vs was tane for to tente,
		Trowe þou þat þou marre hym maye,
		To mustir mightis what he has mente?
175		If he nowe depriue vs of oure praye,
		We will ȝe witte whanne þei are wente.
	Sattan	I bidde ȝou be noȝt abasshed,
		But boldely make youe boune
		With toles þat ȝe on traste,
180		And dynge þat dastard doune.
	Jesus	*Principes, portas tollite,*
		Vndo youre ȝatis, ȝe princis of pryde,

159 *I knowe . . . taile*] 'I know his tricks in and out'.
162 *Lazar*] see John 11:1–46
165 *I . . . Judas*] see John 13:27
171 *Lazar*] see John 11:1–46
181–183 *Principes . . . glorie*] see Psalms 24:7, 9

Et introibit rex glorie,
   Þe kyng of blisse comes in þis tyde.

185   *Sattan*   Owte, harrowe! What harlot is hee
   Þat sais his kyngdome schall be cryed?

   Dauid   Þat may þou in my Sawter see,
   For þat poynte I prophicied.
   I saide þat he schuld breke
190   Youre barres and bandis by name,
   And on youre werkis take wreke –
   Nowe schalle ȝe see þe same.

   Jesus   Þis steede schall stonde no lenger stoken:
   Opynne vppe, and latte my pepul passe.

195   *I Diab.*   Owte! Beholdes, oure baill is brokynne,
   And brosten are alle oure bandis of bras –
   Telle Lucifer alle is vnlokynne.

   Belsabub   What þanne, is Lymbus lorne? Allas,
   Garre Satan helpe þat we wer wroken;
200   Þis werke is werse þanne euere it was.

   Sattan   I badde ȝe schulde be boune
   If he made maistries more.
   Do dynge þat dastard doune
   And sette hym sadde and sore.

205   *Belsabub*   Ȝa, sette hym sore – þat is sone saide,
   But come þiselffe and serue hym soo.
   We may not bide his bittir braide,
   He wille vs marre and we wer moo.

   Sattan   What, faitours, wherfore are ȝe flayd?
210   Haue ȝe no force to flitte hym froo?
   Belyue loke þat my gere be grathed,
   Miselffe schall to þat gedlyng goo.
   Howe, belamy, abide,
   With al thy booste and bere,
215   And telle to me þis tyde
   What maistries makes þou here?

   Jesus   I make no maistries but for myne,
   Þame wolle I saue I telle þe nowe.
   Þou hadde no poure þame to pyne,
220   But as my prisounes for þer prowe
   Here haue þei soiorned, noght as thyne,

---

190 *by name*] 'in particular'
204 *And . . . sore*] 'and set upon him heftily'
208 *and*] 'even if'
213 *belamy*] here used derisively

	But in thy warde – þou wote wele howe.
Sattan	And what deuel haste þou done ay syne
	Þat neuer wolde negh þame nere or nowe?
225 *Jesus*	Nowe is þe tyme certayne
	My fadir ordand before,
	Þat they schulde passe fro payne
	And wonne in mirthe euer more.

Sattan	Thy fadir knewe I wele be sight,
230	He was a write his mette to wynne,
	And Marie me menys þi modir hight –
	Þe vttiremeste ende of all þi kynne.
	Who made þe be so mekill of myght?
Jesus	Þou wikid feende, latte be thy dynne.
235	Mi fadir wonnys in heuen on hight,
	With blisse þat schall neuere blynne.
	I am his awne sone,
	His forward to fulfille,
	And same ay schall we wonne
240	And sundir whan we wolle.

Sattan	God sonne? Þanne schulde þou be ful gladde,
	Aftir no catel neyd thowe crave!
	But þou has leued ay like a ladde,
	And in sorowe as a symple knave.
245 *Jesus*	Þat was for hartely loue I hadde
	Vnto mannis soule, it for to saue;
	And for to make þe mased and madde,
	And by þat resoune þus dewly to haue
	Mi Godhede here, I hidde
250	In Marie modir myne,
	For it schulde noȝt be kidde
	To þe nor to none of thyne.

Sattan	A, þis wolde I were tolde in ilke a toune.
	So, sen þou sais God is thy sire,
255	I schall þe proue be right resoune
	Þou motes his men into þe myre.
	To breke his bidding were þei boune,
	And, for they did at my desire,
	Fro paradise he putte þame doune

223–224 *And what . . . nowe?*] freely: 'And what the devil have you been doing until now, and
why haven't you come earlier to them?'

230 *He . . . wynne*] Joseph earned his living as a carpenter, see Matthew 13:55 and Mark 6:3.

232 *Þe . . . kynne*] 'the last and lowliest of all your kin'

256 *Þou . . . myre*] 'you lead his followers into the mire' (into error).

260   In helle here to haue þer hyre.
                  And thyselfe, day and nyght,
                     Has taught al men emang
                  To do resoune and right,
                    And here werkis þou all wrang.

265 *Jesus*   I wirk noght wrang, þat schal þow witte,
                  If I my men fro woo will wynne.
                Mi prophetis playnly prechid it,
                    All þis note þat nowe begynne.
                Þai saide þat I schulde be obitte,
270   To helle þat I schulde entre in,
                And saue my seruauntis fro þat pitte
                    Wher dampned saulis schall sitte for synne.
                     And ilke trewe prophettis tale
                     Muste be fulfillid in mee;
275   I haue þame boughte with bale,
                    And in blisse schal þei be.

   Sattan   Nowe sen þe liste allegge þe lawes,
                    Þou schalte be atteynted or we twynne,
                For þo þat þou to wittenesse drawes
280   Full even agaynste þe will begynne.
                Salamon saide in his sawes
                    Þat whoso enteres helle withynne
                Shall neuer come oute, þus clerkis knawes –
                    And þerfore felowe, leue þi dynne.
285   Job, þi seruaunte, also
                     Þus in his tyme gune telle
                  Þat nowthir frende nor foo
                    Shulde fynde reles in helle.

   Jesus   He saide full soth, þat schall þou see,
290   Þat in helle may be no reles,
                But of þat place þan preched he
                    Where synffull care schall euere encrees.
                And in þat bale ay schall þou be
                    Whare sorowes sere schall neuer sesse,
295   And for my folke þerfro wer free,
                    Nowe schall þei passe to þe place of pees.
                     Þai were here with my wille,
                     And so schall þei fourthe wende,
                   And þiselue schall fulfille
300   Þer wooe withouten ende.

_____

281 *Salamon . . . sawes*] see Psalms 49:15
285 *Job*] see Job 24:19

Sattan	Owe, þanne se I howe þou menys emang
	Some mesure with malice to melle,
	Sen þou sais all schall noȝt gang,
	But some schalle alway with vs dwelle.

305 *Jesus* Ȝaa, witte þou wele, ellis were it wrang,
　　　　Als cursed Cayme þat slewe Abell,
And all þat hastis hemselue to hange,
　　　　Als Judas and Archedefell,
　　　　　Datan and Abiron,
310　　　　　And alle of þare assente,
　　　　Als tyrantis euerilkone
　　　　Þat me and myne turmente.

And all þat liste noght to lere my lawe
　　　　Þat I haue lefte in lande nowe newe –
315　Þat is my comyng for to knawe,
　　　　And to my sacramente pursewe,
Mi dede, my rysing, rede be rawe –
　　　　Who will noght trowe, þei are noght trewe.
Vnto my dome I schall þame drawe,
320　　　　And juge þame worse þanne any Jewe.
　　　　And all þat likis to leere
　　　　　My lawe and leue þerbye,
　　　　Shall neuere haue harmes heere,
　　　　　But welthe, as is worthy.

325 *Sattan* Nowe here my hande, I halde me paied,
　　　　Þis poynte is playnly for oure prowe.
If þis be soth þat þou hast saide
　　　　We schall haue moo þanne we haue nowe.
Þis lawe þat þou nowe late has laide
330　　　　I schall lere men noȝt to allowe;
Iff þei it take þei be betraied,
　　　　For I schall turne þame tyte, I trowe.
　　　　I schall walke este and weste,
　　　　And garre þame werke wele werre.

---

306 *Cayme . . . Abell*] see Genesis 4:3–8
308 *Judas*] see Matthew 27:5
308 *Archedefell*] refers to Ahitophel, see 2 Samuel 17:23
309 Dathan and Abiram did not hang themselves, but were swallowed by the earth because
　they had rebelled against Moses, see Deuteronomy 16:31.
310 *And . . . assente*] 'and their like'
316 *sacramente*] refers to the sacraments of penance and the Eucharist.
317 *rede be rawe*] 'frequently preached'
325 *I . . . paied*] 'we're even'
333 *este and weste*] 'in every direction'

335	*Jesus*	Naye, feende, þou schall be feste,
		Þat þou schalte flitte not ferre.
	Sattan	Feste? Þat were a foule reasoune –
		Nay bellamy, þou bus be smytte.
	Jesus	Mighill myne aungell, make þe boune
340		And feste yone fende þat he noght flitte.
		And, Deuyll, I comaunde þe go doune
		Into thy selle where þou schalte sitte.
	Sattan	Owt! Ay herrowe! Helpe, Mahounde!
		Nowe wex I woode oute of my witte.
345	*Belsabub*	Sattan, þis saide we are,
		Nowe schall þou fele þi fitte.
	Sattan	Allas for dole and care,
		I synke into helle pitte.

	Adame	A, Jesu, lorde, mekill is þi myght,
350		That mekis þiselffe in þis manere,
		Vs for to helpe as þou has hight,
		Whanne both forfette, I and my feere.
		Here haue we leuyd withouten light
		Four thousand and vi c ȝere;
355		Now se I be þis solempne sight
		Howe thy mercy hath made vs clere.
	Eue	A, lorde, we were worthy
		Mo turmentis for to taste,
		But mende vs with mercye
360		Als þou of myght is moste.

	Baptista	A, lorde, I loue þe inwardly,
		That me wolde make þi messengere
		Thy comyng in erth for to crye,
		And teche þi faith to folke in feere;
365		And sithen before þe for to dye
		And bringe boodworde to þame here,
		How þai schulde haue thyne helpe in hye.
		Nowe se I all þi poyntis appere
		Als Dauid, prophete trewe,
370		Ofte tymes tolde vntill vs;
		Of þis comyng he knewe,
		And saide it schulde be þus.

---

338 *þu ... smytte*] 'you are done for'
343 *Owt ... Mahounde*] Here Satan is so beside himself that he can only cry for help.
346 *Nowe ... fitte*] 'now you will get what you deserve'.
354 *Four ... c ȝere*] i. e. 4600 years

Dauid	Als I haue saide, ȝitt saie I soo,
	Ne derelinquas, domine,
375	*Animam meam in inferno,*
	Leffe noght my saule, lorde, aftir þe
	In depe helle where dampned schall goo;
	Ne suffre neuere þi sayntes to se,
	The sorowe of þame þat wonnes in woo
380	Ay full of filthe, and may not fleye.
Adame	We thanke his grete goodnesse
	He fette vs fro þis place.
	Makes joie nowe, more and lesse.
Omnis	We laude God of his grace.

Tunc cantent.

385 *Jesus*	Adame, and my frendis in feere,
	Fro all youre fooes come fourth with me.
	Ȝe schalle be sette in solas seere
	Wher ȝe schall neuere of sorowes see.
	And Mighill, myn aungell clere,
390	Ressayue þes saules all vnto þe
	And lede þame als I schall þe lere,
	To paradise with playe and plenté.
	Mi graue I woll go till,
	Redy to rise vpperight,
395	And so I schall fulfille
	That I before haue highte.
Michill	Lorde, wende we schall aftir þi sawe,
	To solace sere thai schall be sende.
	But þat þer deuelis no draught vs drawe
400	Lorde, blisse vs with þi holy hende.
Jesus	Mi blissing haue ȝe all on rawe,
	I schall be with youe wher ȝe wende,
	And all þat lelly luffes my lawe,
	Þai schall be blissid withowten ende.
405 *Adame*	To the, lorde, be louyng,
	Þat vs has wonne fro waa.
	For solas will we syng
	Laus tibi cum gloria etc.

374–375 *Ne . . . inferno*] see Psalms 16:10 and Acts 2:27
389 *Mighill*] see Jude 1:9
399 *But . . . drawe*] freely: 'So that these devils cannot triumph over us'.
401 *on rawe*] 'one after the other'

Text 13: Geoffrey Chaucer

The *Canterbury Tales* are perhaps the most well-known English work of the Middle Ages. Written by Geoffrey Chaucer (1343–1400?) near the end of his life, the work is transmitted in several fragments.

The framework of the *Canterbury Tales* is a pilgrimage undertaken to the Shrine of Saint Thomas Becket in Canterbury. A group of 29 pilgrims and the narrator "Chaucer" meet at the Tabard Inn in Southwark, just south of London. Harry Bailey, owner of the inn, suggests that they travel to Canterbury together, and that each pilgrim should tell four stories, two on the way there and two on the way back. Of the 120 tales that should have resulted from this, only twenty-four and a fragment have been preserved; however, to what extent Chaucer later reduced the proportions of his story, and to what extent stories have been lost to us, cannot be determined.

Unlike Boccaccio's *Decamerone*, also a frame narrative in which 10 aristocrats each tell two stories to pass the time, Chaucer's pilgrims are all from different classes. This variety is utilised to tell stories of different moral levels, different genres and in different styles. The lower classes, the Miller, the Reeve and the Shipman, for example, all tell fabliaux tales – short verse tales with a comic twist. The upper classes, including the Knight, his Squire and the Franklin, all tell romances (see M 6 and 9). The members of the clergy all tell more or less religious tales; the Prioress, Monk, Nun, Clerk and the Pardoner use the genres exemplum, hagiography, tragedy, and didactic tale. Not only does Chaucer use the characters for literary diversity, the characters also interact with each other as one would expect from members of these classes. The Miller and the Reeve attack each other's professions through their tales and in the end have to be separated by the Host (see lines 79–90, 133–144 and 542–548). On the other hand, some pilgrims are able to learn from each other's stories: the Pardoner, for example, decides not to marry after hearing a part of the Wife of Bath's prologue.

The *Canterbury Tales* begin with a prologue, which is divided into three main parts. An introduction (ll. 1–42) is followed by the first-person-narrator's ("Chaucer's") impressions of the other pilgrims (ll. 43–714), and finally the narrative switches to the Host, who explains how the stories will be told (ll. 715–858). The host is also the moderator for the rest of the tales. According to the Host's wishes, only *tales of best sentence and moost solaas* ('well-written and interesting', l. 798) are to be told.

The text printed here is taken from Fragment A which contains the 'General Prologue' as well as the tales of the knight, the miller, the reeve and the fragmentary tale of the cook. The first two sections are taken from the 'General Prologue'; section three provides the full text of the Reeve's Prologue and Tale.

Looking at the 'Reeve's Tale', a fabliau, we can see at a glance that this originally aristocratic genre has been transformed by Chaucer in various directions. Whereas most of the Old French fabliaux devote little space to the constitution of character, Chaucer succeeds brilliantly in breathing new life into the stock characters of the genre: clerics, craftsmen, and women as sex objects. In the 'Reeve's Tale', most of the characters are individualised quite intricately. The miller is described on two levels, i.e. his outward appearance and his behaviour, and he even has a proper name. The narrator also dwells on the miller's high social ambitions in respect of the marriage of his daughter. The students (clerics) are presented in a very elaborate way. It is interesting to note that Chaucer uses social and linguistic prejudice in his direct and indirect characterisation of John and Aleyn: they come from the north and use their northern dialect frowned upon by southern speakers. Chaucer is thus one of the first authors to use dialect as a highly efficient means of characterisation.

The story of the 'Reeve's Tale', based on the motif of 'the misplaced cradle', seems to be rather traditional. However, as a close look at the text will reveal, Chaucer is also experimenting with literary conventions and genres. Thus, the brief dialogue between Malyne, the miller's daughter, and Aleyn, her lover for one night, can be seen as a parody of the courtly genre 'aube' or 'Tagelied' with its description of the courtly lover taking leave of his lady at the break of day (see ll. 460–471).

Chaucer's language has been the subject of quite a number of special studies. It is therefore not necessary to point out the special linguistic features of the Ellesmere Manuscript. See Fries (1985), Markus (1990), Samuels (1963, 1972, 1983a, 1983b), Sandved (1985). – *LALME* describes MS Ellesmere 26 C 9 as Linguistic Profile 6400 (partly), London.

Sources: Ellesmere 26 C 9 from the Henry E. Huntington Library, San Marino, California. – Benson (1987); Robinson (1957), Pratt (1974), Fichte/Kemmler (1989). – Secondary literature: Kolve (1984), Mann (1973), Pearsall (1985), Wetherbee (1989), Patterson (1991), Johnston (2001).

Here bygynneth the Book of the Tales of Caunterbury

    Whan that Aprill with his shoures soote
    The droghte of March hath perced to the roote,
    And bathed every veyne in swich licour
    Of which vertu engendred is the flour;
5   Whan Zephirus eek with his sweete breeth
    Inspired hath in every holt and heeth
    The tendre croppes, and the yonge sonne
    Hath in the Ram his half cours yronne,
    And smale foweles maken melodye,
10 That slepen al the nyght with open ye
    (So priketh hem nature in hir corages),
    Thanne longen folk to goon on pilgrimages,
    And palmeres for to seken straunge strondes,
    To ferne halwes, kowthe in sondry londes;
15 And specially from every shires ende
    Of Engelond to Caunterbury they wende,
    The hooly blisful martir for to seke,
    That hem hath holpen whan that they were seeke.

5 *Zephirus*] the west wind of classical literature

7–8 *yonge . . . yronne*] The sun has passed halfway through Aries; i. e. it is the beginning of April, for the sign of Aries starts on March 21st.

13 *palmeres*] a reference to the professional pilgrims who could be hired; they wore a palm-leaf sewn to their clothing to show that they had completed a pilgrimage to the Holy Land.

17 *martir*] Thomas Becket, Archbishop of Canterbury, was murdered by four knights of King Henry II in the cathedral of Canterbury in 1170; he was canonised in 1173.

Bifil that in that seson on a day,
20 In Southwerk at the Tabard as I lay
Redy to wenden on my pilgrymage
To Caunterbury with ful devout corage,
At nyght was come into that hostelrye
Wel nyne and twenty in a compaignye
25 Of sondry folk, by aventure yfalle
In felaweshipe, and pilgrimes were they alle,
That toward Caunterbury wolden ryde.
The chambres and the stables weren wyde,
And wel we weren esed atte beste.
30 And shortly, whan the sonne was to reste,
So hadde I spoken with hem everichon
That I was of hir felaweshipe anon,
And made forward erly for to ryse,
To take oure wey ther as I yow devyse.
35 But nathelees, whil I have tyme and space,
Er that I ferther in this tale pace,
Me thynketh it acordaunt to resoun
To telle yow al the condicioun
Of ech of hem, so as it semed me.
40 And whiche they weren, and of what degree,
And eek in what array that they were inne;
And at a knyght than wol I first bigynne.
[...]
The REVE was a sclendre colerik man.   [I, 587]
His berd was shave as ny as ever he kan;
45 His heer was by his erys ful round yshorn;
His top was dokked lyk a preest biforn.
Ful longe were his legges and ful lene,
Ylyk a staf; ther was no calf ysene.
Wel koude he kepe a gerner and a bynne;
50 Ther was noon auditour koude on him wynne.
Wel wiste he by the droghte and by the reyn
The yeldynge of his seed and of his greyn.
His lordes sheep, his neet, his dayerye,
His swyn, his hors, his stoor, and his pultrye
55 Was hoolly in this Reves governynge,
And by his covenant yaf the rekenynge,

20 *Southwerk*] Southwark, now a London suburb, in Chaucer's time a village on the road to
Canterbury
20 *Tabard*] name of an inn
23 *At nyght*] in the evening
29 *atte beste*] 'perfectly'
45–46 *His heer... biforn*] i. e. the reeve tries to pass for a cleric; see also l. 77.
56 *yaf the rekenynge*] 'he rendered his account'; the subject has to be supplied.

Syn that his lord was twenty yeer of age.
Ther koude no man brynge hym in arrerage.
Ther nas baillif, ne hierde, nor oother hyne,
60   That he ne knew his sleighte and his covyne;
They were adrad of hym as of the deeth.
His wonyng was ful faire upon an heeth;
With grene trees yshadwed was his place.
He koude bettre than his lord purchace.
65   Ful riche he was astored pryvely.
His lord wel koude he plesen subtilly,
To yeve and lene hym of his owene good,
And have a thank, and yet a cote and hood.
In youthe he hadde lerned a good myster:
70   He was a wel good wrighte, a carpenter.
This Reve sat upon a ful good stot
That was al pomely grey and highte Scot.
A long surcote of pers upon he hade,
And by his syde he baar a rusty blade.
75   Of Northfolk was this Reve of which I telle,
Biside a toun men clepen Baldeswelle.
Tukked he was as is a frere aboute,
And evere he rood the hyndreste of oure route.
          [. . .]

The prologe of the Reves Tale.

Whan folk hadde laughen at this nyce cas   [I, 3855]
80   Of Absolon and hende Nicholas,
Diverse folk diversely they seyde,
But for the moore part they loughe and pleyde.
Ne at this tale I saugh no man hym greve,
But it were oonly Osewold the Reve.
85   By cause he was of carpenteris craft,
A litel ire is in his herte ylaft;
He gan to grucche, and blamed it a lite.
      "So theek," quod he, "ful wel koude I thee quite
With bleryng of a proud milleres ye,
90   If that me liste speke of ribaudye.
But ik am oold; me list not pley for age;
Gras tyme is doon; my fodder is now forage;
This white top writeth myne olde yeris;

---

67 *yeve . . . owene good*] i. e. the reeve is a thief.
76 *Baldeswelle*] Bawdeswell, Norfolk
77 *Tukked . . . frere*] This is a reference to the girdle worn by friars to pull up their long coat.
80 *Absolon . . . Nicholas,*] two of the protagonists in the preceding 'Miller's Tale'.
93 *This white . . . yeris*] 'My white hairs signal my old age'

Myn herte is also mowled as myne heris,
95 But if I fare as dooth an open-ers –
That ilke fruyt is ever lenger the wers,
Til it be roten in mullok or in stree.
We olde men, I drede, so fare we:
Til we be roten, kan we nat be rype;
100 We hoppen alwey whil that the world wol pype.
For in oure wyl ther stiketh evere a nayl,
To have an hoor heed and a grene tayl,
As hath a leek; for thogh oure myght be goon,
Oure wyl desireth folie evere in oon.
105 For whan we may nat doon, than wol we speke;
Yet in oure asshen olde is fyr yreke.
    "Foure gleedes han we, which I shal devyse –
Avauntyng, liyng, anger, coveitise;
Thise foure sparkles longen unto eelde.
110 Oure olde lemes mowe wel been unweelde,
But wyl ne shal nat faillen, that is sooth.
And yet ik have alwey a coltes tooth,
As many a yeer as it is passed henne
Syn that my tappe of lif bigan to renne.
115 For sikerly, whan I was bore, anon
Deeth drough the tappe of lyf and leet it gon,
And ever sithe hath so the tappe yronne
Til that almoost al empty is the tonne.
The streem of lyf now droppeth on the chymbe.
120 The sely tonge may wel rynge and chymbe
Of wrecchednesse that passed is ful yoore;
With olde folk, save dotage, is namoore!"
    Whan that oure Hoost hadde herd this sermonyng,
He gan to speke as lordly as a kyng.
125 He seide, "What amounteth al this wit?
What shul we speke alday of hooly writ?
The devel made a reve for to preche,
Or of a soutere a shipman or a leche.
Sey forth thy tale, and tarie nat the tyme.
130 Lo Depeford, and it is half-wey pryme!
Lo Grenewych, ther many a shrewe is inne!
It were al tyme thy tale to bigynne."
    "Now, sires," quod this Osewold the Reve,
"I pray yow alle that ye nat yow greve,
135 Thogh I answere, and somdeel sette his howve;
For leveful is with force force of-showve.

---

112 *coltes tooth*] 'the desire (tooth) of a young man (coltes)'
130 *half-wey pryme*] about 7.30 a.m.
135 *sette his howve*] 'make a fool of him'

"This dronke Millere hath ytoold us heer
How that bigyled was a carpenteer,
Peraventure in scorn, for I am oon.
140 And, by youre leve, I shal hym quite anoon;
Right in his cherles termes wol I speke.
I pray to God his nekke mote to-breke;
He kan wel in myn eye seen a stalke,
But in his owene he kan nat seen a balke."

Heere bigynneth the Reves Tale

145 At Trumpyngtoun, nat fer fro Cantebrigge,
Ther gooth a brook, and over that a brigge,
Upon the whiche brook ther stant a melle;
And this is verray sooth that I yow telle:
A millere was ther dwellynge many a day.
150 As any pecok he was proud and gay.
Pipen he koude and fisshe, and nettes beete,
And turne coppes, and wel wrastle and sheete;
Ay by his belt he baar a long panade,
And of a swerd ful trenchant was the blade.
155 A joly poppere baar he in his pouche;
Ther was no man, for peril, dorste hym touche.
A Sheffeld thwitel baar he in his hose.
Round was his face, and camus was his nose;
As piled as an ape was his skulle.
160 He was a market-betere atte fulle.
Ther dorste no wight hand upon hym legge,
That he ne swoor he sholde anon abegge.
A theef he was for sothe of corn and mele,
And that a sly, and usaunt for to stele.
165 His name was hoote deynous Symkyn.
     A wyf he hadde, ycomen of noble kyn;
The person of the toun hir fader was.
With hire he yaf ful many a panne of bras,
For that Symkyn sholde in his blood allye,
170 She was yfostred in a nonnerye;
For Symkyn wolde no wyf, as he sayde,
But she were wel ynorissed and a mayde,

143–144 *seen a stalke . . . balke*] cf. Matthew 7:3
152 *And turne coppes*] the meaning is ambiguous: either 'produce' wooden cups or 'empty'
cups in a drinking contest.
157 *Sheffeld thwitel*] Sheffield knife
158 *camus . . . nose*] see also l. 198
168–169 *With hire . . . allye*] a reference to the rich dowry necessary to find a suitable husband
for an illegitimate daughter.

To saven his estaat of yomanrye.
And she was proud, and peert as is a pye.
175 A ful fair sighte was it upon hem two;
On halydayes biforn hire wolde he go
With his typet wounde aboute his heed,
And she cam after in a gyte of reed;
And Symkyn hadde hosen of the same.
180 Ther dorste no wight clepen hire but "dame";
Was noon so hardy that wente by the weye
That with hire dorste rage or ones pleye,
But if he wolde be slayn of Symkyn
With panade, or with knyf, or boidekyn.
185 For jalous folk ben perilous everemo –
Algate they wolde hire wyves wenden so.
And eek, for she was somdel smoterlich,
She was as digne as water in a dich,
And ful of hoker and of bisemare.
190 Hir thoughte that a lady sholde hire spare,
What for hire kynrede and hir nortelrie
That she hadde lerned in the nonnerie.
    A doghter hadde they bitwixe hem two
Of twenty yeer, withouten any mo,
195 Savynge a child that was of half yeer age;
In cradel it lay and was a propre page.
This wenche thikke and wel ygrowen was,
With kamus nose and eyen greye as glas,
With buttokes brode and brestes rounde and hye.
200 But right fair was hire heer; I wol nat lye.
    This person of the toun, for she was feir,
In purpos was to maken hire his heir,
Bothe of his catel and his mesuage,
And straunge he made it of hir mariage.
205 His purpos was for to bistowe hire hye
Into som worthy blood of auncetrye;
For hooly chirches good moot been despended
On hooly chirches blood, that is descended.
Therfore he wolde his hooly blood honoure,
210 Though that he hooly chirche sholde devoure.
    Greet sokene hath this millere, out of doute,
With whete and malt of al the land aboute;
And nameliche ther was a greet collegge

---

187 *smoterlich*] 'sullied' because of her illegitimate descent as daughter of the parson (cf. l. 167).
188 *digne . . . dich*] the meaning is 'stinking with pride'.
211 *greet sokene*] i. e. the miller had a profitable monopoly.

Men clepen the Soler Halle at Cantebregge;
215 Ther was hir whete and eek hir malt ygrounde.
And on a day it happed, in a stounde,
Sik lay the maunciple on a maladye;
Men wenden wisly that he sholde dye.
For which this millere stal bothe mele and corn
220 An hundred tyme moore than biforn;
For therbiforn he stal but curteisly,
But now he was a theef outrageously,
For which the wardeyn chidde and made fare.
But therof sette the millere nat a tare;
225 He craketh boost, and swoor it was nat so.
    Thanne were ther yonge povre scolers two,
That dwelten in this halle, of which I seye.
Testif they were, and lusty for to pleye,
And, oonly for hire myrthe and revelrye,
230 Upon the wardeyn bisily they crye
To yeve hem leve, but a litel stounde,
To goon to mille and seen hir corn ygrounde;
And hardily they dorste leye hir nekke
The millere sholde not stele hem half a pekke
235 Of corn by sleighte, ne by force hem reve;
And at the laste the wardeyn yaf hem leve.
John highte that oon, and Aleyn highte that oother;
Of o toun were they born, that highte Strother,
Fer in the north; I kan nat telle where.
240   This Aleyn maketh redy al his gere,
And on an hors the sak he caste anon.
Forth goth Aleyn the clerk, and also John,
With good swerd and with bokeler by hir syde.
John knew the wey – hem nedede no gyde –
245 And at the mille the sak adoun he layth.
Aleyn spak first: "Al hayl, Symond, y-fayth!
Hou fares thy faire doghter and thy wyf?"
    "Aleyn, welcome," quod Symkyn, "by my lyf!
And John also, how now, what do ye heer?"
250   "Symond," quod John, "by God, nede has na peer.
Hym boes serve hymself that has na swayn,
Or elles he is a fool, as clerkes sayn.
Oure manciple, I hope he wil be deed,
Swa werkes ay the wanges in his heed;

---

214 *Soler Halle*] a reference to King's Hall at Cambridge
215 *malt*] Colleges frequently brewed their own ale.
238 *Strother*] a town in either Yorkshire or Northumberland
250 *nede has na peer*] proverbial: 'Necessity knows no law'.

255 And forthy is I come, and eek Alayn,
To grynde oure corn and carie it ham agayn;
I pray yow spede us heythen that ye may."
  "It shal be doon," quod Symkyn, "by my fay!
What wol ye doon whil that it is in hande?"
260   "By God, right by the hopur wil I stande,"
Quod John, "and se howgates the corn gas in.
Yet saugh I nevere, by my fader kyn,
How that the hopur wagges til and fra."
  Aleyn answerde, "John, and wiltow swa?
265 Thanne wil I be bynethe, by my croun,
And se how that the mele falles doun
Into the trough; that sal be my disport.
For John, y-faith, I may been of youre sort;
I is as ille a millere as ar ye."
270   This millere smyled of hir nycetee,
And thoghte, "Al this nys doon but for a wyle.
They wene that no man may hem bigyle,
But by my thrift, yet shal I blere hir ye,
For al the sleighte in hir philosophye.
275 The moore queynte crekes that they make,
The moore wol I stele whan I take.
In stide of flour yet wol I yeve hem bren.
'The gretteste clerkes been noght wisest men,'
As whilom to the wolf thus spak the mare.
280 Of al hir art counte I noght a tare."
  Out at the dore he gooth ful pryvely,
Whan that he saugh his tyme, softely.
He looketh up and doun til he hath founde
The clerkes hors, ther as it stood ybounde
285 Bihynde the mille, under a levesel;
And to the hors he goth hym faire and wel;
He strepeth of the brydel right anon.
And whan the hors was laus, he gynneth gon
Toward the fen, ther wilde mares renne,
290 And forth with "wehee," thurgh thikke and thurgh thenne.
  This millere gooth agayn, no word he seyde,
But dooth his note, and with the clerkes pleyde
Til that hir corn was faire and weel ygrounde.
And whan the mele is sakked and ybounde,
295 This John goth out and fynt his hors away,
And gan to crie "Harrow!" and "Weylaway!

278–279 *The gretteste . . . mare*] proverbial; the reference to the mare is ultimately based on
the genre beast fable.

Oure hors is lorn, Alayn, for Goddes banes,
Step on thy feet! Com of, man, al atanes!
Allas, our wardeyn has his palfrey lorn."
300 This Aleyn al forgat, bothe mele and corn;
Al was out of his mynde his housbondrie.
"What, whilk way is he geen?" he gan to crie.
     The wyf cam lepynge inward with a ren.
She seyde, "Allas! youre hors goth to the fen
305 With wilde mares, as faste as he may go.
Unthank come on his hand that boond hym so,
And he that bettre sholde han knyt the reyne!"
     "Allas," quod John, "Aleyn, for Cristes peyne
Lay doun thy swerd, and I wil myn alswa.
310 I is ful wight, God waat, as is a raa;
By Goddes herte, he sal nat scape us bathe!
Why ne had thow pit the capul in the lathe?
Ilhayl! By God, Alayn, thou is a fonne!"
Thise sely clerkes han ful faste yronne
315 Toward the fen, bothe Aleyn and eek John.
     And whan the millere saugh that they were gon,
He half a busshel of hir flour hath take,
And bad his wyf go knede it in a cake.
He seyde, "I trowe the clerkes were aferd.
320 Yet kan a millere make a clerkes berd,
For al his art; now lat hem goon hir weye!
Lo, wher he gooth! Ye, lat the children pleye.
They gete hym nat so lightly, by my croun."
     Thise sely clerkes rennen up and doun
325 With "Keep! Keep! Stand! Stand! Jossa, warderere,
Ga whistle thou, and I shal kepe hym heere!"
But shortly, til that it was verray nyght,
They koude nat, though they dide al hir myght,
Hir capul cacche, he ran alwey so faste,
330 Til in a dych they caughte hym atte laste.
     Wery and weet, as beest is in the reyn,
Comth sely John, and with him comth Aleyn.
"Allas," quod John, "the day that I was born!
Now are we dryve til hethyng and til scorn.
335 Oure corn is stoln; men wil us fooles calle,
Bathe the wardeyn and oure felawes alle,
And namely the millere, weylaway!"

---

320 *make a clerkes berd*] i. e. 'outwit a clerk'
322 *he*] i. e. the horse
324 *rennen*] Chaucer's use of the historical is similar to the function of the present continous in
    Modern English – 'these poor clerks are running to and fro'.

     Thus pleyneth John as he gooth by the way
     Toward the mille, and Bayard in his hond.
340 The millere sittynge by the fyr he fond,
     For it was nyght, and forther myghte they noght;
     But for the love of God they hym bisoght
     Of herberwe and of ese, as for hir peny.
     The millere seyde agayn, "If ther be eny,
345 Swich as it is, yet shal ye have youre part.
     Myn hous is streit, but ye han lerned art;
     Ye konne by argumentes make a place
     A myle brood of twenty foot of space.
     Lat se now if this place may suffise,
350 Or make it rowm with speche, as is youre gise."
     "Now, Symond," seyde John, "by Seint Cutberd,
     Ay is thou myrie, and this is faire answerd.
     I have herd seyd, 'Man sal taa of twa thynges:
     Slyk as he fyndes, or taa slyk as he brynges.'
355 But specially I pray thee, hooste deere,
     Get us som mete and drynke, and make us cheere,
     And we wil payen trewely atte fulle.
     With empty hand men may na haukes tulle;
     Loo, heere oure silver, redy for to spende."
360 This millere into toun his doghter sende
     For ale and breed, and rosted hem a goos,
     And boond hire hors, it sholde namoore go loos,
     And in his owene chambre hem made a bed,
     With sheetes and with chalons faire yspred
365 Noght from his owene bed ten foot or twelve.
     His doghter hadde a bed, al by hirselve,
     Right in the same chambre by and by.
     It myghte be no bet, and cause why?
     Ther was no roumer herberwe in the place.
370 They soupen and they speke, hem to solace,
     And drynken evere strong ale atte beste.
     Aboute mydnyght wente they to reste.
     Wel hath this millere vernysshed his heed;
     Ful pale he was for dronken, and nat reed.
375 He yexeth, and he speketh thurgh the nose
     As he were on the quakke, or on the pose.
     To bedde he goth, and with hym goth his wyf.

---

339 *Bayard*] a name for a horse
346 *ye han lerned art*] this is a reference to the arts curriculum at a medieval university.
347–348 *argumentes . . . space*] Chaucer alludes to a contemporary prejudice against the art of
  disputation ('argumentes').
364 *chalons*] blankets manufactured at Chalons

As any jay she light was and jolyf,
So was hir joly whistle wel ywet.
380   The cradel at hir beddes feet is set,
To rokken, and to yeve the child to sowke.
And whan that dronken al was in the crowke,
To bedde wente the doghter right anon;
To bedde goth Aleyn and also John;
385   Ther nas na moore – hem nedede no dwale.
This millere hath so wisely bibbed ale
That as an hors he fnorteth in his sleep,
Ne of his tayl bihynde he took no keep.
His wyf bar hym a burdon, a ful strong;
390   Men myghte hir rowtyng heere two furlong;
The wenche rowteth eek, *par compaignye*.
     Aleyn the clerk, that herde this melodye,
He poked John, and seyde, "Slepestow?
Herdestow evere slyk a sang er now?
395   Lo, swilk a complyn is ymel hem alle;
A wilde fyr upon thair bodyes falle!
Wha herkned evere slyk a ferly thyng?
Ye, they sal have the flour of il endyng.
This lange nyght ther tydes me na reste;
400   But yet, na fors, al sal be for the beste.
For, John," seyde he, "als evere moot I thryve,
If that I may, yon wenche wil I swyve.
Som esement has lawe yshapen us,
For, John, ther is a lawe that says thus:
405   That gif a man in a point be agreved,
That in another he sal be releved.
Oure corn is stoln, sothly, it is na nay,
And we han had an il fit al this day;
And syn I sal have neen amendement
410   Agayn my los, I will have esement.
By Goddes sale, it sal neen other bee!"
     This John answerde, "Alayn, avyse thee!
The millere is a perilous man," he seyde,
"And gif that he out of his sleep abreyde,
415   He myghte doon us bathe a vileynye."

----

389 *bar hym a burdon*] 'sang the bass accompaniment', i. e. 'snorted just as he did'.
395 *complyn*] the last canonical hour; here the reference is to the service sung before retiring
  for the night.
396 *wilde fyr*] an acute inflammation of the skin
398 *the flour . . . endyng*] i. e. the worst end possible
399 *tydes me na reste*] 'I will get no sleep'

Aleyn answerde, "I counte hym nat a flye."
And up he rist, and by the wenche he crepte.
This wenche lay uprighte and faste slepte,
Til he so ny was, er she myghte espie,
420   That it had been to late for to crie,
And shortly for to seyn, they were aton.
Now pley, Aleyn, for I wol speke of John.
    This John lith stille a furlong wey or two,
And to hymself he maketh routhe and wo.
425   "Allas!" quod he, "this is a wikked jape;
Now may I seyn that I is but an ape.
Yet has my felawe somwhat for his harm;
He has the milleris doghter in his arm.
He auntred hym, and has his nedes sped,
430   And I lye as a draf-sak in my bed;
And when this jape is tald another day,
I sal been halde a daf, a cokenay!
I wil arise and auntre it, by my fayth!
'Unhardy is unseely,' thus men sayth."
435   And up he roos, and softely he wente
Unto the cradel, and in his hand it hente,
And baar it softe unto his beddes feet.
    Soone after this the wyf hir rowtyng leet,
And gan awake, and wente hire out to pisse,
440   And cam agayn, and gan hir cradel mysse,
And groped heer and ther, but she foond noon.
"Allas!" quod she, "I hadde almoost mysgoon;
I hadde almoost goon to the clerkes bed.
Ey, benedicite! Thanne hadde I foule ysped!"
445   And forth she gooth til she the cradel fond.
She gropeth alwey forther with hir hond,
And foond the bed, and thoghte noght but good,
By cause that the cradel by it stood,
And nyste wher she was, for it was derk;
450   But faire and wel she creep in to the clerk,
And lith ful stille, and wolde han caught a sleep.
Withinne a while this John the clerk up leep,
And on this goode wyf he leith on soore.
So myrie a fit ne hadde she nat ful yoore;
455   He priketh harde and depe as he were mad.
This joly lyf han thise two clerkes lad
Til that the thridde cok bigan to synge.

---

423 *a furlong . . . two*] 'for about five minutes'
424 *maketh routhe and wo*] 'he feels sorry for and pities himself'.
434 *Unhardy is unseely*] proverbial: 'the timid one is unlucky'.
454 *So . . . fit*] 'such a good time'

Aleyn wax wery in the dawenynge,
For he had swonken al the longe nyght,
460 And seyde, "Fare weel, Malyne, sweete wight!
The day is come; I may no lenger byde;
But everemo, wher so I go or ryde,
I is thyn awen clerk, swa have I seel!"
     "Now, deere lemman," quod she, "go, far weel!
465 But er thow go, o thyng I wol thee telle:
Whan that thou wendest homward by the melle,
Right at the entree of the dore bihynde
Thou shalt a cake of half a busshel fynde
That was ymaked of thyn owene mele,
470 Which that I heelp my sire for to stele.
And, goode lemman, God thee save and kepe!"
And with that word almoost she gan to wepe.
     Aleyn up rist, and thoughte, "Er that it dawe,
I wol go crepen in by my felawe,"
475 And fond the cradel with his hand anon.
"By God," thoughte he, "al wrang I have mysgon.
Myn heed is toty of my swynk to-nyght,
That makes me that I ga nat aright.
I woot wel by the cradel I have mysgo;
480 Heere lith the millere and his wyf also."
And forth he goth, a twenty devel way,
Unto the bed ther as the millere lay.
He wende have cropen by his felawe John,
And by the millere in he creep anon,
485 And caughte hym by the nekke, and softe he spak.
He seyde, "Thou John, thou swynes-heed, awak,
For Cristes saule, and heer a noble game.
For by that lord that called is Seint Jame,
As I have thries in this shorte nyght
490 Swyved the milleres doghter bolt upright,
Whil thow hast, as a coward, been agast."
     "Ye, false harlot," quod the millere, "hast?
A, false traitour! False clerk!" quod he,
"Thow shalt be deed, by Goddes dignitee!
495 Who dorste be so boold to disparage
My doghter, that is come of swich lynage?"
And by the throte-bolle he caughte Alayn,
And he hente hym despitously agayn,

---

457 *the thridde . . . synge*] the third crow of the cock, about an hour before dawn
481 *a twenty devel way*] 'in the name of twenty devils'
495–496 *disparage . . . lynage*] 'degrade my daughter's superior lineage'

And on the nose he smoot hym with his fest.
500 Doun ran the blody streem upon his brest;
And in the floor, with nose and mouth tobroke,
They walwe as doon two pigges in a poke;
And up they goon, and doun agayn anon,
Til that the millere sporned at a stoon,
505 And doun he fil bakward upon his wyf,
That wiste no thyng of this nyce stryf;
For she was falle aslepe a lite wight
With John the clerk, that waked hadde al nyght,
And with the fal out of hir sleep she breyde.
510 "Help! hooly croys of Bromeholm," she seyde,
"*In manus tuas!* Lord, to thee I calle!
Awak, Symond! The feend is on me falle.
Myn herte is broken; help! I nam but deed!
Ther lyth oon upon my wombe and on myn heed.
515 Help, Symkyn, for the false clerkes fighte!"
      This John stirte up as faste as ever he myghte,
And graspeth by the walles to and fro,
To fynde a staf; and she stirte up also,
And knew the estres bet than dide this John,
520 And by the wal a staf she foond anon,
And saugh a litel shymeryng of a light,
For at an hole in shoon the moone bright,
And by that light she saugh hem bothe two,
But sikerly she nyste who was who,
525 But as she saugh a whit thyng in hir ye.
And whan she gan this white thyng espye,
She wende the clerk hadde wered a volupeer,
And with the staf she drow ay neer and neer,
And wende han hit this Aleyn at the fulle,
530 And smoot the millere on the pyled skulle,
That doun he gooth, and cride, "Harrow! I dye!"
Thise clerkes beete hym weel and lete hym lye,
And greythen hem, and tooke hir hors anon,
And eek hire mele, and on hir wey they gon.
535 And at the mille yet they tooke·hir cake
Of half a busshel flour, ful wel ybake.
      Thus is the proude millere wel ybete,
And hath ylost the gryndynge of the whete,
And payed for the soper everideel

---

507 *a lite wight*] 'for a short time'
510 *hooly croys of Bromeholm*] A reference to the relic of the true cross kept at the Cluniac
priory at Bromholm in Norfolk.
511 *In manus tuas*] 'Into thy hands (I commend my spirit)', Luke 23:46.

540   Of Aleyn and of John, that bette hym weel.
His wyf is swyved, and his doghter als.
Lo, swich it is a millere to be fals!
And therfore this proverbe is seyd ful sooth,
"Hym thar nat wene wel that yvele dooth."
545   A gylour shal hymself bigyled be.
And God, that sitteth heighe in magestee,
Save al this compaignye, grete and smale!
Thus have I quyt the Millere in my tale.

Heere is ended the Reves Tale

---

544 *Hym thar . . . dooth*] 'He that does evil need not expect well'.
545 *A gylour*] proverbial: 'a deceiver will himself be deceived'.

Text 14: Robert Henryson

Robert Henryson, a Middle Scottish poet, worked as a teacher in the second half of the
15th century in Dunfermline; he composed a collection of fables, probably in the
1470s. Fables were very popular in the Middle Ages and early modern period. Similar
to the homiletic tradition and the Physiologus (see M 2 and 3), fables seek to provide a
moral or exemplum based on a situation from the animal world. Essentially, fables are
allegorical poetry, teaching the reader how to act. Even in the prologue to his
collection, Henryson uses the traditional medieval exegetic tradition when describing
the nut and its shell: *The nuttis schell, thocht it be hard and teuch, / Haldis the kirnell,
sueit and delectabill; / Sa lyis thair ane doctrine wyse aneuch / And full of frute, ynder
ane fenzeit fabill* ('the nut may be hard and tough, but it holds the kernel, sweet and
delectable; likewise do (these stories) hold a wise and fruitful kernel under a feigned
fable'). Henryson is thus able to legitimise his work; although poetry has no claim on
truth, it can nonetheless hide a deeper meaning under the surface. This deeper meaning
is always carefully explained by Henryson at the end of the story.

Most fables express some sort of general truth or moral, applicable to the whole
world; Henryson, though he does employ this strategy, also specifically uses the moral
to express definite social criticism (this is to some extent the case in *The Fox and the
Wolf*), making Henryson's fables much richer than traditional fables.

Though Henryson mentions Aesop in the prologue to his fables, he seems to have
relied more on the Latin fable tradition. Gualterus Anglicus, Archbishop of Palermo,
is also credited with writing a collection of Latin fables around 1175, upon which
Henryson relies strongly. The Old French *Roman de Renart* was of course also a
source, as well as the *Disciplina Clericalis* by Petrus Alphonsi.

The Taill of the Foxe, that begylit the wolff in the schadow of the Mone makes use of
three motifs which can be found in other fables: the angry farmer who gives his ox to
the wolf; the wolf who thinks his reflection is a wheel of cheese; and the fox and the
wolf in the well (see M 8). These three motifs can also all be found in the 23rd
exemplum of the *Disciplina Clericalis*, probably Henryson's main source for the
action in this fable. Unlike the exemplum, however, Henryson interprets the action and
builds a *moralitas* quite different from his source.

A survey of the vowel qualities in Middle Scots can be found in Aitken (1977).
Among the most notable features of the text the following deserve to be mentioned:
Old English $\bar{a}$ is written both <a> and <ai>, as for example in *stanis, sa, ma* (l. 13, 4,
112) and *sair, mair* (l. 9, 22). The present participle ends in *-ande*, as in *hirpilland*
(l. 25), *eirrand* (l. 37), *lourand* (l. 64) and so on. Word-initial *hw-* is written <quh->,
as in *quhilk* (l. 2), *quhy* (l. 34), *quhair* (l. 60) and so on.

Sources: The text is based on an edition printed by the Scottish printer Thomas
Bassandyne in 1571. – Fox (1981); Elliott (1974), Gopen (1987). – Secondary
literature: Gray (1979), Powell (1983).

In elderis dayis, as Esope can declair,   [2231]
Thair wes ane husband quhilk had ane plewch to steir.
His vse wes ay in morning to ryse air:
Sa happinnit him, in streiking tyme off ʒeir,
5   Airlie in the morning to follou furth his feir
Vnto the pleuch, bot his gadman and he.
His stottis he straucht with 'Benedicite!';

The caller cryit: 'How! Haik!' vpon hicht,
'Hald draucht, my dowis,' syne broddit thame full sair:
10   The oxin wes vnwsit, ʒoung, and licht,
And for fersnes thay couth the fur forfair.
The husband than woxe angrie as ane hair,
Syne cryit, and caist his patill and grit stanis:
'The volff,' quod he, 'mot haue ʒou all at anis!'

15   Bot ʒit the volff wes neirar nor he wend,
For in ane busk he lay, and Lowrence baith,
In ane rouch rone wes at the furris end,
And hard the hecht; than Lowrence leuch full raith:
'To tak ʒone bud,' quod he, 'it wer na skaith.'
20   'Weill,' quod the volff, 'I hecht the, be my hand,
ʒone carlis word as he wer king sall stand.'

The oxin waxit mair reulie at the last;
Syne efter thay lousit, fra that it worthit weill lait;
The husband hamewart with his cattell past.
25   Than sone the volff come hirpilland in his gait
Befoir the oxin, and schupe to mak debait.
The husband saw him, and worthit sumdeill agast,
And bakwart with his beistis wald haif past.

The volff said: 'Quhether dryuis thou this pray?
30   I chalenge it, for nane off thame ar thyne!'
The man thairoff wes in ane felloun fray,

---

1 *In elderis dayis*] 'In the days of our forefathers'
4 *in . . . ʒeir*] season for ploughing, either spring or autumn
7 *His . . . straucht*] 'He put his young oxen to work'.
8 *cryit . . . hicht*] 'called loudly "Let's go!"'
9 *Hald . . . dowis*] 'Keep pulling, my doves!'
11 *And . . . forfair*] 'They destroyed the furrow with their vehemence'.
13 *patill*] a small spade used for cleaning the plough
15 *nor he wend*] 'than he suspected'
18 *full raith*] 'immediately'
21 *ʒone . . . stand*] 'This man's word is as good as the king's', i. e. we can rely on him.
23 *lousit*] 'they unharnessed the oxen'.
29 *thou*] The wolf always uses the familiar form 'thou', whereas the farmer uses the formal
'ʒe' (see l. 34); the fox, on the other hand, addresses the farmer with 'thou' (see l. 86) and the
wolf with 'ʒe' (see l. 109).

And soberlie to the volff answerit syne:
'Schir, be my saull, thir oxin ar all myne:
Thairfoir I studdie quhy ȝe suld stop me,
35   Sen that I faltit never to ȝou, trewlie.'

The volff said, 'Carll, gaif thou not me this drift
Airlie, quhen thou wes eirrand on ȝone bank?
And is thair oucht, sayis thou, frear than gift?
This tarying wyll tyne the all thy thank:
40   Far better is frelie for to giff ane plank
Nor be compellit on force to giff ane mart.
Fy on the fredome that cummis not with hart!'

'Schir,' quod the husband, 'ane man may say in greif,
And syne ganesay fra he auise and se.
45   I hecht to steill; am I thairfoir ane theif?
God forbid, schir, all hechtis suld haldin be.
Gaif I my hand or oblissing,' quod he,
'Or haue ȝe witnes or writ for to schau?
Schir, reif me not, bot go and seik the lau.'

50   'Carll,' quod the volff, 'ane lord, and he be leill,
That schrinkis for schame, or doutis to be repruuit –
His sau is ay als sicker as his seill.
Fy on the leid that is not leill and lufit!
Thy argument is fals, and eik contrufit,
55   For it is said in prouerb: "But lawte
All vther vertewis ar nocht worth ane fle."'

'Schir,' said the husband, 'remember of this thing:
Ane leill man is not tane at halff ane taill.
I may say and ganesay; I am na king.
60   Quhair is ȝour witnes that hard I hecht thame haill?'
Than said the volff, 'Thairfoir it sall nocht faill.
Lowrence,' quod he, 'cum hidder of that schaw,
And say na thing bot as thow hard and saw.'

---

35 *Sen . . . trewlie*] 'Since I have never done anything wrong to you'.
40–41 *Far . . . mart*] 'It is better to give a little of your own accord than to have to pay a lot in the end'.
47 *Gaif . . . oblissing*] 'Have I sealed the deal with this handshake?'
50–52 *ane . . . seill*] freely: 'The word of a loyal lord who fears shame or reproof can always be trusted'.
55–56 *But . . . fle*] 'justice is the greatest virtue of all'.
58 *Ane . . . taill*] 'A good man will not be fooled by a half-truth'.
61 *Thairfoir . . . faill*] 'my case shall not fail for that reason'.

Lowrence come lourand, for he lufit neuer licht,
65   And sone appeirit befoir thame in that place:
The man leuch na thing quhen he saw that sicht.
'Lowrence,' quod the volff, 'thow man declair this cace,
Quhairof we sall schaw the suith in schort space.
I callit on the leill witnes for to beir:
70   Quhat hard thou that this man hecht me lang eir?'

'Schir,' said the tod, 'I can not hastelie
Swa sone as now gif sentence finall;
Bot wald ȝe baith submit ȝow heir to me,
To stand at my decreit perpetuall,
75   To pleis baith I suld preif, gif it may fall.'
'Weill,' quod the volff, 'I am content for me.'
The man said: 'Swa am I, how euer it be.'

Than schew thay furth thair allegeance but fabill,
And baith proponit thair pley to him compleit.
80   Quod Lowrence, 'Now I am iuge amycabill:
Ȝe sall be sworne to stand at my decreit,
Quhether heirefter ȝe think it soure or sweit.'
The volff braid furth his fute, the man his hand,
And on the toddis taill sworne thay ar to stand.

85   Than tuke the tod the man furth till ane syde,
And said him, 'Freind, thou art in blunder brocht;
The volff will not forgif the ane oxe hyde.
Ȝit wald my self fane help the, and I mocht,
Bot I am laith to hurt my conscience ocht.
90   Tyne nocht thy querrell in thy awin defence;
This will not throu but grit coist and expence.

'Seis thou not buddis beiris bernis throw,
And giftis garris crukit materis hald full euin?
Sumtymis ane hen haldis ane man in ane kow;
95   All ar not halie that heifis thair handis to heuin.'
'Schir,' said the man, 'ȝe sall haue sex or seuin
Richt off the fattest hennis off all the floik –
I compt not all the laif, leif me the coik.'

---

70 *lang eir*] 'earlier'
78 *Than . . . fabill*] 'Then they explained the case accurately'.
86 *thou . . . brocht*] 'you're in trouble now'.
90–91 *Tyne . . . expence*] 'Do not weaken your case by only thinking of your defence (strategy)
/ You will have to pay a little (in order to win your case)'.
92–93 *'Seis . . . euin?*] freely: 'Do you not see how bribes make things easier, and gifts
straighten out even crooked affairs?'
94 *Sumtymis . . . kow*] 'Sometimes a hen can save you a cow'.
98 *I compt . . . coik*] freely: 'I don't care about the hens, just leave me the cock'.

'I am ane iuge,' quod Lowrence than, and leuch:
100   'Thair is na buddis suld beir me by the rycht.
I may tak hennis and caponis weill aneuch,
For God is gane to sleip, as for this nycht;
Sic small thingis ar not sene in to his sicht.
Thir hennis,' quod he, 'sall mak thy querrell sure:
105   With emptie hand na man suld halkis lure.'

Concordit thus, than Lowrence tuke his leiff,
And to the volff he went in to ane ling;
Syne preuelie he plukkit him be the sleiff:
'Is this in ernist,' quod he, 'ȝe ask sic thing?
110   Na, be my saull, I trow it be in heithing.'
Than said the volff: 'Lowrence, quhy sayis thou sa?
Thow hard the hecht thy selff that he couth ma.'

'The hecht,' quod he, 'ȝone man maid at the pleuch –
Is that the cause quhy ȝe the cattell craif?'
115   Halff into heithing said Lowrence than, and leuch:
'Schir, be the rude, vnroikit now ȝe raif:
The Deuill ane stirk taill thairfoir sall ȝe haif!
Wald I tak it vpon my conscience
To do sa pure ane man as ȝone offence?

120   'Ȝit haif I commonnit with the carll,' quod he.
'We ar concordit vpon this cunnand:
Quyte off all clamis, swa ȝe will mak him fre,
Ȝe sall ane cabok haue into ȝour hand
That sic ane sall not be in all this land,
125   For it is somer cheis, baith fresche and fair;
He sayis it weyis ane stane and sumdeill mair.'

'Is that thy counsell,' quod the volff, 'I do,
That ȝone carll for ane cabok suld be fre?'
'Ȝe, be my saull, and I wer sworne ȝow to,
130   Ȝe suld nane vther counsell haue for me;
For gang ȝe to the maist extremitie,
It will not wyn ȝow worth ane widderit neip:
Schir, trow ȝe not I haue ane saull to keip?'

<hr />

100 *Thair . . . rycht*] 'No bribe can bring me away from the right path'.
107 *in . . . ling*] 'immediately'
112 *that . . . ma*] '(the promise) he made'
116–117 *vnroikit . . . haif*] freely: 'you're raving without reason; you'll get nothing as a result'.
121–122 *We . . . fre*] 'We have agreed on this: if you forget all claims and release from his obligation'.
127 *I do*] '(your advice) that I should follow'
132 *wyn . . . neip*] freely: 'will bring you nowhere'

'Weill,' quod the volff, 'it is aganis my will

135 That ʒone carll for ane cabok suld ga quyte.'

'Schir,' quod the tod, 'ʒe tak it in nane euill,

For, be my saull, ʒour self had all the wyte.'

'Than,' said, the volff, 'I bid na mair to flyte,

Bot I wald se ʒone cabok off sic pryis.'

140 'Schir,' said the tod, 'he tauld me quhair it lyis.'

Than hand in hand thay held vnto ane hill;

The husband till his hous hes tane the way,

For he wes fane he schaippit from thair ill,

And on his feit woke the dure quhill day.

145 Now will we turne vnto the vther tway:

Throw woddis waist thir freikis on fute can fair,

Fra busk to busk, quhill neir midnycht and mair.

Lowrence wes euer remembring vpon wrinkis

And subtelteis, the volff for to begyle;

150 That he had hecht ane caboik he forthinkis;

ʒit at the last he findis furth ane wyle,

Than at him selff softlie couth he smyle.

The volff sayis, 'Lowrence, thov playis bellie blind;

We seik all nycht, bot na thing can we find.'

155 'Schir,' said the tod, 'we ar at it almaist;

Soft ʒow ane lytill, and ʒe sall se it sone.'

Than to ane manure place thay hyit in haist;

The nycht wes lycht, and pennyfull the mone.

Than till ane draw well thir senʒeours past but hone,

160 Quhair that twa bukkettis seuerall suithlie hang;

As ane come vp ane vther doun wald gang.

The schadow off the mone schone in the well:

'Schir,' said Lowrence, 'anis ʒe sall find me leill;

Now se ʒe not the caboik weill ʒour sell,

165 Quhyte as ane neip and round als as ane seill?

He hang it ʒonder that na man suld it steill.

Schir, traist ʒe weill, ʒone caboik ʒe se hing

Micht be ane present to ony lord or king!'

---

144 *And . . . day*] 'and stayed on his feet, guarding the door, until daybreak'.

153 *thov . . . blind*] 'you are playing blind man's bluff'.

156 *Soft . . . lytill*] 'Calm down a little'

157 *manure place*] 'manor house'

158 *pennyfull . . . mone*] i. e. full moon

159 *but hone*] 'at once'

'Na,' quod the volff, 'mycht I ȝone caboik haif
170 On the dry land, as I it ȝonder se,
I wald quitclame the carll off all the laif:
His dart oxin I compt thame not ane fle;
Ȝone wer mair meit for sic ane man as me.
Lowrence,' quod he, 'leip in the bukket sone,
175 And I sall hald the ane, quhill thow haue done.'

Lowrence gird doun baith sone and subtellie;
The vther baid abufe and held the flaill.
'It is sa mekill,' quod Lowrence, 'it maisteris me:
On all my tais it hes not left ane naill.
180 Ȝe man mak help vpwart, and it haill:
Leip in the vther bukket haistelie,
And cum sone doun and mak me sum supple!'

Than lychtlie in the bukket lap the loun;
His wecht but weir the vther end gart ryis:
185 The tod come hailland vp, the volff ȝeid doun.
Than angerlie the volff vpon him cryis:
'I cummand thus dounwart, quhy thow vpwart hyis?'
'Schir,' quod the foxe, 'thus fairis it off fortoun:
As ane cummis vp, scho quheillis ane vther doun!'

190 Than to the ground sone ȝeid the volff in haist;
The tod lap on land, als blyith as ony bell,
And left the volff in watter to the waist:
Quha haillit him out, I wait not, off the well.
Heir endis the text; thair is na mair to tell.
195 Ȝit men may find ane gude moralitie
In this sentence, thocht it ane fabill be.

Moralitas

This wolf I likkin to ane wickit man
Quhilk dois the pure oppres in euerie place,
And pykis at thame all querrellis that he can,
200 Be rigour, reif and vther wickitnes.
The foxe, the Feind I call into this cais,
Arctand ilk man to ryn vnrychteous rinkis,
Thinkand thairthrow to lok him in his linkis.

---

172 *His . . . fle*] 'His damn oxen are worth nothing to me'.
182 *and mak . . . supple*] 'and help me a little'
184 *but weir*] 'doubtless'
188–189 *fortoun . . . doun*] The fox is making an ironic reference to the Wheel of Fortune.
199 *And . . . can*] 'And pick as many quarrels as he can'.
202 *Arctand . . . rinkis*] 'forcing everyone to take the crooked path'

The husband may be callit ane godlie man
205 With quhome the Feynd falt findes, as clerkis reids,
Besie to tempt him with all wayis that he can.
The hennis ar warkis that fra ferme faith proceidis:
Quhair sic sproutis spreidis, the euill spreit thair not speids,
Bot wendis vnto the wickit man agane –
210 That he hes tint his trauell is full vnfane.

The wodds waist, quhairin wes the wolf wyld
Ar wickit riches, quhilk all men gaipis to get:
Quha traistis in sic trusterie ar oft begyld,
For mammon may be callit the Deuillis net,
215 Quhilk Sathanas for all sinfull hes set:
With proud plesour quha settis his traist thairin,
But speciall grace lychtlie can not outwin.

The cabok may be callit couetyce,
Quhilk blomis braid in mony mannis ee:
220 Wa worth the well of that wickit vyce,
For it is all bot fraud and fantasie,
Dryuand ilk man to leip in the buttrie
That dounwart drawis vnto the pane of hell –
Christ keip all Christianis from that wickit well!

208–210 *Quhair . . . vnfane*] freely: 'The devil will not succeed where there are good works; he concentrates his efforts on wicked men; he regrets having laboured in vain'.
211 *quhairin . . . wyld*] 'where the wolf was tricked'
213 *Quha . . . trusterie*] 'whoever trusts in such trash'
216–217 *With . . . outwin*] 'Whoever sets his trust therein (i. e. money), can only be saved by God's special grace'.
222 *buttrie*] Storerooms ('buttery') were often in the basement.

7. Glossaries

How to use the glossaries

The glossary for the *Old English* texts contains all forms except for Latin words and Roman numerals. For inflected forms which occur frequently there is a reference to the infinitive or nominative singular under which they are listed and parsed. Nominal forms are listed according to case and number, verbal forms according to person-number-tense-mode. If a form appears frequently in a given text, only the first few text and line references will be given, provided homography can be ruled out.

Nouns, adjectives and verbs which only appear in the texts in inflected forms will be listed as they appear; the form of the nominative singular or infinitive is given in square brackets at the end of the list.

Proper names glossed in the explanatory notes accompanying the texts are listed in the glossaries but not glossed.

When using the glossary for the Old English texts you should be aware of the following rules:
1. *æ* follows *a* and *þ, ð* follow *t*.
2. Long vowels follow short vowels.
3. Negative contractions of verbs as well as complex collocations such as 'for ðan þe' are listed at the end of the respective entry. The individual forms are listed in alphabetic order with a reference to the main entry: for example 'næs' directs you to 'bēon', 'for þām' to 'for'.
4. Forms only appearing with the prefix *ge-* are listed alphabetically under 'ge-'; forms which appear both with and without 'ge-' are listed under the root word.

The glossary for the *Middle English* texts is structured parallel to the Old English glossary; however, there are no glosses for entries which can easily be derived from Modern English. Pronominal and verbal forms appearing frequently are listed and discussed under the Modern English form of the nominative or infinitive, which is given in quotation marks. The Modern English form is also used when there is considerable dialectal variation: for example, "sæ" (2 instances), "se" (2 instances), "see" (2 instances) and "ze" (also 2 instances) are referenced to "sea", although this form is not found in the texts. Although this is not the standard method, it has the decided advantage of offering readers the form they are already familiar with.

Observe the following guidelines in using the Middle English glossary:
1. *æ* follows *a*, *ȝ* follows *g* and word initial *ð, þ, th* follow *t*.
2. Negative and pronominal contractions of verbs are listed at the end of a given entry.
3. Vocalic *v* and consonantal *u* are not differentiated.

The abbreviations used in both glossaries are found below. The reference to the text is shown by text number/line number. The Middle English poems in text 10 are delineated by a decimal point, e. g. '10.1/5' means text ten, poem one, line five. References to a new text are signalled by an asterisk.

Please note, the category *case* is indicated in the following way: nominative, accusative, genitive, dative, and instrumental are shortened to the first letter of the case and the number is appended to this. For example, nasg. = nominative or accusative singular and so on.

Similarly, cases governed by prepositions or verbs are indicated in brackets; for example, (d.a.) = dative or accusative preposition or verb.

adj.	adjective	perspron.	personal pronoun
adv.	adverb	pl.	plural
art.	article	pn.	place name
aux.	auxiliary verb	poss.	possessive
col.	collocation	prep.	preposition
comp.	comparative	prn.	proper name
compd.	compound form	pron.	pronoun
conj.	conjunction	prps.	preterite present
contr.	contracted form	ps.	present (indicative)
dempron.	demonstrative pronoun	psp.	present participle
f.	feminine	pt.	past (indicative)
imp.	imperative	ptp.	past participle
impv.	impersonal verb	refl.	reflexive
inf.	infinitive	rel.	relative use
infl.	inflected form	relpart.	relative particle
infl. inf.	inflected infinitive	sb.	substantive
init.	word initial	sg.	singular
interj.	interjection	subj.	subjunctive
irr.	irregular	sup.	superlative
m.	masculine	vb.	verb
n.	neuter	voc.	vocative
neg.	negated form	I–III	weak verb classes
num.	numeral	1–7	strong verb classes
obj.	object case	1., 1.sg.	1st person etc.
ord.	ordinal	1, 2	conjugation according to
part.	particle		class 1 and 2

Old English Glossary

ā (adv.) *always, (for)ever, continuously* 2/155 *6/27, 180 *7/9 *8/109 *10/315; **aa** 7/4

abbod (nsg. m.) *abbot* 2/96

abbudisse (nsg. f.) *abbess* 3/118; **abbudissan** (gdsg.) 3/66, 108

ābēod (imp.sg.) *to announce* 10/49; **ābēad** (sg.pt.) 10/27 [ābēodan 2]

ābīdan (1) *to (a)wait, remain behind* 6/158

Abraham (prn.) 1/3, 7, 9–10 etc.; **Abrahames** (gsg.) 1/1

ābrēoðe (sg.ps. subj.) *to fail, degenerate* 10/242; **ābroþene** (ptp.) 7/113 [ābrēoþan]

ac (adv., conj.) *but, however, moreover; and* 1/27 *2/17, 108, 126 etc. *3/27, 56, 74 etc. *4/19 *5/29, 35 *6/9, 50, 113–114 etc. *7/10, 29, 43 etc. *8/3, 10, 21 etc. *10/82, 193, 247 etc. *11/11, 43, 115 etc.

ācwele (imp.sg.) *to kill* 1/18; **ācwealde** (sg.pt.) 7/60 [ācwellan I]

ācwehte (sg.pt.) *to shake* 10/255, 310 [ācweccan I]

ācwencan (I) *to quench, extinguish* 7/18

āde (dsg. m.n.) *(funeral) pyre* 4/26 [ād]

ādlig (adj. nsg. m.) *sick, diseased* 6/170; **ādligum** (dpl.) 6/128

ādliga (nsg. m.) *sick person* 6/23; **ādligan** (dsg.) 6/166

Adomes (prn. gsg.) *Adam* 11/100

ādrāf (sg.pt.) *to drive out/away* 2/103 [ādrīfan 1]

ādrǣfan (I) *to drive out/away* 2/6; **ādrǣfde** (sg.pt.) 2/3

ādrēah → **ādrēogað**

ādrēd (sg.pt.) *to dread, fear* 8/79 [ādrǣdan I]

ādrēogað (pl.ps.) *to practise, commit, pass time* 7/69; **ādrēah** (sg.pt.) 6/154 [ādrēogan 2]

ādruncen (ptp.) *to drown* 2/115 [ādrincan 3]

ādwǣscte (sg.pt.) *to put out* 6/8 [ādwǣscan I]

āēode (sg.pt.) *to happen* 2/102 [āgān irr.]

afaran (napl. m.) *successor, offspring* 9/7, 52

āfeallen (ptp.) *to fall (down)* 5/53 *10/202 [āfeallan 7]

āfirsa (imp.sg.) *to drive away* 8/39 [āfeorsian II]

āflīgde (ptp.) *to expell* 6/125 [āflīegan I]

āflȳmde (sg.pt.) *to put to flight* 10/243 [āflīeman I]

āfyllan (I) *to kill* 6/13; **āfylle** (sg.ps. subj.) 7/82, 84

āfyrhte (ptp.) *to frighten, terrify* 6/119, 146 [āfyrhtan I]

āfȳsan (I) *to drive away, impell* 10/3; **āfȳsed** (ptp.) 11/125

āgan (prps.) *to own, have* 1/29 *10/87; **āh** (sg.ps.) 10/175 *11/107; **āht** (2.sg.ps.) 3/91; **āhte** (sg.pt.) 7/83 *10/189; **āhton** (pl.pt.) 2/62, 74, 75 etc. ◆ neg.: **nāh** (sg.ps.) 11/131

āgeaf (sg.pt.) *to deliver* 3/117 *10/44; **āgyfen** (ptp.) 10/116 [āgiefan 5]

āgen (adj. asg. n.) *own* 5/27, 35, 41, 43–44; **āgenum** (dsg. n.m.) 6/41 *7/49; (dpl.) 7/80; **āgenne** (asg. m.) 2/24 *7/72

āgēted (ptp.) *to kill* 9/18 [āgētan I]

āginnan (pl.ps. subj.) *to begin* 7/135 [āginnan 3]

āgoten (ptp.) *to empty, shed* 6/124 [āgēotan 2]

āgyfen → **āgeaf**

āh; āhafen; āhangen → **āgan; āhefde; āhēng**

āhēawen (ptp.) *to cut down* 11/29 [āhēawan 7]

āhefde (sg.pt. (weak)) *to lift (up), raise* 1/22; **āhōf** (sg.pt. (strong)) 10/130, 244 *11/44; **āhōfon** (pl.pt.) 10/213 *11/61; **āhafen** (ptp.) 10/106 [āhebban 7]

āhēng (sg.pt.) *to hang* 6/142; **āhangen** (ptp.) 6/147 [āhōn 7]

āhōf, āhōfon → **āhefde**

āhrǣrde → **ārǣrende**

āhreddene (infl.inf.) *to save, rescue* 6/14; **āhredde** (sg.ps. subj.) 6/13 [āhreddan I]

āhsode → **(ge)āscian**

āht → **āgan**

āhte, āhton → **ōwiht; āgan**

āhwār (adv.) *anywhere* 7/152

Aidan (prn.) 6/33, 43, 56; **Aidanus** 6/62, 64; **Aidanes** (gsg.) 6/176

āīdligan (II) *to profane* 3/46

alda → **eald**

aldorman, aldormen, aldormon, aldormonnes → **ealdormann**

Aldred (prn.) 2/131

ālecgað (pl.ps.) *to lay down; kill* 4/28, 40; **ālēdon** (pl.pt.) 6/17 *11/63; **ālēd** (ptp.) 4/29 [ālecgan I]

ālīhð (sg.ps.) *to deny* 6/170 [ālēogan 2]

all, alle, alne → **eall**

ālȳfan (I) *to allow, grant* 10/90; **ālȳfed** (ptp.) 3/52 *8/34

Amen (interj.) 6/180 *7/163

āmyrde (sg.pt.) *to injure* 10/165 [āmyrran I]

ān (adj. nasg. m.n.) *a, one, a single, alone* 2/4, 85 *3/25, 27, 78 *4/42, 44 *5/13, 62 *6/57,

115, 135, 153 *7/69, 89, 137, 142 *8/103;
āna (nsg. m.) 6/147 *8/43, 45 *10/94
*11/123, 128; āne (asg. f.) 5/62 *6/11
*7/68–69; ānre (dsg. f.) 1/3 *4/28, 30 *6/124
*8/101, 103; ānne (asg. m.) 1/21 *2/7 *5/15
*10/117, 226; ǣnne 5/21 *6/143 *8/51, 107;
ānra (gpl.) 11/86, 108; ānum (dsg. m.n.) 2/17,
32 *6/57, 141, 146, 152; (adv.) 7/70
anbīdiað (imp.pl.) *to stay, remain* 1/7;
  geanbīdode (sg.pt.) 2/136 [anbīdian II]
āncennedan (dasg. m.) *only-begotten* 1/2, 20,
26
and (conj.) *and, but* and . . . and, ond . . . ond
  both . . . and
andefn (nsg. f.) *amount* 4/28
andette (sg.ps.) *to confess, acknowledge* 3/11;
  ondette 3/37; (sg.pt.) 3/41 [andettan I]
andgit (nsg. n.) *meaning* 5/57; andgiete (dsg.)
  5/57
andgitfullīcost (adv. sup.) *(most) meaningful*
  5/61
Andred (pn.) 2/3
andsund (adj. nsg. m.) *healthy, whole* 6/110;
  ansund (nsg. f.) 6/137; (nsg. m.) 6/147
andsware (asg. f.) *answer* 3/93 *10/44
andswarode (sg.pt.) *to answer* 3/1, 9;
  ondswarade 3/157; ondswarede 3/89;
  andswerode 8/103; ondsworede 3/47;
  ondswaredon (pl.pt.) 3/155, 162;
  ondswarodon 3/151 [andswarian II]
andwearde (adj. nsg. n.) *present* 3/21; (npl.)
  8/56; ondweardum (dpl.) 3/110
andwlitan (dsg. m.) *face, countenance* 8/11,
  18 [andwlita]
andwyrde (sg.pt.) *to answer* 1/11, 18 *5/36
  [andwyrdan I]
āne → ān
anforht (adj. nsg.) *terrified* 11/117
ānforlēte (sg.pt. subj.) *to abandon* 3/119
  [ānforlǣtan 7]
Angelcynn (prn.) *England, the English* 5/3–4,
  24, 34, 54; Angelcynne (dsg.) 5/11, 48
angin (nsg. n.) *enterprise* 10/242
Angle (npl. m.) *Angles* 6/67; Engle 2/116
  *7/87, 95 *9/70; Engla (gpl.) 7/144; Englum
  (dpl.) 7/152
Anlāf (prn.) 9/46; Anlāfes (gsg.) 9/31; Anlāfe
  (dsg.) 9/26
ānlipig (adj. nsg. m.) *single* 2/83; ānlēpne (asg.
  m.) 5/15
ānne, ānra, ānre → ān
ānrǣd (adj. asg. m.) *resolute* 10/44, 132
ansund → andsund

Antecrīstes (prn. gsg.) *Antichrist* 7/5
ānum → ān
Anwealda (nsg. m.) *God, ruler* 11/153
Apollines (prn.) *Apollo* 8/53
Apollonius (prn.) 8/1, 3, 6, 25 etc.; Apolloni
  (voc.) 8/36, 44, 49 etc.; Apollonige (dsg.)
  8/50, 87, 91; Apollonio (dsg.) 8/11, 16, 22
  etc.; Apollonium (asg.) 8/79, 92
apostatan (npl. m.) *apostate* 7/113
apostola (gpl.) *apostle* 3/131 [apostol]
apuldran (dsg. f.) *apple tree* 2/125
ār (nsg. m.) *messenger* 10/26
ārās → ārīsan
ārǣdan (I) *to read* 5/51, 54; ārēdodne (ptp.)
  to choose 8/108
ārǣrende (psp.) *to raise, erect, spread* 6/86;
  ārǣrde (sg.pt.) 1/14 *6/11, 19; āhrǣrde
  6/54; ārǣred (ptp.) 6/26 *11/44 [ārǣran I]
arcebiscop (nsg. m.) *archbishop* 2/131, 140,
  146, 151; ærcebiscep 2/56; ærcebiscepe
  (dsg.) 5/58
Arcestrates (prn.) 8/11, 48, 65, 98
āreccean (I) *to translate, explain, tell* 5/13,
  61; ārece (imp.sg.) 8/25; ārehte (sg.pt.) 8/29
ārēdodne → ārǣdan
ārehte → āreccean
ārfæstnisse (dsg. f.) *piety* 3/68 [ārfæstnes]
ārhwate (adj. npl.) *eager for glory* 9/73
ārian (II (d.)) *to spare, pardon* 1/26
āriht (adv.) *rightly, properly* 7/98
ārīsan (1) *to arise, rise* 3/161; ārās (sg.pt.) 1/3
  *3/83, 104 *6/133 *11/101; ārison (pl.pt.)
  8/73
arodlīce (adv.) *quickly* 1/17
ārwurðlīce (adv.) *solemnly* 6/38, 109, 121
ārwurðne (adj. asg. m.) *honourable* 6/33
ārwurðnysse (dsg. f.) *honour, reverence*
  6/106, 120 [ārwurðnes]
ārwurðode (sg.pt.) *to honour* 6/92
  [ārweorðian II]
āsǣde (sg.pt.) *to tell, say* 10/198 [āsecgan III]
āsænde (1.sg.ps.) *to send* 8/110 [āsendan I]
Ascanmynster (pn.) *Axminster, Devon* 2/35
(ge)āscian (II) *to ask, demand; discover* āscie
  (1.sg.ps.) 1/11; āxsast (2.sg.ps.) 8/26; āxsa
  (imp.sg.) 8/21; āscode (sg.pt.) 1/10; āhsode
  3/44; geāscode 2/8; geāxode 6/112
āsceōc (sg.pt.) *to shake* 10/230 [āscacan 7]
āsette (sg.ps. subj.) *to set, put, erect* 4/46
  *11/142; āsetton (pl.pt.) 11/32 [āsettan I]
āslēan (6) *to cut off* 6/102; āslagen (ptp.)
  6/110
āsmēagan (I) *to consider* 7/138

āsmiþod (ptp.) *to forge* 6/109 [āsmiðian II]

āsolcennesse (asg. f.) *laziness* 7/146
  [āsolcennes]

āsong → singan

āspended (ptp.) *to spend* 4/38 [āspendan I]

āsprang (sg.pt.) *to spread* 6/151 [āspringan 3]

Assere (prn.) 5/58

assum (dpl. m.) *ass, donkey* 1/5, 8 [assa]

āstāg (sg.pt.) *to rise, ascend* 11/103 [āstīgan 1]

āstirian (I) *to stir, move* 8/55; āstyred 11/30

āstrece (imp.sg.) *to stretch (out), reach* 1/19;
  āstreht (ptp.) 6/117 [āstreccan I]

āstyred → āstirian

āswefede (ptp.) *to kill* 9/30 [āswebban I]

ātēah (sg.pt.) *to draw, pull* 1/16; ātuge (sg.pt.
  subj.) 3/134 [ātēon 2]

āð (asg. m.) *oath* 7/158; āðas (apl.) 2/119, 143

āðbricas (apl. m.) *oath-breaking* 7/111
  [āðbrice]

āðume (dsg. m.) *son-in-law* 8/107 [āðum]

āþwōh (sg.pt.) *to wash* 6/123 [āðwēan 6]

Augustīnus (prn.) 6/1

āwǣgan (I) *to annul* 6/169

āwearp (sg.pt.) *to throw away, cast aside,
  depose* 3/50 *6/34; āworpenne (ptp. nsg. m.)
  2/38 [āweorpan 3]

āweg (adv.) *away* 6/146

āwehte (sg.pt. subj.) *to awake, rouse, raise
  (up)* 3/135; āwehton (pl.pt.) 8/90 [āweccan I]

āwendan (I) *to turn (from, to); translate*
  6/159; āwende (sg.pt.) 5/61; āwend (ptp.)
  6/39; āwendum (ptp.) 6/74

āwōc (sg.pt.) *to awake* 6/137 [āwacan 6]

āworpenne → āwearp

āwrītað (pl.ps.) *to write (down)* 8/109; āwrāt
  (sg.pt.) 7/142; āwritene (ptp.) 5/27

āxsa, āxsast → (ge)āscian

Æ

ǣ (nsg. f.) *law* 5/40

ǣfæst (adj. nsg. m.) *pious, religious* 3/136;
  ǣfæste (apl.) 3/74; ǣfestan (asg. f.) 3/78

ǣfæstnes (nsg. f.) *religion, piety* 3/12;
  ǣfæstnisse (dsg.) 3/68; ǣfestnesse 3/78

ǣfen (asg. m.) *evening* 2/96; ǣfenne 3/145

ǣfentīde (asg. f.) *eventide* 11/68

ǣfestan → ǣfæst

æfestful (adj. nsg. m.) *full of envy* 8/9

æfestig (adj. nsg. m.) *envious* 8/6

æfestigað (sg.ps.) *to envy* 8/10 [æfestigian II]

ǣfestnesse → ǣfæstnes

ǣfre (adv.) *ever, always, constantly* 2/119,
  133 *5/36 *6/68, 74 *7/116 *9/66 *10/271

æftan (adv.) *(from) behind* 7/54 *9/63

æfter (adv., prep. (d.)) *after, afterwards, behind*
  2/76, 92, 154 *3/69, 73, 102 *4/5, 26, 34
  *5/30 *6/7, 72, 104, 178 *7/10, 70, 90, 90
  *8/2, 26, 57 etc. *10/65 *11/65 ♦ col.: æfter
  þām (adv.) 7/60, 80; æfter ðan ðe (conj.)
  after 6/1

æfterfylige (sg.ps. subj.) *to follow after,
  succeed* 3/29

æftergengan (gpl. m.) *follower, successor* 6/6
  [æftergenga]

Ægelnāð (prn.) 2/151

ǣghwǣr (adv.) *everywhere, completely* 7/22,
  47, 115

ǣghwæþer ge ge → ǣgþer

ǣghwylc (pron., adj. nsg. m.f.) *each, every, all*
  10/234 *11/120; ǣghwylcan (dsg. m.) 7/30;
  ǣghwylcne (asg. m.) 11/86

ǣgþer (pron., adj.) *every one, either (of both)*
  7/59 *10/133; ǣgðer 10/224; ǣgðre (dsg. f.)
  2/127 ♦ col.: ǣgþær ge (conj.) *both . . . and,
  as well as* 2/98; ǣgðer ge . . . ge 5/7, 30;
  ǣgþer ge . . . ge 5/3; ǣgðer ge . . . ge . . . ge
  5/5, 8; ǣghwæþer ge . . . ge 3/2

ǣgylde (adj. nsg. m.) *unpaid, without
  compensation* 7/83

Ǣgypta londe (pn.) *Egypt* 3/128

ǣlc (adj., pron. nsg. m.n.) *any, all, every, each*
  4/34, 36 *7/53–54, 70, 90 *8/59; ǣlces (gsg.
  m.) 4/41; ǣlcere (dsg. f.) 4/15 *6/108; ǣlcre
  5/62; ǣlcum (dsg. m.) 5/61 *6/61; ǣlcra
  (gpl.) 7/32

Ælfere (prn.) 10/80

Ælfnōð (prn.) 10/183

Ælfred (prn.) *King Alfred* 2/48, 59, 63 etc.
  *5/1

Ælfrīces (prn., gsg.) 10/209

Ælfwine (prn.) 10/211, 231

Ællan (prn.) 2/39

ælmæsriht (nsg. m.) *right to alms* 7/37

ælmesgeorn (adj. nsg. m.) *charitable* 6/53

ælmihtig (adj. nsg. m.) *almighty* 3/103 *11/39,
  93, 98, 106, 153, 156; ælmihtigan (dsg. m.)
  6/169, 175; ælmihtegum (dsg. m.) 5/16;
  ælmihtigne (asg. m.) 11/60

Ælmihtiga (nsg. m.) *the Almighty (God)* 1/26
  *6/68; Ælmihtigan (dsg.) 6/12, 180

ælmyssan (dasg. f.) *almsgiving* 6/58–59

ænde; ænglas → ende; engel

ǣnig (adj. nsg. m.n.) *any, any one* 2/149 *3/151
  *6/162 *7/23, 49, 52, 101 *10/70, 195
  *11/110, 117; ǣnige (dasg. f.) 3/16 *7/12, 26,
  98; ǣnigre (dsg. f.) 3/40; ǣnigum (dsg. m.)
  7/122 *11/47; ǣnigne (asg. m.) 5/16

ǣnlice (adj. asg. n.) *singular, splendid* 6/69
 [ǣnlic]

ǣnne → **ān**

ǣr (adv., conj.) *before that, formerly; soon;*
 earlier 2/9, 21, 28 etc. *3/45, 50, 63 etc.
 *5/28, 53 *6/69, 95, 120 etc. *7/5, 83, 92–93
 etc. *8/35, 64, 101 *10/60–61, 158, 198 etc.
 *11/114, 118, 137 etc.; **ǣror** (comp.) 2/142;
 ǣrur 11/108 ♦ col.: **ǣr þām** (adv.) 7/63; **ǣr**
 þan 11/88; **ǣr þysan** 7/13, 41; **ǣr þan þe**
 (conj.) 2/147 *6/11; **ǣr ðǣm ðe** 5/23

ǣra (gpl. m.) *wave, sea* 9/26

ǣrcebiscepe, ǣrcebiscepe → **arcebiscop**

ǣrænde (asg. n.) *message* 10/28

ǣrendfæst (adj. nsg. m.) *bound on an errand*
 6/140

ǣrendgewrit (asg. n.) *letter* 5/13

ǣrendwrecum (dpl. m.) *messenger* 5/5

ǣrest (adv.) *first* 2/96 *3/46, 99, 126 *4/6
 *5/40 *10/5, 186 *11/19; **ǣrost** 10/124

ǣreste (adj. nsg. f. sup.) *first* 3/127; **ǣrestan**
 (dsg. m.) 4/34

ǣrgewin (asg. n.) *former strife, trouble* 11/19

ǣrnað (pl.ps.) *to run, ride* 4/32, 41; **ǣrndon**
 (pl.pt.) 10/191 [ǣrnan I]

ǣrne (adj. asg. m.) *early* 6/15

ǣror, ǣrur → **ǣr**

ǣrost → **ǣrest**

ǣrwacol (adj. nsg.) *early awake* 8/89

æsc (asg. m.) *spear* 10/43, 310

Æscesdune (pn.) *Ashdown, Berkshire* 2/63

Æscferð (prn.) 10/267

æschere (nsg. m.) *Viking army* 10/69

æscholt (asg. n.) *spear* 10/230

ǣses (gsg. n.) *carrion* 9/63 *10/107 [ǣs]

æstel (nasg. m.) *bookmark* 5/62–63

ǣswicas (apl. m.) *offence, fraud* 7/109

æt (prep. (d.)) *at, near, by, in, on, upon, with*
 2/4, 34–35, 40 etc. *3/15, 23, 87 etc.
 *5/58–59, 66 *6/95, 142 *7/15, 143, 157
 *8/29, 87, 93, 100 *9/4, 8, 42, 44 *10/10, 39,
 48, 55 etc. *11/8, 63

ǣt (sg.pt.) *to eat* 8/3, 7; **ǣton** (pl.pt.) 8/3
 [etan 5]

ætēawed, ætēowde → **ætȳweð**

ætforan (prep. (d.)) *before* 2/149 *10/16

ætgædere (adv.) *together, at the same time*
 3/150 *6/56 *7/141 *11/48

æthlēape (sg.ps. subj.) *to run away from,*
 escape 7/80 [æthlēapan 7]

ǣton → **ǣt**

ætsamne (adv.) *together, united* 9/57;
 ætsomne 3/4, 145

ætstōd (sg.pt.) *to remain* 6/147 [ætstandan 6]

ǣtterne (adj. nsg. m.) *poisonous, deadly*
 10/146; **ǣttrenne** (asg. m.) 10/47

ætwītan (1) *to blame, reproach* 10/220, 250

ætȳweð (sg.ps.) *to show, reveal, display,*
 appear 3/28; **ætēowde** (sg.pt.) 2/96;
 ætēawed (ptp.) 3/60 [ætīewan I]

æðela, æþelan → **æðele**

æþelborene (adj. npl.) *of noble birth* 8/100

æðelborennesse (asg. f.) *nobility of birth* 8/24,
 27

æðele (nsg. m.f.) *noble, excellent, famous* 6/1;
 æþele 9/16 *10/280; **æðela** 6/62; **æþelan**
 (asg. m.) 10/151; **æðelum** (dpl.) 8/106

Æþelgāres (prn. gsg.) 10/320

æþeling (nasg. m.) *man of royal blood,*
 nobleman 2/7, 12, 16, 21, 31 *9/3, 58;
 æþelinges (gsg.) 2/35; **æþelinge** (dsg.) 11/58;
 æðelingum (dpl.) 3/64

æþelo (asg. f.) *noble origin* 10/216

Æþelred (prn.) 7/61; **Æþelredes** (gsg.) 10/53,
 151, 203

Æþelstān (prn.) 9/1

Æþelwulf (prn.) 2/58, 61; **Æþelwulfing** 2/79

Æþered (prn.) 2/47, 59, 63 etc.

Æþerīc (prn.) 10/280

ǣwbrycas (apl. m.) *adultery* 7/110

ǣwiscmōde (adj. npl.) *ashamed, abashed* 9/56

B

bā → **bēgen**

Bachsecg (prn.) 2/64; **Bagsecg** 2/66

baldlīce (adv.) *boldly* 10/311; **baldlīcost** (sup.)
 10/78

bān (asg.) *bone* 4/42; (napl.) 6/89, 112, 115 etc.

bana (nsg. m.) *killer, slayer* 10/299; **banan**
 (dasg.) 2/27 *11/66

band (sg.pt.) *to bind* 6/138; **geband** 1/15
 *6/140 [bindan 3]

Bardanīge (pn.) *Bardney, Lincolnshire* 6/113

Basengum (prn.) *Old Basing, Hampshire* 2/71

Bastard → **Wyllelm**

bæc → **ofer**

bæcbord (asg. n.) *larbord* 4/3, 5, 7

bæd, bǣde, bǣdon → **(ge)biddan**

bær → **beran**

bærnað (pl.ps.) *burn (down)* 7/100 [bærnan I]

bærnette (dsg. n.) *burning* 1/15 [bærnett]

bǣron; bærst → **beran; berstan**

bæðe (dsg. n.) *bath* 3/65 [bæð]

be (prep. (d.)) *by, near, in, on, upon* 1/22
 *3/34, 82, 88, 126, 133 *4/40 *5/15, 57
 *6/78, 94, 96, 110, 140, 152 *7/121, 142,

151, 154 *8/6, 66 *10/9, 152, 318–319; **bī**
3/126–132 *5/67; **big** 10/182 ♦ col.: **be**
fullan (adv.) *completely* 5/34
bēacen (nasg. n.) *sign, token, beacon* 11/6, 21;
  bēacne (dsg.) 11/83; **bēacna** (gpl.) 11/118
beadurǣs (nsg. m.) *onslaught* 10/111
beaduwe (dsg. f.) *battle* 10/185 [beadu]
beaduweorca (gpl. n.) *operation in a war* 9/48
bēagas (apl. m.) *ring, armlet* 10/31, 160 [bēag]
bēah → **(ge)būgan**
bēahgifa (nsg. m.) *ring-giver, king* 9/2;
  bēahgifan (asg.) 10/290
bealuwara (gpl. m.) *evildoer* 11/79 [bealuware]
bēam (nsg. m.) *tree, cross* 11/97; **bēame** (dsg.)
  11/114, 122; **bēama** (gpl.) 11/6
bearh → **beorgan**
bearn (nsg. m.) *child, son* 7/49, 73 *10/92,
  155, 186, 209, 238, 267, 300, 320 *11/83;
  bearne (dsg.) 7/49; **bearnum** (dpl.) 3/99
bearnmyrðran (npl. m.) *child-murderer* 7/132
bearnum → **bearn**
beæftan (prep. (d.)) *after, behind* 2/19, 21
Bebbanbyrig (pn.) *Bamburgh,*
  Northumberland 6/110
bebēodan (2) *to command, commend* **bebīode**
  (1.sg.ps.) 5/17, 63; **bebēodende** (psp.) 3/170;
  bibēad (sg.pt.) 3/148; **gebēad** 2/16, 24;
  bebudon (pl.pt.) 3/114; **beboden** (ptp.) 3/86,
  117 *8/83; **geboden** (ptp.) *offer* 2/28
beboda (apl. n.) *commandment, order* 6/154
  [bebod]
beboden, bebudon → **bebēodan**
bebyrged (ptp.) *to bury* 6/88 [bebyrgan I]
bēc → **bōc**
becōm, becōman, becōmon → **becuman**
becuman (4) *to come* 8/13; **becōm** (sg.pt.) 6/1,
  35, 81, 132 *8/15; **becwōm** 3/168; **becōmon**
  (pl.pt.) 5/20 *10/58; **becōman** 9/70
Bēda (prn.) *the Venerable Bede* 6/21, 171
bedǣlde (ptp.) *to deprive* 7/25 [bedǣlan I]
bedde (dsg. n.) *bed* 6/22 *8/88 [bedd]
bedealf (sg.pt.) *to bury* 11/75 [bedelfan 3]
bedrifenne (ptp.) *to cover* 11/62
beēode (sg.pt.) *to practice, perform, surround*
  2/9 *3/48, 50; **beēodon** (pl.pt.) 3/13;
  beēodan 3/36; **biēodon** 3/45
befæstan (I) *to apply, use, entrust* 5/19;
  befæste (sg.ps. subj.) 5/19 *8/91
befēolan (3) *to apply oneself* 5/49
beforan (adv., prep. (d.a.)) *before, in front of,*
  earlier 8/70, 88 *9/67
began → **beginnan**
begēatan, begēaton → **begietan**

bēgen (adj. npl.) *both* 2/43, 69, 106 *6/97
  *9/57 *10/182–183, 191 etc.; **bā** (dpl.) 2/112
begeondan (prep. (d.)) *beyond* 2/110 *3/61;
  begiondan 5/14; **begeonde** 2/97
begietan (5) *to get, gain, acquire* 5/10;
  begitan 2/98; **begēaton** (pl.pt.) 5/29;
  begēatan 9/73
beginnan (3) *to begin* 1/17; **began** (sg.pt.)
  6/135; **begunnon** (ptp.) 6/70
begiondan → **begeondan**
begitan → **begietan**
begoten (ptp.) *to cover, shed* 11/7, 49
  [begēotan 2]
begunnon → **beginnan**
behātan (7) *to promise* **behǣt** (sg.ps.) 6/169;
  behēt (sg.pt.) 2/143 *6/79 *8/69; **behēton**
  (pl.pt.) 2/133; **behētan** 7/156
behǣt → **behātan**
behēold (sg.pt.) *to behold, gaze at* 8/4–5, 7
  *11/25, 58; **behēoldon** (pl.pt.) 6/118 *11/9,
  11, 64 [behealdan 7]
behēt, behētan, behēton → **behātan**
behindan (prep. (d.a.)) *behind* 9/60
behionan (prep. (d.)) *on this side of* 5/12
belifen (pl.pt.) *to remain* 2/154 [belīfan 1]
belimpeð (sg.ps.) *to pertain, belong* 4/9;
  belumpon (pl.pt.) 3/78; **belumpen** 3/68
  [belimpan 3]
belocen (ptp.) *to lock* 2/22 [belūcan 2]
belumpen, belumpon → **belimpeð**
benam → **benimð**
bence (dsg. f.) *bench* 10/213 [benc]
benimð (sg.ps. (g.)) *to deprive* 4/13; **benam**
  (sg.pt.) 2/1 [beniman 4]
bēnum (dpl. f.) *prayer, request* 6/31 [bēn]
bēo → **bēon**
bēodas (apl. m.) *table, dish* 8/4 [bēod]
bēodaþ (pl.ps.) *to offer, announce, proclaim*
  7/116; **budon** (pl.pt.) 2/27
bēon (irr.) *to be* 2/133, 144, 149 *4/24, 30–31,
  42 *8/74, 76, 94 *10/185 ♦ 1.sg.ps.: **eom**
  3/158 *6/159 *10/179, 317 ♦ 2.sg.ps.: **eart**
  3/153 *8/36, 49, 89 *10/36 ♦ 3.sg.ps.: **bið**
  3/26–27 *4/15–16, 18–20, 24 etc. *5/62
  *6/170 *7/23–24, 57–58 *11/86; **is** 1/11,
  24–25 *3/11, 21–22, 30 etc. *4/8, 11, 15 etc.
  *5/48, 56 *6/24, 65, 160–161 *7/3–4, 18, 21
  etc. *8/8, 17, 19 etc. *10/31, 93, 223, 233
  *11/80, 97, 126 etc. ♦ sg.ps. subj.: **bēo** 8/12;
  sī 11/144; **sīe** 1/11 *3/10, 24 *5/16, 67
  *11/112; **sȳ** 4/47 *6/180 *8/21, 23 *10/215 ♦
  pl.ps.: **bēoð** 1/29 *4/23, 37; **siendon** 5/65;
  synd 4/6 *7/76; **syndan** 7/25, 31–32, 34, 74,
  110, 129–133; **syndon** 3/14, 19 *8/105

272   **bēon** (OE)

*11/46 ♦ pl.ps. subj.: **sīen** 5/45, 49, 65; **sȳn** 7/55–56, 84, 112 ♦ sg.pt.: **wæs** 1/27 *2/7, 18, 20 etc. *3/7, 9–10 etc. *4/2–3, 5, 8 *5/11, 40, 53 *6/1, 23, 30 etc. *7/43, 46, 86 etc. *8/1, 34, 59 etc. *9/7, 40 *10/23, 75–76, 103–104 etc. *11/6, 10, 13 etc.; **was** 2/7, 42 ♦ sg.pt. subj.: **wǣre** 2/28, 95, 126 *3/8, 111–112, 148 etc. *6/153 *8/53 *10/195, 240 ♦ pl.pt.: **wǣron** 2/25, 31, 65 etc. *3/46, 73, 124, 144 etc. *4/6 *5/2, 4, 8 etc. *6/40, 126 *8/3, 57 *10/110 *11/8; **wǣran** 2/17 *3/5 *7/8, 157; **wǣrun** 2/10, 13, 19 etc. ♦ pl.pt. subj.: **wǣren** 5/22, 66 ♦ neg.: **nis** (sg.ps.) 3/162 *7/103; **nys** 6/171; **næs** (sg.pt.) 7/9 *10/325; **nǣre** (sg.pt. subj.) 2/26 *8/53; **nǣron** (pl.pt.) 5/27; **nǣren** (pl.pt. subj.) 5/14

beorg (asg. m.) *mountain, hill* 11/32; **beorge** (dsg.) 11/50

beorgan (3) *to protect, save, seek a cure for* 7/127, 140, 160; **beorge** (sg.ps. subj.) 7/40; **bearh** 7/48; **burgon** (pl.pt.) 10/194

beorge → **beorg**; **beorgan**

Beorhhāmstede (pn.) *Great Berkhamstead, Hertfordshire* 2/139

beorht (adj. nsg.) *bright, radiant, white* 9/15; **beorhtan** (dsg. m.) 11/66; **beorhtost** (sup.) 11/6

beorn (nsg. m.) *man, warrior* 9/45 *10/270 *11/42; **beornes** (gsg.) 10/131, 160; **beorne** (dsg.) 10/154, 245; **beornas** (npl.) 10/17, 62, 92, 111, 182, 277, 305, 311 *11/32, 66; **beorna** (gpl.) 9/2 *10/257; **beornum** (dpl.) 10/101

bēorscipes → **gebēorscipe**

bēot (asg. n.) *vow, boast* 10/15, 213 ♦ col.: **on bēot** (adv.) *threateningly* 10/27

bēotode (sg.pt.) *to boast, vow* 10/290 [bēotian II]

bēoð → **bēon**

berād (sg.pt.) *to ride up to, overtake* 2/9 [berīdan 1]

beran (4) *to carry, bear, bring* 1/9 *4/26 *10/12, 62; **bereð** (sg.ps.) 11/118; **byrð** 4/38; **berað** (imp.pl.) 3/153 *8/69; **bær** (sg.pt.) 1/10 *6/56, 121; **bǣron** (pl.pt.) 10/99 *11/32; **bēron** (pl.pt. subj.) 10/67; **geboren** (ptp.) 8/2; **geborene** 8/106

berēafian (II) *to rob, deprive of* 8/82

bereð, bēron → **beran**

berstan (3) *to burst* 11/36; **bærst** (sg.pt.) 10/284

berȳpte (ptp.) *to rob, plunder* 7/24, 32 [berȳpan I]

beseah (sg.pt.) *to look* 1/21 *8/11, 76, 102 [besēon 5]

beslagen (ptp.) *to strike, kill* 9/42 [beslēan 6]

besorgað (sg.ps.) *to regret* 8/18 [besorgian II]

bestēmed (ptp.) *to drench, make wet* 11/22, 48 [bestēman II]

bestōdon (pl.pt.) *to surround* 10/68 [bestandan 6]

bestrȳpte (ptp.) *to strip, plunder* 7/32 [bestrȳpan I]

beswīce (sg.ps. subj.) *to betray, deceive* 7/57; **beswicene** (ptp.) 7/34 *10/238 [beswīcan 1]

beswyled (ptp.) *to drench* 11/23 [beswylian II]

besyrwde (ptp.) *to deceive, ensnare* 7/34 [besyrwan I]

bet (adv. comp.) *better* 7/13; **betre** 5/45

(ge)bētan (I) *to amend, atone for, compensate, make good, restore, satisfy* 2/142 *7/126, 155; **gebētan** 4/43 *6/158; **bēttan** (pl.pt.) 7/42

betǣhte (sg.pt.) *to entrust* 6/100; **betǣht** (ptp.) 7/24

betera (adj. nsg. m. comp.) *better* 10/276; **betere** (nsg. n.) 10/31; **beteran** (napl.) *better* 3/18 *9/48 [see gōd]

betre; betst, betstan → **bet; gōd**

betst (adv. sup.) *best* 2/149

bēttan → **(ge)bētan**

betwēonan (prep. (d.)) *between* 4/18 *7/159

betweox (prep. (d.)) *between, among* 1/21; **betwux** 6/51 ♦ col.: **betwux þām** (adv.) *while* 6/4

betȳnde (sg.pt.) *to close, conclude* 3/139, 170 [betȳnan I]

beþencan (I) *to bring to mind, reflect on* 7/137; (pl.ps. subj.) 7/153

bewænde (sg.pt.) *to turn* 8/31 [bewendan I]

beweaxen (ptp.) *to cover* 6/23 [beweaxan 7]

bewiste (sg.pt.) *to guard* 6/58 [bewitan prps.]

bewrigen (ptp.) *to cover over* 11/17, 53 [bewrēon, 1, 2]

bewunden (ptp.) *to envelop* 11/5 [bewinden 3]

bī; bibēad → **be; bebēodan**

bicgað (pl.ps.) *to buy* 7/69; **gebōhte** (sg.pt.) 7/72 [bycgan I]

(ge)bīdan (1) *to await, remain; experience* 3/163; **gebīdan** 7/12; **gebād** (sg.pt.) 8/87 *10/174 *11/125; **gebiden** (ptp.) 7/12 *11/50, 79

(ge)biddan (5) *to bid, ask, pray* 6/13; **gebiddan** 6/72; **gebiddenne** (infl.inf.) 1/8; **bidde** (1.sg.ps.) 6/162 *8/33, 90, 106; **gebiddaþ** (pl.ps.) 11/83; **bæd** (sg.pt.) 3/50, 145 *6/30, 65 *10/20, 128, 170, 257; **gebæd**

3/163 *6/99 *11/122; **bæde** (sg.pt. subj.)
3/147; **bædon** (pl.pt.) 2/47; 3/157 *6/119
*8/74, 104 *10/87, 262, 306
biēodon → **beēode**
bifian (II) *to shake, tremble* 11/36; **bifode**
(sg.pt.) 11/42
big → **be**
bīgong (nsg. m.) *worship* 3/9; **bīgonges** (gsg.)
3/59; **bīgange** (dsg.) 3/14, 37
bigwiste (asg. f.) *food, sustenance* 6/174
bilgeslehtes (nsg. n.) *battle* 9/45
bill (asg. n.) *sword* 10/162; **billum** (dpl.)
10/114
bilwitre (isg. m.) *innocent* 3/166 [bilewit]
binnan (prep. (d.)) *within, in* 2/42, 121 *6/6,
89, 109 etc.; **binnon** 8/98
Birinus (prn.) 6/76, 78; **Birine** (dsg.) 6/85
bisceop (nasg. m.) *bishop* 2/44 *3/5, 33 *6/33,
42, 62 etc.; **biscep** 2/76 *5/1, 66; **biscop**
2/153 *3/62 *6/45; **bisceopes** (gsg.) 6/41,
176; **biscepe** (dsg.) 5/58; **biscope** 3/42, 44,
52; **biscoppe** 2/117; **biscepas** (npl.) 5/65;
biscopa (gpl.) 7/146
bisceoprīce (asg. n.) *diocese* 2/44
bisceopstōle (dsg. m.) *episcopal see* 6/85;
biscepstōle 5/61
bisgum (dpl. f.) *occupation* 5/55 [bisgu]
bisy (adj. nsg. f.) *busy* 8/108
biter (adj. nsg. m.) *bitter* 10/111; **biteres** (gsg.)
11/114; **bitere** (npl.) 10/85
bið → **bēon**
blandenfeax (adj. nsg. m.) *grey-haired* 9/45
Blēcingaēg (pn.) *Blekinge (Sweden)* 4/6
blēdum (dpl. m.) *glory* 11/149 [blǣd]
blēom (dpl. m.) *colour* 11/22 [blēo]
blētsie (1.sg.ps.) *to bless* 1/27; **geblētsode**
(ptp.) 1/30 *6/64 [bētsian II]
blētsunge (dsg. f.) *blessing* 1/31 [blētsung]
blis (nsg. f.) *bliss, joy* 11/139, 141; **blisse** (gsg.)
3/82 *11/149, 153; **blysse** (dsg.) 6/63
blissigende (psp.) *to be glad, rejoice* 6/143;
blissode (sg.pt.) 8/38; **geblissod** (ptp.) 8/92
blīðe (1) (adv.) *friendly, cheerfully, joyously*
6/138, 177 *8/66
blīðe (2) (adj. nasg. m.) *friendly, cheerful,*
joyous 3/155 *8/12; (isg. m.) 11/122; (napl.)
3/157 *8/3 *6/142; **blīðum** (dsg. m.) 8/11;
blīþum 6/41; **blīþra** (nsg. m. comp.) 10/146
blīðemōd (adj. nsg. m.) *friendly* 3/158;
blīðemōde (npl.) 3/156
blīþra, blīþum → **blīðe** (2)
blōde (dsg. m.) *blood* 11/48 [blōd]
blōdgyte (nsg. m.) *bloodshed* 7/43

blōdigne (adj. asg. m.) *bloody* 10/154 [blōdig]
blysse → **blis**
bōc (nasg. f.) *book* 5/55, 64 *6/171; **booc** (nsg.)
3/127; **bēc** (dsg.) 2/147 *5/64; (napl.) 5/34,
42, 45 *7/126, 135 *9/68; **bōca** (gpl.) 3/129
*5/25–26
bōceras (apl. m.) *scholar, scribe* 3/69
boda (nsg. m.) *messenger* 10/49; **bodan** (npl.)
7/116
bodad, bodade → **bodian**
bodian (II) *to preach* 6/79; **bodigende** (psp.)
6/45, 50; **bodade** (sg.pt.) 3/34; **bodad** (ptp.)
3/11, 19
bodunge (asg. f.) *preaching* 6/41 [bodung]
bogan (npl. m.) *bow* 10/110 [boga]
bolstre (dsg. m.) *pillow* 3/164 [bolster]
booc → **bōc**
bord (nasg. n.) *shield* 10/15, 42, 62 etc.;
bordes (gsg.) 10/284; **borda** (gpl.) 10/295;
bordum (dpl.) 10/101
bordweall (asg. m.) *shield-wall* 10/277;
bordweal 9/5
bōsme (dsg. m.) *bosom* 9/27 [bōsm]
bōt (nsg. f.) *remedy, relief, compensation,*
atonement 7/17; **bōte** (dsg.) 6/125; (asg.) 7/9,
12, 15, 135; (gsg.) 7/29
brād (adj. nasg. m.) *broad* 4/11 *9/71 *10/15,
163
bræc (sg.pt.) *to break* 10/277; **brǣcon** (pl.pt.)
2/41; **brǣcan** 7/41, 155; **brocen** (ptp.) 10/1
[brecan 4]
brǣd (sg.pt.) *to draw, pull out* 10/154, 162
[bregdan 3]
bregu (nsg. m.) *lord* 9/33
brēmelum (dpl. m.) *bramble* 1/22 [brēmel]
brenge (sg.ps. subj.) *to bring* 3/30 [brengan I;
see (ge)bringan]
brēostum (dpl.) *breast* 10/144 *11/118 [brēost]
Bretwālum (prn. dpl.) *the (Celtic) British* 2/6
bricge (asg. f.) *bridge, causeway* 10/74, 78
[brycg]
bricgweardas (apl. m.) *guardians of the*
causeway 10/85
brimlīþendra (gpl. m.) *Viking, seafarer* 10/27
[brimlīðend]
brimmen (npl. m.) *Viking, seafarer* 10/295;
brimmanna (gpl.) 10/49 [brimman]
brimu (asg. n.) *sea, water* 9/71 [brim]
(ge)bringan (I) *to bring, lead, carry, present*
bryng (imp.sg.) 8/113; **gebringeð** (sg.ps.)
7/123; **gebringe** (sg.ps. subj.) 11/139;
gebrōhte (sg.pt.) 6/113; **gebrōht** (ptp.) 6/155,
178; **brōht** 7/23

broce (dsg. n.) *disease, sickness* 6/138 [broc]

brocen; brōht → bræc; (ge)bringan

brosnunge (dsg. f.) *decay, corruption* 6/64, 108 [brosnung]

brōþor (nasg. m.) *brother* 2/99 *7/49, 73 *9/2; **brōðor** 2/107, 128–129 *3/66 *6/104 *10/282; **brōþur** 2/8, 48, 59 etc.; **brōður** 2/71; **brōþor** (gsg.) 6/112; **brōðor** 6/105; **brōðru** (npl.) 10/191; **brōðor** 3/158, 161; **gebrōþer** 9/57; **gebrōþru** 10/305

brūcan (2 (g.)) *to use, enjoy* 9/63 *11/144

Brunanburh (pn.) 9/5

brūnecg (asg. n.) *bright-bladed* 10/163

bryce (dsg. m.) *breach, violation* 7/17

bryhtm (nsg. m.) *blink* 3/27

bryne (asg. m.) *burning, fire* 7/18, 43, 161 *11/149

bryng → (ge)bringan

Brytene (pn.) *Britain* 9/71

Bryttas (prn.) *the British* 6/67; **Brytta** (gpl.) 6/5 *7/142, 144; **Bryttan** (dpl.) 7/152

bryttian (II) *to enjoy* 9/60

Bryttiscum (adj. dsg. m.) *British* 2/18

budon → bēodaþ

bufan (prep. (d.)) *above* 4/23

(ge)būgan (2) *to bend, turn, submit, withdraw* 2/136 *10/276 *11/36, 42; **gebūgan** 7/154; **bēah** (sg.pt.) 2/50; **bugon** (pl.pt.) 2/141 *10/185

būr (asg. m.) *chamber, cottage* 2/9; **būre** (dsg.) 8/70

Burgenda land (pn.) *Bornholm* 4/4; **Burgenda lande** (dsg.) 4/5

burgon → beorgan

Burgrǣd (prn.) 2/47

burh (nasg. f.) *enclosure, settlement, town* 4/15 *6/85 *10/291; **byrig** (dsg.) 2/22 *4/16 *6/88

burhwaru (nsg. f.) *citizenry, population* 2/131

būrþēne (dsg. m.) *chamberlain* 10/121 [būrþēn]

būtan (prep. (d.), conj.) *except (that, for) unless, but, only* 2/17, 32, 83 *6/35, 108 *7/40, 102, 159; **būton** 2/2 *3/40, 53, 154 *5/66 *6/146, 160 *10/71; (adv.) *without, outside* 2/42

butsacarlas (npl. m.) *boatman* 2/103 [butsecarl]

būtū (adj. apl.) *both* 2/73 *11/48

bydela (gpl.) *messenger, priest* 7/147 [bydel]

bylde (sg.pt.) *to encourage* 10/169, 209, 234, 320 [byldan I]

byre (asg. m.) *opportunity* 10/121

Byrhtelmes (prn.) 10/92

Byrhtnōð (prn.) 10/17, 42, 101 etc.; **Byrhtnōðes** (gsg.) 10/114

Byrhtwold (prn.) 10/309

byrig → burh

byrigde (sg.pt.) *to taste* 11/101 [byrigan I]

byrne (nsg. f.) *corslet* 10/144, 284; **byrnan** (asg.) 10/163

byrst (nsg. m.) *loss, injury* 7/39; **byrsta** (gpl.) 7/12

byrð → beran

bysene (dsg. f.) *example* 3/48 [bysen]

bysige (adj. npl.) *busy* 10/110

bysmara → bysmor

bysmeredon (pl.pt.) *to mock* 11/48 [bysmerian II]

bysmor (asg. m.) *disgrace, shame, insult* 7/39, 99; **bysmore** (dsg.) 7/90; **bysmara** (gpl.) 7/12

C

cāflīce (adv.) *bravely* 10/153

cāfne (adj. asg. m.) *brave* 10/76 [cāf]

cald (adj. asg. n.) *cold* 10/91

Calesti (prn. gsg.) *Calixtus* 2/135

campe (dsg. m.) *combat, battle* 9/8; **gecampe** 10/153 [camp]

campstede (dsg. m.) *battlefield* 9/29, 49

canōnes (gsg. m.) *canon, rule* 3/129

canst → cunnan

castel (asg. m.) *castle, fort* 2/123; **castelas** (apl.) 2/154

ceaflum (dpl. m.) *jaw* 7/148 [ceafl]

ceallian (II) *to call, shout* 10/91

cēap (asg. m.) *purchase, bargain* 7/72; **cēape** (dsg.) 7/69

ceastergewaran (npl.) *citizens* 8/106

ceastre (gsg. f.) *castle, stronghold, town* 8/99 [ceaster]

Cedmon (prn.) 3/88

Cedwalla (prn.) 6/6–7; **Cedwallan** (asg.) 6/17, 96

Cēfi (prn.) 3/10, 33

cellod (adj. asg. n.) *concave (?), embossed (?)* 10/283

cempa (nsg. m.) *champion, warrior* 10/119

cēne (adj. nsg. m.) *brave, keen, bold* 10/215; (npl.) 10/283; **cēnre** (nsg. f. comp.) 10/312

cēnlīce (adv.) *boldly* 6/9

Cēolan (prn.) 10/76

Ceolnoþ (prn.) 2/56

ceorl (nsg. m.) *man, peasant, commoner, husband* 10/256; **ceorle** (dsg.) 7/33 *10/132

Cerdice (prn.) 2/35

cild (nasg. n.) *child, infant, young man* 1/8, 18 *2/132, 140, 152

cirice (f.) *church* **cyrce** (asg.) 6/27; **cyrcan**
  (dsg.) 6/73, 106, 121, 123; (apl.) 6/54;
  ciricean (npl.) 5/24
clāþe (dsg. m.) *cloth* 6/141 [clāð]
clǣne (1) (adj. npl.) *clean, pure* 3/123 *5/11
clǣne (2) (adv.) *entirely* 7/24, 31
clǣnsian (II) *to purify* 7/158
cliopodon, clipode → **clypian**
clufan (pl.pt.) *to cleave, split* 9/5; **clufon**
  10/283
clumedan (pl.pt.) *to mumble* 7/148 [clumian II]
clypian (II) *to speak, cry out, call* 7/148;
  clypode (sg.pt.) 3/35 *6/12, 63, 101, 155
  *10/25, 256; **clipode** 1/1, 17, 25; **cliopodon**
  (pl.pt.) 8/57
clyppan (I) *to embrace, clasp, honour* 3/118
cnapa (nsg. m.) *child, youth; servant* 6/175;
  cnapum (dpl.) 1/4, 7, 31
cnear (nsg. m.) *small ship* 9/35
cnēomǣgum (dpl. m.) *kinsman, ancestor* 9/8
  [cnēowmǣg]
cniht (nsg. m.) *young man* 10/9, 153; **cnihtas**
  (npl.) 8/111
cnyt (sg.ps.) *to bind* 7/93 [cnyttan I]
cōlode (sg.pt.) *to grow cold* 11/72 [cōlian II]
cōm, cōman, cōme → **cuman** (2)
cometa (nsg. m.) *comet* 2/95
cōmon → **cuman** (2)
con → **cunnan**
condel (nsg. f.) *candle, lamp* 9/15
corōna (asg. f.) *crown* 2/93
Costontīnus (prn.) 9/38
coþum (dpl. f.) *disease, sickness* 6/123 [coðu]
cradolcild (npl. n.) *child in the cradle* 7/35
crǣfte (dsg. m.) *physical strength, might; skill,
  art* 8/55; **crǣftum** (dpl.) 8/62 [crǣft]
Crēacas (prn.) *the Greeks* 5/41
crēad (sg.pt.) *to press, hasten* 9/35 [crūdan 2]
crincgan (3) *to fall, die in battle, perish*
  10/292; **gecranc** (sg.pt.) 10/250, 324;
  cruncon (pl.pt.) 10/302; **crungun** 9/10
Crīst (prn.) 6/5, 10 *11/56; **Crīstes** (gsg.)
  2/147 *3/43, 65, 129, 163; **Crīste** (dsg.) 3/5
  *6/88, 96, 160 *11/116
crīsten (adj., sb.) *Christian* **crīstenes** (gsg.)
  7/64; **crīstene** (npl.) 7/27; **Crīstne** 5/21;
  Crīstenan 6/98; **crīstenra** (gpl.) 7/96, 115;
  Crīstna 5/44
crīstendōme (dsg. m.) *Christianity* 7/81
  [crīstendōm]
**crīstene, crīstenes, crīstenra, crīstna,
  crīstne** → **crīsten**
cruncon, crungun → **crincgan**

cuǣdon → **cweðan**
cuman (1) (dsg. m.) *guest* 8/91 [cuma]
cuman (2) (4) *to come* 2/137 *3/51; (ptp.)
  3/111; (pl.ps. subj.) 8/81; **cymeð** (sg.ps.) 3/28
  *4/11, 33; **cumað** (pl.ps.) 1/9 *4/12; **cume**
  (sg.ps. subj.) 3/25; **cōm** (sg.pt.) 2/91, 97,
  102–103 etc. *3/107 *5/2 *6/9, 76, 168
  *9/37 *10/65 *11/151; **cuōm** 2/57, 77;
  cwōm 3/116 *11/155; **cōme** (sg.pt. subj.)
  6/11; **cōmon** (pl.pt.) 1/13 *2/106 *6/97
  *8/100, 105; **cōman** 2/114; **cwōman** 11/57;
  cumen (ptp.) 6/83 *10/104 *11/80; **cumene**
  6/59
cumbolgehnāstes (nsg. n.) *crash of banners,
  battle* 9/49
Cumbran (prn.) 2/5
cume, cumen, cumene → **cuman** (2)
cunnan (prps.) *to be able to, know, can* **con**
  (1.sg.ps.) 3/89; **canst** (2.sg.ps.) 8/93; **cunne**
  (sg.ps. subj.) 7/39, 78, 85; **cunnon** (pl.ps.) 3/29
  *5/30; **cunnen** (pl.ps. subj.) 5/51; **cūðe** (sg.pt.)
  3/91 *6/96; **cūþe** 6/42; **cūðon** (pl.pt.) 5/39,
  54; **cūþon** 7/98; **cūðen** (pl.pt. subj.) 5/12
cunnian (II (g.a.)) *to test, try* 10/215
cunnon → **cunnan**
cuōm → **cuman** (2)
curfon (pl.pt.) *to cut, carve* 11/66 [ceorfan 3]
Cūðberht (prn.) 6/175
cūðe, cūþe, cūðen, cūðon, cūþon → **cunnan**
cūðlīce (adv.) *certainly* 3/11
cūðlicre (adj. asg. comp.) *certain, true* 3/30
cwalu (nsg. f.) *death* 7/44
**cwǣdan, cwǣde, cwǣden, cwǣdon, cwǣð,
  cwǣðende, cwēdon** → **cweðan**
cwēn (nsg. f.) *queen, princess, woman* 6/112
  *8/75, 78; **cwēne** 8/71; (asg.) 8/74
cwenan (asg. f.) *wife* 7/69, 91 [cwene]
cwēne → **cwēn**
cweðan (5) *to say, speak, name, call* 11/116;
  cweþenne (infl.inf.) 7/38, 134; **cwæðende**
  (psp.) 6/63; **cweðende** 8/112; **cwyð** (sg.ps.)
  11/111; **cwæð** (sg.pt.) 1/2, 7, 18, 25 *3/1–2,
  5, 21 etc. *5/36 *6/153, 156, 171 *8/7, 9, 12,
  16 etc. *10/211, 255; **gecwæð** 6/108 *8/14
  *10/168; **cwǣde** (2.sg.pt.) 8/82; **cwǣdon**
  (pl.pt.) 3/152, 155; **cwǣdan** 7/111; **cuǣdon**
  2/26, 28–29; **cwēdon** 2/94; **cwǣden** (pl.pt.
  subj.) 5/27
cwīðdon (pl.pt.) *to bewail* 11/56 [cwīðan I]
cwōm, cwōman → **cuman** (2)
cwyð; cȳdde → **cweðan; cȳðan**
cyle (asg. m.) *cold, chill* 4/44–45
cyme (dsg. m.) *coming, arrival* 3/131; **cymes**
  (gsg.) 6/38

cymeð → cuman (2)
cynedōm (asg. ·m.) *kingdom, government* 6/91
cynegas → cyning
Cynegyls (prn.) 6/77, 85; Kynegyls 6/82;
   Cynegylse (dsg.) 6/83
Cyneheard (prn.) 2/7
cynehelm (asg. m.) *royal crown* 8/51
cynelic (adj. nsg. m.) *kingly, royal* 8/2;
   cynelices (gsg.) 8/85; cynelice (apl.) 6/57;
   cynelican 8/5
cynerīce (nsg. n.) *kingdom* 6/66; kynerīces
   (gsg.) 5/55
Cynewulf (prn.) 2/1, 3, 5, 34
cyng, cyngc, cynge, cynges, cynincg →
   cyning
cyning (nasg. m.) *king, ruler* 2/8, 11, 13 etc.
   *3/1, 5, 10, 21 etc. *4/5, 16 *6/1, 14, 38, 40
   etc. *8/14, 48 *9/1, 35, 58 *11/44, 133;
   cynincg 6/5, 26, 53 etc.; cyningc 4/16 *8/16,
   19, 44, 80, 91; kyning 5/1; cyng 2/91–92,
   99–100, 105 etc., *8/50, 65, 102; cyngc 8/1,
   8–9, 11 etc.; kyncg 2/94; kyng 2/61, 71, 73;
   cyninges (gsg.) 2/14, 19, 83–84 *3/20, 31, 54
   *6/36, 58–59, 62, 95 *8/101 *11/56; cynges
   2/117 *8/15, 61; cyninge (dsg.) 2/29–30
   *6/5, 33, 57; kyninge 2/10, 63 *6/77; cynge
   2/108, 124 *8/6, 8, 63; kynge 2/77, 91;
   cyningas (npl.) 2/43, 65 *9/29; cynegas
   6/84; kyningas 4/22 *5/4; cyninga (gpl.)
   2/66
cynn (nasg. n.) *kind, family, generation* 11/94;
   cynnes (gsg.) 10/217, 266; cynne (dsg.) 10/76
cyrcan, cyrce → cirice
cyrichatan (npl. m.) *opponent of the church*
   7/114 [cyrichhata]
cyrm (nsg. m.) *cry, shout, uproar* 10/107
cyst (nsg. f.) *best* 11/1
cyste (sg.pt.) *to kiss* 8/15 [cyssan I]
cystig (adj. nsg. m.) *generous, liberal* 6/54
cȳðan (I) *to proclaim, tell, relate* 5/2;
   gecȳþan 10/216; cȳð (sg.ps.) 8/10; cȳðde
   (sg.pt.) 2/108 *3/109; cȳþde 2/25; cȳdde
   6/156, 168; gecȳdd (ptp.) 2/69; gecȳðd 2/101
cȳþþe (dasg. f.) *native land* 9/38, 58 [cyðð]

D

daga, dagum → dæg
daroð (asg. m.) *spear, javelin* 10/149, 255;
   daraða (gpl.) 9/54
dǣde (gsg. f.) *deed, act, action* 7/53, 104;
   dǣda (ngapl.) 3/136 *7/74, 152; dǣdum
   (dpl.) 2/2 *6/92, 157 [dǣd]

dæg (nasg. m.) *day, time* 2/74, 81, 93 etc.
   *4/25 *8/88 *9/21 *10/198; dæge (dsg.) 1/6
   *2/134 *3/61; daga (gpl.) 11/136; dagum
   (dpl.) 3/141 *4/1
dæghwāmlīce (adv.) *daily* 7/10, 100
dægweorces (gsg. n.) *day's work* 10/148
   [dægweorc]
dǣl (nasg. m.) *portion, part* 4/28, 30, 35 *5/35,
   44 *6/23, 61 *8/68; dǣle (dsg.) 4/34 *7/122,
   154
dǣlde (sg.pt.) *to divide, part, deal out,
   distribute* 6/36; dǣlon (pl.ps. subj.) 10/33
   [dǣlan I]
dænnede (sg.pt.) *to stream* 9/12
dēad (adj. nsg. m.) *dead* 4/20; dēada 4/30;
   dēadan (gsg.) 4/40, 45
dēah (sg.ps.) *to be of use, avail* 10/48; dohte
   (sg.pt.) 7/42, 86 [dugan prps.]
dear → durran
dēað (nasg. m.) *death* 11/101; dēaðes (gsg.)
   11/113; dēaðe (dsg.) 3/167; dēaþe 6/157
dēman (I) *to judge, determine, decree* 11/107;
   gedēmed (ptp.) 3/82
Denemearcan (pn.) *Denmark* 4/4
Deniscan (prn.) *the Danes, Vikings* 2/54, 62,
   71, 75, 81
Denon (prn.) *the Danes, Vikings* 10/129
dēofol (nsg. m.) *devil* 7/7; dēofla (apl.) 6/125
dēofolgyld (napl. n.) *devil-worship, idol* 3/51;
   dēofolgilda (gpl.) 3/46; dēofulgilda 3/60;
   dēofolgildum (dpl.) 3/42; dēofulgeldum
   3/55
dēop (adj. asg. n.) *deep* 9/55; dēopan (dsg.)
   11/75
dēor (nsg. n.) *animal, beast* 9/64
deorcan (adj. dpl.) *dark, wicked* 11/46 [deorc]
dēore (adv.) *dearly, at great cost* 7/72
Deorwentan (pn.) *the River Derwent* 3/61
dēorwurðan (adj. gsg. f.) *precious, dear*
   6/141; (apl.) 8/4; (gsg. m.) 8/68
derian (I (d.)) *to injure, harm* 10/70; dereð
   (sg.ps.) 7/74; derede (sg.pt.) 7/45, 53
dēst, dēð, dide, didon → (ge)dōn
Difelin (pn.) *Dublin* 9/55
Dinges mere (pn.) 9/54
disc (asg. m.) *dish, plate* 6/60–61; disce (dsg.)
   6/57
dō → (ge)dōn
dohte → dēah
dohtor (nsg. f.) *daughter* 6/112 *7/91 *8/15,
   19, 32, 61, 89, 92, 108; (gsg.) 8/38, 104;
   (asg.) 8/44, 46, 101; (dsg.) 8/31, 110
dolg (npl. n.) *wound, scar* 11/46

dōm (nasg. m.) *judgement, ordeal, sentence, decree, law* 2/24 *7/160 *10/38, 129; **dōmes** (gsg.) 3/131 *11/107; **dōme** (dsg.) 3/111; **dōmum** (dpl.) 3/134

dōmdæge (dsg. m.) *doomsday* 11/105

dōme, dōmes, dōmum → **dōm**

(ge)dōn (irr.) *to do, make, act, perform* 3/34, 74, 137 *5/9, 52 *7/140, 151, 154; **gedō** (1.sg.ps.) 8/37; **dēst** (2.sg.ps.) 8/44; **gedēst** 8/8; **dēð** (3.sg.ps.) 7/27, 79, 122; **dō** (sg.ps. subj.) 5/17, 64 *7/54; **dōð** (pl.ps.) 7/68; **gedōð** 4/46; **gedōn** (pl.ps. subj.) 5/47; **dyde** (sg.pt.) 2/100, 142, 149 *3/5, 85, 148 *6/61, 139 *10/280 *11/114; **dide** 8/83; **dydon** (pl.pt.) 6/128; **dydan** 7/13; **didon** 8/111; **gedōn** (ptp.) 2/135, 142 *8/35, 71 *10/197

Dorcanceaster (pn.) *Dorchester-on-Thames* 6/86

dorste → **durran**

dōð → **(ge)dōn**

drāfe (asg. f.) *drove, herd* 7/96 [drāf]

drǣfde (sg.pt.) *to drive* 7/61 [drǣfan I]

drēam (nasg. m.) *joy, gladness, delight* 11/140; **drēames** (gsg.) 11/144; **drēamum** (dpl.) 11/133

drenga (gpl. m.) *warrior* 10/149 [dreng]

drēogað (pl.ps.) *to suffer* 7/68 [drēogan 2]

drēorig (adj. nsg.) *bloody, blood-stained* 9/54

drīfað (pl.ps.) *to drive* 7/96; **drīfe** (sg.ps. subj.) 7/59 [drīfan 5]

Drihten, Drihtne, Drihtnes → **Dryhten**

drincað (pl.ps.) *to drink* 4/17 [drincan 3]

drohtnunga (dsg. f.) *condition, way of life* 6/34 [drohtnung]

dryhten, Dryhten (nasg. m.) *ruler, king; God* 9/1 *11/64, 101, 105, 144; **Drihten** 3/98, 102 *6/92 *10/148; **Drihtnes** (gsg.) 9/16; **Dryhtnes** 11/9, 35, 75, 113, 136, 140; **Drihtne** (dsg.) 3/112, 166

dugeþe (asg. f.) *army; benefit, honour* 7/144; **duguþe** (dsg.) 10/197 [duguð]

dūne (dsg. f.) *height, mountain* 1/3, 6, 25 [dūn]

Dunnere (prn.) 10/255

durran (prps.) *to dare* **dear** (sg.ps.) 7/20, 22, 26; **dorste** (sg.pt.) 11/35, 42, 45, 47

duru (asg. f.) *door* 2/11 *3/25

dūst (nasg. n.) *earth, dust* 6/143, 147; **dūste** (dsg.) 6/125, 141, 147

dwǣsan (adj. dpl.) *fool* 7/127 [dwǣs]

dwelode (sg.pt.) *to lead astray* 7/7 [dwelian II]

dydan, dyde, dydon → **(ge)dōn**

dȳre (adj. npl.) *precious, costly* 4/37

dysige (adj. npl.) *ignorant, foolish* 7/115 [dysig]

dysignesse (dasg. f.) *folly, madness* 3/48, 50 [dysignes]

dyslicum (adj. dpl.) *foolish, stupid* 6/155 [dyslic]

E

ēa (nsg. f.) *water, stream* 3/61 *4/9

ēac → **swelce**

ēac (adv.) *also, and, likewise, moreover* 2/100, 115, 147 *5/6–7, 20, 23 etc. *6/76, 140, 151 *7/7, 11, 56 etc. *8/76 *9/2, 19, 30, 37 *10/11 *11/92 ♦ col.: **ēac swā** 6/64; **ēac swelce** 3/73, 170; **ēac swilce** 6/20, 127, 151 *8/74; **ēac swylce** 3/166

Ēadgār (prn.) 2/76, 85, 97

ēadiga (adj. nsg. m.) *blessed, happy* 6/8

ēadignesse (gsg. f.) *blessedness, bliss, prosperity* 3/38 [ēadignes]

ēadmōd → **ēaðmōd**

Ēadmund (prn.) 2/54 *9/3

Ēadric (prn.) 10/11

Ēadweard (prn.) 7/60 *10/117, 273; **Ēadweardes** (gsg.) 9/7, 52

Ēadwine (prn.) 2/103, 107, 132 etc. *3/64 *6/5, 69; **Ēadwines** (gsg.) 6/95

ēagan (gsg. n.) *eye* 3/27; **ēagum** (dpl.) 8/30 [ēage]

eahta (num.) *eight* 6/94

eal → **eall**

ēalā (interj.) *alas, oh, lo* 7/137 *8/45

ealað → **ealo**

Ealchstān (prn.) 2/44

eald (adj. nsg. m.) *old* 8/5 *9/46 *10/310; **ealda** (nsg. m.) 10/218; **alda** 2/68; **ealdan** (asg. f.) 1/14, 16; **ealde** (asg. f.) 8/33; (npl.) 9/69; (asg. n.) 10/47; **ealdra** (gpl.) 7/32; **ieldran** (npl. comp.) *ancestors, elders* 5/28

ealde, ealdan → **eald**; **mynster**

ealdgewyrhtum (dpl. n.) *deed of old, former action* 11/100 [ealdgewyrht]

ealdor (nsg. m.) *lord, prince; God* 10/202, 222, 314 *11/90; **ealdres** (gsg.) 10/53; **ealdre** (dsg.) 10/11 *11/90

ealdorbisceop (nsg. m.) *high-priest* 3/9

ealdorlangne (adj. asg. m.) *life-long, eternal* 9/3 [ealdorlang]

ealdormann (nasg. m.) *nobleman, ruler, officer* 3/20; **ealdorman** 8/6 *10/219; **ealdormon** 3/107; **aldormon** 2/3, 5, 20 etc.; **aldorman** 2/58; **aldormonnes** (gsg.) 2/32; **aldormen** (npl.) 3/31; **ealdormannum** (dpl.) 3/23

ealdra → eald
ealdre, ealdres → ealdor
Ealdred (prn.) 2/140, 146
Ealdwold (prn.) 10/304
ealgodon (pl.pt.) *to defend* 9/9 [ealgian II]
Ealhelm (prn.) 10/218
eall (1) (adv.) *entirely* 6/145, 159 *10/314
  *11/20, 48, 62; eal 7/87; ealles 7/11, 30, 62,
  114, 120, 124, 140 ♦ col.: mid ealle 7/125,
  144
eall (2) (adj. nsg. n.) *all* 2/134 *4/29, 34, 38
  *6/77, 96 *11/6; (asg. n.) 2/93, 144 *4/36
  *5/23–24, 33 *6/45, 54 *10/256 *11/58, 94;
  (nsg. f.) 5/48 *11/12, 82; (npl. n.) 4/4; eal (nsg.
  n.) 7/65, 74, 89, 95 *11/55; (asg. n.) 3/126
  *7/122, 127 *8/5; (apl. n.) 3/104, 122; ealle
  (asg. f.) 3/142 *4/24 *6/117–118 *7/11
  *10/304; (dsg. f.) 7/65, 138; (npl.) 1/29
  *2/141 *3/4, 82, 154–156 *4/31, 33 *5/46
  *6/15, 48 *7/38, 141, 160 *8/3, 42, 44, 52,
  56, 71, 73, 101 *10/63, 203, 207 *11/9, 128;
  (apl.) 2/97 *3/109 *4/39 *5/9, 41–42 *6/34,
  82 *8/7, 29 *10/196, 231, 320 *11/37, 74;
  (dpl.) 11/93; eallum (dsg. m.) 3/155; eallon)
  2/137; (dpl.) 2/117; eallra (dsg. f.) 6/167;
  eallre (dsg. f.) 7/40; ealre 7/83; ealne (asg.
  m.) 2/138 *3/59 *7/98; ealla (napl.) 5/34, 43;
  ealra (gpl.) 3/111 *7/56, 134 *10/174
  *11/125; eallum (dpl.) 3/8, 15, 42, 64 etc.
  *5/46 *6/54, 92, 133, 137 *7/41, 97, 101
  *8/49, 59, 61 *10/216, 233 *11/154; all (asg.
  n.) 2/55; alle (npl.) 2/13, 17, 32; alne (asg. m.)
  2/63, 80
ealles → eall (1) gelōme
eallinga (adv.) *altogether, entirely* 3/11
eallon, eallra, eallre → eall (2)
eallswā (adv., conj.) *just as, even as* 2/46, 75,
  77, 79
eallum, ealne → eall (2)
ealne, ealneg → weg
ealo (nsg. n.) *ale* 4/18; ealað (gsg.) 4/46
ealra, ealre → eall (2)
ēam (nsg. m.) *uncle* 6/5
eard (asg. m.) *native place, country* 7/144, 149
  *9/73 *10/53, 58, 222; earde (dsg.) 6/161
  *7/34, 46, 56 etc.
earh (adj. nsg. m.) *cowardly* 10/238 ♦ neg.:
  unearge (npl. m.) *brave* 10/206
earhlice (adj. npl.) *shameful* 7/84
earm (1) (nasg. m.) *arm* 2/99 *6/21, 102, 108
  *10/165
earm (2) (adj. asg. n.) *poor, miserable,
  wretched* 2/154; earman (dsg. f.) 7/136;
  earme (npl.) 7/34 *11/68; earmra (gpl.) 8/75
  *11/19

earmlīce (adv.) *miserably, wretchedly* 7/138
earmlicum (dsg. m.) *miserable, pitiable* 6/157
  [earmlic]
earmra → earm (2)
earn (asg. m.) *eagle* 9/63 *10/107
(ge)earnung (f.) *deserts, merit, favour*
  geearnunga (apl.) 6/24, 148 *10/196;
  geearnunge 6/122; geearnungum (dpl.)
  6/68; earnungan (dpl.) 7/14–15
eart → bēon
ēast (adv.) *eastwards* 3/61
Ēast Englum (pn.) *East Anglia* 2/36;
  Eastengle 2/53
ēastan (adv.) *from the east, easterly* 4/11–12
  *9/69
Ēasterdæge (dsg. m.) *Easter Sunday* 6/56
ēasteðe (dsg. n.) *river bank* 10/63 [ēasteð]
Ēastran (ndpl. f.) *Easter* 2/92–93; Ēastron
  (dpl.) 2/77
Ēastseaxena (pn. gpl.) *East Saxons* 10/69
ēaðe (adv.) *easily* 5/47; ēaþe 7/137
ēaðmōd (adj. nsg. m.) *humble-minded,
  obedient* 11/60; ēadmōd 6/53
ēaðmōdlīce (adv.) *humbly, meekly* 3/137
eaxlgespanne (dsg. n.) *crossbeam* 11/9
eaxlum (dpl. f.) *shoulder* 11/32
ebban (dsg. m.) *ebb-tide* 10/65 [ebba]
Ebriscgeðīode (dsg. f.) *the Hebrew language*
  5/40
ēce (adj. nsg. m.) *eternal, everlasting* 3/98,
  102; ēcan (dsg. f.) 6/174, 177; ēces (gsg. m.)
  3/39 *9/16; ēcre (gsg. f.) 3/38
ecg (nsg. f.) *edge, sword* 10/60; ecgum (dpl.)
  9/4, 68
Ecglāfes (prn.) 10/267
ecgum → ecg
ēcnysse (dsg. f.) *eternity* 6/27 [ēcnes]
ēcre; Eferwīc → ēce; Eoforwīc
efne (adv.) *even* 3/47, 78 *8/8
efstan (I) *to hasten, hurry* 11/34; efston (pl.pt.)
  10/206
eft (adv.) *again, afterwards* 1/9, 25 *2/52, 136
  *3/28, 91, 116 etc. *5/35, 40, 42 *6/39, 89,
  112 etc. *7/81 *8/79 *9/56 *10/49, 156, 201
  *11/68, 101, 103
ege (nsg. m.) *fear, terror* 1/27 *3/131 *7/121
egesa (nsg. m.) *awe, fear, horror* 11/86
egeslic (nsg. n.) *awful, terrible* 7/6, 66 *11/74;
  egeslican (dsg. n.) 6/138; egeslice (npl.) 7/74
ēiglande (asg. n.) *island* 9/66
elcor (adv.) *otherwise* 3/53
elcunge (dsg. f.) *delay* 8/104
ellen (asg. n.) *courage, zeal* 10/211; elne (dsg.)
  11/34, 60, 123

ellenwōdnisse (dsg. f.) *zeal* 3/138 [ellenwōdnes]
elne → ellen
embe → ymb
ende (nsg. m.) *end, conclusion; region* 2/134,
    138, 155 *6/155 *7/4, 43, 87 *8/29 *11/29;
    ænde (dsg.) 3/138 *7/30
endebyrdnesse (nasg. f.) *order, succession*
    3/82, 94
endlyftan (ord. isg. n.) *eleventh* 3/65
engel (nsg. m.) *angel* 1/17–18, 25 *11/9;
    englas (npl.) 11/106; ænglas 6/176; engla
    (gpl.) 10/178; englum (dpl.) 11/153
engla → engel; Engle; Englaland
Englafelda (pn.) *Englefield, Berkshire* 2/58
Englaland (pn.) *England* 2/93; Englalande
    (dsg.) 2/98; Engla lande 6/1
englas → engel
Engle (prn.) *the English* 2/116 *7/87, 95
    *9/70; Engla (gpl.) 2/108; Englum (dpl.)
    7/152
Englisc (asg.) *the English language* 5/13, 51,
    54 etc. *6/25
engliscan (npl. m.) *the English* 2/114
englisces (adj. gsg. n.) *English* 2/111
Engliscgereorde (dsg. n.) *the English
    language* 3/71
englum → engel; Engle
ēode, ēodon → gān
eodorcende (psp.) *to chew the cud* 3/123
Eoforwīc (pn.) *York* 2/91, 107, 111;
    Eoforwicceastre 2/36, 41, 52 *3/61
eoh (asg. m.) *horse* 10/189
eom → bēon
eorl (nsg. m.) *nobleman* 2/67–69, 97, 102–103
    etc. *10/6, 51, 89 etc.; eorles (gsg.) 10/165;
    eorle (dsg.) 2/117 *10/28, 159; eorlas (napl.)
    2/58, 65, 85 *9/31, 73; eorla (gpl.) 2/67 *9/1
eornost (f.) on eornost (adv.) *in earnest,
    seriously* 7/98
ēorodcistum (dpl. f.) *troop* 9/21 [ēoredcist]
eorðe (nsg. f.) *ground, earth* 6/124; eorðan
    (gsg.) 3/99 *11/37; (dsg.) 3/22 *4/23 *11/42,
    74, 137, 145; (asg.) 6/127, 130 *10/126, 233,
    286; eorþan (dsg.) 10/107, 157, 303
eorðwege (dsg. m.) *earthly way* 11/120
ēow, ēower → gē
Ēowland (pn.) *Öland* 4/7
ēowre, ēowrum → gē
ernian → geearnian
Estland (pn.) *Estonia* 4/15; Estlande (dsg.)
    4/12
Estmere (pn.) *Frisches Haff* 4/10–12
Estum (prn.) *Estonians* 4/10, 19–20, 41, 44

ēðel (nasg. m.) *homeland, territory* 5/7
    *11/156; ēþel (asg.) 10/52

F

fadian (II) *to arrange, order* 7/158; fadode
    (sg.pt.) 7/50
fāh (adj. nsg. m.) *stained* 11/13
Falster (pn.) *Falster* 4/3
fandian (I) *to try, tempt* 1/1
faran (6) *to set forth, go, travel, journey; die*
    2/120 *6/157 *10/88, 156; far (imp.sg.) 1/2;
    fare (sg.ps. subj.) 8/81; fōr (sg.pt.) 2/36, 46,
    52 etc.; gefōr *died* 2/44, 55, 77; fōron (pl.pt.)
    2/106, 118; gefōre (sg.pt. subj.) 4/1; gefaren
    (ptp.) 2/109 *7/138
fæc (nasg. n.) *space of time, moment* 3/27, 164;
    fæce (dsg.) 3/28, 69
fæder (nsg. m.) *father* 1/11–12 *7/48, 73
    *8/17, 63; (gsg.) 8/36, 67, 88 *10/218; (dsg.)
    7/49 *8/16, 35, 80; (asg.) 1/10 *8/15
fǣge (adj. npl.) *doomed to death, fated* 9/12,
    28 *10/105, 119; fǣges (gsg. m.) 10/297;
    fǣgean (dsg. m.) 10/125
fægen (adj. nsg. m.) *glad, joyful* 6/84
fæger (adj. nsg. m.) *fair, lovely, beautiful*
    11/73; fægran (dsg. f.) 11/21; fægre (isg. m.)
    3/138; fægere 11/8, 10; fægera (gpl.) 8/58
fægere (adv.) *suitably* 10/22
fæges → fǣge
fægnode (sg.pt.) *to rejoice, be glad* 6/38, 134
    [fægnian II (g.)]
fægran, fægre → fæger
fǣhðe (asg. f.) *hostility, feud* 10/225 [fǣhðu]
fǣringa (adv.) *suddenly* 8/14
fǣrlīce (adv.) *suddenly* 6/145
fǣrsceaðan (dsg. m.) *(sudden) attacker* 10/142
fæste (adv.) *fast, firmly* 3/57, 104 *7/93
    *10/21, 103, 171, 301 *11/38, 43
fæsten (asg. n.) *place of safety* 10/194
fæstenbrycas (npl. m.) *non-observance of
    fasts* 7/112 [fæstenbryce]
fæstlīce (adv.) *firmly* 3/42 *10/82, 254
fæstnian (II) *to secure* 10/35
fǣtels (apl. m.) *vessel* 4/46
fǣxedon (ptp.) *long-haired* 2/95
fēa (adv.) *hardly* 11/115
feaht; feala → feohtan; fela
fealene (adj. asg. m.) *fallow* 9/36 [fealu]
(ge)feallan (7) *to fall, decay, die* 6/12 *10/54,
    105 *11/43; feallende (psp.) 6/100; fēol
    (sg.pt.) 6/127, 130 *10/126, 303; fēoll 6/21,
    132 *10/119, 166, 286; gefēol 8/47, 62;
    fēollon (pl.pt.) 6/15, 98 *8/29 *10/111;
    fēollan 9/12

fealohilte (nsg. n.) *golden-hilted* 10/166

fēawa (adj. npl.) *few* 5/12, 14, 22; **fēawum** (dpl.) 8/98

feccan (II) *to fetch* 8/39, 41, 92; **gefeccan** 10/160; **feccende** (psp.) 6/149; **fette** (sg.pt.) 6/22

fela (npl.) *many, much* 2/69, 76, 129 *6/20, 58, 122, 179 *7/7, 9, 12 etc. *8/10, 58 *10/73, 90; **feala** 11/50, 125, 131

feld (nasg. m.) *field, area, battlefield* 6/129, 131 *9/12; **felda** (dsg.) 10/241

fēng (sg.pt.) *to catch, seize* 2/79 *3/21 *5/16 *6/104 *10/10; **fēngon** (pl.pt.) 6/98 ♦ col.: **fēng tō rīce** *succeeded to the throne* 5/15–16 *6/104 [fōn 7]

feoh (asg. n.) *money, property, prize; cattle* 2/16, 99 *4/26, 35 *10/39; **fēos** (gsg.) 2/24 *4/27; **fēo** (dsg.) 4/32–33, 36

feohtan (3) *to fight, attack* 2/133 *10/16, 261; **gefeohtan** 10/129; **feohtende** (psp.) 2/13, 17, 31; **feaht** (sg.pt.) 2/5, 54, 126 *10/254, 277, 281, 298; **gefeaht** 2/59, 63, 65 etc.; **fuhton** (pl.pt.) 2/107; **gefuhton** 2/49, 60; **gefohten** (ptp.) 2/82

feohte (nsg. f.) *fighting, battle* 10/103 [see gefeoht]

feohtende → **feohtan**

fēol, fēoll, fēollan, fēollon → **(ge)feallan**

fēolhearde (adj. apl.) *sharpened* 10/108

fēond (asg. m.) *enemy, foe, devil* 6/13; **fȳnd** 6/17 *10/82; **fēondas** (napl.) 11/30, 33, 38; **fēonda** (gpl.) 1/29 *6/10; **fēondum** (dpl.) 7/71 *10/103, 264

feor (adv.) *far (away)* 3/60, 162 *10/3, 57

fēore, fēores → **feorh**

feorgbold (nsg. n.) *body* 11/73

feorh (asg. n.) *life* 2/16, 32 *9/36 *10/125, 142, 184; **fēores** (gsg.) 10/260, 317; **fēore** (dsg.) 10/194, 259

feorhhūs (asg. n.) *body* 10/297

feorran (adv.) *from afar* 11/57

fēos → **feoh**

fēower (num.) *four* 6/66 *8/67

fēowertȳnum (num. dpl.) *fourteen* 3/141

fēran (I) *to go, journey, depart* 10/41, 221; **fērde** (sg.pt.) 1/4 *3/55 *6/2, 45, 129, 134, 138, 140; **gefērde** *happened* 2/135; **fērdon** (pl.pt.) 1/31 *2/49 *6/50

fēre (adj. npl.) *ready, prepared* 2/123

ferian (II) *to carry, convey, go* 10/179; **ferode** (sg.pt.) 6/89, 106, 136; **feredon** (pl.pt.) 6/176

fers (apl. n.) *verse* 3/94

fēseð (sg.ps.) *to drive away* 7/89 [fēsan I]

fette → **feccan**

fēþan (npl. m.) *foot-soldier* 10/88 [fēða]

fierd (asg. f.) *army, campaign* 2/40, 60; **fierde** (dsg.) 2/49; **fyrde** 10/221

fierlenan (adj. dsg. n.) *far away, distant* 1/4; **fyrlenum** (dpl.) 6/80 [fierlen]

fīf (num.) *five* 2/121 *4/27, 32; **fīfe** (npl.) 9/28 *11/8

fīftegum (num. dpl.) *fifty* 5/63

fīftēne (num.) *fifteen* 4/11

findan (3) *to find, meet* 8/82; **findeð** (sg.ps.) 4/42; **fundon** (pl.pt.) 10/85; **funden** (ptp.) 5/40

fiorme (asg. f.) *use, profit* 5/26

first (asg. m.) *space of time, duration* 5/50; **fyrstes** (gsg.) 6/160; **fyrste** (dsg.) 6/87

firum (dpl.) *men, people* 3/103 [fīras, pl.]

fiscað (nsg. m.) *fishing* 4/16

flān (asg. m.) *arrow* 10/269; **flānes** (gsg.) 10/71

flǣsce (dsg. n.) *flesh* 6/108 [flǣsc]

flēam (asg. m.) *flight* 10/81, 254; **flēame** (dsg.) *flight* 2/113 *9/37 *10/186

flēogan (2) *to fly* 10/7, 109, 150; **flee** 10/275

flēon (2) *to flee* 10/247; **flugon** (pl.pt.) 6/146 *10/194

flōd (asg. m.) *flood, sea, stream* 9/36 *10/65, 72; **flōdan** (dsg.) 2/4

flot (asg. n.) *sea* 9/35 *10/41

flotan (gpl. m.) *sailor* 9/32; (npl.) 10/72; (asg.) 10/227 [flota]

flotmen (npl.) *sailor, pirate* 7/88 [flotmann]

flōwende (psp.) *to flow* 10/65 [flōwan 7]

flugon → **flēon**

flyht (asg. m.) *flight* 10/71

folc (nasg. n.) *people, nation, tribe; army* 2/126, 154 *3/55 *6/87, 97, 100 *10/22, 45, 54, 241 *11/140; **folces** (gsg.) 2/111, 130 *3/128 *5/5 *6/93 *7/5, 64, 148 *9/67 *10/202; **folce** (dsg.) 3/65 *6/39, 50–51 *8/58 *10/227, 259, 323

folcgefeoht (npl. n.) *pitched battle* 2/82, 120

folclaga (npl. f.) *public law* 7/30 [folclagu]

folcstede (dsg. m.) *battlefield* 9/41

foldan (asg. f.) *earth* 3/103; (gsg.) 11/8; (dsg.) 10/54, 166, 227 *11/43, 132 [folde]

folgian (II) *to follow, obey* 2/26

folman (dsg. f.) *hand, palm* 10/21, 108, 150 [folma]

fōr → **faran**

for (prep. (d.a.i.)) *for, because of, before, in* 1/20, 23 *2/1, 130, 141, 143 *3/71, 83 *5/20, 37 *6/17, 68, 70 etc. *7/5, 36, 55 etc. *8/9, 25 *11/21, 93, 99 etc. *10/64, 89, 96, 259 ♦ col.: **for hwī** 8/89; **for hwon** 3/147 ♦

causal: **forðām** 8/20, 22, 91, 105; **forðāmþe**
8/44; **for þām** *because, because of,*
wherefore 7/12–13, 29, 41 etc.; **for þām þe**
1/30 *2/45; **forþan** 10/241; **for þan** 11/84;
for ðan þe 6/172; **for þan þe** 6/42; **for ðǣm**
5/30–31; **for ðǣm ðe** 5/26–27; **for ðon** 3/13,
29, 77, 138 *5/17; **for þon** 3/17, 36, 39 etc.;
forðȳ 5/44, 65; **for ðȳ** 4/14, 36; **for þȳ** 6/168
forbærnan (I) *to burn down, cremate* 3/60
*6/149; **forbærneð** (sg.ps.) 4/38; **forbærnað**
(pl.ps.) 4/25; **forbærnen** (pl.ps. subj.) 3/41;
forbærned (ptp.) 4/42 *5/24; **forbærnde**
2/115 *7/60
forbēah (sg.pt.) *to avoid* 10/325 [forbūgan 2]
forburnon (ptp.) *to burn down* 6/146
[forbeornan 3]
ford (asg. m.) *ford* 10/88; **forda** (dsg.) 10/81
fordōn (irr.) *to destroy* 7/144; **fordyde** (sg.pt.)
3/63
foregange (sg.ps. subj.) *to precede* 3/29
[foregangan 7]
foresǣdon (pl.pt.) *to mention before* 6/107;
foresǣdan 6/133; (ptp.) 6/22, 137
forescēawað (sg.ps.) *to provide, preordain*
1/12 [forescēawian II]
forespecan (npl.) *sponsor* 7/157 [forespeca]
foresprecenan (ptp.) *to mention before* 3/44
forfarene (ptp.) *to destroy* 2/115
forgeaf (sg.pt.) *to give* 8/78 *10/139, 148
*11/147; **forgifen** (ptp.) 3/113 *8/77 [forgifan
5]
forgrunden (ptp.) *to grind down, destroy* 9/43
[forgrindan 3]
forgyldon (pl.ps. subj.) *to buy off* 10/32
[forgieldan 3]
forhæfednysse (asg. f.) *temperance,*
continence 6/47 [forhæfednes]
forhealdan (7) *to withhold* 7/20; **forhealdað**
(pl.ps.) 7/21
forheardne (asg. m.) *very hard* 10/156
[forheard]
forhēawen (ptp.) *to cut down* 10/115, 223,
288, 314 [forhēawan 7]
forhergod (ptp.) *to harry, plunder* 5/24
[forhergian II]
forhogdnisse (dsg. f.) *contempt* 3/72
[forhogodnes]
forhogode (sg.pt.) *to scorn* 10/254
[forhogian II]
forht (adj. nsg. n.) *afraid, timid* 11/21
forhtiað (pl.ps.) *to be afraid, fear* 11/115;
forhtedon (pl.pt. subj.) 10/21 [forhtian II]
forhwæga (adv.) *somewhere, about* 4/28, 32

forlǣtan (7) *to let go, relinquish, surrender,*
abandon, neglect 7/154 *10/2, 208;
forlǣtende (psp.) 3/167; **forlǣt** (imp.sg.)
8/36; **forlēt** (sg.pt.) 3/85 *8/27, 57 *9/42
*10/149, 156, 187, 321; **forlēton** (pl.pt.) 5/38
*11/61; **forlǣten** (ptp.) 5/30
forlēas → **forlēosen**
forlegene (ptp.) *fornicator* 7/132 [forlicgan 5]
forlēosen (pl.ps. subj.) *to lose, abandon, let go*
3/41; **forlēas** (sg.pt.) 8/26; **forlure** (2.sg.pt.)
8/95; **forloren** (ptp.) 7/112 *8/11
forlēt, forlēton → **forlǣtan**
forliden (ptp.) *to suffer shipwreck* 8/19
[forlīðan 1]
forligru (apl. n.) *fornication* 7/110 [forliger]
forlogen (ptp.) *to lie, perjure oneself* 7/112;
forlogene 7/76 [forlēogan 2]
forloren, forlure → **forlēosen**
forman (adj. asg. m.) *first* 10/77; **fyrmest** (nsg.
m. sup.) 10/323
formoni (adj. npl.) *too many* 10/239
fornumene (ptp.) *to take away* 7/37
[forniman 4]
fornȳdde (ptp.) *to force, compell* 7/33
[fornȳdan I]
foroft (adv.) *very often* 7/46, 48, 104
fōron → **faran**
forrǣde (sg.ps. subj.) *to betray* 7/58;
forrǣdde (sg.pt.) 7/60 [forrǣdan I]
forrotige (sg.ps. subj.) *to decay* 6/63
[forrotian II]
forsawene (ptp.) *to despise, scorn* 7/38
[forsēon 5]
forsōcon (pl.pt.) *to reject, oppose, deny* 6/120;
forsōcan 2/49 [forsacan 6]
forspendað (pl.ps.) *to spend, squander* 4/39
[forspendan I]
forspilde (sg.pt.) *to kill* 7/62 [forspillan I]
forstōd (sg.pt.) *to understand* 5/60
[forstandan 6]
forsworene (ptp.) *to forswear, swear falsely*
7/76 [forswerian 6]
forsyngod (ptp.) *to sin greatly* 7/105;
forsyngodan 7/136 [forsyngian II]
forð (adv.) *forth, forwards, onwards* 6/134,
141 *7/123 *8/58, 60 *9/20 *10/3, 12, 150
etc. *11/132
forðām, forðāmþe, forþan → **for**
forþbrōhte (sg.pt.) *to bring forth, produce*
3/71 [forðbringan I]
forðearle (adv.) *very much, greatly* 6/22
forðēode (sg.pt.) *to go forth, conquer* 11/54
[forðgān irr.]

forðfērde (sg.pt.) *to die* 2/37 [forðfēran I]
forðfōr (nsg. f.) *departure, death* 3/148;
  forðfōre (gsg.) 3/140, 171; (dsg.) 3/144;
  forþfōre (dsg.) 3/152
forðgeorn (adj. asg. m.) *eager to advance*
  10/281
forðgesceaft (asg. f.) *eternal decree* 11/10
forðlīcor (adv. comp.) *further* 2/78
forðwege (dsg. m.) *way forth, departure*
  11/125
forðȳ → **for**
forwandigendre (ptp.) *hesitating* 8/23
forwegen (ptp.) *to destroy* 10/228 [forwegan 5]
forweorðan (3) *to perish* 7/141; **forwurdan**
  (ptp.) 7/63, 150
forworhtan → **forwyrcan**
forwundod (ptp.) *to wound sorely* 11/14, 62
  [forwundian II]
forwurdan → **forweorðan**
forwyrcan (I) *to forfeit, destroy* 7/125;
  forworhtan (pl.pt.) 7/149
forwyrnde (sg.pt.) *to prohibit* 8/85
  [forwiernan I]
foryrmde (ptp.) *to reduce to poverty* 7/33
  [foryrman I]
fōtes (gsg. m.) *foot* 10/247; **fōtum** (dpl. m.)
  6/51, 139 *10/119, 171 [fōt]
fōtmæl (asg. n.) *footstep* 10/275
fracodes (adj. gsg. m.) *bad, evil* 11/10;
  fracodum (dpl.) 6/157 [fracod]
fram (prep. (d.)) *from, of, since, concerning,*
  on 2/97, 134, 138 *3/7 *4/28, 32 *6/3, 5, 34,
  39 etc. *7/97 *8/34, 39 *10/185, 187, 193
  etc. *11/69; **from** 2/25, 28, 87 *3/44, 49, 75
  etc. *5/64 *9/8
francan (dsg. m.) *spear, javelin* 10/77; (asg.)
  10/140
Franclande (pn.) *the Frankish kingdom* 6/152
frægn → **frignende**
Fræna (prn.) 2/68
frēa (nsg. m.) *ruler, God* 3/103; **frēan** (asg.)
  10/12, 16, 184, 259, 289 *11/33
fremdan (adj. npl.) *foreign, strange* 4/40
  *7/48; **fremdum** (dpl.) 7/35, 74 [fremde]
fremsumnesse (asg. f.) *benefit, gift* 3/15;
  fremsumnessum (dpl.) 3/133 [fremsumnes]
Frencyscan (prn. npl.) *'the French'* 2/129
frēode (asg. f.) *peace* 10/39 [frēod]
frēolsbricas (npl.) *non-observance of festivals*
  7/112 [frēolsbrice]
frēond (nsg. m.) *friend* 11/144; **frēondas** (npl.)
  11/76; **frȳnd** (apl.) 8/39 *10/229; **frēonda**
  (gpl.) 6/150 *9/41 *11/132; **frēondum** (dpl.)
  3/3 *4/21 *6/3 *8/70

frēondlīce (adv.) *friendly* 5/1
frēondscype (asg. f.) *friendship* 2/64
frēondum → **frēond**
frēoriht (npl.) *rights of freemen* 7/37
frignende (psp.) *to ask (for), enquire* 3/8;
  frīneð (sg.ps.) 11/112; **frægn** (sg.pt.) 3/151,
  154, 160; **gefrūnon** (pl.pt.) 11/76
frīora (adj. gpl.) *free* 5/48 [frēo]
friþ (asg. m.n.) *peace* 2/43, 51, 86 etc.; **frið**
  10/39; **frȳð** 2/119; **friþes** (gsg.) 10/41; **friþe**
  (dsg.) 10/179
frōd (adj. nsg. m.) *old, mature, wise* 10/140,
  317; **frōda** (nsg. m.) 9/37
frōfres (gsg. f.) *joy, consolation* 8/85 [frōfor]
from → **fram**
fruman (dsg. m.) *origin, beginning* 3/126
  [fruma]
frumsceaft (asg. f.) *creation* 3/92
frymdi (adj. nsg. m.) *desirous* 10/179
frȳnd → **frēond**
frȳð; fuhton → **friþ; feohtan**
ful (adv.) *fully, completely* 7/17, 58, 84 etc.
  *10/253, 311; **full** 10/153
fūle (adj. npl.) *foul, disgusting* 7/132; **fūlne**
  (asg. m.) 7/148 [fūl]
fulgon (pl.pt.) *to penetrate* 2/30 [fēolan 3]
fūliað (pl.ps.) *to rot, decay* 4/45 [fūlian I]
full → **ful**
full (adj.) *full* 4/46
fullan → **be**
fullīce (adv.) *fully, completely* 7/82–83
fulluht, fulluhte → **fulwihte**
fūlne → **fūle**
fultume (dsg. m.) *help, support* 5/47
fultumian (II) *to help, support* 3/17;
  gefultumadon (pl.pt.) 2/48; **gefultumed**
  (ptp.) 3/76
fulwihte (gsg. f.m.) *baptism* 3/65; **fulluht** (asg.)
  6/45 *7/156; **fulluhte** (dsg.) 6/84 *7/157
fulworhte (sg.pt.) *to finish* 6/69 [fulwyrcan I]
fundaþ (sg.ps.) *to be eager for; set out,*
  journey 11/103; **fundode** (sg.pt.) 6/142
  [fundian II]
funden, fundon → **findan**
fundode → **fundaþ**
furðor (adv.) *further* 10/247; **furður** 5/51–52
furðum (adv.) *even* 5/13, 15
fūs (adj. nsg. m.) *eager, ready* 10/281; **fūse**
  (asg. n.) 11/21; (npl.) 11/57
fyl → **fyll**
fylgean (I) *to follow, observe* 7/156; **fylgen**
  (pl.ps. subj.) 3/31
fyll (asg. m.) *fall, death (in battle)* 11/56; **fyl**
  10/71, 264; **fylle** (dsg.) 6/8, 101

fyllan (I) *to fell, strike down* 11/73; **gefyllan** 11/38; **gefylled** (ptp.) 9/41, 67

fylle → **fyll**

fylstan (I) *to support, help* 10/265; **fylste** (sg.pt.) 6/96; **gefylste** 6/10

fȳlþe (dasg. f.) *foul sin* 7/69–70 [fȳð]

fȳnd → **fēond**

fȳr (nasg. n.) *fire* 1/10–11 *3/24 *6/144, 148 *7/18; **fȳre** (dsg.) 3/41 *6/145

fyrde → **fierd**

fyrdrinc (nsg. m.) *warrior* 10/140

fyrhtu (dsg. f.) *fear* 3/132

fyrlenum → **fierlenan**

fyrmest → **forman**

fyrste, fyrstes → **first**

fȳsde (sg.pt.) *to send forth* 10/269 [fȳsan I]

G

Gaddes (prn. gsg.) 10/287

gaderade (sg.pt.) *to gather, assemble* 2/124; **gegædrade** 2/99; **gegadrodon** (pl.pt.) 2/40 [gad(e)rian II]

gafole → **gofol**

galan (6) *to sing, call* 11/67

gān (irr.) *to go, come, move, proceed, advance* 8/78, 100 *10/247; **gǣþ** (sg.ps.) 2/35; **gāð** (pl.ps.) 1/8; (imp.pl.) 10/93; **ēode** 2/11 *3/84, 90, 115, 149 *6/57 *8/1, 14, 22 etc. *10/132, 159, 225 etc.; **ēodon** 2/23, 28 *6/16, 49 *8/99 *10/229, 260

gangan *to go, move* 10/3, 40, 62, 170; **gongan** 3/143; **gegangan** *to win* 10/59; **gangon** (pl.ps. subj.) 10/56; **gongende** (psp.) 3/85, 146; **gangǣnde** 6/139

gange (dsg.) *flow* 11/23 [gang]

gār (nasg. m.) *spear* 10/13, 134, 154 etc.; **gāre** (dsg.) 10/138; **gāras** (napl.) 10/46, 67, 109; **gārum** (dpl.) 9/18

gārberend (npl. m.) *spear-bearer, warrior* 10/262

gārmittinge (dsg. f.) *battle* 9/50

gārrǣs (asg. m.) *attack* 10/32

gārum → **gār**

gāst (asg. m.) *ghost, spirit, soul* 3/170 *11/49; **gāste** (dsg.) 10/176; **gāstas** (npl.) 11/11; **gāsta** (gpl.) 11/152

Gāstes → **hālig**

gatu (apl. n.) *gate, door* 1/29 *2/22, 30 [geat]

gāð → **gān**

gǣlsan (asg. m.) *pride, wantonness* 7/148 [gǣlsa]

gǣþ; ge → **gān; ǣgþer**

ge (conj.) *and* 4/21; **ge . . . ge** *both . . . and* 3/142

gē (perspron. 2.npl.) *you* 8/76, 103, 108 *10/32, 34, 56–57, 59; **ēower** (gpl.) 8/111; **ēow** (dapl. refl.) 1/7, 9 *3/158 *8/69, 77, 109 *10/31, 41, 46, 48, 93; **īow** 5/45 ♦ poss. adj.: **ēowre** (npl.) 2/29 *8/109; **ēowrum** (dsg. m.) 6/161

geaf, gēafon → **gifan**

geald → **gylde**

gealga (nsg. m.) *gallows, cross* 11/10; **gealgan** (asg.) 11/40

gealgian (II) *to defend* 10/52

gealgtrēowe (dsg. m.) *gallows-tree, cross* 11/146 [gealgtrēow]

geanbīdode → **anbīdiað**

geānlǣhte (sg.pt.) *to unite* 6/68 [ānlǣcan I]

gēar (asg. n.) *year* 2/52, 78 *4/23; **gēares** (gsg.) 2/82, 85; **gēare** (dsg.) 2/39, 44, 55 etc. *3/65 *6/93–94; **gēara** (gpl.) 7/7, 47, 104; **gēarum** (dpl.) 6/6, 178

gēara (adv.) *formerly* 11/28

geare (adv.) *readily, clearly* 3/35 *6/14

gearo (adj. nsg. m.) *ready, prepared* 2/15 *10/274; **gearowe** (npl.) 10/72, 100

gēarum → **gēar**

geāscode, geāxode → **(ge)āscian**

geǣmetige (sg.ps. subj.) *to free, disengage* 5/18 [ǣmetian I]

geǣrneð (sg.ps.) *to gallop, run* 4/35 [ǣrnen I]

geæþele (adj. nsg.) *natural, congenial* 9/7

gebād; geband; gebǣd → **(ge)bīdan; band; (ge)biddan**

gebǣrum (dpl. n.) *behaviour* 2/14 [gebǣre]

gebēad → **bebēodan**

gebēded (ptp.) *to force* 9/33 [gebǣdan I]

gebedum (dpl. n.) *prayer* 6/15, 70, 73

gebēoras (napl. m.) *pot-companion, guest* 6/142, 145; **gebēorum** (dpl.) 6/143–144

gebeorge (dsg. n.) *protection* 10/31, 131, 245 [gebeorg]

gebēorscipe (dsg. m.) *feast, beer party* 3/81, 90 *8/2, 20, 73; **gebēorscipes** (gsg.) 3/85; **bēorscipes** 8/63

gebēorum → **gebēoras**

gebētan → **(ge)bētan**

gebīdan → **(ge)bīdan**

gebiddan, gebiddaþ, gebiddenne → **(ge)biddan**

gebiden → **(ge)bīdan**

gebīgan (I) *to turn, bend, convert* 6/29, 43; **gebīgde** (sg.pt.) 6/46, 81

gebland (asg. n.) *confusion* 9/26

geblētsode → **blētsie**

geblissod → **blissigende**
geboden → **bebēodan**
gebōhte → **bicgað**
geboren, geborene → **beran**
gebræc (nsg. n.) *breaking, smashing* 10/295
gebringe, gebringeð → **(ge)bringan**
gebrocod (ptp.) *to crush, hurt* 6/22, 135
  [brocian II]
gebrōht, gebrōhte → **(ge)bringan**
gebrōþer, gebrōþru → **brōþor**
gebrowen (ptp.) *to brew* 4/19 [brēowan 2]
gebūgan → **(ge)būgan**
gebyrdum (dpl. f.) *birth, descent* 8/106 [byrd]
gebyriað (pl.ps.) *to be fitting, appropriate*
  7/117 [byrian II]
gebysnode (sg.pt.) *to set an example* 6/46
  [bysnian II]
gecampe → **campe**
gecēose (sg.ps. subj.) *to choose, decide* 8/106,
  110; **gecēas** (sg.pt.) 10/113; **gecoren** (ptp.)
  3/111 [cēosan 2]
gecierde → **gecyrran**
gecīg (imp.sg.) *to call, name, summon* 8/39;
  gecīged (ptp.) 6/6 [cīegan I]
gecirdon → **gecyrran**
gecnāwan (7) *to know, perceive* 5/47;
  gecnāwað (imp.pl.) 7/3; **gecnāwe** (sg.ps. subj.)
  7/39, 78
gecneordnessan (npl. f.) *diligence, study* 8/90
  [cneordnes]
gecoren → **gecēose**
gecranc → **crincgan**
gecwæð → **cweðan**
gecwēmde (sg.pt.) *to please* 8/19 [cwēman I]
gecŷdd → **cŷðan**
gecynde (adj. nsg.) *natural, innate* 2/77 ♦neg.:
  ungecyndne (asg. m.) *unnatural, alien* 2/38
gecyrran (I) *to turn, change, come back*
  6/158; **gecierde** (sg.pt.) 1/31; **gecirdon** 2/39
gecyrrednysse (gsg. f.) *conversion* 6/84
  [gecyrrednes]
gecŷþan, gecŷðd → **cŷðan**
gedafenað (sg.ps.) *to befit* 8/22; **gedafenade**
  (sg.pt.) 3/79 [dafenian II]
gedēmed; gedēst → **dēman; (ge)dōn**
gedihte (sg.pt.) *to compose* 6/171 [dihtan I]
gedō, gedōn, gedōð → **(ge)dōn**
gedrēfed (ptp.) *to trouble, afflict* 11/20, 59
  [drēfan]
gedrehtan (pl.pt.) *to afflict* 7/45; **gedrehte**
  (ptp.) 6/126 [dreccan I]
gedrync (nsg. n.) *drinking* 4/24; **gedrynce**
  (dsg.) 4/27

gedwolgoda (gpl. m.) *false god* 7/21, 25;
  gedwolgodan (dpl.) 7/23 [gedwolgod]
gedwylde (dsg. n.) *heresy* 6/114
geearnian (II) *to earn, deserve* 7/161; **ernian**
  7/13; **geearnaþ** (sg.ps.) 11/109; **geearnode**
  (sg.pt.) 6/177; **geearnedan** (pl.pt.) 7/14
geearnunga, geearnunge, geearnungum →
  (ge)earnung
geednīwod (ptp.) *to renew* 8/33 [ednīwan II]
geendian (II) *to end, finish, complete* 6/157;
  geendode (sg.pt.) 8/73; **geendade** 3/139, 165
geendunge (dasg. f.) *end, ending* 6/99 *8/63
geēode (sg.pt.) *to happen* 6/64 [gegān irr.]
geēodon (pl.pt.) *to conquer* 2/55 [gegān irr.]
gefaren → **faran**
gefæstnodon (pl.pt.) *to fasten* 11/33;
  gefæstnod (ptp.) 6/105 [gefæstnian II]
gefe → **gifu**
gefeaht → **feohtan**
gefeccan → **feccan**
gefeoht (nsg. n.) *action of fighting, fight, battle*
  2/51, 109, 112, 135; **gefeohte** (dsg.) 2/76
  *6/16, 97, 127, 132 *7/89 *9/28 *10/12;
  gefeohtum (dpl.) 2/5
gefeohtan → **feohtan**
gefēol → **(ge)feallan**
gefēonde (psp.) *to rejoice* 3/58, 149
  [fēon 5 (g.)]
gefēra (nsg. m.) *companion, comrade* 10/280;
  gefēran (napl.) 2/30 *3/59 *6/4, 49 *10/170,
  229; **gefērum** (dpl.) 2/28 *6/12
gefērde → **fēran**
gefērum → **gefēra**
gefetige (sg.ps. subj.) *to fetch* 11/138 [fesian II]
gefirn → **gefyrn**
geflīemde (sg.pt.) *to put to flight* 2/81; (ptp.)
  2/69; **geflīemdon** (pl.pt.) 2/74; **geflēmed**
  (ptp.) 9/32 [flīeman I]
gefohten → **feohtan**
gefōr, gefōre → **faran**
geforþod (ptp.) *to carry out, accomplish*
  10/289 [geforðian II]
gefremman (I) *to advance, further*
  accomplish 6/79; **gefremmede** (ptp.) 2/120
gefrūnon → **frignende**
gefuhton → **feohtan**
gefullod (ptp.) *to baptise* 6/4 [fulwian II]
gefultumadon, gefultumed → **fultumian**
gefylced (ptp.) *to marshal troops* 2/126 [fylcian
  I,II]
gefylcum (dpl. n.) *army, host* 2/64; **gefylcium**
  2/73
gefylda (ptp.) *to fill* 5/25 [fyllan I]

gefyllan, gefylled → **fyllan**
gefylled (ptp.) *to fulfil* 6/107
gefylste → **fylstan**
gefyrn (adv.) *formerly, long ago* 6/139; **gefirn**
    8/104
gegadrodon, gegædrade → **gaderade**
gegangan → **gangan**
gegearwode (sg.pt.) *to prepare, equip* 3/146,
    160; **gegearwod** (ptp.) 7/162 [gegearwian II]
geglængde (ptp.) *to adorn, decorate* 3/70;
    geglenged 3/116 [glengan I]
gegōdod (ptp.) *to make rich* 8/81 [gōdian II]
gegremode (sg.pt.) *to enrage, provoke,*
    infuriate 10/296; **gegræmedan** (pl.pt.) 7/143;
    gegremod (ptp.) 10/138 [gremian II]
gegrēteð → **grētan**
gegrundene (ptp.) *to grind, sharpen* 10/109
    [grindan 3]
gegyred, gegyrwed → **gyrde**
gehādode (ptp.) *to ordain* 7/50 [hādian II]
gehālgade, gehālgode → **hālgode**
gehāte, gehāten → **hātan**
gehātlandes (gsg. n.) *promised land* 3/128
    [gehātland]
gehæft (ptp.) *to catch, hold captive* 1/22
    [hæftan I]
gehǣlde, gehǣle, gehǣled, gehǣlede →
    hǣlan
gehealdan → **healdan**
gehelpan (3) *to help* 6/173; **helpe** (sg.ps. subj.)
    7/163
gehende (prep. (d.)) *near, close by* 10/294
gehēold, gehēolde → **healdan**
gehēt → **hātan**
gehīerdun → **gehȳran**
gehīersumnesse (asg. f.) *obedience* 1/1
    [gehīersumnes]
gehīersumodest (2.sg.pt.) *to obey* 1/30;
    hīersumedon (pl.pt.) 5/5 [hīersumian II]
gehiht (imp.sg.) *to hope* 8/12 [hyhtan I]
gehīoldon → **healdan**
gehīrde → **gehȳran**
gehlēop → **hlēop**
gehlyston (pl.pt.) *to listen* 10/92 [hlystan I]
gehwā → **hwā**
gehwanon → **hwanon**
gehwæne, gehwæs → **hwā**
gehwæþere, gehwæðere, gehwæþre → **hand**
gehwelcum → **hwelc**
gehwerfde → **gehwyrfde**
gehwilcum, gehwylc, gehwylce, gehwylcum
    → **hwelc**
gehwyrfde (sg.pt.) *to turn, change* 3/115;
    gehwerfde 3/124 [gehwierfan I]

gehȳnede → **hȳnan**
gehȳran (I) *to hear (of), understand, serve,*
    obey 3/34 *11/78; **gehȳranne** (infl.inf.)
    3/125; **gehȳrst** (2.sg.ps.) 10/45; **hȳrað** (pl.ps.)
    4/4, 7; **hȳrde** (sg.pt.) 3/17; **gehȳrde** 3/1, 35,
    94 *8/87, 90, 96 *10/117 *11/26; **gehīrde**
    8/34; **hȳrdon** (pl.pt.) 3/171; **gehȳrdan** 7/152;
    gehīerdun 2/19
gehȳrnesse (dsg. f.) *hearing, listening* 3/122
gehȳrst → **gehȳran**
gehȳrsum (adj. nsg.) *obedient* 8/94
geinseglode (sg.pt.) *to seal* 8/112 [inseglian II]
gelagod (ptp.) *to appoint by law, ordain* 7/21
    [lagian II]
gelamp → **gelimpan**
gelaðode (sg.pt.) *to invite* 8/20 [laðian II]
gelǣdde, gelǣddon → **lǣdan**
gelǣred, gelǣrede, gelǣredestan → **lǣran**
gelǣstan (I) *to support, perform, fulfil* 2/127
    *7/156 *10/11; **gelǣste** (sg.ps. subj.) 7/20;
    (sg.pt.) 10/15
gelēafa (nsg. m.) *belief, faith* 6/10, 30, 39;
    gelēafan (dasg.) 3/2, 43, 65 *6/17, 29, 45–46,
    63 etc.
gelēaffulla (adj. asg. m.) *pious* 6/40, 83
gelēd → **lecgað**
geleornad, geleornade, geleornede,
    geleornian, geleornode → **leornian**
gelette (sg.pt.) *to hinder* 10/164 [lettan I]
gelēwede (ptp.) *to blemish, hurt* 7/129
    [lēwian II]
gelīce (adj., adv.) *like, similar* 3/74 *7/126;
    gelīcost (sup.) 6/131; **gelīccast** 7/70; **gelīcum**
    (dpl.) 3/31
gelīefan (I) *to believe, trust in* **gelȳfan** 6/163;
    gelīefe (1.sg.ps.) 5/17; **gelīfst** (2.sg.ps.) 8/46;
    gelȳfe (sg.ps. subj.) 7/65; **gelȳfed** (sg.pt.) 6/2,
    5
gelimp (asg. n.) *fortune* 8/33; **gelymp** 8/25,
    29; **gelimpum** (dpl.) 7/102
gelimpan (3) *to happen, befall* 7/79; **gelimpð**
    (sg.ps.) 7/85; **gelamp** 6/40, 55, 82 *8/98
gelimplice (adv.) *properly, suitable* 3/86
gelimpð; gelimpum → **gelimpan; gelimp**
geliornod, geliornode, geliornodon →
    leornian
gelōgode (sg.pt.) *to place, arrange* 1/14 *6/89
    *7/63; **gelōgodon** (pl.pt.) 6/121 [lōgian II]
    7/63
gelōme (adv.) *often, constantly* 7/39, 80, 160 ◆
    col.: **ealles tō gelōme** *only too often* 7/22,
    51, 121, 147; **oft and gelōme** *very often*
    7/43–44, 77, 86–87, 113

gelpan (3) *to boast* 9/44
gelustfullīcor (adv. comp.) *readily* 3/13
gelȳfan, gelȳfe, gelȳfed → **gelīefan**
gelȳfdre (adj. dsg. f.) *advanced* 3/80
gelymp → **gelimp**
geman (1.sg.ps. (g.)) *to remember* 11/28;
   gemunað (imp.pl.) 10/212; **gemunde** (sg.pt.)
   5/23, 33, 40, 53 *10/225; **gemundon** (pl.pt.
   subj.) 10/196 [gemunan prps.]
gemānan (dsg. m.) *clashing* 9/40 [māna]
gemanigfealde (sg.ps.) *to multiply* 1/28
   [manigfealdan I]
gemanode → **manian**
gemǣlde → **mǣlde**
gemǣne (adj., adv.) *common, in common* 7/40,
   69, 82, 85; **gemǣnum** (dsg. m.) 7/69
gemængde (sg.pt.) *to mix* 8/42, 56 [mengan I]
gemǣnum → **gemǣne**
gemǣred (ptp.) *to celebrate, glorify* 3/67
   [mǣran I]
gemǣtte (sg.pt.) *to dream* 11/2 [mǣtan I]
gēmde → **gȳme**
gemet (asg. n.) *metre* 3/105
gemetlīce (adv.) *moderately* 3/142
gemētte → **mētte**
gemiltsa (imp.sg. (d.)) *to pity* 6/101;
   gemiltsigend (psp.) 8/75 [miltsian II]
gemōt (nasg. n.) *meeting, encounter* 10/199,
   301; **gemōtes** (gsg.) 9/50
gemunað, gemunde, gemundon → **geman**
gemynd (asg. n.) *mind, memory, remembrance*
   5/2; **gemynde** (dsg.) 3/104
gemyndgade (sg.pt.) *to remember* 3/123
   [myndgian II]
gemynt (ptp.) *to intend* 6/134 [myntan I]
gēn (adv.) *yet, still* 3/33, 61
genam, genāman, genāme, genāmon →
   niman
geneahhe (adv.) *enough* 10/269
genēalǣhton, genēalēcan → **nēalēcan**
genēat (nsg. m.) *follower* 10/310
genemned → **nemnde**
generede (sg.pt.) *to save* 2/32 *9/36 [nerian I]
Genesis (prn.) 3/127
genīwad (ptp.) *to renew* 11/148 [nīwian II]
genōh (adj. nsg. m.) *enough, sufficient* 4/19
   *7/92; **genōge** (npl.) 11/33
genumen → **niman**
genyrwde (ptp.) *to narrow, restrict* 7/37
   [nyrwan I]
geoffra (imp.sg.) *to sacrifice* 1/3; **geoffrode**
   (sg.pt. subj.) 1/16 [offrian II]
geond (prep. (a.)) *through, throughout, over,
   across* 2/93, 154 *6/45, 54, 59 etc.; **giond**
   5/3–4, 24, 34, 53; **gynd** 7/11, 36, 62, 139

geong (adj. nsg. m.) *young* 10/210 *11/39;
   geonga 10/155; **gioncga** 2/68; **iunga** 8/9, 12,
   17, 19; **iungan** (dsg. m.) 8/39; **giungne** (asg.
   m.) 9/44; **giunge** (npl. m.) 9/29; **iunge** (apl.
   m.) 6/48 *8/15
georn (adj. nsg. m.) *eager* 10/107; **georne** (npl.)
   10/73
georne (adv.) *eagerly, readily* 6/48 *7/7, 10,
   17, 19 etc. *10/84, 123, 206; **giorne** 5/8;
   geornost (sup.) 7/141
geornful (adj. nsg. m.) *eager* 10/274
geornfulnesse (dsg. f.) *yearning, desire, zeal*
   3/135; **geornfulnysse** 6/55 [geornfulnes]
geornlīce (adv.) *eagerly, carefully* 3/134
   *10/265; **geornlīcor** (comp.) 3/17, 33, 36
geornost → **georne**
gerǣcan (I) *to reach, attain, obtain, strike*
   7/15; **gerǣhte** (sg.pt.) 10/142, 158, 226
gerǣdest (2.sg.ps.) *to agree* 10/36 [gerǣdan I]
gerǣdum (dpl. n.) *harness, trappings* 10/190
   [rǣde]
gerǣhte; gerehte → **gerǣcan; reccenne**
gerēnod (ptp.) *to adorn* 10/161 [rēnian II]
gereorde (dsg. n.) *speech, voice* 6/41, 43
   [reord]
gerestan (I) *to rest* 3/146 *8/78, 83; **reste**
   (sg.pt.) 11/64, 69
geriht (ptp.) *to direct* 11/131 [rihtan I]
gerihta → **riht**
gerihtlǣcende (psp.) *to direct, guide* 6/86
   [rihtlǣcan I]
gerisena (gpl. n.) *what is decent* 7/32 [risen]
gerisenlecor (adv. comp.) *fittingly* 3/48
gerisenlice (adj. apl.) *fitting, proper* 3/67;
   gerisenlicre (comp.) 3/30
gerȳmde (sg.pt.) *to open, clear, extend* 11/89;
   rȳmdon (pl.pt.) 5/7; **gerȳmed** (ptp.) 6/66
   *10/93 [rȳman I]
gesamnode → **gesomnian**
gesāwe, gesawen, gesāwon → **gesīon**
gesǣd, gesǣde, gesægd → **secgan**
gesǣlig (adj. nsg. m.) *blessed, happy* 6/87;
   gesǣligan (dsg. m.) 6/32 *8/93
gesǣliglica (adj. npl.) *blessed, happy* 5/3
gesǣne → **gesīene**
gesæt → **sit**
gescēadwīsnysse (dsg. f.) *discrimination,
   reason* 6/52 [scēadwisnes]
gesceaft (nsg. f.) *creation, creature* 9/16
   *11/12, 55, 82; **gesceafte** (asg.) 7/71
gesceape (dsg. n.) *creation* 3/126
gescyrpedne (ptp.) *to equip* 3/56
geseah; gesealde, gesealdon → **gesīon; sillan**

goda; gōda, gōdan → god; gōd

godbearn (apl. n.) *godchild* 7/61

godcundan (npl. m.) *divine, religious* 3/133
  *5/8; **godcundre** (gdsg. f.) 3/66, 114;
  godcundra (gpl.) 5/3 *7/115; **godcundum**
  (dpl.) 3/69

godcundlīce (adv.) *divinely* 3/76

godcundnesse (gsg. f.) *divine nature, godhead*
  3/9 [godcundnes]

godcundra, godcundre, godcundum →
  godcundan

gōddǣda (apl. f.) *good deed* 7/120;
  gōddǣdan (dpl.) 7/119 [gōddǣd]

Gode, Godes → God

gōde, gōdena, gōdes → gōd

godfyrhte (dsg. f.) *fear of God* 7/120

gōdiende (psp.) *to improve* 7/16 [gōdian II]

Gōdmundingahām (pn.) *Goodmanham,
  Yorkshire* 3/62

gōdne → gōd

gōdnysse (dsg. f.) *goodness, virtue* 6/175

godo; gōdra → god; gōd

Godrīc (prn.) 10/187, 237, 321, 325

godsibbas (apl. m.) *godfather* 7/61 [godsibb]

godsunu (nsg. m.) *godson* 2/32

gōdum → gōd

Godwīg (prn.) 10/192

Godwine (prn.) 10/192

gofol (asg. n.) *tribute* 10/61; **gafole** (dsg.)
  10/32, 46

gold (asg. n.) *gold* 8/4 *11/18; **goldes** (gsg.)
  8/67; **golde** (dsg.) 10/35 *11/7, 16, 77

goldhorde (dsg. m.) *treasure of gold* 8/65

gongan, gongende → gangan

Gotland (pn.) 4/7

grame (adj. npl.) *fierce, angry* 10/262;
  gramum (dpl.) 10/100 [gram]

grǣdigne (adj. asg. m.) *greedy, hungry* 9/64
  [grǣdig]

grǣge (adj. asg. n.) *grey* 9/64 [grǣg]

grēote (dsg. n.) *grit, earth* 10/315 [grēot]

grēotende (psp.) *to lament* 11/70 [grēotan 2]

grētan (I) *to greet* 5/1; **gegrēteð** (sg.ps.) 7/121;
  grētte (sg.pt.) 3/88; **grētton** (pl.pt.) 8/73,
  102–103

grim (adj. nsg. m.) *fierce, severe* 10/61;
  grimme (npl.) 7/114

Grimbolde (prn.) 5/59

grimlic (adj. nsg. n.) *cruel, grim, terrible* 7/6

grimme → grim

grimme (adv.) *cruelly* 10/109

grið (asg. n.) *truce, peace, sanctuary* 10/35;
  gryð 2/116; **griðe** (dsg.) 7/64

griðian (II) *to protect* 7/28

griðlēase (adj. npl.) *unprotected* 7/31 [griðlēas]

grund (asg. m.) *ground, earth* 10/287;
  grundas (apl. m.) 9/15

gryrelēoða (gpl. n.) *terrible song* 10/285

gryð; gū → grið; gīu

guma (nsg. m.) *man, warrior* 9/18; **guman**
  (gsg.) 11/49; (npl.) 10/94; (gpl.) 11/146;
  gumena (gpl.) 9/50

gūðe (dsg. f.) *battle, combat* 9/44 *10/285,
  296, 325; **gūþe** 10/13, 94, 187 etc. [gūð]

gūðhafoc (asg. m.) *war-hawk* 9/64

gūðplega (nsg. m.) *battle* 10/61

gūðrinc (nsg. m.) *warrior* 10/138

gyf; gyfe → gif; gifu

gyld (asg. n.) *tax* 2/150

gylde (sg.ps. subj.) *to pay, offer* 7/84; **gyldað**
  (pl.ps.) 7/99–100; **geald** (sg.pt.) 2/98
  [gieldan 3]

gylpwordum (dpl. n.) *boast* 10/274 [gylpword]

gȳme (sg.ps. subj. (g.)) *to care for, take heed*
  7/19; **gȳmde** (sg.pt.) 6/153; **gēmde** 3/134;
  gȳmdon (pl.pt.) 10/192 [gīeman I]

gynd → geond

gyrde (sg.pt.) *to prepare, deck, dress, adorn*
  3/54; **gyredon** (pl.pt.) 11/77; **gegyred** (ptp.)
  11/16; **gegyrwed** 11/23 [gyrwan I]

Gyrð (prn.) 2/129

gȳsel (nsg. m.) *hostage* 10/265; **gīsle** (dsg.)
  2/18

gȳsledan (pl.pt.) *to give hostages* 2/143
  [gīslian II]

gystas (npl. m.) *stranger* 10/86 [gist]

gȳt, gȳta → gīet

H

habban (III) *to have, possess* 1/15 *2/131
  *3/3 *4/36 *5/11, 67 *7/159 *8/107
  *10/236; **habbe** (1.sg.ps.) 8/37; **hæbbe** 3/11
  *6/163 *11/50, 79; **hafast** (2.sg.ps.) 8/33
  *10/231; **hæfst** 6/162; **hafað** (3.sg.ps.) 3/12
  *4/33; **hæfð** 6/174 *7/162 *8/10 *10/237;
  habbað (pl.ps.) 4/5, 23, 31 *5/16, 30, 48
  *7/12, 24, 38, 95, 121; **hæbben** (pl.ps. subj.)
  5/49; **hæfde** (sg.pt.) 2/2, 6, 44 *3/7, 105, 115,
  154 *5/60 *6/70, 135 *8/77, 86 *10/13, 22,
  121, 197, 199, 289 *11/49; **hæfdon** (pl.pt.)
  2/14, 23 *3/12, 16, 151, 155 *5/4, 34
  *11/16, 52; **hæfdun** 2/38 ♦ neg.: **næfð**
  (3.sg.ps.) 8/47; **nabbe** (2.pl.ps.) 8/108

hāda, hādas → hāde

hādbrycas (apl. m.) *violation of holy orders*
  7/109 [hādbryce]

hāde (dsg. m.) *order, office, rank* 5/52; **hādas** (npl.) 5/8; **hāda** (gpl.) 5/3 [hād]

hafast, hafað → **habban**

hafenode (sg.pt.) *to raise* 10/42, 309 [hafenian II]

hafoc (asg. m.) *hawk* 10/8

hāl (adj. nsg.) *whole, sound, safe* 6/107, 133, 164; **hāle** (npl.) 10/292

haldan → **healdan**

hālette (sg.pt.) *to greet, salute* 3/88 [hālettan I]

Halfdene (prn.) 2/64

halfe → **healfe**

hālga, hālgan → **hālig**

hālgode (sg.pt.) *to sanctify, consecrate, ordain* 2/146; **hālgodon** (pl.pt.) 3/40; **gehālgode** (ptp.) 3/63; **gehālgade** 3/5 [hālgian II]

hālgum → **hālig**

hālig (adj. nsg. m.) *holy, divine, saintly* 3/100 *6/116, 161; (asg. n.) 3/113 *6/165; **hālige** (apl. f.) 6/48; (nsg. n.) 6/147; (npl. f.m.) 7/62 *11/11; **hālga** (adj., sb., nsg. m.) *saint* 6/160, 171–172, 175; **hālgan** (gsg.) 3/122, 129 *6/148, 162, 176, 178; (dsg.) 6/56, 85, 99, 141, 166; (apl.) 6/115, 120, 122; (asg.) 6/129, 180; **hālgum** (dpl.) 6/168 *11/143, 154 ◆ col.: **Hālgan Gāstes** (gsg.) *Holy Ghost* 3/130

hālignessa (npl. f.) *sanctuary* 7/31; **hālignesse** (gsg.) *religion* 3/45, 52 [hālignes]

hals (asg. m.) *neck* 10/141

hālwende (adj. apl.) *salutary* 3/168

hām (1) (adv.) *homewards, home* 1/31 *2/120 *3/84, 115 *6/138 *8/74 *10/251

hām (2) (asg. m.) *home* 11/148; **hāme** (dsg.) 10/292; **hāmas** (apl.) 9/10

hamora (gpl. m.) *hammer* 9/6 [hamor]

Hamtūnscīre (pn.) *Hampshire* 2/2

hand (nasg. f.) *hand* 1/19 *2/147 *6/62, 65, 106–107 *8/51, 99 *10/112, 141; **hond** 3/54; **handa** (dapl.) 8/99 *10/149 *11/59; **honda** 3/154, 170; **handon** (dsg.) 10/7; **handum** (dpl.) 10/4, 14 ◆ col.: **on gehwæþere hond** *on both sides* 2/75; **on gehwæðere hand** 10/112; **on gehwæþre hond** 2/61

handbredum (dpl. n.) *palm of the hand* 6/75 [handbred]

handon, handum → **hand**

hār (adj. nsg. m.) *hoary, grey* 9/39 *10/169; **hāran** (dsg. f.) 2/125

Hareld (prn.) 2/69

Harold (prn.) 2/91, 99, 105 etc.; 128; **Harolde** (dsg.) 2/108, 124

Harold Harfagera (prn.) 2/112

hasewanpādan (asg. m.) *the grey-coated one* 9/62

hātan (7) *to command, bid, be called* **hāte** (1.sg.ps.) 5/2 *11/95; **gehāte** 10/246; **hāteð** (3.sg.ps.) 5/1; **hǣt** 4/14; **hāt** (imp.sg.) 8/38, 47, 82; **hātað** (pl.ps.) 2/95; **hēt** (sg.pt.) 1/9, 23 *3/34, 110 *6/60, 101 *8/41, 50, 92 *10/2, 62, 74, 101; **gehēt** 10/289; **hēht** 3/59, 109, 121; **hēton** (pl.pt.) 10/30 *11/31; **hāten** (ptp.) 2/7 *3/10 *10/75, 218; **gehāten** 6/2, 24, 33, 76–77, 161; **hātene** 4/6; **hātte** (passive) *was called* 7/142

hæbbe, hæbben → **habban**

Hædde (prn.) 6/88

hæfde, hæfdon, hæfdun, hæfst, hæfð → **habban**

hǣlan (I) *to heal, cure* 11/85; **gehǣle** (sg.ps. subj.) 6/172; **gehǣlde** (ptp.) 6/20, 122; **gehǣled** 6/24; **gehǣlede** 6/129

hǣle → **hǣlo**

Hǣlendes (gsg. m.) *Saviour* 6/80 *11/25; **Hǣlende** (dsg.) 6/160

hæleð (nsg. m.) *man, hero, warrior* 11/39, 78, 95; (npl.) 10/214, 249; **hæleþa** (gpl.) 9/25; **hæleða** 10/74

hǣlo (gsg. f.) *health, salvation* 3/39; **hǣle** (asg.) 6/149

hǣse (dsg. f.) *bidding, command* 1/30 *8/71 [hǣs] 78, 95

Hǣstingan (pn.) *Hastings, Sussex* 2/136; **Hǣstingaport** 2/123

hǣt → **hātan**

hǣðen (adj., sb. nsg. m.) *heathen* 6/77; **hǣþen** 6/81; **hǣþena** 6/102; **hǣðenan** (npl.) 6/98; **hǣþnan** 2/65; **hǣþene** (apl.) 7/107; (npl.) 10/55; **hǣðene** (npl.) 10/181; **hǣþenra** (gpl.) 8/53; **hǣþenum** (dpl.) 6/80 *7/20, 23, 26

Hǣðum (pn.) *Hedeby, Jutland* 4/1

hē (pron. 3.nsg. m.) *he* 1/10, 13–16, 18 etc. *2/2, 4, 6 etc. *3/1–3, 5, 7 etc. *4/1, 20 *6/11, 13, 28 etc. *7/19, 50, 53 etc. *8/3, 5–8, 10 etc. *9/40 *10/7, 10, 13–16 etc. *11/34, 40–41, 49; **his** (gsg.) 1/1, 10, 15–16, 19 etc. *2/1, 20–21, 27 etc. *3/3, 7, 9 etc. *4/21, 26, 38 *5/1, 5 *6/2, 4–6, 8–10 etc. *7/48–49, 57–58, 61 etc. *8/29, 32–33, 38–39 etc. *9/2, 38, 40, 42 *10/11, 16, 24, etc. *11/49, 63, 92 etc.; **hys** 4/36–37, 39; **him** (dsg.) 1/2, 11–13, 18, 20 *2/3, 19, 21, 24, 32, 54, 83, 98, 100, 105, 124–127, 132–133, 136–139, 143, 147–149, 151 *3/1, 9, 50–51, 53, 73–74, 83, 86–87, 107, 112–114, 117, 146–147, 155–156, 160, 163 *4/2–3 *5/66 *6/4, 9–10, 17–18, 22, 31–32, 35, 46, 49, 63–65, 82, 85, 94, 136, 142, 156, 163, 173 *7/93 *8/1, 29, 33, 65, 77, 82, 85,

92 *10/7, 11, 23, 44, 119–120, 139, 145, 148, 152, 182, 188, 191, 198, 265, 267, 300 *11/63, 65, 67, 86, 88, 108, 118, 133; **hym** 8/84; **hine** (asg.) 1/3, 16, 23 *2/9, 11–13, 48–49 etc. *3/4, 13, 54–55 etc. *4/25, 38, 45 *6/10, 38, 66, 72 etc. *7/92, 139 *8/20–21, 26, 31, etc. *10/164, 181 *11/11, 39, 61, 64; **hiene** 2/3–4 *5/19

hēafdum → **hēafod**

hēafod (asg. n.) *head* 3/164 *6/102, 105–106, 138, 163 *8/51; **hēafode** (dsg.) 2/148; **hēafdum** (dpl.) 11/63

hēafodmenn (apl. m.) *commander* 6/30 [hēafodmann]

Hēahfædere (dsg. m.) *God* 11/134 [Hēahfæder]

Hēahmund (prn.) 2/76

hēahne (adj. asg. m.) *high* 6/143; **hēanne** 11/40; **hīerran** (dsg. m. comp.) 5/52 [hēah]

hēahðungene (adj. nsg. m.) *of high rank* 4/22

healdan (7) *to hold, keep, maintain, possess, preserve* 7/27, 159 *10/14, 19, 41, 74, 102, 236; **gehealdan** 10/167; **haldan** 2/119, 149; **hēold** (sg.pt.) 8/99; **gehēold** 6/91; **gehēolde** (sg.pt. subj.) 6/71; **hēoldan** (pl.pt.) 7/51; **hīoldon** 5/28; **gehīoldon** 5/6; **hēoldon** (pl.pt. subj.) 10/20

healf (adj. asg. n.) *half* 4/23

healfe (dsg. f.) *side, part* 2/128 *10/152, 318 *11/20; **halfe** 2/112 [healf]

hēalic (adj. nsg. m.) *intense* 6/117

heall (asg. f.) *hall, palace* 3/24; **healle** (dsg.) 8/54 *10/214

hēanlic (adj. nsg. n.) *low, despicable* 10/55

hēanne → **hēahne**

heard (adj. nsg. m.) *hard, fierce, severe* 10/130; (asg. n.) 10/214; **heardes** (gsg. m.n.) 9/25 *10/266; **hearde** (asg. f.) 10/33; **heardne** (asg. m.) 10/167, 236; **heardra** (nsg. comp.) 10/312; **heardost** (nsg. sup.) 11/87

heardlīce (adv.) *fiercely* 2/126 *10/261

heardne, heardost, heardra → **heard**

hearme (dsg. m.) *damage, harm* 2/86; **hearma** (gpl.) 10/223 [hearm]

hearpan (gdasg. f.) *harp* 3/83 *8/39, 41–42, 48 etc. [hearpe]

hearpe-strengas (apl. m.) *harp-string* 8/55 [hearpestreng]

hearpenægl (asg. m.) *plectrum* 8/54

hearpian (II) *to harp* 8/41

hearra (nsg. m.) *lord* 10/204

heaþolinde (apl. f.) *linden-wood shield* 9/6 [heaðulind]

hēaweþ (sg.ps.) *to hack, stab* 7/54; **hēow** (sg.pt.) 10/324; **hēowon** (pl.pt.) 10/181; **hēowan** 9/6, 23 [hēawan 7]

hebban (6) *to lift up* 11/31

hefelic (adj. nsg. n.) *heavy, severe* 2/50

hefgad (ptp.) *to weigh down* 3/142 [hefigan II]

hefian → **hefig**

hefig (adj. nsg. n.) *heavy* 8/24; **hefian** (dsg. n.) 11/61

hegum (dpl. m.) *fence, enclosure* 3/46 [hege]

hēht → **hātan**

helle (gdsg. f.) *hell* 6/157 *7/161 [hell]

helpe → **gehelpan**

helpe (dsg. f.) *help* 11/102

helsceaðan (nsg. m.) *fiend* 10/180 [helsceaða]

hēo → **hīe**

hēo (perspron. 3.nsg. f.) *she* 3/109, 119–120 *6/23, 113, 137, 139 *8/15–16, 35, 41–42, 47, 66, 68, 79–80, 87, 93, 110–111; **hīo** 4/9 *5/11, 67; **hire** (gdsg.) 3/108 *4/13 *6/138 *8/16, 34–35, 37 etc.; **hyre** 8/15, 28, 35, 38 etc.; **hīe** (asg.) 5/10–11, 40–41, 58, 60–61; **hī** 8/43, 45; **hīg** 8/27, 72

heofenas, heofenes, heofenum → **heofon**

heofon (nasg. m.) *heaven* 3/100; **heofones** (gsg. m.) 6/75; **heofenes** 11/64; **heofonan** (gsg. f.) 6/70; **heofonas** (apl.) 3/130; **heofenas** 11/103; **heofona** (gpl.) 11/45; **heofonum** (dpl.) 1/17, 28 *6/117, 172, 177 *11/140, 154; **heofenum** 2/39 *10/172 *11/85, 134

Heofonfeld (pn.) 6/25

heofonlecan → **heofonlic**

heofonlic (adj. nasg. f.n.) *heavenly* 3/113 *6/116; **heofonlican** (gsg. n.) 3/72; **heofonlecan** (gdsg. n.) 3/132, 159; **heofonlicre** (dsg. f.) 1/31; **heofonlicne** (asg. m.) 11/148

heofonrīces (gsg. n.) *heavenly kingdom* 3/95 *11/91 [heofonrīce]

heofonum → **heofon**

hēold, hēoldan, hēoldon → **healdan**

heom → **hīe**

heonanforð (adv.) *henceforth* 7/16, 19

heonon (adv.) *hence* 8/81 *10/246 *11/132

heora → **hīe**

heord (asg. f.) *care, custody* 3/86

heorte (nsg. f.) *heart* 10/312; **heortan** (dsg.) 6/34, 167 *10/145

heorðgenēatas (npl. m.) *hearth-companion, retainer* 10/204 [heorðgenēat]

heorðwerod (asg. n.) *body of household retainers* 10/24

hēow, hēowan, hēowon → **hēaweþ**

hēr (adv.) *here* 1/7, 11 *2/1, 36, 46 etc. *5/29, 38 *6/107, 173 *7/55–56, 111, 129–133 *8/10 *9/1 *10/36, 51, 241 etc. *11/108, 137, 145

here (dasg. m.) *army, host* 2/36, 39–40, 43 etc. *7/43, 86, 144 *10/292; **heriges** (gsg.) 9/31

heredon → **herian**

herefleman (apl. m.) *fugitive from an army* 9/23

heregeatu (asg. f.) *war-gear, heriot* 10/48

heregian → **herian**

herelafum (dpl. m.) *remnants of an army* 9/47

herenesse (dsg. f.) *praise* 3/93; **herenisse** 3/169[herenes]

hergade → **hergiað**

hergas; hergedan → **herig; hergiað**

hergiað (pl.ps.) *to plunder, lay waste* 7/100; **hergade** (sg.pt.) *to plunder, lay waste* 2/83; **hergedan** (pl.pt.) 2/144 [hergian II]

herian (I) *to praise* 8/43; **heregian** 7/123; **herigean** 3/95; **heriað** (pl.ps.) 8/44; **heredon** (sg.pt.) 8/57, 71

herig (asg. m.) *temple, sanctuary* 3/59; **herige** (dsg.) 3/57–58; **hergas** 3/45

herigean; heriges → **herian; here**

hertoēacan (adv.) *besides* 7/137

hēt → **hātan**

hete (nsg. m.) *hatred, malice* 7/45, 86

hetelīce (adv.) *terribly, violently* 2/59 *7/78

hetole (adj. npl.) *hating, hostile* 7/114 [hetol]

hēton → **hātan**

hettend (nsg. m.) *enemy* 9/10

hī → **hēo; hīe**

hicgan (III) *to think, consider, desire* 10/4; **hogode** (sg.pt.) 6/71, 154 *10/128, 133; **hogodon** (pl.pt.) 10/123

hider (adv.) *hither, here* 2/101 *3/90 *8/105 *9/69 *10/57 *11/103; **hieder** 5/10

hīe → **hēo**

hīe (perspron. 3.napl.) *they* 1/6, 13 *2/13, 17, 20, 24, 26–31, 38–41, 48–49, 58, 64, 73 *3/17 *5/5, 8–9, 26–28, 35–37, 41–42, 49–51, 66 *11/32, 48, 60, 63–64, 66–68, 115–116, 132; **hī** 2/106, 110, 114, 118–120, 123, 133, 144–145, 149 *3/4 *4/22–23, 25–26, 42, 44 *6/15, 30, 32, 40, 50, 56, 68, 97, 102, 113, 119–121, 128, 147 *8/101, 112 *9/8, 48, 51 *10/19, 46, 63, 67–68, 82–85, 87, 108, 127, 180, 185, 196, 207, 209, 229, 260, 263, 283, 291, 307, 320 *11/46; **hȳ** 3/155 *4/32, 39–40, 45–46 *7/8, 100, 104, 124–127, 143, 148–149 *8/100; **hēo** (napl.) 3/45–46, 56, 82, 113, 144, 151, 154–156, 162; **hīg** (napl.) 2/114 *8/74; **hiera** (gpl.) 2/16, 24–28, 35, 38; **hiora** 5/5–6, 12, 14, 26–27, 29, 35, 43–44; **hira** 1/29 *11/47; **hyra** 4/24 *10/20, 38, 70, 133, 184, 194, 204, 263–264, 299, 306; **heora** 2/117

*3/45–46, 52, 111, 143, 161 *5/41 *6/7, 17, 39, 41, 61, 100, 149–150 *7/126–127, 142–144, 149 *8/103 *9/47 *11/31, 155;

him (dpl.) 1/31 *2/22, 24–26, 37, 48, 58 *3/8, 17, 42, 110, 112, 116, 144, 149, 157 *4/5, 18 *5/7, 29 *7/99 *9/7, 53, 60 *10/66, 197 *11/31, 83; **heom** 2/107, 130, 143–144 *8/59, 77, 102

hieder → **hider**

hiene; hiera → **hē; hīe**

Hierdebōc (prn.) 5/57

hīerran → **hēahne**

hīersumedon → **gehīersumodest**

hīg → **hēo; hīe**

hige (nsg. m.) *mind, thought* 10/4, 312

hiht → **hyht**

hilde (dasg. f.) *war, battle* 10/8, 33, 48 etc. [hild]

hilderinc (nsg. m.) *warrior* 9/39 *10/169; **hilderincas** (npl.) 11/61; **hilderinca** (gpl.) 11/72

him → **hē; hīe**

hindan (adv.) *from behind* 2/59 *9/23

hine; hīo → **hē; hēo**

hīoldon → **healdan**

hiora → **hīe**

hira; hire → **hīe; hēo**

hīredmen (npl. m.) *household follower* 10/261 [hīredman]

his → **hē**

hit (perspron. 3.nasg. n.) *it* 1/14 *2/17, 95, 101 etc. *3/24, 37, 57 etc. *4/14, 28, 34 etc. *5/20, 23, 37 *6/40, 55, 82, 94 etc. *7/3–5, 15, 41–42 etc. *8/28, 87–88, 113 *10/66, 137, 190 etc. *11/19, 22, 26, 97; **hyt** 4/29, 36 *8/98

hlāford (nasg. m.) *lord, master, ruler* 2/26, 144 *6/134 *7/58, 93 *10/135, 189, 224, 240 *11/45; **hlāfordes** (gsg.) 6/7 *7/57; **hlāforde** (dsg.) 6/67 *7/80 *10/318

hlāfordlēas (adj. nsg. m.) *lordless* 10/251

hlāfordswican (npl. m.) *traitor of a lord* 7/56 [hlāfordswica]

hlāfordswice (nsg. m.) *treachery against a lord* 7/57–58

hlehhan (6) *to laugh, rejoice* 9/47; **hlōh** (sg.pt.) 10/147

hlēo (nsg. m.) *protector* 10/74

hlēop (sg.pt.) *to leap onto, mount* 3/54; **gehlēop** 10/189 [hlēapan 7]

hlēoðrode (sg.pt.) *to speak, proclaim* 11/26 [hlēoðrian II]

hlīfige (sg.ps.) *to rise up* 11/85 [hlīfian II]

hlīsa (nsg. m.) *glory* 6/151
hlīsfullīce (adv.) *gloriously* 6/91
hlōh → **hlehhan**
hlūttre (adj. isg. n.) *pure* 3/166 [hlūttor]
hnāg (sg.pt.) *to bend down* 11/59 [hnīgan 1]
hōcere (dsg. n.) *insult, derision* 7/119 [hōcor]
hōcorwyrde (adj. npl.) *derisive, scornful* 7/115
hogode, hogodon → **hicgan**
hōl (nsg. n.) *slander, malice* 7/44
hold (adj. nsg. m.) *friendly, loyal* 2/144; **holde** (npl.) 2/149; **holdost** (asg. m. sup.) 10/24
holtes (gsg. n.) *wood, forest* 10/8 *11/29 [holt]
holtwudu (asg. m.) *tree* 11/91
hond, honda → **hand**
hondplegan (gsg. m.) *combat* 9/25 [hondplega]
hord (asg. m.) *hoard, treasure* 9/10
hōringas (npl. m.) *fornicator* 7/132 [hōring]
hornum (dpl. m.) *horn* 1/22
hors (nasg. n.) *horse* 4/31, 33, 37 *6/130 *10/2
hraðe (adv.) *quickly, soon* 1/3 *6/36; **hraþe** 3/40 *6/43; **raðe** 8/79 *10/30, 288; **raþe** 10/164; **radost** (sup.) 2/16
hrædest (adj. nsg. n. sup.) *brief, quick* 7/37, 134
hrædinge (dsg. f.) *haste* 7/138
hrædlīce (adv.) *quickly* 3/25
hræfn (asg. m.) *raven* 9/61; **hremmas** (npl.) 10/106
hrægle (dsg. n.) *dress, garment* 4/39 [hrægl]
hrǣw (nasg. n.) *body, corpse* 9/60 *11/53, 72
hrēam (asg. m.) *clamour* 10/106
hrēman (I) *to boast* 9/39
hrēmige (adj. npl.) *boasting, triumphant* 9/59 [hrēmig]
hremmas → **hræfn**
hrēowcearig (adj. nsg. m.) *sorrowful* 11/25
hrēowlīce (adv.) *cruelly, wretchedly* 7/34
hrepode (sg.pt.) *to touch* 6/133 [hrepian II]
hrinen (ptp.) *to touch* 3/26 [hrīnan 1]
hringas (apl. m.) *ring, ring-mail* 10/161; **ringe** (dsg.) 8/112 [hring]
hringlocan (apl. m.) *linked rings of a corslet* 10/145
hrōfe (dsg. m.) *roof* 3/100; **rōfes** (gsg.) 6/145
hū (adv., conj.) *how* 3/160 *5/3–4, 7–10, 23–24 etc. *6/71, 136, 176 *7/79, 138, 143 *10/19
Humbran (pn.) *the River Humber* 2/102, 106; **Humbre** 2/36 *5/12, 14
hund (num.) *hundred* 2/105 *8/67
hundum (dpl. m.) *hound, dog* 7/70 [hund]
hunger (nsg. m.) *hunger* 7/43
hunig (nsg. n.) *honey* 4/16
hūru (adv.) *certainly, indeed* 4/11 *7/5, 53, 139 *11/10

hūs (nasg. n.) *house* 3/25, 85, 143 *6/145–146 *7/24, 31; **hūse** (dsg.) 3/84, 116, 146 *6/142; **hūsum** (dpl.) 4/24
hūsl (asg. n.) *eucharist, host* 3/151, 153; **hūsles** (gsg.) 3/152
hūsum → **hūs**
hwā (pron. nsg.) *who* 3/45, 47 *5/67 *10/71, 95, 124, 215; **gehwā** *each, every, everyone* 7/139; **hwæne** (asg. m.) 10/2; **gehwæne** 9/9; **gehwæs** (gsg.) 3/97
hwanon (adv.) *whence, from where* 8/21; **gehwanon** 6/59; **hwonon** 3/111
hwār; hwæne → **hwǣr; hwā**
hwænne (adv.) *when* 10/67 *11/136
hwǣr (adv.) *where* 1/11 *5/67 *7/72 *11/112; **hwār** 8/82; **swā hwǣr swā** *wherever* 6/74
hwæt (1) (pron. nsg. n.) *what* 3/29, 92, 111 *7/17, 101, 104 *8/17–18, 21, 103 *11/2, 116; (asg.) 10/45 ◆ col.: **swā hwæt swā** *whatever* 3/68 *6/35 *8/34, 64–65, 94
hwæt (2) (interj.) *what, behold, listen* 3/16, 26 *10/ 231 *11/1, 90 ◆ col.: **hwæt ðā** 6/28, 38; **hwæt þā** 6/91, 116, 165; **ono hwæt** 3/41
hwæthwugu (pron. asg.) *something* 3/89
hwæðer (conj.) *whether* 2/136 *3/151; **hwæþer** 3/154
hwæðere (adv.) *nevertheless, yet, still* 11/57, 70, 101; **hwæþere** 3/2; **hwæðre** 3/74, 91, 142, 148 *11/18, 24, 38 etc.
hwelc (adj., pron. nsg. f.) *which, what kind of* 3/10 *5/19; **hwilcne** (asg. m.) 8/107, 111; **hwelce** (npl.) 5/2; **gehwelcum** (dsg.) *each, every, all* 2/16; **gehwilcum** 6/150 *7/19; **gehwylce** 11/136; **gehwylcum** 11/108; **hwylc** (nasg.) 3/8, 152 *7/80; **gehwylc** 10/128, 257; **hwylce** (asg. f.) 3/108 ◆ col.: **swā hwelc swā** *whoever* 2/15
hwī → **for**
hwider (adv.) ◆ col.: **swā hwider swā** *whithersoever* 6/49, 168
hwilcne → **hwelc**
hwīle (asg. f.) *while, period, space of time* 1/8 *4/24 *7/65, 138 *10/304 *11/24, 64, 70, 84 ◆ col.: **ðā hwīle ðe** (conj.) 5/50 *10/272; **þā hwīle þe** 10/14, 83, 235; **þā wīle** (adv.) 2/47 [hwīl]
hwīlum (adv.) *at times, sometimes* 4/21, 23 *5/57 *7/49, 89, 91, 96 *11/22–23; **hwȳlum** 4/27; **hwīlon** 10/270
hwīlwendlican (adj. asg. f.) *transitory* 6/71 [hwīlwendlic]
hwīt (adj. asg. m.) *white* 9/63
hwon → **for**

hwōnlīce (adv.) *moderately, little* 6/72
hwonon → hwanon
hwylc, hwylce → hwelc
hwȳlum; hȳ → hwīlum; hīe
hyht (nsg. f.) *hope* 11/126; hiht 11/148
hyldan (I) *to bow, bend* 11/45
hym → hē
hȳnan (I) *to lay low, harm, humiliate* 10/180;
   hȳnað (pl.ps.) 7/100; hȳnde (sg.pt.) 10/324;
   gehȳnede (ptp.) 7/33
hyra → hīe
hȳrað, hȳrde, hȳrdon → gehȳran
hyre → hēo
hyrnan (dsg. f.) *corner* 6/124 [hyrne]
hyrnednebban (asg. m.) *horny-billed, horn
   beaked* 9/62 [hyrnednebba]
hyrweð (sg.ps.) *to abuse, deride* 7/120, 122
   [hyrwan I]
hys → hē
hyse (nsg. m.) *young man, young warrior*
   10/152; hysses (gsg.) 10/141; hysas (npl.)
   10/123; hyssas (napl.) 10/112, 169; hyssa
   (gpl.) 10/2, 128
hyt → hit
hytte (sg.pt.) *to hit, conquer* 2/110 [hittan I]

I

ic (perspron. 1.nsg.) *I* 1/8, 11, 19, 25, 27 *3/11,
   14–17, 35–37 etc. *5/13, 15, 17, 23 etc.
   *6/157–159, 162–163 *7/29, 151 *8/18,
   20–21, 23, 26–28 etc. *10/117, 173–175,
   179 etc. *11/1, 4, 13–14, 18, 20–21 etc.; mīn
   (gsg.) 1/11–12, 27 *6/159 *8/17, 92, 108
   *10/177, 218, 222, 224, 250 *11/78, 95, 130;
   mē (dasg.) 1/26 *3/17–18, 21, 88, 91–92, 153
   *5/2, 36, 44 *6/160, 162 *8/19, 24–25, 28,
   46–47 etc. *10/29, 55, 220, 223, 249 ect.
   *11/2, 4, 30–34, 42 etc. ♦ poss. adj.: mīne
   (npl.) 3/158 *8/26, 44; (asg. f.) 10/216; mīnes
   (gsg. m.n.) 8/36, 66, 94 *10/53; mīnre (gsg.
   f.) 1/30 *8/110; mīnum (dsg. m.n.) 5/58–59,
   62 *8/26, 70 *10/176, 318 *11/30; mīnne
   (asg. m.) 10/248
īdelan (adj. dpl.) *worthless, vain, idle* 7/125;
   īdles (gsg. n.) 3/77; īdlan (asg. f.) 3/50 [īdel]
ieldran → eald
īhte (sg.pt.) *to add, increase* 7/10 [īecan I]
ilce (adj., pron. nsg. n.) *the same* 2/28 *3/105;
   ylce (nsg. f.) 6/19; ilcan (dsg. f.) 1/4; ylcan
   (isg. m.) 4/25; (asg. f.) 6/20; (dsg. f.) 6/24, 88,
   140; (dsg. m.) 6/76 [ilca]
Ilfing (prn.) *the River Elblag* 4/11, 12, 13

in (1) (prep. (d.a.)) *in, on* 1/24 *3/15, 66,
   69–70, 73, 80–81, 86, 93, 104–105, 114,
   118, 120, 122, 124, 130, 134, 137, 143, 146,
   168–170 *4/10–12 *11/154
in (2) (adv.) *into, within, inside* 2/97 *3/25
   *8/1, 2, 14, 52, 84 *10/58, 157; inn 6/57
inbryrdnesse (asg. f.) *inspiration, incitement*
   3/62; inbryrdnisse 3/70 [inbryrdnes]
incan (dasg. m.) *grievance, grudge* 3/155–156
   [inca]
ingeþanc (asg. m.) *conscience, inner thought*
   7/158
ingong (asg. m.) *entrance, entry* 3/160;
   ingonge (dsg.) 3/128
inlǣdan (I) *to bring in* 3/144
inn → in (2)
innan (adv., prep. (d.)) *in, into, within* 2/46, 49,
   53 *7/30, 32; innon 8/54, 70
innanbordes (adv.) *at home* 5/6
inne (adv.) *inside, within* 2/41 *3/26, 150–151
   *4/20, 24, 40 *7/23–24, 42, 86
innon → innan
intinga (nsg. m.) *cause* 3/82
intō (prep. (d.)) *into, to* 2/97, 102, 106 etc.
   *6/121, 179
inwidda (nsg. m.) *adversary* 9/46
inwidhlemmas (npl. m.) *malicious wound*
   11/47 [inwidhlemm]
Iōhanne (prn.) 5/59
īow → gē
Īraland (pn.) 9/56; Īrlande (dsg.) 6/151, 153
īren (nsg. n.) *iron* 10/253
irnan (3) *to run, hasten* yrnende (psp.) 4/2;
   urnon (pl.pt.) 2/15
is → bēon
Īsaac (prn.) 1/2, 4, 7, 9–10, 23
īse (dsg. n.) *ice* 6/21
Israhēla (prn. gpl.) *Israelites* 3/127
iū; iugoðe → giū; gioguð
iunga, iungan, iunge → geong

K

kyncg → cyning
Kynegyls → Cynegyls
kynerīces → cynerīce
kyng, kynge, kyning, kyningas, kyninge →
   cyning

L

lā (interj.) *lo, behold* 7/17, 79, 101, 140
lāce (dsg. n.) *sacrifice, offering* 1/23; lācum
   (dpl.) 7/24 [lāc]

lāf (nsg. f.) *remnant* 2/43 ∗9/54; lāfe (dsg.)
  2/113, 116, 118, 138 ∗4/26; lāfan (dpl.) 9/6
laga (npl. m.) *law* 7/38, 84; lage (dasg.) 7/19,
  27, 51, 117; lagum (dpl.) 7/156 [lagu]
lāgon → licgan
lagustrēamas (npl. m.) *tidal stream* 10/66
  [lagustrēam]
lahbrycas (apl. m.) *breach of the law* 7/108
  [lahbryce]
lahlīce (adv.) *lawfully* 7/50
land (nasg. n.) *land, country, earth, region*
  2/46 ∗4/4, 6–7 ∗6/151 ∗9/9, 27; lond 2/55
  ∗5/10; landes (gsg.) 10/90, 275; londes 2/24;
  lande (dsg.) 1/3–4 ∗2/45, 64 ∗4/32 ∗7/9, 55,
  59, 71 ∗8/95 ∗10/99; londe 5/38; landum
  (dpl.) 6/81
landhere (asg. m.) *army* 2/100
landum → land
lanferde (dsg. f.) *army* 2/103 [landfyrd]
lang → ymb
lang (adj. nsg. n.) *long* 10/66; langa (nsg. m.)
  10/273; langan (dsg. n.) 4/39; (asg. m.) 6/25;
  lange (dsg. f.) 11/24; langum (dsg. m.) 6/87
  [lang]
Langaland (pn.) *Langeland* 4/3
langan, lange → lang
lange (adv.) *long, for a long time* 4/45 ∗6/135,
  167 ∗7/30, 42, 86–87, 140 ∗8/101; longe
  3/47 ∗5/64; lencg (comp.) 4/22; leng 7/4
  ∗8/87, 109 ∗10/171; lengest (sup.) 2/3
langum → lang
langunghwīla (gpl. f.) *time of longing or
  spiritual desire* 11/126 [langunghwīl]
lār (nsg. f.) *teaching, doctrine* 3/8, 10, 30
  ∗5/37, 53; lāre (asg.) 3/38 ∗5/10 ∗7/51 ∗8/76,
  93; (gsg.) 3/114 ∗6/153; (dsg.) 3/131 ∗5/8
  ∗6/48, 87 ∗8/91, 96; lāra (npl.) 7/38
lārēow (nasg. m.) *teacher* 6/31 ∗8/66, 113;
  lārēowe (dsg.) 8/70; lārēowas (npl.) 3/125;
  lārēowa (gpl.) 5/16
lāst (asg. n.) *track* 9/22
late (adv.) *late* 2/39
latige (sg.ps. subj.) *to delay, hesitate* 7/139
  [latian II]
lāð (adj. nsg. n.) *hostile, loathesome* 7/65;
  lāðost (nsg. sup.) 11/88; lāþere (dsg. f.) 10/90;
  lāðe (npl.) 7/38 ∗10/86; lāþre (asg. n. comp.)
  10/50; lāþra (gpl.) 9/9; lāþum (dpl.) 9/22
lāðet (sg.ps.) *to loath, hate* 7/123 [lāðettan I]
lāðost, lāþra, lāþum → lāð
lǣdan (I) *to lead, bring* 10/88 ∗11/5; lǣdaƌ
  (pl.ps.) 7/101; lǣdde (sg.pt.) 6/141; gelǣdde
  3/108; gelǣddon (pl.pt.) 2/60

Lǣden (asg. n.) *the Latin language* 5/56;
  Lǣdene (dsg.) 5/13
Lǣdengeðīode (dsg. n.) *the Latin language*
  5/51; Lǣdengeðīodes (gsg.) 5/53
Lǣdenware (npl.) *the Romans* 5/42
lǣfde (sg.pt.) *to leave, bequeath* 2/21; lǣfdon
  (pl.pt.) 5/29; lēfdon 5/21 [lǣfan I]
lǣg, lǣge, lǣgon, lǣgun → licgan
Lǣland (pn.) *Lolland* 4/3
lǣnan (adj. dsg. n.) *transitory* 11/109, 138
  [lǣne]
lǣne (dsg. n.) *loan* 5/67 [lǣn]
lǣran (I) *to teach, advise* 3/122 ∗5/52; lǣre
  (1.sg.ps.) 3/39; (sg.ps. subj.) 5/51; lǣrde
  (sg.pt.) 3/2, 119 ∗6/47 ∗10/311; lǣred (ptp.)
  3/9; gelǣred 3/75 ∗6/153 ∗8/49; gelǣrede
  (npl.) 5/65 ∗8/100; gelǣredestan (apl. sup.)
  3/109
lǣrig (nsg. m.) *rim* 10/284
lǣringcmǣdene (dsg. n.) *female pupil* 8/113
lǣs (adv. comp.) *less* 3/37 ∗7/89 ♦ col.: þē̆ lǣs
  lest 7/140; þē lǣs þe 6/170; þē̆lǣsþe 8/109;
  nōht þon lǣs *nonetheless, nevertheless* 3/14
lǣsste, lǣsta, lǣstan → lȳtel
lǣt (sg.ps.) *to let, allow, cause* 7/91; lēt (sg.pt.)
  2/65 ∗7/143 ∗10/7, 140; lēton (pl.pt.) 10/108;
  lētan 9/60 [lǣtan 7]
lǣtre (adj. nsg. comp.) *slack, lax* 2/134 [lǣt]
lǣwede (adj. npl.) *lay* 7/50; lǣwedum (dsg. n.)
  6/51
lēafe (asg. f.) *leave, permission* 8/37, 67 [lēaf]
lēasunge (gsg. f.) *lie* 3/77; lēasunga (apl.)
  7/111
lecgað (imp.pl.) *to lay, set, place* 8/70; leide
  (sg.pt.) 2/150; legdun (pl.pt.) 9/22; gelēd (ptp.)
  6/109 [lecgan I]
lēfdon → lǣfde
leg → licgan
legdun → lecgað
legere (dsg. n.) *lying, illness* 4/39 [leger]
lehtreð (sg.ps.) *to blame* 7/120 [leahtrian II]
leide → lecgað
lencg, leng, lengest → lange
lengtene (dsg. m.) *lent, spring* 2/150 [lencten]
lēode (napl. f.m.) *people* 6/7, 15, 46, 82
  ∗7/146; lēoda 6/29, 31, 118 ∗9/11 ∗10/37;
  lēodum (dpl.) 7/26 ∗10/50 ∗11/88; lēodon
  10/23
lēodhatan (npl. m.) *persecutor, tyrant* 7/114
  [lēodhata]
lēodon, lēodum → lēode
lēofa (nsg. m.) *dear, beloved* 8/63 ∗11/78, 95;
  lēofe (nsg. f.) 8/19, 32, 38, 89; lēofne (asg.
  m.) 10/7, 208; lēofan (npl. m.) 3/158 ∗7/3;

(dsg. m.) 10/319; **lēofra** (nsg. m. comp.) 2/26; **lēofesta** (nsg. m. sup.) 8/17; **lēofost** (nsg. n.) 10/23

leofað (sg.ps.) *to live* 6/172; **lifiaþ** (pl.ps.) 11/134; **lifiendne** (psp. asg. m.) 7/59; **lifigendan** (dsg. m.) 6/29; **leofode** (sg.pt.) 6/47, 51, 167 [libban III]

lēofe, lēofesta, lēofne → **lēofa**
leofode; lēofost, lēofra → **leofað**; **lēofa**
Lēofsunu (prn.) 10/244
Lēofwine (prn.) 2/73
lēoht (nsg. n.) *light* 6/116 *8/88; **lēohte** (dsg.) 11/5
leomu → **limum**
leornade → **leornian**
leorneras (apl. m.) *scholar* 3/110 [leornere]
leornian (II) *to learn, study* 6/49 *8/93; **geleornian** 3/123; **leornade** 3/76; **geleornode** (sg.pt.) 3/69; **geleornade** 3/81; **geleornede** 8/97; **geliornode** 5/58; **leornodon** (pl.pt.) 3/125; **geliornodon** 5/41–42; **geleornod** (ptp.) 8/47; **geleornad** 3/11; **geliornod** 5/34, 60
leornunga (dsg. f.) *learning* 8/109; **liornunga** 5/8, 50 [leornung]
lēoð (asg. n.) *song* 3/81, 110, 124, 133; (apl.) 3/67, 74; **lēoþes** (gsg.) 3/77; **lēoðe** (dsg.) 3/116
lēoðcræft (asg. m.) *poetic art* 3/75
lēoðe, lēoþes → **lēoð**
lēoþsonges (gsg. m.) *song, poem* 3/115; **lēoþsongum** (dpl.) 3/71 [lēoþsong]
lēt, lētan, lēton → **lǣt**
lēwe (dsg. f.) *blemish, injury* 7/127 [lēw]
līc (nsg. n.) *body, corpse* 2/34, 45, 78 *4/24 *6/88; **līces** 11/63
līcað (sg.ps.) *to please* 8/80; **līcode** (sg.pt.) 8/59 [līcian II]
līces → **līc**
licgan (5) *to lie, lie dead* 10/319; **ligeð** (sg.ps.) 4/14 *10/222; **līð** 4/10, 20, 30 *6/110 *10/232, 314; **līþ** 2/34, 45, 78; **licge** (sg.ps. subj.) 7/83; **licgende** (psp.) 6/135 *11/24; **licgað** (pl.ps.) 4/23, 45; **læg** (sg.pt.) 2/22 *6/21 *9/17 *10/157, 204, 227, 294; **leg** 10/276; **lǣge** (sg.pt. subj.) 10/279, 300; **lǣgon** (pl.pt.) 2/17; **lǣgun** 9/28; **lāgon** 10/112, 183
līchomlicre (dsg. f.) *bodily* 3/141 [līchomlic]
līcode → **līcað**
līcreste (dsg. f.) *hearse* 6/115 [līcrest]
lides (gsg. n.) *ship* 9/27, 34 [lid]
lidmen (npl. m.) *sailor, shipman* 10/99; **lidmanna** (gpl.) 10/164 [lidmann]

līf (nasg. n.) *life* 1/27 *3/22, 28, 138, 165 *6/154, 159 *7/49 *10/208 *11/147; **līfes** (gsg.) 3/4, 39, 72, 160 *6/33, 99 *11/88, 126; **līfe** (dsg.) 6/173 *7/58 *11/109, 138
lifiaþ, lifiendne, lifigendan → **leofað**
ligeð → **licgan**
līhte (sg.pt.) *to dismount* 10/23 [līhtan I]
limum (dpl. m.n.) *limb* 6/133, 138; **leomu** (apl.) 3/87 [lim]
limwērigne (adj. asg. m.) *weary of limb, exhausted* 11/63 [limwērig]
linde (apl. f.) *linden-wood shield* 10/99; (asg.) 10/244 [lind]
Lindesīge (pn.) *Lindsey* 6/113; **Lindesse** 2/89
Lindisfarnēa (pn.) *Lindisfarne* 6/106
liornunga → **leornunga**
līthwōn (adv.) *little* 6/153
lītle → **lȳtel**
lītle (adv.) *little* 8/64
līð, līþ → **licgan**
liðe (dsg. n.) *fleet* 2/43 [lið]
lōcað (sg.ps.) *to look, see, gaze* 7/91; **lōcude** (sg.pt.) 2/12 [lōcian II]
lof (asg. n.) *praise, glory* 3/161, 168 *6/86
lond, londe, londes → **land**
longe → **lange**
losige (sg.ps. subj.) *to perish* 6/170 [losian II]
lucon (pl.pt.) *to lock, close* 10/66 [lūcan 2]
lufan → **lufe**
lufast → **lufian**
lufe (dsg. f.) *love* 8/62, 86; **lufan** (dsg.) 3/135 [lufu]
lufian (II) *to love, cherish* 7/123, 155; **lufigean** 3/118; **lufast** (2.sg.ps.) 1/2; **lufiað** (pl.ps.) 7/121; **lufigend** (psp.) 8/76; **lufode** (sg.pt.) 6/47, 72, 113; **lufodon** (pl.pt.) 5/20–21, 28
luflīce (adv.) *affectionately* 5/1
lufode, lufodon → **lufian**
Lundenbyrig (pn.) *London* 2/87; **Lundene** 2/131, 141
lust (asg. m.) *pleasure* 7/51
lȳfdest (2.sg.pt.) *to allow* 8/64 [līefan I]
lyft (asg. f.) *air, sky* 11/5
lȳsan (I) *to release, redeem* 10/37 *11/41
lȳt (nsg. n.) *little* 2/115
lytegian (II) *to use guile, deceive* 10/86
lȳtel (adj. asg. n.) *little* 7/21; **lȳtelre** (dsg. f.) 7/36; **lītle** (isg. m.) 9/34; **lȳtle** 2/8, 80; (asg. f.)5/26; (npl.) 7/8; **lȳtlum** (dsg. m.) 6/9 ◆ sup.: **lǣsste** (nsg. n.) 3/27; **lǣsta** (nsg. m.) 4/30; **lǣstan** (asg. m.) 4/35
lȳtlað (sg.ps.) *to diminish* 10/313 [lȳtlian II]

lȳðre (asg. f.) *wicked, base* 7/147

M

mā → **micel**
Maccus (prn.) 10/80
magan (prps.) *to be able to, can* 7/127, 137,
   141; **mæg** (sg.ps.) 3/38, 47 *5/15, 29 *7/47,
   79, 105, 129 *10/215, 258, 315 *11/85, 110;
   miht (2.sg.ps.) 11/78; **mæge** (sg.ps. subj.)
   5/18–19 *7/55 *8/28, 83 *10/235; **magon**
   (pl.ps.) 4/44 *5/47 *8/78; **mægen** (pl.ps. subj.)
   5/47, 49–50; **mihte** (sg.pt.) 2/98 *6/18, 31,
   43, 148 *10/9, 14, 64, 70, 124, 167, 171
   *11/37; **meahte** (sg.pt.) 3/51, 74, 78, 114,
   123, 142, 147 *5/61 *11/18; **mehte** (sg.pt.
   subj.) 7/138; **meahton** (pl.pt.) 5/26
māgum; man → **mǣg; mann**
man (imp.pron.) *one, someone, anyone* 2/94,
   98, 108, 136–137, 142 *4/14, 38, 42, 46 *5/9
   *6/22, 54, 56, 61, 90, 114, 120, 123, 144
   *7/10, 18, 20, 22, 26–27, 40, 57–58, 60–61,
   63–64, 119–120, 122–123, 137 *10/9
   *11/73, 75; **mon** 5/29, 51–52
māna (gpl. n.) *evil deed, crime* 7/134 [mān]
mancessa (gpl. m.) *mancus (silver coin)* 5/63
mancynn (asg. n.) *humankind, mankind,*
   people 11/104; **mancyn** 11/41; **mancynnes**
   (gsg.) 11/33, 99; **moncynnes** 3/126;
   monncynnes 3/101
māndǣda (gpl. f.) *evil deed* 3/135; (apl.) 7/106
   [māndǣd]
manega, manege, manegum → **manig**
manian (II) *to urge, admonish* 10/228;
   gemanode (ptp.) 10/231
manig (adj., pron. nsg. f.) *many* 4/15; **mænig**
   (nsg. m.) 9/17 *10/282; **manigne** (asg. m.)
   10/243; **mænigne** 10/188; **manega** (npl.)
   6/149 *10/200; **mænege** 7/33, 62; **mænige**
   7/76; **monige** 3/14, 73 *5/14, 54; **monig**
   (napl.) 3/105, 132–133, 168; **manege** 2/153
   *7/11, 56, 68, 114 etc.; **manigra** (gpl.) 11/41;
   monigra 3/71; **manegum** (dpl.) 6/125, 178
   *11/99; **monegum** 3/128
manigeo → **mengeo**
manigfealdum (dpl. f.) *manifold, various*
   5/55; **mænigfealde** (apl.) 7/105, 149;
   mænigfealdre (nsg. n. comp.) 7/75
manigne, manigra → **manig**
mann (nasg. m.) *person, man* 6/136, 169; **man**
   2/106, 51 *4/20, 30, 33, 42 *6/21, 33, 129
   *7/64 *8/8, 10, 12, 17, 19 *10/77, 147, 239,
   243 *11/112; **mon** 3/75, 80, 87, 136 *5/63;
   mannes (gsg.) 4/40 *6/165; **men** (dsg.) 3/109

*6/152 *10/319; **menn** (napl.) 4/31 *5/36
   *6/122, 149 *7/118 *11/82, 93; **men** 2/9, 21,
   32, 94–95, 141, 153 *3/118, 134 *4/17, 22,
   45 *6/48, 127 *7/3, 34, 63 *8/3, 43–44, 71,
   73, 82 *10/105, 125, 206 *11/12, 128;
mænn 7/104; **manna** (gpl.) 2/129 *3/22
   *6/20, 36 *7/9, 19, 52, 97 *8/20, 68
   *10/195; **monna** 2/76 *3/28, 48, 72, 143
   *5/49; **mannum** (dpl.) 2/127, 150 *6/125,
   128 *7/8, 48, 79 *8/69, 76 *11/96, 102;
   monnum 3/75, 159 *5/21, 46
mannslagan (npl. m.) *manslayer* 7/130
   [mannslage]
mannsylena (apl. f.) *selling of people* 7/107
   [mannsylen]
mannum → **mann**
manslyhtas (apl. m.) *manslaughter, murder*
   7/109 [mansliht]
mānsworan (npl. m.) *perjurer* 7/131
   [mānswora]
māra, māran, māre → **micel**
Marīan (prn.) *St Mary* 11/92
Maserfelda (pn.) 6/97
Mathei → **sanct**
maþelode (sg.pt.) *to make a speech* 10/42, 309
   [maðelian II]
māðma (gpl. m.) *treasure* 5/25 [māðum]
mǣca → **mēce**
mǣden (nasg. n.) *maiden, virgin* 6/135–136
   *8/22, 27, 34, 63, 77, 79, 83, 86, 89;
   mǣdene (dsg.) 8/96
mæg → **magan**
mǣg (nsg. m.) *kinsman, kin, parent* 2/26 *6/69
   *10/5, 114, 224, 287; **mǣges** (gsg.) 6/95;
   mǣgas (npl.) 2/25; **mǣga** (gpl.) 9/40;
   mǣgum (dpl.) 2/27; **māgum** 4/21 *6/3
mǣge, mǣgen → **magan**
mǣgen (nsg. n.) *might, strength, power; army*
   10/313; **mǣgenes** (gsg.) 3/12; **mǣgna** (apl.)
   8/94; **mǣgnum** (dpl.) 6/52
mǣges → **mǣg**
mǣgna, mǣgnum → **mǣgen**
mǣgrǣsas (apl. m.) *attack on kinsmen* 7/109
   [mǣgrǣs]
mǣgslagan (npl. m.) *slayer of a kinsman*
   7/130 [mǣgslaga]
mǣgð (nsg. f.) *tribe* 4/44; **mǣgðe** (dsg.) 7/83
mǣgum → **mǣg**
mǣla (gpl. n.) *speech* 10/212 [mǣl]
mǣlde (sg.pt.) *to speak* 10/26, 43, 210;
   gemǣlde 10/230, 244 [mǣlan I]
mǣnege, mǣnig, → **manig**
mǣnige → **manig; mengeo**

mænigfealde, mænigfealdre →
  manigfealdum

mænigne → **manig**

mænn → **mann**

mǣre (adj. nsg. f.n.) *famous, renowned* 6/27
  *9/14 *11/12, 82; **mǣres** (gsg. n.) 6/33;
  mǣran (dsg. m.) 11/69

mǣrþa (apl. f.) *glory* 7/161 [mǣrðu]

mæsseæfen (asg. m.) *eve of a festival* 2/123

mæsseprēost (nsg. m.) *mass-priest* 6/152, 165;
  mæsseprēoste (dsg.) 5/59; **mæsseprīoste**
  5/59

mæsserbanan (npl. m.) *murderer of a priest*
  7/130 [mæsserbana]

mǣst, mǣstan, mǣste → **micel**

mǣte (adj. isg. n.) *small, inferior* 11/69, 124

mǣð (nsg. f.) *respect, honour, fitness* 10/195;
  mǣþe (gsg.) 7/25; (asg.) 7/64

mē → **ic**

meahte → **magan; mihte**

meahton → **magan**

mearh (asg. m.) *horse* 10/188; **mēare** (dsg.)
  10/239

mēce (asg. m.) *sword* 10/167, 236; **mǣca** (gpl.)
  9/40; **mēcum** (dpl.) 9/24

medmicel (asg. n.) *short, moderate* 3/164;
  medmiclum (dsg.) 3/28, 69

medo (nasg. m.) *mead* 4/18–19; **meodo** (dsg.)
  10/212

mehte; men → **magan; mann**

mengeo (nsg. f.) *multitude* 5/25; **manigeo**
  (dsg.) 11/151; **mænige** (dsg.) 11/112

menn → **mann**

menniscnesse (dsg. f.) *incarnation* 3/129
  [menniscnes]

menniscum (adj. dsg. n.) *human* 6/114

meodo → **medo**

meolc (asg. f.) *milk* 4/17

Mēore (pn.) *Möre (Sweden)* 4/6

mēoses (gsg. n.) *moss* 6/23

Meotodes → **metod**

Merantūne (pn.) *Merton* 2/8; **Meretune** 2/73

mere (dsg. m.) *mere, lake, pool* 4/11, 14 *9/54

Meretune → **Merantūne**

mergen → **morgenne**

Metod (nsg. m.) *God, Lord, Creator* 10/175;
  Meotodes (gsg. m.) 3/96; **Metode** (dsg.)
  10/147

metsunge (asg. f.) *provisions* 2/99 [metsung]

mētte (sg.pt.) *to meet* 3/37; **gemētte** 2/58, 104
  *6/142; **mētton** (pl.pt.) 2/22, 50 [mētan I]

mettrume (adj. apl.) *sick* 6/122 [medtrum]

mēðe (adj. asg. m.) *worn out* 11/65; (npl.) 11/69

meþelstede (dsg. m.) *meeting-place* 10/199

micclan, miccle, miccles, micclum → **micel**

micclum (adv.) *much* 6/113, 119; **miclum**
  2/12 *4/43

micel (adj. nasg.) *much, great, big* 2/37, 61, 74,
  127, 142 *5/25 *6/144 *7/17–18, 21, 58,
  137, 153; **mycel** 4/9, 15–16, 18 *11/130,
  139; **miccles** (gsg. n.) 10/217; **mycelne** (asg.
  m.) 2/124; **micelne** 2/99; **micle** (dsg. n.) 3/36
  *11/34; (nsg. f.) 2/40, 60; (npl.) 7/55, 74;
  miccle (isg. n.) 10/50; **mycle** 11/60, 123;
  micclan (dsg. m.n.) 2/56 *6/18; **micclum**
  (dsg. m.) 6/92; **miclum** (dpl.) 2/5; (dsg.) 2/43;
  micelre (dsg. f.) 3/138 *6/55 *8/57; **mycelre**
  (dsg. f.) 6/51; **miclan** (asg. m.) 7/160 *11/65,
  102; (dsg. m.) 7/17–18; (dpl.) 7/14; **micelan**
  (dpl.) 7/15 ♦ comp.: **mā** 3/17 *4/27 *5/38
  *7/89, 112 *9/46 *10/195; **māra** 5/38;
  māran 3/15–16 *4/22; **māre** 1/27 *7/54, 75,
  79 *9/65 *10/313 ♦ col.: **þē mā þe** *any more
  than* 7/48; **þon mā þe** 2/29 ♦ sup.: **mǣst**
  2/86 *7/53–54, 57 *10/223; **mǣste** (asg. f.)
  10/175; **mǣstan** 3/70 *4/28, 34 *8/68

Michǣles → **Sanct**

miclan, micle → **micel**

micle (adv.) *much* 3/36 *4/22

miclum → **micclum; micel**

mid → **eall** (1)

mid (prep. (d.a.i.)) *with, together with, amid,
  among, by* 1/4, 8, 31 *2/9, 25, 28–29 etc.
  *3/3–4, 7, 23, etc. *4/19–21, 36, 38–39 etc.
  *5/7, 31, 47, 66 *6/4, 9, 15, 18 etc. *7/8, 14,
  26, 47 etc. *8/5, 12, 18, 22, 42 etc. *9/26,
  37, 47 *10/14, 21, 23, 32, 40 etc. *11/7, 14,
  16, 20, 22–23 etc. ♦ col.: **mid ealle** (adv.)
  entirely 6/60; **mid þām þe** (conj.) *when, as*
  1/16 *6/131; **mid þȳ þe** 3/44; **mid þȳ** 3/148;
  midþīðe 8/14; **midþīþe** 8/6; **midþȳþe**
  8/31–32, 61

middangeard (nasg. m.) *middle earth, world*
  3/101, 167 *11/104; **middangeardes** (gsg.)
  3/126

middanwintre (dsg. m.n.) *midwinter,
  Christmas* 2/92; **midwintres dæg** *Christmas*
  2/146 [middanwinter]

middeneaht (asg. f.) *midnight* 3/150; **midre
  nihte** 11/2

midþīðe, midþīþe, midþȳþe → **mid**

midwintres → **middanwintre**

Mierce (pn.) *Mercia, the Mercians* 2/46, 49,
  51 etc.; **Myrce** 9/24; **Miercna** (gpl.) *(of the)
  Mercians* 2/47; **Myrcena** 6/95–96; **Myrcena
  lande** 6/179; **Myrcan** (dpl.) 6/112; **Myrcon**
  10/217

miht, mihte → **magan**

mihte (asg. f.) *might, power, strength, virtue* 3/16; (dsg.) 11/102; **meahte** (asg.) 3/96 [miht]

mihtig (adj. nsg. m.) *mighty, powerful* 11/151

mīla → **mīle**

milde (adj. nsg. m.) *merciful* 10/175

mīle (dsg. f.) *mile* 4/28, 30; **mīla** (gpl.) 4/11; **mīlum** (dpl.) 4/32 [mīl]

mīn, mīne, mīnes, mīnne, mīnre, mīnum → **ic**

misbēodan (2) *to ill-treat, harm* 7/26

misdǣda (ngapl. f.) *misdeed* 7/106, 126, 134; **misdǣdum** (dpl.) 7/142; **misdǣdan** 7/119 [misdǣd]

mislīce (adv.) *variously* 2/115

mislicum (adj. dpl.) *various* 5/55 *6/122; **mistlice** (apl.) 7/56, 110–111 [mislic]

mislīcyge (sg.ps. subj. impv.) *to displease* 8/113 [mislīcian II]

mislimpe (sg.ps. subj.) *to go wrong* 7/103 [mislimpan 3]

mistlice → **mislicum**

misðingð (sg.ps. impv.) *to err* 8/9 [misðyncan II]

mōd (nasg. n.) *heart, mind, spirit* 3/72, 154 *8/62 *10/313; **mōde** (dsg.) 3/149, 166 *5/31 *6/37, 42 *11/122, 130

mōdgeþanc (asg. m.) *plan* 3/96

mōdig (nsg. m.) *spirited, brave, proud* 11/41; **mōdi** 10/147; **mōdigan** (asg. m.) 6/13, 17; **mōdige** (npl.) 10/80

mōdiglīce (adv.) *bravely* 10/200

mōdor (asg. f.) *mother* 7/73 *11/92

mōdsefa (nsg. m.) *mind, spirit* 11/124

moldan (asg. f.) *earth* 6/148 *11/12, 82 [molde]

moldern (asg. n.) *tomb* 11/65

mon → **man; mann**

monade (sg.pt.) *to admonish* 3/119 [manian II]

mōnaþ (apl. m.) *month* 2/72, 80; **mōnað** (asg.) 4/21

moncynnes, monncynnes → **mancynn**

monegum, monig, monige, monigra → **manig**

monna, monnum → **mann**

morgengife (asg. f.) *morning gift* 8/110 [morgengifu]

morgenne (dsg. m.) *morning* 2/19 *3/107, 116; **mergen** (asg.) 6/16, 119 [morgen]

morgentīd (asg. f.) *morning* 9/14

Morkere (prn.) 2/107, 132, 140, 152

morðdǣda (apl. f.) *murder, deadly deed* 7/106 [morðdǣd]

morþorwyrhtan (npl. m.) *murderer* 7/131 [morðorwyrhta]

mōst, mōste, mōston → **mōt**

mōt (prps. 1.sg.ps.) *to be able, be allowed to, must* 11/142; **mōst** (2.sg.ps.) 10/30; **mōton** (pl.ps.) 10/180; **mōtan** 4/36 *7/15; **mōte** (sg.ps. subj.) 7/13 *8/12, 93 *10/95, 177 *11/127; **mōste** (sg.pt.) 3/52 *6/158 *8/64 *10/272; **mōston** (pl.pt.) 6/119 *10/83, 87, 263

Moyses (prn. gsg.) *Moses* 3/127

mundbyrd (nsg. f.) *hope* 11/130

munde (dsg. f.) *security, protection* 7/25 [mund]

munuchād (asg. m.) *monastic orders, monastic life* 3/119

munuclīce (adv.) *monkishly* 6/51

munuclicre (adj. dsg. f.) *monastic* 6/34

murcnunge (asg. f.) *grief* 8/36 [murcnung]

murnan (3) *to care about, reck* 10/259; **murnon** (pl.pt.) 10/96

mūðe (dsg. m.) *mouth* 3/125 [mūð]

mycel, mycelne, mycelre, mycle → **micel**

mylenscearpan (dpl. m.) *sharpened on a grindstone* 9/24

myltestran (npl. f.) *whore* 7/131 [myltestre]

mynster (asg. n.) *monastery, church* 3/120 *6/69; **mynstre** (dsg.) 3/66 *5/64 *6/109, 113 ◆ col.: **Ealdan Mynstre** 6/90

mynsterhatan (npl. m.) *persecutor of monasteries* 7/130 [mynsterhata]

mynsterlice (apl. f.) *monastic* 6/55

mynstermen (npl. m.) *monk* 6/119; **mynstermenn** 6/114

mynstre → **mynster**

mȳran (dsg. f.) *mare* 3/53 *4/17 [mȳre]

Myrcan, Myrce, Myrcena, Myrcon → **Mierce**

myrcelse (dsg. m.f.) *trophy* 6/103 [myrcels]

myrhða (apl. f.) *mirth, joy* 7/162 [myhrð]

N

nā (adv.) *no, not (at all)* 2/84 *7/124, 135 *8/47, 87, 108 *10/21, 258, 268, 325 ◆ col.: **nā ne** 7/63, 104, 127, 139

nabbe → **habban**

nāh → **āgan**

nāht (adv.) *not* 3/90; **nōht** 3/60, 77, 89 *5/14

nales (adv.) *not at all* 3/75

nam → **niman**

nama (nsg. m.) *name* 10/267; **naman** (gdasg.) 1/1 *4/13 *5/21, 63 *6/80 *7/140 *8/25–26, 32 *11/113; (apl.) 8/109; **noman** (dsg.) 3/88

nāmon → **niman**

nān (adj., pron. nasg. m.n.) *none, not one, not any* 2/50, 94, 100 *5/63 *6/18, 96, 169, 171 *7/103 *8/3, 7; **nānes** (gsg. n.) 6/34; **nānre** (dsg. f.) 5/50; **nānum** (dpl. m.) 8/10; (dsg. m.) 9/25

nānwuht (adj., pron. asg. n.) *nothing* 5/26; **nāwiht** 3/12; **nōwiht** 3/36

nāst, nāt → **witan**

nāþor (conj.) *neither* 7/51

nāwiht → **nānwuht**

nǣfre (adv.) *never* 2/27 *3/77, 81, 94 *8/79

nǣfð → **habban**

nægledcnearrum (dpl. m.) *nailed ship* 9/53 [nægledcnearr]

næglum (dpl. m.) *nail* 11/46 [nægl]

nǣnig (adj., pron. nasg. m.n.) *no* 2/16, 26 *3/13, 74, 81 *4/18; **nǣnigne** (asg. m.) 3/156; **nǣnne** 5/35

nǣre, nǣren, nǣron, næs → **bēon**

ne → **nā**

ne (adv., part.) *not* 1/19 *2/29, 51, 84 etc. *3/12–13, 26, 29 etc. *4/18, 45 *5/15, 20–21, 26 etc. *6/18, 43, 63, etc. *7/20–23, 26, 40, etc. *8/3, 7, 10, 21, etc. *9/24, 39, 44, 46 etc. *10/21, 34, 48, 59 etc. *11/10, 35, 42, 45 etc.; **ne ... ne** (conj.) *neither ... nor* 1/18 *5/64; **nōhwæðer ne ... ne** 5/20

nēah (adj., adv.) *near* 3/148, 152, 160; **nēh** 10/103; **nȳhst** (sup.) 4/30, 35; **nȳhstan** 7/144 *8/100

neahte → **niht**

nēalǣcte, nēalǣcð → **nēalēcan**

nēalēcan (I) *to draw near, approach* 3/83; **genēalēcan** 6/99; **nēalǣcð** (sg.ps.) 7/3; **nēalǣcte** (sg.pt.) 3/140; **nēalēhte** 3/57; **genēalǣhton** (pl.pt.) 6/98

nēata (gpl. n.) *animal* 3/85 [nēat]

nēaweste (dsg. f.) *neighbourhood* 3/143

nēde → **nēod**

nēh → **nēah**

nellað, nelle → **willan** (2)

nemnde (sg.pt.) *to call, name, appoint* 3/88; **nemned** (ptp.) 3/62; **genemned** 5/56 [nemnan I]

nēod (nsg. f.n.) *need* 7/140; **nēode** (dsg.) 2/141 *8/25; **nēde** (dsg. n.) 9/33

nēodlīcor (adv. comp.) *diligently* 3/13

nēotan (II (g.)) *to use* 10/308

nēten (npl. n.) *animal* 3/123; **nȳtena** (gpl.) 6/20

nīedbeðearfosta (adj. npl. sup.) *necessary* 5/45

nigoðan (ord.) *ninth* 6/93

niht → **seofon**

niht (asg. f.) *night* 2/57, 59, 62, 70 *6/118 *8/86; **neahte** (gdsg.) 3/86, 145; **nihte** (dsg.) 1/4 *6/24; **nihtum** (dpl.) 4/2; **nihtan** 2/66

nihte → **middeneaht**

niman (4) *to take (away), grip, seize* 10/39, 252; **nim** (imp.sg.) 1/2 *8/112; **nimð** (sg.ps.) 4/35; **nimað** (pl.ps.) 4/41 *8/77; **nam** (sg.pt.) 2/43, 59, 87 etc. *6/84 *8/51, 111; **nom** 3/54; **genam** 6/62, 105 *8/54; **genāme** (sg.pt. subj.) 10/71; **nāmon** (pl.pt.) 2/47, 51, 53 etc. *6/127; **genāman** 11/30; **genāmon** 11/60; **genumen** (ptp.) 4/35

nis → **bēon**

nīwan (adv.) *newly* 3/18

nīwe (adj. nsg. f.) *new* 3/8, 30

nōht → **lǣs; nāht**

nōhwæðer → **ne**

nolde, noldest, noldon → **willan** (2)

nom; noman → **niman; nama**

Norhymbra land → **Norðhymbra**

Normandīge (pn.) *Normandy* 2/122, 151

Normen (prn.) 2/108, 113; **Normenn** (apl.) 2/110; **Norna** (gpl.) 2/116

norð (adv.) *north* 4/14 *9/38

Norþanhymbra →**Norþhymbre**

norþerna (nsg. m.) *northern* 9/18

Norþhymbre (pn.) *Northumbria, Northumbrians* 2/37, 89; **Norþanhymbra** (gpl.) 2/42; **Norðhymbra** (prn.) 6/5, 83, 104; **Norðhymbran** (adj.) 6/7; **Norðhymbriscum** (dsg.) 6/43; **Norðhymbron** (dpl.) 10/266 ♦ col.: **Norhymbra land** 6/45; **Norðhymbra lande** 6/2

Norþmen (prn.) *norsemen* 9/53; **Norðmanna** (gpl.) 9/33

Norwegon (prn.) *Norwegians* 2/105

note (dsg. f.) *occupation* 5/50 [notu]

nōwiht → **nānwuht**

nū (adv., conj.) *now, now that* 1/19–20, 26–27 *3/10, 37, 39, 47 etc. *5/10, 16, 30, 48, 65 *6/157–158, 160–161 etc. *7/7, 27, 42, 47–48 etc. *8/24, 33, 36, 44 etc. *10/57, 93, 175, 215 etc. *11/78, 80, 84, 95 etc.

nȳde (adv.) *of necessity, necessarily* 7/5, 17

nȳdgyld (npl. n.) *forced tax* 7/84

nȳdmāgan (asg. f.) *close kinswoman* 7/91

nȳdþearf (nsg. f.) *need, necessity* 7/19

nȳhst, nȳhstan → **nēah**

nys; nȳtena → **bēon; nēten**

nytnisse (gsg. f.) *usefulness, benefit* 3/40; **nyttnesse** (asg.) 3/12 [nyttnes]

O

Ōda (prn.) 2/153

Oddan (prn.) 10/186, 238

of (prep. (d.)) *from* 1/17 *2/36, 91, 105, 117
etc. *3/27, 68, 90, 128 etc. *4/1, 10–14
*5/13, 57 *6/22, 35, 73, 102 etc. *7/34,
58–59, 61 etc. *8/29, 64, 106–107 *10/7,
108, 149–150 etc. *11/30, 49, 61, 66 etc.

ofer (prep. (d.a.)) *over, after* 1/19 *2/36, 53,
77, 138, 150 *3/150 *6/115, 117 *7/102
*9/15, 19, 26, 55, 71 *10/88, 91, 97–98, 256,
276 *11/12, 35, 82, 91, 94 ♦ col.: **ofer bæc**
(adv.) *backwards* 10/276

ofercōman (pl.pt.) *to overcome* 9/72
[ofercuman 4]

oferfērde (sg.pt.) *to traverse, cross* 2/139
[oferfēran I]

oferfōron (pl.pt.) *to pass through, cross* 2/145
[oferfaran 6]

oferfroren (ptp.) *to freeze over* 4/47
[oferfrēosan 2]

oferfylla (apl. f.) *gluttony* 7/149 [oferfyllu]

oferhogan (npl. m.) *despiser* 7/114 [oferhoga]

oferlīce (adv.) *excessively* 7/143

ofermōde (dsg. n.) *great courage or pride*
10/89 [ofermōd]

oferwan (sg.pt.) *to overcome* 6/26
[oferwinnan 3]

Offa (prn.) 10/198, 230, 286, 288; **Offan** (gsg.)
10/5

offrung (nsg. f.) *offering, oblation, sacrifice*
1/11; **offrunge** (dasg.) 1/12, 22

ofhrēow (sg.pt.) *to feel pity* 6/165 [ofhrēowan 2]

ōfre (dsg. m.) *shore* 10/28 [ōfer]

ofscēat (sg.pt.) *to shoot, kill* 10/77 [ofscēotan 2]

**ofslagen, ofslægen, ofslægene, ofslægenne,
ofslægenra** → **ofslēan**

ofslēan (6) *to strike off, cut down* 1/20;
ofslēanne (infl.inf.) 1/7; **ofslōg** (sg.pt.) 2/2;
ofslōgon (pl.pt.) 2/31, 55; **ofslagen** (ptp.) 6/4,
93, 127; **ofslægen** 1/15 *2/20, 22, 62, 66
etc.; **ofslægenne** (asg. m.) 2/14; **ofslægene**
(npl.) 2/30, 43, 85; **ofslægenra** (gpl.) 2/69

ofsnāð (sg.pt.) *to cut off, kill* 1/23 [ofsnīðan 1]

ofspring (nasg. m.) *offspring, descendant*
1/28–29

ofstang (sg.pt.) *to stab* 2/4 [ofstingan 3]

ofste (dsg. f.) *haste, speed* 7/3 [ofost]

ofstlīce (adv.) *hastily* 10/143

oft → **gelōme**

oft (adv.) *often, frequently* 2/5, 33, 84 *3/72,
81 *5/2 *6/179 *7/67, 88–89, 91, 95 etc.
*9/8 *10/188, 212, 296, 321; **oftor** (comp.)
7/41 *11/128; **oftost** (sup.) 5/18 *6/72 *7/116

oftrǣdlīce (adv.) *frequently* 8/104

Ōlāfe (prn.) 2/116

olle (dsg. n.) *contempt* 7/121 [oll]

on (prep. (d.a.)) *in, on, against* 1/3, 5–6, 14 etc.
*2/3, 8, 11–14 etc. *3/4, 22–23, 26 etc. *4/1,
3, 5, 7–8 etc. *5/2, 10–13, 27, 35 etc. *6/2–3,
5, 15, 19 etc. *7/3–4, 6, 9 etc. *8/10, 12, 17,
20 etc. *9/14, 22, 27, 29 etc. *10/25, 27–28,
38, 41 etc. *11/5, 9, 20, 29 etc.

onǣled (ptp.) *to kindle, enflame* 3/24 *8/86
[onǣlan I]

onbærnde (ptp.) *to fire, inspire* 3/73;
onbærned 3/138 [onbærnan I]

onbryrdnysse (dsg. f.) *inspiration* 6/74
[onbryrdnes]

onbyrigan (I (g.)) *to taste* 11/114

oncnāwan (7) *to recognise* 10/9; **oncnāwe**
(1.sg.ps.) 8/49; **oncnēow** (sg.pt.) 1/19

oncwæð (sg.pt.) *to answer* 10/245 [oncweðan 5]

ond; ondette → **and; andette**

ondlongne (asg. m.) *long* 9/21 [ondlong]

ondrǣtst (2.sg.ps.) *to be afraid, dread* 1/20
[ondrǣdan I]

**ondswarade, ondswarede, ondswaredon,
ondswarodon, ondsworede** → **andswarode**

ondweardum → **andwearde**

onemn (prep. (d.)) *alongside of* 10/184

onfēng, onfēngc, onfēnge, onfēngon →
onfōn

onfeohtende (psp.) *to attack* 2/70 [onfeohtan 3]

onfōn (7) *to receive, accept* 3/2, 43; (pl.ps.
subj.) 3/19; **onfēng** (sg.pt.) 3/49, 64, 77, 93,
108, 120 *8/84 *10/110; **onfēngc** 8/96;
onfēnge (sg.pt. subj.) 3/120; **onfēngon** (pl.pt.)
3/15; **onfongne** (ptp.) 3/115

onfunde (sg.pt. subj.) *to discover, perceive,
find out* 10/5; **onfundon** (pl.pt.) 2/14;
onfunden (pl.pt. subj.) 2/9 [onfindan 3]

ongan, ongann → **onginnen**

ongēan (adv.) *again, back, against, opposite*
2/70, 81, 84 *8/1, 16–17, 100 *10/49, 100,
137, 156

ongeat, ongēaton → **ongietan**

Ongelþēode (prn.) *England* 3/73

ongemang (prep. (d.)) *among, next* 5/55

ongietan (5) *to know, understand, perceive*
5/26; **ongytan** (5) 11/18; **ongite** (1.sg.ps.)
8/46; **ongeat** (sg.pt.) 2/11, 137 *3/35;
ongēaton (pl.pt.) 10/84

onginnen (pl.ps. subj.) *to begin* 11/116; **ongan**
(sg.pt.) 3/118 *5/54 *8/41, 55 *10/12, 17, 89,
91 etc. *11/19, 27, 73; **ongann** 6/28; **ongon**
3/93; **ongunnon** (pl.pt.) 3/74 *8/42 *10/86,
261 *11/65, 67 [onginnan 3]

ongite → **ongietan**

ongon, ongunnon → **onginnen**

ongyrede (sg.pt.) *to unclothe, strip* 11/39
[ongierwan I]

ongytan → **ongietan**

ongytenesse (gsg. f.) *knowledge* 3/58
[ongietenes]

onhylde (sg.pt.) *to lower, incline* 3/164
[onhyldan I]

onlūtan (2) *to bow, bend down* 5/32

onlȳsde (sg.pt.) *to redeem* 11/147 [onlȳsan I]

onmang þisan (adv.) *meanwhile* 2/144

onmunden (pl.pt. subj.) *to pay attention to*
2/29 [onmunan prps. (g.)]

ono → **hwæt** (2)

onridon (pl.pt.) *to ride (on a raid)* 2/84
[onrīdan 1]

onsǣge (gsg.) *assailing, attacking* 7/42

onscytan (dpl. m.) *attack, calumny* 7/54, 126
[onscyte]

onsendan (I) *to send forth, yield up* 5/62;
onsended (ptp.) 11/49

onslēpte (sg.pt.) *to fall asleep* 3/87, 164
[onslǣpan I]

onstal (asg. m.) *supply* 5/16

onstealde (sg.pt.) *to institute* 3/98 [onstellen I]

onweald (asg. m.) *authority, power* 5/6;
onwald 5/4

onwrēoh (imp.sg.) *to reveal, disclose* 11/97
[onwrēon 1,2]

opene (adj. npl.) *open* 11/47 [open]

openlīce (adv.) *openly* 3/37, 41

ōr (asg. n.) *beginning* 3/98

Orcanēge (prn.) *Orkney* 2/117

ord (nasg. m.) *point, spear, front line* 10/47,
60, 69, 110 etc.; **orde** (dsg.) 10/124, 226, 273

orfcwealm (nsg. m.) *cattle-plague* 7/44

Ōsbearn (prn.) 2/68

Ōsbryht (prn.) 2/38

Ōsrīc (prn.) 2/20

Ōswīg (prn.) 6/104

Ōswold (prn.) 6/2, 8–10, 19 etc. *10/304;
Ōswoldes (gsg.) 6/17, 24, 66, 68 etc.;
Ōswolde (dsg.) 6/15, 99

oð (prep. (a.), conj.) *up to, as far as, until* 3/12,
80 *4/8, 25 *5/50 *6/65 *9/16 *10/324; **oþ**
2/2, 12, 17, 49, 70 *4/34; **oð ðæt** 6/155
*11/26, 32; **oð þæt** 2/51, 59, 84 *6/8, 22,
87–88, 92, 98, 145; **oþ þæt** 2/4, 13, 31;
oðþæt 10/278; **oþ þe** 4/29

ōðer (adj., pron. nsg. m.) *other, another, next*
3/133 *4/46 *7/101 *10/207; **ōþer** 3/20
*10/282; **ōðres** (gsg. n.) 3/160; **ōðerre** (dsg.
f.) 5/50; **ōþrum** (dsg. m.n.) 2/64, 65 *7/10,
49, 53, 89; **ōðrum** 10/64, 70, 133; **ōðerne**

(asg. m.) 4/29; **ōþerne** 7/52, 54, 74 *10/143,
234; **ōþre** (asg. f.) 3/25–26; **ōðre** (napl.) 2/153
*3/31, 73 *4/22 *5/42 *8/3; (dsg. f.) 3/137
*5/67; **ōðerra** (gpl.) 3/48; **ōðra** 5/43; **ōðrum**
(dpl.) 3/128 *4/34 *5/21, 55 *6/47 *7/70;
(dsg.) 7/10 ♦ col.: **ōðer twēga** *one of two*
10/207

oðfæste (ptp.) *to set* 5/50 [oðfæstan I]

oðfeallan (7) *to fall away, decline* 5/37;
oðfeallenu (ptp.) 5/11

ōðra, ōðre, ōþre, ōðres, ōðrum, ōþrum →
ōðer

oðþæt → **oð**

oððe (conj.) *or* 3/29, 111 *4/27, 32, 46 *5/13,
67 *6/36, 49, 154 *7/90–91, 96, 104
*10/208, 292 *11/36; **oððon** 7/59, 157

ōwiht (pron. asg.) *something, anything* 3/30; **to
āhte** *at all* 7/18

P

Pantan (pn.) *the River Blackwater* 10/68, 97

pāpan (gsg. m.) *pope* 6/78; **pāpe** (gsg.) 2/135

paralisyn (asg.) *paralysis* 6/135

Paulīnus (prn.) 3/33

Pefnesēa (pn.) *Penvensey, Sussex* 2/122

Penda (prn.) 6/95–96

Peohtas (pn.) *the Picts* 6/67

Pētres → **sanct**

plega (nsg. m.) *play, festivity, game, sport*
4/25; **plegan** (dsg.) 4/27 *8/20

Plegmunde (prn.) 5/58

plegode (sg.pt.) *to play, amuse oneself* 8/58;
plegodan (pl.pt.) 9/52 [plegian II]

post (nasg. m.) *post* 6/143, 147; **poste** (dsg.)
6/146

prasse (dsg. m.) *proud array, pomp* 10/68
[prass]

prēost (nasg. m.) *priest* 6/152, 156, 163

Pryfetes (pn.) *Privett, Hampshire* 2/4

prȳtan (dsg. f.) *pride* 7/127 [prȳte]

punda (gpl.) *pound* 8/67

R

rād → **rīdan**

rāde (dsg. f.) *ride* 2/84 *6/136 [rād]

radost → **hraðe**

ramm (nsg. m.) *ram* 1/21–22

rancne (adj. asg. m.) *proud, brave* 7/92 [ranc]

randas (apl. m.) *shield* 10/20 [rand]

raðe → **hraðe**

rǣdde (sg.pt.) *to advise, direct* 10/18 [rǣdan I]

rǣde (dsg. m.) *advice, counsel* 6/78 [ræd]

rǣdinge (asg. f.) *reading* 6/48–49 [ræding]

rǣran (I) *to rear, establish* 3/161; **rǣrde** (sg.pt.) 7/11

rǣsde (sg.pt.) *to rush* 2/12 [rǣsan I]

Rēadingum (pn.) *Reading* 2/57, 60, 87

rēaf (apl. n.) *garment, vestment* 8/4 *10/161; **rēafes** (gsg.) 8/68

rēaferas (npl. m.) *robber, plunderer* 7/133 [rēafere]

rēafes → **rēaf**

rēafiað (pl.ps.) *to rob, plunder* 7/101 [rēafian II]

rēaflāc (nasg. n.) *robbery, plunder* 7/45, 145

reccelēase (adj. npl.) *negligent, careless* 5/37

reccenne (infl.inf.) *to relate, narrate, explain* 6/136; **rehte** (sg.pt.) 6/21; **gerehte** 6/41; **rehton** (pl.pt.) 3/113

regollecum (adj. dpl.) *regular, according to the monastic rule* 3/136 [regollic]

regollīce (adv.) *according to the rule* 7/50

rehte, rehton → **reccenne**

reliquium (gpl.) *relics* 6/162

reordberend (npl. m.) *person, speach-bearer* 11/3; **reordberendum** (dpl.) 11/89

reste → **gerestan**

reste (dasg. f.) *rest, resting* 3/87, 149 *11/3

rēðan (adj. asg. m.) *cruel* 6/14 [rēðe]

rīce (nsg. n.) *kingdom, realm, rule* 11/119; (dasg.) 2/6, 79 *5/15, 62 *6/54, 70, 104 *11/119, 152; **rīces** (gsg.) 2/1, 24 *3/65, 132 *6/28, 93 *8/94

ricene (adv.) *quickly* 10/93

rīcne (adj. asg. m.) *rich, powerful* 7/92 *11/44; **rīcra** (gpl.) 6/36 *7/145 *11/131; **rīcost** (nsg. sup.) 10/36; **rīcostan** (npl.) 4/17 [rīce]

rīcsode (sg.pt.) *to reign* 2/34, 78 *7/9 [rīcsian II]

rīdan (1) *to ride* 3/53 *6/50 *10/291; **rīdeð** (sg.ps.) 4/36; **rīdende** (psp.) 1/5; **rād** (sg.pt.) 6/104 *10/18, 239; **ridon** (pl.pt.) 2/20, 57

ridda (nsg. m.) *rider* 6/134, 140

rīdende, rīdeð, ridon → **rīdan**

riht (asg. n.) *justice, law, right* 7/121 *10/190; **rihte** (dsg.) 7/154; **gerihta** (napl.) 7/20, 22, 29; (gpl.) 7/32 ♦ col.: **mid rihte** *rightfully, lawfully* 7/20, 117

rihte (adv.) *rightly, justly, correctly* 7/52 *10/20

rihtlaga (gpl. f.) *just law* 7/115 [rihtlagu]

rihtlīce (adv.) *justly, properly* 6/14 *7/158

rihtne (adj. asg. m.) *right, proper* 11/89

rīmde (sg.pt.) *to count* 2/84 [rīman I]

rincum (dpl. m.) *warrior* 10/18 [rinc]

rīne (sg.ps. subj.) *to rain* 3/24 [rīnan I]

ringe → **hringas**

rōd (nsg. f.) *cross, rood* 6/19 *11/44, 136; **rōde** (dasg.) 6/11–12, 20, 22 *11/56, 119, 131

rōdetācne (dsg. n.) *sign of the cross* 3/164 [rōdetācen]

rōfes → **hrōfe**

rōhton (pl.pt.) *to care about, care for* 10/260; **rōhtan** 7/104 [reccan I]

Rōmaniscan (prn.) *the Romans* 6/25

Rōme (pn.) 6/78–79; **Rōmebyrig** 6/76

rōtlīce (adv.) *gladly, cheerfully* 3/153

ryhtfæderencyn (nsg. n.) *direct paternal ancestry* 2/35

rȳmdon → **gerȳmde**

rȳpaþ (pl.ps.) *to rob, plunder* 7/101 [rȳpan I]

rȳperas (npl. m.) *robber, plunderer* 7/133; **rȳpera** (gpl.) 7/45 [rȳpere]

S

sāh (sg.pt.) *to sink* 9/17 [sīgan 1]

saluwigpādan (adj. asg. m.) *dark-coated* 9/61 [saluwigpād]

sam ... sam (conj.) *whether ... or* 4/47

same → **swā**

samod (adv.) *too, at the same time* 1/5 *4/12 *6/4, 143

sanct (nasg. m.) *saint* 6/114, 116, 120; **Sancte Michæles** (prn.) 2/122; **Sancte Pētres** (prn.) 6/109; **Sancti Mathei** (prn.) 2/109

sandcēosol (nsg. m.) *sand* 1/28

sandum (dpl. f.) *food, victuals* 6/60 [sand]

sang → **singan**

sanga, sange → **song**

sār (asg. n.) *wound, pain* 8/33

sāre (adv.) *sorely, grievously* 7/34, 129 *11/59

sārlīce (adv.) *mournfully* 8/7

sārlicre (adj. dsg. f.) *sad, grievous* 6/156; **sārlicum** (dsg. m.) 8/18 [sārlic]

sārnesse (dasg. f.) *suffering, pain* 8/5, 40 [sārnes]

sārra (adj. gpl.) *painful* 11/80

sāule → **sāwul**

sāwul (nsg. f.) *soul* 10/177; **sāwl** (nsg. f.) 11/120; **sāwle** (asg.) 6/154, 176; **sāule** 7/57; **sāwla** (apl.) 6/100; **sāwlum** (dpl.) 6/101

sǣ (ndasg. f.m.) *sea* 1/29 *2/97, 138, 150 *4/14 *6/3 *7/97 *8/26, 95; (gsg.) 6/110

sæcce (dsg. f.) *battle* 9/4, 42 [sacu]

sǣd (adj. nsg. m.) *sated with, weary* 9/20

sǣde → secgan
sǣde (dsg. n.) *seed, offspring* 1/29 [sǣd]
sægde, sægdon → secgan
sǣl (nsg. f.) *time, occasion* 11/80; (dsg.) 6/55
sǣlida (nsg. m.) *seafarer* 10/45; **sǣlidan** (asg.) 10/286
sǣmen (npl. m.) *sailor, Viking* 7/96 *10/29; **sǣmannum** (dpl.) 10/38, 278 [sǣmann]
sǣrinc (nsg. m.) *sea-warrior, Viking* 10/134
sæt, sǣtan, sǣton → sit
scamað (sg.ps.) *to be ashamed of* 7/119, 124, 126, 135 [scamian II]
scamu (nsg. f.) *shame* 7/79; **scome** (dsg.) 3/84; **sceame** 6/7
scān → scīnan
scandlic (adj. nsg. n.) *shameful* 7/67; **scandlice** (npl.) 7/84; **sceandlican** (dpl.) 7/54
sceadu (nsg. f.) *shadow, darkness* 11/54
scēaf (sg.pt.) *to push, thrust* 10/136 [scūfan 2]
sceaft (nsg. m.) *shaft* 10/136
sceal (sg.ps.) *shall* 1/29 *3/92 *4/24, 41 *7/4, 15, 17–18 *10/60, 252, 312–313 *11/119; **sceall** 4/30 *6/157, 169; **sceolon** (pl.ps.) 4/31 *10/54, 220; **sceolan** 4/42; **sceole** 10/59; **sculon** 3/95 *7/160; **scylan** 7/13; **sceolde** (sg.pt.) 2/133 *3/2 *10/16 *11/43; **scolde** 3/47 *7/10, 50, 53, 63, 112, 123; **sceoldon** (pl.pt.) 3/82, 144 *5/10–11 *6/49 *10/19, 105, 291, 307; **scolden** 3/161; **scoldon** 1/6 *5/9; **scoldan** 7/27, 52, 148; **sceolden** (pl.ps. subj.) 5/36 [sculan prps.]
scealcas (npl. m.) *man, warrior* 10/181
sceall; sceame → sceal; scamu
sceandlican → scandlic
sceard (adj. nsg. m.) *bereft* 9/40
scēat → scēotað
scēatas (apl. m.) *corner, region* 11/37; **scēatum** (dpl.) 11/8, 43 [scēat]
sceattum (dpl. m.) *money* 10/40, 56 [sceatt]
scēawode (sg.pt.) *to see, behold* 11/137 [scēawian II]
scendað (pl.ps.) *to shame, insult* 7/90, 99 [scendan I]
sceolan, sceolde, sceolden, sceoldon, sceole, sceolon → sceal
scēōp (sg.pt.) *to create, shape* 3/99 [scieppan 6]
scēotað (pl.ps.) *to shoot, throw, hit* 7/68; **scēat** (sg.pt.) 3/57 *10/143, 270; **scoten** (ptp.) 9/19
Sceotta → Scottas
scēðe (dsg. f.) *sheath* 10/162 [scēað]
sceððan (6) *to injure, harm* 11/47
scild (asg. m.) *shield* 9/19; **scylde** (dsg.) 10/136; **scyldas** (npl.) 10/98

scīman (asg. m.) *splendour* 11/54 [scīma]
scīnan (1) *to shine, flash, gleam* 11/15; **scīneð** 3/38; **scān** 2/96
scip (nsg. n.) *ship* 4/2; **scipe** (dsg.) 7/101; **scype** 2/114 *10/40, 56; **scipum** (dpl.) 2/102; **scypum** 2/105, 118, 120
scipene (dsg. f.) *cattle-shed* 3/86 [scipen]
scipflotan (npl. m.) *sailor* 9/11 [scipflota]
sciphere (asg. m.) *fleet* 2/100
scipum → scip
scīr (adj. asg. n.) *bright, gleaming* 10/98; **scīrne** (asg. m.) 11/54
scīre (asg. f.) *region* 6/118 [scīr]
Scīreburnan (pn.) *Sherborne, Dorset* 2/45
scīrne → scīr
Scittisc (adj. nsg.) *Scottish* 9/19; **Scyttysc** 6/42
scōf (sg.pt.) *to shave, scrape* 6/165 [scafan 6]
scoldan, scolde, scolden, scoldon → sceal
scome → scamu
Scōnēg (pn.) *Skåne, Sweden* 4/4
scopgereorde (dsg. n.) *poetical language* 3/70 [scopgereord]
scoten → scēotað
Scotlande (pn.) *Scotland* 2/104 *6/3, 30
Scottas (prn.) 6/67; **Sceotta** (gpl.) 9/11, 32
scrīdde (sg.pt.) *to clothe, dress* 8/50 [scrȳdan I]
scrīfað (pl.ps.) *to care about* 7/70 [scrīfan 1]
scrīne (dsg. n.) *chest, shrine* 6/109, 121 [scrīn]
sculon, scylan → sceal
scyldas, scylde → scild
scyldburh (asg. f.) *shield-wall* 10/242
scype → scip
Scyppend (asg. m.) *creator, God* 3/100; **Scyppendes** (gsg.) 3/93, 168 *6/154
scypum → scip
Scyttysc → Scittisc
sē (dempron. nsg. m.) *the* 1/12, 18, 25–26 *2/5, 7, 11, 16 etc. *3/1, 5, 34, 41 etc. *5/62, 66 *6/2, 6, 8, 16 etc. *7/39, 57, 65, 75 etc. *8/9, 11, 14, 17 etc. *9/37 *10/6, 9, 27, 69, etc. *11/13, 42, 78, 95 etc. ♦ gsg.: ðæs 3/31, 62 *5/5 *6/78 *8/14 *10/141, 148; þæs 2/7, 14, 19, 24 etc. *3/20, 27, 30, 54 etc. *4/27, 39 *6/23, 32, 35, 41 etc. *7/13, 21, 38, 90 etc. *8/37, 61, 63, 101 *9/51 *10/8, 120, 131, 160 etc. *11/49 ♦ dsg.: ðām 6/11, 68, 93 *8/7, 13, 20, 63 *10/136 *11/61, 65, 114, 129; þām 1/2, 4, 6 *2/10, 29–30, 39, 50, 92, 134, 150 *3/2, 34, 36, 41, 52, 164 *6/16, 29, 32, 39, 50; 56–57, 76, 85, 94, 99, 108, 125, 127, 132, 138, 141–142, 146–147, 160, 163, 166, 169, 174, 177, 180 *7/4 *8/2, 6, 39, 58, 96 *9/29 *10/9–10, 28, 34–35, 63–64, 81, 121, 132, 142, 154, 159, 193, 199, 227, 240,

245, 268, 300, 323 *11/9, 50, 58, 69, 111,
122, 146, 150; **ðǣm** 4/11 *5/18, 31, 49, 64;
þǣm 3/44, 49, 57–58, 84, 104, 107, 118,
131, 143, 146, 171 *4/14, 25–27, 29–35;
ðān 4/36; **þān** 2/117 *4/39 ◆ asg.: **ðone** 4/25
*5/4, 18, 21, 28 etc. *8/1 *10/77, 151; **þone**
1/9, 14, 22 *2/2, 5, 8–9, 12–13, 21 etc.
*3/28, 33, 50, 59, 75–76 *4/28, 35, 45
*6/12–13, 17, 25–26 etc. *7/160–161 *8/68,
73, 102 *9/61 *10/19, 88, 102, 187 etc.
*11/127; **þane** 9/62; **þæne** 4/29 *7/82–83,
93, 98 ◆ isg.: **þon** 2/29 *3/142, 162; **ðȳ** 5/38;
þȳ 2/43, 54–55, 82, 85 *3/26, 57, 65, 116,
159 *4/25, 44 *7/4, 42, 118, 153 *9/46 ◆
npl.: **ðā** 3/45 *4/31 *5/4, 8, 24–25, 28, 45
*8/111 *10/82; **þā** 2/9, 21–22, 25, 42, 54,
62, 64–65, 71, 75, 81, 92, 103, 108, 113,
129, 141 *3/14, 47, 67, 125, 137, 158, 161
*4/5–6, 17, 21–22, 37, 40, 45 *6/25, 84, 98,
113, 118–119, 125, 144–145 *8/42, 52, 71,
73, 90, 100 *9/57 *10/72, 182, 305 *11/61 ◆
gpl.: **ðāra** 5/26, 33, 49 *8/53; **þāra** 2/66–67
*3/45, 60, 86, 121, 131 *8/59, 86 *10/212
*11/86; **þǣra** 7/23 *9/26 *10/174 ◆ dpl.:
ðām 6/51, 144 *8/29, 69, 76 *11/154; **þām**
1/7–8, 21–22 *2/83, 91, 118, 126 *3/19, 42
*6/60–61, 80, 143 *7/99, 101, 126, 162
*10/40, 190, 278 *11/59, 143, 149, 154;
ðǣm 3/137; **þǣm** 3/55, 64, 105, 133–134
*4/40; **þān** 2/117 ◆ apl.: **ðā** 5/9, 22, 34, 46,
49, 52 *6/30 *8/4, 15, 111 *10/145, 277; **þā**
2/30–31, 69, 97, 110 *3/18, 39–40, 45, 59,
63, 78, 94, 104, 109, 144, 169 *6/7, 46, 115,
120, 123 *7/14, 116, 121, 157, 161–162
*8/4, 55, 110 *10/196, 322 *11/46
sealde → **sillan**
sealmas (apl. m.) *psalm* 6/49 [sealm]
searacræftas (apl. m.) *fraud* 7/108 [searacræft]
sēaþe (dsg. m.) *pit* 11/75 [sēað]
seaxe (prn.) *Saxons* 9/70
sēcan (I) *to seek, seek out* 8/78 *9/55 *11/104,
127; **gesēcan** 10/222 *11/119; **sōhte** (sg.pt.)
3/37, 44 *5/10; **gesōhte** 10/287; **sōhton**
(pl.pt.) 2/40 *9/58 *10/193 *11/133; **sōhtan**
9/71; **gesōhton** 6/149; **gesōhtun** 9/27
secg (nsg. m.) *man, warrior* 9/17 *10/159;
secgas (apl.) 10/298; **secga** (gpl.) 9/13;
secgum (dpl.) 11/59
secgan (III) *to say, tell, declare* 3/110, 171
*10/30 *11/1; **secge** (1.sg.ps.) 7/29, 151
*8/26, 46; (imp.sg.) 11/96; **segeð** (sg.ps.)
10/45; **sege** (imp.sg.) 8/24, 28 *10/50; **secgað**
(pl.ps.) 9/68; **sǣde** (sg.pt.) 4/1 *6/58, 152, 162
*7/145 *10/147; **gesǣde** 10/120; **sægde** 1/26

*3/107, 109; **sǣgdon** (pl.pt.) 3/113; **gesǣgd**
(ptp.) 1/24; **gesǣd** 6/161
secgas, secgum → **secg**
secgað, secge, sege, segeð → **secgan**
segle (dsg. m.n.) *sail* 4/2 [segl]
segniende (prps.) *to cross oneself, bless* 3/170;
gesegnode (sg.pt.) 3/163 [segnian II]
seldon (adv.) *seldom* 6/50
sēlest (adj. asg. n. sup.) *best* 11/118; **sēlesta**
(nsg. m.) 11/27 [see gōd, sēlran]
self (adj., pron. nsg. m.) *self* 1/10, 12; **silf** 8/12,
35, 56, 96; **sylf** (nsg. f.m.) 6/13, 47, 94, 170
*8/110; (dpl.) 4/5; **sylfe** 3/37–38 *11/92;
seolfa (nsg. m.) 3/49, 63; **sylfa** 11/105;
seolfes (gsg. m.) 3/171; **selfum** (dsg. m.) 5/36;
sylfum 3/112 *7/141; **selfne** (asg. m.) 1/26;
seolfne 3/169; **sylfne** 3/13 *6/100 *7/92,
125, 139, 153; **selfe** (npl. m.) 5/20 *7/149;
seolfan 3/125; **sylfra** (gpl.) 10/38; **selfum**
(dpl.) 2/37
sēlran (adj. dsg. n. comp.) *better* 8/13 [see gōd,
sēlest]
sendan (I) *to send* 10/30; **sende** (sg.pt.) 6/30,
59 *10/134; **sendon** (pl.pt.) 6/31–32 *10/29
sēo (dempron. nsg. f.) *the* 1/11 *2/131 *3/60,
118, 127, 168 *4/8, 10 *6/19, 24, 124 *7/72
*8/2, 78 *10/104, 144, 284 *11/121; **sīo** 2/43
*3/12 *5/37, 40, 48, 53 *9/16 ◆ gdsg.: **ðāre**
8/31, 54, 99; **þāre** 8/29, 42, 55, 71, 84, 86;
ðǣre 3/140 *5/37, 64, 66 *6/12, 22, 24, 88,
140; **þǣre** 1/4, 9, 13, 22 *2/22, 37, 125 *3/9,
21–22, 30, 58, 61, 86, 94, 108, 145, 160, 163
*4/29 *6/110, 115, 121, 123, 136, 141, 174
*7/29, 95 *10/8, 95, 220 *11/21, 112, 131 ◆
asg.: **ðā** (asg.) 5/48, 55, 64 *6/20, 117, 130
*8/74, 93 *11/119; **þā** 1/6, 12, 14, 16, 23
*2/2, 11, 15, 41, 148 *3/26, 38, 49–50, 70,
80, 83, 115, 118, 142 *4/24 *6/59, 71, 85,
118, 127, 133, 148 *7/9, 15, 69–69, 96
*8/47, 50–51, 58 *10/74, 78, 139, 163
*11/20, 68
seofon (num.) *seven* 2/42; **syfan** 4/1; **seofene**
(npl.) 9/30 ◆ col.: **seofon niht** (asg. f.) *week*
2/97
seolfa, seolfan, seolfes, seolfne → **self**
seolfor (asg. n.) *silver* 8/4; **seolfres** (gsg.) 8/67;
seolfre (dsg.) 6/109 *11/77
setle (dsg. n.) *throne, resting-place* 8/18 *9/17
[setl]
settan (I) *to set (up, down), place* 2/148
*6/102; **sette** (sg.pt.) 8/51; **gesette** 3/87, 169;
gesetton (pl.pt.) 11/67; **geseted** (ptp.) 3/80
*11/141

sī → bēon
sibbe (asg. f.) *peace* 5/6 [sibb]
siblegeru (apl. n.) *incest* 7/110 [sibleger]
Sībyrhtes (prn.) 10/282
sīdan (asg. f.) *side* 11/49 [sīde]
sīde → wīde
Sīdroc (prn.) 2/67–68
sīe, sīen, siendon → bēon
sige (asg. m.) *victory* 2/54, 59, 71, 74, 108
  *6/16
sigebēam (nasg. m.) *tree of victory, cross*
  11/13, 127
Sigebryht (prn.) 2/1; Sigebryhtes (gsg.) 2/7
sigelēase (adj. npl.) *without victory* 7/87
  [sigelēas]
sigora (gpl. m.) *victory* 11/67 [sigor]
sigorfæst (adj. nsg. m.) *victorious* 11/150
silf → self
sillan (I) *to give, give up, supply, sell* 8/47, 50;
  syllan 3/38 *6/61, 174 *10/38, 46; syle
  (imp.sg.) 6/162; syllað (pl.ps.) 7/71; syllon
  (pl.ps. subj.) 10/61; sealde (sg.pt.) 2/147
  *3/20, 51, 53 *5/19 *6/166 *7/73 *8/112
  *10/271; gesealde (sg.pt.) 10/188; gesealdon
  (pl.pt.) 10/184; gesealde (ptp.) 7/35, 65, 73
simle (adv.) *always, continuously* 2/17; symle
  6/47
sinc (asg. n.) *treasure* 10/59; since (dsg.) 11/23
sincgyfan (asg. m.) *giver of treasure* 10/278
  [sincgyfa]
sing → singan
singāl (adj. nsg. f.) *perpetual, everlasting*
  11/141; singālum (dpl. n.) 6/70
singāllīce (adv.) *continuously, incessantly*
  7/100
singālum → singāl
singan (3) *to sing, recite* 3/79, 83, 89–93, 110,
  162; sing (imp.sg.) 3/88, 92; sang (sg.pt.)
  10/284; song 3/104, 126; āsong (sg.pt.) 3/117
sīo → sēo
siodu (asg. m.) *custom, morality* 5/6
sit (sg.ps.) *to sit, dwell, occupy* 7/78 *8/18;
  sittað (pl.ps.) 7/14; sitte (sg.ps. subj.) 3/23;
  sæt (sg.pt.) 2/52 *6/143 *8/5, 7; gesæt 8/1,
  88; sǣton (pl.pt.) 6/56; sǣtan 6/58 [sittan 5]
sīþedon, sīðode, sīþode → sīðian
sīðfate (dsg. m.) *journey* 11/150 [sīðfæt]
sīðian (II) *to travel, go* 10/177 *11/68; sīðie
  (sg.ps.) 10/251; sīðode (sg.pt.) 6/50; sīþode
  6/87; sīþedon (pl.pt.) 6/4
siððan (adv., conj.) *afterwards, after, later,
  when* 1/9 *5/42, 51, 60 *6/19, 112, 140, 149
  *11/49; siðþan 9/13; siþþan 6/26, 124
  *9/69; syððan 1/15 *2/47, 83, 100 *6/167

*7/60, 71; syðþan 11/3; syþþan 6/15
  *11/142
sixtigum (num. dpl.) *sixty* 2/47
slæce (sg.ps. subj.) *to slacken* 8/109 [slæccan I]
slǣpe (dsg. m.) *sleep* 3/104 *6/23, 137 [slǣp]
slǣpende (psp.) *to sleep* 3/104 [slǣpan 7]
slēan (6) *slay, kill, strike, conquer* slōh (sg.pt.)
  6/7, 114 *10/163, 285; slōge (sg.pt. subj.)
  10/117; slōgon (pl.pt.) 2/114; geslōgon (pl.pt.)
  9/4; geslægen (ptp.) 2/42, 61, 127
slege (dsg. m.) *slaying* 6/10, 95, 104
slōge, slōgon, slōh → slēan
smēade, smēage → smēagenne
smēagenne (infl.inf.) *to consider* 6/28; smēage
  (sg.ps. subj.) 7/139; smēade (sg.pt.) 7/9
  [smēagan I]
smercode (sg.pt.) *to smile* 8/102 [smearcian II]
smolt (adj. asg. n.) *peaceable* 3/154
smylte (adj. isg. m.) *peaceable* 3/167; smyltre
  (dsg. f.) 3/166
snaccum (dpl. m.) *cutter* 2/104 [snacc]
snelle (adj. npl.) *bold, keen* 10/29
snīwe (sg.ps. subj.) *to snow* 3/24 [snīwan I]
Snotengahām (pn.) *Nottingham* 2/46, 49
snytro (asg. f.) *wisdom* 3/49
sōfte (adv.) *easily* 10/59
sōhtan, sōhte, sōhton → sēcan
sōna (adv.) *at once, directly, soon* 1/9, 18, 21,
  31 *2/97 *3/27, 49, 93, 105, 108 *5/35 *6/3,
  11, 23, 28, 32 etc. *8/41, 88 ♦ col.: sōna þæs
  as soon as 2/123; sōna þæs þe 3/56
song → singan
song (nsg. m.) *song, poem* 3/124; songes (gsg.)
  3/106; sange (dsg.) 8/42, 56; sanga (gpl.)
  8/87
songcræft (asg. m.) *poetic art* 3/76
songes → song
sorga (gpl. f.) *sorrow, grief, trouble* 11/80;
  sorgum (dpl.) 11/20, 59 [sorg]
sorhlēoð (asg. n.) *dirge, song of sorrow* 11/67
sōð (nasg. n.) *truth* 3/37–38 *7/3, 29; sōþ
  7/151; sōþes (gsg.) 7/147
sōðan (adj. dgsg. m.) *true* 3/49, 58, 62; (asg. m.)
  6/80; sōþum (dpl.) 6/52
sōðlīce (adv.) *truly* 1/19 *3/11 *8/9, 28, 36, 46
  etc.
sōþum → sōðan
spǣcan → specenne
spearcan (npl. m.) *spark* 6/144 [spearca]
spearwa (nsg. m.) *sparrow* 3/25
specenne (infl.inf.) *to speak* 7/67; spǣcan
  (pl.pt. subj.) 7/8 [specan 5]
spēda (apl. f.) *means, opportunity* 4/22, 39
  *5/49 [spē]

spēdaþ (pl.ps.) *to be wealthy* 10/34 [spēdan I]
spēdig (adj. nsg. m.) *successful* 11/151
spell (asg. n.) *story, message* 3/113 *10/50; **spelles** (gsg.) 3/122; **spellum** (dpl.) 3/129
spēow (sg.pt.) *to succeed* 5/7 [spōwan 7]
spere (ndasg. n.) *spear* 3/54, 57 *10/137; **speru** (apl.) 10/108
spillan (I) *to destroy* 10/34
spore (dsg. n.) *track* 5/31 [spor]
sprang (sg.pt.) *to spring away* 10/137 [springan 3]
spræc, sprǣcan, sprǣcon → **sprǣce; sprecan**
sprǣce (dsg. f.) *speech, utterance* 3/21 *6/43 *8/23; **sprǣcan** (gsg.) 8/29 [sprǣc]
sprecan (5) *to speak, say* 3/142 *11/27; **sprecende** (psp.) 3/34, 91, 149, 153; **spræc** (sg.pt.) 10/211, 274; **sprǣcon** (pl.pt.) 10/200, 212; **sprǣcan** 3/32
sprengde (sg.pt.) *to break, shiver* 10/137 [sprengan I]
spyrigean (I) *to follow* 5/30
stacan (dsg. m.) *pin, stake* 6/105 [staca]
stafum (dpl. m.) *letter* 3/69 [stæf]
stalu (nsg. f.) *stealing, theft* 7/44; **stala** (apl.) 7/107
standan (6) *to stand* 6/73 *10/19 *11/43, 62; **gestandan** 10/171; **standeð** (sg.ps.) 4/12; **stynt** 10/51; **stōd** (sg.pt.) 3/87 *6/19, 105, 117, 163 *8/52 *10/25, 28, 145, 152, 273 *11/38; **stōdon** (pl.pt.) 5/24 *10/63, 72, 79, 100 etc. *11/7, 71; **gestōdon** 11/63
stāne (dsg. m.) *stone* 11/66 [stān]
stang (sg.pt.) *to stab* 10/138 [stingan 3]
staðe (dsg. n.) *shore* 4/12; **stæðe** 10/25 [stæð]
staðole (dsg. m.) *position* 11/71 [staðol]
stædefæste (adv.) *firmly* 10/127
stæfne → **stefn**
stær (nsg. n.) *history* 3/127; **stǣres** (gsg.) 3/122
stæðe → **staðe**
stēame (dsg. m.) *moisture* 11/62 [stēam]
stēdan (asg. m.) *stallion* 3/55 [stēda]
stede (asg. m.) *place* 6/149 *10/19
stedefæste (adj. npl.) *steadfast, firm* 10/249
stefn (nsg. f.) *voice* 11/71; **stefne** (dasg.) 8/101, 103; **stæfne** (dsg.) 8/57; **stemne** 6/156
stefne (dsg. m.) *prow, place* 9/34 *11/30
Stemfordbrygge (pn.) *Stamford Bridge, Yorkshire* 2/111
stemne → **stefn**
stemnetton (pl.pt.) *to stand firm* 10/122 [stemnettan I]

stēorbord (asg. n.) *starboard* 4/3, 8
steorfa (nsg. m.) *pestilence* 7/44
steorra (nsg. m.) *star* 2/95; **steorran** (napl.) 1/28; (asg.) 2/95
sticode (sg.pt.) *to stick* 3/57 [stician II]
Stīgand (prn.) 2/151
stihte (sg.pt.) *to incite* 10/127 [stihtan I]
stilli (adj. nsg. m.) *quiet* 8/23 [stille]
stilnes (nsg. f.) *quiet, peace* 8/53; **stilnesse** (dasg.) 3/165 *5/48
stīð (adj. asg. n.) *heavy* 2/150 *10/301
stīðhicgende (adj. npl.) *resolute* 10/122
stīðlīce (adv.) *stoutly, sternly* 10/25
stīðmōd (adj. nsg. m.) *resolute, brave* 11/40
stocce (dsg. m.) *stake, post* 6/163 [stocc]
stōd → **standan**
stōdhors (asg. m.) *stallion* 3/51
stōdon → **standan**
stōp (sg.pt.) *to step, advance* 10/8, 78, 131 [steppan 6]
storme (dsg. m.) *storm* 3/26 [storm]
stōw (nsg. f.) *spot, station, locality* 3/60 *6/24; **stōwe** (gdasg.) 1/10, 13, 23 *3/146 *5/66 *6/133, 137, 140–141; **stōwa** (gpl.) 5/28 *7/62
strande (dsg. n.) *sea-shore* 6/110 [strand]
strang (adj. nsg. m.) *powerful, mighty, strong* 11/40; **strange** (npl.) 7/88 *11/30; **strangran** (apl. comp.) 3/18
stranglic (adj. nsg. n.) *fierce, heavy* 2/112
strangran → **strang**
strǣlum (dpl. m.) *arrow, dart* 11/62 [strǣl]
strǣt (asg. f.) *street* 6/59; **strǣte** (dsg.) 8/99
strēam (asg. m.) *stream* 10/68
strīc (nsg. n.) *sickness (?)* 7/44
strūdunga (apl. f.) *robbery, spoliation* 7/107 [strūdung]
stunde (dsg. f.) *time* 10/271 [stund]
Stūrmere (prn.) 10/249
stynt → **standan**
styrme (sg.ps. subj.) *to storm* 3/24 [styrman I]
sum (adj., pron. nsg. m.n.) *a certain, some* 3/66, 87, 113 *6/1, 21, 76, 129, 140, 152, 160–161 *8/5–6 *10/149, 164, 285; **suman** (dsg. m.) 7/154; **sume** (asg. f.) 1/8 *10/271; (napl.) 2/41–42, 94–95, 114–115 *5/45 *6/49 *7/63, 159; **sumne** (asg. m.) 5/44 *6/22, 31, 33, 55; **sumre** (dsg. f.) 3/84; **sumu** (apl. n.) 3/149
sumor (nsg. m.) *summer* 4/47
sumorlida (nsg. m.) *summer army* 2/77
sumre, sumu → **sum**
suna; sunnan → **sunu; sunne**

sunnbēam (nsg. m.) *sunshine* 6/117

sunne (nsg. f.) *sun* 9/13; **sunnan** (gsg.) 6/73

sunu (nasg. m.) *son* 1/2, 12, 15, 20, 23 *9/42
  *10/76, 298 *11/150; **suna** (gdsg.) 1/15, 27
  *2/117

sūpenne (infl.inf.) *to drink* 6/166

sūþ (adv.) *southwards* 6/152

sūþan (adv.) *from the south, south of* 2/82;
  sūðan 4/13 *5/15

sūþerne (adj. asg. m.) *southern* 10/134

swā → **ēac; hwǣr; hwæt; hwelc; hwider**

swā (adv., conj.) *so (that), thus* 1/24, 31 *2/96,
  98–100, 115 etc. *3/28, 34, 36–37 etc.
  *4/22, 34, 45 *6/28, 40, 43, 47 etc. *7/4, 10,
  40, 46 etc. *8/6, 8, 17, 41 etc. *9/7 *10/33,
  59, 122, 132 etc. *11/108, 114; **swǣ** 5/11,
  14, 17–18, 36–37 etc. ◆ col.: **swā swā** 1/14,
  28 *3/5, 112, 123, 148, 165 *4/27 *6/16, 21,
  47, 64, 67, 132, 152 *7/26, 50, 52, 126, 135;
  swǣ swǣ 5/57, 60, 65; **swǣ same** (adv.)
  similarly, likewise 5/42; **swā þæt** 6/48, 66,
  116 *7/124; **swāþēah** (adv.) *however, yet*
  2/150

swān (nsg. m.) *swineherd* 2/4

swanc (sg.pt.) *to labour, work* 6/70 [swincan 3]

swātes (gsg. m.) *sweat, blood* 11/23; **swāte**
  (dsg.) 9/13

swāþēah, swǣ, swǣ same → **swā**

swǣsendum (dpl. n.) *banquet* 3/23 [swǣsende]

swǣtan (I) *to bleed* 11/20

swæð (asg. n.) *track, footprint* 5/29

sweartan (adj. asg. m.) *black* 9/61

swefn (asg. n.) *dream, vision* 3/87, 110;
  swefna (gpl.) 11/1

swēg (asg. m.) *sound* 8/42, 55

swēgcræft (asg. m.) *music, musician's art*
  8/47; **swēgcræfte** (dsg.) 8/43, 45

swelce → **ēac**

swelce (adv., conj.) *likewise, as if* 5/27; **swilce**
  (adv.) 9/37, 57; (conj.) 6/117 *9/19, 30;
  swylce (adv.) 11/8; (conj.) 2/39 ◆ col.: **swelce**
  ēac (adv.) *likewise* 3/133, 169; **swylc swā**
  3/22; **swylce swā** 11/92

sweltan (3) *to die* 10/293

swencte (sg.pt.) *to vex, trouble* 2/155;
  geswænctest (2.sg.pt.) 8/105 [swencan I]

swenges (gsg. m.) *stroke, blow* 10/118 [sweng]

sweolt (sg.pt.) *to die, perish* 6/100 [sweltan 3]

Swēon (prn.) *the Swedes* 4/7

swēoran (asg. m.) *neck* 1/19 [swēora]

sweord (asg. n.) *sword* 1/10, 16 *3/53; **swurd**
  (nasg.) 10/15, 47, 161, 166, 237; **sweordes**
  (gsg.) 9/68; **swurde** (dsg.) 10/118; **sweorda**
  (gpl.) 9/4; **sweordum** (dpl.) 9/30

swerie (1.sg.ps.) *to swear* 1/26; **swerige** 8/94;
  swōr (sg.pt.) 2/147; **swōron** (pl.pt.) 2/118,
  143 [swerian 6]

swēteste (adj. asg. n. sup.) *sweet* 3/124 [swēte]

swētnesse (dsg. f.) *sweetness* 3/132; **swētnisse**
  3/70 [swētnes]

swicdōmas (apl. m.) *deception, fraud* 7/108
  [swicdōm]

swicode (sg.pt.) *to deceive, betray* 7/53
  [swician II]

swiftan (adj. npl.) *swift* 4/37; **swiftoste** (asg. n.
  sup.) 4/33; **swyftoste** 4/31

swīge (nsg. f.) *silence* 8/54

swīgende (psp.) *to be or become silent* 8/45;
  swīgode (sg.pt.) 8/43 [swīgian II]

swilcan (pron. dpl.) *such* 7/151; **swylc** (adj. nsg.
  n.) *such* 2/93; **swylce** 2/94

swilce → **ēac; swelce**

swinsunge (dsg. f.) *melody* 3/114 [swinsung]

swīðe (adv.) *very much, fiercely* 1/19 *2/112,
  126,150, 155 *3/58, 156, 158 *5/2, 12, 22,
  25, 33, 47 *6/27, 53, 118 *8/8, 66, 108
  *10/115, 118, 282; **swīþe** 2/18 *3/136;
  swȳðe 4/8, 15–16, 18 *6/66, 145, 148 *7/45,
  125; **swȳþe** 6/2 *7/5, 8, 15, 31, 33, 35, 45,
  76, 88, 93, 105, 120, 135, 143, 155–156;
  swīþor (comp.) 6/71; **swȳþor** 7/118; **swīðost**
  (sup.) 4/39; **swȳþost** 7/116, 120

swīðlicre (adj. dsg. f.) *exceeding, strong* 6/62;
  swȳðlicre 6/73

swīþor, swīðost → **swīðe**

swīðre (adj. nsg. m. comp.) *right (hand)* 6/65,
  107; **swȳðra** 6/64; **swīðran** (asg.) 6/102, 106
  *11/20; **swȳþran** 6/62

swōr, swōron → **swerie**

swurd, swurde → **sweord**

swustersunu (nsg. m.) *sister's son* 10/115

swutol (adj. nsg. n.) *clear, evident* 7/41, 102

swyftoste → **swiftan**

swylc, swylce → **ēac; swelce; swilcan**

swȳðe, swȳþe → **swīðe**

swȳðlicre → **swīðlicre**

swȳþor, swȳþost → **swīðe**

swȳðra, swȳþran → **swīðre**

sȳ → **bēon**

syfan → **seofon**

syle → **sillan**

sylf, sylfa, sylfe, sylfne, sylfra → **self**

sylfrenan (adj. dasg. m.) *silver* 6/57, 60

sylfum → **self**

sylfwylles (adv.) *voluntarily* 6/169

syllan, syllað, syllon → **sillan**

syllic (adj. nsg. m.) *marvellous, wondrous*
  11/13; **syllicre** (asg. n. comp.) 11/4

symble (dsg. n.) *feast* 3/84; **symle** 11/141 [symbel]

symle → **simle**; **symble**

sȳn, synd, syndan, syndon → **bēon**

syndriglīce (adv.) *individually, specially* 3/7, 66

syndrigum (adj. dpl.) *separate, special* 6/73 [syndrig]

syngian (II) *to sin, transgress* 7/125; **gesingodest** (2.sg.pt.) 8/32

synlēawa (apl. f.) *injury caused by sin* 7/129 [synlēaw]

synna (gpl. f.) *sin* 3/135 *7/105, 149; **synnan** (dpl.) 7/5; **synnon** 2/130; **synnum** 2/143 *7/90, 143 *11/13, 99, 146

syððan, syðþan, syþþan → **siððan**

syx (num.) *six* 4/27, 32

T

tācen (nsg. n.) *sign, portent* 2/94

tǣcan (I) *to teach, instruct* 7/126, 135; **tǣhte** (sg.pt.) 8/96 *10/18; **getǣht** (ptp.) 8/1, 84

tǣleð (sg.ps.) *to slander, wrong* 7/120; **tǣlst** (2.sg.ps.) 8/45 [tǣlan I]

tǣsde (sg.pt.) *to rive, tear* 10/270 [tǣsan I]

tæt → **þæt** (1)

tēah (sg.pt.) *to drag, draw, bring* 6/48 *8/58, 60; **getogen** *instructed* 8/62 [tēon 2]

teala (adv., interj.) *well, properly* 3/162; **teola** 3/56

tealte (adj. npl.) *unstable* 7/47 [tealt]

tēaras (npl. m.) *tear* 8/29 [tēar]

Temese (pn.) *the River Thames* 2/83 *5/15

templ (asg. n.) *temple* 3/39

tēode (sg.pt.) *to create, prepare, adorn* 3/102

teola → **teala**

Tharsum (pn.) *Tarsus, Turkey* 8/27

tīd (nasg. f.) *time, season, occasion* 3/26, 142 *10/104; **tīde** (gdasg.) 3/22, 80, 84, 87, 140, 161, 163; **tīda** (npl.) 5/4; **tīdum** (dpl.) 7/142 *8/98

tīman (dasg. m.) *time* 6/76 *8/108 [tīma]

tintreglican (adj. gsg. n.) *infernal* 3/132 [tintreglic]

tīr (asg. m.) *glory* 9/3 *10/104

tō (1) (adv.) *too* 7/7, 9, 11, 27, 29–31, 33, 61–62, 64, 67–68, 87, 114, 119–120, 123–124, 129, 140 *10/55, 66, 90, 150

tō (2) (adv.) *there* 1/6

tō (3) (prep. (d.)) *to, into, in, of*

tōætȳhte (sg.pt.) *to add* 3/33 [tōætȳcan I]

tōbærst (sg.pt.) *to burst* 6/21 *10/136, 144 [tōberstan 3]

tōbrocen (ptp.) *to break up, violate* 10/242; **tōbrocene** (npl. n.) 7/77

tōceorfan (3) *to cut into pieces* 6/60

tōcyme (dsg. m.) *arrival* 7/5

tōdæg (adv.) *today* 8/81, 105

tōdǣlað (pl.ps.) *to share out* 4/26 [tōdǣlan I]

tōgædere (adv.) *together* 6/98 *7/68, 97 *8/101, 105 *10/67

tōgēnes (adv.) *towards, to* 2/125

tōlīð (sg.ps.) *to separate* 4/9 [tōlicgan 5]

tōmiddes (prep. (d.)) *amidst, among* 6/144

Tosti (prn.) 2/113; **Tostig** 2/97, 102, 105

tōtwǣmed (ptp.) *to divide* 10/241 [tōtwǣman I]

tōweard (prep. (d.)) *towards* 4/33

tōweardan (adj. gsg. m.) *future* 3/131

tōwearp → **tōweorpan**

tōweorpan (3) *to throw down, demolish* 3/47–48, 52, 59; **tōwearp** (sg.pt.) 3/63

trēow (asg. n.) *tree, cross* 11/4, 14, 17, 25; **trēowe** (dsg.) 6/166

Trūsō (pn.) 4/1, 12

trym (asg. n.) *step, pace* 10/247

trymian (I) *to encourage, exhort* 10/17; **trymedon** (pl.pt.) 10/305

tuǣm → **twā**

tūcode (sg.pt.) *to ill-treat, torment* 6/7 [tūcian II]

tūne (dsg. m.) *place* 2/45 *4/29–30, 35 [tūn]

tunge (nsg. f.) *tongue* 3/168; **tungan** (dsg.) 3/78

tūngerēfan (dsg. m.) *town-reeve, bailiff* 3/107 [tūngerēfa]

tungol (nsg. m.n.) *star* 9/14

Tureces iege (pn.) *Torksey, Lincolnshire* 2/90

twā (num. napl.) *two* 2/120 *8/67; **twām** (dpl.) 1/4, 7 *6/6; **twǣm** 2/64; **tuǣm** 2/73; **twēgen** (napl.) 4/21, 46 *6/6 *7/96 *10/80

twēga; twēgen → **oðer; twā**

twelfe (num. npl.) *twelve* 7/90 [twelf]

twēntig (num.) *twenty* 8/68

tȳne (num. napl.) *ten* 7/89–90 [tȳn]

Þ, Ð

þā, ðā → **sē; sēo**

ðā (adv., conj.) *then, at that time, after that time; when, because* **þā** ◆ col.: **ðāðā** 8/5, 95; **ðā ðā** 5/15, 20 *8/34; **þā þā** 6/93, 173, 175; **ðāgīt** 6/77; **þāgīt** 6/44; **ðāgȳt** 6/81

þafode; þafunge → **geþafian; geþafunge**

ðāgīt, ðāgȳt → **ðā**

ðām, þām, ðān, þān → **sē**

þanc (nasg. m.) *thanks* 10/120, 147; **ðonc** 5/16, 65

þancie (sg.ps.) *to thank* 10/173; þancigende
  (psp.) 8/85; þancode (sg.pt.) 8/37 [ðancian II]
þane → sē
ðār, þār → ðǣr
ðāra, þāra → sē
ðāre, þāre → sēo
þās, þās → ðēos, ðes
ðāðā → ðā
ðǣm, þǣm, þǣne → sē
þǣnne → ðonne (1)
ðǣr (adv.) *there, where* 2/128 *4/18 *5/19, 64
  *10/205, 287 *11/10, 30, 63–64 etc.; þǣr
  1/3, 6, 13, 21, 23 *2/4, 9, 22, 37 etc. *3/9,
  29, 62, 82 etc. *4/15–16, 18–20, 24 etc.
  *6/3, 16, 19, 25–26 etc. *7/27, 91, 148
  *9/17, 32, 37 *10/17, 23–24, 28 etc. *11/8–9,
  11, 24 etc.; ðār 8/1, 84, 100; þār 2/112
  *4/42 *8/1, 14, 56, 58
þǣra → sē
þǣrbinnan (adv.) *therein* 6/86
ðǣre, þǣre → sēo
þǣrinne (adv.) *therein* 2/30
ðǣron (adv.) *therein* 11/67
þǣrtō (adv.) *thereto* 2/23
ðæs, þæs → sē
þæs (adv.) *therefore, then* 2/77 *6/119, 180
  *7/13, 38 *10/239 ♦ col.: þæs þe (conj.) *as,
  because, when* 2/6 *4/40 *7/137, 145 *9/68;
  þæs ymb (adv.) *afterwards, later* 2/57, 59,
  62, 70, 72, 79
ðæt, þæt → oð
ðæt (1) (pron. nasg. n.) *that* 3/36, 55 *5/17, 46
  *8/27, 89 *11/66; þæt 1/8, 17–18, 24–25
  *2/11, 19, 44, 55, 142, 145 *3/4–5, 25, 27,
  35–39, 69, 74, 84–85, 105, 110–111, 115,
  117, 120, 122, 124, 127, 170 *4/2, 9, 15, 24,
  26, 33, 35, 41 *6/36, 69, 87, 105, 117,
  123–124, 136, 143, 145–146, 148, 151,
  169–170 *7/3, 18, 29, 63, 65, 74–75, 77, 92,
  122–123, 135, 145, 151, 155–156 *8/4, 22,
  31, 34–35, 46, 48, 63, 76, 79, 83, 86, 95, 103
  *9/64 *10/5, 22, 32, 36, 51, 56, 63, 76, 84,
  102, 105, 119, 135, 137, 142, 144, 168,
  176–177, 180, 194, 200, 217, 221, 223, 226,
  234, 243, 246, 251, 263, 275, 289, 291, 307,
  324–325 *11/6, 18, 21, 28, 39, 58, 74; tæt
  2/28
ðæt (2) (conj.) *that, so that* þæt; ðætte; þætte
  þe → oð
ðe (relpart.) *who, which* 3/40, 67, 78, 91, 137,
  144 *4/11, 30–31 *5/4, 9, 12, 18, 28, 31, 34,
  45–46, 48–49, 51–52, 56 *8/10, 60, 72,
  84–85, 93 *10/316 *11/98, 113, 145; þe 1/2,
  13 *2/3, 9, 19, 21 etc. *3/2, 9–10, 12 etc.

*4/24–25, 40 *6/4, 13, 18–19 etc. *7/9, 14,
  21, 23 etc. *8/8, 17, 56, 58 etc. *9/26
  *10/36, 48, 52, 77–78 etc. *11/86, 111, 118,
  121 etc.
þe (art.) *the* 8/73
ðē, þē → lǣs; ðū; micel
ðēah (adv., conj.) *nevertheless, even so, yet;
  though, although* 5/54 *8/23 *10/289; þēah
  2/33, 40, 126, 144 *4/46 *7/8, 103 *8/23;
  ðēh 7/80; þēh 7/40, 125, 127 *10/190;
  ðēahðe 8/3
þearf (1) (nsg. f.) *need, hardship, distress*
  3/152 *7/29, 151, 153–154 *10/233; ðearfe
  (dsg.) 6/39 *10/307; þearfe 10/175, 201,
  232; þearfa (apl.) 6/154
þearf (2) (sg.ps.) *to need, have occasion to*
  11/117; þurfe (pl.ps.) 10/34; þurfon 10/249;
  þorfte (sg.pt.) 9/39, 44; þorftun (pl.pt.) 9/47
  [ðurfan prps.]
þearfa → þearf (1)
þearfan (npl. m.) *pauper* 6/58 [ðearfa]
þearfum (dpl.) 6/36, 60–61, 173
ðearfe → þearf (1)
þearfum → þearfan
þearle (adv.) *very much, keenly* 7/45 *8/59, 92
  *9/23 *10/158 *11/52
ðēaw (nsg. m.) *custom, practice* 4/20; þēaw
  3/143 *4/41; ðēawas (apl.) 5/22; þēawa (gpl.)
  7/115; þēawum (dpl.) 6/53, 159
þegen, þegenas, þegene, þegenes → þegn
þegengylde (asg. n.) *payment for a thegn* 7/84
ðegenlīce (adv.) *in thanely fashion* 10/294
þegn (nasg.) *thegn, nobleman, retainer;
  warrior, attendant* 2/21 *3/145, 147; þegen
  (nasg.) 7/82–83, 93 *10/151; þegenes (gsg.)
  7/91; þegene (dsg.) 7/82; þegnas (napl.) 2/15,
  19 *11/75; þegenas 10/205, 220, 232; þegna
  (gpl.) 3/13 *6/58; þegnum (dpl.) 3/23; þēnan
  7/26
þegnian (II) *to serve, minister* 3/145
þegnum → þegn
ðēh, þēh → ðēah
þēlǣsþe; þēnan → lǣs; þegn
þencaþ, þence, þenceð → geðencean
þenian (I) *to stretch out* 11/52
ðēninga (apl. f.) *divine service, mass book*
  5/12 [ðēning]
þēnung (nsg. f.) *service, food* 8/2; þēnunga
  (apl.) 6/57 *8/5
þēoda → þēode (1)
þēodde → þēode (2)
þēode (1) (gdsg. f.) *people, nation* 2/37, 154
  *3/64, 166 *7/7, 11, 30, 36, 40, 42, 62,
  76–77, 86, 97, 102, 116, 136, 139 *10/220;

ðēode 10/90; geðēodes (gsg.) 4/41; þēoda (npl.) 1/30 *6/66; ðēoda 10/173; ðīoda 5/44; þēodum (dpl.) 7/20, 23 *9/22 [ðēod]

þēode (2) (sg.pt.) to serve 3/166; þēodde 3/17 [ðēowan I]

ðēoden (nsg. m.) lord, ruler 10/120; þēoden (nasg.) 10/158, 178, 232; ðēodne (dsg.) 10/294; þēodne 11/69

Þēodforda (pn.) Thetford 2/54

þēodne → ðēoden

þēodscipe (nsg. m.) nation, discipline, law 7/105; þēodscype (asg.) 2/93; þēodscipum (dpl.) 3/136

þēodum → þēode (1)

þēodwita (nsg. m.) learned man 7/142

ðēos (dempron. nsg. f.) this 7/3; þēos 3/8, 10, 29 *6/64 *11/12, 82; ðeosse (gsg.) 3/66; ðisse (dsg.) 5/20 *10/221; þysse 3/38 *7/30, 40, 42, 76–77, 85, 136; ðās (asg.) 6/171; þās 2/99 *3/93 *6/168 *7/7, 11, 36, 62, 97, 102, 139 *11/96

þeossum → þes

þēowas (napl. m.) servant 7/25, 28; þēowan (npl.) 4/17; ðēowa (gpl.) 8/68; þēowa 3/121; ðīowa 5/25; þēowum (dpl.) 7/27 *8/69, 76

þēræfter (adv.) thereafter 2/97

þes (dempron. nsg. m.) this 7/105 *8/8–9, 17, 19; þysan (dsg.) 7/34, 46, 59, 65; ðysum 8/20; þisne (asg.) 2/148 *10/32; þysne 6/14 *10/52 *11/104; þīs (isg.) 10/316; ðās (napl.) 5/28; þās 2/120 *3/1 *4/4, 6–7 *8/14, 69, 77 *10/298; ðissa (gpl.) 5/17; þeossum (dpl.) 3/31; (dsg.) 3/90

þicgenne (infl.inf.) to drink 6/128 [ðicgan 5,I]

þider (adv.) thither, there, to that place 2/15, 20 *6/134

þīn → ðū

þincan (I imp.) to seem, appear, think 7/47, 105, 129; þynceð (sg.ps.) 3/18; ðyncð 5/44–45; þinceð 10/55; þince (sg.ps. subj.) 8/24; þūhte (sg.pt.) 3/8, 147 *10/66 *11/4

þincg → þing

þīne → ðū

þing (nasg. n.) thing, object 3/18; (napl.) 3/149 *7/116 *8/77; þinges (gsg.) 6/35; þincg (asg.) 6/96, 162; ðingc 8/3, 7; þingc 8/7, 69; þinga (gpl.) 7/23 *8/58–59; ðingum (dpl.) 8/10; þingum 3/15 *6/54 *8/49, 94

þingian (II) to pray, intercede 7/153; þingie (sg.ps. subj.) 6/160

þingum → þing

þīnne, þīnra, þīnre, þīnum, ðinum → ðū
ðīoda → þēode (1)

ðīowa → þēowas

ðīowotdōmas (apl. m.) service 5/9 [ðēowotdōm]

þīs → þes

ðis (dempron. nasg. n.) this 2/46 *3/12 *5/23, 33; þis 2/108–109, 123, 135 *3/21, 28, 94 *6/65 *8/5, 70 *9/66 *10/45; ðisses (gsg.) 5/55; ðissum (dsg.) 5/53; þissum 2/76, 91 *9/67; þisum 8/57, 94, 98; (dpl.) 8/94; þyssum 11/83, 109; þisan (dsg.) 2/119; þysson 11/138

þisan → onmang; ðis

þisne, ðissa → þes

ðisse → ðēos

ðisses, ðissum, þissum, þisum → ðis

þōhte → geðencean

þolian (II) to suffer 10/201, 307; geþolian 10/6; þoliað (pl.ps.) 7/99; þolodan (pl.pt.) 11/149

þon → sē

ðonc → þanc

ðone, þone → sē

ðonne (1) (adv.) then, now, therefore 4/28–29, 31, 33; þonne 2/15 *3/28, 37, 39, 81, 83 *4/4–5, 11, 13, 20, 25–26, 29, 32, 36–38 *8/24, 48, 110 *11/107, 115, 117, 139, 142; þænne 7/6

ðonne (2) (conj.) when, while 8/87; þonne 2/155 *3/16, 83 *6/170 *7/13 *10/213, 195; þonne than 1/27 *2/26 *3/14–15, 48 *6/71 *7/13, 42, 79, 112, 119, 152 *10/33 *11/128

þorfte, þorftun → þearf (2)

þræl (nasg. m.) slave 7/82–83, 92; þrǣle (dsg.) 7/82, 93; þrǣla (gpl.) 7/80

þrǣlriht (npl. m.) right of a slave 7/37

þrēom, þrēora → þrȳ

þriddan (ord. dasg. m.) third 1/6 *4/29

þrittig (num.) thirty 6/94

þrōwode (sg.pt.) to suffer, endure 11/84, 98, 145 [ðrōwian II]

þrōwunge (dsg. f.) suffering, passion 3/130 [ðrōwung]

þrȳ (num. npl.) three 7/96 *8/100–101; þrēora (gpl.) 10/299; þrēom (num. dpl.) three 2/105; þrȳm 8/107

þrycced (ptp.) to oppress 3/141 [ðryccan I]

þrȳm → þrȳ

þrymfæst (adj. nsg. m.) illustrious, mighty 11/84

ðū (perspron. 2.nsg.) you 5/17–19 *8/8, 12, 16, 21 etc. *11/78, 96; þū 1/2, 18–20, 26, 30 *3/10, 18, 21, 23, 91, 152 *6/161, 163–164 *8/8, 12, 22, 32–33 etc. *10/30, 36–37, 45 etc.; þīn (gsg.) 1/29 *3/24 *8/25, 46 *10/178; ðē (dasg.) 3/152 *5/2, 17–18 *8/9, 17, 24, 37

etc. *10/30, 177; **þē** 1/27 *3/11, 15 *6/162
*8/22, 26, 33, 39 etc. *10/29, 146, 173, 179
etc. *11/95 ♦ poss. adj.: **þīnne** (asg. m.) 1/2,
20, 27 *8/24; **þīne** (asg. f.) 1/19 *8/23, 36
*10/37; (apl.) 8/39; **þīnre** (gsg. f.) 3/152;
þȳnre (gsg. f.) 8/104; **ðīnum** (dsg. n.) 8/9;
þīnra (gpl.) 3/13; **þīnum** (dsg. m.n.) 1/26, 29
*8/64, 113; (dpl.) 3/23 *10/50; **þȳne** (npl.)
8/105

þūhte → **þincan**
þurfe, þurfon → **þearf**
ðurh (prep. (a.)) *through, by, by means of* 5/28,
43 *7/146 *11/119; **þurh** 1/26 *3/25, 49, 62,
69 etc. *6/20, 24, 122, 129, 180 *7/36, 39,
63, 79 etc. *8/81, 94 *10/71, 141, 145, 151
*11/10, 18
þurhdrifan (pl.pt.) *to drive through, pierce*
11/46 [ðurhdrīfan 1]
þurhflēo (sg.ps. subj.) *to fly through* 3/25
[ðurhflēon 2]
þurhwōd (sg.pt.) *to pass through* 10/296
[ðurhwadan 6]
Þurstānes (prn.) 10/298
þus (adv.) *thus, in this way* 1/2, 7, 30 *2/53
*3/21, 35, 152–153 *4/37 *6/63, 101, 156
*8/68, 71, 81, 89 etc. *10/57
þūsenda (gpl.) *thousand* 2/69 [ðūsend]
ðwōh (sg.pt.) *to wash, cleanse* 6/120 [ðwēan 6]
þȳfþe (dsg. f.) *theft* 7/36 [ðȳfð]
ðȳ, þȳ → **sē**
ðyncð, þynceð → **þincan**
þȳne, þȳnre → **ðū**
þysan → **þes**
þyslic (adj. nsg. n.) *such* 3/21
þysne → **þes**
þysse → **ðēos**
þysson, þyssum → **ðis**
þȳstro (npl. f.) *darkness, shadow* 11/52
ðysum → **þes**

U

ūhtsong (asg. m.) *Matins* 3/161; **ūhtsange**
(dsg.) 6/72
unbefohtene (ptp.) *unopposed* 10/57 [see
feohtan]
unc (perspron. dual 1.a.) *we two* 1/8 *11/48 [wit]
uncoþu (nsg. f.) *disease* 7/44
uncræftan (dpl. m.) *evil practice, deceit* 7/159
[uncræft]
uncūð (adj. nsg. m.) *unknown* 3/22 *5/64
undǣde (dsg. f.) *wicked deed, crime* 7/124
[undǣd]

under (prep. (d.a.)) *under* 4/2 *11/55, 85
underbæc (adv.) *backwards, behind* 1/21
underfēng, underfēngan, underfēngon →
underfōn
underfōn (7) *to receive, accept* 6/114, 120;
underfēng (sg.pt.) 6/38, 124; **underfēngon**
(pl.pt.) 2/39 *6/67; **underfēngan** 7/157
understandan (6) *to understand, comprehend*
7/98, 160 *8/28; **understondan** 5/12;
understande (sg.ps. subj.) 7/75, 85;
understandað (imp.pl.) 7/7
underþēodde (sg.pt.) *to subject* 3/14;
underþēoded (ptp.) 3/137 [underðēodan I]
unearge → **earh**
unforbærned (ptp.) *unburned, uncremated*
4/20, 23, 42 [see forbærnan I]
unforcūð (adj. nsg. m.) *noble, excellent* 10/51
unforht (adj. nsg. m.) *unafraid, fearless*
11/110; **unforhte** (npl.) 10/79
unforworhte (adj. npl.) *innocent* 7/35
ungecnāwe (adj. npl.) *unknown* 8/59
ungecyndne → **gecynde**
ungefōge (adv.) *excessively* 4/37
ungefullod (adj. nsg. n.) *unbaptized* 6/97
ungelimpa (gpl. m.) *misfortune* 7/85 [ungelimp]
ungemetlic (adj. nsg. n.) *immense* 2/42
ungerīm (nsg. n.) *countless number* 7/134
ungetrȳwþa (npl. f.) *treachery, disloyalty* 7/55
[ungetrȳwð]
ungewunelic (adj. nsg. n.) *unknown* 8/59
ungylda (npl. n.) *excessive tax* 7/45 [ungyld]
unhēanlīce (adv.) *not ignobly* 2/11
unlaga (npl. f.) *unlawful act, abuse of law*
7/11, 36, 146 [unlagu]
unlȳtel (adj. nsg. n.) *not a little* 7/18
unorne (adj. nsg. m.) *plain, simple* 10/256
unrǣd (nsg. m.) *folly* 2/142
unriht (asg. n.) *injustice, wrong* 7/11, 33, 154;
unrihta (npl.) 7/47; (gpl.) 7/9
unrihtlīce (adv.) *unjustly, wrongly* 7/54
unrīm (nsg. n.) *countless number* 9/31
unrōt (adj. nsg. m.) *sad, dejected* 8/23
unryhtum (adj. dpl.) *unjust, wrongful* 2/2
[unriht]
unsida (apl. m.) *abuse* 7/108 [unsidu]
unspēdigan (adj. npl.) *poor* 4/17 [unspēdig]
unstille (adj. asg. f.) *inquiet* 8/86
unstilnesse (asg. f.) *uproar* 2/15 [unstilnes]
untrumnysse (apl. f.) *infirmity, disease* 6/172;
untrymnesse (dsg.) 3/141 [untrumnes]
untrumra (adj. gpl.) *sick, infirm* 3/143 *6/20;
untrumran (apl. comp.) 3/144 [untrum]
untrymnesse → **untrumnysse**

unwāclīce (adv.) *strongly* 10/308
unwær (adv.) *unexpectedly* 2/110, 125
unwæstma (gpl. m.) *crop failure* 7/46
 [unwæstm]
unweaxen (ptp.) *not grown up* 10/152
unwedera (gpl. n.) *bad weather, storm* 7/46
 [unweder]
ūp → ūpp
ūpāstīgnesse (dsg. f.) *ascension* 3/130
 [ūpāstīgnes]
ūpgangan (asg. m.) *passage* 10/87 [ūpganga]
ūpgange (dsg. m.) *rising* 6/73 [ūpgang]
ūpp (adv.) *upwards* 2/63, 82 *6/121; ūp 2/58
 *6/74, 117 *9/13, 70 *10/130 *11/71
uppan (prep. (d.a.)) *upon, on* 1/3; uppon 8/51
uppe (adv.) *above* 11/9
uppon → uppan
ūra, ūran, ūre, ūrne → wē
urnon → irnan
ūrum, ūs → wē
ūt (adv.) *out, outside* 2/12, 103 *3/26, 85, 90
 *4/10, 12, 38 *5/6 *7/34, 61, 65, 97 *8/41,
 50, 66, 99 *9/35 *10/72
utan → uton
ūtan (adv.) *outside, from outside* 2/9
ūtanbordes (adv.) *from abroad* 5/9
ūte (adv.) *out, outside, abroad* 3/24 *5/10
 *7/23–24, 43, 86
ūtgonge (dsg. m.) *exitus, exodus* 3/127 [ūtgong]
uton (irr.) *let us* 6/12; utan 7/140, 154–155,
 157, 159; wutan 7/151; wuton 3/162 [see
 gewīte]
ūðe, ūþon → geunne
ūðwitan (npl. m.) *scholar, authority* 9/69
 [ūðwita]
uuiþ → wið

W

wācian (II) *to weaken, grow weak* 10/10
wācne (adj. asg. m.) *slender* 10/43 [wāc]
wadan (6) *to go, advance* 10/140; wōd (sg.pt.)
 10/130, 253; gewōd 10/157; wōdon (pl.pt.)
 10/96, 295
wālā (interj.) *alas, woe* 7/95
Waldend; wand → Wealdend; windan
wandian (II) *to hesitate* 10/258; wandode
 (sg.pt.) 10/268
wanedan (pl.pt.) *to lessen, dwindle, wane* 7/29
 [wanian 2]
wanhālum (dpl.) *sick, weak* 6/128;
 wannhālum 6/173 [wanhāl]
wann → gewinnan

wann (adj. nsg. f.) *dark, black* 11/55
wannhālum → wanhālum
ware (dsg. f.) *protection* 6/93 [waru]
warnian (2) *to warn* 7/151
was → bēon
wāst, wāt → witan
wǣdlum (dpl. m.) *beggar* 6/36 [wǣdla]
wǣdum (dpl. f.) *clothing, covering* 11/15, 22
 [wǣd]
wǣfersȳne (dsg. f.) *spectacle* 11/31 [wǣfersȳn]
wæl (nsg. n.) *slaughter, carnage* 2/42, 61, 127
 *9/65 *10/126, 303; wæle (dsg.) 10/279, 300
wælcyrian (npl. f.) *sorceress* 7/133 [wælcyrie]
wælfelda (dsg. m.) *battlefield* 9/51 [wælfeld]
wælhrēowan (asg. m.) *cruel, savage* 6/26;
 wælhrēowe (apl. f.) 7/36 [wælhrēow]
wælrǣste (asg. f.) *death in battle* 10/113
 [wælrǣst]
wælsliht (nsg. m.) *slaughter, carnage* 2/74
wælspere (asg. n.) *slaughterous spear* 10/322
wælstōwe (gsg. f.) *battlefield* 2/62, 75, 81,
 116, 129 *10/95; (dsg.) 9/43 *10/293
 [wælstōw]
Wælþēof (prn.) 2/152
wælwulfas (npl. m.) *slaughterous wolf,*
 warrior 10/96 [wælwulf]
wǣpen (nasg. n.) *weapon* 3/51, 53 *10/130,
 235, 252; wǣpnes (gsg.) 10/168; wǣpne
 (dsg.) 10/228; wǣpna (apl.) 10/83, 272, 308;
 wǣpnum (dpl.) 4/38 *10/10, 126
wǣpngewrixl (nsg. n.) *exchange of weapons,*
 armed encounter 7/81; wǣpengewrixles
 (gsg.) 9/51
wǣpnum → wǣpen
wǣran, wǣre, wǣren → bēon
Wǣrferð (prn.) 5/1
wǣrlīce (adv.) *warily, carefully* 7/158
wǣron, wǣrun, wæs → bēon
wæstmum (dpl. m.) *fruit* 3/40 [wæstm]
wǣtan (dsg. m.) *moisture, blood* 11/22 [wǣta]
wæter (nasg. n.) *water* 6/123–124, 128, 165
 *7/18 *9/55 *10/91, 98; wæteres (gsg.) 4/46;
 wætere (dsg.) 10/64, 96
wē (perspron. 2.npl.) *we* 1/8 *3/12, 19, 29–30,
 36, 40 etc. *5/10–11, 16, 20–21, 29–31, 38
 etc. *6/14, 107, 132 *7/11–15, 17, 21, 24, 38
 etc. *8/78, 104–106 *10/33–35, 40, 61,
 212–213 *11/70; ūre (gpl.) 2/110 *3/16
 *5/28, 31 *6/14 *7/49, 157–158, 163 *8/36,
 78 *10/232, 234, 240, 313–314; ūs (dapl.)
 3/10, 18, 22, 38, 153 *4/5–6, 8 *5/19, 29
 *6/13, 21, 160 *7/14, 41, 44, 46, 51 etc.
 *8/12, 78, 81, 104, 107 *9/68 *10/34, 39–40,
 60, 93, 233, 237 *11/73, 75, 147 ♦ poss. adj.:

ūran 2/118; **ūrne** (asg. m.) 10/58; **ūra** (gpl.)
3/14; **ūrum** (dpl.) 2/143 ∗6/101 ∗7/89 ∗8/91
∗10/56; (dsg. m.) 8/20

Wēalas (prn.) *the Welsh* 9/72

wealdan (7) *to rule, govern, control, cause*
10/83, 95, 168, 272; **gewēold** (sg.pt.) 6/29,
93; **wēoldan** (pl.pt.) 7/46

wealde (dsg. m.) *forest, wood* 9/65 [weald]

Wealdend (nasg. m.) *ruler, lord, God* 6/16
∗11/67, 111, 155; **Waldend** 10/173;
Wealdendes (gsg.) 11/17, 53; **Wealdende**
(dsg.) 11/121

wealhstod (nsg. m.) *interpreter, translator*
6/42; **wealhstodas** (npl.) 5/43

weall (asg. m.) *wall* 6/25

weallendan (psp. asg. m.) *to well up, seethe,
boil* 7/161 [weallan 7]

wealwigende (psp.) *to roll* 6/130; **wealweode**
(sg.pt.) 6/131 [wealwian II]

Weard (nasg. m.) *guardian, God* 3/95, 101
∗6/75 ∗11/91

wearð, wearþ → **weorðan**

wed (asg. n.) *pledge, oath* 7/158; (apl.) 7/76
[wedd]

wedbrycas (apl. m.) *pledge-breaking* 7/111
[wedbyrce]

wēdde (sg.pt.) *to rage* 3/56 [wēdan I]

weg (asg. m.) *way* 6/134 ∗11/88; **weges** (gsg.)
4/36; **wegum** (dpl.) 4/40 ♦ col.: **ealne weg**
(adv.) *always, continuously* 4/2, 8; **ealneg**
5/66

wegan (5) *to carry, bear* 3/53; **wēgon** (pl.pt.)
10/98

weges → **weg**

wegfarende (adj. nsg. m.) *wayfaring* 6/129

wegneste (dsg. n.) *viaticum, provision for a
journey* 3/160 [wegnest]

wēgon; wegum → **weg; wegan**

wel (adv.) *well, fully, properly* 2/132, 148
∗3/71, 120, 163 ∗5/51 ∗6/42, 46 ∗7/8 ∗8/8,
47, 49, 62, 80, 82, 96; **well** 11/129, 143

welan (asg. m.) *prosperity, riches* 5/29, 31
[wela]

welhwǣr (adv.) *(nearly) everywhere* 5/65;
gewelhwǣr 7/25

weligne (asg. m.) *rich* 8/37 [welig]

well → **wel**

welme (dsg. m.) *zeal* 3/138 [welm]

welwillendnesse (dsg. f.) *benevolence, good-
will* 8/38 [welwillendnes]

welwillendum (adj. dsg. n.) *benevolent* 6/37
[welwillende]

wendan (I) *to turn, go, change, translate* 5/35,
56 ∗10/316 ∗11/22; **wende** (1.sg.ps.) 10/252;

wenden (pl.ps. subj.) 5/46; **gewende** (sg.pt.)
6/78, 167; **gewænde** 8/16; **wendon** (pl.pt.)
5/41, 43–44 ∗10/193, 205; **gewændon** 8/74;
gewende (ptp.) 6/40

wēnde → **wēne**

wenden, wendon → **wendan**

wēndon → **wēne**

wēne (1.sg.ps.) *to think, believe, imagine* 5/14
∗11/135; (sg.ps. subj.) 7/40; **wēnde** (sg.pt.)
6/18 ∗10/239; **wēndon** (pl.pt.) 3/56 ∗5/36
∗8/52

wēofod (asg. n.) *altar* 1/13; **wīgbed** (apl.) 3/45,
63; **wīgbedo** 3/40

wēoldan → **wealdan**

Weonodland (pn.) *country of the Wends* 4/7,
9; **Weonoðland** 4/2; **Weonodlande** (dsg.)
4/10; **Winodlande** 4/13

wēop (sg.pt.) *to weep* 11/55 [wēpan 7]

weorc (asg. n.) *work, action, deed* 1/17 ∗3/97
∗7/158 ∗11/79; **weorcum** (dpl.) 6/46, 155,
168

weorode → **werod**

weorðan (3) *to become, be, happen* 5/37
∗7/16; **wurþest** (2.sg.ps.) 6/164; **wyrð** (sg.ps.)
7/5, 39; **weorþe** (sg.ps. subj.) 7/81; **weorðe**
7/82; **geweorþe** 7/81; **wurðe** 2/155; **wearð**
(sg.pt.) 2/93, 106, 111–112, 124 etc. ∗6/3–4,
23, 26, 32, 53, 66 etc. ∗7/104 ∗8/2, 53, 71,
91 ∗9/32, 65 ∗10/106, 113–114, 116, 135,
138, 202, 241, 288, 295; **wearþ** 2/15, 51, 61,
66–67 etc. ∗6/88, 146; **gewearð** 6/94 ∗7/72;
wurde (sg.pt. subj.) 1/15 ∗6/39 ∗10/1;
gewurde (sg.pt. subj.) 7/92; **wurdon** (pl.pt.)
2/41, 82, 113 ∗6/20, 118, 122, 125, 128, 178
∗10/186; **wurdun** 9/48; **geworden** (ptp.)
3/165 ∗7/59, 67, 118, 145 ∗8/54 ∗11/87

weorðe, weorþe → **weorðan**

weorðe (dsg. n.) *price* 7/71, 82; **weorþe** 7/73,
81 [weorð]

weorþe (adj. nsg. f.) *worthy, valuable, dear*
3/30; **wyrðe** 6/160; **wyrðes** (gsg. m.) 3/105

weorþian (II) *to honour, worship* 11/129;
wurðað (sg.ps.) 6/90; **weorðiað** (pl.ps.) 11/81;
wurðode (sg.pt.) 6/69, 74; **geweorþode**
11/90; **geweorðod** (ptp.) 11/15; **geweorðode**
11/94; **geweorðad** 3/67

weorðlīce (adv.) *worthily, honourably, nobly*
11/17; **wurðlīce** 10/279; **wurðlīcost** (sup.)
8/83

weorðscipe (dsg. m.) *honour, dignity* 7/99;
wurðscipes (gsg.) 8/85 [weorðscip]

weorðunge (dsg. f.) *honour, veneration* 7/21

weoruldhāde → **woruldhād**

wer (nasg. m.) *man* 6/129, 153, 180; **weres** (gsg.) 6/148; **weras** (npl.) 8/100

werede → **werod**

werede (sg.pt.) *to protect, defend* 2/12; **weredon** (pl.pt.) 10/82, 283 [werian II]

weres → **wer**

wergas (apl. m.) *criminal* 11/31 [wearg]

wērig (adj. nsg. m.) *weary, exhausted* 9/20; **wērige** (npl.) 10/303

werod (nasg. n.) *host, troop, army* 6/18 *10/64, 97, 102; **werode** (dsg.) 2/8 *6/9, 18, 105 *10/51; **weorode** 9/34 *11/69, 152; **werede** 2/80 *11/124; **weruda** (gpl.) 11/51

wesan (5) *to be* 11/110, 117 [see bēon]

Wesseaxe, Wesseaxna → **Westseaxan**

west (adv.) *westwards* 4/14 *10/97

Westmynstre (pn.) *Westminster* 2/91, 146

Westseaxan (prn.) *West Saxons* 6/81; **Westseaxe** 2/57, 86; **Westseaxna** (gpl.) 2/1, 47 *6/77; **Westsexena land** *kingdom of the West Saxons* 6/78

wiccan (npl. m.) *wizzard* 7/132 [wicca]

wicge (dsg. n.) *horse* 10/240 [wicg]

wīcing (asg. m.) *Viking* 10/139; **wīcinge** (dsg. m.) 7/81; **wīcinga** (gpl.) 10/26, 73, 97; **wīcingas** (apl.) 10/322; **wīcingum** (dpl.) 10/116

wīde (adv.) *widely, far and wide* 2/154 *6/151 *7/6, 11, 27, 31 etc. ♦ col.: **wīde and sīde** 7/118 *11/81

wīdgillan (adj. asg. m.) *wide-spread, extensive* 6/131 [wīdgil]

wīfa → **wīfes**

wīfcȳþþe (dsg. f.) *company of a woman* 2/8 [wīfcȳðu]

Wīferþ (prn.) 2/21

wīfes (gsg. n.) *woman* 2/14; **wīfa** (gpl.) 11/94 [wīf]

wiga (nsg. m.) *warrior* 10/210; **wigan** (asg.) 10/75, 235; (npl.) 10/79, 126, 302; **wigena** (gpl.) 10/135

wīgbed, wīgbedo → **wēofod**

wīge (dsg. n.) *war, battle* 5/7 *10/128, 193, 235, 252; **wigge** 10/10; **wīges** (gsg.) 9/20, 59 *10/73, 130 [wīg]

Wīgelmes (prn.) 10/300

wigena → **wiga**

wīgend (npl. m.) *warrior* 10/302

wīges, wigge → **wīge**

wīgheardne (adj. asg. m.) *brave in war* 10/75 [wīgheard]

wīgplegan (dsg. m.) *battle* 10/268, 316 [wīgplega]

wīgsmiþas (npl. m.) *warrior* 9/72 [wīgsmið]

wīhagan (asg. m.) *line of defence* 10/102

Wiht (pn.) *the Isle of Wight* 2/98

wiites → **wīte**

wīle → **hwīle**

wile → **willan** (2)

willa (nsg. m.) *will, desire, volition* 11/129; **willan** (gdasg.) 6/28, 35, 79, 159 *7/162

willan → **willa**

willan (1) (dsg. f.) *well, fountain* 3/4 [wille]

willan (2) (irr.) *to wish, desire, will* 7/128; **wille** (sg.ps.) 5/52, 62, 67 *7/66, 75 *8/111 *10/37, 221, 247, 317; **wylle** 10/216; **wylt** (2.sg.ps.) 6/164 *5/52, 62, 67 *7/65, 74 *8/111; (sg.ps. subj.) 5/17 *8/21, 34, 65, 107; **wilt** (2.sg.ps.) 8/26, 93; **wile** (sg.ps.) 6/13 *10/52 *11/107; **wylle** (sg.ps. subj.) 2/100 *11/1; **willað** (pl.ps.) 10/35, 46; **wyllað** 4/26 *10/40; **wolde** (sg.pt.) 1/1, 14, 17 *2/6, 101, 136 etc. *3/2–3, 33, 42 *5/66 *6/29, 50, 72, 79, 158, 173 *7/64 *8/35, 64, 80 *10/11, 129, 160 *11/34, 41, 113; **woldest** (2.sg.pt.) 1/20 *8/32; **woldon** (pl.pt.) 2/119, 127, 131, 133, 149 *3/137 *5/38 *10/207 *11/68; **woldan** 3/4, 17 ♦ neg.: **nelle** (1.sg.ps.) 10/246; **nellað** (pl.ps.) 7/127; **nolde** (sg.pt.) 2/17, 137, 143 *10/6, 9, 275; **noldest** (2.sg.pt.) 1/26; **noldon** (pl.pt.) 2/25, 27 *5/31, 35 *6/114 *10/81, 185, 201

wilnigende (psp.) *to desire* 6/35 [wilnian II]

wilnunga (dsg. f.) *desire, wish* 5/37

wilsumnesse (dsg. f.) *devotion* 3/166 [wilsumnes]

wilt → **willan** (2)

Wiltūne (pn.) *Wilton, Wiltshire* 2/80

winas → **wine**

Winburnan (pn.) *Wimborne, Dorset* 2/78

windan (3) *to fly, fly up, brandish* 10/322; **wand** (sg.pt.) 10/43; **wundon** (pl.pt.) 6/144 *10/106

wine (nsg. m.) *lord, friend* 10/250; **winas** (apl.) 10/228

winedrihten (asg. m.) *lord* 10/248, 263

winemāgas (apl. m.) *dear friend* 10/306 [winemæg]

winnað, winnende → **gewinnan**

Winodlande → **Weonodland**

winsumum → **wynsumu**

Wintanceastre (pn.) *Winchester* 2/34 *6/89

winter (nasg. m.) *winter; year* 3/28 *4/47; **wintres** (gsg.) 3/27; **wintre** (dsg.) 2/54; **wintra** (gpl.) 2/6, 34, 44 *3/27; **wintrum** (dpl.) 10/210

wintersetl (asg. n.) *winter-quarters* 2/46, 53, 87, 89

wintertīde (dsg. f.) *winter-time* 3/23 [wintertīd]

wintra, wintre, wintres, wintrum → **winter**

wiotan, wiotena → **wita**

wiotonne → **witan**

wīs (adj. nsg. m.) *wise, learned* 10/219; **wīse** (apl.) 5/43

wīsan (dasg. f.) *way, fashion, order* 1/14, 16 *3/115, 137 *7/26, 56 [wīse]

wīsdōm (nasg. m.) *knowledge, learning, wisdom* 5/10, 18, 28, 31, 38; **wīsdōme** (dsg.) 5/7

wīse → **wīs**

Wīsle (pn.) *the River Vistula* 4/8, 10, 13

Wīslemūða (pn.) *the mouth of the Vistula* 4/14; **Wīslemūðan** 4/8

wīslic (adj. nsg. n.) *wise* 3/18

wīsode (sg.pt.) *to guide* 10/141 [wīsian II]

Wīstān (prn.) 10/297

wiste, wiston → **witan**

wita (nsg. m.) *counsellor, adviser* 3/20; **witan** (dpl.) 6/41; **wiotan** (npl.) 2/1, 47 *5/2; **wiotena** (gpl.) 5/33; **witum** (dpl.) 3/7; **wytum** 3/3

wīta; witan → **wīte; wita**

witan (prps.) *to know, understand, perceive* 7/64 *8/21, 27, 32; **witanne** (infl.inf.) 7/67; **wiotonne** 5/46; **wite** (2.sg.ps. subj.) 8/22, 27; **witan** (pl.ps.) 7/17, 72, 103, 152; **wāt** (1.sg.ps.) 3/16 *6/14, 159; (3.sg.ps.) 10/94; **wāst** (2.sg.ps.) 8/48; **wiste** (sg.pt.) 3/56 *10/24; **wiston** (pl.pt.) 3/156 *5/26 ♦ neg.: **nāt** (1.sg.pt.) 8/18, 21; **nāst** (2.sg.pt.) 8/48

wīte (dasg. n.) *punishment, torment* 11/61; **wītes** 7/161; **wiites** 3/132; **wītu** (napl.) 5/19; **wīta** (gpl.) 11/87

Wītland (pn.) 4/9

witodlīce (adv.) *certainly* 6/78

wītu → **wīte**

witum → **wita**

wið (prep. (a.g.d.i.)) *to, towards, with, against* 2/107, 126 *3/91, 137 *6/13–14, 25, 129, 144 *7/52, 69, 71, 73 etc. *8/8 *10/8, 31, 35, 39 etc.; **wiþ** 2/39, 43, 48, 51 etc. *6/75 *9/9, 52; **uuiþ** 2/6

wiþerlēan (nsg. n.) *requital* 10/116

wiþersæce (dsg. f.) *apostasy* 6/40 [wiðersæc]

wiðfeaht (sg.pt.) *to fight against* 6/9 [wiðfeohtan 3]

wiðmetenesse (dsg. f.) *comparison* 3/22 [wiðmetennes]

wiðsacan (6 (d.a.)) *to renounce, forsake* 3/42

wiðstandan (6) *to resist* 6/18

wlance (adj. npl.) *proud, exulting* 9/72 *10/205; **wlancan** (dsg. m.) 10/240; **wlancne** (asg. m.) 10/139 [wlanc]

wlāt (sg.pt.) *to look* 10/172 [wlītan 1]

wōd → **wadan**

wōdnysse (dsg. f.) *madness* 6/126 [wōdnes]

wōdon → **wadan**

wōdum (dpl. m.) *madman* 6/131 [wōda]

wōhdōmas (apl. m.) *unjust judgement* 7/146 [wōhdōm]

wōhgestrēona (gpl. n.) *ill-gotten gains* 7/146 [wōhgestrēon]

wolcnum (dpl. m.n.) *cloud* 11/53, 55 [wolcen]

woldan, wolde, woldest, woldon → **willan** (2)

wommum (dpl. m.) *stain, sin* 11/14 [womm]

word (nasg. n.) *word, command, speech* 5/57 *7/157 *10/168 *11/35; **wordes** (gsg.) 7/53, 104; **worde** (dsg.) 5/57 *11/111; **word** (napl.) 3/1, 35, 94, 105, 114, 168–169 *8/14 *11/27; **worda** (gpl.) 8/86; **wordum** (dpl.) 3/20, 31, 105 *5/1 *10/26, 43, 210, 250 *11/97; **wordon** 10/306

worhtan, worhte, worhton → **wyrcan**

worold (nsg. f.) *world* 7/3; **worolde** (dsg.) 7/4, 6, 55, 57–58, 162; **worulde** 3/72, 145 *5/20 *6/71, 91, 167, 174, 177, 180 *10/174 *11/133

woroldscame (dsg. f.) *public disgrace* 7/95, 98 [woroldscamu]

worolstrūderas (npl. m.) *pillager, spoliator* 7/133 [worolstrūdere]

woruldcara (apl. f.) *worldly care* 6/34 [woruldcearu]

woruldcundra (adj. gpl.) *worldly* 5/3 [woruldcund]

worulde → **worold**

woruldgesǣlig (adj. nsg. m.) *prosperous* 10/219

woruldhād (asg. m.) *secular life* 3/119; **weoruldhāde** (dsg.) 3/80

woruldðinga (gpl. n.) *worldly affair* 5/18 [woruldðing]

wrāðra (adj. gpl.) *wrathful, cruel* 11/51 [wrāð]

wræc, wrǣce, wrec → **wrecan**

wrecan (5) *to avenge* 10/248, 258; **gewrecan** 10/208, 263; **wræc** (sg.pt.) 2/5; **wrec** 10/279; **wrǣce** (sg.pt. subj.) 10/257

wreoton → **wrīte**

wrīte (sg.ps. subj.) *to write (down)* 5/67; **wreoton** (pl.pt.) 3/125 [wrītan 1]

wrixendlīce (adv.) *in turn* 3/157

wudu (nasg. m.) *wood; cross, tree* 1/9, 11, 14, 10/193 *11/27

wuldor (nsg. n.) *wonder, glory, splendour, heaven* 6/180; **wuldres** (gsg.) 11/14, 90, 97, 133; **wuldre** (dsg.) 6/177 *11/135, 143, 155

wuldorfæder (gsg.) *father of glory, God* 3/97

wuldre, wuldres → **wuldor**

wulf (asg. m.) *wolf* 9/65

Wulfmǣr (prn.) 10/113, 155; **Wulmǣr** 10/183

Wulfstān (prn.) 4/1 *10/75; **Wulfstānes** (gsg.) 10/155; **Wulfstāne** (dsg.) 10/79

wunade, wunað → **wunian**

wund (adj. nsg. m.) *wounded* 10/113, 144

wunde (asg. f.) *wound* 10/139, 271; **wundum** (dpl.) 10/293, 303; **wundun** 9/43 [wund]

wundon → **windan**

wundor (nsg. n.) *marvel, miracle* 6/171 *7/103; **wundra** (gpl.) 3/97 *6/168, 179

wundrigende (psp.) *to wonder, be astonished at* 6/118; **wundrode** (sg.pt.) 3/147; **wundrade** 5/33; **wundroden** (pl.pt.) 6/148 [wundrian II]

wundum, wundun → **wunde**

wunedon → **wunian**

wunian (II) *to dwell, live, remain* 11/121, 143; **wunað** (sg.ps.) 6/27, 107; **wuniaþ** (pl.ps.) 11/135; **wunode** 2/3 *6/86; **wunade** (sg.pt.) 2/4; **wunedon** (pl.pt.) 11/3, 155

wununge (dsg. f.) *dwelling* 8/84 [wunung]

wurde, wurdon, wurdun → **weorðan**

wurðað → **weorþian**

wurðe, wurþest → **weorðan**

wurðlīce, wurðlīcost → **weorðlīce**

wurðlicum (adj. dsg. n.) *honourable, worthy* 8/18 [weorðlic]

wurðmynt (asg. f.) *dignity, esteem, honour* 6/174; **wurðmynte** (dsg.) 6/11, 19, 27, 89 [weorðmynd]

wurðode → **weorþian**

wurðscipes → **weorðscipe**

wutan, wuton → **uton**

wydewan (npl. f.) *widow* 7/32 [wuduwe]

wyllað, wylle → **willan** (2)

Wyllelm (pn.) *William the Conqueror* 2/101, 122, 125, 135, 153; **Wyllelm Bastard** 2/101

wylt → **willan** (2)

wynna (gpl. f.) *joy, pleasure, delight* 10/174; **wynnum** (dpl. f.) 11/15 [wynn]

wynsumu (adj. npl.) *pleasant, delightful* 3/124; **winsumum** (dsg. m.) 8/42, 56

wyrcan (I) *to do, make, prepare, perform, cause* 3/67, 74, 77 *10/102 *11/65;

gewyrcan 4/44 *10/81, 264; **wyrcð** (sg.ps.) 7/93; **wyrcað** (pl.ps.) 4/45; **gewyrcað** 7/162; **worhte** (sg.pt.) 6/144; **worhton** (pl.pt.) 2/123, 154; **worhtan** 6/25 *7/50, 104; **geworhton** 11/31; **geworhte** 3/133–134; (ptp.) 7/113; **geworht** (ptp.) 3/71

wyrd (nsg. f.) *event, fate* 11/74; **wyrda** (gpl.) 11/51

wyrnde (sg.pt.) *to refuse, withhold* 10/118; **wyrndon** (pl.pt.) 9/24 [wiernan I (g.)]

wyrre, wyrsan → **wyrse**

wyrse (adj. nsg. n. comp.) *worse* 7/4; **wyrre** 2/134; **wyrsan** (apl. f.) 7/152

wyrsedan (pl.pt.) *to grow worse* 7/30 [wyrsian II]

wyrð → **weorðan**

wyrðe, wyrðes → **weorþe**

wytum → **wita**

Y

yfel (asg. n.) *evil, wickedness* 7/10; **yfeles** (gsg.) 10/133

yfelan (adj. dsg. m.n.) *evil, wicked* 7/118, 124; **yfele** (npl.) *evil, wicked* 8/81 [yfel]

yfele (adv.) *wrongly* 8/44

yfeles → **yfel**

yfelian (II) *to become bad, grow worse* 7/5; **yflade** (sg.pt.) 2/155

yfelnysse (asg. f.) *wickedness, depravity* 6/8 [yfelnes]

yflade; ylcan, ylce → **yfelian; ilca**

ylde (dasg. f.) *age* 3/80 *6/94

ymb (prep. (a.)) *about, with regard to, after* 2/6, 30 *5/8–9; **ymbe** 7/9 *8/108 *9/5 *10/214; **embe** 6/28, 132, 154 *10/249, 271
   ♦ col.: **embe lang** (adv.) *finally* 6/132

ymbclypte (sg.pt.) *to embrace* 11/42 [ymbclyppan I]

ymbe → **ymb**

ymbsette (ptp.) *to surround* 3/46 [ymbsettan I]

ymbsittendan (npl.) *neighbour* 8/15, 52 [ymbsittend]

yrhðo (asg. f.) *cowardice* 10/6; **yrhðe** (dsg.) 7/147

yrmð (nsg. f.) *misery, hardship, crime* 7/72; **yrmþe** (gsg.) 7/68; **yrmðe** (asg.) 7/95; **yrmða** (apl.) 7/14

yrnende → **irnan**

yrre (1) (nasg. n.) *anger* 7/39, 77, 79, 85 etc.

yrre (2) (adj. nsg. m.) *angry, fierce* 10/44, 253

ȳtmǣstan (adj. apl.) *last* 3/169 [ȳtmǣst]

Middle English Glossary

a → God; he; ilk; on

a (1) (art., pron.) *a, an* **an** 1/42, 46, 62, 75, 84
*2/39 *4/57 *5/14, 175 *6/27, 29, 74, 82 etc.
*7/3, 51, 131, 169 etc. *8/4 *10.1/5, 10, 14,
18 *12/88 *13/62, 95, 102, 159 etc.; **ane** 3/3
*4/19 *5/18, 28, 81, 96–97 *8/5 *11/4, 34,
36, 38 *14/2, 12, 16–17 etc.; **anne** 8/15; **o**
8/133 *10.2/14 *13/238, 465

a (2) (interj.) *ah, oh* 4/24, 26 *8/66, 86
*12/357

abasshed (adj.) *abashed* 12/177

abbeie (sb.) *abbey* 5/82, 98; **abbeiȝe** 5/97

abbot (sb.) 1/68; **abbotes** (gsg.) 1/60

abbotrice (sb.) *abbacy* 1/68; ◆ contr. art.:
þabbotrice 1/75

abegge → abugge

Abell (prn.) 12/306

a-bide (inf.) *to wait (for), remain, stay* 5/226;
tabide 9/93; **abide** (imp.) 12/213; **abyt**
(sg.ps.) 4/23

abill (adj.) *able* 11/101

Abiron (prn.) 12/309

abite (sb.) *attire, garb* 7/3

abiten (ptp.) *to bite to death* 8/102

abof, a-boue → above

abought → about

'about' (adv., prep.) **abought** 10.10/17;
a-boute 5/33; **aboute** 6/67, 91, 118, 138,
227 *7/31, 41 *10.6/14 *12/7 *13/77, 177,
212, 372; **a-bouten** 5/183, 215; **abouten**
8/8; **abute** 9/19; **abuten** 1/3; **abuton** 1/40,
46; **obout** 11/74

'above' abof 6/265; **a-boue** 5/33; **abufe**
14/177; **oboue** 11/48

abreyde (sg.pt.) *to wake up* 13/414; **breyde**
13/509

Absolon (prn.) 13/80

Abstinence (sb.) 7/241

abufe → above

abugge (inf.) *to pay for, atone for* 8/104;
abuggen 10.7/19; **abegge** 13/162

abute, abuten, abuton → about

abyt → a-bide

ac (conj.) *but, and* 1/23, 31, 60 *3/18, 24
*4/21, 42, 47, 61 etc. *5/198 *7/6, 62, 78,
212 *8/30, 33, 42, 53 etc.; **ak** 4/48; **ake**
5/13, 77, 83, 100–101 etc.; **hac** 3/8; **oc** 1/48,
58, 63, 87 *2/10, 48

accidie (sb.) *fit of sloth* 7/218

acorden (inf.) *to agree (on)* 7/187; **acordaunt**
(psp.) 13/37; **acordede** (sg.pt.) 1/17

acoursed (ptp.) *to curse* 8/28

Adam (prn.) 4/17; **Adame** 12/45, 49, 385

a-doun (adv.) *down, below* 5/16; **adoun** 6/41
*7/64 *8/19, 29, 38, 43, 59, 87, 97 *10.1/10
*10.8/16 *13/245; **adun** 9/115; **adune** 9/114

a-dounward → dounward

a-drad (ptp.) *to be afraid (of), fearful* 5/108;
adrad 13/61

adrenche (inf.) *to drown* 4/12 *9/76;
adrencheþ (pl.ps.) 4/13; **adreynten** (pl.pt.)
4/10

adun, adune; afalle → a-doun; fall

a-feng (sg.pt.) *to receive, accept* 5/54

a-ferde (sg.pt.) *to frighten* 5/68; **aferd** (ptp.)
13/319; **afered** 10.6/16

affers (sb.pl.) *affair* 11/96

affies (pl.ps.) *to put* 12/29

afingret (ptp.adj.) *very hungry* 8/1–2, 55, 95,
129

a-forcede (sg.pt.) *to apply oneself* 5/56

after (adv., prep.) *after, afterwards* 5/46, 161
*6/42, 161, 169 *8/26, 31, 54 *9/85, 117
*13/178, 438; **aftir** 7/14, 16, 50, 52 *12/26,
242, 376, 397; **aftur** 5/8, 154, 163, 206
*7/162, 179, 193, 202, 218; **efter** 1/13; **efter**
1/5, 36 *4/25, 70, 75 *11/102 *14/23; ◆
compd.: **efterþan** 4/27

'again' agane 14/209; **agayn** 6/173 *13/256,
291, 344, 440, 498, 503; *in return for*
13/410; **agayne** 12/11, 33; **ogayne** 11/99;
a-ȝein 5/89, 166, 171, 187; **aȝein** 5/186;
aȝeyn 10.3/43; **a-yen** 4/87; **ayen** 4/88

'against' aganis 14/134; **agaynste** 12/92,
280; **agænes** 1/32; **agenes** 1/15–16, 18;
a-ȝein 5/24, 70, 105, 117, 167, 170; **aȝeinest**
5/76; **aȝen** 9/78; **aȝenes** 9/28

aganis → against

agast (adj.) *afraid, fearful* 13/491 *14/27;
a-gaste 5/37, 150; **gast** 6/112

agayn, agayne; agaynste → again; against

agænes → against

age (sb.) 9/32 *13/57, 91, 195

agenes → against

ago → go

agraiþi (inf.) *to prepare* 4/66; **agrayþed** (ptp.)
4/68

agreved (ptp.) *to injure* 13/405

agrise (inf.) *to be afraid* 8/120
a-ȝein, aȝein → again; against
aȝeinest → against
aȝen, aȝenes → against
aȝeyn → again
ah (interj.) *ah, oh* 10.3/34, 40, 46
ahte (sb.) *danger* 10.3/42
ai → ay
Ailmer (prn.) 8/136
air, airlie → early
ak, ake → ac
akelþ (sg.ps.) *to cool, make cold* 3/27
a-knowe → know
akþ (sg.ps.) *to ache* 4/29
al → all (1, 2)
alas (interj.) *ah, alas* 5/77, 83 *10.4/31
    *10.6/36, 55; allas 4/28 *11/105 *12/198,
    347 *13/299, 304, 308, 333, 425, 442
Alayn → Aleyn
albidene (adv.) *entirely* 11/113
ald → old
alday (adv.) *all the time* 13/126
Aldewingle (pn.) 1/80
Aldred (prn.) 5/46, 50
ale (sb.) 7/43, 158, 176, 194, 235 *13/361,
    371, 386
Alexander (prn.) 1/27
Aleyn (prn.) 13/237, 240, 242, 246 etc.; Alayn
    13/255, 297, 313, 412, 497
algate (adv.) *at least* 13/186
al-huet (pron.) *so much* 4/29
a-liue (adj.) *alive* 5/222; aliue 8/92 *9/51, 90
all (1) (adj., pron.) al; alle; ælle 1/28; ♦ col.: al
    hayl (interj.) *good day* 13/246; alre fyrst
    (adv.) *first of all* 1/16 [see alþeruerst]
all (2) (adv.) *all, entirely* 12/57, 139, 264; al
    2/4, 13, 29 *9/22, 55, 84, 97 *10.1/12, 15
    *10.3/43 *10.4/5, 8, 10 *10.5/3 *10.6/25,
    33–34, 49 *11/83, 104 *12/120 *13/118,
    366, 476
allas; alle → alas; all (1)
allegeance (sb.) *agreement* 14/78
allegge (inf.) *to expound* 12/277
all-if (conj.) *even if* 11/93
allowe (inf.) *to embrace, accept* 12/330
all-thing (pron.) *in every respect* 11/101
allway → alway
allye (inf.) *to make an alliance* 13/169
almaist (adv.) *almost* 14/155
almes → sake
almichti (adj.) *almighty* 3/35; almyhty 7/228
almoost (adv.) *almost* 13/118, 442–443, 472
almus; almyhty → ælmes; almichti

almichti (adj.) *almighty* 3/35; almyhty 7/228
aloft (adv.) *up, above* 7/211, 225; alofte 6/222
along (prep.) 5/224
alpi (adj.) *single* 8/66
alre → all (1)
als, alse → also; as; as-tit
also (adv.) 2/2 *3/17, 27 *5/55, 79, 87, 176,
    181, 205 *7/46 *8/77, 109 *12/87, 118, 285
    *13/94, 242, 249, 384, 480, 518; al-so 5/21,
    47, 83, 91, 109, 119, 128, 168, 185, 193,
    209, 216; als 6/57 *12/28; alsuo (adv.) *just
    as* 4/15, 47; alswa 13/309
alsuic (adj.) *just as* 1/22
alsuo, alswa → also
al-to (adv.) *entirely, (all) too* 5/74, 78; alto 2/4
alþeruerst (adv.) *first of all* 4/30 [see alre fyrst]
alway (adv.) *always* 12/150, 164, 304; alwey
    13/121, 199; allway 12/168
Alysoun (prn.) 10.1/6
am → be
Amen (interj.) 9/136 *10.4/51 *10.5/61
amend (inf.) 11/20; a-mende 5/162; a-mendi
    5/170
amendement (sb.) *compensation* 13/409
amidde (adv.) *half-way down* 8/121
amidward (adv.) *in the middle of* 8/137
among (adv., prep.) 6/253, 260 *7/88, 236
    *8/133 *9/40, 129, 134 *10.4/44; a-mong
    5/147, 221; emang 12/262, 301; enmang
    1/12
amounteth (sg.ps.) *to amount to* 13/125
amycabill (adj.) *friendly* 14/80
an → a (1) and; on
Anaball (prn.) 12/113
and (conj.) ande 6/20, 57, 95; ant 10.1/1, 6, 8,
    10–11, 14 *10.2/5, 8, 12 *10.3/3, 26, 45
    *10.4/2, 6, 9 etc. *10.5/5, 7, 11 etc. *10.6/5,
    9, 17 etc. *10.7/4, 6–7, 11 etc. *10.8/6–7,
    10, 15 etc.; an 1/2–3 *4/3, 37 *5/35
Andreas → Saints
ane; aneuch → a (1) enough
anger (sb.) 13/108
angerlie (adv.) *angrily* 14/186
angrie (adj.) *angry* 14/12
anhet (sg.ps.) *to warm, make hot* 3/33; anheet
    (ptp.) 3/34, 40
anhongeþ (sg.ps.) *to hang* 4/32
a-niȝt (adv.) *at night* 5/216
ani; anis → any; at; ones
ani-þing → anything
ankeres (sb.pl.) *anchorite* 7/30
anne; anodir → a (1) another
a-non (adv.) *immediately, at once* 5/108, 155,
    191; anon 7/111, 113 *9/46 *10.8/16

*13/32, 115, 162, 241 etc.; **anoon** 13/140;
onane 11/77
another (adj., pron.) 13/406, 431; **anodir**
12/87
anoureden (pl.pt.) *honoured* 5/185
'answer' (vb.) **answerien** (inf.) 5/110;
onsware 6/62; **answere** (sg.ps.) 13/135;
ansuereþ (sg.ps.) 4/73; **onswarez** 6/173;
answerd (sg.pt.) 11/49; (ptp.) 13/352;
answerde (sg.pt.) 3/7 *13/264, 412, 416;
answerit 14/32
answere (sb.) *answer* 5/126
answerien, answerit → **answer**
ant → **and**
any (pron., adj.) 6/24, 44, 72, 78, 87, 124
*10.7/1 *10.8/1 *11/53 *12/320 *13/150,
194, 378; **ani** 1/35 *5/172 *6/120; **eni** 9/100;
enie 5/106; **eny** 4/25 *7/159, 239 *10.1/16
*13/344; **ony** 14/168, 191
anything (adj., pron.) 11/116; **ani-þing** 5/181
apart (adv.) 7/185
ape (sb.) 13/159, 426
aperseiuede (sg.pt.) *to observe, notice* 8/107
apert (adj.) *clear, telling* 5/184
appeirit → **appere**
appere (inf.) *to become clear, appear* 12/368;
appeirit (sg.pt.) 14/65
Aprill (prn.) *April* 13/1; **Aueril** 10.1/1
aquenche (inf.) *to satisfy, assuage* 8/7, 56
ar → **be; er**
arbitreres (sb.pl.) *arbiter, judge* 7/183
Archedefell (prn.) 12/308
Architriclin (prn.) 3/16, 19
arctand (psp.) *to incite, induce* 14/202
are, aren → **be; er**
a-rere (inf.) *to raise up, erect, build* 5/31, 97,
99; **arerde** (sg.pt.) 5/67; **arered** (ptp.) 10.6/15
arere (adv.) *backwards* 7/206
arered → **a-rere**
argument (sb.) 14/54; **argumentes** (pl.)
13/347
aright (adv.) *properly, truly* 13/478; **aryht**
10.4/24
arise (inf.) 4/22 *8/120 *13/478; **arisen** 8/132;
a-risen 5/167; **aryse** 7/188, 193; **arist**
(sg.ps.) 4/15, 24; **ariseþ** (pl.ps.) 4/92, (imp.)
8/135; **arizeþ** (pl.ps.) 4/79; **a-ros** (sg.pt.) 5/41,
222; **aros** 5/155 *9/27 *10.5/46
ariue (inf.) *to arrive, land* 9/18, 123; **ariuede**
(sg.pt.) 9/127
arizeþ → **arise**
arm (sb.) 13/428
armes (sb. pl.) *arms, weapon* 6/68

arn → **be**
Arnoldin (prn.) 9/92, 117, 119
a-ros, aros → **arise**
arowe (adv.) *one after the other* 9/115
array (sb.) *clothing, outfit, appearance* 13/41
arrerage (sb.) *arrears* 13/58
art → **be**
art (sb.) *knowledge, arts* 13/280, 321, 346
Arthur (prn.) *King Arthur* 6/26; **Arthure**
6/117; **Arthurez** (gsg.) 6/29; **Arthour** (prn.)
6/37, 40; **Arthour** (prn.) 6/37, 40; **Arþer**
6/254; **Arþour** 6/62; **Arþures** 6/96
aryht; aryse → **aright; arise**
as → **that**
as (conj.) **ase** 3/14, 29, 31 *4/3, 16, 36–37 etc.
*5/2, 8, 31, 36–37 etc. *10.3/8 *10.5/1, 52
*10.8/32; **als** 1/3 *11/2, 10, 22, 26 etc.
*12/73–74, 78, 80, 306 etc. *13/401, 541
*14/52, 165, 191; **alse** 1/22, 38, 76
ascuth; ase → **ask; as**
asemoche (pron., adj.) *as much* 4/96
ashamed (ptp.) 7/223
ask (inf., sg.ps.) 6/60 *11/15, 119 *14/109;
esche (inf.) 5/146; **ascuth** (sg.ps.) 7/21; **aske**
11/112; **axe** (sg.ps.) 8/26; **asked** (pt.) 6/180
*11/57, 59, 110; **askede** 7/155; **axede** 9/105;
askyng (sb.) 6/110, 136
askapie (inf.) *to escape* 4/74; **schaippit** (sg.pt.)
14/143
aske, asked, askede → **ask**
askez (sb.pl.) *ashes* 6/2
askyng; aslaȝe → **ask; a-slouȝ**
aslepe (adj.) *asleep* 9/22 *13/507
a-slouȝ (sg.pt.) *to slay, kill* 5/74, 99; **aslaȝe**
(ptp.) 9/116
aspele (inf.) *to spare, save* 7/233
assaut (sb.) *assault* 6/1
assay (inf.) *to taste, try* 10.10/20; **assaye** 7/158
assende (inf.) *to ascend* 12/32
assente (sb.) *assent, agreement* 12/170, 310
asshen (sb.) *ashes* 13/106
assoylen (inf.) *to assoil* 7/68
as-tit (adv.) *immediately* 6/31; **als tit** 11/77;
tite 6/86; **tyte** 12/332
astored (ptp. adj.) *provided* 13/65
astrangli (inf.) *to strangle, kill* 4/16
Astrotte (prn.) 12/113
asyde (adv.) *sidewards* 7/206
at → **best; full** (2)
at (prep.) 1/3 *3/6, 20 *4/83 *5/23, 230 *6/1,
51, 55 etc. *7/38, 43, 132, 201, 209, 230
*8/11, 113 *9/89, 102, 107 *10.3/33
*10.4/48 *11/90, 95, 106 *12/258 *13/20,
23, 42, 79 etc. *14/17, 22, 58, 74 etc.; **æt**

1/1, 26; **at** *to, from* 11/3, 79; ♦ col., compd.:
at anis (adv.) *at once* 14/14; **atanes** 13/298; ♦
contr.: **ate** *at the* 4/31, 54 *5/82; **atþe** 5/86,
179; **atþon** 5/223
aton (adv.) *together* 13/421
a-trayt (adv.) *with pleasure* 4/22
atte → **best, full, last**
atteynted (ptp.) *to test* 12/278
attle (sg.ps.) *to intend* 6/27
atþon → **at**
atwene (adv.) *in(to) two parts, a-two* 7/114
atywede (sg.pt.) *to reveal* 1/87
athel (sb.) *nobleman* 6/5
Aþelbrus (prn.) 9/121, 124
athes → **othþ**
Aþulf (prn.) 9/16, 20, 40–41, 45, 80, 128;
  Aþulfes (gsg.) 9/92
aþurst (ptp.) *thirsty* 8/33
auditour (sb.) *auditor* 13/50
auen; auenture → **owen; aventure**
Aueril → **Aprill**
auise (sg.ps.subj.) *to take counsel* 14/44
auncetrye (sb.) *(noble) lineage* 13/206
aune → **owen**
aungell (sb.) *angel* 12/339, 389
aunte (sb.) *aunt* 7/241
aunter → **aventure**
auntre (inf.) *to take a risk* 13/433; **auntred**
  (sg.pt.) 13/429
auter (sb.) *altar* 5/14, 17
avauntyng (sb.) *boasting* 13/108
aventure (sb.) *adventure, incident* 13/25;
  auenture 3/5 *6/37, 276 *8/35; **aunter** 6/27;
  awenture 6/29
avyse (sg.ps.) *be careful* 13/412
awake (inf.) 7/196 *13/439; (imp.) 9/23; **awak**
  (imp.) 13/486, 512
away (adv.) 12/154 *13/295; **awaye** 12/171;
  a-wei 5/198; **oway** 11/80, 86
awecche (inf.) *to wake up* 8/134; **a-weiȝhte**
  (sg.pt.) 5/223, 225
a-wei → **away**
a-weiȝhte → **awecche**
awen → **owen**
awenture → **aventure**
awin, awne → **owen**
awonderd (ptp.) *to wonder* 11/52
awreke (ptp.) *to avenge* 8/32 [see wreke]
ax (sb.) *axe* 6/76, 203, 208, 264; **axe** 6/117
axe, axede; ay → **ask; ey**
ay (adv.) *always, continuously* 5/201 *6/26
  *11/80, 111 *12/223, 239, 243, 293, 380
  *13/153, 254, 352, 528 *14/3, 52; **ai** 2/6

a-yen, ayen → **again**
ayenward (adv.) *contrariwise* 4/85
ayled (ptp.) *to trouble* 6/225
Aylmare (prn.) 9/117

Æ

æie (sb.) *fear* 1/8
ælc; ælle → **each; all** (1)
ælmes (sb.pl.) *almes* 1/56; **almus** 11/77
ær (adv.) *before, earlier* 1/81
ærcebiscop → **erchebischop**
æt → **at**
æure; æuric → **ever; every**

B

baar → **bear**
bachelers (sb.pl.) *bachelor (acad.)* 7/85
bad, badde, bade → **bid**
bagge (sb.) *bag* 7/42
baid → **bide**
baill (sb.) *stronghold, prison* 12/195
baillif (sb.) 13/59
baine (adj.) *quick, ready* 11/99
baith → **both**
bakbiteres (sb.pl.) *backbiter, slanderer* 3/30
bakeres (sb.pl.) *baker* 7/140
bakwart (adv.) *backwards* 14/28
baldeliche → **boldely**
Baldeswelle (pn.) *Bawdeswell, Norfolk* 13/76
baldly → **boldely**
Balduin (prn.) 1/17; **Balduin de Reduers**
  1/16
bale (sb.) *suffering, prison* 12/161, 275, 293
balke (sb.) *balk* 13/144
Bamburn (pn.) *Bamburgh, Northumberland*
  11/36
bandis → **bonde**
banere (sb.) *banner, signal* 5/67 *9/57
banes → **God**
bank (sb.) *river bank, field* 11/48 *14/37;
  bonkkes (pl.) 6/14
baptiste (sg.pt.) *to baptise* 12/75
bar, bare, baren → **bear**
bare (adj.) *plain, simple, naked* 6/64, 77; (adv.)
  plainly 6/252
baret (sb.) *fighting, strife* 6/21, 140
bargaynes (sb.pl.) *strife, conflict* 7/196
barlay (adv.) *in return (?)* 6/83
baronage (sb.) *country* 9/11
barones (sb.pl.) *baron, nobleman* 5/79 *7/138
baronie (sb.) *barony* 5/71

barre (sb.) *court* 7/132
barres (sb.pl.) *bolt* 12/190
Bastard → **Willam**
bataile (sb.) *battle, war* 5/81, 92; **bataille**
  5/82, 97–98; **batayl** 6/64; **batayle** 7/108,
  112; **batailes** (pl.) 12/131
bathe → **both**
bathed (sg.pt.) *to bathe* 13/3
baþieres (sb.pl.) *bath-tub* 3/13
baundoun (sb.) *control, power* 10.1/4
Bayard (prn.) 13/339
bayst (sg.pt.) *to be dismayed* 6/163
bayþen (inf.) *to grant* 6/114
bæron → **bear**
be → **by; nihtes; smit**
be (inf.) **bee** 12/7 *13/411; **been** 13/110, 207,
  268, 432; **ben** 1/22, 86 *2/24 *7/87, 180
  *8/29, 53, 59, 81, 86, 91 *10.5/59; **bene**
  10.5/52; **beo** 5/76, 160, 232 *9/13 *10.4/20;
  beon 5/18, 154 *9/130; **buen** 10.1/9; **by**
  4/29, 53, 58; ◆ 1.sg.ps.: **am** 4/22, 73 *5/130
  *6/141, 143, 175 *8/52, 67, 80, 95 etc.
  *10.2/1–2 *10.6/52 *10.9/1–2 *11/7, 9–10,
  19 *12/111, 237 *13/91, 139 *14/45, 59,
  76–77 etc.; **is** 13/255, 269, 310, 426, 463; ◆
  2.sg.ps.: **art** 3/41 *5/44, 128 *7/225 *8/65,
  70, 75, 125 *10.4/27 *14/86; **ert** 11/66; **is**
  13/313, 352; ◆ 3.sg.ps.: **is ys** 4/81 *7/214
  *10.3/26, 28 *10.6/40 *10.8/23 *10.10/5,
  15; **es** 11/10, 12, 26, 28, 30, 37, 61, 63, 67,
  70, 122–123; **his** 3/39; **hiis** 8/53; ◆ pl.ps.: **ar**
  6/46, 58, 71, 143 *13/269 *14/30, 33, 56, 84,
  95, 103, 121, 155, 207, 212–213; **are**
  10.3/10, 19 *10.6/32 *12/110, 134, 176, 196,
  209, 318 *13/334; **aren** 2/40, 51 *7/93
  *10.6/16; **arn** 2/3, 41, 49, 59 *6/67; **been**
  13/278; **ben** 7/94, 97 *9/45, 132 *13/185;
  bene 12/40; **beoþ** 10.3/16 *10.6/35; **beothþ**
  5/90; **beþ** 8/25, 77, 83–84 *10.3/8, 41
  *10.6/31, 55 *10.8/33–34; **bied** 3/34; **bueþ**
  10.3/37; **senden** 2/14; ◆ sg.pl.ps.: **byeþ** 4/36,
  43–44, 49, 64, 70–71, 80, 89, 95–96; ◆
  imp.sg.: **be** 8/18, 97, 110 *10.2/3 *10.3/34
  *12/1; **by** 4/40; ◆ sg.ps. subj.: **by** 4/25
  *6/137; ◆ pl.ps. subj.: **err** 11/115; **be** 11/32
  *12/24, 331 *13/99; **by** 4/68; ◆ sg.pt.: **ves**
  8/129; **was; watz** 6/1, 4–5, 20, 26, 44, 248,
  252, 265; **wæs** 1/55, 74, 81–82; **wes** 1/8, 15,
  22–23, 57 *4/28 *8/1, 3, 6, 9–10 etc.
  *10.4/15, 17 *10.5/30, 32–33, 35 etc.
  *10.7/17 *14/2–3, 10, 15 etc. ◆ pl.pt.:
  uuaren 1/34; **uuæren** 1/37; **uueron** 1/64;
  wæron 1/16, 31, 38, 41, 44–45, 62; **war**
  11/35, 96; **ware** 3/13 *11/89; **waren** 1/56;

were 3/12 *5/33, 75, 168, 214 *6/88, 107
  *7/53, 82, 106, 108, 112, 116, 181, 186
  *9/47, 105–106 *10.3/13 *12/17, 88, 257,
  297 *13/18, 26, 41, 47, 61, 226, 228, 238,
  316, 319, 421; **weren** 2/22 *4/10 *5/37, 40,
  107, 117, 123, 150, 163, 190 *8/14, 21, 145
  *9/116 *10.3/48 *13/28–29, 40; ◆ sg.pt.
  subj.: **uuare** 1/3; **war** 11/40; **were** 2/13, 37
  *5/22, 48, 141, 148, 177, 220, 222, 228–229
  *6/68, 225, 230 *7/2, 11, 66, 76, 80, 136,
  189 *8/4, 22, 29–30, 88, 109, 110 *10.2/14
  *10.8/3 *12/253, 305, 337, 357 *13/84, 132,
  172, 376, 455; ◆ pl.pt. subj.: **weren** 8/32, 102
  *9/106; ◆ pt. and subj.: **wer** 12/170, 199,
  208, 295 *14/19, 21, 129, 173; ◆ ptp.: **be**
  7/62, 203; **been** 13/420, 491; **ben** 6/36
  *8/93, 100; **bene** 10.9/16 *11/14, 95, 106,
  112, 115; **iben** 8/44, 50; **i-beo** 5/57, 208;
  y-by 4/28; ◆ contr. a) 1.sg.ps.: **icham** 10.1/4,
  15 *10.2/5 *10.8/7; ◆ contr. b) 2.sg.ps.:
  hertou 8/60; ◆ contr. c) 1.sg.ps. neg.: **i-nam**
  5/130, 174; ◆ neg.: **nam** (1.sg.ps.) 13/513; **nis**
  (3.sg.ps.) 8/73, 82, 92 *10.3/31; **nys** 4/23
  *13/271; **nas** (3.sg.pt.) 5/61, 111, 152, 177,
  183 *13/59, 385; **nes** 8/2 *10.4/16; **nere**
  (pt.subj.) 5/41, 173 *10.3/15, 38
'bear' (vb.) **bæron** (inf.) 1/45, 48; **beir** 14/69,
  100; **bere** 4/87 *9/13; **bere** (sg.ps.) 6/52;
  bereþ 10.2/12 *10.5/36; **bereþ** (pl.ps.)
  10.5/36; **bere** (imp.) 11/69; **bereth** 3/16;
  beiris (pl.ps.) 14/92; **bar** (sg.pt.) 1/64 *5/62
  *13/389; **baar** (sg.pt.) 13/74, 153, 155, 157,
  437; **bare** 1/10; **bare** (pl.pt.) 11/78; **baren**
  7/217; **bere** 5/34, 213; **bore** (ptp.) 8/58
  *10.3/40 *10.5/28, 33 *13/115; **born** 11/80
  *13/238, 333; **i-bore** 5/129, 204
bebirieden (pl.pt.) *to bury* 1/8; **bebyried** 1/88;
  byrieden 1/86; **i-bured** (ptp.) 5/230
bec (sb.) *beak* 2/4, 13–14, 17
becaȝt (ptp.) *to catch* 4/44
becom → **come** (2)
'become' becomþ (sg.ps.) 4/30–31; **bicumeð**
  2/20; **bycommes** *is fitting* 6/258; **bi-cam**
  (sg.pt.) 5/8; **bicome** (pl.pt.) 6/6 *10.5/27, 42;
  bi-comen 5/79
bed → **bede** (1)
bed (sb.) 7/217 *11/90, 97, 103 *13/363,
  365–366, 430, 443, 447, 482; **bedde** 5/13
  *7/44 *8/107–108 *13/377, 383–384;
  beddes (gsg.) 13/380, 437
bede → **bid**
bede (1) (inf.) *to offer, give* 6/161; **bede**
  (sg.ps.) 6/169; **bed** 10.3/17; **boden** (pl.pt.)
  5/170; (ptp.) 6/114

bede (2) (sb.) *prayer, request* 11/21; **beden** 5/20; **bedes** 11/32

Bede → **Saints**

beden, bedes → **bede** (2);

bee, been → **be**

beest (sb.) *beast, animal* 13/331; **beste** 4/1–2; **beistis** (pl.) 14/28

beete → **bete** (1)

beete (inf.) *to repair* 13/151

before (adv., prep.) 6/209 *12/19, 226, 365, 396; **beforen** 1/84; **befoir** 14/26, 65; **bifor** 11/83; **bi-fore** 5/14; **bifore** 5/17, 28, 117–118, 136, 144, 199 *6/37, 119, 134, 155, 184 *7/235 *10.3/41; **biforn** 2/14, 17 *13/100, 235; **byfore** 10.5/35

begæt (sg.pt.) *to get* 1/75, 77

beggers (sb.pl.) 7/41

'**begin**' **begynne** (inf.) 12/20, 280; (sg.ps.) 12/268; **biginne** (inf.) 9/9; **bigynne** 13/42, 132; **bigynnes** (sg.ps.) 6/11; **begynþ** 4/24; **biginneþ** 8/40 *10.1/1; **bygynneth** 7/151; **bi-gan** (sg.pt.) 5/27, 196, 223; **bigan** 8/54 *9/17, 76, 122 *11/41 *13/44, 307, 371, 376, 391, 406; **bigon** 8/8; **bygan** 7/196; **bigunne** (pl.pt.) 9/87; **bi-gonne** (ptp.) 5/29

begyle (inf.) *to beguile, betray, trick* 14/149; **bigyle** (inf.) 13/272; **begyld** (ptp.) 14/213; **bigilid** 11/123; **giled** 9/96; **bigyled** 13/138, 545

begynne, begynþ → **begin**

beȝete (sb.) *profit, gain* 8/124

beheld → **behold**

'**behold**' **biholde** (sg.ps.) 10.6/4, 21; **beholdes** (imp.pl.) 12/195; **byholdez** 6/37; **beheld** (sg.pt.) 7/14; **biheld** 8/8; **bi-heold** 5/38; **bi-heolden** (pl.pt.) 5/148

behoueþ (sg.ps.) *to behove, be obliged to* 4/23, 38, 83; **behoues** 6/111, 243; **behoued** (pl.pt.) 1/70

beir, beiris → **bear**

beire (pron., adj. gpl.) *of both* 5/30

beistis → **beest**

bel (sb.) *fire* 2/53

belamp (sg.pt.) *to happen* 1/83

belamy (sb.) *friend* 12/213; **bellamy** 12/338

Bele-Berit (prn.) 12/115

beleue (sg.ps.subj.) *to remain* 8/99

beleuede → **believe**

bel-hous (sb.) *belfry* 5/32

Belial (prn.) 12/115

beliaue (sb.) *belief, faith* 3/24; **leue** 2/59–60

'**believe**' **bileue** (inf.) 9/31; **ylefth** (sg.ps.) 4/20; **lef** 10.8/19; **leue** 7/17, 78, 103 *10.2/9 *10.3/19; **leueð** 2/25; **beleuede** (pl.pt.) 3/23; **leued** 7/70

bell (sb.) 14/191; **bellen** (pl.) 5/32; **belles** 9/61

bellamy → **belamy**

bellen, belles → **bell**

bellie blind (sb.) *blind-man's-buff* 14/153

belongeth (sg.ps.) *to concern, belong (to)* 3/7; **belongeþ** 4/3; **longest** (2.sg.ps.) 9/25; **longen** 13/109

Belsabub (prn.) 12/97, 137

belt (sb.) 13/153

bely (sb.) *belly, stomach* 7/42

belyue; ben → **bliue; be**

bench (sb.) 6/67, 124, 138; **benche** 6/131 *7/163 *9/108

bende (sg.pt.) *to bend, incline* 5/164, *wrinkle* 6/92

bene → **be**

benedicite (interj.) *(the Lord) bless you* 13/444 *14/7

benes (sb.pl.) *prayer* 4/24

benissowne (sb.) *grace, blessing* 11/57

bent (sb.) *battlefield* 6/140

beo → **be**

beom (sb.) *beam* 1/46

beon, beothþ, beoþ → **be**

berd (sb.) *beard* 13/44, 320; **berde** 6/93, 121

berdlez (adj.) *beardless* 6/67

bere → **bear**

bere (1) (sb.) *bier* 5/221

bere (2) (sb.) *behaviour* 12/214

bereth, bereþ → **bear**

bernis (sb.pl.) *man* 14/92

besæt (sg.pt.) *to besiege* 1/17

besech (imp.) *to beg, entreat* 3/42; **beseche** (sg.ps.) 6/128; **besouhte** (pl.pt.) 7/188; **bisoght** 13/342; **bysechynge** (sb.) 10.5/10

besie (adj.) *busy* 14/206

besouhte → **besech**

best (adj., adv. sup.) 6/46 *10.2/13 *10.3/11 *10.5/21; **beste** 3/20–21 *10.3/13 *10.5/15 *13/371, 400; ♦ col.: **atte beste** (adv.) *perfectly* 13/29; (adj.) *best* 13/371; **mid þe beste** *one of the best* 9/2; **wiþ þe beste** 9/33 [see good; well]

beste → **beest**

bet → **bete** (1) **better**

Betannye (pn.) 12/162

bete (1) (inf.) *to beat* 8/145; **bet** (sg.pt.) 7/115; **beete** (pl.pt.) 13/532; **bette** 13/540; **ybete** (ptp.) 13/537

bete (2) (inf.) *to amend, better* 8/138 *10.4/46; **beteð** (sg.ps.) 2/28

Betene (prn.) 7/154

betere; beteð → **better; bete** (2)

betidde (ptp.) *to happen* 12/100
betokned (sg.ps.) *to betoken* 3/34; **bitockned**
  3/26
betraied → **bi-traiȝe**
betre; bette → **better; bete** (1)
better (adj., adv. comp.) 6/140 *11/30, 53
  *14/40; **bettere** 7/183; **betere** 1/81 *10.1/17
  *10.5/17; **bet** 5/145, 172 *13/368, 519;
  betre (adv.) *sooner* 7/135; **bettre** (adv.)
  13/64, 307; ♦ col.: **þe betere** 10.5/17; **þe**
  better 6/197; **þe bettre** 7/33
'between' bituene (prep.) 10.6/27; **bi-twene**
  5/34; **bitwene** 11/71; **bytuene** 10.1/1;
  bytwene 7/19; **betwyx** 1/19
beþ → **be**
beuereges (sb.) *drinking* 7/196
bewepþ (sg.ps.) *to cry for, lament* 4/27
bey (sg.pt.) *to bend* 8/97
bi → **by; God; siþe**
bibbed (sg.pt.) *to imbibe* 13/386
bi-cam → **become**
bicharde (sg.pt.) *to betray* 8/147
bicome, bi-comen, bicumeð → **become**
bid (imp.sg.) *to bid, request, pray* 6/131
  *11/70; **bidde** (inf.) 8/90, (imp.) 12/118;
  (sg.ps.) 12/177; **bidden** (inf.) 2/33; (sg.ps.)
  14/138; **biddes** 6/157; **bad** (sg.pt.) 7/154 *9/1
  *10.2/3 *11/68, 84 *13/318; **badde** 12/201;
  bade 7/180; **bede** 5/169; **beden** (pl.pt.)
  5/171, 176; **ibede** (ptp.) 8/68, 128
bidde, bidden → **bid**
bidders (sb.pl.) *beggar* 7/41
biddes → **bid**
bidding (sb.) *prayer* 12/257
bide (inf.) *to wait for, abide, rest* 6/77
  *12/207; **byde** 13/461; **byden** 6/161; **bidis**
  (sg.ps.) 12/23; **bydez** 6/163; **baid** (sg.pt.)
  14/177
bie; bied → **by; be**
bieste (adv.) *in the east* 9/33
bi-falle (inf.) *to happen* 5/20, 200; **bifallez**
  (sg.ps.) 6/169; **bifalle** (ptp.) 13/344; **bi-fel**
  (sg.pt.) 5/49; **bi-feol** 5/45; **bifil** 13/19; **biful**
  7/7
biflette (sg.pt.) *to flood* 9/68
bifor, bi-fore, bifore, biforn → **before**
biful → **begin**
biges (sg.ps.) *to build* 6/9; **bigged** (ptp.)
  founded 6/20
bigilid → **begyle**
biginne, biginneþ → **begin**
bigo (sg.ps.subj.) *to betide, come upon* 8/27
Bigog (interj.) *by God* 6/177

bigon, bi-gonne, bigonne → **begin**
bigripen (inf.) *to seize* 2/43 [see grip]
bigunne → **begin**
bigyle, bigyled → **begyle**
bigynne, bigynnes → **begin**
biheld, bi-heold, beheolden → **behold**
bihind (adv., prep.) *behind* 11/13; **bihynde**
  13/285, 388, 467
biholde → **behold**
bihynde → **behind**
bile (sb.) *bill* 2/18
bi-leue (sg.ps.) *to remain* 5/131, 201; **blefte**
  (pl.pt.subj.) 4/77
bileue, bileued → **believe**
billeð (sg.ps.) *to peck* 2/16–17
biloken (pl.ps.) *to look about* 2/50
bind (sg.ps.) *to bind, fasten, fetter* 8/127;
  bynde (inf.) 10.3/9 *12/97; **boond** (sg.pt.)
  13/306, 362; **ybounde** (ptp.) 7/97 *10.3/36
  *10.7/2 *13/284, 294; ♦ neg.: **vnbynde** (inf.)
  12/8
bi-neoþe (adv.) *beneath* 5/86; **bi-nethe** 5/33;
  bineþe 8/127
biniȝte (adv.) *in the evening* 9/85
bi-nome (ptp.) *to deprive* 5/186; **binome** 8/87
bischop, bischopes, bischopis → **bishop**
bischop-riche (sb.) *office of bishop, bishopric*
  5/120; **bischopriche** 5/51, 55, 109, 187
biscop, biscopes → **bishop**
bisemare (sb.) *scorn* 13/189
bi-sette (sg.pt.) *to institute, conquer* 5/93, 101
'bishop' bischop 5/1, 6–7, 9, 45–46 etc.
  *7/76, 78, 81; **biscop** 1/27; **bischopes** (pl.)
  7/85; **bischopis** (gsg.) 7/67; **biscopes** (pl.)
  1/60, 63
biside (prep.) *beside* 9/22, 83 *11/44 *13/76
bisily (adv.) *eagerly* 13/230
bisoght → **besech**
bistowe (inf.) *to bestow* 13/205
biswiken (inf.) *to betray* 2/43; **byswyken** (ptp.)
  10.3/23
bit (sb.) *blade, cutting edge* 6/213
bi-take → **bi-tok**
bitere → **bittir**
bitockned → **betokned**
bi-tok (sg.pt.) *to entrust* 5/136–137; **bi-take**
  (ptp.) 5/143
bi-traiȝe *to betray* 5/80; **bitraide** (sg.pt.) 9/5;
  betraied (ptp.) 12/331
Bitte (prn.) 7/180
bittir (adj.) *bitter* 12/207; **bittre** 10.6/46;
  bitere 9/111
bituene, bi-twene, bitwene → **between**

bitwixe (prep.) *betwixt* 13/193
biþenche (inf.) *to consider, deliberate* 8/42;
  biðenken 2/22; **biþout** (ptp.) 8/41
biþine *from your* 9/25 [bi+þine]
biþout → **biþenche**
blade (sb.) 13/74, 154
Blais → **Stephne**
blake (adj.) *black* 9/30 *10.1/7
blame (sb.) 6/148 *9/3
blamed (sg.pt.) 13/87
ble (sb.) *colour* 10.6/24
blede (inf.) *to bleed* 10.7/28; **bledest** (sg.ps.)
  10.6/33; **bledeþ** (pl.ps.) 10.7/30; **bledde**
  (sg.pt.) 6/228
blefte → **bileue**
blenche (inf.) *to capsize* 9/76
blere (inf.) *to deceive, trick* 13/273; **blered**
  (sg.pt.) 7/72; **bleryng** (sb.) 13/89
blessing (sb.) 9/135; **blessyng** 6/157; **blissing**
  12/401
bleþeliche (adv.) *gladly, willingly* 4/16 *8/86
bleu, blew → **blowe**
blind → **bellie**
blinde (sb.pl.) *blind person* 5/193; **blynde**
  4/84
blis, blisce → **bliss**
blisful (adj.) *blessed* 13/17
'**bliss**' **blisse** 4/60, 67, 75 *7/29 *8/70, 72,
  117, 147 *10.1/4 *10.4/9 *12/16, 184, 236,
  276, 400; **blis** 10.5/20; **blisce** 3/32, 43;
  blysse 6/18 *10.5/60
blissid; blissing → **iblessed; blessing**
bliþe (adj.) *glad, happy* 8/125 *9/44; **blyith**
  14/191
bliue (adv.) *immediately, quickly* 8/55; **belyue**
  12/211
blo (adj.) *blue* 10.6/24
blod, blode → **blood**
blody (adj.) *bloody* 10.4/15 *13/500
blomis (sg.ps.) *to bloom, flower* 14/219
blonk (sb.) *horse* 6/221
blood (sb.) 13/169, 206, 208–209; **bloode**
  12/12; **blod** (sb.) *blood* 5/96 *6/73, 104, 144,
  216 *8/20, 26 *10.4/38 *10.5/7, 11 *10.6/6
  *10.7/9, 35; **blode** 9/73 *10.6/25
blomis (sg.ps.) *to bloom, flower* 14/219
blosmes (sb.pl.) *blossom* 10.3/4 *10.4/1
blowe (inf.) *to blow* 9/56; **bleu** (sg.pt.) 9/17,
  126; **blew** 7/201
blunder (sb.) *turmoil, trouble* 6/18 *14/86
blycande (psp.) *to shine, gleam* 6/92; **blykked**
  (sg.pt.) 6/216
blyith → **bliþe**

blykked → **blycande**
blynde → **blinde**
blynne (inf.) *to end, cease* 12/16, 236
blysse; bo → **bliss; both**
bobbaunce (sb.) *pomp, pride* 6/9
bochere (sb.) *butcher* 7/180; **bochers** (pl.)
  7/140
bodé; boden → **body; bede**
body (sb.) 6/216 *10.5/50–51 *11/93 *12/89;
  bodye 4/39, 41–42; **bodi** 4/54 *5/196, 198,
  213, 221, 231 *6/228 *10.6/23; **bodie** 12/23;
  bodé 6/144; **bodyes** (pl.) 6/140 *13/396
boes (sg.ps., imp.) *must* 13/251
boȝ (sb.) *bough, twig* 4/45, 56, 63; **bowes** (pl.)
  10.3/4
boȝe (inf.) *to turn, go* 6/131; **boȝez** (sg.ps.)
  6/221; **boȝed** (pl.pt.) 6/268
boȝte, boht, bohte, bohton → **buy**
boidekyn (sb.) *dagger* 13/184
bok (sb.) *book* 5/17; **boke** 2/2 *5/217
bokeler (sb.) *buckler* 13/243
boket (sb.) *bucket* 8/39–40, 44, 116; **bukket**
  14/174, 181, 183; **boketes** (pl.) 8/37;
  bukkettis 14/160
bold (adj.) 6/59; **bolde** 6/21, 73, 138 *12/145;
  boold 13/495
boldely (adv.) *boldly* 12/178; **baldeliche**
  5/105, 156; **baldly** 6/163
bolle (sb.) *drinking-bowl* 7/221
bolt bolt upright (col.) *lying flat (on the back)*
  13/490
bon (sb.) *bone* 10.5/46; **bones** (pl.) 6/211
  *8/32
bonde (sb.) *bonds, chains* 10.2/4; **bandis** (pl.)
  12/190, 196
bondemen (sb.pl.) *slave, bondman* 7/138
bone (sb.) *prayer, request* 2/33 *6/114
bones; bonkkes → **bon; bank**
boodworde (sb.) *message, tidings* 12/366
boold; boond → **bold; bind**
boost (sb.) *boast, boasting* 13/225; **booste**
  12/214; **bost** 4/61
bord (sb.) *table* 11/82; **borde** 6/268 *9/113;
  burdes (pl.) 11/86
bore, born → **bear**
borȝ; bost → **burȝ; boost**
bot, bote → **but**
bote (1) (sb.) *fulfilment* 10.2/3
bote (2) (inf.) *to compensate* 7/183
both (adj., adv., conj.) 11/20, 115 *12/352;
  bothe 7/10, 76, 85, 140 *10.10/16 *12/34,
  75 *13/203, 219, 300, 315, 523; **boðe** 2/6;
  boþe 6/18, 55, 158, 271 *8/84 *9/45, 132
  *10.5/22; **boþen** 8/13; **baith** 14/16, 73, 75,

79, 125, 176; **bathe** 1/35 *13/311, 336, 415;
  bo 10.6/22
bought, boughte, bouhte → **buy**
bounchede (sg.pt.) *to tap* 7/72
boune (adj.) *ready* 12/178, 201, 257, 339
bounté (sb.) *worth, virtue* 6/144; **bounte**
  10.1/13
bour (sb.) *chamber, bower* 10.3/8 *10.8/25;
  bure 9/89
bourded (sg.pt.) *to joke* 11/95
bout; bowes → **but; boʒ**
bowsum (adj.) *meek* 11/2, 21, 32; ◆ neg.:
  vn-bouʒhsome 5/133
box (sb.) *chest, box* 10.10/13; **boxes** (pl.) 7/97
boy (sb.) *young man, rascal, fellow* 7/78;
  boyes (pl.) 12/97, 145
braid → **brode**
braid (sg.pt.) *to draw, pull, turn, shoot, extend*
  14/83; **brayd** 6/216; **brayde** 6/227
braide (sb.) *attack* 12/207
brake → **breke**
bras (sb.) *brass* 12/196 *13/168
braunch (sb.) *branch* 6/52
brayd, brayde → **braid**
brayn (sb.) *brain* 6/73
bræcon → **breke**
bredale (sb.) *wedding* 3/2, 4, 6, 21
bredden; brede → **bredeþ; breed**
bredeþ (sg.ps.) *to flower* 10.3/4; **bredden**
  (pl.pt.) *to multiply* 6/21
bredgume (sb.) *bridegroom* 3/19
breed (sb.) *bread* 13/361; **brede** 11/76, 79
breeth (sb.) *breath* 13/5
breke (inf.) *to break* 12/189, 257; **brake**
  (sg.pt.) 7/114; (inf.) *to vomit* 7/232; **bræcon**
  (pl.pt.) 1/44; **broken** (ptp.) 13/513; **brokynne**
  12/195; **ybrokene** 7/69
bren (sb.) *bran* 13/277
brennen (inf.) *to burn, burn down, kindle*
  2/53; **brenden** (pl.pt.) 1/59; **brendon** 1/53;
  brent (ptp.) 6/2
breres (sb.pl.) *briar* 7/203
bresed (adj.) *bristling* 6/92
brest (sb.) *breast* 8/26, 97 *13/500; **breste**
  11/16; **brestes** (pl.) 13/199
Bretaygne (pn.) 6/25; **Bretayn** 6/14, 20
bretful (adv.) *brimful* 7/42 *13/236
bretheren, breþerne, breþren → **brother**
breued (ptp.) *to declare* 6/252
breuh-wyf (sb.) *alewife* 7/155
breweres (sb.pl.) *brewer* 7/140
brewestere (sb.) *alewife* 7/154
breyde → **abreyde**

brigge (sb.) *bridge* 13/146
bright (adj.) 13/522; **briʒt** 2/10; **briʒte** 9/85;
  briht 10.5/8; **brihtest** (sup.) 10.2/13; **bryʒt**
  6/56; **bryht** 10.3/8 *10.4/27; **bryhte** 10.6/22
Briʒtei (prn.) 5/7; **Briʒtey** 5/45; **Briʒttey** 5/6
briht, brihtest → **bright**
brim (sb.) *brook, river, water* 11/44
'bring' bringe (inf.) 9/37 *10.1/4 *10.5/29
  *12/118, 366; **brynge** 13/58; **brynges**
  (sg.ps.) 13/354; **bring** (sg.ps.subj.) 10.6/59;
  brohte (sg.pt.) 1/71 *10.5/34 *10.7/23;
  brought 12/161; **brouʒte** 5/78, 123, 191;
  brohute 8/35; **broute** 8/52, 130; **brouth**
  7/67; **brohten** (pl.pt.) 1/7; **brouʒten** 5/60;
  brouhten 7/217; **browt** 10.9/11; **brocht**
  (ptp.) 14/86; **broght** 11/80, 82; **broʒt** 6/124;
  broht 10.2/4; **ibrocht** 3/19; **i-brouʒt** 5/84,
  86–87, 134; **ibrout** 8/41, 61; **ybroht** 10.7/33
brittened (ptp.) *to destroy* 6/2
broches (sb.pl.) *brooch* 7/73
brocht → **bring**
broddit (sg.pt.) *to goad, prick* 14/9
brode (adj.) *broad, large* 6/14 *13/199; **brood**
  13/348; (adv.) *wide open* 6/233; **braid** (adv.)
  14/219
broght; broʒez → **bring; browe**
broʒt, broht, brohte, brohten, brohute →
  bring
broken, brokynne → **breke**
Bromeholm (pn.) *Bromholm, Norfolk* 13/510
brondeʒ (sb.pl.) *piece of burned wood* 6/2
brood → **brode**
brook (sb.) 13/146–147
brosten (ptp.) *to burst* 12/196
brother (sb.) 7/107; **broþer** 9/16; **bretheren**
  (pl.) 12/37; **breþerne** 5/214, 228; **breþren**
  5/199
brought, brouʒte, brouʒten, brouhten →
  bring
broun (adj.) *brown* 6/213; **broune** 10.1/7
broute, brouth → **bring**
browe (sb.) *eyebrows* 10.1/7; **broʒez** (pl.) 6/92
browt → **bring**
bruche (sb.) *breach, opening* 8/11, 117
Brutus → **Felix**
brydel (sb.) *bridle* 6/221 *13/287
bryʒt, bryht, bryhte → **bright**
brynge, brynges → **bring**
bryniges (sb.pl.) *coat of mail* 1/39
bud (sb.) *bribe* 14/19; **buddis** (pl.) 14/92, 100
buen, bueþ → **be**
buffet (sb.) *buffet, blow* 6/169
bukket, bukkettis → **boket**

bulk (sb.) *trunk, body* 6/227
bulle (sb.) *papal bull* 7/67; **bulles** (pl.) 7/71–72
bult (sg.pt.) *to reign* 6/25
bur (sb.) *blow* 6/77, 161
burde (sb.) *young woman* 10.2/13
burdes → **bord**
burdes (sb.pl.) *joke* 4/71
burdon (sb.) *bass* 13/389
bure → **bour**
burgeys (sb.) *burgess, citizen* 7/138
burʒ (sb.) *town, castle* 6/46; **burʒe** 6/9; **borʒ** 6/2
burn (sb.) *man, knight* 6/20; **burne** 6/124; **burnes** (pl.) 6/46, 268; **burnez** 6/59
bus (sg.ps.) *to deserve* 12/338
busk (sb.) *bush, thicket* 14/16, 147
busshel (sb.) *bushel* 13/317, 468, 536
but (adv., conj., prep.) 7/64 *12/60, 178, 206, 217 etc. *13/35, 82, 84, 91 etc. *14/55, 78, 91, 217; **bute** 1/11 *9/26, 69–70; **buten** 2/30; **bot** 6/25, 30, 45, 58–59 etc. *11/2, 23, 27, 50 etc. *14/6, 15, 49, 63, 73 etc.; **bote** 4/63–64 *5/20, 22, 126 *7/36 *8/20, 22, 25, 82, 96, 127 *10.1/9 *10.3/32 *10.6/38 *10.8/3, 13, 27; **bout** 6/148; ♦ col.: **but weir** (adv.) *doubtless* 14/184
butere (sb.) *butter* 1/55
buttokes (sb.pl.) *buttock* 13/199
buttrie (sb.) *pantry* 14/222
'buy' boʒte (sg.pt.) 9/64; **bohte** 10.6/58 *10.7/4, 8–9; **boughte** 12/275; **bouhte** 7/161; **bohton** (pl.pt.) 1/84; **boht** (ptp.) 10.6/60; **bought** (ptp.) 12/8; **yboht** 10.4/34, 40; **bying** (sb.) 12/12
by → **be; God**
by (prep.) 4/18 *6/61, 110, 120, 131 etc. *7/78, 103, 154, 175 etc. *10.2/13 *10.3/10, 45 *10.5/2, 56 *10.6/56 *11/34, 81, 99, 105, 108 *12/190, 248 *13/25, 45, 51, 56 etc. *14/100; **bi** 1/38–39 *2/6 *4/18 *5/34–35, 171 *6/20, 52, 108, 126 etc. *8/25, 57, 59, 105 *9/8, 14, 20, 86 etc. *11/121; **be** 1/35–36 *4/8, 14–15, 22, 35, 49, 51–52 *7/183 *11/2 *12/229, 255, 317, 355 *14/20, 33, 108, 110, 116, 129, 137, 200
byche (sb.) *bitch* 7/205
bycommes → **become**
byde, byden, bydez → **bide**
byeþ; byfore → **be; before**
bygan, bygynneth → **begin**
byholdez; bying → **behold; buy**
byleyn (ptp.) *to deflower* 10.3/44
bynde → **bind**

bynethe (adv.) *beneath* 13/265
bynne (sb.) *bin* 13/49
byrieden → **bebirieden**
byrthen (sb.) *load* 1/10
bys (sb.) *garment* 10.2/14
bysechynge → **besech**
bysihede (sb.) *activity, sedulity* 4/63, 65
bysinesse (sb.) *care, effort* 4/68
byswyken → **biswiken**
bytuene, bytwene → **between**

C

caboik (sb.) *cheese* 14/150, 164, 167, 169; **cabok** 14/123, 128, 135, 139, 218
cacche (inf.) *to catch* 13/329; **cachchez** (sg.ps.) 6/221; **cachez** 6/155; **caughte** (pl.pt., sg.pt.) 13/330, 485, 497; **cauhte** (sg.pt.) 7/210; **caught** (ptp.) 13/451; **ikaut** 8/43, 52
cace → **case**
cachchez, cachez → **cacche**
cais; caist → **cace; cast**
cake (sb.) *loaf (of bread)* 13/318, 468, 535
cald, calde → **calle**
calde (sb.) *cold* 11/104
calf (sb.) *calf (of the leg)* 13/48
calle (inf.) *to call (out)* 10.7/20 *12/113, 138, 141 *13/335, 511; **call** (sg.ps.) 14/201; **calles** 12/135; **callis** 12/126; **cald** (sg.pt.) 11/96, 102, 110; **callit** 14/69; **called** (ptp.) 13/488; **calde** 6/243; **callit** 14/204, 214, 218
caller (sb.) 14/8
calles, callis, callit → **calle**
cam → **come** (2)
camus (adj.) *short, stubby* 13/158; **kamus** 13/198
can → **gynneth**
can (vb., ps.) *can, to be able to, understand, know* 1/49 *2/22 *7/227 *14/1, 71, 154, 199, 206, 217; **canne** 12/100; **kan** 4/83 *7/233 *13/44, 99, 143–144, 239, 320; **kanne** 12/74; **con** 8/49 *10.1/13 *10.4/31; **conne** (sg.ps.) 5/175; (pl.ps.) 10.4/37; **conneth** 7/35; **konne** 13/347; **cunne** 2/9; ♦ pt. and subj.: **couthe** 7/187; **couþe** 5/121; **koude** 13/49–50, 58, 64, 66, 88, 151, 328; **kouþe** 8/92; **cowd** 10.9/7; **kowthe** 13/14; **cuþe** 9/100
canceler (sb.) *chancellor* 1/28
Cane (pn.) *Cana, Galilee* 3/3
canne → **can**
Cantebregge (prn.) *Cambridge* 13/214; **Cantebrigge** 13/145

caponis (sb.pl.) *capon* 14/101
capul (sb.) *horse* 13/312, 329
care (sb.) 10.6/52 *12/292, 347; **kare** 8/17,
71, 82; **cares** (pl.) 12/84
carie (inf.) *to carry* 13/256
carited → **charite**
carll (sb.) *man, churl* 14/36, 50, 120, 128, 135,
171; **carlis** (gsg.) 14/21
carlmen (sb.pl.) *man* 1/36
caroles (sb.pl.) *carol* 6/260
carp (inf.) *to speak, talk* 6/50, 94, (sg.ps.)
6/147; **carppez** 6/164
carpenter (sb.) 13/70; **carpenteer** 13/138;
carpenteris (gsg.) 13/85
carppez → **carp**
case (sb.) 12/114; **cas** 13/79; **cace** 14/67; **cais**
14/201
'cast' kastes (sg.ps.) 11/29; **cast** (sg.pt.) 7/177;
caste 5/220 *7/122 *13/241; **caist** 14/13;
ycast (ptp.) 10.7/6, 32
castel *castle, fortress* 1/78 *4/94 *9/68, 91,
103; **castles** (pl.) 1/18, 29, 32–34, 44
castelweorces (sb.) *the building of castles*
1/34
castles → **castel**
catel (sb.) *property, cattle* 12/242 *13/203;
catell 11/12; **cattell** 14/24, 114
caudel (sb.) *mixture, mess* 7/213
caught, caughte, cauhte → **cacche**
Caunterburi (pn.) *Canterbury* 5/115;
Caunterbury 13/16, 22, 27
cause (sb.) 13/368 *14/114; ◆ col.: **by cause**
because 13/85, 448
Cayme (prn.) *Cain* 12/306
cayren (inf.) *to go, wander* 7/31; **kayres**
(sg.ps.) 7/152
cæse (sb.) *cheese* 1/55; **cheis** 14/125
cellerer (sb.) *cellarer* 8/30
certayne (adv.) *certainly* 12/46, 225; **sarteyne**
12/94
certes → **no**
cęste (sb.) *chest, box* 1/42
cete (sb.) *whale* 2/42
Cethegrande (prn.) 2/35
chaere → **chayere**
chaffare (sb.) *commerce, trade, bargain* 7/33,
181
chald → **cold**
chalenge (sg.ps.) *to lay claim to* 14/30;
chalengen (pl.ps.) 7/91
chalons (sb.pl.) *blanket* 13/364
chamber (sb.) 11/87, 90; **chambre** 13/363,
367; **chaumber** 11/72; **chambres** (pl.) 13/28

chancerye (sb.) *chancery* 7/91
chapel (sb.) 6/238, 241 *13/107; **chapele**
4/82; **chapeles** (pl.) 9/60
chapman (sb.) *tradesman, merchant* 7/62;
chapmen (pl.) 7/181
charge (sg.ps.) *to command, order* 6/238;
charged (ptp.) 7/87
charite (sb.) *charity* 7/62, 64, 87; **carited** 1/70
chaste (adj.) 3/38
chastisid (sg.pt.) *chastise* 7/110
chaueles (sb.pl.) *jaw* 2/42
chaumber → **chamber**
Chauntecler (prn.) 8/23; **Sire Chauntecler**
8/19
chayere (sb.) *throne, chair* 7/114; **chaere** 9/1
cheastes → **cheste**
cheere (sb.) *jollity; expression, face* 13/356;
chere 7/176 *10.1/8 *11/17, 84; **schere**
6/121
cheis → **cæse**
cheker (sb.) *exchequer* 7/91
cheosen (inf.) *to choose* 10.4/33; **chose** (sg.ps.)
to go 6/238; **chesen** (pl.pt.) 7/33; **i-chose**
(ptp.) 5/52; **ychose** 7/181
cherche; chere → **churche; cheere**
cherl (sb.) *man, churl* 7/212; **cherles** (gsg.)
13/141 [see carl]
chesen → **cheosen**
cheste (sb.) *strife, fighting* 7/105; **cheastes**
(pl.) 4/92
cheueth (pl.ps.) *to be successful* 7/33
chide (inf.) 5/225; **chidde** (sg.pt.) 13/223
chief (sb.) 7/62
child (sb.) *young man, child* 5/3 *9/40–41, 50,
128 *13/195, 381; **childe** 8/114 *10.4/29;
cild 1/84; **childre** (pl.) 9/48; **children** 5/4
*7/105, 111, 115 *8/58, 78 *13/322; **chylder**
6/67
chinne (sb.) *chin* 4/18
chirche, chirches → **churche**
chold → **cold**
choppe (sg.ps.) *to remove* 7/64
chose → **cheosen**
Christ → **Jesus Christ**
christianis (sb.pl.) *Christian* 14/224
churche (sb.) *church* 5/4, 112, 133, 213
*7/156, 167; **cherche** 4/23, 83; **chirche**
7/64, 87, 116 *9/60; **circe** 1/58, 70; **cyrce**
1/59; **kirke** 2/21; ◆ col.: **holi chirche** *Holy
Church* 7/64; **holy chirche** 7/87, 116; **hooly
chirche** 13/210; **hooly chirches** (gsg.)
13/207–208; **holie churche** 5/133; **holy
churche** 7/156

chylder → **child**
chymbe (1) (inf.) *to chime* 13/120
chymbe (2) (sb.) *rim* 13/119
cild; **circe** → **child**; **churche**
circewican (sb.) *sacrist* 1/76
cite (sb.) *town* 3/3
clamis (sb.pl.) *claim* 14/122
clanly (adv.) *completely* 6/180
Claryce (prn.) 7/167
clater (inf.) *to clatter* 11/98
clay (sb.) 10.6/17
cledd (ptp.) *to clothe* 11/73
clemb (sg.pt.) *to climb* 5/35; **cloumben** (pl.pt.)
 5/34
Clement (prn.) 7/177, 191, 210; **Clementis**
 (gsg.) 7/213
clenche (inf.) *to seize, take* 9/108
clene (adj.) *clean, pure* 5/3, 189 *8/114, 125
 *11/115; **klene** 8/89
clenesse (sb.) *cleanliness, purity* 3/13
cleopeden → **clepe**
clepe (inf.) *to call, name* 10.7/20; **clepen**
 13/180; **clepeþ** (sg.ps.) 10.5/38; **clepen**
 (pl.ps.) 13/76, 214; **clepede** (sg.pt.) 3/11;
 clepeden (pl.pt.) 1/52; **cleopeden** 5/46, 169;
 i-cleoped (ptp.) 5/98; **icleped** 3/3; **iclepede**
 3/13
clerc → **clerk**
clere (adj.) *clear, bright, pure* 11/84 *12/128,
 356, 389
clerekes → **clerk**
clerk (sb.) *cleric, scribe* 5/46, 111 *13/147,
 389; **clerc** 7/167; **clerekes** (pl.) 1/61; **clerkes**
 11/35; 13/252, 278, 284, 292 etc.; **clerkis**
 12/283 *14/205; **clerkus** 7/120
cleuiinde (psp.) *to tempt* 4/44
cloke (sb.) *cloak, coat* 7/177, 182, 190
clothed (pl.pt.) 7/54
clothes (sb.pl.) *sheet* 11/94
clothyng (sb.) *clothing* 7/26
cloumben → **clemb**
clumsed (ptp.) *to be numb, stiff* 11/104
clyngeþ (pl.ps.) *to shrink* 10.6/17
cnokez (sg.ps.) *to knock, deal a blow* 6/201;
 knokked (sg.pt.) 11/16
cnotted (ptp.) *knotted* 1/40
coblere (sb.) *cobbler* 7/177, 210
Cockes-lane (prn.) 7/167
coȝed (sg.pt.) *to cough* 6/94
coik → **cok**
coist (sb.) *costs* 14/91
cok (sb.) *cock* 13/457; **coik** 14/98; **kok**
 8/15–17, 27

cokenay (sb.) *weakling* 13/432
cokes (sb.pl.) *cook* 7/145
cold (adj.) 8/127; **colde** 8/128 *10.6/23; **calde**
 (sb.) 11/104; **chald** 3/28; **chold** 3/41; **schald**
 3/27
colerik (adj.) *choleric* 13/43
collegge (sb.) *college* 13/213
coltes (sb. gsg.) *young person* 13/112
com, coman → **come** (2)
comaunde (sg.ps.) *to command, order* 12/341;
 comaunded (sg.pt.) 6/153
come (1) (sb.) *coming* 8/67
come (2) (inf.) 5/13 *9/70, 98 *12/22, 33, 283;
 coman 1/61; **com** 6/134; **comen** 8/68, 90,
 115, 118; **cum** 11/81; **cumen** (inf.) 1/4;
 kome 8/87; ◆ ps.: **comes** 12/57, 84, 184;
 comþ 4/75, 87–88; **comth** 13/332; **comeþ**
 4/26, 62, 78 *9/36 *10.3/35; **cumen** 2/41;
 cummis 14/42, 189; **cumeð** 2/3, 8, 13, 29,
 45; ◆ ps. subj.: **come** 13/306; ◆ psp.:
 cummand (psp.) 14/187; **comyng** 12/315,
 363, 371; ◆ imp.: **come** 12/206, 386; **com**
 6/243 *8/19 *13/298; **cum** 10.10/9 *14/62,
 182; **komeþ** (imp.pl.) 8/135; ◆ pt.: **com** 1/12,
 26 *8/13, 46, 54, 57 etc. *9/29, 53, 62, 129;
 cam 5/66, 89, 94, 113, 117, 197, 206 *7/95,
 118, 120 *10.5/26, 50 *13/178, 303, 440;
 come 5/82 *8/9 *10.5/39 *14/25, 64, 161,
 185; **kom** 8/62; **becom** 6/247; ◆ pl.pt.:
 comen 1/19 *5/60, 192, 194, 211 *7/71
 *8/144 *9/57; ◆ ptp.: **come** 13/23, 255, 461,
 496; **cumen** 1/12; **i-come** 5/75, 167; **icome**
 9/94; **icomen** 8/30; **y-come** 4/70; **ycomen**
 13/166
comlych (adj.) *beautiful* 6/256
comlyly (adv.) *fittingly, graciously* 6/147
commencement (sb.) 3/22
commonnit (ptp.) *to talk, speak* 14/120
communliche (adv.) *commonly* 4/79
compaignye (sb.) *company, party* 13/24, 547;
 ◆ col.: **par compaignye** *for company's sake*
 13/391
compellit (ptp.) *to compell* 14/41
compleit (adv.) *completely* 14/79
complyn (sb.) *compline* 13/395
compt (sg.ps.) *to count, care (for)* 14/98, 172
comth, comþ → **come** (2)
comune (sb.) *people, commonwealth;
 sustenance* 7/95, 123, 126; **comunes** (pl.)
 7/122
comyng; con → **come** (2) **can; gynneth**
concordit (ptp.) *to agree* 14/106, 121
condicioun (sb.) *circumstances* 13/38

conne, conneth → can; gynneth
conquestes (sb.pl.) *conquest* 6/98
conscience (sb.) 7/121 *14/89, 118; consience
  7/95, 130, 187
contacky (inf.) *to fight* 4/92
content (adj.) 14/76
continance (sb.) *bearing; face* 7/26;
  countenaunce 6/122
contrarie (sb.) *contrary* 3/21
contraryed (pl.pt.) *to contradict* 7/59
contreued (pl.pt.) *to contrive, fabricate,*
  concoct 7/123; contrufit 14/54
contreys → cuntre
contrufit → contreued
copis (sb.pl.) *hooded cloak* 7/54, 59
coppe (sb.) *cup* 7/191, 195; coppes (pl.)
  13/152
corage (sb.) *heart, spirit, disposition* 13/22;
  corages (pl.) 13/11
corn (sb.) 1/54, 65 *9/63 *13/163, 219, 232,
  235 etc.
cort → court
cortays (adj.) *courteous, polite* 6/63, 256
cortaysye (adj.) *courtly conduct, courtliness*
  6/50
cosin (sb.) *cousin, relative* 9/92; cosyn 6/159
cote (sb.) *coat, cloak* 6/122 *13/68
Cotingham (pn.) 1/78
cou (sb.) *cow* 4/76; kow 14/94
couenaunt → covenant
couent (sb.) *convent, community* 5/25, 188
couerd (pl.pt.) *to cover* 11/109
couetyce → coueytise
coueyten (pl.ps.) *to desire, covet* 7/31
coueytise (sb.) *covetousness* 7/59, 103;
  couetyce 14/218; coveitise 13/108
counsaille → counsell
counseileþ (sg.ps.) *to counsel, advise* 10.5/21
counsell (sb.) *counsel, advice, support,*
  agreement 14/127, 130; counsaille 12/114,
  163; counseyl 6/134; cownsell 10.9/6
counte (sg.ps.) *to count, consider* 13/280, 416
countenaunce → continance
cours (sb.) *course, path* 13/8
court (sb.) 5/166–167 *6/70 *7/130; cort
  6/134, 147, 187
couth; couthe, couþe → can; gynneth
coveitise → coueytise
covenant (sb.) *agreement, contract* 13/56;
  couenaunt 6/180 *7/191
covyne (sb.) *treachery* 13/60
coward (sb.) 13/491
cowd → can

cowed (sg.pt.) *to retch, throw up* 7/213
cownsell → counsell
cowpe (sb.) *sin, guilt* 7/152
cradel (sb.) *cradle* 13/196, 380, 436, 440 etc.
craft (sb.) 2/56 *6/258 *13/85; craftes (pl.)
  7/123
craif → crave
craketh (sg.ps.) *to protest* 13/225
crane (sb.) *crane (bird)* 4/76
craue → crave
crave (inf.) 12/242; craue (sg.ps.) 6/64, 70;
  craif (sg.pt.) 14/114
crede (sb.) *creed* 2/31
creep → crepen
crekes (sb.pl.) *trick* 13/275
crepen (inf.) *to creep* 13/474; creep (sg.pt.)
  13/450, 484; crepte (sg.pt. (weak)) 13/417;
  cropen (ptp.) 13/483; icrope 8/14
criand, cride, crie, crien → crye
Crist, Criste → Jesus Christ
Cristeman (sb.) *Christian* 3/28; Cristeneman
  3/27
Cristen (adj., sb.) *Christian* 1/84 *2/20
  *13/55; cristene 9/29; Cristine 8/60
cristene → Cristen
Cristeneman → Cristeman
Cristes → Jesus Christ
Cristesmasse → Cristmasse
Cristine → Cristen
Cristmasse (sb.) *Christmas* 6/258;
  Cristesmasse 10.5/32; Crystemas
croce (sb.) *cross* 5/129, 148, 151, 171,
  180–181; crois 9/25; croiz 5/140, 155, 157;
  croys 13/510; croyz 5/39
crokede (adj.) *crooked, bent* 4/84; crukit
  14/93
croos (sb.pl.) *water-pot* 3/12
cropen → crepen
croppes (sb.pl.) *blossom, tip, shoot* 13/7
croun (sb.) *crown, head* 6/151, 206; croune
  5/62; crune 9/13, 114
crouni (inf.) *to crown* 5/92
crowke (sb.) *crock* 13/382
crownyng (sb.) *tonsure* 7/86
croys, croyz → croce
crucethur (sb.) *torture-box* 1/42
crude (inf.) *to move fast* 9/17
crukit → crokede
crune → croun
crye (inf.) *to call, announce, proclaim* 12/363;
  (pl.ps.) 13/230; crie (inf.) 13/296, 302, 420;
  (ps.) 10.8/17 *12/107, 141; crien 10.7/14;
  cryis (sg.ps.) 14/186; criand (psp.) 12/73;
  cride (sg.pt.) 13/531; cryit 14/8, 13; cryede
  (pl.pt.) 7/145; cryed (ptp.) 12/186

Crystemas → Cristmasse
cuddest → kiðen
cum, cumen, cumeð, cummand, cummis →
  come (2)
cunde → kinde
cunnand (sb.) *covenant, agreement* 14/121
cunne, cunnen → can; kin
cuntre (sb.) *country* 11/58; contreys (pl.) 7/31
Curbuil → Willelm
cure (sb.) *cure of souls* 7/86
cursede (sg.pt.) *to curse, excommunicate* 1/63
  *8/130; cursed (ptp.) 12/306
curtaisly (adv.) *courteously, perfectly* 11/83;
  curteisly *in a polite way* 13/221
curtiler (sb.) *gardener* 8/136
cused (sg.pt.) *to accuse* 7/95
custome (sb.) *custom* 3/14
Cutberd → Saints
cuþe → can
cuynde (adj.) *natural* 5/94; cuyndeste (sup.)
  5/106
cyrce → churche
cyrceiærd (sb.) *churchyard*

D

daf (sb.) *fool* 13/432
dai, daies → day
dale (sb.) *valley, dale* 7/17
dalt → dele
dame (sb.) 4/72 *6/257 *7/144 *13/180
dampned (ptp.) *to damn* 12/272, 377
dare (vb.) 12/145; dar 6/74, 87; dorste (sg.pt.)
  3/8 *9/72 *10.8/10 *13/156, 161, 180, 182
  etc.; durste 1/9–10 *7/215
dares (pl.ps.) *to cower* 6/102
dart (adj.) *inferior, darned (?)* 14/172
dastard (sb.) 12/180, 203
Datan (prn.) 12/309
Dauid (prn.) 1/18 *12/369; Dauiþ 4/43
daunced (pl.pt.) *to dance* 11/88
Dawe (prn.) 7/170
dawe, dawed → dawen
dawen (inf.) *to dawn* 10.5/44; dawes (sg.ps.)
  10.3/1; dawe (ps.subj.) 13/473; dawed (sg.pt.)
  11/108
dawenynge (sb.) *dawn* 13/458
dawes, dawse → dawen; day
day (sb.) 4/25 *5/113 *6/85, 272 *10.2/9
  *10.5/1, 14, 17, 32, 35 *10.7/7, 15 *10.10/16
  *11/44, 108 *12/31, 261 *13/19, 149, 216,
  333 etc. *14/144; daye 5/82 *12/148; dai
  2/6 *5/81, 146 *9/84; dæi 1/2, 5; dei 1/2;
  dæis (gsg.) 1/53; (pl.) 1/69; dayes (gsg.)

10.5/20; (pl.) 11/11; days (pl.) 7/144; daies
  8/24, 77; dayis 14/1 *9/18; dawes 5/19, 21,
  208; dawse 11/35; ◆ col.: be dæies (adv.)
  during the day 1/36; ender day (adv.)
  recently 10.5/1; enþer day 10.9/3
dayerye (sb.) *dairy cattle* 13/53
dayes, dayis → day
dayntyez (sb.pl.) *dainty* 6/270
days; dædes → day; deed
dæi, dæies, dæis → day; Midewintre
dær (sb.) *animal, beast* 1/10; dueres (gpl.)
  10.3/2
dære → dear
'dear' dære 1/54; deore 10.7/8; dere (adj.,
  adv.) 6/257 *9/42, 64 *10.9/1, 14; deere
  13/355, 464; duere (adv.) 10.4/34 *10.6/60;
  derrest (sup.) 6/232, 270
debait → debat
debat (sb.) *contention, strife* 7/189; debait
  14/26
debate (inf.) 12/142
dece (sb.) *dais* 6/37, 232, 265; dese 11/75
deciples (sb.pl.) *disciple, student* 3/5, 23 *4/81
declair (inf.) *to state; lay down* 14/1, 67
decreit (sb.) *judgement, decision* 14/74, 81
ded → deth
ded (adj.) *dead* 1/5 *5/45, 49, 211, 221, 228
  *8/75, 96; dede 5/15 *9/132 *12/148; deed
  13/253, 494, 513; dyad 4/28
dede → ded; deth; do
dede (sb.) *deed* 2/23 *5/30, 104, 161 *8/112
  *10.7/24 *11/28 *12/72, 133; deden (pl.)
  3/30; dedis 7/143 *12/24; dædes (pl.) 1/65
deed; deere → ded; dear
deeth → deth
defence (sb.) 14/90
deffie (sg.ps.) *defy* 12/158
deffye (inf.) *to digest* 7/231; defye 7/149;
  defyen 7/240
degree (sb.) 13/40
deȝe; dei → die; day
deide, deie → die
del (sb.) *part, portion* 1/83; deles (pl.) 4/5; ◆
  compd.: somdeel (adv.) *partly, considerably*
  13/135; somdel 13/187; sumdeill 14/27,
  126; sumdel 5/225 *8/119
dele (inf.) *to deal out, give, deal with* 6/82
  *12/63; deles (2.sg.ps.) 6/184; dalt (ptp.)
  6/239
deles → del; dele
delit (sb.) *delight, joy* 4/63; delite 12/63
deluers (sb.pl.) *delver, digger* 7/143
demay (sg.ps.) *to be perturbed* 6/257

deme (inf.) *to judge, deem* 12/34; demen (pl.ps.) 7/94

deolful (adj.) *terrible* 5/73

deope; deore → depe; dear

deoules → devel

depe (adj., adv.) *deep, deeply* 7/17 *8/55 *12/377 *13/455; deope 5/142, 149 *10.4/35 *10.7/30; ◆ neg.: undep *shallow* 1/43

Depeford (pn.) *Deptford* 13/130

depreced (pl.pt.) *to subjugate* 6/6

depriue (sg.ps.subj.) *to deprive* 12/175

dere → dear

derk (adj.) *dark* 13/449

derke (sb.) *darkness* 9/86

dern (adj.) *secret, hidden* 2/20; derne 10.8/2

derrest → dear

des (sb.) *dice* 4/31

descended (ptp.) 13/208

dese → dece

deseritede (ptp.) *to depose* 5/107

deseyte (sb.) *deceit* 7/77

desgysed (ptp.) *to disguise* 4/69

desire (sb.) 12/258

desireth (sg.ps.) *to desire* 13/104

despendeþ (pl.ps.) *to spend* 4/57; despended (ptp.) 13/207

despenses (sb.pl.) *expenditure* 4/59

despitously (adv.) *angrily* 13/498

dest → do

destrueth (pl.ps.) *to destroy* 7/24; destruyde (sg.pt.) 5/68

dettes (sb.pl.) *debt* 7/91

deþ; deþe → do; deth

deth (sb.) *death* 7/17; deþ 10.7/23; deeth 13/61, 116; deþe 10.2/9; ded 2/49; dede 12/317

deue (adj.pl.) *deaf* 5/193; dyaue 4/85

deuel (sb.) *devil, fiend* 2/56 *8/52, 141 *12/133, 223; devel 13/127, 481; deuill 14/117; deuyll 12/341; dyeuel 4/7–8, 11, 15, 34, 85, 90; dyeule 4/81, 83; deueles (gsg.) 2/61; deuillis 14/214; dyeules (gsg.) 4/94; deuelis (pl.) 12/399; deoules 1/34; dyeulen (pl.) 4/10

deuyll, devel → deuel

devoure (inf.) *to devour* 13/210

devout (adj.) 13/22

devyse (sg.ps.) *to describe* 13/34

Dew (prn.) 7/144

dewes (sb. gsg.) *dew* 10.8/33

dewly (adv.) *duly* 12/248

deye → die

deynous (adj.) *haughty* 13/165

dich (sb.) *lair, ditch* 4/94 *13/188; dych 13/330

did, dide, diden → do

'die' deie (inf.) 9/43; deye 10.7/21; dye 12/164, 365 *13/218; (sg.ps.) 13/531; deȝe (sg.ps.) 10.2/9; dyen (pl.ps.) 7/102; deide (sg.pt.) 5/199; died 11/64

digne (adj.) *haughty* 13/188

dignete (sb.) *dignity, office* 5/54, 121, 144

dignitee → God

diȝt (inf.) *to ajudge, condemn* 6/82; diht (ptp.) 10.2/9

dikere (sb.) *ditcher* 7/170; dykers (pl.) 7/143

dim (adj.) 2/62; dimme 2/5

dint (sb.) *blow* 6/176; dunt 6/239; dynt 6/102; dintes (pl.) 8/148; dintez 6/123

dipped (ptp.) 11/103

discende (sg.pt.) *to descend* 12/77

discomfited (ptp.) *to defeat* 7/108; disconfit 7/112

discouerez (sg.ps.) *to uncover, reveal* 6/205

dismayd (ptp.) *to dismay* 6/123

disordeneliche (adv.) *unduly, over-much* 4/48

disparage (inf.) *to degrade* 13/495

disport (sb.) *entertainment, disport* 13/324

disserued (ptp.) *to deserve* 6/239

disshere (sb.) *dish-maker or seller* 7/173

diueð (sg.ps.) *to dive* 2/55

diverse (adj.) 13/81

diversely (adv.) 13/81

do (inf.) 3/43 *4/42, 83, 99 *5/14, 17, 132, 165 etc. *7/109 *8/69, 115, 126 *9/81 *11/91 *12/263 *14/119; don 1/76 *5/116, 124, 171 *8/23 *10.2/10 *10.5/9 *10.7/10; done 5/72 *8/118; doon 13/105, 259, 415; ◆ ps.: do 3/9 *4/12 *5/127, 138 *8/22, 25–26, 96 *9/12 *10.7/26 *12/203 *13/249 *14/127; doon 13/502; dooth 13/95, 292, 544; dois 14/198; dose 11/28–29; dest 4/42 *5/44 *8/17–18, 76; deþ 3/36 *4/45, 82, 85, 97; dost 10.8/20; doð 2/54, 57; doþ 3/10, 20, 29 *4/68, 99 *8/109; dothe 10.10/3; ◆ sg.ps. subj.: do 3/42–43; ◆ pt.: dede 4/17, 36, 96 *8/34; did 6/107 *12/258; dide 1/5, 24, 28, 30, 39, 43 *13/328, 519; diden 1/30, 36, 41–42, 46, 49, 58; dude 5/41, 66 *9/30, 65, 67, 107 etc. *10.7/24; duden 5/212, 215; ◆ ptp.: do 8/34 *10.4/47; don 6/265 *8/20, 27; done 5/212 *11/81 *12/24, 223 *14/175; doon 13/92, 258, 271; i-do 5/48, 92, 104; ido 3/21 *8/111; idon 8/53 *9/81; y-do 4/80, 96; ydon 10.7/13

doctours (sb.pl.) *authority in theology, scholar*
   7/59, 85
doghter (sb.) *daughter* 13/193, 247, 360, 366
   etc.
dois → **do**
dokked (ptp.) *cut short* 13/46
dole (sb.) *pain, sorrow* 12/347
dom (sb.) *judgement, doom* 5/118 *6/82;
   dome 12/319
dombe (sb.pl.) *the dumb* 4/85; **doumbe** 5/193
don, done → **do**
dong (sb.) *dung* 4/20
doon, dooth → **do**
dor (sb.) *door* 6/245; **dore** 7/208 *8/14
   *13/281, 467; **dure** 14/144
dorste; dose → **dare; do**
doser (sb.) *wall-tapestry* 6/265
dosoyne (sb.) *dozen* 7/170
dost → **do**
dotage (sb.) 13/122
doth, doð, doþ dothe → **do**
dou (sb.) *dough* 8/128
double (adv.) 6/270
doumbe → **dombe**
doun (adv.) *down, downwards* 5/34 *6/122,
   155, 210 *8/124 *13/266, 283, 309, 324 etc.
   *14/161, 176, 182, 185, 189; **doune** 11/57,
   77 *12/78, 180, 203, 259, 341; **downe**
   11/56; **dun** 2/11, 55
doune → **doun**
doune (sb.) *down, hill* 10.6/11; **dounes** 10.3/2
dounward (adv.) *downwards, down* 5/37;
   dounwart 14/187, 223; **a-dounward** 5/38
doute (sb.) *fear, doubt* 6/229 *13/211
doutis (sg.ps.) *to fear* 14/51
douþe (sb.) *assembled company* 6/184
dowis; downe → **dowue; doun**
dowue (sb.) *dove* 12/78; **dowis** (pl.) 14/9
draf-sak (sb.) *sack of chaff* 13/430
draȝe, draȝen → **drawe**
drapen → **drepeð**
draucht (sb.) *line (?)* 14/9
draught (sb.) *draft* 12/399
draw → **well**
drawe (inf.) 5/151, 181 *12/319, 399; **draȝe**
   9/15, 80; **drawes** (2.sg.ps.) 12/279; **drawis**
   (3.sg.ps.) 14/223; **draȝen** (pl.ps.) 2/40, 51, 59;
   droȝ (sg.pt.) 6/122; **drou** 8/139; **drough**
   13/116; **drouȝ** 5/4, 25, 157, 187; **drow**
   7/208 *13/528; **drogh** (pl.pt.) 11/74; **drawin**
   (ptp.) 11/97
drawes, drawin, drawis → **drawe**
draye (sb.) *noise* 12/146

dreccheð (sg.ps.) *to stay* 2/26; **dreccheþ** *to
   torment* 10.8/21
drede (1) (sg.ps.) *to dread* 13/98
drede (2) (sb.) *dread, fear* 4/50–51 *5/105
   *6/102 *8/45 *12/137, 146
dreȝe (inf.) *to suffer, experience* 10.4/25
   *10.6/46
drepeð (sg.ps.) *to kill* 2/55; **drapen** (pl.pt.)
   1/42, 48
drery (adj.) *dreary, sad* 11/13
dres (inf.) *to turn, direct, make ready* 6/261;
   dresses (sg.ps.) 6/204; **dressez** 6/232
dri (inf.) *dry* 11/100
drift (sb.) *drove, team* 14/36
Driȝte (sb.) *lord, God* 9/25; **Driȝtin** 2/34;
   Drihten 1/85; **Drihtin** 1/88; **Drihtines** (gsg.)
   1/86; **Dryhtin** 1/87
drink (sb.) 11/117; **drinke** 4/4, 6 *8/72;
   drynke 13/356; **drunche** 8/7
drinke (inf.) *to drink* 4/13 *8/40; **drynk**
   6/124; **drink** (imp.) 4/37; **drinkeþ** (pl.ps.)
   3/28; **drynken** 13/371; **drinked** 3/34;
   drinken 2/54; **dronk** (sg.pt.) 8/47; **dronke**
   (pl.pt.) 7/164; **dronken** (ptp.) 13/374, 382;
   ydronke 4/29 *7/220; **idrunke** 3/17
driue; drogh → **dryue; drawe**
droghte (sb.) *drought* 13/2, 51
droȝ → **drawe**
dronk, dronke, dronken → **drinke**
dronke (adj.) *drunken* 13/137
dropes (sb.pl.) *drop* 10.8/33
droppeth (sg.ps.) *to drip* 13/119
drou, drough, drouȝ → **drawe**
droui (adj.) *stirred-up* 2/47
drow; drunche → **drawe; drink**
dry (adj.) 14/170; **dryȝe** *unmoved* 6/122
Dryhtin → **Driȝte**
drynk, drynken → **drinke**
drynke → **drink**
dryue (inf.) *to drive, spend* 6/176; **dryuis**
   (sg.ps.) 14/29; **driue** (sg.ps.subj.) 9/37, 82;
   dryueth (pl.ps.) 7/144; **dryuand** (psp.)
   14/222; **dryve** (ptp.) 13/334
dude, duden → **do**
duere → **dear**
dueres; dun → **dær; doun**
dunt; dure → **dint; dor**
durste → **dare**
dwale (sb.) *sleeping potion* 13/385
dwelle (inf.) 7/83, 12/304, (pl.ps.) 12/102;
   dwellynge (psp.) 13/149; **dweld** (sg.pt.)
   11/58; **dwelten** (pl.pt.) 13/227
dweole miengyngue (sb.) *trance* 5/18

dweolkningue (sb.) *trance* 5/220
dyad; dyaue → **ded; deue**
dych; dye, dyen → **dich; die**
dyeuel, dyeule, dyeulen, dyeules → **deuel**
dykers → **dikere**
dymmede (pl.pt.) *to grow dim* 7/208
dyne (inf.) *to dine* 7/146
dynge (imp.) *to beat* 12/180, (inf.) 12/203
dynne (sb.) *din, noise* 12/234, 284
dynt → **dint**

E

'each' ælc 1/80; **ech** 4/69 *5/8, 48 *13/39;
  eche 5/43, 192, 194; **euch** 8/112, 143; **euche**
  8/51; **vch** 10.3/29 *10.6/13 *10.8/12; **ech-on**
  5/158; **echon** 13/369; **echone** 5/90
'early' erly 13/33; **air** 14/3; **airlie** 14/5, 37;
  herly 7/175
'eat' ete (inf.) 4/12, 25; **eten** 5/19; **ethe**
  4/48–49; **ett** 11/86; **ette** 11/45; **est** (2.sg.ps.)
  4/42; **et** (imp.) 4/21; **eth** 4/37; **heten** (pl.ps.)
  2/54; **eat** (sg.pt.) 5/21; **eet** 7/232; **hete** 8/78;
  i-ete (ptp.) 8/49, 85; **etinge** (sb.) 4/75
ech, eche, ech-on, echone → **each**
eddre-blod (sb.) *blood in the veins* 8/23
ede; Edward → **go; Saints**
edwitede (pl.pt.) *to accuse, reproach* 7/222
ee → **eye**
eek (adv.) *also, likewise, too* 13/5, 41, 187,
  215 etc.; **eik** 14/54; **eke** 10.4/9 *10.5/15–16
eelde → **elde**
eet → **eat**
eft (adv.) *again* 11/50, 103
ęfter, efter, efterþan → **after**
efterward (adv.) *afterwards, later* 4/59–60,
  66–67, 76
egen, eghe, eghen → **eye**
egre (adj.) *eager* 8/145
eȝe, eȝen, eiȝene → **eye**
eik; eir → **eek; long**
eirrand (psp.) *to plough* 14/37
eke → **eek**
elde (sb.) *age* 2/3 *5/195; **eelde** 13/109
elde, elder, elderis → **old**
elles (adv.) *else, otherwise* 5/48 *7/89; **ellez**
  6/82, 171; **ellis** 12/305 *13/252
elleswer (adv.) *elsewhere* 8/104
ellez, ellis → **elles**
em (sb.) *uncle* 6/143; **eom** 1/22
emang → **among**
emell (prep.) *among* 12/104; **ymel** 13/395
Emme (prn.) 7/144

empty (adj.) 13/118, 358; **emptie** 14/105
encenȝ (sb.) *incense* 10.5/41
enclyne (inf.) *to incline* 6/127
encrees (inf.) *to increase* 12/292
end (sb.) 14/17, 184; **ende** 5/223 *6/272
  *7/29, 201 *10.4/48 *10.8/12 *12/52, 232,
  300, 404 *13/15; ◆ contr. art.: **þende** 9/59
endeþ (sg.ps.) *to end* 9/133–134; **endis** 11/27
  *14/194; **endyng** (sb.) 13/398
ender; endis → **day; endeþ**
endles (adj.) *eternal, endless* 12/35; **yendles**
  (adj.) 12/124
endyng; enes → **endeþ; ones**
Engelond, Engelonde → **England**
engendred (ptp.) *to produce* 13/4
'England' Engelond (pn.) 5/59 *13/16;
  Engelonde 5/1; **Englaland** 1/26; **Engleland**
  1/8, 12; **Enguelond** 5/60, 64, 78, 84 etc.;
  Enguelonde 5/62, 66, 69, 71, etc.; **Ingland**
  11/35
Englische (adj.) *English* 5/79, 81, 106
eni, enie; enmang → **any; among**
Ennias (prn.) *Aeneas* 6/5
'enough' aneuch 14/101; **onoh** 1/45; **innogh**
  6/76, 191, 264; **inogh** 11/74, 112; **inou** 8/12,
  40, 42, 46, 74, 130, 139; **i-nouȝ** 5/26, 65,
  142, 188; **i-novȝ** 5/3, 40, 73; **inowe** 8/144;
  ynoȝe 9/70; **ynoh** 10.1/7
ensaumpill (sb.) *example, exemplum* 11/65;
  ensaumple 11/2, 121
entent (sb.) *intent* 11/72
entered, enteres → **entre**
enterludez (sb.pl.) *interlude* 6/259
entre (inf.) *to enter* 12/270; **entered** (sg.pt.)
  12/165; **enteres** (sg.ps.) 12/282
entree (sb.) *entry* 13/467
entremes (sb.) *appetizer* 4/71
enþer; eny; eom → **day; any; em**
eorl (sb.) *ruler, earl* 5/63
eorþe → **erth**
eou, eoure, eouwer, eov, eower → **ȝe** (2)
eppel (sb.) *apple* 4/36
Epyphany (prn.) 10.5/38
er → **other** (1)
er (adv., conj.) *before, early, already* 5/27, 29,
  113, 153, 180, 182, 186 *6/165 *9/87–88
  *10.2/5, 9 *13/36, 394, 419, 465, 473; **ar**
  7/136; **are** 5/178, 207, 210 *12/38, 98, 345;
  or 2/20, 22 *9/84 *12/154, 156, 224, 278;
  erour (comp.) 8/2; **eroust** (sup.) 8/8, 62; **erst**
  13/325
erchebischop (sb.) *archbishop* 5/49–50, 119,
  128, 155, 160, 168, 176; **ærcebiscop** 1/13

erde (sb.) *land, earth, world* 6/27
eremites → **hermit**
eres (sb.pl.) *ear* 7/76; **erys** 13/45
erly → **early**
ermit → **hermit**
ern (sb.) *eagle* 2/19; **ernes** (gsg.) 2/1
ernde (1) (sg.ps.) *to obtain* 10.4/30
ernde (2) (sb.) *business, mission* 6/44
erne (inf.) *to run* 8/8
ernes → **ern**
ernist (sb.) *earnest, seriousness* 14/109
erour, eroust → **er**
err, ert → **be**
erth (sb.) *earth, world* 12/363; **erthe** 1/64
  *7/142, 209; **erþe** 3/4, 23 *6/4, 214; **eorþe**
  5/36, 195; **vrþe** 5/204
erthely (adj.) *earthly* 12/10, 134
erys → **eres**
es; esche → **be; ask**
ese (sb.) *ease, comfort, quiet* 7/55 *13/343;
  eyse 4/29
esed (ptp.) *to entertain* 13/29
esely (adv.) *easily* 11/114
esement (sb.) *easement* 13/403, 410
Esope (prn.) 14/1
espie (inf.) *to discover, perceive* 13/419; **espye**
  13/526
est → **eat**
estaat (sb.) *state* 13/173
este → **west**
Estermorewe (sb.) *Easter Sunday morning*
  10.5/44
Estren (sb.) *Easter* 1/84
estres (sb.) *interior of a room* 13/519
Estun (pn.) *Great Easton, Leicestershire* 1/79
estward (adv.) *eastwards* 7/14
et, ete, eten, eth, ethe, etinge, ett, ette → **eat**
eþe (sg.ps.) *to conjure, entreat* 6/166
euch, euche → **each**
eue (sb.) *eve* 5/202
euel (adj., adv., sb.) *evil, bad, vile* 3/42; **euele**
  3/27–28, 30, 37, 42 *4/92; **euil** 11/29; **euill**
  14/136, 208; **yfel** 1/15; **yuele** 1/35, 68; **vuele**
  (adv.) 5/48; **yvele** 13/544
euen → **even**
Euen (prn.) *Eve* 4/17, 36
euensong (sb.) *evensong* 7/197
euer, euere → **ever**
euer-ech-on, euerech-on, euerech-one,
  euerich, euerie, euerilkone → **every**
euermore (adv.) *evermore, forever* 10.1/17
  *12/15; **euremo** 4/50; **everemoo** 13/185,
  462

Euerwicke (pn.) *York* 5/49
euery → **every**
Eugenie → **Pape**
euil, euill → **euel**
euin; eure → **even; ever**
euremo → **euermore**
euyn → **even**
euyn (sb.) *evening* 11/90
even (adj., adv.) 12/52, 280; **evene** 13/83; **euen**
  6/231 *12/76, 80; **euin** 14/93; **euyn**
  11/90–91
ever (adv.) 13/44, 96, 117, 516; **evere** 13/78,
  101, 371, 394 etc.; **euer** 6/80 *7/46 *10.7/7,
  14–15, 22 etc. *10.8/7, 15, 22, 29, 36
  *12/228 *14/77, 148; **euere** 5/100, 225
  *8/71 *12/200, 292; **eure** 2/44 *9/134; **æure**
  1/50, 63; ♦ col.: **æure um wile** *repeatedly*
  1/51; **evere in oon** (adv.) *continuously*
  13/104
everemo → **euermore**
everichon → **every**
everideel (adv.) *completely* 13/539
every (adj., pron.) 13/3, 6, 15; **euerich** 3/39;
  euerie 14/198; **euery** 10.10/4; **æuric** 1/6, 32,
  61; ♦ compd.: **everichon** *everyone* 13/31;
  euer-ech-on 5/223; **euerech-on** 5/136;
  euerech-one 5/146; **euerilkone** 12/311;
  heuereuchon 8/135
exces (sb.) *excess* 7/218
Execestre (pn.) *Exeter* 1/16
expence (sb.) *cost* 14/91
extremitie (sb.) *extreme severity* 14/131
ey (interj.) *ah, oh* 13/444; **ay** 12/343
eye (sb.) 13/143; **ee** 14/219; **eghe** 11/24; **ye**
  13/10, 89, 273, 525; **eȝe** 10.1/7; **egen** (pl.)
  2/5, 10; **eghen** 11/15; **eȝen** 2/22, 26
  *10.4/12; **eiȝene** 5/220; **yes** 7/72, 208; **eyen**
  13/198; **euȝen** 10.6/22; **uȝen** 6/91
euȝen → **eye**
eyr (sb.) *heir* 5/61; **eyres** (pl.) 5/89–90
eyse → **ese**
eyþur (pron.) *either* 5/74

F

Fabianes → **Saints**
fabill (sb.) *fable* 14/78, 196
face (sb.) 6/104, 232 *12/90 *13/158
fader (sb.) *father* 9/12, 38 *10.7/16 *13/100,
  330; **fadir** 12/5, 25, 79, 226, 229, 235;
  fadris (gsg.) 12/36; **uader** 4/97–98
faȝen → **fain**
faile (inf.) *to fail, be at fault, be wanting, lack*
  12/157; **faill** 14/61; **faillen** 13/111; **faylez**

(2.sg.ps.) 6/65, 242; **failede** (sg.pt.) 3/6;
failleden (pl.pt.) 5/85
fain (adj., adv.) *glad, gladly, joyful, joyfully*
5/132; **fayn** 6/175 *10.9/1; **faine** 11/120;
fayne 10.10/16; **faȝen** 2/40, 51; **fane** 14/88,
143; ◆ neg.: **vnfane** 14/210
fair (adj.) 5/231 *7/19 *9/133 *13/175, 200
*14/125, 146; **faire** 5/162, 188–189 *11/74,
92, 109 *13/62, 247, 286, 293 etc.; **fayr**
10.1/7; **fayre** 6/154, 214 *7/178; **feir**
10.3/26 *13/201; **feyr** 10.3/37 *10.5/8; **feyre**
10.3/34, 40; **uayre** 4/36; **fairer** (comp.)
13/303; **feireste** (sup.) 10.8/11; **feyrest**
10.1/14; **ffayrest** 10.8/30
fairis → **fare** (2)
faith (sb.) 12/29, 364 *14/207; **fayþ** 6/66; ◆
col.: **by my fayth** *on my good word* 13/433;
by my fay 13/258; **in god fayth** 6/168;
y-faith *truly* 13/268; **y-fayth** 13/246
faitour (sb.) *liar, trickster* 12/157; **faitours**
(pl.) 12/209
fal (sb.) *fall* 13/509
fall (inf.) *to fall, happen, occur* 14/75; **falle**
6/270; (ptp.) 7/63; (sg.ps. conj.) 13/396; (ptp.)
13/507, 512; **falleð** (sg.ps.) 2/12, 29; **falles**
(sg.ps.) 6/145 *13/266; **fallen** (pl.ps.) 2/11;
(ptp.) 6/23; (inf.) 10.1/10; **fel** (sg.pt.) 5/8
*6/217 *10.8/16; **fell** 12/14; **feol** 5/39–40, 43
*9/110 *10.4/38; **fil** 13/505; **ful** 5/37 *7/106,
113; **iuel** 3/5; **yfalle** (ptp.) 10.7/17 *13/25;
afalle (ptp.) *fallen down* 8/9
fals (adj.) *false, treacherous, deceiving* 7/106
*13/542 *14/54; **false** 5/79 *10.3/15
*10.8/19 *13/492–493, 515; **falsly** (adv.)
7/229
falsnesses (sb.pl.) *offence* 7/69
falt (sb.) *fault* 14/205
faltered (sg.pt.) *to falter* 6/217
faltit (sg.pt.) *to commit a fault* 14/35
fand, fande; fane → **find; fain**
fange (inf.) *to receive* 6/178
fantasie (sb.) *lie, fiction* 14/221; **fantasyes**
(pl.) 7/37
far → **fare** (2)
far (adj., adv.) 14/40; **fer** 6/13 *13/145, 239;
ferre (comp.) 12/156, 336; **fyrre** 6/165, 198
fare (1) (sb.) *journey; use, practice; behaviour*
1/53 *6/196 *10.3/27 *12/158 *13/223
fare (2) (inf.) *to go, turn, journey, fare* 8/71,
(sg.ps.) 8/101; (sg.ps.subj.) 2/32 *13/95; (ptp.)
9/48; **far** (sg.ps.subj.) 13/464; **faren** (inf.)
1/53; **fares** (sg.ps.) 13/247; **fairis** 14/188; **for**
(sg.pt.) 1/1, 21, 74; ◆ col.: **fare weel** *farewell*
13/460

faren, fares → **fare** (2)
farleis → **ferlyes**
fast (1) (adv.) *fast, securely, safely* 7/41
*10.7/30; **faste** 5/38, 70, 85, 149, 157, 180,
219 *7/65 *12/107 *13/305, 314, 329, 418,
516
fast (2) (vb.) *to fast* 11/11; **ueste** (inf.) 4/21;
fastyng (psp.) 7/153; **fastynges** (sb.pl.)
fasting 7/69
fastyng, fastynges → **fast** (2)
fastyng-dayes (sb.pl.) *day of fasting* 7/161,
235
faten → **fatt**
fatt (sb.) *vat* 11/97; **faten** (pl.) 3/12, 14
fattest (adj. sup.) 14/97
fay → **faith**
faylez → **faile**
fayn, fayne → **fain**
fayr, fayre → **fair**
fayteden (pl.pt.) *to dissemble* 7/43
fæstned (ptp.) *to fasten* 1/46
feblesse (sb.) *feebleness* 5/196
feblest (adj. šup.) *feeblest, least capable* 6/141
fedde (sg.pt.) *to feed, drink* 7/235; **fed** (ptp.)
11/89
feele → **fele** (1)
feend (sb.) *fiend, devil, enemy* 13/512; **feende**
(sb.) *fiend, devil, enemy* 12/9, 14, 234, 335;
feind 14/201; **fende** 12/340; **feynd** 14/205
feere → **fere; in**
feersly; feet → **ferse; foot**
feȝtyng → **fight**
feind; feir → **feend; fair**
feir (sb.) *companion (?)* 14/5
feireste → **fair**
feit; fel → **foot; fall**
felaȝe, felaȝes, felaw → **felowe**
felaweshipe (sb.) *company, party* 13/26, 32
felaws → **felowe**
feld (1) (sb.) *field, battle field* 7/19; **felde** 9/21
feld (2) (ptp.) *to fell, chop down* 11/43; **ifulde**
(sg.pt.) 9/114; **yueld** 4/14
felde → **feld** (1)
fele (1) (adj., sb.) *many* 6/215 *8/83 *9/35
*10.8/32; **feele** 12/61; **feole** 10.3/15; **uele**
4/34, 58, 62, 69, 92
fele (2) (inf.) *to feel, experience* 12/346; **feleð**
(sg.ps.) 2/54; **felen** (pl.ps.) 2/40; **feled** (sg.pt.)
11/93–94; **fielde** 5/196
feled, felen, feleð → **fele** (2)
Felix Brutus (prn.) 6/13
fell → **fall**
felle (adj.) *bold, fierce* 6/78

felloun (adj.) *fierce, extreme* 14/31
felowe (sb.) *fellow, friend, companion* 12/284;
  felaȝe 9/80; **felaw** 11/25; **felaws** (gsg.) 11/23;
  uelaȝe 4/14; **felaȝes** (pl.) 9/15, 39, 101;
  uelaȝes 4/95
fen (sb.) 13/289, 304, 315
fende → **feend**
fende (inf.) *to defend* 12/30
fenge *to receive (?), gain (?)* 10.3/18
fenkelsedes (sb.pl.) *fennel-seeds* 7/161
feol; feole → **fall; fele** (1)
feorden → **ferd**
fer; fere → **far; fir; in**
fere (sb.) *companion, friend* 8/60 *9/45
  *10.3/18, (sb.) **feere** 12/352; **ifere** 8/86, 93;
  feren (pl.) 9/83
ferd (sg.pt.) *to go, happen* 11/102; **ferde** 9/84;
  feorden (pl.pt.) 1/19 [see fare (2)]
feren → **fere**
ferly (adj.) *amazing* 13/397
ferly (adv.) *exceedingly* 6/175
ferlyes (sb.) *marvel, wonder* 6/23 *7/63;
  farleis 12/61
ferme (adj.) *firm* 14/207
ferne (adj.) *distant, far* 13/14
ferre → **far**
ferse (adv.) *fiercely* 12/131; **feersly** *proudly*
  6/116
fersnes (sb.) *impetuosity, unruliness* 14/11
ferst → **first**
ferther (adv. comp.) *far, further* 13/36; **forther**
  13/341, 446
ferthyng-worth (sb.) *amounting to a farthing*
  7/161
fest (1) (sb.) *feast* 9/87; **feste** 9/63
fest (2) (sb.) *fist* 13/499; **fust** 6/178
feste → **fest** (1)
feste (ptp.) *to fasten, make secure, rely on*
  12/335, 337, (sg.ps.) 12/340; **festeð** 2/62
festen (sb.) *firm ground* 2/52
festeð; fet, fete → **feste; foot**
fette (inf.) *to fetch, summon* 5/199; (sg.pt.)
  12/382; **fotte** (inf.) 6/238; **foch** (imp.) 6/183
feðres (sb.pl.) *feather* 2/11
feuere (sb.) *fever* 5/197
fewe (adj.) *few* 5/190 *7/63 *9/101
feye (adj.) *doomed* 10.1/10
feynd → **feend**
feyr, feyre, feyrest, ffayrest → **fair**
ffor; fielde → **for; fele** (2)
fierd (sb.) *army* 5/67
fif (num.) *five* 10.5/24; **fiue** 5/57 *8/15 *9/18,
  82

fifte (ord.) *fifth* 10.5/49; **vifte** 4/63
fight (inf.) 12/131; **fiȝte** 9/36; **fyȝt** 6/65; **fighte**
  (pl.ps.) 13/515; **foughten** (pl.pt.) 7/43, (ptp.)
  13/62; **fuȝten** (pl.pt.) 9/58; **feȝtyng** (sb.) 6/54
Fikenhild (prn.) 9/65, 71, 78, 81 etc.;
  Fikenhildes (gsg.) 9/114
fil → **fall**
filthe (sb.) *filth* 12/380; **fulþe** 8/83; **uelþe** 4/90
finall (adj.) *final* 14/72
find (inf.) 14/154, 163, 195; **finden** 1/54;
  fynde 6/111, 242 *7/122 *12/6, 288
  *13/468, 518, (sg.ps.subj.) 6/236; **uynde** 4/25;
  findes (sg.ps.) 14/205; **fyndes** 13/354; **findeð**
  2/58; **findis** 14/151; **vind** 8/127; **fynt**
  13/295; **fyndeth** (pl.ps.) 7/37; **fand** (sg.pt.)
  1/69; **fond** 5/68 *7/19 *8/11, 47, 81, 147
  *9/92 *13/340, 445, 475; **fonde** 7/56; **foond**
  13/441, 447, 520; **founde** 8/37, 46, 56, 107,
  (pl.pt.) 9/21; (ptp.) 13/283; **fande** (pl.pt.)
  12/62; **funde** 6/183
Fines (prn. gsg.) *Phinehas* 7/107
fir (sb.) *fire* 2/54; **fer** 3/31; **fyr** 6/246 *13/106,
  340, 396
first (adj., adv.) 13/42, 246; **ferst** 3/17, 20;
  furst 10.5/25; **furste** 7/221; **fyrst** 6/9, 77,
  88, 146, 166; **uerst** 4/7, 35; **verst** 4/58, 65
fis (sb.) *fish* 2/35, 38, 44, 50; **fysch** 7/240; **viss**
  4/18; **fissches** (pl.) 11/44, 46, 60; **fisses** 2/40,
  42
fisshe (inf.) *to fish* 13/151
fit (sb.) *experience* 13/408, 454
fitte (sb.) *punishment* 12/346
fiue; flaȝe → **fif; fleȝeð**
flaill (sb.) *crank* 14/177
Flaundres → **Purnele**
flayd (adj.) *afraid* 12/209
fle → **fleȝeð**
fle (1) (sb.) *flea* 14/56, 172
fle (2) (inf.) *to flay, skin* 9/55
fleȝeð (sg.ps.) *to fly* 2/7; **fle** (imp.) 8/19; **flaȝe**
  (sg.pt.) 6/246; **flowen** (ptp.) 8/16
fleme (inf.) *to flee* 9/6
flesc (sb.) *flesh* 1/55; **fles** 2/60; **fless** 11/101;
  fleysh 10.5/11, 46
flesliche (adv.) *bodily, materially* 3/4, 22, 36
fless → **flesc**
flet (1) (sb.) *floor* 6/81
flet (2) (sg.ps.) *to swim, float* 2/36
fleye (inf.) *flee, esacpe* 12/380
fleysh → **flesc**
fliȝt (sb.) *flight, flying* 2/4; *wings* 2/10; **fliȝte**
  9/69
flitte (inf.) *to flit, escape* 12/210, 336, (sg.ps.)
  12/340

flod (sb.) *sea, flood* 6/13; **floode** 12/76
flok (sb.) *flock* 8/15; **floik** 14/97
floode → **flod**
floor (sb.) 13/501
flour (1) (sb.) *flour* 13/277, 317, 536
flour (2) (sb.) *flower, blossom* 10.3/7 *13/4, 398
flowe (inf.) *to flow* 9/122
flowen → **fleȝeð**
flugæn (pl.pt.) *to flee* 1/62; **flugen** 1/56
flum (sb.) *river* 11/103; **flume** 12/76
flye (sb.) *fly* 13/416
flynt (sb.) *flint* 6/246
flyte (inf.) *to quarrel* 14/138
fnorteth (sg.ps.) *to snort* 13/387
foch → **fette**
fodder (sb.) 13/92
fode → **foode**
fode (sb.) *being, child* 9/40 *10.8/30
foȝel (sb.) *bird, fowl* 9/69; **foul** 10.1/2; **fowel** 13/126; **foules** (pl.) 7/207 *10.4/2; **foweles** 13/9
fois; fol; folc → **foo; fool; folk**
folde (sb.) *earth, ground* 6/23, 183, 209
foldez (sg.ps.) *to befit, be proper* 6/146
fole (1) (sb.) *horse* 6/246
fole (2) (adj.) *foolish* 4/6
folegeð → **folȝen**
foles → **fool**
folȝen (inf.) *to follow* 2/62; **follou** 14/5; **folegeð** (sg.ps.) 2/58; **folowd** (sg.pt.) 11/45
folie (sb.) *folly, sin* 13/104; **foly** 6/111 *11/8; **folies** (pl.) 3/38
folk (sb.) 5/36, 65, 68 etc. *7/19 *9/56, 131 *10.6/12 *11/58 *13/12, 25, 79, 81 etc.; **folc** 1/13; **folke** 12/6, 53, 73, 295, 364; **uolk** 4/35, 58; **uolke** 4/65; **folkes** (pl.) 12/70
folliche (adv.) *foolish* 5/124
follou, folowd → **folȝen**
folvellet → **fulfill**
folwd; foly → **folȝen; folie**
fomen (sb.pl.) *foe* 8/144 [see foo]
fond, fonde → **find**
fonde (inf.) *to try, test, experience* 6/78; **founde** 10.3/27; **fondede** (sg.pt.) 9/127; **fondeden** (pl.pt.) 5/182; **fonde** (ptp.) 10.8/4; **founded** 6/54
fonne (sb.) *fool* 13/313
foo (sb.) *foe, enemy* 12/287 *13/63; **fooes** 12/386; **fois** (pl.) 12/30
foode (sb.) *food, sustenance* 12/10; **fode** 2/15, 34 *7/43
fooes → **foo**

fool (sb.) 13/252; **fol** 5/123; **fooles** (pl.) 13/335; **foles** 5/123 *7/37
foond → **find**
foot (sb.) 13/348, 365; **fot** 6/209 *10.4/13; **fote** 6/116; **uot** 4/87; **fute** 14/83, 146; **feet** (pl.) 13/298, 380, 437; **fet** 1/38, 40 *5/36; **fete** 6/215; **feit** 14/144
for → **fare** (2)
for (conj., prep.) **ffor** 10.7/34; **fore** 3/24; **uor** 4/16, 34–35, 39–40 etc.; **vor** 4/19, 30, 46, 50 etc. ♦ compd.: **forte** *in order to* 10.1/9 *10.2/2 *10.5/54; **for-to** 5/12, 14, 70, 72, 121, 151, 159, 179, 227; **forto** 8/133; **forþi** 1/22, 82 *6/27, 242 *10.1/11; **forthy** 13/255; **forþy** 6/70; ♦ col.: **for soþe** (adv.) *truly, indeed* 6/190, 202; **uor zoþe** 4/96; **uor þet** *so that* 4/76
forage (sb.) 13/92
forbaren → **fur-bere**
forbid → **God**
force (sb.) 12/210 *13/136, 235 *14/41; **na fors** *no matter* 13/400
forcursæd (ptp.) *to excommunicate* 1/64
fordon (ptp.) *to destroy* 1/65
fordriuen (ptp.) *to go astray* 2/49
fore → **for; to** (1)
forfair (inf.) *to destroy* 14/11
forfette (sg.pt.) *to forfeit* 12/352
forgat → **fur-ȝite**
forgif (inf.) *to forgive, excuse* 14/87; **forȝeue** (inf.) 8/88, (sg.ps.) 8/113; **forȝef** (sg.ps.subj.) 8/105
forȝelde (sg.ps.subj.) *to repay, reward* 8/113
forȝeue → **forgif**
forȝeuenesse (sb.) *remission, respite* 7/237 *8/148; **for-ȝiuenesse** 5/169
forholen (ptp.) *to conceal* 1/87
forlete (inf.) *to shed* 10.6/6
forlore (ptp.) *to lose* 10.5/30; **forloren** 1/32, 64 *2/17; **uorlore** 4/89
formest (adv.) *foremost* 5/123
fors → **force**
forsake (inf.) 6/262 *9/30 *10.1/10, (ptp.) 8/89; **forsaket** (sg.ps.) 2/23
forstode (sg.pt.) *to avail* 1/20
forsuoren, forsworen → **uorzuerie**
fort → **forth**
forte → **for**
for-to → **for**
forto → **for**
fortoun (sb.) *fortune* 14/188
forth (adv.) 5/100, 147, 179 *6/215, 218 *7/4, 49, 67, 97 etc. *13/129, 242, 290, 445, 481; **forthþ** 5/169; **forþ** 3/20; **fort** 8/9; **fourth**

12/386; **fourthe** 12/298; **furth** 11/120 ∗14/5,
78, 83, 85, 151; **furthe** 12/140
forther; forþi → **ferther; for**
forthinkis (sg.ps.) *to repent of, be sorry for*
14/150
forthy, forþy → **for**
forthþ → **forth**
forwake (ptp.) *very tired* 10.1/15
forward (sb.) *agreement, promise, contract*
12/5, 238 ∗13/33; **forwarde** 12/166;
forwardes (pl.) 6/165; **forwardez** 6/196
fot, fote; fotte → **foot; fette**
foughten; foul → **fight; foȝel**
foul (adj.) 11/16; **foule** 7/37, 234 ∗12/337;
(adv.) 13/444; **ful** 1/38; **uoule** 4/70
foules → **foȝel**
founde; founded → **find; fonde**
four (num.) 5/57, 208 ∗12/354; **foure** 5/203,
207 ∗7/56 ∗11/96 ∗12/39 ∗13/107, 109
four-score *fourscore* 5/209
fourth, fourthe → **forth**
fourti (num.) *forty* 5/36
foweles → **foȝel**
foxe (sb.) *fox* 14/188, 201; **vox** 8/1, 8, 41, 48
etc.; **wox** 8/6, 17, 19, 147
foyned (pl.pt.) *to kick, thrust at* 6/215
fra → **fro**
fra (conj.) *since, because* 14/23, 44
fram → **from**
fraud (sb.) 14/221
fray (sb.) *fear, alarm* 14/31
frayn (inf.) *to ask, enquire, look for* 6/276;
frayned (sg.pt.) 6/146 ∗11/60
frayst (inf.) *to ask, enquire, look for* 6/196,
(sg.ps.) 6/66, (ptp.) 6/111, 178; **fraystez**
(sg.ps.) 6/242 [see frayn]
fre, frear → **free**
fredome (sb.) *liberality* 14/42
free (adj.) *free, liberal, noble* 12/5, 295
∗13/401; **fre** 7/106 ∗10.4/27 ∗10.5/7 ∗10.8/3
∗14/122, 128; **freo** 10.4/17; **frear** (comp.)
14/38
freikis; freind → **freke; frend**
freke (sb.) *man, warrior* 6/78, 116, 217;
freikis (pl.) 14/146
frelie (adv.) *freely, liberally* 14/40; **frely**
11/117
French (adj.) 6/13
frend (sb.) *friend* 1/7 ∗8/67, 80 ∗10.6/37;
frende 11/47 ∗12/287; **freind** 14/86;
frendes (pl.) 10.6/16 ∗10.7/24; **frendis**
12/29, 62, 385
freo → **free**

freoli (adv.) *beautiful, noble* 10.3/7; **freoly**
10.3/26, 40 [see free]
frere (sb.) *friar* 8/133, 136, 140 ∗13/77;
freren (pl.) 8/131; **freris** 7/56; ◆ col.:
mendenant freres *mendicant friars* 7/60
fresche (adj.) *fresh, refreshing* 14/125
frewte (sb.) *fruit* 12/10
Friday (sb.) 7/153; **Fryday** 7/240; ◆ col.:
Lang Fridæi *Good Friday* 1/85
fro (1) (adv., prep.) *from, away from, to and fro*
6/131, 214, 216, 246 ∗7/114 ∗11/78–79
∗12/30, 77, 96, 159 etc. ∗13/145, 517; **froo**
12/210; **fra** 13/263 ∗14/147, 207
fro (2) (adv.) *later* 6/8
from (prep.) 6/248 ∗9/32 ∗10.1/5–6 ∗10.3/12,
30 ∗10.5/26 ∗10.6/13 ∗10.7/23 ∗13/15, 365
∗14/143, 224; **fram** 1/74 ∗5/36, 43 ∗7/54
∗9/57
froo → **fro** (1)
fruyt (sb.) *fruit* 13/96
Fryday; fuȝten → **Friday; fight**
ful → **fall; foul; full**
fulfill (inf.) *to fulfil, fill up* 11/101; **fulfille**
12/27, 166, 238, 299, 395; **folvellet** (imp.pl.)
3/11; **fulfulde** (sg.pt.) 5/29; **uuluelden** (pl.pt.)
3/14; **fulfillid** (ptp.) 12/6, 72, 274
full (1) (adj.) *full (of)* 12/289, 380; **ful** 1/33
∗7/19 ∗9/73 ∗11/78 ∗13/189; **uol** 4/19, 23,
73
full (2) (adv.) *fully, completely* 11/117 ∗12/48,
82, 107, 151, 280 ∗14/9, 18, 93, 210; **ful**
5/197 ∗6/14, 19, 94–95, 154, 179, 233, 252,
255 ∗7/22–23 ∗8/108, 119 ∗9/28, 48 ∗11/19,
21, 66, 89, 119–120 ∗12/241 ∗13/22, 45, 47,
62, 65, 71, 88, 121, 154, 168, 175, 281, 310,
314, 374, 389, 451, 454, 536, 543; ◆ col.: **at
the fulle** *fully, completely* 13/529; **atte fulle**
13/160, 357; **full yoore** *long ago, for a long
time* 13/121, 454
fulle (inf.) *to fill* 7/191; **uelle** 4/57; **uelþ** (sg.ps.)
4/53; **fylden** (pl.pt.) 1/33–34; **ueld** (ptp.) 4/58
fulliche (adv.) *fully* 5/57
fulþe; funde → **filthe; find**
funde (sg.ps.) *to hasten* 9/10
funt-fat (sb.) *baptismal font* 2/29
fur (sb.) *furrow* 14/11; **furris** (gsg.) 14/17
fur-bere (inf.) *to forbear, refrain* 5/219;
forbaren (pl.pt.) 1/58, 60
fur-ȝite (inf.) *to forget* 5/228; **uoryet** (sg.ps.)
4/72; **forgat** (sg.pt.) 13/300
furlong (sb.) 13/390, 423
furmest (adj.) *foremost, first* 8/11
furres (sb.pl.) *fur* 10.10/21

furris → **fur**
furst, furste → **first; þurst**
furth, furthe → **forth**
furþe (ord.) *fourth* 10.5/43; **uerþe** 4/56
fust → **fest** (2)
fute → **foot**
fy (interj.) *fie!* 14/42, 53
fyȝt → **fight**
fyȝt (sb.) *fight* 6/66
fyke (inf.) *to flatter* 10.3/26
fylden → **fulle**
fynde, fyndes, fyndeth → **find**
fyneste (adj. sup.) *finest* 10.10/21
fynt; fyr → **find; fir**
fyrre; fyrst; fysch → **far; first; fis**

G

ga → **go**
gabbe (imp.) *to deceive, lie* 8/61
Gabriel (prn.) 10.5/26
gadered → **gederes**
gadering (sb.) *council* 1/26
gadman (sb.) *ox-driver* 14/6
gaffe, gaif → **give**
gaipis → **gapeð**
gait → **gate** (2)
galon (sb.) *gallon* 7/194; **galoun** 7/198
game (sb.) 6/152 *13/487; **gamin** 11/88;
  gome 8/12; **gomen** 6/60, 70; **gamys** (pl.)
  12/20; **gomenes** 10.8/26
gan → **gynneth**
gane → **go**
ganesay (inf.) *to contradict, unsay* 14/44, 59
gang (inf.) *to go, leave* 11/119 *12/303
  *14/161, (sg.ps.subj.) 14/131; **gange** (inf.)
  12/144; **gangen** (pl.ps.) 2/52
gapeð (sg.ps.) *to gape; be eager* 2/38; **gaipis**
  (pl.ps.) 14/212; **gapeand** (psp.) 11/45
garlek (sb.) *garlic* 7/160
garlek-monger (sb.) *seller of garlic* 7/174
garre (inf.) *to make, cause* 12/20, 164, (imp.)
  12/144, 100, 334; **garris** (pl.ps.) 14/93; **gart**
  (sg.pt.) 14/184
gas → **go**
Gascoyne (pn.) *Gascony* 7/148
gast → **agast; gost**
gate (1) (sb.) *gate, door* 9/107; **ȝat** 8/10; **ȝates**
  (pl.) 12/139; **ȝatis** 12/124, 182
gate (2) (sb.) *street, way* 12/144; **gait** 14/25
Gauan → **Gawan**
gaudis (sb.pl.) *trick* 12/160
Gawan (prn.) 6/126, 152, 162 etc.; **Sir Gawan**
  6/164, 174, 177, 274; **Sir Gawen** 6/263;
  Gauan 6/185, 208; **Wawan** 6/130

gay (adj.) *fine, colourful* 13/150
gaynly (adv.) *appropriately, appositely* 6/263
gæde → **go**
gældes (sb.pl.) *tax* 1/51
gær, gære; gæt → **yeer; yet**
gederes (sg.ps.) *to gather, raise* 6/208;
  gadered (ptp.) 1/24
gedlyng (sb.) *rascal, villain* 12/212
geen → **go**
gees (sb.pl.) *goose* 7/146
gef → **give**
gere (sb.) *garment, clothing* 11/118 *12/211
  *13/240
gerner (sb.) *granary* 13/49
geserne → **giserne**
gest (sb.) *guest* 10.2/14; **gestes** (pl.) 1/69
gestend (ptp.) *to stay (as guest)* 11/106
get → **yet**
get (1) (sb.pl.) *goat* 8/84
get (2) (inf.) 14/212; (imp.) 13/356; **gete** (inf.)
  7/136 *11/45; (pl.ps.) 13/323; **gettes** (sg.ps.)
  11/31; **getyn** (ptp.) 12/11
geþ; geuen, geuyth → **go; give**
geynest (adj. sup.) *most friendly* 10.1/18
gif → **give; if**
giff, giffe → **give**
gift (sb.) 11/15 *14/38; **gyft** 6/75; **giftis** (pl.)
  14/93; **yefþes** 4/52
gigours (sb.pl.) *fiddler* 9/106
giled → **begyle**
gilery (sb.) *deceit, trick* 12/160
ginne (sb.) *craft, trick; mechanism* 8/36, 39,
  41, 43 etc. *9/98; **ginnes** (pl.) 4/34
gird (sg.pt.) *to spring* 14/176
gise (sb.) *manner, custom* 13/350; **gyse** 7/26
giserne (sb.) *battle-axe* 6/75, 162; **geserne**
  6/113
gistninge (sb.) *feast* 8/128
giues; Gius → **give; Jewe**
'give' ◆ inf.: **gif** 6/75, 84, 152 *11/11 *14/72;
  giff 11/117 *14/40–41; **giffe** 12/114; **gyuen**
  1/52; **yeve** 13/67, 231, 277, 381; ◆ sg.ps.:
  geuyth (sg.ps.) 10.10/19; ◆ imp.: **gif** 6/113;
  ȝef 10.4/22; **giues** 11/111; **gyue** 7/74; ◆
  sg.ps. subj.: **ȝeue** 8/17 *9/135 *10.3/20; ◆
  sg.pt.: **gaffe** (sg.pt.) 12/163; **gaif** 14/36, 47;
  ȝaf 9/66, 125; **yaf** 4/9 *13/56, 168, 236; **ȝef**
  10.7/35; **gef** 6/157; ◆ pl.pt.: **geuen** 7/176;
  ȝeuen 9/119; **iafen** 1/28; ◆ ptp.: **ȝeue** (ptp.)
  7/241

glad (adj.) 7/176 *8/125 *11/85; **gladde**
  12/42, 241; **glade** 9/134; ◆ neg.: **vnglad**
  10.2/2

gladieþ (sg.ps.) *to gladden* 10.4/7
gladly (adv.) 6/157, 202
glas (sb.) *glass* 13/198
gleedes (sb.pl.) *embers* 13/107
glemans (sb. gsg.) *minstrel, gleeman* 7/205
gleme (sb.) *gleam* 12/42
glent (sg.pt.) *to glance, look* 6/263
gleowes (sb. pl.) *entertainment* 10.8/26
gleowinge (sb.) *entertainment* 9/104
glorious (adj.) 12/42
glosede (pl.pt.) *to gloss* 7/58
Gloton (prn.) 7/212
glotons → **glotoun**
glotony (sb.) *gluttony, drunkenness* 7/24;
  glotonye 4/57 *7/44; **glotounye** 4/5, 7, 78,
  91
glotoun (sb.) *glutton* 4/19, 86 *7/151, 158,
  162, 176 etc.; **glotouns** (pl.) 4/11; **glotons**
  7/74; **glotuns** 4/63
go (inf.) 5/14 *6/235 *7/151, 195, 205 *8/1, 82
  *12/341, 393 *13/176, 305, 318, 362, 474;
  gon 5/15, 112, 156 *8/142 *9/46 *10.6/50
  *13/116, 228; **goo** 12/212, 377; **goon** 13/12,
  232, 321; **guo** 4/10–11; **ga** 14/135; **ȝonge**
  8/31; ◆ sg.ps.: **ga** 13/478; **gas** 13/261; **geþ**
  4/71, 86–87; **goo** 12/120; **gotz** 6/162; **gooth**
  13/146, 281, 291, 322, 338, 445, 531; **goth**
  7/162 *13/242, 286, 295, 304, 377, 384, 481;
  goð 2/16; ◆ sg.ps. subj.: **go** 12/156 *13/462,
  465; ◆ pl.ps.: **gon** 13/534; **goon** 13/503; **goth**
  7/44; ◆ imp.: **go** 8/17, 27–28, 124 *13/464
  *14/49; **ga** 7/146 *13/326; ◆ sg.pt.: **ede** 8/35;
  hede 8/138; **gæde** 1/40; **ȝede** 7/41, 219
  *9/19–20, 113 *11/3; **ȝeid** 14/185, 190;
  ȝeode 5/112; **yede** 3/4; ◆ pl.pt.: **ȝeden** 9/103;
  ȝeoden 5/13; **ieden** 1/56; **wenten** 7/49, 52; ◆
  pt.: **went** 11/22, 71–72, 87, 108, 120
  *14/107; **wente** 7/4, 130 *9/39 *13/181,
  372, 383, 435, 439; ◆ ptp.: **ago** 8/25, 77;
  gane 10.9/2 *14/102; **gon** 8/54 *13/316;
  goon 13/103, 443; **geen** 13/302; **vend** 8/80;
  wente 12/176
god → **good**
God (sb.) 1/82 *3/35 *4/8–9, 18–22 etc.
  *5/12, 26, 56, 126, 232 *7/117, 226, 228,
  237, 239 *9/36 *10.5/27, 33 *10.9/1, 14
  *11/3, 5, 7, 15 etc. *12/50, 56, 241, 254, 384
  *13/142, 250, 260, 313 etc. *14/46, 102;
  Gode 2/27, 33 *3/28, 41 *8/86; **Goddez**
  (gsg.) 6/157; **Godes** 3/4, 31, 41 *4/53 *5/193
  *7/228 *8/28; ◆ col.: **a Godes nome** *by God*
  8/18; **bi Godes nome** 8/29; **God forbid**
  14/46; **God waat** *by God* 13/310; **Gode**
  þonk *thank God* 8/79; **vpon Godez halue**

for God's sake 6/113; **by Goddes sale** *for
  the soul of God* 13/411; **by Goddes dignitee**
  for God's dignity 13/494; **for Goddes banes**
  for the bones of God 13/297; **for Goddes**
  herte *for God's heart* 13/311
gode → **good**
goded (sg.pt.) *to improve* 1/71
Godefray (prn.) 7/174
Godes, Godez → **God**
Godhede (sb.) *divine nature* 12/249
Godhild (prn.) 9/50
godlie (adj.) *godly* 14/204
godly (adv.) *kindly, willingly* 6/60
godspel, godspell, godspelle → **gospel**
goed → **good**
gold (sb.) 1/10, 24, 37 *7/74 *10.5/41 *11/69
gome → **game**
gome (sb.) *man, knight* 6/112, 162, 192;
  gomus (pl.) 7/44
gomen, gomenes → **game**
gomus → **gome**
gon → **go; gynneth**
Gondolf of Roucestre (prn.) *Gundulf of
  Rochester* 5/116, 153
gonne, gonnen → **gynneth**
goo → **go**
good (adj., sb.) 3/37 *7/29, 58, 154, 158, 176
  *10.7/11 *10.9/8 *13/67, 69–71, 207 etc.;
  goode 6/168 *7/146 *12/34 *13/453, 471;
  god 1/8, 11, 24, 29 etc. *6/168 *10.5/9; **gode**
  1/82 *2/15 *3/43 *6/269 *7/237 *8/74, 110
  *9/27, 40, 113, 121, 124 *10.8/31; **goed**
  8/20, 23, 81, 87; **gude** 11/16, 61, 72, 76,
  84–85 *14/195; **guod** 4/26 *5/48, 146;
  guode 4/27, 48–49 *5/26, 137, 142; **guodes**
  (pl.) 4/42
goodnesse (sb.) *goodness* 12/381; **guodnesse**
  5/25
goon → **go**
goos (sb.) *goose* 13/361
gooth → **go**
gore (sb.) *garment* 10.1/18
gospel (sb.) 7/58; **godspel** 3/2 *11/1; **godspell**
  11/27; **godspelle** 4/9
gossip (sb.) *kinsman, friend* 7/158 *8/58, 105,
  110, 122
gost (sb.) *ghost* 10.7/6; **holy goste** *Holy
  Ghost/Spirit* 12/77; **gast** 2/60
gostliche (adv.) *in a spiritual way* 3/37
gottes (sb.pl.) *guts* 7/199
gotz, goth, goð → **go**
gothly (inf.) *to rumble, bubble, sputter* 7/199
governynge (sb.) *rule* 13/55

grace (sb.) 2/34 *3/37 *5/191, 193 *12/20, 384 *14/217

gradde → **grede**

graid (sg.pt.) *to clothe* 11/118

gramery (sb.) *magic* 10.9/7

grant (inf.) 6/60; **graunte** (sg.ps.subj.) 7/237; **graunti** 5/232

gras (sb.) *grass* 7/232; **grases** (pl.) 10.8/34

graspeth (sg.ps.) *to grope* 13/517

grat → **greate**

grathed; grathely → **greiþi; grayþely**

graue (sb.) *grave* 12/23, 393

grauel (sb.) *sand, gravel* 9/103

graunte, graunti → **grant**

grayþe (adj.) *ready* 6/235

grayþely (adv.) *readily, promptly, at once* 6/204; **grathely** 12/92

greate (adj.) *great* 4/59, 65; **greet** 7/212 *13/211, 213; **gret** 5/10, 59, 65–66, 111, 169, 187, 214 *6/9 *8/84; **grete** 2/43 *5/114, 119, 123, 170, 188, 195–196 *6/99, 112 *7/36, 53, 162 *8/36, 78, 145 *10.4/14 *10.8/7 *11/31 *12/104, 137, 381 *13/547; **grat** 4/9, 19, 59–60, 66; **grit** 14/13, 91; **gretteste** (sup.) 13/278

grece (1) (sb.) *grease* 6/212

grece (2) (sb.) *step* 5/17

grede (sg.ps.) *to cry out, weep* 10.2/2; **gradde** (sg.pt.) 8/141

greet, grééte → **greate; grete**

greif (sb.) *anger* 14/43

greiþi (inf.) *to prepare, make ready* 5/65; **greiþie** 5/70; **greythen** (pl.ps.) 13/533; **grathed** (ptp.) 12/211

greme (sb.) *wrath* 6/99

grene (adj., adv., sb.) *green, fresh* 6/92, 164, 177, 192 etc. *10.5/2 *10.7/28 *13/63, 102

Grenewych (pn.) *Greenwich* 13/131

grenne (pl.ps.) *to grin* 6/251

gret, grete → **greate; grete**

grete (sg.ps.) *to greet* 10.4/43, (sg.pt.) 7/194; **grééte** (sg.ps.) 10.8/31; **gret** 4/72; **grette** (sg.pt.) 9/46

gretteste; greued → **greate; greve**

greve (ps.) *to take offence; give trouble* 13/83, 134; **greued** (sg.pt.) 6/103 *7/212

grey (adj.) 13/72; **greye** 13/198

greyn (sb.) *grain crop* 13/52

greythen → **greiþi**

grimly (adj., adv.) *fierce, grim; heavily* 10.7/6, 28

grin → **lof**

gripped; grit → **grypez; great**

gromes (pl.) *servant, groom* 4/97

grone (sg.ps.) *to groan* 10.2/2

gropeth (sg.ps.) *to grope* 13/446; **gropith** 10.10/17; **groped** (sg.pt.) 13/441

gros (sg.pt.) *to be afraid* 9/27

ground (sb.) 14/190; **grounde** 5/39, 60, 74, 78, 83–84, 87 *6/204, 213 *8/37, 46 *10.4/38 *10.7/6; **grund** 2/12, 47; **grunde** 2/55

grucche (inf.) *to complain* 13/87

grund, grunde → **ground**

grydy (adj.) *greedy* 7/199

Gryffyth (prn.) 7/174

grymme (adj.) *grim* 6/200

grynde (inf.) *to grind* 13/256; **ygrounde** (ptp.) 13/215, 232, 293; **gryndynge** (sb.) 13/538

gryndellayk (sb.) *fierceness* 6/99

gryndynge → **grynde**

grypez (sg.ps.) *to grip, grasp* 6/117; **gripped** (sg.pt.) 6/208

grys (sb.) *pig, piglet* 7/146

gude → **good**

gult (sb.) *guilt* 5/164

gulty (adj.) *guilty* 7/226

gune, gunne → **gynneth**

guo → **go**

guod, guode, guodes → **good**

guodnesse → **goodnesse**

gyde (sb.) *guide* 13/244

gyft → **gift**

gyle (sb.) *deception, guile, trickery* 7/12

gylle (sb.) *gill* 7/198

gylour (sb.) *deceiver* 13/545

gynneth (aux. sg.ps.) *to begin, start* 13/288; **gan** (pt.) *to begin, start* 5/156, 181, 224–225 *7/153, 199, 205, 220, 232 *9/15, 18, 23, 46, 56, 71–72, 74, 83–84, 101, 105, 122, 126 *11/14, 56, 92, 98, 104 *13/87, 124, 296, 302, 439–440, 472, 526; **gon** 8/1, 42, 98, 120 *10.5/44 *10.7/20; **gonne** 7/124; **gonnen** 8/142; **gune** 12/47, 286; **gunne** 9/104, 123; **can** 6/127 *14/146; **con** 6/62, 149; **conne** 10.7/28; **couth** 14/11, 112, 152

gyrdyll (sb.) *girdle* 10.9/13

gyse → **gise**

gyte (sb.) *gown* 13/178

gyue, gyuen → **give**

ʒ

ʒa → **ʒe** (1)

ʒaf; ʒare → **give; ʒore**

ʒat, ʒates, ʒatis → **gate** (1)

ȝe (1) (interj.) *yeah* 8/88, 104 *14/129; **ȝa** 12/109, 205; **ȝaa** 12/305

ȝe (2) (perspron. 2.pl.; also polite form) 2/19 *5/129, 131, 134–135 etc. *6/30, 52, 130, 137 etc. *7/74, 96, 101, 139 *9/48–49 *12/122, 124, 176, 179 etc. *14/34, 48, 73, 81–82 etc.; **ye** 3/26 *13/134, 249, 257, 259, 269, 345–347; **youe** 12/178, 402; ♦ poss.: **eoure** 5/127, 138; **eouwer** 5/132; **eower** 5/175; **ȝour** 14/60, 123; **ȝoure** 7/74, 103; **your** 6/98–99, 134, 136, 144; **youre** 12/124, 182, 190–191, 386 *13/140, 268, 304, 345, 350; ♦ obj.: **eou** 5/135; **eov** 5/136, 144; **ou** 8/107–108 *10.3/36, 41 *10.5/5; **yow** 6/131, 138, 145–146, 257 *13/34, 38, 134, 148, 257; **yu** 3/9; ♦ refl.: **ȝourself** 6/137; **ȝour sell** 14/164; **yourseluen** 6/137

ȝede, ȝeden → **go**

ȝederly (adv.) *promptly* 6/240

ȝef → **give; if**

ȝeid; ȝeir → **go; yeer**

ȝelde, ȝelden → **yelde**

ȝeode, ȝeoden → **go**

ȝeonde (adv.) *over there* 5/137

ȝeot → **yet**

ȝep (adj.) *brave, bold* 6/71

ȝer, ȝere, ȝeres → **yeer**

ȝerne (1) (adv.) *eagerly* 8/8, 47

ȝerne (2) (inf.) *to desire, covet* 9/72; **yȝyrned** (ptp.) 10.1/16

ȝet; ȝeue, ȝeuen → **yet; give**

ȝeynchar (sb.) *return, way back* 10.3/35

ȝif; ȝit, ȝitt → **if; yet**

ȝol (sb.) *Christmas* 6/71

ȝolden → **yelde**

ȝonder (adv.) *over there* 14/166, 170

ȝone (dempron.) *that* 14/19, 21, 37, 113, 119, 128, 135, 139, 167, 169, 173; **yon** 13/402; **yone** 12/340

ȝong, ȝonge → **yonge; go**

ȝore (adv.) *for a long time, long* 10.1/16; **ȝare** 5/129 *8/85 *9/48

ȝou; → **ȝe** (2)

ȝoung → **yonge**

ȝour, ȝoure, ȝourself, ȝow → **ȝe** (2)

ȝut, ȝutt → **yet**

ȝuðhede (sb.) *youth* 2/2

ȝuyt → **yet**

ȝwam; ȝwane → **who; when**

ȝwat; ȝwile → **what; while**

ȝwuche; ȝwyle; ȝynge → **such; while; yonge**

H

ha → **have; he**

habbe, habbes, habbet, habbeþ, habbez → **have**

hac → **ac**

hackenayman (sb.) *one who hires out horses* 7/166, 179

had, hadde, hadden, hade, haf → **have**

haȝerer (adj. comp.) *fit, ready* 6/139

haif → **have**

haik (interj.) 14/8

haill → **hole** (2)

haill (inf.) *to pull, haul* 14/180; **hailland** (psp.) 14/185; **haillit** (sg.pt.) 14/193

hailsed → **hals** (2)

hair → **hare**

'hair' (sb.) **heer** 13/45, 200; **her** 10.1/7; **here** 6/223; **heris** (pl.) 13/94

haire (sb.) *hair-shirt* 11/109

haist (sb.) *haste* 14/157, 190

haistelie → **hastily**

haiward → **hayward**

hal; halce → **hall; hals** (1)

hald, halde, halden, haldez, haldin, haldis → **hold**

halechede (sg.pt.) *to consecrate* 1/14

halechen (sb.pl.) *saint* 1/66; **halȝen** 4/95, 98; **halwes** 13/14

halely → **hoolly**

half (adj., adv., sb.) 1/68 *4/55 *8/2, 4 *13/8, 195, 234, 317, 468, 536; **halff** 14/58, 115; **half-wey** 13/130

halȝen → **halechen**

hali, halie, halier, haliest → **holy**

halkis (sb.pl.) *hawk* 14/105

hall (sb.) 11/73; **hal** 6/245; **halle** 6/89, 237 *9/62, 107 *12/136 *13/227

halled (sg.pt.) *to go, depart* 6/245

halme (sb.) *shaft, handle* 6/117

halp → **help** (2)

hals (1) (sb.) *neck* 1/47; **halce** 6/214

hals (2) (inf.) *to embrace, greet* 11/92; **halsed** (sg.pt.) 12/64; **hailsed** 11/57

halt; halue → **hold; God**

halwes; haly → **halechen; holy**

halydayes (sb.pl.) *holy day* 13/176

ham; hame → **they; home**

hamewart, hamward → **homward**

han → **have**

hand (sb.) 13/161, 306, 358, 436, 475 *14/20, 47, 83, 105, 123, 141; **hond** 13/339, 446; **hande** 6/245 *12/64, 325 *13/259; **honde** 5/88 *6/115, 156, 158, 162, 223, 231, 277

*8/51 *9/20, 34, 77, 120 *10.2/5 *10.4/13;
hend 11/20; **handes** (pl.) 7/141 *11/79;
handis 14/95; **hende** 12/75, 400
hange (inf.) *to hang* 12/307; **hanguy** 5/32;
honge 10.6/45; **hongi** 4/93 *8/44, 116;
hangeth (sg.ps.) 7/99; **hang** (pt.) 14/160, 166
hangeman (sb.) *hangman* 7/169
hangeth, hanguy → **hange**
hansull (sb.) *present, gift, han(d)sel* 7/176
hap (sb.) *lot, hap, fortune* 10.1/5, 10; ◆ neg.:
vnhap *misfortune* 6/225
happed (sg.pt.) *to happen* 13/216; **happinnit**
14/4
hard → **harde; hear**
harde (adj., adv.) *hard, heavily, strict* 5/16, 43
*7/23, 28 *8/98 *12/151; **hard** 11/104;
hardely 12/143
hardi (adj.) *bold, brave* 6/158; **hardy** 6/72
*13/181; ◆ neg.: **unhardy** 13/434
hardily (adv.) *certainly* 13/233
hardy; hare → **hardi; they**
hare (sb.) 4/23; **hair** 14/12
harke, harkens → **herke**
harlot (sb.) *rascal, knave* 12/185 *13/492;
harlotes (pl.) 7/170
harm (sb.) *harm, injury, misfortune* 13/427;
harme 5/43; **harmes** (pl.) 12/323
harmles (adv.) *unhurt, uninjured* 5/40
Harold (prn.) *King Harold II* 5/61, 69
harpe (sb.) *harp* 9/101, 108
harpurs (sb.pl.) *harper* 9/106
harrow (interj.) 13/296, 531; **harrowe** 12/98,
185; **herrowe** 12/343
hart → **hert**
hartely (adj.) *hearty* 12/245
has → **have**
hasped (ptp.) *to clasp, fasten* 6/68
hast, haste → **have**
hastily (adv.) 11/82; **hasteliche** 3/15; **hastelie**
14/71; **haistelie** 14/181
hastis (pl.ps.) *to hasten* 12/307
hastou, hastow → **have**
hat (1./3.sg.ps.) *to be called, command,
promise* 4/21–22 *6/10, 40; **hatte** 6/168; **hot**
3/9; **hote** 8/18; **hattes** (2.sg.ps.) 6/166, 188;
hotez (pl.ps.) 5/134; **hatte** (sg.pt.) 1/89; **heiȝte**
5/6; **hettez** 6/235; **heyte** 8/136; **hette** (ptp.)
6/237; **hight** 12/231, 12/351; **highte** 12/396
*13/72, 237–238; **hyht** 10.2/10; **hoote**
13/165
hated (sg.pt.) 7/242
hatte, hattes → **hat**
hatz, hath, haþ → **have**

haþel (sb.) *knight, man* 6/43, 96, 110, 166;
haþeles (pl.) 10.8/24
hauberghe (sb.) *hauberk, coat of mail* 6/55
haue, hauen, haues, hauest, haueð, haueþ
→ **have**
haukes (sb.pl.) *hawk* 13/358
haunten (pl.ps.) *to pursue* 7/75
have → **so**
have (inf., ps.) 8/20 *13/35, 68, 102, 112 etc.;
habbe (inf.) 3/43 *4/47, 51; **haif** (inf., ps.)
14/28, 117, 120, 169; **haue** (inf., ps.) **hauen**
(inf., ps.) **han** 6/23 *7/63, 86 *8/44 *10.2/6
*10.7/13 *13/107, 307, 314, 346 etc. ◆ ps.:
habbe 4/28–29 *5/129, 134, 143
*8/100–102, 105 *9/48; **habbes** 6/114;
habbet 3/7; **habbeþ** 3/20, 26 *4/34, 60,
66–67; **habbez** 5/146 *6/239; **haf** 6/26, 50,
178, 262; **has** 12/67, 167, 174, 243, 262,
329, 351, 406 *13/250–251, 299, 403,
427–429; **hast** 10.6/37 *12/69, 327
*13/491–492; **haste** 12/223; **hatz** 6/17, 19,
36, 51, 111, 117, 179, 194, 237, 239, 264,
277; **hath** 7/38, 62 *12/56, 356 *13/2, 6, 8,
18, 103, 117, 137, 211, 283, 317, 373, 386,
538; **haþ** 9/81, 95–96 *10.1/2 *10.3/22–23,
36 *10.4/34, 40 *10.6/60 *10.7/32; **hes**
14/142, 179, 210, 215; **hest** 3/21 *4/78; **heþ**
4/3, 8, 11, 14, 34, 40, 87–89; **haues** 10.8/13;
hauest 8/24, 27–28, 87, 93, 111, 122
*10.2/3, 9; **haueð** 2/17; **haueþ** 8/61, 84, 128
*10.7/2, 5, 7 *10.8/6; ◆ sg.ps. subj.: **habbe**
10.3/32; ◆ pt.: **had** 6/54, 225, 229 *10.8/4
*10.9/10 *11/14, 39–40, 54, 56 etc. *13/312,
408, 420, 459 *14/2, 137, 150; **hadde**
1/23–24 *5/26, 29, 57, 96 etc. *7/50, 182,
190, 198 etc. *8/12 *9/79 *12/38, 63, 136,
219, 245 *13/31, 69, 79, 123 etc.; **hade**
6/124, 254 *10.9/9 *13/73; **hadden** 1/30, 45,
52 *5/75, 88, 122; **hedde** 3/17–19 *4/26
*8/68, 143; **hedden** 3/23 *4/76; **hede** 8/144;
hefden 1/35, 77; **heuede** 8/34, 67; **heuedest**
8/89; ◆ contr. a) perspron. 1.sg.ps.: **ichabbe**
10.1/5; **ychabbe** 10.1/16; **ichaue** 10.2/10; ◆
contr. b) perspron. 2.sg.ps.: **hastou** 11/113;
hastow 7/159; ◆ neg.: **nabbe** (1.sg.ps.) 8/20;
nadde (3.sg.pt.) 5/126; **nedde** 8/50, 85, 143;
neddi (1.sg.pt.subj.) 8/50; **neuede**
(1.sg.pt.subj.) 8/49
hayl → **all**
hayward (sb.) *hedge-keeper, hayward* 7/169;
haiward 8/13
hærnes (sb.pl.) *brain* 1/41
hæued → **head**

he → she; they
he (perspron. 3.sg. m.) **hee** 12/185; **a** 5/140
∗7/72, 200–201, 219, 223; **ha** 3/11, 18, 36,
39, 42 ∗4/86; ♦ poss.: **his**; **hise** 1/28 ∗2/3, 11,
14, 20 ∗3/5 ∗4/12, 50; **hys** 6/73, 123 ∗10.9/6,
10, 12 ∗10.10/12–13; **is** 5/2, 7, 11–12, 17–18,
24, 41, 54–55, 67, 70, 94, 108–109, 113,
115, 120, 140, 164, 171, 179, 187, 189, 198,
214, 227, 231 ∗10.3/22, 32 ∗10.6/6, 49–50
∗10.7/4, 7, 9, 18; **ys** 10.3/27 ∗10.4/15
∗10.6/8; ♦ obj.: **him hym hine** 4/32 ∗5/142
∗8/62; ♦ refl.: **him selff** 14/152; **himself** 2/15
∗8/63 ∗11/14, 16, 26, 43; **himselue** 3/33;
himseluen 3/40 ∗11/24; **hymself** 7/68
∗13/251, 424, 545; **hym-selfe** 10.10/5;
hymseluen 6/72
'head' (sb.) **hed** 6/220, 245; **hede** 6/40, 73,
120, 205, 214, 223, 231; **heed** 13/102, 177,
254, 373, 477, 514; **hæued** 1/40; **heaued**
4/1–2, 29; **hefed** 1/39; **heued** 5/16 ∗10.4/15
'hear' (vb.) **heer** (imp.) 13/487; **heere** (inf.)
13/390; **here** (inf., ps.) 6/234 ∗7/4, 139, 156,
236 ∗8/64 ∗10.4/2 ∗12/169; **heris** (sg.ps.)
12/101; **hereð** (imp.) 2/5; **herande** (psp.)
6/237; **ihere** (inf.) 8/93 ∗9/1, 105; (sg.ps.)
8/60; **ihereþ** (pl.ps.) 3/26; **y-herþ** (sg.ps.)
4/88; **yhere** (imp.) 10.3/47; ♦ pt.: **hard** 14/18,
60, 63, 70, 112; **heorde** 5/69; **herd** (pt.) 6/50
∗11/21, 23, 60 ∗13/123, 353; **herde** 6/26, 31
∗7/95, 202 ∗8/85 ∗12/98, 138 ∗13/392;
iherde 8/57; ♦ ptp.: **iherd** 3/26; **y-hyerd**
4/78; ♦ contr. 2.sg.: **herdestow** 13/394
heaued → head
hecht (1) (sb.) *promise* 14/18, 112–113;
hechtis (pl.) 14/46
hecht (2) (sg.pt.) *to promise, vow* 14/20, 45,
60, 70, (ptp.) 14/150
hed; hedde, hedden → head; have
heddre (sb.) *blood in the veins* 8/22
hede → go; have; head
hede (sb.) *heed, attention* 10.7/27
hedlez (adj.) *headless* 6/225
hee; heed → he; head
heele; heelp → hele; help (2)
heep (sb.) *heap, crowd* 7/175, 186; **hep** 7/51
heer → hair; hear; here
heeth (sb.) *heath* 13/6
hefden; hefed → have; head
heghind (ptp.) *to exalt* 11/26
heglice (adv.) *with great ceremony* 1/88
heȝe → highe
heifis (sg.pl.) *to raise, hold up* 14/95; **houe**
(sg.pt.) 9/4; **heuened** (ptp.) 6/136

heighe, heiȝ, heiȝe → highe
heiȝte; heil → hat; hole (2)
heir → here
heir (sb.) 13/202
heirefter → heraftur
heithing (sb.) *scorn, mockery* 14/110, 115
held, helde → hold
helde (sg.pt.) *to heal, cure* 5/193
helden; helder → hold; never
hele (sb.) *health, salvation* 5/191 ∗12/67, 106;
heele 12/38
hell (sb.) 14/223; **helle** 2/62 ∗3/31 ∗4/12, 17
∗10.5/29 ∗10.7/32 ∗12/98, 156, 260, 270 etc.
helme (sb.) *helmet* 6/55
help (1) (sb.) 11/102; **helpe** 12/43, 367
help (2) (inf., ps.) 6/43 ∗13/510, 513, 515
∗14/88, 180; **helpe** 5/72 ∗7/74, 228 ∗12/97,
199, 343, 351; **helpeþ** (sg.ps.) 10.5/21; **halp**
(sg.pt.) 8/42; **heelp** 13/470; **holpen** (ptp.)
13/18
helþe (sb.) *health* 4/39–40
Hely (prn.) *Elijah* 12/87
hem, hemself, hemselue, hemsulue → they
hen (sb.) 8/4 ∗14/94; **hennen** (pl.) 8/14, 16, 18,
20; **hennis** 14/97, 101, 104, 207
hend, hende → hand
hende (adj.) *courteous, gracious, courtly, kind*
6/192, 254 ∗9/21 ∗12/45 ∗13/80; **hendest**
(sup.) 6/26; **hendi** 10.1/14, 18; **hendy** 9/38
∗10.1/5, 10
henge (inf.) *to hang* 6/265; **hengest** (sg.ps.)
10.6/25; **heng** (imp.) 6/264; **henged** (pt.)
1/38–39; **hengen** (pl.pt.) 1/39, 86
henne (adv.) *hence, since* 13/113; **heonne**
5/207
hennen, hennis → hen
Henri (prn.) *King Henry I* 1/1, 24
hente (sg.pt.) *to seize, grasp* 13/436, 498;
yhent (ptp.) 10.1/5
heo → she; they
heold, heolden → hold
heom, heom-seolf, heomsulue → they
heonne → henne
heorde; heore → hear; they
heorte; heouene → hert; heuen
heowes (sb.pl.) *servant* 10.8/24
hep → heep
her → hair; here; she; they
heraftur (adv.) *hereafter, later* 7/139;
herefter 1/5; **heirefter** 14/82
herande → hear
herberowe (sb.) *lodging, inn* 12/136;
herberwe 13/343, 369

herbifore (adv.) *before this time, herebefore* 8/111

herd, herde, herdestow → **hear**

here → **hair; hear; she**

here (adv.) 5/1, 129, 134, 144, 195 *6/23, 25, 50, 52, 65, 69, 71, 178 *9/45 *11/28, 33–34, 48, 69, 121 *12/37, 124, 151, 168, 216, 221, 249, 260, 264, 297, 325, 353, 366; **heer** 13/137, 249, 441; **heere** 12/40, 323 *13/326, 359, 480; **heir** 14/73, 194; **her** 5/208 *8/20, 30, 70–74, 83–84, 92 *9/24, 133; **hyer** 4/34

heredmen (sb.pl.) *courtier* 6/89

herefter → **heraftur**

heremite, heremites, heremyte → **hermit**

hereð; herie → **hear; herye**

herinne (adv.) *herein, here* 6/87 *8/52

heris → **hair; hear**

heritage (sb.) 5/94 *9/11

herke (inf.) *to listen, hear, hearken* 10.9/5; **herkne** (sg.ps.) 10.1/18; **harke** (imp.) 12/137; **harkens** 12/37; **herkned** (sg.pt.) 13/397; **herknede** 5/125

herly → **early**

hermit (sb.) 11/52, 59, 64, 71 etc.; **hermite** 11/34; **heremite** 7/3; **heremyte** 7/169; **ermit** 11/38; **hermites** (pl.) 11/48; **heremites** 7/55; **eremites** 7/30, 51

herof (pron.) *hereof* 5/69 *7/237

herre; herrowe → **highe; harrow**

hert (sb.) *heart* 6/158, 254 *11/13, 20, 29, 40; **herte** 4/53, 55 *9/65, 111 *10.4/4, 18 *10.5/3 *10.6/6, 49 *10.7/18, 35 *10.8/35 *13/86, 94, 311, 513; **heorte** 5/164, 227; **hart** 10.10/9 *14/42

Hertfordshyre (pn.) *Hertfordshire* 7/214

hertou → **be**

herye (inf.) *to praise, thank* 4/51; **herie** (sg.ps.) 10.3/11

hes → **have**

hes (sb.) *carrion* 4/46

hest → **have**

heste (sb.) *command, order* 5/127, 132

hete → **eat**

hete (sb.) *heat* 2/11 *4/60 *11/93

heten; hette, hettez → **eat; hat**

heþ → **have**

hethely (adv.) *contemptuously* 11/25

hethen (adj.) *heathen* 1/57

hethyng (sb.) *contempt* 13/334

heu; heué → **hewe; heui**

heued; heuede, heuedest → **head; have**

heuegy (inf.) *to become heavy* 5/196

heuen (sb.) *heaven* 6/110, 139 *12/32, 235; **heuene** 2/7–8 *3/33, 44 *4/98 *5/210

*7/129 *8/117 *9/132, 135 *10.1/5 *10.2/14 *10.3/14 *10.4/30 *10.5/12, 26, 50, 60 *10.7/26 *12/77; **heouene** 5/5, 201, 232; **heuin** 11/5 *14/95

heuened → **heifis**

heuenriche (sb.) *heavenly kingdom* 7/29; **heuyn-rike** 11/7

heuereuchon → **every**

heui (adj.) *heavy* 8/139; **heué** 6/76

heuie (adv.) *heavily* 9/74

heuin → **heuen**

heuyn-rike → **heuenriche**

Hewe (prn.) 7/166

hewe (sb.) *appearance, form, shape* 10.3/37; **heu** 10.1/7

hewen (ptp.) *to hew, cut* 6/264

hey (interj.) 10.10/1

hey, heyȝe; heyte → **highe; hat**

heythen (adv.) *hence* 13/257

hi; hicht → **she; they; highe**

Hicke (prn.) 7/166, 179, 190; **Hickes** (gsg.) 7/192

hidde (sg.pt.) *to hide* 12/249

hidder → **hider**

hide (sb.) 11/100; **hyde** 14/87

hider (adv.) *hither* 6/51 *9/37 *13/221; **hidder** 14/62

hierþe (sb.) *hearing* 4/85

hierde (sb.) *herdsman* 13/59

highe (adj., adv., sb.) *high, highly* 6/5 *11/24; **hiȝ** 6/37; **hyȝ** 6/89; **hyȝe** 6/45, 86, 94, 136, *loudly* 6/255; **heȝe** 6/68 *10.3/14 *10.6/11, 26, 45; **heighe** 13/546; **heiȝ** 5/30; **heiȝe** 5/43, 91; **heyȝe** 10.6/34; **heyȝe** 10.6/34; **hye** 13/199, 205; **hyȝ** 6/89; **hyȝe** 6/45, 94, 136, 255; **herre** (comp.) 6/120; ◆ col.: **an heiȝ** (adv.) *high up, above* 5/210; **on heiȝ** 5/35; **on hey** 8/16; **on hyȝe** 6/43; **on hight** 12/88, 235; **on hyȝt** 6/208; **vpon hicht** (adv.) *loudly* 14/8; **vpon hyȝt** *towering* 6/119

hight, highte → **hat**

hiȝ; hiis → **highe; be**

hill (sb.) 14/141; **hille** 12/88

hilte (sb.) *hilt* 9/78

him, him selff, himself, himselue, himseluen, hine → **he**

hing (inf.) *to hang* 14/167 [see hang; henge]

hir → **she; they**

hirdes (sb.pl.) *herdsman, shepherd* 10.5/36

hire → **she; they**

hire (sb.) *payment, wages, hire* 12/167; **hyre** 12/260

hirselve → **she**

hirpilland (psp.) *to limp* 14/25
hirselve → **she**
his → **be**; **he**
hise; **hit** → **he**; **they**; **it**
hit (sg.pt.) *to fling down (as a wager)* 7/179
hod; **hoe** → **hood**; **they**
hoeld; **hoere** → **hold**; **they**
hof → **of**
hofþurst (ptp.) *thirsty* 8/137
hokede (ptp.) *hooked* 7/51
hoker (sb.) *disdain* 13/189
hol → **hole** (2)
'hold' (vb.) ♦ inf.: **hald** 11/79, 104 *14/93,
  175; **helde** 9/66; **holde** 5/22 *6/196 *7/192;
  holden 5/121; **hyealde** 4/38; ♦ ps.: **hald**
  11/33; **halde** 12/325; **haldez** 6/223, 231;
  haldis 14/94; **halt** 4/14–15 *7/221; **holdeth**
  7/30; **holdez** 6/72; **hyalde** (sg.ps.subj.) 4/39; ♦
  imp.: **hald** 14/9; ♦ pt.: **held** (sg.pt.) 1/16
  *11/16, 43, 58, 80, 92 *14/141, 177; **helde**
  7/202; **helden** (pl.pt.) 1/17; **heold** 1/68, 70,
  78 *5/11, 100; **heolden** 1/31–32; **hoeld** 8/3;
  holden 6/28; ♦ ptp.: **halde** 13/432; **halden**
  11/38, 98; **haldin** 14/46; **holden** 6/46;
  ihialde 3/21
holde (sb.) *keeping* 12/151
holden, holdeth, holdez → **hold**
hole (1) (sb.) 13/522
hole (2) (adj.) *whole, entire, sound* 5/40; **hol**
  5/40 *9/41; **haill** 14/60; **heil** 2/12, 44
holi, holie → **holy**
holpen → **help** (2)
holt (sb.) *wood, coppice* 13/6
holy → **churche**; **gost**; **writ**
holy (adj.) 10.5/59 *10.7/9 *12/400; **holi** 3/2
  *5/2, 227; **holie** 5/23, 31, 53, 58 etc.; **hooly**
  13/17, 209, 510; **hali** 1/87; **halie** 14/95; **haly**
  11/28, 32, 38, 40–41 etc.; **halier** (comp.)
  11/66; **holyiste** (sup.) 4/44; **haliest** 11/58; ♦
  neg.: **vnholy** 7/3
holyer (sb.) *adulterer* 4/32
holyiste; **hom** → **holy**; **home**
homage (sb.) *retinue* 9/119
home (adv., sb.) 6/195; **hom** 8/17; **ham**
  13/256; **homes** (pl.) 6/12; ♦ col.: **at home**
  6/55; **at hame** 11/95, 106
homely (adv.) *friendly* 12/64
homes → **home**
homward (adv.) *homewards* 13/466;
  hamward 11/55; **hamewart** 14/24
hond, honde → **hand**; **hound**
hondele (inf.) *to handle* 6/76
hondred → **hundred**

hone; **honge** → **one**; **hange**
honger; **hongi** → **hungur**; **hange**
honnoure → **honour**
honour (sb.) 5/187, 214; **honoure** 13/209;
  honnoure 12/132–133; **honur** 5/169
hood (sb.) 7/182, 192 *13/68; **hod** 7/179
hoolly (adv.) *entirely, wholly* 13/55; **halely**
  11/65
hooly → **church**; **holy**; **writ**
hoor (adj.) *hoary, grey* 13/102
hoost (sb.) *host, innkeeper* 13/123; **hooste**
  13/355
hoote → **hat**
hope (1) (sb.) 2/27, 62 *7/29 *12/38
hope (2) (sg.ps.) 6/139 *12/43; *expect* 13/253;
  hopes 6/182; **hopede** (sg.pt.) 8/40 *9/67
hoppen (pl.ps.) *to dance* 13/100
hopur (sb.) *hopper (of a mill)* 13/260, 263
horderwycan (sb.) *office of steward* 1/77
Horn (1) (prn.) 9/1, 3, 15, 19 etc.; **Hornes**
  (gsg.) 9/38, 57, 111, 134
horn (2) (sb.) 9/56; **horne** 7/202
hors (sb.) *horse* 13/241, 284, 286, 288 etc.;
  (pl.) 13/54
hose (sb.) 13/157; **hosen** (pl.) 13/179
ho-so → **who**
hostelrye (sb.) *inn, lodging* 13/23
hostiler (sb.) *hostler, stableman* 7/190, 192
hot, hote → **hat**
hot (adj.) 3/33; **hote** 7/145, 159
hotez; **hou** → **hat**; **how**
houe; **houed, houen** → **heifis**; **houeð**
houes → **howve**
houes (sb.pl.) *hoof* 6/246
houeð (sg.ps.) *to stay, circle, swarm* 2/9, 48;
  houen 2/41; **houed** (pt.) 7/131
hound (sb.) 7/214, 232; **hond** 4/45; **houndes**
  (pl.) 8/145; **hundes** 9/54
hounderstod → **vndirstande**
hounger → **hungur**
houpbringe (inf.) *to bring up* 8/63
houre; **hous** → **we**; **house**
housbondrie (sb.) *(careful) management*
  13/301
house (sb.) 8/131 *12/136; **hous** 4/54 *5/10,
  24 *6/72, 96, 120, 195 *7/154 *8/6, 14
  *13/346 *14/142; **hows** 11/22; **hus** 1/70
  *9/121
houssong (sb.) *matins* 8/133, 135; **houssonge**
  8/137
how (adv., conj.) 6/166, 188, 201 *7/227
  *11/3, 53, 60 *12/367 *13/138, 249, 263,
  266 *14/8, 77; **howe** 12/3, 213, 222, 301,
  356; **hou** 4/69 *5/38, 149 *10.7/2 *10.8/2

*13/247; **hu** 2/3 *9/48; **howgates** 13/261; **ou**
8/115; **wu** 2/2, 5
hows → house
howve (sb.) *cap* 13/135; **houes** (pl.) 7/131
hu → how
huader → quhether
huan, huanne → when
hue → she
huer, huere → they; where
huer-of, huerof; huet → where; what
Hugo of Walteruile (prn.) 1/79
hulles → Maluerne
hundereth → hundred
hundes → hound
hundred (num.) 9/35 *13/220; **hundret** 5/203;
   hundrid 7/131; **hondred** 4/57 *5/28;
   hundereth 12/39; **oundred** 8/4
hungær; hungerd → hungur; hungren
hungery → hungry
hungren (inf.) *to hunger, to be hungry* 2/57;
   hungreð (sg.ps.) 2/38; **hungerd** (sg.pt.) 11/89
hungry (adj.) 7/214; **hungery** 11/93
hungur (sb.) *hunger* 7/239; **hungær** 1/48, 56;
   honger 8/56; **hounger** 8/7, 34, 73, 84, 127
huo; hure → who; she
hurt (inf.) 14/89
hus → house
husband (sb.) *husband, farmer* 12/45 *14/2,
   12, 24, 27, 43, 57, 142, 204
husberners (sb.pl.) *burner of houses* 3/30
huy, huyche → they; which
hwer-of; hwylem → where; whilom
hy → in; she; they
hyalde; hyde → hold; hide
hydously (adv.) *hideously* 12/138
hye → highe; in; she
hyealde; hyer → hold; here
hyʒ, hyʒe → highe
hyʒe (imp.) *to hasten* 6/86; **hyis** (sg.ps.)
   14/187; **hyit** (pl.pt.) 14/157
hyʒt; hyht → highe; hat
hyis, hyit → hyʒe
hym, hymself, hym-selfe, hymseluen → he
hyndreste (adj., sup.) *last* 13/78
hyne (sb.) *servant* 13/59
hyre → hire; she
Hyrtlingbyri (pn.) 1/79
hys → he

I

I (perspron. 1.sg.) **i** 9/5, 7–10, 12, 29, 43, 96; **Ic**
   2/2; **ich**; **Ihc** 8/80 *9/9, 28–29, 31, 48; **ik**
   13/91, 112; **ych** 10.3/6; **Y**; ♦ poss.: **mi** 5/128

*8/60, 93–94, 97, 100 *9/3, 11–12 *10.1/6
   *10.2/11–12 *10.4/42 *10.5/13–14 *10.6/54
   *12/37, 235, 249, 267 etc.; **min** 8/93 *9/11,
   40; **mine** 5/132, 165 *8/25, 50, 80, 91, 106
   *9/53 *11/12; **my**; **myn** 6/44, 143, 195
   *7/241 *10.1/11 *10.3/47 *10.4/4, 12, 18
   *12/389 *13/94, 143, 309, 346, 477,
   513–514; **myne** 6/129 *12/217, 250, 312,
   339 *13/93–94 *14/33; ♦ obj.: **me; mee**
   12/274; ♦ refl.: **miselffe** 12/212; **miselue**
   10.4/11; **my self** 14/88; **myself** 11/63;
   myselfe 12/67
iafen → give
Iame → Saints
ibede → bid
iben, i-beo → be
iblessed (ptp.) *to bless* 9/52; **yblessed** 7/76;
   blissid 12/404
i-bore → bear
ibrocht, i-brouʒt, ibrout → bring
i-bured → beberieden
Ic, ich → I
ichabbe; icham → have; be
ichaue; i-chose → have; cheosen
ichot → wit (2)
i-chulle, ichulle → will (2)
i-cleoped, icleped, iclepede → clepe
i-come, icome, icomen → come (2)
icrope → crepen
i-do, ido, idon → do
idrunke; ieden → drinke; go
Ieneuer (sb.) *January* 5/202
Ierusalem (pn.) *Jerusalem* 3/3
Iesu, Iesus → Jesus Christ
i-ete → eat
if (conj.) **iff** 12/331; **gif** 1/61, 76 *13/405, 414
   *14/75; **ʒef** 2/36 *8/49, 102 *10.3/15, 39
   *10.5/23 *10.8/20; **ʒif** 5/124 *6/193 *8/67;
   yef 3/40–41 *4/38, 96; **yf** 7/38, 80
ifaie (adv.) *gladly* 8/100
ifere → fere
iff; ifulde → if; feld (2)
i-ʒolden → yelde
Ihc → I
iherd, iherde, ihere, ihereþ → hear
ihialde → hold
ik → I
ikaut; iknede → cacche; knede
ikneu, iknowe → know
i-kud; il → kiðen; ill
ilc, ilce; iles → ilk; ille
ilhayl (sb.) *bad luck* 13/313
ilk (adj., pron.) *same, every each, every* 2/23
   *6/24 *11/25, 107 *14/202, 222; **ilke** 4/4,

37, 46, 53, 89 *8/24, 50, 136 *12/273
*13/96; **ilc** 1/5; **ilce** 1/85; ♦ col.: **ilk a** *every*
11/11; **ilke a** 12/130; 253; ♦ contr. art.: **þilke**
8/74; **þulke** 5/83, 85

ill (adj.) *bad, poor, evil* 11/16 *12/34; (adv.)
12/139; (sb.) 14/143; **il** 13/398, 408; **ille** (adj.)
2/48 *13/269; (adv.) 6/133 *7/109 *10.6/43;
ylle (adv.) 7/143 *9/28

ille → **ill**

ille (sb.) *island* 9/29; **iles** (pl.) 6/7

iloke → **lok**

i-mad, i-maked, imaked → **make**

imunt → **mene** (2)

in (prep.) **ine** 3/3, 14, 24, 33 etc. *4/5–6, 9–12
etc.; 8/69, 81–82, 132; ♦ col.: **in feere** (adv.)
together 12/364, 385; **in fere** *in company*
6/54; *together* 12/126; **in hy** (adv.)
immediately, at once 11/49, 87; **in hye**
12/367

i-nam; ine → **be; in**

i-nelle → **will** (2)

Ingland → **England**

inne (adv., prep.) *in, inside, within* 1/41 *5/142
*8/12, 36 *9/49, 98 *13/41, 131

innogh, inogh → **enough**

i-nome → **nime**

inou, i-nouȝ, i-novȝ, inowe → **enough**

inspired (ptp.) *to breathe forth, quicken* 13/6

into (adv., prep.) 1/72 *3/15, 43 *5/141 *6/104,
222 *7/2, 101 *9/75, 86 *10.3/12 *11/3
*12/256, 342, 348 *13/23, 206, 267, 360
*14/115, 123, 201; **in-to** 5/66, 88

inward (adv.) *inwards* 13/303

inwardly (adv.) *greatly* 12/361

inwit (sb.) *conscience* 7/222

Iohan → **Saints**

ioie, ioies → **joie**

iolite (sb.) *ease, pleasure* 11/62

ioye, ioyes → **joie**

ire (sb.) *anger* 13/86

i-redie → **redy**

iren (sb.) *iron* 1/46, 48; **yren** 7/97

Irisse (adj.) *Irish* 9/53; **Yrisse** 9/15

Irlond (pn.) *Ireland* 10.3/12; **Yrlonde** 9/127

is → **be; he**

i-sched → **schade**

iseie, i-seiȝ, i-seiȝen, i-seo, iseon, i-seothþ →
   see

iserued; isey, isiist → **serve; see**

i-somoned (ptp.) *to summon* 5/113

Israel (prn.) 7/105, 111

isriue; istounge → **shryue; stong**

istrengþed (ptp.) *to strengthen* 3/25

iswonge (ptp.) *to beat, scourge* 8/146

it (perspron. 3.sg. n.) **itt** 12/147; **hit**

itake; itt → **take; it**

i-þoled → **þolien**

Iudeus → **Jewe**

iuel → **fall**

iuge (sb.) *judge* 14/80, 99

iustise (sb.) *justice* 1/30; *judge* 5/118

iwend → **wene**

i-wende, iwent, i-wiende → **wend**

iwil → **will** (1)

i-wis (adv.) *certainly, indeed, truly* 5/6, 9, 29,
78, 132–133; **iwyis** 6/51; **iwys** 6/39; ♦ col.:
mid iwisse 8/117, 147; **myd iwisse** 10.4/8

iwriten → **writeth**

iwyis, iwys → **i-wis**

J

jalous (adj.) *jealous* 13/185

Jame → **Saints**

jape (sb.) 13/425, 431

jay (sb.) 13/378

'Jesus Christ' Iesu 10.4/21, 41, 50 *10.6/5,
36, 47 *10.7/14, 25; **Iesu Crist** 2/24; **Iesus**
10.5/12; **Iesus Crist** 3/5; **Jesu** (prn.) *Jesus*
12/349; **Jesus** 9/135; ♦ col.: **for Cristes loue**
by the love of Christ 8/97; **for Cristes peyne**
by the pains of Christ 13/308; **for Cristes**
saule *by the soul of Christ* 13/487

Jewe (sb.) *Jew* 12/147, 320; **Jewes** (pl.)
12/163, 170; **Gius** 3/13; **Iudeus** 1/84

Job (prn.) 12/285

John (prn.) 13/237, 242, 244, 249–250 etc.;
Ser John 10.10/2–3, 7, 11, 15, 19

joie (sb.) *joy, happiness* 12/35, 383; **ioie** 9/43,
47, 51 *10.4/9 *10.5/15, 25, 31, 37, 43, 47,
49, 54; **ioye** 5/210, 232; **joies** (pl.) 12/103;
ioies 8/83; **ioyes** 10.5/24

joly (adj.) *merry, cheerful, pretty, attractive*
13/155, 379, 456; **jolyf** 13/378

Jordane (prn.) *the River Jordan* 11/103;
Jordanne 12/76

Jossa (interj.) 13/325

Judas (prn.) 12/147, 165, 308

juge (inf.) *to pass judgement* 12/320

K

kamus → **camus**

kan, kanne → **can**

kare; kastes → **care; cast**

kay (adj.) *left* 6/209

kayres → cayren
keep (1) (sb.) *care, attention* 13/388
'keep' (2) (vb.) keip (inf.) 14/133, (sg.ps.subj.)
   14/224; kepe (inf.) 5/114 *6/94 *9/32
   *13/326, (sg.ps.subj.) 6/80, 159 *7/127
   *13/471; kepest (sg.ps.) 9/24; kep (imp.sg.)
   9/10
keip → keep (2)
kele (inf.) *to alleviate, cool* 12/84
kempe (sb.) *fighter* 4/14
ken (inf.) *to teach, instruct, show* 11/2; kende
   (sg.pt.) 12/50, 73; kend (ptp.) 11/34
kene (adj.) *bold, courageous* 6/108, 269
kenne → kin
kep, kepe, kepest → keep (2)
kid, kidde → kiðen
'kin' kenne 9/129; cunne 8/83; kun 8/62;
   kunne 8/27 *10.8/12; kyn 13/166, 262;
   kyne 7/26; kynne 12/232; kunnes (pl.) 8/73,
   112, 147
kinde (sb.) *kind, nature* 2/1; cunde 9/59;
   kynde 6/5, 48, 108, 260 *7/120–121, 123,
   126, 231; ♦ col.: Kynde Wit *intelligence*
   7/121; Kynde Witt 7/126; Kynde Wytt
   7/120, 123
kinedom (sb.) *royal state, reign* 5/205;
   kynedom 5/100
king (sb.) 1/1, 5, 17–18 etc. *5/53, 69, 72, 85
   etc. *9/2, 5, 13, 34 etc. *11/51, 53–56, 59
   etc. *14/21, 59, 168; kinge 1/14 *9/14, 84;
   kyng 5/5, 58, 80, 176 *6/108, 127, 130, 151,
   153, 155, 159, 250, 254, 269 *7/118 *9/38,
   72 *10.3/14 *12/126, 128, 184 *14/124;
   kynge 6/180 *7/90, 126–127, 130 *10.5/12;
   kinges (gsg.) 1/14, 83 *9/13, 94 *11/73, 119;
   kinges (pl.) 11/35; kingues 5/90; kynges
   6/25 *10.5/39
kirke → church
kitchine (sb.) *kitchen* 11/76
kiðen *to proclaim, tell, announce, make
   known* 2/1; cuddest (2.sg.pt.) 5/42; kid
   (3.sg.pt.) 11/61; kidde (ptp.) 12/251; kydde
   6/50; i-kud 5/184, 229
klene → clene
knaue, knaues → knave
knave (sb.) *servant, young man* 12/244;
   knaue 7/40, 172; knaues (pl.) 7/45, 145, 165
knawe, knawen, knawes, knaws → know
knede (inf.) *to knead* 13/318; iknede (ptp.)
   8/128
knees (sb.pl.) 7/211
kneled (sg.pt.) *to kneel* 6/155; knelede 7/71
kneu, knew, knewe → know

'knight' (sb.) *young man, knight* kniȝt 9/4,
   21–23, 27 etc.; knyght 13/42–43, 64, 72
   etc.; knyȝt 6/63, 153, 164, 168 etc.;
   knightes (pl.) 11/74, 88; kniȝtes 9/102, 125;
   knyȝtes 6/237; knyȝtez 6/260
kniȝthod (sb.) *knighthood* 9/4; knyghthed
   7/121; knyghthede 7/118
knokked → cnokez
know (sg.ps.) 6/112, 187; iknowe (inf.) 9/56;
   knowe (sg.ps.) 6/144 *12/159; (ptp.) 7/54;
   knawe (inf.) 12/315; knawes (ps.) 12/283;
   knaws 11/35; knowen (pl.ps.) 6/241
   *13/279; knew (sg.pt.) 13/60, 244, 519; kneu
   8/57; ikneu 8/62; knwe 6/247; knewe (pl.pt.)
   9/91 *12/229, 371; knawen (ptp.) 6/135;
   a-knowe 5/130; iknowe 8/91
knyf (sb.) *knife* 13/184
knyght → knight
knyghthed, knyghthede → kniȝthod
knyȝt, knyȝtes, knyȝtez → knight
knyt (ptp.) *to tie* 13/307
kok → cok
kom, kome, komeþ → come (2)
konne → can
kors (sb.) *curse* 8/101
koude; kow → can; cou
kowthe, kouþe → can
kueade (adj.) *evil, bad, sinful* 4/2, 6, 30; qued
   8/100, 105; quede 8/112; kueades (sb.pl.)
   4/62
kun, kunne, kunnes → kin
kydde → kiðen
kyn → kin
kynde; kyne → kinde; kin
kynedom → kinedom
kyneriche (sb.) *kingdom* 7/127
kyng, kynge, kynges → king
kyngdome (sb.) *kingdom* 12/186
kynne → kin
kynrede (sb.) *lineage* 13/191
kyrf (sb.) *blow, cut* 6/159
kyrke-ward (adv.) *towards the church* 7/152
kys (inf.) *to kiss* 10.10/3, 9 *11/92; kyssen
   7/71
kyth (sb.) *country* 6/247

L

labour (sb.) *work, toil* 7/125
lacche (inf.) *to catch, seize, grasp* 7/207; lach
   (imp.) 6/79; laȝt (sg.pt.) 6/115, 220; lahte
   10.3/45
lad, ladde → lede

ladde (sb.) *fellow, serving-man* 12/243
laddre (sb.) *ladder* 5/35; **laddren** (pl.) 5/34
ladis → **lady**
lady (sb.) *lady, woman* 11/94 *12/135
*13/190; **ledy** 10.3/44 *10.8/17–18; **leuedi**
3/4, 6 *10.1/12 *10.2/2, 7; **leuedy** 10.2/4
*10.5/37, 55; ♦ pl.: **ladyez** 6/260; **ladis**
11/74, 88; **ledies** 10.3/8; **leuedis** 10.3/34; ♦
col.: **legge lady** *(liege lady)* 6/133; **oure**
lheuedy *St Mary* 4/98; **ure Lauedi** 3/8; **ure**
Leuedi 3/4, 6
lafe (sb.) *loaf* 11/83
laft → **leave**
laʒe → **loʒe**
laʒe (inf., ps.) *to laugh* 6/251, 259; **laʒes**
(sg.ps.) 6/103; ♦ sg.pl.pt.: **loh** (sg.pt.) 10.1/8;
lou 8/12, 74; **loughe** 13/82; **louʒe** 9/110;
leuch 14/18, 66, 99, 115; ♦ ptp.: **laughen**
(ptp.) 13/79; ♦ sb.: **leyhing** 7/195
laʒt, lahte → **lacche**
lai; laid, laide → **lien; lay** (3)
laif (sb.) *remainder, rest* 14/98, 171
lait; laith → **late; loth**
Lammasse (sb.) *Lammas* 1/1
land (sb.) *land, country, state* 1/33, 50, 54–55
etc. *11/38, 42 *13/212 *14/124, 170, 191;
lande 1/57 *12/51, 68, 314; **lond** 9/6, 12;
londe 2/39 *3/3 *5/93 *6/36, 198, 273
*7/125, 128 *8/51 *9/20, 34, 39, 49, 77, 94
*10.2/4 *10.3/19; **landes** (pl.) 1/2, 6, 71,
75–77; **londes** 13/14
Lanfranc (prn.) 5/115
lang → **Friday; long; longe**
Langaberde (prn.) 6/12
lange; lap → **long; lepe**
lape (1) (sb.) *lap* 10.10/17; **lappe** 7/213
lape (2) (inf.) *to lap up, drink* 7/215
lappid (pl.pt.) *to clothe, lap* 11/109
large (adj.) *generous, liberal* 3/38
last (1) (inf.) 11/111; **leste** 10.2/11; **lasteth**
(sg.ps.) 7/125; **lesteþ** 10.8/5; **lastand** (psp.)
12/66; **lastede** (sg.pt.) 1/50; **laste** 5/198
'last' (2) (adv.) ♦ col.: **atte laste** *at last, finally*
13/330; **at the last** 14/22, 151; **atþe laste**
5/86, 179
lastand → **last** (1)
laste → **last** (1, 2)
lastede → **last** (1)
lastes (sb.pl.) *vice* 10.3/17
lasteth → **last** (1)
lat, late → **let**
late (adj., adv.) 8/41 *10.3/35, 43 *12/162, 329
*13/420; **lait** 14/23

lathe (sb.) *barn* 13/312
latte; lau → **let; lawe**
laude (pl.ps.) *to praise, laud* 12/384
laudes (sb.) *lauds* 4/26
Lauedi → **lady**
laughen → **laʒe**
launde (sb.) *clearing, meadow* 7/8
laus; law → **loos; loʒe**
lawe (sb.) *law* 7/133 *12/313, 322, 329, 403
*13/403–404; **lau** 14/49; **lawes** (pl.) 12/277
lawte (sb.) *loyalty, fidelity* 14/55; **lewte** 7/128
lay → **lien**
lay (1) (sb.) *light, splendour* 10.5/33
lay (2) (sb.) *song, lay* 9/109 *10.2/10; **laye**
6/30
lay (3) (imp.) *to lay (down)* 12/143 *13/309;
legge (inf.) 5/16 *13/161; **leye** 13/233; **leith**
(sg.ps.) *work on* 13/453; **layd** (sg.pt.) 6/206;
leyde 7/211; **laid** (ptp.) 11/99, 105; **laide**
12/83, 329; **læiden** (pl.pt.) 1/51
laye → **lay** (2)
laykez (sb.pl.) *sport, entertainment* 6/49
laykyng (sb.) *to play* 6/259
layne (inf.) *to keep secret* 10.9/6
layt (inf.) *to seek* 6/198; **layte** (sg.ps.) 6/236;
laytes 6/142
layth → **lien**
Lazar (prn.) 12/162, 171
læiden → **lay** (3)
læt → **let**
'leave' (vb.) *to leave, leave off* **leffe** (sg.ps.
subj.) 12/376; **leif** 14/98; **leue** 12/284; **leue**
allow, permit 7/128 *10.5/53; **left** (sg.pt.,
ptp.) 14/179, 192; **laft** (sg.pt.) 6/156; **lefte**
(ptp.) 12/314; **ylaft** 13/86
lece → **never**
leche (sb.) *physician* 13/128
lecherie (sb.) *lechery, debauchery* 3/29 *4/61,
75, 78, 91; **lecherye** 7/75; **litchery** 11/8
lechur (sb.) *lecher* 3/38; **lechurs** (pl.) 4/64
led → **lede** (2)
lede (1) (sb.) *man, knight* 6/45; **leid** 14/53;
lude 6/236
lede (2) (inf., ps.) *to lead* 7/128 *9/67, 132
*11/62 *12/391; **let** (sg.ps.) 4/30; **ledeþ**
(sg.pl.) 4/11; **led** (sg.pt., ptp.) 11/54, 73, 90,
119; **ladde** (sg.pt.) 5/3, 189 *7/118 *9/86,
120–121; **lad** (ptp.) 10.2/1 *13/456
ledeþ → **lede** (2)
ledies, ledy → **lady**
leede ♦ col.: **in leede** *on earth* 12/70, 135
leek (sb.) 13/103
leep → **lepe**

leere (inf.) *to learn* 12/321; **lere** 12/313; **leren** 2/32; **lereð** (sg.ps.) 2/25, 27

lees (sb.pl.) *lie* 12/127

leet; lef → **let; believe**

lef (1) (adj., adv.) *dear, beloved, precious* 2/49; **leue** 9/40, 50; **leuer** (comp.) 11/106; **leuere** 8/4

lef (2) (sb.) *leaf* 10.3/3

lefde → **live**

leffe, left, lefte → **leave**

legge → **lady; lay** (3)

legges (sb.pl.) *leg* 13/47

leid → **lede** (1)

leif; leiff → **leave; leue**

leiȝen → **lien**

leill; leip → **lel; lepe**

leith → **lay** (3)

lel (adj.) *loyal, faithful, just, true* 6/35; **lele** 7/88, 125 *12/65; **leill** 14/50, 53, 58, 69, 163

lelly (adv.) *loyally, faithfully* 6/236 *12/403; **lely** 11/11

lemes → **lim**

lemman (sb.) *lover, beloved* 9/76, 95 *13/464, 471; **lemmon** 10.4/33 *10.6/47

lende (inf.) *to come, arrive, descend* 12/47, 54; **lent** (ptp.) 10.1/6; **ylent** 10.1/12

lene (1) (adj.) *lean, thin* 13/47

lene (2) (inf.) *to lend* 13/67; **leneth** (pl.ps.) 7/75

lened (sg.pt.) *to lean, recline* 7/8

leneth → **lene** (2)

leng → **longe**

leng (inf.) *to stay, remain* 6/198; **lenge** (sg.ps.) 6/41

lengar; lenge → **longe; leng**

lenger → **long; longe**

lengour → **longe**

lengðe (sb.) *length* 2/61

lent → **lende**

lenton (sb.) *Lent, spring* 7/89

leof (sb.) *beloved* 10.8/7; **luef** 10.8/31

leose (inf.) *to lose* 10.7/8; **liesed** (pl.ps.) 3/32; **lorn** (ptp.) 7/112 *13/297, 299; **lorne** 12/198; **losten** (pt. (weak)) 7/108; **ylost** (ptp. (weak)) 13/538

leouede → **live**

lepe (imp.) *to leap, run* 6/79; **leip** (inf., imp.) 14/174, 181, 222; **lep** 8/117; (sg.pt.) 8/11, 119; **lepez** (sg.ps.) 6/115; **lepynge** (psp.) 13/303; **lap** (sg.pt.) 14/183, 191; **leep** 13/452; **lop** 8/39

lere → **leere**

lere (1) (adj.) *empty, vacant* 5/51

lere (2) (sb.) *face* 6/105, 205; **lyre** 12/119

lere (3) (inf.) *to teach, tell* 8/116 *12/330, 391; **leres** (sg.ps.) 11/1; **lered** (ptp.) 1/63 *7/88; (sg.pt.) 12/55, 127

leren → **leere**

leres → **lere** (3)

lereð → **leere**

lerned (ptp.) *to learn* 13/69, 192, 346

lernyng (sb.) *tidings, news* 12/85

les, less, lesse → **little**

les (imp.) *to release, set free* 10.2/4

lessouns (sb.pl.) *lesson, reading* 4/90

lest → **little**

lest (conj.) 10.1/16

leste, lesteþ → **last** (1)

let (imp.; pt.) *to let, allow; give up, relinquish* 5/65 *6/86, 147, 201, 207, 210, 255 *8/87 *9/60–61, 63, 68, 97 *10.4/45; **lete** (inf., ps., pt.) 4/74 *5/120 *8/26, 44 *10.2/7 *10.4/45 *10.9/12, 17 *11/52 *13/532; **leten** (ptp.) 8/20, 23; **lette** (inf.) 5/102; **lat** (imp.) 7/195 *11/65, 67 *13/321–322, 349; **late** (imp., pt.) 9/107 *12/65; **latte** (imp.) 12/194, 234; **læt** (sg.pt.) 1/71; **leet** 13/116, 438; **liet** 5/31, 67, 70, 92 etc.

let → **let; lede** (2)

leten, lette → **let**

letteres (sb.pl.) *letter* 6/35

leuand; leuch → **live; laȝe**

leueð → **believe**

leue → **beliaue; believe; lef; leave; live**

leue (sb.) *leave, permission* 7/50, 83, 241 *8/13 *11/111, 119; **leve** 13/140, 231, 236; **leiff** 14/106; **yleaue** 4/9, 11

leued → **believe; live**

leuedi, leuedis, leuedy → **lady**

leuely (adv.) *attentively* 10.3/47

leuer, leuere → **lef** (1)

leuyd, leuys → **live**

leve → **leue**

leveful (adj.) *lawful* 13/136

levesel (sb.) *arbour* 13/285

lewed (adj.) *ignorant, lay, simple* 7/70, 88, 102

lewte → **lawte**

Leycestre (pn.) *Leicester* 10.3/30

leyde, leye → **lay** (3)

leyen; leyhing → **lien; laȝe**

lheuedy; lhorde → **lady; lord**

libbe, libe → **live**

lic (sb.) *body, corpse* 1/7

licence (sb.) 7/83

licht → **light; liȝt**

licour (sb.) *sap, moisture* 13/3

lie (inf.) *to lie, tell lies* 8/66 *9/96; **lye** 7/50 *13/200; **lyeȝe** 4/91; **liyng** (sb.) 13/108

lien (inf.) *to lie (down), belong to* 1/47, 76;
  ligge 9/8, 14; **liggen** 5/18; **layth** (sg.ps.)
  7/207 *13/245; **liht** 5/230 *10.3/44; **lijthþ**
  5/137; **lith** 13/423, 451, 480; **liþ** 4/65; **lye**
  13/430; (inf.) 13/532; **lyis** (sg.ps.) 14/140;
  lyth 13/514; **leyen** (pl.ps.) 7/89; **lai** (sg.pt.)
  1/2 *5/221; **lay** 7/8 *9/22 *11/91, 94 *13/20,
  196, 217, 418, 482· *14/16; **leiȝen** (pl.pt.)
  5/219
liesed; liet → **leose; let**
lif, lif-daie, lif-dayes → **life**
life (sb.) 11/40, 53–54, 60 etc.; **lif** 4/11 *5/2–3,
  189 *7/125 *8/89 *9/64 *10.2/11 *10.5/13
  *13/114; **liffe** 12/66; **liif** 8/94; **lijf** 5/23, 210;
  liue 5/58 *8/106, 114, 125 *9/37; **lyf** 6/142
  *7/238 *10.2/4 *13/116, 119, 248, 456; **lyue**
  6/172 *10.4/46; **lyues** (gsg.) 10.4/48; (pl.)
  7/225; ♦ compd.: **lif-daie** *term of life* 8/100;
  lif-dayes (pl.) 8/25; **lyf-tyme** 7/50, 238, 242
lifes, liff, liffe, liffis, lifing → **life; live**
liflode (sb.) *means of life, sustenance* 7/32
lift (inf.) *to lift, lift up, raise* 11/15; **lyftes**
  (sg.ps.) 6/12; **lyft** (ptp.) 6/45; (sg.pt.) 6/220;
  lyfte (sg.pt.) 6/156, 233; (inf.) 7/211; **luftynge**
  (sb.) 7/212
ligge, liggen; light → **lien; liȝt; liȝte** (2)
light (sb.) 12/21, 47, 54, 57, 69, 83, 85, 92–93,
  353 *13/521, 523; **licht** 14/64; **lyht** (sb.)
  10.4/30
lightly (adv.) *easily* 13/323; **liȝhtliche** 5/181;
  lychtlie 14/183, 217; **lyȝtly** 6/79, 115, 210
liȝt → **liȝte** (2)
liȝt (adj.) *light, easy* 8/118; **liȝte** 9/25; **licht**
  14/10; **light** 10.3/3
liȝte → **liȝt**
liȝte (1) (inf.) *to illuminate* 4/84
liȝte (2) (inf.) *to alight, arrive, land, stand*
  9/69; **light** 11/56; **lyȝt** 6/210; **liȝt** (imp.) 6/41;
  lyȝtis (sg.ps.) 6/116; **liht** (ptp.) 10.2/8; **lyht**
  10.1/6
liht → **lay; liȝte** (2)
liif, lijf; lijthþ → **life; lien**
like (1) (adj.) 11/7, 33, 42, 122 *12/90, 243;
  lyk 13/46; **lyke** 7/205; **ylyk** 13/48
like (2) (sg.ps.subj.) *to like, love, please, prefer*
  10.6/43; **likis** (pl.ps.) 12/321; **lykes** (sg.ps.)
  6/76, 177; **liked** (sg.pt.) 11/82; **lyked** 6/133;
  likede (pl.pt.) 7/58; **lykede** 7/70; **liking** (sb.)
  desire 11/101
likerous (adj.) *luxurious, pleasant* 7/32;
  likerouses (pl.) 4/36
liking, likis → **like** (2)
likkin (sg.ps.) *to compare* 14/197

lim (sb.) *limb* 11/122; **limes** (pl.) 1/44 *2/3, 14
  *5/40; **lemes** 13/110
Lincol (pn.) *Lincoln* 1/27
ling ♦ col.: **in to ane ling** (adv.) *at once,
  immediately* 14/107
linkis (sb.pl.) *fetter, chain* 14/203
list → **lust**
list (sg.ps., impv.) *to desire, long for* 13/91;
  liste (sg.pt.) 12/68, 277, 313; (sg.ps.subj.)
  13/90; **luste** (sg.pt.) 5/218
liste → **list**
liste (sb.) *trick, cunning* 9/100
listen (inf.) 2/19; **lysten** 6/30; **listneð** (sg.ps.)
  2/61; **luste** 9/2
litchery → **lecherie**
lite, litel → **little**
littel → **little**
little (adj., adv.) 2/59; **lite** 4/80 *13/87, 507;
  litel 1/20 *2/30 *9/90 *13/86, 231, 521;
  littel 6/30, 205; **lut** 10.3/19; **lutel** 10.1/2
  *10.8/1; **luitel** 8/130; **luyte** 5/22, 108, 121;
  luytel 5/21; **lvtel** 10.7/1; **lytill** 14/156; ♦
  comp.: **les** 11/12, 47, 50, 123; **less** 11/45;
  lesse 12/383; ♦ sup.: **lest** 6/142
lith, liþ; liue → **lien; life**
liuen, liueð, liuie → **live**
'live' ♦ inf.: **libbe** (inf., ps.) 4/56, 58; **liff**
  11/117; **liffe** 12/68; **liuen** 1/76 *2/49; **liuie**
  8/83; **lyfe** 7/88; **lyue** (inf.) 7/125 *10.8/21;
  lyuen (pl.ps.) 7/102; (inf.) 10.1/10; (sg.ps.)
  10.1/3; **libe** 8/21; **leue** 12/322; **lyueþ** (sg.ps.)
  9/50 *10.3/45; ♦ ps.: **leuys** 12/160; **lifes**
  11/8, 114; **liffis** 12/70; **liueð** 2/44; ♦ psp.:
  leuand 12/55, 127; ♦ pt.: **lefde** 9/59; **leouede**
  5/23, 195; **leuyd** 12/353; **lyueden** 7/28; ♦
  ptp.: **leued** 12/243; ♦ sb.: **lifing** 11/113
liyng → **lie**
lo (interj.) 5/129 *13/130–131, 322, 395, 542;
  loo 13/359
lobies (sb.pl.) *lubber, lout* 7/53
lof and grin (sb.) *fetters and chains* 1/44
lofden → **loue**
loft ♦ col.: **vpo loft** *on high* 10.8/30
loȝe (adj.) *low* 6/89; **laȝe** 2/59; **loȝwe** 5/91;
  law 11/25
loh → **laȝe**
lok (inf.) *to lock (in)* 14/203; **luketh** (sg.ps.)
  2/42; **iloke** (ptp.) 8/10; ♦ neg.: **vnlokynne**
  12/197
loke (inf., ps.) *to look (at)* 3/39 *5/218 *6/235,
  266 *12/92, 152, 211; **looketh** (sg.ps.)
  13/283; **luke** 11/11; **loked** (sg.pt.) 6/233
  *11/78; **lokede** 9/112; **loken** (ptp.) 6/35; **loki**
  (inf.) *to consider* 4/40; *to attribute* 4/43

lokkez (sb.pl.) *locks* 6/206
lond, londe, londes → **land**
Londoun (pn.) *London* 7/83, 89; **Lundene** 1/13; **lundenisce** (adj.) 1/13
long → **ylong**
long (adj.) 10.2/4 ∗13/73, 153; **longe** 6/206 ∗7/53 ∗10.4/36 ∗13/47, 459; **longue** 5/178; **lenger** 13/96; **lang** 11/112, 115, 119; **lange** 13/399; **lang eir** 14/70
longe → **long**
longe (adv.) *long* 4/21 ∗6/36 ∗8/140 ∗10.2/9 ∗10.6/33 ∗10.8/5; **longue** 5/23, 122, 195, 198; **lang** 11/112, 119; ◆ comp.: **leng** 1/76 ∗5/15; **lenger** 4/77 ∗12/193 ∗13/461; **lengar** (comp.) 12/68; **lengour** 8/21; **longe** 10.1/10
longen (inf., ps.) *to long for, desire* 10.4/23 ∗13/12; **longinge** (sb.) 10.1/12; **longyng** 10.2/1
longest; longinge → **belongeth; longen**
longue → **long; longe**
longyng; loo → **longen; lo**
looketh → **loke**
loos (adv.) *loose* 13/362; **laus** (adj.) 13/288
lop → **lepe**
lord (sb.) 3/16, 35 ∗7/28, 103, 134, 225 ∗10.10/3 ∗11/19 ∗13/57, 64, 66, 488, 511 ∗14/50, 168; **lorde** 3/34, 42 ∗6/103, 130 ∗12/65, 120, 129, 135, 349, 357, 361, 376, 397, 400, 405; **lhorde** 4/50; **Louerd** *the Lord, God* 2/25 ∗3/5, 7, 11, 18 ∗5/42, 44, 204; **Louerde** 3/15, 22; **Louerdes** (gsg.) 5/191; **lordes** (gsg., pl.) 7/62, 93 ∗11/113 ∗13/53
lordinges (sb.pl.) *lord, master* 3/35
lordly (adv.) 13/124
lore (sb.) *teaching, advice, knowledge* 2/25, 61 ∗5/111, 121, 145 ∗9/125 ∗10.8/19; **lores** (pl.) 10.3/47
lorelles (sb.pl.) *worthless fellow* 7/75
lores; lorn, lorne → **lore; leose**
los (1) (sb.) *loss* 13/410
los (2) (sb.) *renown, fame* 6/45
lossum (adj.) *lovely, pleasant* 10.1/8
lost; losten → **lust; leose**
loth (adj.) *hateful, loathsome, loath, reluctant* 7/53; **laith** 14/89; **loð** 2/49; **loþ** 8/3, 110
lou → **laȝe**
loude (adv.) *loudly, fiercely* 6/103; **lude** 9/17
loue → **love**
loue (inf., ps.) *to love* 10.2/6 ∗10.3/17 ∗10.5/13, 19 ∗10.8/13 ∗10.10/2, 7–8 ∗11/9 ∗12/361; **louien** (inf.) 5/48; **louye** (inf.; sg.ps.subj.) 4/47 ∗7/128 ∗10.4/24 ∗10.8/27; **loueþ** (sg.ps.) 4/20 ∗10.8/14, 28, 35; **loues**

10.10/7; **luffes** 12/403; **luueþ** 9/42; **louede** (sg.pt.) 5/47; **lufit** (ptp.) *respected* 14/53; (sg.pt.) 14/64; **loueden** (pl.pt.) 9/131; **lofden** 6/21; **luueden** 1/82; **louyng** (sb.) 12/405
loue-longinge (sb.) *love-longing* 10.1/3; **loue-longynge** 10.4/3; **louelongynge** 10.5/16
louely (adj.) *lovely, pleasant* 12/119; **louelych** 6/206; **lufly** 6/220; ◆ neg.: **vnlouely** 7/215
Louerd, Louerde, Louerdes → **lord**
loues; loughe, louȝe → **loue; laȝe**
louien → **loue**
loun (sb.) *rogue* 14/183
Lounde (pn.) *Lound, Lincolnshire* 10.3/30
lourand (psp.) *to lurk* 14/64
louryng (sb.) *frowning* 7/195
lousit (pl.pt.) *to detach, untie* 14/23
louting → **lut**
louye, louyng → **loue**
love (sb.) 13/342; **loue** 5/26 ∗7/28, 88, 103, 134 ∗8/97 ∗10.1/6 ∗10.2/8 ∗10.3/9, 36 ∗10.4/5, 19, 29, 37 ∗10.6/7 ∗10.7/2, 5, 34 ∗10.8/2, 4–5, 14, 21, 28 ∗12/245; **luf** 11/49, 51, 64; **lufe** 11/48; **luue** 1/86 ∗2/27 ∗3/28, 34, 40–41
Lowrence (prn.) 14/16, 18, 62, 64 etc.
Lucifer (prn.) 12/119, 197; **Luciferes** (gsg.) 7/40
lud (sb.) *language, speech* 10.1/2
lude → **lede** (1) **loude**
luef; luf, lufe → **leof; love**
luffes, lufit → **loue**
lufly → **louely**
luflych (adv.) *lovingly, in a friendly manner* 6/41; **luflyly** 6/156
luftynge; luitel → **lift; little**
luke; Luke → **loke; Saints**
luketh → **lok**
Lumbardie (pn.) 6/12
Lundene, lundenisce → **Londoun**
lur (sb.) *loss* 6/142
lurdans (sb.pl.) *rogue, rascal* 12/102
lure (inf.) 14/105
lust (sb.) *desire, longing, lust* 8/48, 50; **list** 2/57; **lost** 4/42, 60, 64, 66, 70
luste → **list; listen**
lusty (adj.) *desirous* 13/228
lut, lutel → **little**
lut (sg.pt.) *to bow, bend* 6/205; **louting** (sb.) 11/57
luþer (adj.) *bad, evil* 5/104; **luyther** 7/238
luue; luueden, luueþ → **love; loue**
luyte, luytel → **little**

luyther; lvtel → **luþer; little**
lycame (sb.) *body* 7/32
lycht (adj.) *bright* 14/158
lychtlie → **lightly**
lyckestre (sb. f.) *licker* 4/73
lye, lyeʒe → **lie; lien**
lyf; lyfe → **life; live**
lyft, lyfte, lyftes → **lift**
lyf-tyme → **life**
lyʒt, lyʒtis → **liʒte** (2)
lyʒtly → **lightly**
lyht → **light; liʒt; liʒte** (2)
lyhtnesse (sb.) *splendour* 10.5/34
lyis → **lien**
lyk, lyke → **like** (1)
lyked, lykede, lykes → **like** (2)
lylie-leor (sb.) *fair-faced one* 10.3/46
lylie-whyt (adj.) *lily-white* 10.2/11
Lymbo (prn.) *Limbo* 12/102; **Lymbus** 12/198
lyn (sb.) *linen* 10.3/46
lynage (sb.) *lineage* 13/496
lynde (sb.) *lime-tree* 10.3/3
lynes (sb.pl.) *line, rope* 7/207
lyppes (sb.pl.) *lip* 7/134
lyre → **lere** (2)
lysten; lyth; lytill → **listen; lien; little**
lyþe (imp.) *listen* 10.5/5
lyue → **life; live**
lyuen; lyues → **live; life**
lyuynge (sb.) *vomit* 7/215

M

ma, maced → **make** (2)
mach (inf.) *to match* 6/69
machouns (sb.pl.) *mason* 5/33
macod → **make** (2)
mad (adj.) 10.2/1 *13/455; **madde** 12/247
made, maden → **make** (2)
madyn → **maiden**
magestee (sb.) *majesty* 13/546
maʒe (sb.) *stomach* 4/72; **mawe** 7/234
maʒt → **miht**
Mahounde (prn.) 12/343
mai; maid → **may** (2) **make** (2)
maiden (sb.) *maiden, girl, virgin* 10.5/7;
  madyn 10.9/2; **maide** 9/128 *10.2/1;
  maidins (pl.) 11/115; **mayde** 13/172;
  mayden 10.4/28 *10.5/48; **maydens** (pl.)
  11/74; **may** 10.1/14 *10.5/3, 13, 31 *10.8/11
maiʒ → **may** (2)
maine (sb.) *strength, might* 8/140 *11/120;
  mayn 10.9/10

mainsum (adj.) *nourishing* 11/75
mair, maist → **much**
maister (sb.) *master* 8/103, 136; **maistres**
  7/60; **maystres** 7/85
maisteris (sg.ps.) *to master* 14/178
maistres → **maister**
maistries (sb.pl.) *master stroke* 12/116, 202,
  216–217
mak → **make** (2)
make (1) (sb.) *mate, wife* 9/75 *10.1/9, 16
make (2) (inf., ps.) *to make, cause, effect* 7/35,
  124 *9/97, 134 *12/42, 103, 142, 146, 178,
  217, 247, 339, 362 *13/275, 320, 347, 350,
  356; **maken** 13/9, 202; ◆ inf.: **ma** (inf.)
  14/112; **mak** 11/46, 50, 84, 101 *14/26, 104,
  122, 180, 182; **maki** 4/69; ◆ ps.: **maked**
  3/36–37; **makes** 11/24, 30 *12/125, 216, 383
  *13/478; **maket** 1/88 *3/39; **maketh** 7/37
  *13/240, 424; **makeð** 2/10; **makeþ** 4/19, 59,
  62, 82, 90 *8/15; **makie** 10.6/42; **mase**
  12/116; ◆ pt.: **macod** 1/26; **made** 3/22 *5/39,
  53, 198 *7/55, 119–120 *11/5, 25, 83, 85
  *12/80, 202, 233, 356 *13/33, 127, 204, 223,
  363; **maid** 14/113; **makede** 1/9, 32, 80–81
  *3/36 *5/9 *9/31, 47, 63, 104, 109, 117, 124,
  130; **makedest** 9/6; **maden** 5/50; ◆ ptp.:
  maced 1/46; **maked** 1/30, 34; **i-mad** 5/101;
  i-maked 5/52; **imaked** 3/3, 18 *5/24 *8/36;
  ymake 10.1/8; **ymaked** 10.7/5 *13/469
maker (sb.) *creator* 12/2
makes, maket, maket, maki, makie → **make**
  (2)
maladye (sb.) *illness* 13/217
Malduit → **Willelm**
malice (sb.) 12/302
malt (sb.) 13/212, 215
Maluerne hulles (pn.) *the Malvern Hills* 7/6,
  135
Malyne (prn.) 13/460
mammon (sb.) 14/214
man → **must**
man (1) (pron.) *one* 3/30 *5/190, 231; **me**
  1/24, 38–39, 64 *4/25, 32, 38, 50–51, 53–54,
  82, 93, 96–97 *8/38 *10.3/17, 20, 41
  *10.5/47; **men** 8/106 *9/5 *10.5/38 *13/434
  *14/195
man (2) (sb.) *man, person, mankind* **manne**
  3/37 *4/9 *12/1, 80; **mon** 6/69, 109, 119
  *8/143 *10.1/13 *10.5/42 *10.7/1, 17
  *10.8/1, 18; **mannes** (gsg.) 1/47 *5/88, 96;
  mannis 12/246 *14/219; **men** (pl.) **menne**
  6/253 *9/53
manciple (sb.) 13/253; **maunciple** 13/217

maner (sb.) *manner, kind, way* 6/271; **manere** 4/71 *5/162 *7/20 *11/5, 17 *12/350; **maneres** 4/58; **manyeres** 4/92

manhede (sb.) *manliness* 5/106

mani, manie → **many**

manifældlice (adj.) *manifold* 1/89

mankynde (sb.) *mankind* 12/15; **monkunne** 10.7/35; **monkyn** 10.5/30

manne, mannes, mannis → **man** (2)

manred (sb.) *homage* 1/30

manslaȝþe (sb.) *murderer* 4/40

manslaȝþes (sb.pl.) *murder* 4/93; **manslechtes** 3/29

manure → **place**

many (adj.) 7/5, 26, 49, 229 *11/75 *12/103 *13/113, 131, 149, 168; **manye** 7/96; **mani** 1/44, 48, 81 *2/57 *3/36 *5/96, 182, 231; **manie** 1/80; **moni** 6/229 *8/87; **mony** 6/14, 22, 71, 97, 138, 241 *7/27, 60, 63 *14/219

manyeres → **maner**

marbre-ston (sb.) *marble* 5/139, 141, 149, 157

March (sb.) 13/2; **Mersh** 10.1/1

marchandise (sb.) *trade* 7/61

marchen (pl.ps.) *to go hand in hand* 7/61

mare → **much**

mare (sb.) 13/279; **mares** (pl.) 13/289, 305

mariage (sb.) *marriage* 13/204

Marie → **Saints**

Marie (prn.) 10.6/10, 19, 29, 39 *12/231, 250; **Marye** 10.4/26

market-betere (sb.) *bully* 13/160

marre (inf.) *to injure, afflict, harm* 12/116, 173, 208; **marreþ** (sg.ps.) 10.2/1

mart (sb.) *fattened ox or cow* 14/41

Martin (prn.) 1/68

martir (sb.) *martyr* 13/17; **martyr** 1/87; **martyrs** (pl.) 1/37

Marye; mase → **Marie; make** (2)

mased (ptp.) *to make dizzy* 12/247

masse (sb.) *mass* 7/156 *8/126; **masses** (pl.) 9/61

massedæi (sb.) *feast-day* 1/6; **mæssedæi** 1/72

masses → **masse**

mate (adj.) *daunted* 6/123

materis (sb.pl.) *matter, affair* 14/93

matynes (sb.pl.) *matins* 4/26; **matyns** 4/24

maugre (prep.) *in spite of* 11/92

maunciple → **manciple**

mawe; mawen → **maȝe; may** (2)

may → **maiden**

May (1) (prn.) 7/6 *10.3/1

may (2) (ps.) *to be able to, may* 4/52 *5/231 *6/52, 167, 183, 196 etc. *7/9 *8/59, 115

*10.1/4 *10.2/8, 11 *10.5/5, 23 *10.6/12, 28 *10.8/2, 14, 21 *11/31, 33–34, 62 etc. *12/6, 187, 207, 290, 380 *13/105, 120, 257, 268 etc. *14/43, 59, 75, 101 etc.; **mai** 1/49 *2/46–47 *8/71 *9/98 *10.5/9, 47; **maiȝ** (sg.ps.) 2/15, 43, 59; **mawen** (pl.ps.) 10.5/43; **maye** (sg.ps.) 10.10/8 *12/173; **mouwen** (pl.ps.) 5/146; **mowe** 13/110; ◆ pt. and subj.: **micht** 14/168; **might** 11/39, 53, 86; **miȝte** 5/102, 152, 158, 160, 185; **miȝten** (pl.) 5/182, 219; **miȝt** 4/34, 42; **miȝte** 4/68 *5/15, 20 *8/29, 44 *9/43, 69–70, 130–131; **miȝten** (pl.) 4/58, 77 *5/218; **miȝtte** 8/21, 56; **mihte** 1/7 *10.3/9; **mocht** 14/88; **moȝe** 4/69, 87; **mycht** 14/169; **myghte** 7/100 *13/341, 368, 390, 415, 419, 516; **myghtest** (2.sg.) 7/135; **myȝt** 6/132, 266, 270; **myhte** 1/47 *7/39, 68, 204, 231, 233; **myhtes** (2.sg.) 1/53

mayde, mayden, maydens → **maiden**

maye; mayn → **may** (2) **maine**

mayn (adj.) *great, strong* 6/123

maystres → **maister**

mæssedæi → **massedæi**

me → **I; man** (1)

mede (sb.) *reward* 2/24 *10.7/26 *11/31

mee → **I**

meel (sb.) *meal* 8/124; **mel** 8/87

meit → **mete** (2)

meke (adj.) *meek* 11/2, 13, 61 *12/1; **meoke** 10.7/11

mekely (adv.) *meekly* 11/20

mekenes (sb.) *meekness* 11/30; **meoknesse** 9/118

mekes (sg.ps.) *to humble* 11/26; **mekis** 12/350

mekill; mekis → **much; mekes**

mel → **meel**

mele (sb.) *flour* 13/163, 219, 266, 294 etc.

meled (sg.pt.) *to speak* 6/234

melle → **mille**

melle (inf.) *to mingle* 12/302

melly (sb.) *contest, battle* 6/129

melodye (sb.) *melody, music* 13/9, 392

melte (inf.) *to melt* 5/198

men → **man** (1, 2)

mende (inf., ps.) *to amend, improve* 12/79, 359; **mendid** (sg.pt.) 11/120

mendenant; mendid → **frere; mende**

mene (1) (adj.) *poor, simple* 7/20, 137

mene (2) (inf., ps.) *to mean, signify; complain; intend; moan* 2/60 *5/190 *11/14, 68, 102; **menes** (sg.ps.) 11/27; **menys** 12/46, 231, 301; **mente** (sg.pt.) 12/174; **imunt** 8/122

menne → **man** (2)

menske (inf.) *to honour, adore* 10.2/8

mente → **mene** (2)

menyng (sb.) *token, reference, mention* 12/103; **menynge** 7/99

menys → **mene** (2)

meoke; meoknesse → **meke; mekenes**

mercy (sb.) 10.8/18 *11/19 *12/356; **merci** 10.5/57; **mercye** 12/359

merie (adj., adv.) *glad, gladly, merry, merrily* 9/63; **murie** 9/64, 104; **mury** 10.8/23; **myrie** 13/352, 454

Mersh → **March**

meruaile (sb.) *marvel, wonder* 11/67; **meruayl** 6/253, 266

merueylousliche (adv.) *wondrously* 7/9

mes (sb., sg.pl.) *dish, buffet* 4/62, 69–70, 75; **mese** 11/75, 82

meschaunce (sb.) *disaster* 7/105

meschief (sb.) *evil* 7/65

mese; messagers → **mes; messengere**

messengere (sb.) *messenger* 12/362; **messagers** (pl.) 5/163

mest → **much**

mesuage (sb.) *house (and its contents)* 13/203

mesure (sb.) *measure, moderation* 4/49 *12/302

met (inf.) *to meet, encounter* 10.9/13; **mete** 8/3; *dream* 9/74; **meten** (inf.) 7/135 *8/4; **mete** (sg.pt.) 10.9/3; **mett** 11/55; **mette** (impv.) *dreamt* 7/9, 137; **mette** *met* 8/121

mete → **met**

mete (1) (adv.) *appropriately* 10.6/9

mete (2) (sb.) *food, provisions, dinner, livelihood* 2/18 *4/3, 5, 45, 52–54, 69 *6/261, 271 *8/7, 49, 72, 85 *11/50, 78, 81, 85, 117 *13/356; **meit** 14/173; **mette** 12/230; **metes** (pl.) 4/27, 36, 48–49, 62, 68

meten; metes → **met; mete** (2)

mett → **met**

mette → **met; mete** (2)

meþ (sb.) *moderation* 8/49

mi; micel → **I; much**

micht; mid → **may** (2) **right**

mid (prep.) *with, by, through* 1/33–34, 38, 48 etc. *2/51, 53, 60 *4/50, 66 *8/7, 15, 28, 31, 36 etc. *9/66, 68 *10.5/3; **mide** 2/11; **myde** 4/8

midday (sb.) 10.6/14; **middæi** 1/3

middel (sb.) *waist* 10.1/8; **myddel** 7/210

middelniȝte → **midnycht**

mide → **mid**

Midewintre Dæi (sb.) *Christmas Day* 1/14

midnycht (sb.) *midnight* 14/147; **mydnyght** 13/372; **middelniȝte** 9/19

miengyngue → **dweole**

Mighill (prn.) *Michael* 12/339, 389

might → **may** (2)

mightis, migt → **miht**

miȝhte, miȝhten → **miht; may** (2)

miȝt → **may** (2)

miȝte, miȝten, miȝtte, mihte → **may** (2)

miht (sb.) *might, force, authority, power, strength* 10.2/7; **migt** 2/51; **miȝhte** 5/123; **miȝte** 4/9 *5/42; **myght** 7/119 *12/86, 129, 233, 349, 360 *13/103, 328; **myht** 10.4/22; **maȝt** 2/56; **mightis** (pl.) 12/174; **myȝtez** 6/69

mikel, mikle → **much**

milce (sb.) *pity* 5/176

milde (adj.) *mild, gentle* 1/29 *10.4/21, 41 *10.5/8 *10.7/11; **mylde** 10.4/28

mildeliche (adv.) *humbly, gently* 5/125, 140, 166, 180, 222

mile (sb.) 10.6/13; **myle** 13/348

milk (sb.) 11/94

mille (sb.) *mill* 13/232, 245, 285, 339, 535; **melle** 13/147, 466

millere (sb.) *miller* 13/137, 149, 211, 219 etc.; **milleres** (gsg.) 13/89, 490; **milleris** 13/428

min, mine → **I**

minstralsy (sb.) *entertainment* 11/87; **mynstralcie** 6/271

mint (sg.pt.) *to intend* 1/76

miracle (sb.) 3/18, 24, 26, 39 *5/150, 184, 229, 231 *11/46; **miracles** 1/89 *3/22 *4/82, 84, 90; **myracles** 7/99

mirke (adj., sb.) *murk* 2/22 *12/53

mirth (sb.) 11/87; **mirthe** 12/79, 104–105, 228; **myrthe** 13/229; **murthes** (pl.) 7/35

mis (sb.) *sin, transgression* 11/20

misdede (sb.) *misdeed, sin* 5/170 *8/91 *11/3

misdon (inf.) *to act unjustly* 1/9; **mis-do** (ptp.) 5/110

miselffe, miselue → **I**

misferdest (2.sg.pt.) *to commit adultery* 8/106

mis-payþ (sg.ps.) *to offend* 4/18

misse (ps.subj.) *to lose, forget, miss* 9/99 *10.5/58; **mysse** (inf.) 13/440

mis-stap (sg.pt.) *to stumble* 5/37

mist (sb.) 2/26; **myst** 7/135

miste → **must**

miszigge (inf.) *to slander* 4/91

mo → **much**

mobils (sb.pl.) *moveable goods* 11/12

moche, mochel → **much**

mocht → **may** (2)

mod (sb.) *mind, state of mind, heart, wrath* 10.5/8; **mode** 9/73 *11/13, 61

moder (sb.) *mother* 4/97 *9/50, 62 *10.4/28;
  modir 12/231, 250
Modi (prn.) 9/123
modir; moʒe → **moder; may** (2)
molde (sb.) *earth, world* 7/65 *10.2/1 *12/1,
  91
mon → **man** (2)
mon (sb.) *moan, plaint* 10.6/42
mone → **moone**
monek (sb.) *monk* 5/9; **munec** 1/82; **monekes**
  (pl.) 5/211, 214; **munekes** 1/60, 69, 80, 87
moneye (sb.) *money* 7/61, 136
moni → **many**
monkunne, monkyn → **mankynde**
monþe (sb.) *month* 5/202; **monþes** (pl.) 5/208
mony; mo, moo → **many; much**
moone (sb.) *moon* 13/522; **mone** 1/3 *14/158,
  162
moore; moot → **much; must**
moralitie (sb.) *moral* 14/195
more; morʒen, morn → **much; morning**
morning (sb.) 14/3, 5; **mornyng** 7/6; **morʒen**
  4/22; **morn** 6/240 *11/110; **morwe** 7/175;
  morwen 7/154
morwe, morwen → **morning**
mosseles (sb.pl.) *morsel, bit* 4/77
most, moste → **much; must**
mot, mote → **must**
motes (sg.ps.) *to lead* 12/256
mounteth (sg.ps.) *to arise* 7/65
mournen (inf.) *to mourn, sorrow* 10.1/17;
  mournynde (psp.) 10.6/38
mouse-trappe (sb.) *mousetrap* 10.10/15
mouth (sb.) 7/136 *13/501; **mouthe** 7/234;
  mouþ 4/3; **mouþe** 4/2 *8/28, 50; **mudh**
  3/31; **muð** 2/30–31, 33, 41; **muthe** 6/234
mouwen → **may** (2)
moveth (pl.ps.) *to pour* 3/16
mowe → **may** (2)
mowled (ptp.) *to mould* 13/94
Moyses (prn.) *Moses* 12/86
much (adj., adv.) *great, important, much, very*
  6/143, 234; **muche** 5/24, 42, 80, 185, 227
  *7/99 *9/47 *10.8/4; **muchel** 8/49; **muchele**
  5/77; **mekill** 12/129, 146, 233, 349 *14/178;
  micel 1/4, 8, 23, 69, 72; **mikel** 2/56; **mikle**
  (sb.pl.) 2/59–60; **moche** 4/8, 12–13, 18, 47;
  mochel 4/98; **mycel** 1/70; ♦ comp.: **mare**
  1/57, 66 *11/47; **mair** 14/22, 126, 138, 147,
  173, 194; **mo** 5/36 *6/23 *8/102 *12/358
  *13/194; **moo** 12/208, 328; **moore** 13/82,
  220, 275–276, 385; **more** 3/25 *4/20, 46, 77
  *5/112, 175 *6/120, 123, 191, 248 *7/137,
  150, 157, 231 *8/34, 103 *10.5/47 *10.6/28

*10.7/10 *10.10/8 *11/12, 27, 45, 49, 114,
  123 *12/106, 142, 202, 228, 383; ♦ sup.:
  maist 14/131; **mest** 9/44 *10.5/19; **most**
  7/124; **moste** 2/35 *7/65 *12/360; ♦ compd.:
  non-more 5/146; **nonmore** 5/122; **þe more**
  3/24–25
mudh → **mouth**
mullok (sb.) *mullock, refuse* 13/97
mum (sb.) *mumbling* 7/136
munec, munekes → **monek**
munne (inf.) *to think, remember, mention*
  10.7/31 *10.8/10; **mynge** 10.5/24
murgeþ (sg.ps.) *to grow merry* 10.3/1
murie → **merie**
Murry (prn.) 9/38
murthes; mury → **mirth; merie**
'must' *must, may* **miste** (sg.subj.) 9/51; **muste**
  12/274; **man** 14/67, 180; **moot** 13/207, 401;
  most 8/104; **mot** 5/165 *6/129, 174 *12/139
  *14/14; **mote** 3/43 *5/232 *9/80 *13/142; ♦
  pt.: **moste** 1/76 *8/43 *10.7/21
mustir (inf.) *to show, demonstrate, muster*
  12/174; **musteres** (sg.ps.) 12/104; **mustered**
  (sg.pt.) 12/86
muð, muthe → **mouth**
my → **I; faith**
mycel; mycht → **much; may** (2)
myddel; myde → **middel; mid**
mydnyght; myght → **midnycht; miht**
myghte, myghtest → **may** (2)
myghty (adj.) *mighty, strong* 12/91
myʒt → **may** (2)
myʒtez, myht → **miht**
myhte, myhtes → **may** (2)
mylde; myle → **milde; mile**
myn → **I**
mynde (sb.) *mind, thought, memory* 12/2
  *13/301
myne; mynge → **I; munne**
mynstralcie → **minstralsy**
mynstre (sb.) *monastery, minster* 1/72, 88
mynstrels (sb.pl.) *minstrel* 7/35
myracles → **miracle**
myre (sb.) *mire, bog* 12/256
myrie → **merie**
myrre (sb.) *myrrh* 10.5/41
myrthe → **mirth**
mysbileue (sb.) *wrong belief* 7/102
myself, myselfe → **I**
mysgo (ptp.) *to go astray* 13/479; **mysgon**
  13/476; **mysgoon** 13/442
mys-nyme (sg.ps.subj.) *to err* 4/51
mysse; myst → **misse; mist**

myster (sb.) *craft* 13/69

N

na; nabbe → no; nothing; have
nacht; nadde → not; have
nadres (sb.pl.) *adder* 1/41
nagulte (sg.pt., neg.) *to sin* 10.7/12
Naȝareth (pn.) 10.7/25
naȝt → not; nouȝt
naht; nai → nouȝt; no
naill (sb.) *nail* 14/179; nayl 13/101; nayles
   (pl.) 10.4/14; naylles 10.6/31
naked (adj., adv.) 2/29 *6/207, 210
nam → be; nime
name (sb.) 5/115 *6/187 *9/3 *12/190
   *13/165; nome 5/81 *6/10, 195
named (ptp.) 11/37
nameliche (adv.) *in particular* 4/65 *13/213;
   namely 13/337
namen → nime
nammore (adv., pron.) *no more; nothing* 1/52;
   namoore 13/122, 362; namore 3/8 *8/33
   *10.8/21
nan, nane → no
nareu (adj.) *narrow* 1/43
nas; nat → be; not
nathelees (adv.) *nevertheless* 13/35
nature (sb.) 13/11
natureliche (adv.) *by nature, naturally* 3/27;
   naturelliche 3/33
nawþer; nay, naye → neyther; no
nayl, nayles, naylles → naill
næure → never
ne (part.) *not* ne ... ne (conj.) *neither ... nor*
   1/47, 49, 60
nec (sb.) *neck* 6/207; nekke 7/114 *13/142,
   233, 485; nykken (pl.) 4/76
nedde, neddi → have
nede (1) (sb.) *need, necessity* 2/32 *7/229
   *8/113, 138 *11/116 *13/250; nedes (pl.)
   13/429
nede (2) (adv.) *needs* 5/165
nedede; nedes → nedes; nede (1)
nedes (sg.ps., impv.) *to be in need of* 6/191;
   nedede (pt.) 13/244, 385
nedlare (sb.) *needle-maker* 7/166
neen; neer → no; neiȝ
neet (sb.pl.) *cattle* 13/53
nefe (sb.) *nephew* 1/12; neues (pl.) 1/28
negh (inf.) *to draw near* 12/224
neiȝ (adv., prep.) *nearly, almost; near, next to*
   5/28; neiȝh 5/107, 209; neiȝh-ȝwat 5/91;
   ney 8/16, 108, 131; nie 5/203; ny 13/44,

419; nyeȝ 4/28; ♦ comp.: neer 13/528; neir
   14/147; neirar 14/15; ner 8/19; nere 6/109
   *12/43, 224
neiȝebore (sb.) *neighbour* 8/58
neiȝh, neiȝh-ȝwat → neiȝ
neilond (sb.) *island* 2/37, 50
neip (sb.) *turnip* 14/132, 165
neir, neirar → neiȝ
nekke → nec
nelle, neltou → will (2)
nemne (inf.) *to name, appoint* 10.8/9; neuenes
   (sg.ps.) 6/10; nempned (sg.pt.) 7/189;
   nempnede 7/178
Neptalym (pn.) *Nephthalim* 12/51
ner → neiȝ; never
nere, nes → be; neiȝ
nesche (adj.) *soft* 5/141
nestes (sg.ps.) *to survive* 8/24
net (sb.) 14/214; nettes (pl.) 13/151
neuede; neuenes → have; nemne
neuer, neuere, neuer-eft, neuereft,
   neuermo, neure → never
neues; neure; neuuæ → nefe; never; newe
never (adv.) 14/35; nevere 13/262; neuer
   6/38, 186, 242, 248, 257 *8/99 *12/98, 106,
   112, 136, 224, 283, 294 *14/64; neuere
   7/240 *8/2, 24 *9/7 *12/16, 38, 236, 323,
   378, 388; næure 1/37, 57; neure 1/54; ner
   10.8/14, 28; ♦ col.: neuer-eft *no more* 5/89;
   neuereft 5/94; neuermo *never more* 8/73;
   neuer þe helder *never the more for that*
   6/163, 217; neuer þe lece *none the less*
   6/261
newe (adj.) *new* 2/13, 29 *7/178 *10.4/5; (adv.)
   recently 5/75 *12/314; nywe (adj.) 9/86, 91;
   neuuæ 1/72
neweð (sg.ps.) *to renew* 2/2, 5, 21
ney → neiȝ
neyd (sg.ps.) *to need* 12/242
neyther ♦ col.: neyther ne (conj.)
   neither ... nor 7/36; nawþer ne 6/217;
   noþer ne 7/204; nouþer ne 8/3; nouther ne
   1/58; nowthir nor 12/287
Nicholas (prn.) 13/80
nie → neiȝ
night (sb.) 11/107; nigt 2/6; niȝht 5/199, 217;
   niȝt 4/28 *9/58, 74, 82; niȝte 8/56; niht 1/3
   *10.7/15; nycht 14/102, 154, 158; nyght
   10.10/16 *12/261 *13/10, 23, 327, 341, 399,
   459, 489, 508; nyht 10.2/14 *10.5/14
   *10.7/7; nyhtes (gsg.) 10.5/20
nihtes (adv.) *at night* 10.1/11; be nihtes 1/35
nime (inf.) *to take* 4/35 *5/171; nimeth (sg.ps.)
   5/175; nimeþ 4/50; nimeð *goes* 2/21; nymþ

4/18, 54; **nim** (imp.) 4/41; **nyme** (sg.ps.subj.) 4/55; **nam** (sg.pt.) 1/27 *5/7, 65, 68, 140, 157, 180, 197 *10.5/51; **nom** 8/39; **namen** (pl.pt.) 1/7, 35, 59, 88; **nomen** (ptp.) 8/125; **i-nome** 5/148

nis; niste → be; wit (2)

niþinge (sb.) *niggard* 3/38

no → nothing

no (adv., pron.) **na** 1/24, 29 *13/250–251, 358, 385, 399–400, 407 *14/19, 59, 63, 66, 100, 105, 110, 138, 154, 166, 169, 194; **non** 2/15 *4/23 *5/61, 135, 152, 160, 177 *6/94, 139, 225, 247 *8/21, 73, 80 *9/16, 59, 110 *10.1/13 *10.2/7 *10.3/7 *10.5/48 *10.6/37, 44 *11/6; **none** 2/15 *5/13, 89 *7/214 *8/2, 42 *9/98 *10.3/38 *11/42, 85, 112 *12/252; **nones** (gsg.) 8/147; **noon** 13/50, 181, 441; **nan** 1/9–10, 31, 37, 55, 65; **nane** 11/9, 33, 86 *14/30, 130, 136; **neen** 13/409, 411; **nay** 6/43, 66 *8/94 *10.10/6, 10, 14, 18, 22 *12/105, 153, 157, 338 *13/407; **naye** 12/335; **nai certes** (adv.) *certainly not* 5/173

nobilly (adv.) *royally, splendidly* 11/89; **nobleliche** 4/56

noble (adj., adv.) 5/10, 98 *13/166, 487

nobleiȝe (sb.) *honour* 5/188

nobleliche; nocht → nobilly; not

noen (sb.) *noon* 7/235; **at nones** 7/230

noght, noȝt, noht, nohut → naȝt; not

nolde, nolden → will (2)

nom → nime

noman (sb.) *nobody* 5/126 *9/98

nome; nomen → name; nime

non, none, none → no

nones → noen; no

non-more, nonmore → much

nonnerie (sb.) *nunnery* 13/192; **nonnerye** 13/170

noon → no

nor (conj.) 12/252 *13/59; *than* 14/15, 41

Noremaundie → Normandi

Noremauns (prn.) *Normans* 5/81

Normandi (pn.) *Normandy* 1/6, 21; **Noremaundie** 5/63

nortelrie (sb.) *education* 13/191

north (sb.) 13/239; **norð** (adv.) *northwards* 2/32

Northfolk (pn.) *Norfolk* 13/75

Northhumberland (pn.) *Northumberland* 11/36

Noruuic (pn.) *Norwich* 1/84

nose (sb.) 7/202 *13/158, 198, 375, 499, 501

noster; not → pater noster; wit (2)

not (adv., pron.) 6/44, 65, 133, 135, 147, 187, 262 *10.9/13, 17 *12/207, 336, 380 *13/91, 234 *14/36, 42, 49, 53, 58, 71, 87, 91–92, 95, 98, 103, 124, 132–133, 164, 172, 179, 193, 208, 217; **nocht** 3/18 *14/56, 61, 90; **nacht** 3/23; **naȝt** 4/38, 40, 42, 61, 74; **noght** 7/110, 115 *11/7, 10, 15, 23, 31, 33, 49, 64, 82 *12/109, 152, 221, 265, 313, 318, 340, 376 *13/278, 280, 341, 365; **noȝt** 2/43 *6/145 *7/31 *9/133 *12/101, 153, 177, 251, 303, 330; **nouȝt** 5/57, 111, 130, 133, 158, 173–174, 197, 219 *7/77–78, 100; **noht** 10.2/7 *10.3/31; **nohut** 8/110; **nout** 8/61, 77 *10.7/8, 12 *10.8/8; **nowyht** 10.8/5; **nat** 7/134, 182, 187, 227, 233 *13/99, 105, 111, 129 etc.

note (sb.) *business, matter, task* 6/145, 207 *12/268 *13/292

nothing (pron., sb.) 11/61, 119; **no-þing** 5/19, 41; **noþing** 8/56, 92, 127; ◆ col.: **na thing** 14/63, 66, 154; **no thyng** 13/506

noþer; nou; nouȝt → neyther; now; not

nou → now

nouȝt (pron.) *nothing, nought* 5/20, 135; **noght** 11/63 *13/447; **noht** 10.4/37 *10.6/57; **nout** 8/20, 39 *10.4/16; **naȝt** 4/37, 40; **naht** 1/10, 63

noumper (sb.) *umpire* 7/189

nout → not; nouȝt

nouþe; nouther, nouþer → now; neyther

now (adv.) 6/10, 86, 98, 100 etc. *7/151 *10.9/2, 8, 13, 17 *11/37, 51, 113 *12/355 *13/92, 119, 133, 222 etc. *14/72, 80, 116, 145, 164; **nowe** 12/7, 30, 41, 56 etc.; **nou** 4/34, 78 *5/111, 143, 232 *8/53, 64, 76, 79, 92–93, 114, 122, 124 *10.5/23 *10.6/37; **nouþe** 5/5, 145–146 *8/28, 50; **nu** 1/83 *2/19 *3/8, 26, 35, 39 *9/99, 132

nowiderwardes (adv.) *in no direction* 1/47

nowthir; nowyht → neyther; not

noyney (interj.) 10.10/1

noyse (sb.) *noise* 12/101

nu → now; what

nul, nulle, nully → will (2)

Nwe ȝer (sb.) *New Year* 6/71, 191; **Nw ȝeres** (gsg.) 6/240

ny → neiȝ

nyce (adj.) *foolish* 13/79, 506; **nys** 6/110, 145

nycetee (sb.) *foolishness* 13/270

nycht → night

nyeȝ; nyght, nyht, nyhtes → neiȝ; night

nykken → nec

nyme, nymþ → nime

nyne (num.) *nine* 13/24
nys → **be; nyce**
nyslye (adv.) *wantonly* 10.10/17
nyste → **wit** (2)
nywe → **newe**

O

o → **a** (1) **on; oo**
o (interj.) 10.10/3
obeien (inf.) *to obey* 5/179
obitte (adj.) *dead* 12/269
oblissing (sb.) *binding contract* 14/47
oboue; obout → **above; about**
oc; ocht → **ac; ought**
of (prep.) *of, off, from, out of, with* **off** 2/34
  *10.10/5, 21 *14/4, 30, 97, 122, 139, 162,
  171, 188, 193; **offe** 5/190; **hof** 8/148
ofdred (ptp.) *afraid* 1/4
ofer; off, offe → **over; of**
offence (sb.) 14/119
offices (sb.pl.) *function* 4/3
Offnies (prn. gsg.) *Hophni* 7/107
offryng (sb.) *offering* 10.10/13
ofreche (inf.) *to reach* 9/12
ofsei (sg.pt.) *to catch sight of* 8/5
ofserueth (sg.ps.) *to merit* 3/31
of-showve (inf.) *to repel* 13/136
oft (adv.) *often, frequently* 6/18, 23 *10.8/32
  *14/213; **ofte** 4/32, 61–62 *5/103, 148
  *7/227 *8/18, 93, 105, 108 *10.4/23, 43
  *10.6/41, 51 *10.8/8
ofte → **time**
oftsithes (adv.) *often* 11/105
ofþinkeþ (sg.ps., impv.) *to regret* 8/103;
  of-þouȝte (pl.pt.) 5/161
ofuundred (ptp.) *astonished* 1/4
of-walked (ptp.) *exhausted from walking* 7/7
ogayne; oghe → **again; owen**
oght → **ought**
oȝen, oȝene → **owen**
oȝt; oht → **ought; othþ**
ohte (subj.) *ought to* 10.4/18 *10.7/31
old (adj.) 2/20 *5/209; **olde** 13/93, 98, 106,
  110, 122; **oold** 13/91; **ald** 1/3; **elde** (pl.) 9/66
  *10.5/22; **elder** (comp.) 11/35; **elderis** (comp.
  gpl.) 14/1
on → **one**
on (prep.) *on, in, near* **o** 1/55 *2/2, 39 *10.5/32
  *10.7/3; **one** 2/37, 53; **onne** 1/45; **a** 5/202;
  an 4/29; **un** 10.9/11
onane → **a-non**
onde (1) (sb.) *enmity* 10.2/6

onde (2) (sb.) *breath* 2/39, 58
onder-fongue → **ounderfonge**
onderstant, onder-stod, onder-stonde →
  vndirstande
onderstondinge (sb.) *understanding* 4/89
one → **on**
one (art., num.) 3/35 *4/55, 69 *5/17, 35 *8/4,
  9, 36, 107 *10.3/11; **on** 4/3, 70 *6/30, 159,
  229 *7/186 *8/6, 10, 14–15, 38, 66, 99, 135
  *10.2/13; **one** (adv.) *alone* 10.6/19; **oon**
  13/139, 237, 514; ◆ col.: **al hone** (adv.) *alone*
  8/138; **but hone** (adv.) *immediately* 14/159
ones (adv.) *once* 7/134 *13/182; **anis** 14/163;
  enes 5/152, 158, 182
onlepiliche (adv.) *only* 4/61
only (adv.) 6/143; **oonly** 13/84, 229
onne → **on**
onneaþe (adv.) *hardly* 4/14
onoh → **enough**
onpayþ (sg.ps.) *to displease* 4/8
on-riȝhte (sb.) *injustice* 5/104
onsware, onswarez → **answer**
on-treowe (adj.) *unfaithful, perfidious* 5/79
ony → **any**
oo (adv.) *always, continuously* 10.7/7, 15, 22,
  29, 36 *10.8/7, 15, 22, 29, 36; **o** 10.3/27
oold; oon → **old; ever; one**
oonly; oother → **only; other** (2)
op → **up**
opdrowe (sg.pt.) *to pull up* 8/144
ope → **open; up**
open (adj.) 13/10; **ope** 8/14
open-ers (sb.) *fruit of the medlar* 13/95
openlice (adv.) *openly, publicly* 1/65
opon → **upon**
oppen (imp.pl.) *to open* 12/122; **opynne**
  12/194
oppres (inf.) *to oppress* 14/198
opriȝt (adv.) *upright* 4/86
opward → **vpwart**
opwinde (inf.) *to wind up* 8/38
opynne → **oppen**
or → **er; other** (1)
ordand → **ordeinie**
orde (sb.) *point (of a sword)* 9/113
ordeinie (inf.) *to prepare, ordain* 5/67;
  ordand (sg.pt.) 11/43 *12/25, 226; (ptp.)
  11/96
ordre (sb.) *order, ordination* 5/7, 11, 227;
  ordres (pl.) 7/56
ore → **we**
ore (sb.) *grace, mercy* 5/176 *9/125; ◆ col.:
  þin ore *have pity* 8/95; **þyn ore** 10.7/14
  *10.8/17

oresones (sb.pl.) *prayer* 5/14; **oreysones** 4/24

orgeilus (adj.) *proud* 3/38

orn, ornen → **ryn**

Osewold (prn.) 13/84, 133

Oseye (pn.) *Alsace* 7/148

ost (sb.) *army, host* 5/70

ostel (sb.) *house, court* 6/40

Oswald (prn.) 11/51, 55

Oswalde, Oswold → **Saints**

other (1) (conj.) *or* 1/39; **oþer** 1/45, 61 *3/8, 12, 32, 41 *4/39, 41–42, 48, 96–97 *6/243 *8/26, 52, 60, 75, 104; **oþur** 5/17; **or** 7/239 *11/24, 116, 123 *12/35, 141 *13/97, 128, 182, 184, 252, 350, 354, 365, 376, 423, 462 *14/47–48, 51, 82, 96, 168; **er** 2/32; ◆ col.: **oþer . . . oþer** *either . . . or* 8/7

other (2) (adj., pron.) 1/61 *6/82 *7/140 *11/7 *13/411; **oðer** 1/9 *2/57; **oþer** 1/2, 5, 7, 75 *3/20 *4/4, 55, 70, 99 *6/24, 49, 57, 74, 116, 170, 173 *7/93 *8/37–38, 73 *9/16 *10.5/31 *11/4, 8, 33, 81, 85, 112; **oother** 13/59, 237; **othir** 12/148; **oþur** 5/4, 8, 21, 29, 48, 61, 160, 172, 175, 177; **othyr** 10.10/21; **oþeres** (gsg.) 5/74 *8/112; **othere** (sg., pl.) 7/54; **oþere** 5/13, 93, 168; **oðre** (pl.) 1/17 *2/40; **oþre** (sg., pl.) 3/30, 38 *4/92 *8/29, 109; **oþure** (pl.) 5/107; **vther** 14/56, 130, 145, 161, 177, 181, 184, 189, 200

oþerhuyl (adv.) *sometimes* 4/44

oþes, othes → **othþ**

othir, oðre, oþre → **other** (2)

othþ (sb.) *oath* 5/108; **oht** 10.7/18; **othes** (pl.) 7/36, 162, 186; **oþes** 10.3/24; **athes** 1/30

oþur → **other** (1, 2)

oþure, othyr → **other** (2)

ou → **how; ʒe** (2)

oucht; ouer → **ought; over**

oueral (adv.) *everywhere* 8/5, 10, 35

ouer-clothes (sb.pl.) *overgarment* 11/109

ouer-come (ptp.) *to overcome* 5/86

ouerdede (sb.) *excess* 4/51

ouer-eode (sg.pt.) *to overpower* 5/15; **ouer-hede** *to pass off* 8/45

ouermyhte (sg.pt.) *to have more power* 1/61

ouer-sopped (sg.pt.) *to eat too much* 7/230

ouerwalt (ptp.) *to overthrow* 6/101

ought (adj., adv., pron.) *anything, something, somehow, at all* 12/100; **oght** 11/59, 110; **ocht** 14/89; **oʒt** 6/87; **oucht** 14/38

ouʒwere (adv.) *anywhere* 5/194

ounder → **under**

ounderfonge (inf.) *to receive, take up* 8/98; **vnder-fongue** 5/118; **vndefong** (sg.ps.) 10.4/50; **underfeng** (sg.pt.) 1/13; **vnder-feng**

5/9, 188; **onder-fongue** (ptp.) 5/124; **underfangen** 1/22, 74

oundred → **hundred**

ounwiis; oup → **wiis; up**

our, oure, ous → **lady; we**

out (adv., prep.) 5/58, 109, 124, 201, 210 *6/219, 245 *7/37, 236 *8/1, 55 *10.2/4 *10.6/58 *10.7/32–33 *11/29, 97, 103 *13/211, 281, 295, 301, 414, 439, 509 *14/193; **oute** 12/112, 161, 283, 344; **owt** 12/343; **owte** 12/18, 185, 195; **ut** 1/56 *2/3, 13, 29; **vt** 2/39 *9/39, 57

outrageously (adv.) *to excess* 13/222

outtrage (adj.) *exceedingly strange* 6/29

outwin (inf.) *to get out, escape* 14/217

over (prep.) 13/146; **ouer** 1/1–2, 58 *6/13, 206 *8/11; **ofer** 1/21

oway → **away**

owe (interj.) 12/149, 301

owen (adj., sb.) *own* 6/195 *10.1/9; **owene** 13/67, 144, 363, 365, 469; **oghe** 3/31; **oʒen** *possessions* 4/31; **oʒene** 4/69, 81 *9/40; **auen** 6/80; **aune** 6/10; **awen** 13/463; **awin** 14/90; **awne** 12/237

owt, owte → **out**

oxe (sb.) *ox* 14/87; **oxin** (pl.) 14/10, 22, 26, 33, 172

Oxeneford (pn.) *Oxford* 1/26

oxin → **oxe**

P

pace → **passe**

pades (sb.pl.) *toad* 1/41

page (sb.) *boy, rascal* 10.9/15 *12/125 *13/196

paied, paies; pais → **pay; pees**

pale (adj.) 13/374

palfrey (sb.) *horse* 13/299; **palfray** 11/56

palmers (sb.pl.) 7/47; **palmeres** 13/13

panade (sb.) *cutlass* 13/153, 184

pane → **payne**

panne (sb.) *pan* 13/168

Pape Eugenie (prn.) *Pope Eugenius* 1/74

papelard (sb.) *sycophant* 4/39

par → **compaignye**

paradise (sb.) 12/48, 259, 392; **paradiis** 8/70; **paradis** 4/98; ◆ col.: **paradys terestre** *the Garden of Eden* 4/17

parayled (pl.pt.) *to dress* 7/25

pardoner (sb.) 7/66, 79

parsche (sb.) *parish* 7/79, 81; **parsches** (pl.) 7/80, 82

part (sb.) 13/82, 345
parten (pl.ps.) *share, divide* 7/79
pas → **passe**
passage (sb.) 9/32
passe (inf., ps.) *to pace, pass, move* 6/53, 165
*12/66, 96, 112, 152, 194, 227, 296; **pace**
(ps.) 13/36; **pas** (inf.) 11/52; **passed** (ptp.)
13/113, 121; **past** (pt., ptp.) 14/24, 28, 159;
paste (ptp.) 12/105
Pater Noster (sb.) *the Lord's Prayer* 2/31;
Pater-noster 7/200
patill (sb.) *small shovel* 14/13
patrounes (sb.pl.) *ruler* 6/6
pay (inf.) 10.10/12; **payen** 13/357; **payꝫe**
5/12; **paies** (sg.ps., impv.) 12/82; **payþ** (sg.ps.)
4/33; **payed** (sg.pt.) 13/539; **paied** 12/325;
ypayd (ptp.) 4/8
payne (sb.) *pain, punishment* 12/96, 227; **pane**
14/223; **peyne** 10.4/40 *12/35; **paynes** (pl.)
12/4, 122; **peynes** 10.4/17, 36
payns (sb.pl.) *pagan* 9/28
payþ → **pay**
pecok (sb.) *peacock* 13/150
peer (sb.) 13/250; **pere** 11/39; **peres** (pl.) 11/1
peert (adj.) *impudent* 13/174
pees (sb.) *peace* 12/296; **pes** 6/53; **pesse**
12/66; **pais** 1/9
pekke (sb.) *peck* 13/234
pelte → **pulte**
penaunces (sb.pl.) *penance* 7/27
peniworths (sb.pl.) *trifle* 7/185
pennyfull (adj.) *round as a penny* 14/158
peny (sb.) *penny* 13/343; **penyes** (pl.) 7/133
people (sb.) 7/77; **peple** 7/57, 80; **pepul**
12/194
pepur (sb.) *pepper* 7/160
peraventure (adv.) *perhaps* 13/139
perced (ptp.) *to pierce* 13/2
pere → **peer**
pereles (adj.) *peerless* 12/4
peres → **peer**
peril (sb.) 13/156
perilous (adj.) 13/185, 413
perpetuall (adj.) *valid for all time* 14/74
pers (sb.) *dark blue* 13/73
person (sb.) *parson, priest* 13/167, 201;
persones (pl.) 7/81
pes → **pees**
pese (sb.) *goblet, mug* 11/84
pesse → **pees**
pestelence (sb.) *plague* 7/82
Petres; peyne, peynes → **Saints; payn;**
Jesus Christ

phariseu (sb.) *pharisee* 11/4–5, 28
philosophye (sb.) *learning* 13/274
pigges (sb. pl.) *pig* 13/502
pikeporses (sb.) *pickpocket* 7/171
pikes (sb.pl.) *pike* 8/31, 142
piled (adj.) *bald-headed* 13/159; **pilede** 7/171;
pyled 13/530
pilgrimages → **pilgrymage**
pilgrimes (sb.pl.) *pilgrim* 13/26; **pilgrymes**
7/47
pilgrymage (sb.) *pilgrimage* 13/21;
pylgrymage 10.9/16; **pilgrimages** (pl.)
13/12
pilgrymes → **pilgrimes**
pine (sb.) *pain, torture* 8/71; **pyn** 10.5/29;
pyne 10.4/25 *10.6/40; **pines** (pl.) 1/49;
pynes 10.6/46
pined, pineden; pines → **pyne; pine**
pining (sb.) *torture* 1/37, 85
pipen (inf.) *to play on a (bag)pipe* 13/151;
pype 13/100
pisse (inf.) *to piss* 13/439; **pissede** (sg.pt.)
7/200
pit → **puttes**
pitte (sb.) *pit, well, hell* 12/271, 348; **put**
8/131; **putte** 8/36, 57, 59–61, 69, 121, 129,
138–139, 141–142, 144
place (sb.) 5/192, 194 *6/39, 185 *12/112,
291, 296, 382 *13/63, 347, 349, 369 *14/65,
157, 198; **places** (pl.) 7/96; ♦ col.: **manure**
place (sb.) *manor house* 14/157
plank (sb.) *penny* 14/40
plantede (sg.pt.) *to plant* 1/80
plawes → **play** (2)
play (1) (inf.) *to play, joke, amuse* 6/49; **pleiꝫe**
5/4; **pley** (inf., ps.) 10.9/18 *10.10/4 *13/91,
422; **pleye** 13/182, 228, 322; **playis** (sg.ps.)
14/153; **playþ** 4/31; **playde** (pl.pt.) 7/22;
pleyde (pt.) 13/82, 292
play (2) (sb.) *play, game, amusement, joy*
10.5/2, 15; **playe** 12/392; **plawes** (pl.) 10.3/2
playde → **play** (1)
playe → **play** (2)
playis → **play** (1)
playne (adv.) *plainly, clearly* 12/48; **playnly**
12/267, 326
playþ → **play** (1)
plededen (pl.pt.) *to plead at law* 7/133
pleiꝫe → **play** (1)
pleis → **plese**
plenté (sb.) *plenty* 12/392
plesant (adj.) *pleasing* 10.10/5
plese (inf.) *to please, satisfy* 7/32; **pleis** 14/75;
plesen 13/66

plesour (sb.) *enjoyment, delight* 14/216; **plesure** 10.10/12, 20

pleuch, plewch → **plogh**

pley → **play** (1)

pley (sb.) *plea* 14/79

pleyde, pleye → **play** (1)

pleyneth (sg.ps.) *to complain, lament* 13/338; **pleyned** 7/81

plighten (pl.pt.) *to agree, pledge, promise* 7/47; **plyht** (ptp.) 10.2/10 *10.8/6; **yplyht** 10.3/22

plogh (sb.) *plough* 7/22, 124; **pleuch** 14/6, 113; **plewch** 14/2

plukkit (sg.pt.) *to pluck* 14/108

plyȝt (sb.) *hostility* 6/53

plyht; poer → **plighten; power**

point (sb.) 5/140 *13/405; **poynte** 12/59, 105, 188, 326; **poyntis** (pl.) 12/368

poke (sb.) *sack, bag* 13/502

poked (sg.pt.) 13/393

pomely (adj.) *dapple* 13/72

poppere (sb.) *small dagger* 13/155

porchaci (inf.) *to purchase, buy* 4/66

pore (adj., sb.) *poor, needy* 7/20, 82; **poure** 4/57; **povre** 13/226; **pure** 14/119, 198

portours (sb.pl.) *porter* 7/171

porueiden (pl.pt.) *to appoint* 5/153

pose (sb.) *suffer from a cold* 13/376

potage (sb.) *potage, soup* 5/22

potel (sb.) *pottle, pot* 7/200

potte, potten → **puttes**

pouche (sb.) *pocket* 13/155

pouert (sb.) *poverty* 11/54

Poule (prn.) *St. Paul* 7/39

pound (sb.) 7/160; **poundes** (pl.) 7/133

poure → **pore; power**

povre → **pore**

power (sb.) 5/186; **powre** 10.10/6, 10, 14, 18, 22; **poer** *army* 5/65; **poure** 12/219

poynte, poyntis → **point**

prai, praied → **pray** (2)

praier (sb.) *prayer* 11/31; **prayere** 11/5; **preiers** (pl.) 7/27

praty (adj.) *pretty* 10.10/20

pray (1) (sb.) *prey* 14/29; **praye** 12/175

pray (2) (inf., ps.) 11/3, 51 *13/134, 142, 257, 355; **praye** (sg.ps.) 6/41 *12/152; **prai** 11/47; **preye** (ps.) 10.4/44 *10.5/55; **praied** (sg.pt.) 11/17, 20, 23; **preiede** 10.7/21; **prayd** 10.9/5

praye → **pray** (1, 2)

prayere → **praier**

prayse (inf.) *to praise, appraise* 6/143; **preyse** 7/181; **preisede** (pl.pt.) 7/185

preche (inf.) *to preach* 13/127; **precheþ** (sg.ps.) 7/78; **prechyng** (psp.) 7/57; **preched** (sg.pt.) 12/291; **prechede** 7/39, 66; **prechid** 12/51, 267

prees (sb.) *turmoil* 12/125

preest (sb.) *priest, parson* 13/46; **preost** 5/8; **prest** 7/66, 79 *8/26, 97; **prestes** (gsg.) 2/25; **preostes** (pl.) 1/60; **prestis** 7/81, 106, 116

preiede → **pray** (2)

preiers; preif → **praier; proue**

preisede → **prayse**

prelates (sb.pl.) *prelate* 7/101

preost, preostes → **preest**

present (sb.) 14/168

presente (inf.) *to donate* 10.5/40

prest → **preest**

prest (adj.) *ready* 5/114

prestes, prestis; preue → **preest; proue**

preue (1) (adj.) *brave* 6/49

preue (2) (adj.) *privy, secret* 11/123

preuelie → **pryvely**

preye → **pray** (2)

preyse → **prayse**

pride (sb.) 11/29, 40, 43, 123; **prude** 10.2/12; **pruyde** 7/25; **pryde** 12/182

priketh (sg.ps.) *to incite* 13/11, 455

prince (sb.) 12/111; **princes** (pl.) 12/122; **princis** 12/182

principall (sb.) *commander* 12/111

principalliche (adv.) *essentially* 4/5

princis → **prince**

prior (sb.) 5/24

priorie (sb.) *priory* 5/10–11, 27, 55, 212

pris (sb.) *price, value, praise* 10.2/12; **pryis** 14/139

prisounes (sb.pl.) *prisoner* 12/220

prisun (sb.) *prison* 1/28, 36

priuilegies (sb.pl.) *privilege* 1/75

proceidis (pl.ps.) *to arise* 14/207

proferyng (psp.) *to suggest* 10.10/11

profitable (adj.) 7/124

profiteþ (sg.ps.) *to be useful* 7/101

profyt (sb.) *profit* 7/57

prophete (sb.) *prophet* 12/369; **prophettis** (gsg.) 12/273; **prophetis** (pl.) 12/267

prophicied (sg.pt.) *to prophesy* 12/188

prophicyes (sb.pl.) *prophecy* 12/27

proponit (pl.pt.) *to propound* 14/79

propre (adj.) *comely* 13/196

propreliche (adj.) *proper* 4/64

proud (adj.) 13/89, 150, 174 *14/216; **proude** 13/537; **prowd** 11/1, 23, 41; **prut** 9/65

proue (inf.) *to prove* 12/255; **preif** 14/75; **preue** 7/39; **proued** (ptp.) 9/4

prouerb → **proverbe**
prouinces (sb.) *realm* 6/6
proverbe (sb.) *proverb* 13/543; **prouerb** 14/55
prowd → **proud**
prowe (sb.) *advantage* 12/220, 326
prude; prut → **pride; proud**
pruyde, pryde → **pride**
pryis → **pris**
pryme (sb.) *first canonical hour* 13/130
pryvely (adv.) *secretly, stealthily* 13/65, 281; **preuelie** 14/108
pulte (inf.) *to pelt, strike* 5/109; **pelte** (sg.pt.) 9/78
pultrye (sb.) *poultry* 13/54
puplican (sb.) *tollkeeper* 11/4, 10; **puplicane** 11/13
puplisshid (ptp.) *to make known* 12/59
purchace (inf.) 13/64
pure → **pore**
pure (adj.) *fair, noble* 6/49
Purnele of Flaundres (prn.) 7/168
purpos (sb.) *purpose* 13/202, 205
pursewe (inf.) *to follow* 12/316
pursward (adv.) *as to the purse* 7/101
purueyed (sg.pt.) *to purvey* 12/69
put, putte → **pitte**
puttes (sg.ps.) *to put* 10.10/13; **putte** (pt.) 7/25 *12/259; **potte** 7/22; **potten** (pl.pt.) 7/27; **pit** (ptp.) 13/312
pye (sb.) *magpie* 13/174
pyes (sb.pl.) *pie* 7/145
pykis (sg.ps.) *to pick* 14/199
pyled; pylgrymage → **piled; pilgrymage**
pyn, pyne → **pine**
pyne (inf.) *to torture, inflict pain* 12/219; **pined** (pl.pt., ptp.) 1/36–37, 85; **pineden** (pl.pt.) 1/84; **pyned** (ptp.) 12/4
pynes → **pine**
pyonie (sb.) *peony* 7/160
pype → **pipen**

Q

quad → **quoþ**
quakke (sb.) *hoarseness* 13/376
quarterne (sb.) *prison, dungeon* 1/41
quat; quath, quaþ → **what; quoþ**
quat-so → **what**
qued, quede → **kueade**
quen → **when**
quene (sb.) *woman, queen* 6/126, 256 *9/130 *11/68, 71, 73, 79, 84, 91, 95–96, 99, 102, 105–106, 108, 110, 113, 118; **quenes** (gsg.) 11/90

queor (sb.) *choir* 5/224
querrell (sb.) *cause, accusation* 14/90, 104; **querrellis** (pl.) 14/199
queþen (adv.) *whence* 6/248
queynte (adj.) *clever, ingenious* 13/275
quha; quhair, quhairin, quhairof → **who; where**
quhat → **what**
quheillis (sg.ps.) *to wheel* 14/189
quhen; quhether → **when; weder** (2)
quhether (conj.) *whether, if* 14/82; **huader** 4/25
quhilk; quhill → **which; whil**
quhome; quhy → **who; why**
quhyte → **white**
quic (adj.) *alive* 9/55
quile → **while**
quitclame (inf.) *to renounce, discharge* 14/171; **quit-clayme** (sg.ps.) 6/80
quite (inf., ps.) *to pay back* 13/88, 140; **quyt** (ptp.) 13/548
quo, quo-so; quod → **who; quoþ**
quoþ (sg.pt.) *to say, speak, talk* 6/43, 96, 130, 159, 168, 177, 185, 192, 203; **quod** 7/156, 159 *8/27, 59, 64, 66 etc. *13/88, 133, 248, 250 etc. *14/14, 19–20, 43 etc.; **quad** 8/17, 100, 104, 111; **quath** 5/173; **quaþ** 8/19, 48
quyle; quyt → **while; quite**
quyte (adj.) *free* 14/122, 135
qwan; qwat → **when; what**

R

raa → **ro**
rachenteges (sb.) *chain* 1/45
rad → **rede** (1)
rad (adj.) *hasty* 6/38 *10.3/16
radly → **redily**
rage (inf.) *to flirt* 13/182
rage (sb.) *passion* 10.9/17
rageman (sb.) *document with seals* 7/73
raȝt → **recche** (2)
raif (sg.ps.) *to rave* 14/116
raith (adv.) *quickly* 14/18; **raþer** (comp.) *earlier* 8/34; **rathest** 7/193; ◆ col.: *þe raþer immediately* 7/117
rakeare (sb.) *street-sweeper* 7/172
Ram (prn.) *Aries* 13/8
ran → **ryn**
rape (1) (adv.) *quickly* 7/184
rape (2) (sb.) *haste* 9/79
rase → **rise**
ratoner (sb.) *rat-catcher* 7/172

raþer, rathest; raughte → raith; recche (2)

rawe ◆ col.: **be rawe** (adv.) *one after the other* 12/317; **on rawe** 12/401

raynez → reyne

ræflac (sb.) *robbery* 1/15

ræuede, ræueden → reue

ræueres (sb.pl.) *robber* 1/62

realte (sb.) *royal power* 11/53

reasoune; rebalde → resoun; ribaud

rebuken (inf.) *to rebuke* 7/110

recche (1) (sg.ps.) *to care* 8/114; **route** (sg.pt.) 8/130

recche (2) (inf.) *to reach, go* 8/134; **raȝt** (sg.pt.) 6/219; **raughte** 7/73

recorder (sb.) *remembrance, recollection* 4/75

recordinge (sb.) *recollection* 4/67

recreaunt (sb.) *coward* 6/243

red → rede (1)

red (sb.) *advice, counsel* 4/99 *10.3/16; **rede** 5/171 *8/25; **reed** 8/96

redde; redden → redeþ; rede (1)

rede → red; redeþ; so

rede (1) (inf., ps.) *to counsel* 5/126 *10.7/13; **red** (sg.ps.) 10.2/8; **redes** 11/32; **redez** 6/160; **redden** (pl.pt.) 6/150; **rad** (ptp.) 10.2/3

rede (2) (adj.) *red* 5/206 *6/91; **reed** 13/178, 374

redes → rede (1)

redeþ (pl.ps.) *to read* 4/9; **rede** (sg.ps.) 2/2; (ptp.) 12/317; **ret** (sg.ps.) 4/54, 90; **reids** (pl.ps.) 14/205; **redde** (ptp.) 6/230

redez; redi → rede (1) **redy**

redily (adv.) *readily, willingly, promptly* 6/179; **redly** 6/160; **radly** 6/154

Redinge (pn.) *Reading* 1/8

redly → redily

redy (adj.) *ready* 12/120, 394 *13/21, 240, 359; **redi** 5/71; **i-redie** 5/163

redyngkynge (sb.) *thatcher* 7/173

reed → red; rede (2)

refen (inf.) *to roof* 1/71

refourme (pl.ps.) *to restate* 6/165

regne (inf.) *to reign* 7/119

rehersed (ptp.) *to repeat* 6/179

reids; reif → redeþ; reue

reif (sb.) *robbery* 14/200

rekenly (adv.) *courteously* 6/38

rekenynge (sb.) *account* 13/56

reled (sg.pt.) *to roll* 6/91

reles (sb.) *release* 12/288, 290

releved (ptp.) *to compensate* 13/406

religion (sb.) 4/54; **religiun** 3/14

reluys (adj.) *glittering* 10.10/19

reme (inf.) *to quit* 9/6

remember (ps.) 14/57; **remembring** (psp.) 14/148

ren (sb.) *run* 13/303

Reneuard (prn.) 8/67

reneye (inf.) *to renege* 4/91

renk (sb.) *knight, man* 6/90; **renkkez** (pl.) 6/219

renne (inf., ps.) *to run; be current* 13/114, 289; **rennes** (sg.ps.) 6/97; **rennen** (pl.ps.) 13/324

renoun (sb.) *renown, glory* 6/100

rentes (sb.pl.) *revenues* 1/71

reowe, reowen → rewe

repentaunce (sb.) *repentance* 7/224

repentede (sg.pt.) *to repent* 7/193

repruuit (ptp.) *to reprove, censure* 14/51

rerde (sb.) *voice* 8/57

rered (ptp.) *to raise* 6/140

resaiued → ressayue

resoun (sb.) *reason, argument* 6/179 *7/236 *13/37; **resoune** 12/248, 255, 263; **reasoune** 12/337; **resounz** (pl.) 6/230

respite (sb.) 6/84

ressayue (sg.ps.) *to receive, accept* 12/390; **resaiued** (ptp.) 11/22

rest (sb.) *rest, repose, quiet* 10.2/12 *10.5/20; **reste** 7/219 *10.2/6 *13/30, 372, 399

resting (sb.) *rest, quiet* 10.2/5

restore (inf.) 12/13

ret; reue → redeþ; reve

reue (inf., sg.ps.) *to rob* 10.1/16 *11/9; **reif** (sg.ps.) 14/49; **reueþ** 10.2/12; **ræuede** (sg.pt.) 1/7; **ræueden** (pl.pt.) 1/53, 60

reuel (sb.) *revel, revelry* 6/100

reuerenced (sg.pt.) *to salute* 6/38

reueþ → reue

Reule (pn.) *La Reole* 7/149

reuliche (adv.) *piteously* 8/54

reulie (adj.) *orderly* 14/22

reuthe (sb.) *pity* 7/224; **reuþe** 5/59

reve (sb.) *reeve* 13/43, 71, 75, 84, 127, 133, 235; **reue** 8/13 *9/31; **reves** (gsg.) 13/55

revelrye (sb.) *delight, pleasure* 13/229

reves; rew → reve; rewe

rewardid (ptp.) *to reward* 7/129

rewe (inf., ps.) *to sorrow for* 9/131 *10.2/3; *cause grief* 10.8/27; **rewen** (inf.) *cause grief* 2/61; **rew** (sg.ps.) *have pity on* 10.2/8; **reweþ** (pl.ps.) 10.6/10; **reowe** (inf.) *cause grief* 10.8/20; **reowen** (pl.ps.) *sorrow for* 10.7/13

rewe (sb.) *row* 5/224

reyn (sb.) *rain* 13/51, 331

reyne (sb.) *reins* 13/307; **raynez** (pl.) 6/244

Reynild (prn.) 9/128

ribaud (sb.) *ribald, worthless creature* 4/32;
  rebalde 12/99; **rybaudes** (pl.) 7/236

ribaudye (sb.) *ribaldry* 13/90; **rybaudrye**
  joke 7/45, 236

ribe (sb.) *rib* 8/21

ricchis (sg.ps.) *to journey* 6/8

rice → **riche**

riche (adj.) *rich, nourishing, beautiful* 4/62
  *6/8 *7/137 *11/76 *13/65; **rych** 6/20, 147;
  ryche 6/75, 134, 149, 184; **rice** 1/15, 32, 56,
  77

richely (adv.) *stately* 6/95

riches (sb.pl.) *wealth, riches* 14/212; **richesses**
  4/47

richt → **right**

ride (inf.) 9/83, 126; **ryde** (inf., sg.ps.) 6/47
  *13/27, 462; **ridend** (psp.) 1/61; **rod** (sg.pt.)
  10.5/1; **rood** 13/78

right (adj., adv., sb.) *right, just (as)* 11/46, 70,
  85, 91, 95, 99 *12/255, 263 *13/141, 200,
  260, 287, 367, 383, 467; **richt** 14/97; **rycht**
  14/100; **riȝht** 5/88, 127, 213, 215, 229;
  riȝhte 5/89, 124, 186, 226; **riȝt** 5/72 *8/137
  *9/84, 107; **riȝte** 2/18, 60 *9/19, 36; **ryght**
  10.10/12 *12/31; **ryȝt** 6/61, 95, 160; **ryht**
  7/224 *10.2/8; **riȝhtest** (sup.) *most rightful*
  5/61; ♦ col., neg.: **mid vnriȝhte** *wrongfully*
  5/96; **with vnriȝhte** 5/99

rightful (adj.) *just* 7/129

rightwis (adj.) *righteous* 11/22; ♦ neg.:
  vnrychteous 14/202

rigour (sb.) 14/200

riȝht, riȝhte → **right**

riȝhtes (sb.) *last rites* 5/200

riȝhtest → **right**

riȝt → **so**

riȝt, riȝte → **right**; **riȝten**

riȝten (inf.) *to put right, straighten* 2/33; **riȝte**
  4/84

rime (sb.) *speech* 9/52

rimed (sg.pt.) *to draw oneself up* 6/95

ring (sb.) 5/54 *11/69; **ringe** 9/112; **rynges**
  (pl.) 7/73 *10.10/19

ringe → **ring**

ringe (inf.) *to ring* 8/126 *9/61; **rynge** 13/120

rinkis (sb.) *course* 14/202

rise (inf.) *to rise* 12/394; **rysc** 6/93, 153
  *13/33 *14/3; **ryis** 14/184; **rist** (sg.ps.)
  13/417, 473; **ryseþ** (pl.ps.) 7/45; **roos** (sg.pt.)
  13/435; **ros** 9/87; **rase** 11/108; **risen** (pl.pt.)
  1/15; **rysen** 7/184

ro (sb.) *roe* 10.2/6; **raa** (sb.) *roe* 13/310

rob (inf.) 11/9

Robardus (prn. gsg.) 7/45

roberie (sb.) *robbery* 3/29

Robyn (prn.) 7/188

roche (sb.) *rock* 9/62

Rochele (pn.) *La Rochelle* 7/149

rod → **ride**

rode (1) (sb.) *cross, rood* 1/85 *10.6/15, 18,
  26, 56 *10.7/3, 27; **rude** 14/116

rode (2) (sb.) *complexion* 10.2/11

Roger (prn.) 1/27; **Roger of Serebyri** *Roger
  of Salisbury* 1/2728

Rogingham (pn.) *Rockingham Castle* 1/78

rokken (inf.) *to rock* 13/381

roled (sg.pt.) *to roll* 6/215

Rome (pn.) 1/74 *6/8 *7/48

Romulus (prn.) 6/8

ron (sg.pt.) *to bleed* 10.7/3

rone (sb.) *thicket, undergrowth* 14/17

rood → **ride**

rooris (sg.ps.) *to roar* 12/99

roos → **rise**

roost (sb.) *roast meat* 7/149

roote (sb.) *root* 13/2

ropere (sb.) *rope-maker* 7/173, 188

ros → **rise**

Rose (prn.) 7/173

rose (1) (sb.) 10.2/11

rose (2) (sb.) *pride, arrogance* 11/29

rosed (sg.pt.) *to boast* 11/23

rosted (sg.pt.) *to roast* 13/361

roten (ptp.) *to rot* 13/97, 99

Roucestre → **Gondolf**

Roucestre (pn.) *Rochester* 5/116

rouch (adj.) *rough, wild* 14/17

roumer → **rowm**

roun (1) (sb.) *whispered message* 10.1/18

roun (2) (inf.) *to whisper* 6/149; **rounned**
  7/184

rouncé (sb.) *horse* 6/90

round (adj.) 13/45, 158 *14/165; **rownd**
  7/201; **rounde** 13/199; ♦ col.: **Rounde
  Table** 6/100

rounned → **roun** (2)

rous (sb.) *fame* 6/97

rout (sb.) *jerk* 6/244

route → **recche** (1)

route (sb.) *company* 13/78

routhe (sb.) *pity, sorrow* 13/424; **rouþe** 10.2/3

rowe (inf.) *to row* 9/122

rowm (adj.) *large* 13/350; **roumer** (comp.)
  13/369

rownd → **round**
rowteth (sg.ps.) *to snore* 13/391
rowtyng (sb.) *snoring* 13/390, 438
royis (sg.ps.) *to talk nonsense* 12/99
ruchched (sg.pt.) *to turn, move* 6/154; **ruched** 6/90
rude → **rode** (1)
ruet (sb.) *small horn* 7/201
runisch (adj.) *rough, violent* 6/244; **runischly** (adv.) 6/91; **runyschly** 6/219
rusty (adj.) 13/74
ruylynge (sb.) *rule* 7/129
ry (sb.) *rye* 11/83
ryalmes (sb.pl.) *realm, kingdom* 6/97
rybaudes; rybaudrye → **ribaud; ribaudye**
rybibour (sb.) *player on the rubible* 7/172
rych, ryche → **riche**
rycht → **right**
ryd (inf.) *to relieve* 6/151
ryde → **ride**
rygebones (sb. gsg.) *backbone* 7/201
ryght, ryȝt, ryht → **right**
ryis → **rise**
Rymenhild (prn.) 9/8, 64, 71, 73, 75, 77, 81, 85, 90, 95, 99, 105, 110, 120, 130; **Rymenhilde** 9/14, 89, 109, 112
ryn (inf.) *to run* 14/202; **ran** (sg.pt.) 13/329, 500; **orn** 5/183; **ornen** (pl.pt.) 5/4, 159; **yronne** (ptp.) 13/8, 117, 314
rynge; rynges → **ringe; ring**
rype (adj.) *ripe, mature* 13/99
rys (sb.) *branch* 10.2/11
ryse, rysen, ryseþ → **rise**
rysing (sb.) *resurrection* 12/317

S

sa → **so**
sacramente (sb.) *sacrament* 12/316
sacrefice (sb.) *offering* 7/98
sad (adj.) *sated, weary, sad* 10.2/2; **sadde** 12/44, 204
sadel (sb.) *saddle* 6/90, 224
sadly (adv.) *steadily, firmly* 6/224
saet; saf → **sitten; save**
saȝez → **sawe**
sahte (ptp.) *to reconcile* 10.3/48; **sæhte** 1/20
sai, said, saide, saie → **say**
sair; sais → **sore; say**
saisi (inf.) *to take, seize* 5/155
'Saints': Sancte Andreas (gsg.) 1/5–6; **Saint Bede** 11/28; **Seint Cutberd** 13/351; **Seint Edward** 5/5, 53, 58; **Seint Edwardes** (gsg.) 5/139; **Seint Fabianes** (gsg.) 5/202; **Seynt**

Iame 7/48; **Seint Iohan** 10.6/38; **Seint Jame** 13/488; **Saint Luke** 11/1; **Seint Marie** 5/12, 56; **Seinte Marie** 3/5–6; **Saint Oswalde** 11/37; **Seint Oswold** 5/27; **Sancte Petres** (gsg.) 1/72; **Sanct Willelm** 1/89; **Seint Wolstan** 5/161; **Seint Wolston** 5/1, 7, 28, 31, 38, 47, 52, 103, 117, 125, 154, 173; **Seint Wulston** 5/111
sak (sb.) *sack* 13/241, 245; **zeche** 4/19
sake (sb.) ♦ col.: **for almes sake** *for the sake of charity* 8/22; **for þine sake** *because of you* 9/97 *10.1/12
sakked (ptp.) *put in a sack* 13/294
sal → **shall**
Salamon (prn.) *Solomon* 12/281
sale → **God**
sale (sb.) *hall* 6/136
sall; same → **shall; samin**
same (pron., sb.) 7/147 *11/107 *12/56, 71, 85, 93, 192 *13/179, 367
samin (adv.) *together, entirely* 11/83, 88, 115; **samyn** 11/98; **same** 6/150 *12/170, 239
Sanct, Sancte → **Saints**
sandes (sb.pl.) *messenger* 1/19
sang → **song**
Sarazins (prn.) *Saracen* 9/30, 59
sare, sarily → **sore**
sarteyne; sat, sate → **certayne; sitten**
Satan (prn.) 12/117, 199; **Satanas** 2/23; **Sathanas** 14/215; **Sattan** 12/345; **Sir Sattanne** 12/169
Saturday (prn.) 7/219
sau; saue → **sawe; saven**
saugh → **see**
saul, saule, saules, saulis, saull → **Jesus Christ; soule**
saus → **sawe**
sause (sb.) *sauce* 4/50
sauter (sb.) *psalter, psalm* 5/44; **sawter** 12/187; **sauteres** 5/216
save → **saven**
save (prep.) *save, except for* 13/122; **saf** 6/181; **savynge** 13/195
saven (inf.) *to save* 13/173; **save** (sg.ps. subj.) 13/471, 547; **saue** (inf., ps.) 7/144 *12/58, 108–109, 218, 246, 271
savynge; saw → **save; see**
sawe (sb.) *saying, word, psalm* 12/397; **sau** 14/52; **sawes** (pl.) 12/281; **saȝez** 6/128; **saus** 11/23
sawter; say → **sauter; see**
say (inf.) 6/87 *10.10/6, 10, 14, 18, 22 *14/43, 59; **sayn** 10.9/14 *13/252; **sægen** 1/83; **sæin** 1/66; **seggen** 5/216; **seien** 2/36; **seyn** 13/421,

426; **sey** (inf., ps.) 10.9/15 *13/129; **siggen**
(inf.) 3/40; **sigge** (inf., ps.) 3/8, 12, 23; **sugge**
(inf.) 8/104; **suggen** 8/133; ◆ ps.: **sai** 11/25;
saie 12/169, 373; **sei** 1/10 *8/115; **seie** 9/3,
24; **seye** 13/227; **sais** 11/21, 28 *12/60, 108,
186, 254, 303; **says** 10.10/9 *13/404; **sayis**
14/38, 111, 126, 153; **sayth** 13/434; **seith**
5/44; **seiþ** 10.6/20; **zayþ** 4/21–22, 24, 26–28,
30, 37, 39, 41, 43, 72, 74; **zigge** 4/7; **say**
(imp.) 8/61 *12/117 *14/63; ◆ pt.: **said** 11/19,
47, 49, 51 etc. *14/29, 36, 57, 61 etc.; **saide**
7/126, 224 *12/54, 65, 71, 81, 189, 269, 281,
289, 345, 372; **sayd** 6/63; **sayde** 6/39, 110,
255, 263 *7/68 *13/171; **sede** 3/7 *5/125
*8/65, 75, 123 *9/2, 23, 28, 48, 50, 52, 80,
94, 106; **zede** 4/96; **sæden** (pl.pt.) 1/4, 65;
seid 3/31; **seide** 3/6, 16, 19 *5/127, 143,
165, 172, 200 *7/96 *8/91, 106, 113, 135
*9/5 *10.5/27 *10.7/18 *13/125; **seyde** 3/9,
11, 20 *13/81, 291, 304, 319, 344, 351, 393,
401, 413, 460, 486, 510; **seiden** 5/174, 177,
217; ◆ ptp.: **said** 11/52 *14/55; **saide** 12/205,
327, 373; **sehid** 8/105; **seyd** 13/353, 543;
yzed (ptp.) 4/34
sayntes (pl.) *saints* 12/378; **seyntes** 7/48;
  sontes 10.5/56
says, sayth; sæ → **say; se** (2)
sæden, sægen → **say**
sæhte; sæin → **sahte; say**
scape (inf.) *to escape* 13/311
scatered (sg.pt.) *to squander* 1/23
scærp → **scharp** (1)
scele, sceles → **skill**
schade (sb.pt.) *to sever, shed* 6/212; **i-sched**
  (ptp.) 5/96
schadow (sb.) *shadow* 14/162
schaippit; schal → **askapie; shall**
schald → **cold**
schalk (sb.) *man, knight* 6/211
schall, schalle, schalte → **shall**
scham, schame → **shame**
scharp (1) (adj.) *sharp* 6/56; **scærp** 1/46;
  scærpe 1/43
scharp (2) (sb.) *sharp blade* 6/211
schau, schaw → **shewe**
schaw (sb.) *thicket* 14/62
schawe → **shewe**
schelde (sb.) *shield* 6/56 *9/21
schende (inf.) *to shend, put to shame* 9/71
  *12/155
schere → **cheere**
schete (sb.) *(bed) sheet* 10.9/11; **sheetes** (pl.)
  13/364

schinande; schir → **shynyng; sir**
scho; scholde → **she; shall**
schone → **shynyng**
schonkes (sb.pl.) *shank* 6/218
schorn (ptp.) *to cut* 11/83
schort; schot → **scort; sheete**
schrank → **schrinkis**
schrinkis (sg.ps.) *to shrink, recoil mentally*
  14/51; **schrank** (sg.pt.) *sunk* 6/212
schrudde (pl.pt.) *to clothe* 9/102
schuld, schulde, schulle → **shall**
schup, schupe → **scip; shappis**
schyire → **schyre**
schyndered (sg.pt.) *to cleave* 6/211
schyre (adj.) *bright, fair, white* 6/104; **schyire**
  6/212
scip (sb.) *ship* 1/2; **schup** 9/17–18, 76, 89;
  schupe 9/15, 75, 80, 83
sclendre (adj.) *slender, lean* 13/43
scole (sb.) *school* 4/81 *5/112
scolers (sb.pl.) *scolar, student* 13/226
scorn (sb.) 13/139, 334
scorne (sg.ps. subj.) *to scorn* 4/38
scort (adj.) *short* 1/42; **schort** 14/68; **shorte**
  13/489
scot (1) (sb.) *punishment, price* 4/32
Scot (2) (prn.) 4/32 *13/72
Scotland (pn.) 1/18
sculde, sculdest → **shall**
se → **see**
se (1) (art. m.) *the, this* 1/1 *3/17, 27–28; **si**
  3/39
se (2) (sb.) *sea* 2/45, 49 *5/66 *9/122; **see**
  9/68, 70; **ze** 4/10, 12; **sees** (gsg.) 2/47
seche; sede → **seke; say**
see → **se** (2)
see (inf., ps.) 12/41, 72, 187, 192, 289, 388; ◆
  inf.: **seen** 13/143–144, 232; **sene** 10.5/54;
  seo 5/159; **i-seo** (inf.) 5/231; **iseon** 9/43; **ysi**
  4/34; ◆ inf., ps.: **se** (inf., ps.) 6/86, 201
  *10.2/2 *10.4/1 *10.6/2, 5, 12, 45 *11/62,
  67, 121 *12/56, 93, 301, 355, 368, 378
  *13/261, 266, 349 *14/44, 139, 156, 164,
  167, 170; **seis** 14/92; **seo** 10.4/12 *10.8/8;
  seð 2/7; **siht** 10.6/30; **y-zycþ** (sg.ps.) 4/88;
  isiist (2.sg.ps.) 8/116; **i-seothþ** (pl.ps.) 5/129;
  sen 2/50; ◆ pt.: **saugh** (sg.) 13/83, 262, 282,
  316, 521, 523, 525; **saw** 11/44 *14/27, 63,
  66; **say** 7/5, 13, 15, 139, 150; **seghe** 3/24;
  seȝ 9/48; **seh** 10.7/16; **sei** 8/141; **seigh** 7/17;
  sey 7/109 *8/108; **sigh** 7/11; **iseie** 8/109;
  i-seiȝ 5/36; **soȝe** (sg.pt. subj.) 2/36; **i-seiȝen**
  (pl.) 5/160; **isey** 8/140; ◆ ptp.: **seie** 10.5/35;
  sen 6/262; **sene** 6/255 *11/113 *12/67
  *14/103; **ysene** 13/48

seed (sb.) 13/52; seede 12/58

seeke (adj.) *sick, ill* 13/18; seke 8/21; sik 13/217; sike 5/192

seel → so

seel (sb.) *seal* 7/77; seill 14/52, 165; selys (pl.) 7/67

seen; seere → see; sere

sees → se (2)

sééte (adj.) *satisfied* 10.8/35

sege (sb.) *siege* 6/1

segge (sb.) *man, knight* 6/181, 224

seggen; seghe → say; see

se-grund (sb.) *seabed, sea bottom* 2/44

seʒ, seh → see

sehid → say

sei → say; see

seid, seide, seiden → say

seie, seien → say; see

seigh; seik → see; seke

seill; seis → seel; see

seith, seiþ → say

seke → seeke

seke (inf.) *to seek, search* 7/48 *13/17; seken (inf.) 13/13; seche (inf., ps.) 6/53, 182 *10.5/2; seik 14/49, 154; sekeð (sg.ps.) 2/6; zecheþ (pl.ps.) 4/61, 63–64; sohvte (sg.pt.) 8/35

seker → siker (1)

sekeð → seke

selde (adv.) *seldom* 7/22 *10.8/35; selden 10.2/2

selke → silk

selkouthe (adj.) *strange, marvellous* 7/5

sell → ʒe (2)

selle (sb.) *cell* 12/342; selles (pl.) 7/30

selleþ (sg.ps.) *to sell* 10.6/57; sull (inf.) 7/178; zelþ (sg.ps.) 4/31; solde (sg.pt.) 12/147

selles; sellies → selle; selly

selly (sb.) *marvel, wonder* 6/28, 262; sellies (pl.) 7/5

selþe (sb.) *happiness* 10.3/48

selue; seluer → thu; silver

sely (adj.) *wretched, poor* 13/120, 314, 324, 332

selys → seel

sembland (sb.) *appearance, looks* 11/85; semblaunt 6/255

semed, semede → semeþ

semeþ (sg.ps. impv.) *to seem* 7/34; semed (sg.pt.) 13/39; semede 7/132

semly (adj.) *fair, beautiful* 6/135 *10.2/2; semlokest (sup.) 10.1/3

sen → see; siðen

send (imp.) *to send, send for* 11/116; sent 10.2/5; sende (sg.ps.) 9/36 *12/19; sende (pt.) 5/161 *13/360; sente 9/39; senden (pl.pt.) 1/13; ◆ ptp.: send 10.3/43; sende 12/56, 398; sent 10.1/5; ysent (ptp.) 7/77

senden → be; send

sene → see

sene (adj.) *plain, clear* 6/128

seneschalles (sb.pl.) *high steward* 7/93

senʒeours (sb.pl.) *lord* 14/159

sennes → siðen

sent, sente → send

sentence (sb.) *judgement, meaning* 14/72, 196

seo; Ser → see; John

sere (adj.) *various, manifold, different* 11/8, 62 *12/122, 294, 398; seere 12/41, 387

Serebyri → Roger

serewe → sorowe

serganz (sb.pl.) *servant, official* 3/9, 11, 14, 16, 18; seriantz 7/132

serie (inf.) *to become dry, ripen* 9/63

sermonyng (sb.) *argument* 13/123

sertes (adv.) *certainly* 11/66

seruaunt (sb.) *servant* 12/65; seruaunte 12/285; seruauntis (pl.) 12/271

serue, serued, seruede, seruen → serve

seruese → seruis

serueth, serueþ, serui → serve

seruis (sb.) *service, meal* 11/76; seruise 5/215 *11/107; seruese 4/82

serve (inf.) 13/251; serui 4/43 *5/56; serue (imp.) 12/206; serueþ (sg.ps.) 4/21; seruen (pl.ps.) 7/90, 93; serueth 7/132; serued (pl.pt.) 6/269; seruede (pl.pt.) 3/9; serued (ptp.) 11/75, 107; iserued (ptp.) 3/17; yserued 7/192

sesed → sesse (1)

seson (sb.) *season* 13/19; sesoun 7/1

se-sond 2/37

sesoun → seson

sesse (1) (inf.) *to end, seize* 12/44, 294; sesed (ptp.) 6/1

Sesse (2) (prn.) 7/163

set; sete, seten → sette; sitten

sett → sette

sette (inf.) *to set, put, build, treat* 9/68; settez 6/14; settis 14/216; sette (sg.ps. subj.) 6/159 *13/135; sette (imp.) 12/140, 204–205; sette 1/71 *6/209, 224 *9/108 *13/224; ◆ ptp.: set 14/215 *13/380; sett 11/55, 75; sette 12/387; yset (ptp.) 7/97

settynge (sb.) *planting* 7/23

seð; seþin, sethþe → see; siðen

seue (num.) *seven* 5/199; **seuin** 14/96; **seuyn** 7/150 *11/35–36; **seuene** (infl.) 2/8 *5/209

seuerall (adj.) *separate* 14/160

seuin, seuyn → **seue**

sex (num.) *six* 12/39 *14/96; **sexe** (infl.) 2/8

sey → **say; see**

seyd, seyde, seye, seyn → **say**

seyntes → **sayntes**

shall (ps.) 12/283, 323; **shal** 7/13, 139, 240 *8/94, 103, 115 *13/107, 111, 140, 258, 273, 326, 345, 545; **schal** 5/201 *6/31, 42, 75, 77, 81, 114, 161, 176, 178, 181–182, 189 *9/9, 12–14, 26, 96 *12/108, 265, 276; **schall** 12/13, 16, 19, 22 etc.; **schalle** 12/15, 96, 192, 304, 387; **schulle** 9/54–55; **shul** 13/126; **shule** 10.3/18 *10.4/49; **sal** 2/24, 32, 61–62 *13/267, 311, 353, 398, 400, 406, 409, 411, 432; **sall** 11/25–26, 37, 111 *14/21, 61, 68, 81, 96, 104, 117, 123–124, 156, 163, 175; **ssel** 4/29, 50–51, 53; **ssolle** 4/25; **xal** (1.sg.) 10.9/14; **xall** 10.9/8, 15; ♦ 2.sg.ps.: **schalte** 12/278, 336, 342; **shalt** 8/118 *13/468, 494; **sselt** 4/21–22, 39, 41, 43; ♦ pt. and subj.: **scholde** 5/18, 112, 120, 154, 200 *9/76; **sholde** 7/77, 80, 122, 182–183, 186, 191, 193 *13/162, 169, 190, 210, 218, 234, 307, 362; **schuld** 12/189; **schulde** 6/158, 185 *9/43 *12/26, 54, 164, 201, 227, 241, 251, 269–270, 367, 372; **shuld** 8/82, 91; **shulde** 8/38, 69, 134 *10.5/27 *10.7/10, 19 *12/288; **shulden** (pl.) 8/132, 134; **sculde** 1/4, 22, 86; **suld** 11/68, 81, 121 *14/34, 46, 75, 100, 105, 128, 130, 135, 166; **sholdest** (2.sg.) 8/68, 90; **ssoldest** 4/74; **sculdest** 1/54

shame (sb.) 7/233; **scham** 6/104; **schame** 5/116 *11/86 *14/51; **ssame** 4/19, 30, 97; **shome** 8/18, 29, 50

shappis (sg.ps.) *to make ready, create, prepare* 12/155; **shope** (sg.pt.) 7/2, 225; **schupe** 14/26; **shup** 10.3/14; **yshapen** (ptp.) 13/403

shave (ptp.) *to shave* 13/44

she (perspron. 3.sg. f.) 13/170, 172, 174, 178; **scho** 11/70, 72, 80, 85, 91–92, 99 *14/189; **he** 9/51, 73, 107 *10.1/4, 8–9; **heo** 5/142, 149, 198 *9/51, 90, 109 *10.5/9, 21 *10.8/6, 11, 13, 27; **hi** 3/8; **hue** 10.2/11–12; **hy** 4/23; **hye** 3/8; ♦ poss.: **here** 3/6 *7/242; **hir** 11/93, 108 *13/167, 191, 204, 379–380, 390, 438, 440, 446, 509, 525; **hire** 9/77–78 *10.1/2, 4, 7, 9, 13–14 *10.2/11, 14 *10.5/10, 50 *10.8/12 *13/191, 200; **hyre** 10.1/2 *10.5/40, 45 *10.8/23, 25; ♦ obj.: **hir** 11/70

*13/190; **hire** 3/7 *5/134, 152, 158, 180, 182 *9/85 *10.3/24 *10.5/11, 18–19, 28, 56 *10.8/5, 8, 10, 16 *13/168, 176, 180, 182, 190, 202, 205; **hure** 9/10, 72, 86, 120; **hyre** 10.8/9; ♦ refl.: **hire** 10.1/9 *10.6/19 *13/439; **hirselve** 13/366

sheep (sb.) 13/53; **shep** 7/2 *8/84, 102; **ssepe** 4/16

sheete (inf.) *to shoot* 13/152; **schot** (sg.pt.) 6/104

sheetes → **schete**

Sheffeld (pn.) *Sheffield* 13/157

shep → **sheep**

shewe (inf.) *to show, demonstrate, confess* 7/152; **schewe** 6/207 *9/26, 101 *12/22; **schawe** 6/27; **schaw** 14/68; **schau** 14/48; **sseawy** (inf.) 4/83; **sseaweþ** (sg.ps.) 4/35; **schew** (pl.pt.) 14/78; **schewed** (ptp. (weak)) 6/102; **shewed** 7/136

shipman (sb.) *shipman, shipowner* 13/128

shires (sb. gsg.) *shire, region* 13/15

sholde, sholdest → **shall**

shome; shoon → **shame; shynyng**

shope; shorte → **shappis; scort**

shortly (adv.) 13/30, 327, 421

shoures (sb.pl.) *shower* 13/1

shrewe (sb.) *wicked person, rascal* 7/223 *13/131

shrofe → **shryue**

shroudes (sb.pl.) *outer garment* 7/2

shryfte (sb.) *shrift* 7/151; **srift** 8/93, 98

shryuars (sb.pl.) *confessor* 7/64

shryue (inf.) *to shrive* 7/62; (ptp.) 7/157; **sriue** (inf.) 8/92; **shrofe** (sg.pt.) 7/223; **isriue** 8/88

shul, shuld, shulde, shulden, shule → **shall**

shup → **shappis**

shymeryng (sb.) *shimmer* 13/521

shynyng (psp.) *to shine, glimmer* 12/94; **schinande** 6/56; **schone** (sg.pt.) 14/162; **shoon** 13/522

si; sic → **se** (1) **such**

siccurly (adv.) *securely, safely* 10.9/9

sicht; sicker → **sight; siker** (1)

sides; sigge, siggen → **syde; say**

sigh; sighand → **see; siken**

sight (sb.) 11/24, 56 *12/90, 229, 355; **sighte** 7/34 *13/175; **si3t** 6/28; **si3te** 2/28; **sicht** 14/66, 103

signe (sb.) *sign* 5/39 *12/19, 41

signefiance (sb.) *meaning* 3/26, 39

signefied (pl.ps.) *to signify* 3/31

Sigrim (prn.) 8/64

si3t, si3te; siht → **sight; see**

sijknesses (sb.pl.) *sickness* 5/190
sik, sike → **seeke; siken**
siken (inf.) *to sigh* 8/98; **sike** 10.4/20
*10.6/41; **syke** (inf., ps.) 10.6/1, 28, 51;
sighand (psp.) 11/17
siker (1) (adj.) *sure, certain, confident* 8/29;
sicker 14/52; **seker** 6/52, 190
siker (2) (inf.) *to assure* 6/181
sikerlike (adv.) *certainly* 2/28; **sikerly** 13/115,
524
silk (sb.) 11/94; **selke** 7/131
silver (sb.) *silver, money* 13/359; **siluer** 1/37
*7/90; **syluer** 1/24; **sylure** 1/10; **seluer** 7/79,
84
simpill → **symple**
sin (sb.) 11/8; **sunne** 8/83 *10.7/33 *10.8/13;
syn 11/63; **synne** 7/107, 222 *10.6/58
*12/14, 272; **zenne** 4/2, 4–8, 15, 18, 30,
45–48, 56, 65, 79; **sinnes** (pl.) 1/67 *2/20;
sunnen 8/89, 99; **sunnes** 10.4/45; **zennen**
4/95; **zennes** 4/27, 78–80, 92
sinful (adj.) 2/23, 57 *11/10, 14, 19; **sinfull**
11/10 *14/215; **synffull** 12/292
singe (inf., ps.) *to sing* 8/126 *9/61, 104
*10.6/1; **syng** 6/259 *12/407; **synge** 7/84
*10.1/2 *10.4/42 *10.5/18 *13/457; **songen**
(pl.pt.) 7/197
sinke (inf.) *to sink* 8/40, 120; **sinken** 2/54;
synke (sg.ps.) 12/348
sinnes → **sin**
sipes (sb.pl.) *sailor* 2/49, 52
sir, sire → **Chauntecler; Gawan; Satan**
sir (sb.) 6/63, 202, 264; **sire** 5/128, 153 *9/123
*12/117, 254; *father* 13/470; **schir** 14/33,
43, 46, 49, 57, 71, 96, 116, 133, 136, 140,
155, 163, 167, 188; **syre** 7/109, 194; **Syre**
Peres of Prydie 7/168; **sires** (pl.) 5/127, 173
*13/133
sitten (inf., ps.) *to sit (down)* 1/47 *7/94; **sitte**
(inf., ps.) 6/77 *7/157 *8/141 *12/272, 342;
sytten (inf.) 6/138; **sitteth** (sg.ps.) 13/546;
syttes 6/43 *11/48; **sittende** (psp.) 1/54;
sittinde 9/92; **sittynge** 13/340; **saet** (sg.pt.)
7/163; **sat** 7/114 *8/15, 59 *9/1 *11/44
*13/71; **sate** 6/126; **sete** 2/37; **seten** 7/197
*8/16
sith, sithe, sithen, siþen → **siðen**
sithon (sb.pl.) *custom* 1/58
siþe (sb.) *time, occasion* 9/44; **sythe** 7/229;
syþe 10.8/32; **sythes** (pl.) 7/150; ♦ col.: **bi**
syþez (adv.) *at times* 6/17
siðen (adv., conj.) *since, thereafter, later* 2/3–4,
18; **siþen** 6/1, 6; **sithen** 12/33, 365; **sith**
7/62; **sithe** 7/82 *13/117; **sythen** 1/59, 86;

syþen 6/145, 150, 221; **sen** 11/54 *12/169,
254, 277, 303 *14/35; **seþin** 11/60; **sethþe**
5/9, 49, 60, 95; **siððan** 1/17; **syn** 6/24
*13/57, 114, 409; **syne** 12/223 *14/9, 13, 23,
32, 44, 108; **synne** 6/19
siððan → **siðen**
skaith (sb.) *harm, damage* 14/19
sker (adj.) *free* 5/43
skete (adv.) *quickly* 6/19
skies (sb.pl.) *cloud* 2/8
skill (sb.) *argument, cause, reason* 11/26, 81;
skyll 10.9/8; **scele** 4/49, 72, 89; **sceles** (pl.)
4/43
skulle (sb.) *head, skull* 13/159, 530
skyfted (ptp.) *to shift* 6/19
skyll → **skill**
sla; slape → **sle; sleep**
slawe, slawen, slayn → **sle**
sle (inf.) *to slay, kill* 9/49, 55; **sla** 11/9; **slo**
(inf.) 10.2/6; **ssast** (2.sg.ps.) 4/73; **slewe**
(sg.pt.) 12/306; **sloȝe** (pl.pt.) 9/34; **sloȝen**
9/38, 58; **slowen** 5/83; **slawe** (ptp.) 7/113;
slawen 10.5/45; **slayn** 13/183
sleep → **slepe**
sleep (sb.) 13/387, 414, 451, 509; **slep** 5/15,
18, 226 *7/46 *8/134; **slape** 9/79
sleiff (sb.) *sleeve* 14/108
sleighte (sb.) *cunning, skill* 13/60, 235, 274
sleip, slep → **slepe**
slep; slepþ → **sleep; slepe**
slepe (inf.) *to sleep* 4/23 *5/218 *7/7; **slepen**
1/48; (pl.pt.) 5/219; (pl.ps.) 13/10; **sleip**
14/102; **slepþ** (sg.ps.) 4/72; **slepest** (2.sg.ps.)
9/24; **sleping** (psp.) 7/150; **slepynge** 7/13,
139; ♦ pt.: **sleep** 7/219; **slep** 1/2, 66; ♦ pt.
(weak): **slepte** 7/8 *13/418; ♦ contr. 2.sg.ps.:
slepestow 13/393
slete (inf.) *to bait* 8/145
slewe → **sle**
slewthe (sb.) *sloth* 7/46
sley, sleye → **sly**
slike (adj.) *such, so* 11/33, 42; **slyk** 13/354,
394, 397 [see such]
slo, sloȝe, sloȝen → **sle**
slokes (imp.) *to stop* 6/199
slouȝ (adj.) *slow* 5/197
slowen → **sle**
sly (adj.) *sly, crafty, skilful* 13/164; **sley** (adj.)
sly 8/131; **sleye** 10.6/32
slyk → **slike**
smac (sb.) *taste* 4/69
small (adj.) 14/103; **smal** 8/124 *10.1/8;
smale (pl.) 2/43 *8/78 *13/9, 547

smartly (adv.) *immediately* 6/194
smauhte (sg.pt.) *to smell* 7/215
smere (adv.) *derisively* 8/12
smerte (inf., pt.) *to smart, feel pain* 9/65, 111
  *10.4/19 *10.6/48
smit (sg.ps.) *to throw, stab, hit* 2/39; **smoot**
  (sg.pt.) 13/499, 530; **smot** 5/140 *9/111;
  smiten (pl.pt.) 5/83; **smyten** (ptp.) 6/194; ◆
  col.: **be smytte** *done for* 12/338
smoke (sb.) 1/38
smoked (pl.pt.) 1/38
smoot, smot → **smit**
smoterlich (adj.) *sullied* 13/187
smoþely (adv.) *neatly* 6/194
smyle (inf.) *smile* 14/152; **smyled** (sg.pt.)
  13/270
smyten, smytte → **smit**
smyþes (sb.pl.) *smith* 10/6/32
snakes (sb.pl.) 1/41
snelle (adj.) *agile, quick* 9/102
snowe (sb.) *snow* 12/89
so (adv., conj.) *so, so that, as* **soo** 12/99, 206,
  373; **sa** 14/4, 111, 119, 178; **sua** 1/5, 46; **swa**
  1/37, 42 *13/254, 264 *14/72, 77, 122; **zuo**
  4/2, 4, 12–13 etc. ◆ col.: **so God me rede** *so*
  help me God 8/123; **so God þe rede** *so help*
  you God 8/65, 75; **so riʒt so** *as soon as* 2/9;
  so theek *as I may prosper* 13/88; **swa have I**
  seel *as I may prosper* 13/463
soberlie (adv.) *gravely* 14/32
soffren → **suffre**
soft (1) (imp.) *to soften* 14/156
soft (2) (adj.) *soft, mild* 11/94; **softe** 1/29 *7/1
  *10.4/21; **softer** (comp.) 6/58
softe → **soft** (2)
softe (adv.) *softly, quietly* 5/147 *13/437, 485
softely (adv.) *cautiously, quietly* 13/282, 435;
  softlie 14/152
softer; softlie → **soft** (2) **softely**
soʒe, sohvte → **see; seke**
soiorned (ptp.) *to stay* 12/221
sokene (sb.) *monopoly* 13/211
solace (sb.) 11/62 *12/28, 41, 398 *13/370;
  solas 10.5/14 *12/46, 387, 407
solde → **selleþ**
solempne (adj.) *solemn* 12/355
Soler Halle (prn.) *King's College, Cambridge*
  13/214
solidos (sb.pl.) *shilling* 1/80
som → **some; time**
somdeel, somdel → **del**
some (adj., pron.) 5/79, 150–151, 219–220
  *12/19, 302, 304; **som** 5/145 *7/230 *8/9
  *13/206, 356, 403; **somme** 7/22, 59; **soum**

8/52; **sum** 1/56 *7/206 *11/ 40, 81 *14/182;
  sume 1/42, 56, 83 *9/106; **summe** 6/28
  *7/25, 33, 35, 90, 93; **sommne** (asg. m.) 8/63;
  somne 8/96
somer → **sumer**
somme, sommne, somne → **some**
somoune 5/109
somur → **sumer**
somwhat (adv.) *somewhat* 13/427
sona → **sone** (2)
sonde (1) (sb.) *destruction, death* 2/58
sonde (2) (sb.) *sand* 5/141
sonde (3) (sb.) *message* 10.2/5
sondry (adj.) *different, various* 13/14, 25;
  sondrye 7/96
sone (1) (sb.) *son* 9/94 *10.5/40, 45 *10.7/20
  *12/81, 237; **sonne** 12/241; **sune** 1/7 *3/4, 6;
  sones (pl.) 7/113
sone (2) (adv.) *soon* 1/7 *2/55 *5/52, 71, 101,
  151, 163, 184, 211, 229 *6/220 *8/26, 31,
  100, 118 *10.2/5 *11/59, 75, 86, 95,
  102–103 *12/22, 44, 96, 205 *14/25, 65, 72,
  156, 174, 176, 182, 190; **soone** 13/438; **sona**
  1/6, 15; **sune** 11/73, 97
Sonenday (prn.) *Sunday* 7/219
sones → **sone** (1)
song (sb.) 9/134 *10.4/2, 7, 42; **sang** 13/394
songen → **singe**
sonne → **sunne; sone** (1)
sontes → **sayntes**
soo; soone → **so; sone** (2)
soore; soote → **sore; sweete**
sooth → **soth**
soper (sb.) *supper, meal* 7/230 *13/539
sor (adj.) *painful, sore* 10.7/18; **sore** 10.4/36
sore (adv.) *very, sorely* 2/61 *5/37, 68, 150
  *8/33, 95, 103, 120 *10.1/17 *10.4/23
  *10.6/29, 48 *10.7/13 *10.8/20, 27
  *12/204–205; **soore** 13/453; **sair** 14/9; **sare**
  11/17, 89; **sarily** 11/14
sore → **sor**
sorowe (sb.) *sorrow, grief* 12/244, 379;
  sorewe 10.6/2; **serewe** 8/45 *10.6/54; **sorwe**
  7/113; **sorowes** 12/44, 294, 388
sort (sb.) 13/268
sorwe → **sorowe**
sory (adj.) *sad* 10.4/20
sostinonce (sb.) *sustenance* 4/41
sostyeni (inf.) *to support, sustain* 4/87;
  sustyeneþ (pl.ps.) 4/95
sotlice (adv.) *foolishly* 1/23
soth (adj., adv., sb.) *true, truly, truth* 5/174
  *12/289, 327; **soþ** 6/135 *8/61, 65, 79, 109;
  sooth 13/111, 148, 543; **suith** 14/68; **sothe**
  13/163; **soþe** 6/142

soþe → for; soth
sothly (adv.) *truly* 13/407; **suithlie** 14/160
souerein (sb.) *ruler, lord* 5/128; **souereines**
  (pl.) 5/132, 165; **souereins** 5/179
souhteres → soutere
soule (sb.) *soul* 7/228 *8/126 *10.5/51
  *12/246; **saul** 11/122; **saule** 1/24 *12/376;
  saull 14/33, 110, 129, 133, 137; **soulene** (pl.)
  5/99; **sowles** 2/34; **saules** 12/378, 390; **saulis**
  12/272
soule-cnul (sb.) *death-knell* 8/126
soulene; soum → soule; some
sounde (adj.) *healthy, sound* 5/40 *10.7/5;
  sund 2/12, 44 *9/41
soupen (pl.ps.) *to dine* 13/370
sour (adj.) 10.8/34; **soure** 14/82
sourquydrye (sb.) *pride* 6/98
soutere (sb.) *cobbler* 13/128; **souhteres**
  female cobbler 7/163
Southwerk (pn.) *Southwark* 13/20
sowes (sb.pl.) *sow* 7/199
sowke (inf.) *to suck* 13/381
sowles → soule
sowynge (sb.) *sowing (seed)* 7/23
spac → speke
space (sb.) 12/110 *13/35, 348 *14/68
spak, spake → speke
spare (inf.) 11/47, 49, 51 *13/190; **sparede**
  (sg.pt.) 5/105
sparkles (sb.pl.) 13/109
specþ → speke
speche (sb.) *speaking, speech* 4/4, 85 *6/101,
  197, 256 *8/112 *9/54 *13/350
speciall (adj.) *special* 12/110 *14/217
specially (adv.) 13/15, 355
spede (inf., ps.) *to succeed, prosper, satisfy,*
  hurry 9/67 *11/31 *12/139 *13/257; **spedez**
  (sg.ps.) 6/197; **speids** 14/208; **sped** (ptp.)
  13/429; **ysped** 13/444
speke (inf., ps.) *to speak, talk* 6/95 *7/233
  *13/90, 105, 124, 126, 141, 370, 422;
  speken (inf.) 5/20 *8/85 *9/54; (pl.pt.) 5/119;
  specþ (sg.ps.) 4/88; **speketh** 13/375; **spac**
  (sg.pt.) 3/9 *5/105; **spak** 5/21 *8/33 *11/46,
  50 *13/246, 279, 485; **spake** 7/221 *12/28,
  53; **spoken** (ptp.) 13/31; **spekinge** (sb.) 4/6
spende (inf., ps.) *to spend* 6/197 *12/28
  *13/359
sperde → spere (2)
spere (1) (sb.) *spear* 6/56 *10.6/49; **speres**
  (pl.) 8/146
spere (2) (imp.) *to lock, block* 12/139; **sperde**
  (ptp.) 12/110

speres → spere (1)
spilde (sg.pt.) *to waste* 7/233
spird (sg.pt.) *to enquire* 11/79
spiritus (sb.pl.) *spirit, ghost* 7/18
splen (sb.) *spleen* 8/24
spoken → speke
sporned (sg.pt.) *to stumble* 13/504
spray (sb.) *shoot, twig* 10.1/1
spreidis (sg.ps.) *to grow* 14/208
spreit (sb.) *spirit* 14/208
springe (inf.) *to grow, move, flow* 9/84
  *10.1/1 *10.4/1; **springeð** (sg.ps.) 2/6
sproutis (sb.pl.) *sprout, bud* 14/208
spusbreche (sb.) *adultery* 3/29
spyces (sb.pl.) *spice* 7/159
squiers (sb.pl.) *squire, servant* 11/74; **swiers**
  (pl.) 11/96
srift; sriue → shryfte; shryue
ssame; ssast → shame; sle
sseaweþ, sseawy → shewe
ssel, sselt → shall
ssepe → sheep
ssoldest, ssole → shall
stables (sb.pl.) 13/28
stad (ptp.) *to place, set down* 6/33 *11/40
staf (sb.) *staff, stick* 5/54, 141 *7/204 *13/48,
  518, 520, 528; **staues** (pl.) 7/51 *8/31, 142,
  146
stal → stele
stalke (sb.) *piece of straw* 13/143
stand (inf., ps.) 5/98 *13/325 *14/21, 74, 81,
  84; **stande** (inf.) 7/204 *13/260; **stonde** (inf.,
  ps.) 5/70, 142 *6/81, 131 *10.4/11 *10.8/2
  *12/193; **stant** (sg.ps.) 13/147; **stond**
  10.6/18; **stont** 10.6/19; **stod** (sg.pt.) 5/38,
  125, 148–149 *6/109, 119, 121 *8/129
  *9/89; **stode** 11/13; **stood** 13/284, 448;
  stoden (pl.pt.) 6/219
stane, stanes → stone
Stanewig (pn.) *Stanwick* 1/79
stanis; stant → stone; stand
start (sg.pt.) *to start, go* 6/218
staues; stedde → staf; stede (2)
stede (1) (sb.) *horse, steed* 6/68; **stedes** (pl.)
  6/47
stede (2) (sb.) *place* 3/35 *11/21; **stedde**
  6/226 *12/40; **steede** 12/13, 193; ♦ col.: **in**
  stede (adv.) *instead (of)* 7/94; **in stide** (adv.)
  instead 13/277
stedefast (adj.) *steadfast* 2/60
stedes → stede (1)
steede → stede (2)
steill → stele

steir (inf.) *to steer* 14/2

stel (sb.) *steel* 2/53 *6/213

stelbawe (sb.) *stirrup* 6/222

stele (inf.) *to steal* 4/93 *13/164, 234, 276,
  470; **steill** 14/45, 166; **stal** (sg.pt.) 13/219,
  221; **stoln** (ptp.) 13/335, 407

stel-gere (sb.) *armour* 6/47

step (imp.) 13/298

Stephne (prn.) *King Stephen* 1/21, 26, 50;
  Stephnes (gsg.) 1/83; **Stephne de Blais** 1/12

steppe (inf.) *to go, step* 7/204; **steppez** (sg.ps.)
  6/222

ster (sb.) *star* 10.5/35; **sterres** (pl.) 1/3
  *10.8/34

stere (1) (adj.) *devoted* 9/42

stere (2) (sb.) *battlefield* 9/57

sterres → **ster**

steuenyng (sb.) *meeting* 10.3/33

stewardus; stide → **stuard; stede** (1)

stif (adj.) *stiff, brave, firm* 6/34, 81, 109, 119;
  styf 6/218; **stifest** (sup.) 6/47

stifly (adv.) *bravely* 6/74

stiketh (sg.ps.) *to stick* 13/101; **stikede** (sg.pt.
  (weak)) 5/180

stille (adj., adv.) *still, quiet, quietly* 2/48 *5/23,
  137, 166 *8/18, 33, 44 *10.6/9 *12/168
  *13/423, 451; **stiller** (comp.) 6/88

stireð (sg.ps.) *to stir, move* 2/45, 48; **sturez**
  6/118

stirk (sb.) *young bullock or heifer* 14/117

stirte (sg.pt.) *to start up* 13/516, 518

stod, stode, stoden → **stand**

stoken (ptp.) *to lock, close* 6/33 *12/193

stoln → **stele**

ston; stond, stonde → **stone; stand**

stone (sb.) 3/13 *10.6/18; **ston** 2/16, 53 *5/16
  *8/142 *9/67; **stoon** 13/504; **stane** 14/126;
  stones 8/31 *10.6/35; **stanes** 1/43; **stanis**
  14/13

stong (sg.pt.) *to sting, pierce* 10.4/4; **istounge**
  (ptp.) 8/146

stonk (sg.pt.) *to stink* 8/47

stont, stood; stoon → **stand; stone**

stoor (sb.) *livestock* 13/54

stop (inf.) 14/34

stori (sb.) *story, history* 6/34

storm (sb.) 2/45

storue (sg.pt.) *to die* 8/76; **sturuen** (pl.pt.) 1/55

stot (sb.) *horse* 13/71

stottis (sb.pl.) *steer, castrated ox* 14/7

stounde → **stund**

stoure (sb.) *battle* 12/130 [see stere (2)]

stowned (sg.pt.) *to astonish* 6/88

strang → **strong**

straucht (sg.pt.) *to put to work* 14/7

straunge (adj.) *strange, foreign, difficult* 5/60,
  75, 102 *13/13, 204

strayues (sb.pl.) *stray animal* 7/92

stree (sb.) *straw* 13/97

streem (sb.) *stream* 13/119, 500

streiking (psp.) *to plough* 14/4

streit (adj.) *narrow* 13/346

strencþe → **strengthe**

strenges (sb.pl.) *rope* 1/40

strengthe (sb.) *strength, power, violence,
  army* 1/77; **strengþe** 4/43; **strencþe** 5/64,
  66, 75; **streynþe** 10.4/22

strepeth (sg.ps.) *to strip off* 13/287

strete (sb.) *street, way* 8/3

streynþe → **strengthe**

strife (sb.) 11/60; **stryf** 13/506; **strifs** (pl.) 4/93

strike (inf.) 6/74; **stryke** 6/118; **strok** 8/5

strok → **strike**

strok (sb.) *stroke* 6/74, 81

strokes (sg.ps.) *to stroke* 6/203; **stroked**
  (sg.pt.) 6/121

stronde (sb.) *strand, shore* 9/120; **strondes**
  (pl.) 13/13

strong (adj.) 2/14 *5/30, 32, 73, 152 *9/68
  *13/371, 389; **stronge** (adj., adv.) 6/34 *8/31,
  98, 137 *10.4/35 *10.6/31 *12/130;
  strongue (adj., adv.) 5/117, 197; **strang** 4/28;
  ◆ neg.: **unstrong** 2/4

Strother (pn.) 13/238

strydez (sg.ps.) *to stride* 6/222

stryf; stryke → **strife; strike**

stuard (sb.) *steward, deputy* 9/121; **stewardus**
  (pl.) 7/94

studdie (sg.ps.) *to study, reflect, consider*
  14/34; **studieþ** (pl.ps.) 4/81

stund (sb.) *time, space of time, occasion* 2/47;
  stunde 9/10; **stounde** 5/18, 59, 83 *8/107
  *13/216, 231; ◆ col.: **vmbe stounde**
  occasionally 10.3/33

sturez → **stireð**

sturne (adj.) *stern, grim* 6/121

sturnely (adv.) *grimly* 6/118

sturuen; styf → **storue; stif**

styþly (adv.) *stoutly, undismayed* 6/218

suð (adv.) *south* 2/32

sua → **so**

submit (inf.) 14/73

subtellie (adv.) *dexterously, craftily* 14/176;
  subtilly 13/66

subtelteis (sb.pl.) *stratagem, trick* 14/149

subtilly → **subtellie**

such (pron., adj.) 6/136, 183, 239, 258 *12/47,
   98; **suche** 7/34, 46, 64; **suilc** 1/3, 66; **suilce**
   1/65; **swch** 5/123; **swich** 13/3, 345, 496,
   542; **swiche** (pl.) 3/43; **swilk** 11/96 *13/395;
   swilke 12/38, 116; **swuch** 5/104, 121, 123;
   sic 14/103, 109, 124, 139, 173, 208, 213;
   zuich 4/58; **zuiche** 4/82; **zuych** 4/8; **zuyche**
   4/65, 79, 89; **ȝwuche** 5/62
Suddene (pn.) 9/9, 53, 129
suencten (pl.pt.) *to oppress* 1/33
suerdes; suereþ → **swerd; swere**
suete, suetest → **sweete**
sueth (sg.ps.) *to follow, accompany* 7/46
suffise (inf.) *to suffice* 13/349
suffre (sg.ps.) *to allow, suffer* 12/378; **soffren**
   (pl.ps.) 7/96, 101; **suffred** (sg.pt.) 7/109
sugge, suggen → **say**
suikes → **swyke**
suilc, suilce → **such**
suinc; suith → **swinke; soth**
suiðe, suiþe; suithlie → **swiþe; sothly**
sukeð (sg.ps.) *to suck* 2/42
suld → **shall**
sull; sum → **selleþ; some**
sumdeill, sumdel; sume → **del; some**
sumer (sb.) *summer* 2/46; **somer** 14/125;
   somur 7/1
summe; sumtyme, sumtymis → **some; time**
sund → **sounde**
sundir (adv.) *separately* 12/240
sune → **sone** (1, 2)
sunne → **sin**
sunne (sb.) *sun* 1/3 *2/9–10, 28 *9/87–88;
   sonne 7/1, 14, 219 *12/90 *13/7, 30
sunnen, sunnes; suoren → **sin; swere**
supple (sb.) *help* 14/182
surcote (sb.) *surcoat* 13/73
sure (adj.) 14/104
sustyeneþ → **sostyeni**
suythe, suyðe → **swiðe**
swa → **so**
swayn (sb.) *servant* 13/251
swch → **such**
sweete (adj.) *sweet, precious* 13/5, 460; **swete**
   5/204 *7/84 *9/95 *10.4/26; **swett** 10.10/9;
   (adv.) 10.10/3; **suete** 9/135 *10.3/23 *10.4/3,
   6, 39, 41 *10.5/6–7 *10.6/5, 36 *10.7/20, 25
   *10.8/34; **soote** 13/1; **sweit** 14/82; **suetest**
   (sup.) 10.5/4; **swetteste** 2/39
swerd (sb.) *sword* 13/154, 243, 309; **swerdes**
   (gsg.) 9/78; **suerdes** 9/113
swere (sg.ps.) *to swear (an oath)* 6/190
   *10.3/24; **sweren** (pl.ps.) 7/36; **suereþ**
   10.6/56; **zuerie** (inf.) 4/91; **swoor** (sg.pt.)

13/162, 225; **swor** 5/108; **sworn** (ptp.) 7/228;
   sworne 14/81, 84, 129; **suoren** 1/30
swete → **sweete**
swete (inf.) *to sweat* 7/36 *9/74
swett, swetteste → **sweete**
swich, swiche → **such**
swiers → **squiers**
swike (sb.) *treason, guile* 2/41
swikele (adj.) *deceptive, treacherous* 8/43, 52
swikes → **swyke**
swilk, swilke → **such**
swim (inf.) 11/44; **swimand** (psp.) 11/47
swinke (sb.) *labour, toil* 8/72; **swynk** 13/477;
   suinc 1/69
swiðe (adv.) *very, heavily, much, strongly*
   2/51; **swiþe** 5/2, 32, 196, 198, 218 *8/2, 5–6,
   55, 84, 95, 131, 137; **swythe** 7/28, 223;
   swyþe 5/11, 25, 189 *6/8; **suiðe** 1/4; **suiþe**
   9/102; **suyðe** 1/33; **suythe** 1/71
swiðeð (sg.ps.) *to brighten, illuminate* 2/10
swithly (adv.) *fast, quickly* 11/44
swon (sb.) *swan* 10.1/14
swonken → **swynke**
swoor, swor, sworn, sworne → **swere**
swuch → **such**
swyke (sb.) *deceiver, traitor* 10.3/25; **swikes**
   (pl.) 1/16; **suikes** 1/29
swyn (sb.pl.) *swine, pig* 13/54; **zuyn** 4/10–11
swynes-heed (sb.) *pig's head* 13/486
swynk → **swinke**
swynke (inf.) *to work, toil* 7/36, 53; **swonken**
   (pl.pt.) 7/23; (ptp.) 13/459
swyre (sb.) *neck* 10.1/14
swythe, swyþe → **swiðe**
swyve (inf.) *to copulate with* 13/402; **swyved**
   (ptp.) 13/490, 541
syde (sb.) *side* 7/180 *13/74, 243 *14/85;
   sydes (pl.) 10.6/50; **sides** 7/228
syke; syluer, sylure → **siken; silver**
Symeon (prn.) *Simeon* 12/60
Symkyn (prn.) 13/165, 169, 171, 179, 183,
   248, 258, 515
Symond (prn.) 13/246, 250, 351, 512
symonye (sb.) *simony* 7/84
symple (adj.) *simple, sad* 12/244; **simpill**
   11/17
syn; syne → **sin; siðen**
synege → **synne**
synffull → **sinful**
syng, synge → **singe**
synke → **sinke**
synne → **sin; siðen**
synne (inf.) *to sin* 7/109; **synege** 7/157;
   zeneȝeþ (pl.ps.) 4/58

syre → **sir**
sytten, syttes → **sitten**
sythe, syþe → **siþe**
sythen, syþen → **siðen**
sythes, syþez → **siþe**

T

ta, taa → **take**
Tabard (prn.) 13/20
tabide → **a-bide**
table → **rounde**
table (sb.) 6/132
tahte → **teche**
taile; taill → **top; tale**
taill (sb.) *tail* 14/84, 117; **tayl** 13/102, 388
tais (sb.pl.) *toe* 14/179
tak → **take**
take (inf.) 4/80 *5/135 *6/137, 170 *9/23
*10.1/9 *12/191, 331 *13/34, 276, 317; **tak**
(inf., ps.) 11/65 *14/19, 101, 118, 136; **taa**
(inf.) 13/353–354; **taken** (inf., ptp.) 5/138
*10.7/27 *10.10/15; **takeð** (sg.ps.) 2/18, 24;
ta (imp.) 6/200; **takez** (pl.ps.) 5/145; ♦ sg.pt.:
toc 1/18; **tok** (sg.pt.) 5/54, 143, 186 *9/20,
101, 120 *10.5/11; **took** (pt.) 7/117 *13/388;
tuke 14/85, 106; ♦ pl.pt.: **tocan** 1/17; **token**
(pl.pt.) 5/135; **tooke** 13/533, 535; ♦ ptp.: **tan**
6/277; **tane** 11/77, 86, 99, 103 *12/172
*14/58, 142; **itake** 8/22, 89 *9/75
takin → **tokene**
tald, talde → **tell**
tale (sb.) 9/2, 133 *11/34 *12/61, 149, 273
*13/36, 83, 129, 132, 548; **taill** 14/58; **tales**
(pl.) 7/49
talenttyf (adj.) *desirous* 6/137
tales → **tale**
talking (sb.) 11/80
tan, tane → **take**
tanners (sb.pl.) 7/142
tape (sb.) *tap, knock* 6/193
tappe (sb.) *tap, plug* 13/114, 116–117
tare (sb.) *weed* 13/224, 280
tarie (sg.ps.) *to tarry, delay, waste* 13/129;
tarying (sb.) 14/39
taste (inf.) 12/358
tauerne (sb.) *inn, tavern* 4/79–81, 86, 94;
tauernes 4/95–96
tauerners; tauernes → **tauernyer; tauerne**
tauernyer (sb.) *inn-keeper, taverner* 4/31;
tauerners 7/147
taught → **teche**
tauld → **tell**

tayl → **taill**
taylers (sb.pl.) *tailor* 7/142
te → **the**
teche (inf., ps.) *to teach* 6/188, 194 *9/54
*12/364; **tekþ** (sg.ps.) 4/91, 93; **tahte** (sg.pt.)
10.3/39; **taught** (ptp.) 12/262; **teching** (sb.)
9/124
tegædere → **togeder**
tekþ → **teche**
tel → **tell**
teldes (sb.pl.) *dwelling* 6/11
tell (inf.) 11/27 *14/194; **telle** (inf., ps.) 4/68,
92 *5/69 *6/26, 31, 66, 78, 167, 188, 193,
267 *7/9, 13, 227 *8/66, 94 *10.1/13
*10.5/5, 43 *10.9/8 *12/100, 145, 197, 215,
218, 286 *13/38, 75, 148, 239, 465; **tellen**
(inf., ps.) 1/49 *6/59 *7/90 *8/103; **telleth**
(sg.ps.) 7/104; **telþ** 3/2; **tel** (imp.) 8/99; **talde**
(sg.pt.) 11/59, 71; **tauld** 14/140; **tolde** (pt.,
ptp.) 7/111, 147 *10.2/14 *12/149, 253, 370;
tald (ptp.) 13/431; **ytoold** 13/137
temp → **tempt**
temple (sb.) 11/3 *12/62
tempt (inf.) 14/206; **temp** 11/100
ten (num.) 8/24 *13/365
tendre (adj.) *tender* 13/7
tene (sb.) *harm, trouble* 6/22
tenserie (sb.) *protection money* 1/52
tente (inf.) *to guard* 12/172
teoþe (ord.) *tenth* 5/205
teres (sb.pl.) *tear* 9/73
terestre → **paradise**
termes (sb.) *term, word* 13/141
testif (adj.) *testy, headstrong* 13/228
teth → **tooth**
teð (sg.ps.) *to pull, draw* 2/7; **tey** 8/140
teue (adv.) *last night* 4/28
text (sb.) 14/194
tey → **teð**
Ticius (prn.) 6/11
tide (sb.) *time, occasion* 9/93 *11/100; **tyde**
12/184, 215
til → **till** (1, 2)
tiled, tilede → **tilen**
tilen (inf.) *to till, cultivate, order* 2/15, 34;
tylie 7/87; **tilede** (sg.pt.) 1/64; **tiled** (ptp.)
1/54
till (1) (conj.) *till, until* 11/80–81; **tille** 12/24;
til 1/28 *2/7–8, 17, 45 *6/236, 272 *7/42,
188, 197–198, 204, 219, 241 *9/9 *13/97,
99, 118, 263, 283, 293, 327, 330, 334, 419,
445, 457, 504
till (2) (prep.) *to, unto* 11/7 *12/393 *14/85,
142, 159; **tille** 12/32, 35, 172; **til** 7/147

tille → **till** (1, 2)

time (sb.) 1/9, 15, 68, 83–84 *2/45 *3/4, 14,
  36 *8/132 *9/52; **tyme** 4/72 *5/31, 226
  *6/22, 24, 51, 170 *7/82, 206 *10.10/4
  *11/115 *12/149, 225, 286 *13/35, 92, 129,
  132, 220, 282 *14/4; ◆ col.: **som tyme** (adv.)
  sometimes 7/230; **sumtymis** 14/94;
  sumtyme *once* 11/34; **ofte tymes** (adv.)
  frequently 12/370

tint; tis; tit, tite → **tyne; this; as-tit**

tiþandes (sb.pl.) *news* 11/79

tithes (sb.pl.) *tithe* 11/11

to (1) (prep.) **to fore** (conj.) *before* 9/88

to (2) (adv.) *too, to* 4/19, 22, 28, 30, 47–48,
  56, 59–60 *5/122 *8/41, 49 *10.3/16, 35, 43
  *10.6/31–34 *13/420

tobreke (inf.) *to break, break to pieces* 8/32;
  to-breke 13/142; **tobroke** (ptp.) 8/10
  *13/501

toc, tocan → **take**

to-cleue (inf., ps.) *to burst* 4/13, 73–74

tod (sb.) *fox* 14/71, 85, 136, 140, 155, 185,
  191; **toddis** (gsg.) 14/84

today (adv.) 3/2 *9/95; **to-day** 6/184, 257
  *10.8/9

toddis → **tod**

to-delþ (sg.ps.) *to divide, part* 4/4; **todeld**
  (sg.pt.) 1/23

to-draȝe (inf.) *to draw (and quarter)* 9/116

togeder (adv.) *together* 6/149, 268; **togedere**
  8/78, 107–108; **togedres** 7/121; **to-gadere**
  5/82, 220; **togadere** 9/47; **togædere** 1/19;
  togidere 3/16; **togyderes** 7/47, 61, 184;
  tegædere 1/59

toȝeines (prep.) *against* 8/48

tohewe (inf.) *to hack to pieces* 9/26

tok, token → **take**

tokene (sb.) *token, sign* 7/86; **takin** 11/71

tokining (sb.) *token* 11/69; **tokninge** 4/11

tol (sb.) *tribute* 7/98

tolde → **tell**

tole (sb.) *weapon* 6/200; **toles** (pl.) 12/179;
  tolleð (sg.ps.) *to lure* 2/58

tonge (sb.) *tongue, language* 4/6, 73 *6/32
  *7/227 *13/120

toniȝt (adv.) *tonight* 8/96; **to-nyght** *this night*
  13/477

tonne (sb.) *barrel* 13/118

to-nyght; took, tooke → **toniȝt; take**

tooth (sb.) 13/112; **teth** (pl.) 11/98

top (sb.) 13/46, 93; ◆ col.: **fro toppe to taile**
  completely 12/159

tornez → **turne**

toth-draweres (sb.) *tooth-drawer* 7/171

toty (adj.) *dizzy* 13/477

touche (inf.) *to touch* 13/156

toumbe (sb.) *tomb, grave* 5/139

toun (sb.) *dwelling, court, place, town, village*
  6/31 *13/76, 167, 201, 238, 360; **toune**
  10.1/14 *10.3/29 *10.6/13 *12/253; **tun**
  1/62, 81; **tune** 1/54 *9/13; **tunes** (pl.) 1/51,
  53

tour (sb.) *tower, castle, house* 7/15 *10.8/23;
  tur 9/97; **ture** 9/89

toward (prep.) *towards, to* 3/40 *5/4 *13/27,
  289, 315, 339; **to-ward** 5/39; **ward** 2/27

traist (1) (imp.) *to trust* 14/167; **traistis** (sg.ps.)
  14/213; **traste** (pl.ps.) 12/179 [see truste]

traist (2) (sb.) *trust* 14/216

traitour (sb.) *traitor* 13/493; **traytoure**
  12/150

trammes (sb.) *machination* 6/3

trantis (sb.pl.) *trick* 12/159

traste → **traist** (1)

trauell (sb.) *labour* 14/210

traueses (sg.ps.) *to counter* 12/150

traweþ, trawþe → **truth**

trayne (sb.) *guile* 12/9

traytoure → **traitour**

tre (sb.) *cross* 10.6/4, 34 *11/64; **trees** (pl.)
  tree 13/63

trenchant (adj.) *sharp* 13/154

treothes → **truth**

tresor (sb.) *royal treasury* 1/23

tresoun (sb.) *treason* 5/84 *6/3 *7/12

trespas (sb.) *sin, trespass* 5/162

trespased (ptp.) *to trespass* 7/227

treuthe, treuþe → **truth**

trewage (sb.) *oath of obedience* 9/119

trewe (adj.) *true, obedient, honest, faithful*
  5/76 *7/100 *9/131 *10.3/20, 38 *10.4/6
  *10.8/28 *12/273, 318, 369; **trwe** 6/179,
  267; **trewest** (sup.) 6/4; ◆ neg.: **vntrewe** 7/98
  *10.3/29 *10.8/35; **untrewe** *warped* 2/13, 30

trewely; trewest → **truly; trewe**

trewlie, trewly → **truly**

tricherie (sb.) *treachery, guile* 5/64, 77 *6/4
  *10.3/21; **tricherye** 7/12

trichour (sb.) *deceiver, cheat* 10.3/22, 31, 39

tried (ptp.) *to try (for crime)* 6/4

trouþe → **truth**

trough (sb.) 13/267

trow (inf., ps.) *to trust, rely on, believe in*
  10.9/7 *11/37, 114 *14/110, 133; **trowe**
  6/160 *12/95, 173, 318, 332 *13/319;
  trowed (sg.pt.) 7/15; ◆ contr. 1.sg.: **trowy**
  10.3/38

Troye (pn.) *Troy* 6/1
trufles (sb.pl.) *trifle, idle talk* 4/71
truly (adv.) 6/167, 188; **trewely** 13/357;
 trewlie 14/35; **trewly** 12/95; **trwly** 6/193
Trumpyngtoun (pn.) *Trumpington* 13/145
truste (sg.pt.) *to trust* 5/80, 85; **tryst** (inf.)
 6/167
trusterie (sb.) *trash* 14/213
'truth' (sb.) **traweþ** 6/190; **trawþe** 6/181;
 treothes (pl.) 1/31; **treuthe** 1/31 *7/12, 15,
 187; **treuþe** 10.2/10 *10.3/31; **trouþe**
 10.3/20, 22
trwe, trwly → **trewe; truly**
trym (adv.) *properly* 10.10/9
tryst; tu → **truste; thu**
tueie; tuelf → **two; twelve**
tuke → **take**
tukked (ptp.) *to hitch up* 13/77
tulk (sb.) *man, knight* 6/3
tulle (inf.) *to lure* 13/358
tulyers (sb.pl.) *tiller, cultivator* 7/142
tun → **toun**
tunder (sb.) *tinder* 2/53
tune, tunes → **toun**
tunscipe (sb.) *villagers* 1/62
tuo; tur, ture → **two; tour**
turmente (pl.ps.) *to torment, plague* 12/312
turmentis (sb.) *torment* 12/358
turne (inf.) *to turn* 10.4/32 *12/332 *13/152
 *14/145; **tornez** (sg.ps.) 6/244; **turned** (ptp.)
 6/22
tus → **thus**
Tuskan (pn.) *Tuscany* 6/11
twa, tway → **two**
twelmonyþ (sb.) *year* 6/85; **twelmonyth**
 6/170
twelve (num.) 13/365; **tuelf** 9/39
twenty (num.) 13/24, 57, 194, 348, 481
tweyne → **two**
twie (adv.) *twice* 9/96
two (num.) 7/106, 199 *8/16 *11/46 *13/175,
 193, 226, 390, 423, 456, 502, 523; **tuo** 4/3–4
 *8/37 *10.6/27; **tueie** 9/43; **twa** 1/45, 61
 *11/3, 11, 44 *13/353 *14/160; **tway**
 14/145; **tweyne** 7/165; ♦ col.: **in twynne**
 6/212
twynne → **two**
twynne (pl.ps.) *to part* 12/278
Tybourne (pn.) *Tyburn* 7/169
tyde → **tide**
tydes (sg.ps., impv.) *to get* 13/399
tylie → **tilen**
tyme, tymes → **time**

Tymme (prn.) 7/165
tyne (inf., ps.) *to lose* 14/39, 90; **tint** (ptp.)
 14/210
tynekare (sb.) *tinker* 7/165
typet (sb.) *(dangling) tip of a hood* 13/177
tyrantis (sb.pl.) *tyrant* 12/311
tyte → **as-tit**
tytel (sb.) *evidence* 6/267

TH, Þ, Ð

þa (1) (adv., conj.) *then, when* 1/2, 6–7, 17–18,
 26, 29–30, 34–35, 50, 52, 54; **tha** 1/34; **þo**
 3/6, 15, 19, 23 *4/10 *5/5, 35, 58, 61, 63, 73,
 77–78, 92, 106, 112, 122, 142, 160, 167,
 211, 217 *8/8, 12, 41, 47, 62, 85, 111,
 120–121, 132, 144 *9/29; **tho** 7/196; **ðo**
 8/116
þa (2) (art., dempron.) *the, this* 1/15, 17, 35, 46
 *3/3–4 *4/15 *11/9, 36; **þo** 3/3, 9, 13–16,
 18–19, 22, 27–28, 31–34, 37, 39–40, 43
 *4/95 *7/44–45 *10.2/7 *12/279; **ðo** 2/59;
 tho 6/253 *7/18, 119, 184
þabbotrice → **abbotrice**
þaʒ, þah → **though**
þai, thai → **they**
thair, þaire → **there; they**
thairfoir, thairin, thairoff, thairthrow →
 there
þam, þame, thame, þamseluen → **they**
þan, than → **that; then; they**
than (conj.) 7/136 *13/64, 105, 220, 519
 *14/38; **þan** 1/58, 81 *11/30, 53, 66, 106;
 þane 5/36, 172 *9/88; **þanne** 1/66 *4/20, 99
 *12/200, 320, 328; **then** 7/231; **þen** 6/24,
 120, 124, 248 *8/4, 34 *10.1/14, 17
þane → **than**
þane (dempron., asg.m.) *this* 4/18, 36 [see the]
thank (1) (sb.) *thanks* 13/68 *14/39; **þonkes**
 (pl.) 4/52; ♦ neg.: **unthank** 13/306
thank (2) (sg.ps.) 11/7; **thanke** (pl.ps.) 12/381;
 thankid (sg.pt.) 11/42
þanne, thanne → **than; then**
ðanne → **when**
þar, thar, þarby → **there**
þare, thare → **there; they**
þare-a-boute, þare-bi, þare-bi-fore, þare-to,
 þare-vnder → **there**
þarfore, þarin, þarinne, þarof, tharof,
 þar-on, þar-to, þarto, ðarto, → **there**
þas → **thes**
that (conj., pron.) **þat; ðat; þet;** ♦ col.: **þat as**
 (rel.) *who* 5/136–137; **þet yef** (conj.) *if* 4/36;
 to þan þet (conj.) *so that* 4/68; **mid þan þat**

with that 8/28; **after þan** (adv.) *thereafter* 8/54

þay, thay; þæ → they; the

þær, þærinne → there

ðe, þe → the; thu

the → **full** (2)

þe, the → **better; much; while; worse; wroth**

þe (part.) *who, which* 1/7, 15, 35, 56, 61, 76, 78

the þe ðe (art.) **þæ** 1/78; **te** 1/1, 13, 17, 28, 69, 87 *2/28, 47; ◆ infl.: **þene** (asg.m.) 5/50 *8/57, 63, 121, 140–141, 144

þeder; thee → þider; thu

theef (sb.) *thief* 13/163, 222; **þef** 8/51; **theif** 14/45; **þeof** 5/118; **þyef** 4/32; **þeues** (pl.) 10.6/27; **þieues** 4/94

theek; þef → so; theef

thei, þei → they; though

theif → theef

þen, then → than

then (adv., conj.) 6/153 *7/220; **þen** 6/109, 116, 164, 196; **þene** 8/32; **þenn** 6/37; **þenne** 6/96, 197, 249, 268; **thenne** 7/118, 120, 126, 162, 205, 208; **than** 13/42 *14/12, 18, 25, 61, 78, 85, 99, 106, 111, 115, 138, 141, 152, 157, 159, 183, 186, 190; **þan** 11/4, 22, 38, 50, 52, 58, 71, 96, 99, 102–103, 105, 108–109, 120 *12/143, 291; **thanne** 13/12, 226, 265, 444; **þanne** 4/31–32, 71 *5/138 *6/88 *9/14, 44, 90 *12/78, 198, 241, 301; **ðanne** 2/16, 42

þenche; þende → think; end

þene → the; then

þenk; þenn → think; then

thenne, þenne → then; þunne

þeof → theef

þer, ðer, ther → there; thes; they

þer-aftir, þerbefore, therbiforn, þerby, þerbye → there

there (adv.) 7/99, 181, 186, 195, 229; **þere** 5/32, 42, 52, 60–61, 98, 167, 177, 230 *6/131, 215, 219, 247 *8/47, 64, 76, 116 *9/47 *12/125; **þer** 12/20, 114, 220, 260, 300; **ðer** 2/12, 44, 47; **þer** 3/12 *4/82, 90–93, 99 *5/114 *6/3, 107, 121, 136, 140, 266 *7/19, 56, 84, 114 *8/10, 14, 37, 46, 54, 81–82, 99, 117, 131, 133, 141 *9/49, 59, 67, 69, 93, 98, 110, 114, 123–124, 127–128 *10.3/17 *10.6/12; **ther** 1/22 *7/66, 113, 118 *13/34, 48, 50, 58–59 etc.; **thair** 14/2, 38, 100, 194, 208; **þar** 1/27, 41 *5/50; **thar** 13/544; **þare** 5/30, 33, 35, 82, 84, 97, 99, 152, 168, 180, 190, 201, 221, 231 *6/250

*8/17, 86 *9/117 *11/39, 76, 87 *12/15; **thare** 1/75; **þær** 1/74; **ðore** 2/23, 26; ◆ col.: **ther as** (adv.) *where* 13/284, 482; ◆ compd.: **þer-aftir** *thereafter* 7/25; **þare-a-boute** *thereabout* 5/159; **þare-bi** *thereby, near* 5/216; **þarby** (adv.) 11/84, 114; **þerby** 12/161; **þerbye** 12/322; **þare-bi-fore** *before now* 5/203; **þerbefore** 3/24; **therbiforn** 13/221; **thairfoir** *therefore* 14/34, 45, 61, 117; **þarfore** 11/21, 32, 40, 67; **ðerfore** 2/40; **þerfore** 6/243 *8/101, 110 *10.7/12 *12/7, 163, 167, 284; **therfore** 13/209, 543; **þeruore** 4/4, 15, 53, 80; **þeruore þet** 4/2, 79; **þerfro** *therefrom* 12/295; **thairin** *therein* 14/216; **þarin** 11/104; **þarinne** 1/59; **þærinne** 1/44; **þerin** 4/87; **ðerinne** 2/46; **þerinne** 1/43 *6/17, 21 *8/14, 39, 43, 63, 117; **there-ynne** 7/15; **þer-ynne** 7/217; **thairoff** *thereof* 14/31; **þarof** 1/63 *11/86; **tharof** 1/25; **ðerof** 2/51; **þerof** 6/267 *7/110 *8/9, 12, 125, 130 *9/35 *12/157; **therof** 13/224; **þar-on** *thereon* 5/140; **ðeron** 2/16; **ðerouer** *thereover* 2/7; **þare-to** *thereto* 5/172, 174, 177; **þar-to** 5/13, 88, 151; **þarto** 1/71; **ðarto** 2/51; **þer-to** 5/22, 130; **þerto** 6/188; **thairthrow** *therethrough* 14/203; **þare-vnder** *thereunder* 5/17

thes (dempron. pl.) *these* 12/24; **þes** 12/102, 390; **þas** 1/6; **þer** 12/97, 399; **thir** 14/33, 104, 146, 159; **þis** 5/75, 81, 91; **thise** 13/109, 314, 324, 456, 532; **ðise** 2/42; **þise** 4/26, 43, 64 *6/237, 260, 268 *7/60

þestrede (sg.pt.) *to grow dark* 1/2; **þestreden** (pl.pt.) 1/6

þet → for; that

þeues → theef

they (perspron. 3.pl.) 7/187–188 *12/110, 227, 258 *13/16, 18, 26, 40–41 etc.; **þei** 7/33, 38, 44, 80, 116, 124 *9/91 *10.6/9 *12/21, 103, 106–107, 112, 164, 176, 221, 257, 276, 296, 298, 318, 331; **thei** 7/108; **þai** 11/78, 87, 89, 104, 109 *12/269, 297, 367, 404; **thai** 12/398; **þay** 6/150, 248, 251, 268, 272; **thay** 14/11, 23, 78, 84, 141, 157; ◆ init. 'h–': **he** 1/31 *2/40–41, 50–51; **heo** 10.3/16, 18 *10.5/57; **hi** 1/19, 22, 28, 30–31, 33–35, 38, 40, 42, 48–49, 51, 53, 58, 60, 62–63, 65 *3/6, 20, 23–24, 29 *4/10, 12, 59–61, 67–68, 76, 98–99 *9/21, 31, 34, 38–39, 45, 47, 57–58, 87, 103–106, 115–116, 123, 132; **hise** 4/10; **hoe** 8/132, 134; **huy** 5/50, 76, 81–83, 90, 122–125, 153, 162, 167, 169, 172, 185, 194, 215–218, 220, 226; **hy** 4/13, 66, 69 *8/21, 102, 142, 144; ◆ poss., init.

'th–': **thair** 13/396 *14/78–79, 95, 143;
þaire 11/3, 32; **þare** 12/310; **thare** 12/18;
ther 12/30; ◆ poss., init. 'h–': **hare** 4/57,
63–64, 68, 70, 96–97; **heore** 5/30, 80, 99,
161–162, 170–171, 178, 216–217, 220, 226;
her 1/17, 39 *6/215; **here** 1/19, 28, 31, 40
*2/51, 56 *3/20, 24 *7/30, 32, 42–43, 49–50,
52, 55, 61, 72, 82, 109, 122, 134, 136,
143–145, 187, 202, 236 *8/22, 133–134, 137
*9/34, 104; **hir** 13/11, 32, 215, 232–233,
243, 270, 273–274, 280, 293, 317, 321,
328–329, 343, 533–535; **hire** 4/97 *13/186,
229, 362, 534; **hoere** 8/136; **huere** 10.3/16,
28; ◆ obj., init. 'th–': **þam** 11/33, 71; **þame**
12/9, 11, 18, 30, 54, 71, 104, 108–109, 116,
118, 218–219, 224, 259, 275, 319–320, 332,
334, 366, 379, 391; **thame** 12/22 *14/9, 30,
60, 65, 172, 199; **þan** 4/15, 56, 59; ◆ obj.,
init. 'h–': **hem** 2/49–50, 54–55 *3/9, 11, 13
*5/25 *6/88, 269 *7/22, 25, 27, 30 etc.
*8/15, 23, 81, 134 *9/1, 37, 40, 43 etc.
*10.3/9, 11, 17, 20, 39 *10.7/31 *10.10/16
*13/11, 18, 31, 39 etc.; **heom** 1/19, 36, 38,
41–42 etc. *5/76, 80, 107, 117 etc.; **ham**
4/10, 12–13, 35, 49, 96, 99; ◆ refl.:
þamseluen 11/33; **hemself** 7/55; **hemselue**
12/307; **hemsulue** 7/185; **heom-seolf** 5/80;
heom-sulue 5/72
þhis; þi → this; thu
þicke (adv.) *numerously, densely* 5/159, 183,
192
þider (adv.) *thither, in that direction* 8/6, 130;
þidere 8/134; **þeder** 6/189; **þuder** 9/82
þieues → theef
thikke (adj.) *thick* 13/197, 290
þilke → ilk
þin; þine → ore; sake; thu
thing → nothing
thing (sb.) 11/112 *14/57, 109; **þing** 1/4 *4/25
*10.3/13; **ðing** 2/39; **þinge** 10.5/4, 19;
thinge 10.5/6; **thyng** 7/183 *13/397, 465,
525–526; **þynge** 10.1/3; **þinges** (pl.) 4/65
*10.3/40; **thingis** 14/103; **þinkes** 3/30;
thynges 7/5 *10.10/21 *13/353
þink (sg.ps., impv.) *to seem* 6/135; **þinke** 9/25;
thynketh 13/37; **thoughte** (sg.pt.) 13/190;
þoute (impv.) 8/47
think (inf., ps.) 11/25, 121 *14/82; **þenche**
(inf., ps.) 4/53 *10.8/8; **thynke** (imp.) 12/3;
þenk 6/274; **thinkand** (psp.) 14/203; **thoght**
(sg.pt.) 11/81, 88; **thoghte** 13/271, 447; **þoȝt**
6/118; **þoȝte** 9/7, 112; **þohte** 10.5/3; **þohute**
8/7; **thoughte** 13/473, 476; **þouȝte** 5/64;
þoute 8/63

þinke; þinkes → þink; thing
thir → thes
thirde (ord.) *third* 12/31; **þridde** 4/45
*10.5/37; **thridde** 13/457
þis → thes
this; þis ðis (dempron.) **þise** 3/6, 17 *4/45, 56,
71; **þisse** 8/113; **þhis** 12/61; **tis** 2/19
thise, ðise, þise → thes
þiself, þiselffe, þiselue → thu
þisse → this
tho, þo, ðo → þa (1, 2)
þo → thu
thocht, thogh → though
thoght, thoghte → think
ðoȝ → though
þoȝt, þoȝte → think
þoht (sb.) *thought, thinking* 10.4/32 *10.6/54;
þohte 10.7/7 *10.8/7; **þohut** 8/112
þohte → think
þohut; þohute → þoht; think
þohuuethere (adv.) *nevertheless* 1/19;
þoþwethere 1/70
þolien (inf.) *to suffer, endure* 10.1/17; **þolie**
10.4/25; **tholid** (sg.pt.) 12/3; **þoleden** (pl.pt.)
1/66; **i-þoled** (ptp.) 5/122
þonk → God
þonkes → thank (1)
ðore → there
þoro (adj.) *shining* 10.5/33
thorpes (sb.pl.) *village* 7/138
þoruȝ, thorwe → throu
þos (dempron.) *those* 3/12
þoþ → though
þoþwethere → þohuuethere
thou, þou → thu
though (adv., conj.) *though, although* 13/210,
328; **thocht** 14/196; **thogh** 13/103, 135; **ðoȝ**
2/14; **þoþ** 1/20; **þaȝ** 4/74 *6/137, 225, 254;
þah 10.2/6 *10.3/20, 24 *10.6/43; **þei** 5/222,
228
thoughte, þouȝte → think; þink
þourh → throu
þourhout (adv.) *throughout* 10.4/4
þourhsoht (ptp.) *to permeate* 10.6/52
þous → thus
thousand (num.) 12/354; **þousend** 5/203;
þousent 8/102; **thowsande** 12/39; **þusen**
1/48
þoute → think; þink
thov, þow, thow, thowe → thu
thowsande → thousand
thrall (sb.) *slave* 12/134
thrawin → þrowe

thre (num.) *three* 1/3, 45; **þre** 8/77; **þreo** 5/19;
  threo 10.4/14; **þri** 4/65
þrengde (sg.pt.) *to press, force* 1/43
þreo, threo → **thre**
thresfold (sb.) *threshold* 7/209
threty (num.) *thirty* 11/39; **þritti** 5/207
threw; þri → **þrowe; thre**
þridde, thridde → **thirde**
thries (adv.) *thrice* 13/489; **thrise** 11/107
thrift ♦ col.: **by my thrift** *by my welfare*
  13/273
thrise; ðrist → **thries; þurst**
þritti → **threty**
thromblede (sg.pt.) *to stumble* 7/209
throte (sb.) *throat, neck* 1/47; **ðrote** 2/39;
  þrote 4/14, 16, 18, 35, 77
throte-bolle (sb.) *Adam's apple* 13/497
throu (adv., prep.) *through* 14/91; **throw**
  14/92, 146; **þoruʒ** 5/30, 64, 84, 191, 193,
  224; **thorwe** 7/106; **þourh** 10.6/50; **þurch**
  3/30, 32, 37; **þurgh** 12/10; **thurgh** 12/12
  *13/290, 375; **ðurʒ** 2/8, 34; **þurʒ** 6/97, 212;
  þurh 1/88 *10.5/10
throw → **throu**
þrowe (inf.) *to throw* 9/115; **threw** (sg.pt.)
  7/209; **thrawin** (ptp.) 11/97
þryue (inf.) *to thrive* 6/174; **thryve** 13/401;
  ythryueth (pl.ps.) 7/34
thu (perspron. 2.sg.) *you* 1/54; **þu** 1/53 *3/21,
  41, 43 *9/2, 4, 6–7, 10, 24–26, 94, 99; **ðu**
  2/36; **þou; thou** 6/196 *11/51 *13/313, 326,
  352, 466, 468, 486 *14/29, 36–38, 70, 86,
  92, 111; **thov** 14/153; **þow** 12/265; **thow**
  7/135, 225 *13/312, 465, 491, 494 *14/63,
  67, 112, 175, 187; **thowe** 12/242; **tu** 2/36;
  þo 4/22, 73; ♦ poss.: **þi** 5/42 *6/181, 187
  *8/67, 77, 124, 126 *9/6, 50, 95 *10.2/5
  *10.6/23–24 *11/65, 67 *12/2, 231–232,
  284–285, 346, 349, 362, 364, 368, 378, 397,
  400; **þy** 6/42, 46, 112–114, 178, 185, 187,
  198, 200 *7/128 *10.8/18; **thy** 7/127, 129
  *12/2, 65, 67, 214, 222, 229, 234, 254, 342,
  356, 363 *13/129, 132, 247, 298, 309
  *14/39, 54, 90, 104, 127; **þine** 4/39, 41–43
  *8/20, 25, 32, 67, 78, 99, 106, 126 *10.4/29;
  þyn 6/110, 264; **thyn** 13/463, 469; **thyne**
  12/221, 252, 367 *14/30; ♦ obj.: **þe** 3/8,
  42–43 *4/38, 39 *6/41, 45, 66, 111, 159,
  166, 169–170, 183, 185, 187, 190, 193–194,
  200, 238, 243 *7/127–128 *8/17, 23, 26–27,
  31, 61, 66, 68–69, 87–88, 90, 94, 105, 107,
  113, 115–116 *9/5, 26, 51, 96, 99 *10.2/4, 8,
  10 *10.3/25 *10.4/24, 26, 42–44 *10.6/21,
  40 *10.8/31 *11/7, 9, 47, 50–51, 69–70, 112,

117 *12/3, 152, 169, 218, 233, 247, 252,
  255, 277, 280, 339, 341, 361, 365, 376,
  390–391; **the** 7/128, 226 *12/405 *14/20,
  39, 69, 87–88; **thee** 13/88, 355, 412, 465,
  471, 511; ♦ refl.: **þe selue** *yourself* 4/40;
  þiself 6/182; **þiselffe** 12/206, 350; **þiselue**
  12/299; **thyselfe** 12/261; **thy selff** 14/112
þuder → **þider**
þudere-ward (adv.) *thither, in that direction*
  5/156
þulke → **ilk**
þumbes (sb.pl.) *thumb* 1/39
þunne (adj.) *thin* 10.7/34; **thenne** 13/290
þurch, þurgh, thurgh, ðurʒ, þurh → **throu**
þurled (ptp.) *to pierce* 10.4/13
þurst (sb.) *thirst* 8/34, 45; **ðrist** 2/57; **furste**
  7/239
thus (adv.) 7/74, 224 *13/279, 338, 404, 434,
  537, 548 *14/106, 187–188; **ðus** 2/28, 43;
  þus 6/234 *8/46, 79 *9/134 *11/20, 43, 118
  *12/36, 59, 248, 283, 286, 372; **þous** 4/30;
  tus 2/21, 33
þusen → **thousand**
thwitel (sb.) *knife* 13/157
thy, þy; þyef → **thu; theef**
þyn, thyn, thyne → **thu**
thyng, þynge, thynges → **thing**
thynke; thynketh → **think; þink**
thyselfe → **thu**

U

uader; uayre → **fader; fair**
uelaʒe, uelaʒes → **felowe**
uelaʒrede (sb.) *company* 4/38
ueld → **fulle**
uele → **fele** (1)
uelle, uelþ → **fulle**
uelþe → **filthe**
uerliche (adv.) *hastily* 4/45, 48
uerlichhede (sb.) *haste* 4/46
uerst → **first**
uertu; uerþe → **vertu; furþe**
ueste → **fast** (2)
uirtues → **vertu**
umble (adj.) *humble* 3/38
un → **on**
uncuð (adj.) *unfamiliar, unaware, foreign,*
  strange 2/41; **unkuð** 2/31; **vnecouþe** 5/88
undep → **depe**
under (prep.) 13/285; **ounder** 8/21, 24, 26;
  vnder 6/47, 139 *7/86 *9/21, 81, 89
  *10.1/18 *10.2/14

underfangen, underfeng → **ounderfonge**
undergæton (pl.pt.) *to perceive* 1/29
unfrið (sb.) *strife, discord* 1/15
unhardy; unkuð → **hardi; uncuð**
unseely (adj.) *unlucky* 13/434
unstrong → **strong**
untellendlice (adj.) *unspeakable* 1/37
unthank → **thank** (1)
unto (prep.) *unto, to* 13/109, 436–437, 482;
  vnto 11/22, 67, 69, 87, 90, 116, 118 *12/87,
  246, 319, 390 *14/6, 141, 145, 209, 223
untrewe → **trewe**
unweelde (adj.) *weak, infirm* 13/110; **unwelde**
  2/3
uol; uolk, uolke → **full** (1) **folk**
uor → **for**
uorlore → **forlore**
uoryet → **fur-ʒite**
uorzuelʒe (inf.) *to swallow* 4/77
uorzuerie (inf.) *to forswear* 4/91; **forsuoren**
  (ptp.) 1/64; **forsworen** 1/31
uot; uoule → **foot; foul**
up (adv., prep.) *up, upward* 1/28, 38 *2/7, 48,
  52 *5/34–35, 41, 67, 134, 138, 140, 151,
  155, 181, 222 *13/283, 324, 417, 435, 452,
  473, 503, 516, 518; **vp** 6/12, 45, 156, 220,
  231, 233, 264 *7/65, 184, 213 *9/20, 27, 77,
  113 *10.5/29 *10.6/15 *11/15, 108 *14/161,
  185, 189; **vppe** 12/113, 122, 194; **op** 5/144;
  ope 5/17; **oup** 8/123
upon (prep.) 13/62, 71, 73, 147, 161, 175, 230,
  396, 500, 505, 514; **vpon** 6/9, 88, 116, 124,
  138, 183, 204, 218, 258, 263 *10.2/9
  *10.3/16 *10.6/4, 11, 26 *10.7/27 *14/118,
  121, 148, 186; **opon** 5/16
upright → **bolt**
uprighte (adv.) *flat* 13/418
ure → **lady; we**
us → **we**
usaunt (adj.) *accustomed* 13/164
ut; uuan → **out; winne**
uuard → **wurðeð**
uuare, uuaren, uuæren → **be**
uuenden; uueron → **wene; be**
uerrien; uuerse → **werri; worse**
uuluelden; uurecce → **fulfill; wrecce**
uurythen (pl.pt.) *to twist* 1/40
uynde → **find**

V

vacaunt (adj.) *vacant* 5/51
vch; vend → **each; go**

vengeance (sb.) 7/115, 117
vernysshed (ptp.) *to polish* 13/373
verray (adj.) *true, genuine* 7/239 *13/148, 327
verst; vertewis → **first; vertu**
vertu (sb.) *power, strength, ability, virtue*
  13/4; **uertu** 3/42; **vertues** (pl.) 12/128;
  vertewis 14/56; **uirtues** 4/83
ves → **be**
veyne (sb.) *vein* 13/3
vggely (adj.) *ugly, terrible* 12/101; **vgly** 6/228
vʒten (sb.) *morning* 9/58
vice (sb.) 4/7; **vyce** 14/220
vifte → **fifte**
vileynye (sb.) *shame, dishonour, ill-breeding*
  13/415; **vylanye** 6/132; **vilony** 7/234
vind; viss → **find; fis**
vissere (sb.) *fisher* 4/17
vmbe → **stund**
vmbywhile (adv.) *from time to time* 7/197
vn-bouʒhsome → **bowsum**
vnbynde; vndefong → **bind; ounderfonge**
vnder → **under**
vnder-feng, vnder-fongue → **ounderfonge**
vnderfynde (sg.ps.) *to perceive* 10.3/6
vnder-stonde → **vndirstande**
vndertake (inf.) *to receive* 7/98
vndirstande (inf.) *to understand* 12/49;
  onderstant (sg.ps.) 4/88; **onder-stonde** 5/94;
  vnder-stonde 5/2; **onder-stod** (sg.pt.) 5/95;
  hounderstod 8/39
vndo (imp.) *to open, unlock* 12/182
vnecouþe → **uncuð**
vnfane → **fain**
vnglad → **glad**
vnhap; vnholy → **hap; holy**
vnkuynde (adj.) *unnatural* 5/90
vnlokynne → **lok**
vnlose (pl.ps.) *to open* 7/134
vnlouely → **louely**
vnneþes (adv.) *hardly* 5/218
vnorn (adj.) *plain, ugly* 9/133
vnride (adj.) *enormous* 2/38
vnriʒhte → **right**
vnroikit (adv.) *groundless* 14/116
vnrychteous → **rightwis**
vntill (conj., prep.) *against, towards, until* 11/1,
  98, 104, 122 *12/52, 370
vnto; vntrewe → **unto; trewe**
vnwsit (adj.) *untrained* 14/10
vnwurþe → **worthy**
voice (sb.) 12/79; **voyce** 12/73
volf, volff → **wolf**
volupeer (sb.) *nightcap* 13/527

vor → **for**
vowe (sg.ps.) *to vow* 7/239
vowes (sb.pl.) *vow* 7/69
vox; voyce → **foxe; voice**
voyde (inf.) *to leave, vacate* 6/132
vp → **up**
vphalderes (sb.pl.) *second-hand clothes dealers* 7/175
vpo → **loft**
vpon; vppe → **God; upon; up**
vpperight (adv.) *immediately* 12/394
vprise (inf.) *to rise (up)* 12/31; **vpros** (sg.pt.) 6/154; **vpriste** (sg.pt. (weak)) 9/88
vpwart (adv.) *upwards* 14/180, 187; **opward** 8/121
vre, vs → **we**
vse (sb.) *use, custom* 14/3
vses (sg.ps.) *to practice, use* 11/8; **vseþ** (pl.ps.) 4/49, 59
vt; vther → **out; other** (2)
vttiremeste (adj. sup.) *last, utmost* 12/232
vrþe; vuele → **erth; euel**
vuolf; vyce → **wolf; vice**
vylanye → **vileynye**

W

wa, waa; waat → **woo; God**
wages (sb.pl.) 6/183
wagges (sg.ps.) *to wag* 13/263
waist (adj.) *waste, uninhabited* 14/146, 211
waist (sb.) 14/192
wait → **wit** (2)
wake (inf., ps.) *to wake up, guard* 7/220 *10.1/11 *10.6/53; **wakeand** (psp.) 11/92; **wok** (sg.pt.) 9/79; **woke** 14/144; **woken** (pl.pt.) 5/216; **waked** (ptp.) 13/508
wakkest; wal → **wayke; wall**
walaway → **weylaway**
wald, walde → **will** (2)
wale (inf.) *to find* 6/185
walke (inf.) *to walk* 12/333; **walkand** (psp.) 12/53
walkeres (sb.pl.) *cloth-fuller* 7/141
wall (sb.) 12/140; **wal** 8/5, 10 *13/520; **walle** 8/6, 9 *9/62; **walles** (pl.) 13/517
Walshe (prn.) *Welshman* 7/174
Walsyngham (pn.) *Walsingham* 7/52
walt → **welde**
Walteruile → **Hugo**
walwe (pl.ps.) *to wallow* 13/502
wan → **when; winne**
wandryng (psp.) *to wander* 7/21

wane (sb.) *quantity, supply* 11/76
wanges (sb.pl.) *teeth* 13/254
wanne → **when; winne**
wanne (adj.) *pale* 7/220; **won** 10.1/11
war → **be; where**
war (1) (adj.) *wary, cautious* 10.2/12 *10.3/41; **ware** 12/154; ◆ col.: **on war** 10.3/34
war (2) (imp.) *to beware (of)* 10.3/25
ward → **toward**
warde (sb.) *ward* 12/222
wardemotis (sb.) *ward-meetings* 7/92
warderere (interj.) *watch out behind* 13/325
wardeyn (sb.) *warden* 13/223, 230, 236, 299, 336
wardus (sb.pl.) *wardship* 7/92
ware, waren → **be; war** (1)
ware (inf.) *to employ* 6/189
warkis → **werk**
warmen (pl.ps.) *to warm up* 2/54
warne (inf.) *to refuse* 10.9/10
warth → **wurðeð**
warto; was → **where; be**
wasche → **wesse**
wasteþ (pl.ps.) *to waste* 4/57
wastors (sb.pl.) *waster* 7/24
wat → **what**
watches (sb.pl.) *watch, guard* 12/140
wate → **wit** (2)
water (sb.) 2/35 *3/19, 26–27, 32, 41 *8/36, 46–47, 127 *10.1/15 *11/84, 97–98, 100 *13/188; **watere** 3/12, 15, 18, 36, 39; **watter** 14/192
wath → **what**
Watte (prn.) 7/164
watter; watz → **water; be**
Wawan → **Gawan**
wawe (inf.) *to stir, move* 5/152, 182; **wawien** 5/158
waxe (sg.ps.) *to grow, become* 10.2/1; **waxeþ** 10.1/11 *10.6/24 *10.7/34; **wex** 12/344; **waxen** (pl.ps.) 10.6/8; **wax** (sg.pt.) 7/223 *13/458; **wex** 6/106; **woxe** 14/12; **waxit** (pl.pt. (weak)) 14/22
way → **weyis**
way (sb.) 7/49 *9/22 *11/55, 108, 111 *12/133 *13/302, 338, 481 *14/142; **wei** 8/27; **wey** 8/3; *13/34, 244, 423, 534; **weye** 13/181, 321; **wayis** (pl.) 14/206; **weyes** 12/74
wayke (adj.) *weak* 6/69; **wakkest** (sup.) 6/141
wayned (ptp.) *to bring* 6/51
wayte (inf.) *to look, expect, wait* 6/93; **waytede** (sg.pt.) 7/16

wayued (sg.pt.) *to wave* 6/93

wayues (sb.pl.) *lost property* 7/92

wæl → **wel**

wæron, wæs → **be**

we (perspron. 2.pl.) ♦ poss.: **houre** 8/18, 30; **ore** 5/90, 191, 204; **our** 10.10/2 ∗13/299; **oure** 4/50 ∗6/165 ∗7/28, 34, 103, 134 ∗8/27 ∗10.3/14 ∗10.4/48 ∗10.5/55 ∗11/1, 27 ∗12/43–44, 84, 117 etc. ∗13/34, 78, 101, 103–104 etc.; **ure** 1/67, 85–88 ∗2/25, 34 ∗3/11, 15–17, 22, 34–35, 42; **vre** 9/25, 54; ♦ obj.: **ous** 10.7/32; **us** 3/2 ∗4/67 ∗10.9/11 ∗13/137, 257, 311, 335 etc.; **vs** 9/134–135 ∗10.4/30, 34, 40, 50 ∗10.5/9, 34, 53, 57 ∗10.6/58–60 ∗10.7/3–5, 7, 9–10 etc. ∗11/1, 32 ∗12/42, 47, 58, 83 etc.

webbesteres (sb.pl.) *female weaver* 7/141

wecht (sb.) *weight* 14/184

wedden (inf.) *to marry* 9/85, 128; **ywedde** 9/95

wede (sb.) *garment* 11/73; **wedez** (pl.) 6/58

weder (1) (sb.) *weather* 2/48

weder (2) (adv.) *whither* 8/122–123; **quhether** 14/29

wedez → **wede**

weel → **wel; fare** (2)

weet, wééte → **wete** (2)

wehee (interj.) 13/290

wei → **way**

weilawei → **weylaway**

weill; weir → **wel; but**

wel (adv.) *well* 1/53 ∗2/31, 54 ∗3/18 ∗4/8, 14, 23, 61, 68, 88 ∗5/11, 21, 23, 25 etc. ∗6/57, 258, 261, 274 ∗7/70, 100, 117, 220 ∗8/8, 32–33, 44 etc. ∗9/19, 94, 126, 130 ∗10.1/8 ∗10.3/6 ∗10.4/18 ∗10.6/43 ∗13/24, 29, 49, 51 etc.; **weel** 13/293, 464, 532, 540; **weill** 14/20, 23, 76, 101 etc.; **wele** 11/21, 37, 106 ∗12/49, 74, 82, 222, 229, 305, 334; **well** 10.10/12; **wæl** 1/74

welcome (adj., interj.) 13/248; **welcum** 6/39

welde (inf.) *to wield* 6/57; **walt** (pl.pt.) *spent* 6/272

wele → **wel**

wele (sb.) *wealth, joy* 6/7, 272

welkne (sb.) *sky* 10.8/34

welkumd (sg.pt.) *to welcome* 11/72

well → **wel**

well (sb.) 14/162, 193, 220, 224; **welle** 2/6, 12 ∗4/79; ♦ col.: **draw well** (sb.) 14/159

welneȝe (adv.) *almost* 6/7

welth (sb.) *wealth, possessions* 11/54, 63; **welthe** 7/10 ∗12/324

wen → **when**

wenche (sb.) *maidservant, wench* 7/216 ∗13/197, 391, 402, 417–418; **wenches** 7/52

wend → **wene**

wend (inf.) *to go* 11/68, 111; **wende** 7/153 ∗9/71 ∗10.4/49 ∗12/26, 153, 298, 397; **wenden** 13/21; **i-wiende** 5/224; **wende** (ps.) 12/402 ∗13/16; **wendis** 14/209; **wendest** (2.sg.ps.) 13/466; **wende** (pt.) 5/58, 139, 141, 147, 166, 179, 201, 210 ∗8/37; **i-wende** 5/207; **wenden** (pl.pt.) 5/151, 163; ♦ 2nd meaning: **wende** (sg.ps.) *to turn* 10.1/11; ♦ 3rd meaning: **wende** (sg.ps. subj.) *to change, make, turn* 3/42; **wende** (sg.pt.) 1/81; **iwent** (ptp.) 3/15

wene (inf.) *to think, believe, assume* 13/544; **wene** (sg.ps.) 6/57 ∗8/64 ∗13/272; **weneþ** 9/90; **wenes** 11/123; **wenen** (pl.ps.) 2/50; **wend** (sg.pt.) 11/34, 39 ∗14/15; **wende** 8/109, 138 ∗13/483, 527, 529; **wendest** (2.sg.pt.) 9/7; **wenen** (pl.pt.) 1/35, 62, 86 ∗13/186, 218; **uuenden** 1/22; **iwend** (ptp.) 8/67

wenne → **when**

went, wente, wenten → **go**

weork, weorkes → **werk**

weorre → **werre**

wepe (inf.) *to weep* 13/472; **wepeþ** (sg.ps.) 10.6/29; **wepen** (pl.ps.) 10.6/9; **wepynde** (psp.) 10.6/39; **wep** (sg.pt.) 8/54 ∗9/73

weppen (sb.) *weapon* 6/79, 155, 171; **wepne** 8/143; **weppenes** (pl.) 6/57

weps (sb.) *sprig* 7/203

wepynde → **wepe**

wer → **be; where**

were → **be; werre**

wered (ptp.) *to wear* 13/527

weren → **be**

wereð (sg.ps.) *to wear off* 2/26

werk (sb.) *work, deed, castle* 11/24; **werke** 10.9/4 ∗12/17, 200; *castle* 9/86; **weork** 5/30, 32, 34, 41; **werkes** (pl.) 3/29, 32, 43 ∗7/3; **werkis** 12/191; **weorkes** 1/81; **warkis** 14/207

werke (inf.) *to work, act, do* 12/334; **wirk** 11/70 ∗12/265; **wurche** 9/60; **werkes** (pl.ps.) 13/254; **werkis** 12/264; **wroȝt** (sg.pt.) 6/3, 186; **wroȝte** 9/7, 64; **wrohte** 1/70; **wroȝten** (pl.pt.) 6/22

werkemen (sb.pl.) *workman* 12/17

werkes, werkis → **werk; werke**

werldes; wermide → **world; where**

wernare (sb.) *gamekeeper* 7/164

werne (inf.) *to refuse* 9/72
werre → worse
werre (sb.) *war* 6/16; weorre 5/73; were 6/58
werri (inf.) *to wage war* 4/94; uuerrien 1/18
wers, werse → worse
werþ → wurðeð
wery (adj.) *weary* 10.1/15 *10.5/39 *13/331, 458
werynesse (sb.) *weariness* 7/7
wes; wesched → be; wesseþ
wessche → wesse
wesse (pl.ps.) *to wash* 3/13; wessche (sg.pt.) 11/75; wuschen (pl.pt.) 5/213; wasche (ptp.) 7/203
wesseþ (pl.ps.) *to wish, desire* 4/76; wesched (pl.pt.) 7/203
west (adj., sb.) 6/7; ◆ col.: by west *in the west* 10.2/13 *10.3/10; este and weste *in all directions* 12/333
weste → west; wit (2)
Westernesse (pn.) 9/118
Westmunstre (pn.) *Westminster* 5/110, 113
westward (adv.) 7/16
wete (1) (sb.) *water* 2/11
wete (2) (adj.) *wet* 2/11 *10.6/8, 35; weet 13/331; wééte 10.8/33
weterly → witterliche
wex → waxe
wex (sb.) *wax* 7/99
wey, weye, weyes → way
weyis (sg.ps.) *to weigh* 14/126; way 8/119
weylaway (interj.) 10.6/20 *13/296, 337; weilawei (interj.) *woe* 5/59; walaway 9/109
wha → who
whan, whanne; whare → when; where
what (pron.) 6/96, 171, 249 *7/105 *9/24, 105 *10.7/10 *11/27, 68 *12/60, 100–101, 125, 133, 145, 174, 185, 198, 209, 216, 223 *13/40–41, 125–126, 191, 249, 259, 302; ȝwat 5/200; huet 4/25–26, 90; quat 6/247 *10.9/14; quhat 14/70; qwat 10.9/1, 9; wat 1/83 *3/7 *8/17, 45, 59, 65, 69, 76, 82, 115, 122; ◆ compd.: quat-so *whatever* 6/42, 169; ◆ col.: wath nu (adv.) *until now* 3/21; wat is tat (sb.) *trifle* 2/30
when (adv., conj.) 6/94 *7/208 *10.1/1, 11 *10.2/8 *10.3/1, 18, 22, 36, 41, 44 *10.4/1, 11, 49 *10.5/26, 33, 39, 44, 50 *10.6/1, 3, 21, 41, 45, 51, 53 *10.10/4 *11/39, 52, 56, 77 *13/431; whan 7/1 *12/240 *13/5, 30, 79, 105, 115, 276, 288, 294, 316, 526; whanne 9/70, 116 *12/176, 352; wan 2/36, 40; wanne 3/37; wen 8/38, 134; wenne 8/76; ȝwane 5/4, 13, 15, 131, 194; huan

4/88; huanne 4/14, 19, 23, 54, 70, 86–87; quen 6/20, 193; quhen 14/37, 66; qwan 10.9/11; ðanne 2/21, 38, 46; ◆ col.: whan that 13/1, 18, 123, 282, 382, 466
where (adv.) 6/16, 98, 185–186 *7/131 *12/292, 342, 377 *13/239; wher 12/88, 272, 388, 402 *13/322, 449, 462; whare 12/294; wer 3/13; huer 4/82; huere 4/81; quhair 14/60, 140, 160, 208; ◆ compd.: wherfore 12/43, 95, 209; hwer-of *whereof* 4/57; huer-of 4/9, 62; huerof 4/3; quhairof 14/68; quhairin *wherein* 14/211; wermide *wherewith* 8/56; where-so *wherever* 6/182; war sæ 1/64; warto 8/69
whete (sb.) *wheat* 13/212, 215, 538
whi → why
which (pron.) 13/4, 75, 107, 219, 223, 227, 470; whiche 13/40, 147; whuch 10.3/42; wyche 3/30; huyche 4/68; quhilk 14/2, 198, 212, 215, 219; whilk 13/302; whilke 12/14
whil (conj.) *while* 6/138 *10.2/10 *13/35, 100, 259, 491; while 7/84, 125; wile 1/50, 56; wiles 2/26, 48; quhill 14/144, 147, 175
while → whil
while (sb.) *while, space of time* 7/16 *9/29 *13/452; whyle 7/200; quile 6/30; quyle 6/44; ◆ col.: þe ȝwile *while, as long as* 5/3; þe ȝwyle 5/76; þe while 9/47
whilk, wilke → which
whilom (adv.) *once, formerly* 13/279; hwylem 3/35
whils (conj.) *while, as long as* 11/117 *12/55, 111
whistle (1) (inf.) 13/326
whistle (2) (sb.) *pipe, throat* 13/379
white (adj.) 11/94 *12/78 *13/93, 526; whit 7/148 *13/525; whyte 12/89; quhyte 14/165; whittore (comp.) 10.1/14
who (pron.) 7/221 *10.3/9 *10.6/28 *12/233, 318 *13/495, 524; wo 8/61, 64; huo 4/40, 67; quha 14/193, 213, 216; quo 6/142; wha 13/397; ◆ obj.: whome 12/82; wom 8/91; quhome 14/205; ȝwam 5/145, 175; ◆ compd.: whoso *whoever* 12/282; whose 10.8/35; wo so 2/58, 61–62; wua sua 1/10; ho-so 7/182, 193, 207; quo-so 6/93
whodeward (adv.) *whither* 7/155
whome, whose, whoso → who
whuch → which
why (adv.) 10.7/27 *12/99 *13/312, 368; whi 9/24; wy 10.9/8; quhy 14/34, 111, 114, 187
whyle → while
whyle (adv.) *for a while* 10.1/17

whyte → **white**

wicches (sb.pl.) *witch* 2/56

wickit (adj.) *wicked, evil, bad* 14/197, 209, 212, 220, 224; **wikid** 12/234; **wikked** 13/425; **wikkede** 7/18

wickitnes (sb.) *wickedness* 14/200

widderit (ptp.) *to wither* 14/132

wide (adj., adv.) *wide, spacious, far, far and wide* 2/38 *5/184 *9/126; **wyde** 10.3/28 *13/28

widewene (sb.gpl.) *widow* 8/101

wife (sb.) *wife, woman* 11/54; **wif** 7/222 *8/77; **wyf** 7/164, 216 *10.5/48 *13/166, 171, 247, 303, 318, 377, 389, 438, 453, 480, 505, 541; **wiue** 8/106, 114; **wyves** 13/186

wight (sb.) *being* 13/161, 180, 310, 460, 507; **wyht** 10.3/23; **wyhtes** (pl.) 10.3/5

wiis (adj.) *wise* 8/53; **wys** 10.2/12; **wyse** 7/49; **wisest** (sup.) 13/278; **wyseste** 4/44; ◆ neg.: **ounwiis** *unwise* 8/70

wiit; **wikid** → **wit** (1) **wickit**

wikked, wikkede → **wickit**

wil → **will** (1, 2)

wilde (adj.) *wild* 13/289, 305, 396; **wylde** 10.3/5

wile, wiles → **whil**; **will** (2)

will (1) (sb.) *will, volition* 11/16, 26, 54 *12/26, 36 *14/134; **wille** 3/15 *5/12, 24, 138, 165, 175, 178 *7/38 *8/44, 48 *9/28, 102 *10.3/32 *12/297; **wil** 2/56; **wyl** 10.1/2 *13/101, 104, 111; **wyll** 10.9/10, 12–13, 17 *10.10/2; **wylle** 6/42, 139; **iwil** 3/32

will (2) (ps.) *will, desire* 11/2, 27, 49–51, 117 *12/153, 176, 266, 280, 318, 407 *13/410 *14/87, 91, 122, 132, 145; **wille** 2/1 *8/66, 116, 123 *12/208; **willen** 1/83; **wil** 13/253, 260, 265, 309, 335, 357, 402, 433; **wile** 2/18, 43 *8/126; **wyl** 6/30, 60, 82; **wyll** 14/39; **wylle** 4/80; **wylleþ** 4/56; **wylt** 4/38 *6/171; **wol** 10.8/20, 27 *12/18 *13/42, 100, 105, 141, 200, 259, 276–277, 422, 465, 474; **wole** 5/48 *8/88 *10.5/23; **woll** 12/7, 21, 393; **wolle** 10.1/9 *12/218, 240; **wolleth** (pl.) 7/36; **wollez** 5/131, 145; **wolt** 8/122; **wule** 9/26; **wulle** 5/138 *9/49; ◆ pt. and subj.: **wold** 10.10/16; **wolde** 5/14, 16, 22, 102, 178, 190 *6/58, 93–94, 130, 134 *7/38, 155, 220 *8/23, 31–32, 38, 86, 90 *9/31, 77 *10.3/46 *10.8/9 *10.10/4 *12/224, 253, 362 *13/171, 176, 183, 186, 209, 451; **wolden** (pl.) 4/99 *5/76, 124, 162 *13/27; **wulde** 2/19; **wuldes** 2/36; **wald** 11/15, 45–46, 68, 110 *14/28, 73, 88, 118, 139, 161, 171; **walde** 11/59; ◆ neg.: **nelle** 4/74

*5/135 *8/66, 94; **nul** 10.7/8 *10.8/28; **nulle** 10.7/27; **nolde** (sg.pt.) 5/13, 19, 228 *7/110 *8/81 *9/16; **nolden** 5/122, 226; ◆ neg. and contr. 1.2.sg.: **nuly** 10.2/7; **i-nelle** 5/133; **neltou** 8/95; ◆ contr. 1.sg.: **i-chulle** 5/132; **ichulle** 10.1/10; ◆ contr. 2.sg.: **wiltow** 13/264; **woltou** 8/93, 98; **woltow** 7/158

Willam (prn.) *William I* 5/92 *William II* 5/206; **Willam Bastard** *William I* 5/95, 206; **Willame Bastard** 5/63

wille → **will** (1, 2)

Willelm → **Saints**

Willelm Curbuil (prn.) 1/14

Willelm Malduit (prn.) 1/78, 89

willen, wiltow → **will** (2)

wimmen; **win** → **wommon**; **wine**

win (sb.) *riches, possession* 11/63

wind (sb.) 9/17, 37, 126; **wynde** 6/106

winde (inf.) *to go* 8/38; **wond** (sg.pt.) *jumped* 8/11

wine (sb.) 11/76; **win** 3/40; **wyn** 3/5, 7, 20–21, 33, 36, 39 *4/26, 28 *7/148 *14/132; **wyne** 3/9, 15, 17 *6/125; **wynes** (pl.) 4/35

winiærd (sb.) *vineyard* 1/81

winne (inf.) *to win, conquer, fight, come* 5/64 *9/9, 49; **wynne** 6/189 *10.5/60 *12/18, 132, 230, 266 *13/50; **ywynne** 10.8/14; **winnen** (pl.ps.) 2/46; **wan** (sg.pt.) 1/78; **wanne** 12/9, 171; **uuan** 1/79; **wonne** (pl.pt.) 7/24; (ptp.) 12/406; **wonnen** (ptp.) *come* 6/248

winter (sb.) *winter, year* 2/46; **wintre** 1/50, 67–68

Wirecestre (pn.) *Worcester* 5/23, 154, 212, 230; **Wiricestre** 5/10, 51; **Wyrecestre** 5/1; **Wyricestre** 5/6, 27, 45

wirk → **werke**

wise (sb.) *manner, wise* 8/2 *12/25; **wyse** 6/54

wisely (adv.) *surely, certainly* 13/386; **wisly** 13/218

wisest; **wisly** → **wiis**; **wisely**

wisse (sg.ps. subj.) *to guide* 9/99

wiste → **wit** (2)

wit (1) (sb.) *wit, understanding* 7/121 *13/125; **witte** 12/344; **wiit** 8/35, 62; **wyt** 4/89 *6/141, 189; **wytt** 7/38; **wyttes** (pl.) 4/84

wit (2) (inf., ps.) *to know* 11/65, 68, 114; **witte** 12/176, 265, 305; **wyt** 6/42; **wytene** (infl. inf.) 4/5; **wait** (1.sg.ps.) 14/193; **wate** 11/66; **woot** 13/479; **wot** (1./3.sg.ps.) 5/130, 174 *6/24, 141, 186 *7/100 *8/96 *10.4/8 *10.7/1 *10.8/1; **wote** (2.sg.ps.) 12/222; ◆ pt.: **wiste** 3/19 *9/51, 88, 100 *13/51, 506; **weste**

(sg.pt.) 8/30, 119; **wotte** 12/171; **wyste**
6/248; ◆ contr. 1.sg.: **ichot** 10.1/5; ◆ neg.:
not (sg.ps.) 8/80 *10.3/7; **niste** (sg.pt.) 3/18;
nyste 13/449, 524

wite (inf.) *to guard* 5/227; **wuste** (sg.pt.) 5/25,
55

witnes (sb.) *witness* 14/48, 60, 69; **wittenesse**
12/279; **wytnesse** 10.5/36

Witt → **kinde**

witte → **wit** (1, 2)

wittenesse → **witnes**

witterliche (adv.) *truly, for certain* 7/11;
weterly 11/66

with → **right**

with (prep.) *with, against, by, of, near, to,
through* **wið** 1/9 *2/18, 31, 44, 56, 58; **wiþ**
8/124 *9/15–16, 34–35, 39, 53, 69, 77–78,
98, 113, 121 *10.1/8 *10.2/1, 6–7 *10.3/2, 9,
25, 48 *10.4/12, 14, 35–36 *10.5/13, 41, 53
*10.6/3, 22, 52 *10.7/4, 9, 17–18 *10.8/26;
wyth 6/15, 103, 118, 121–122, 151, 171,
271–272; **wyþ** 6/49, 101 *10.8/6, 24; ◆
compd.: **with-alle** (adv.) *at all* 5/19;
with-inne *within* 5/217; **withinne** 13/452;
wiþinne 8/6 *9/18; **withynne** 12/282;
withoute *without* 6/102; **withouten** 12/127,
300, 353 *13/194; **withowten** 12/404;
wiþute 9/41; **wiðuten** 2/55; **wiþouten** 8/13,
71–72; **wyþ-oute** 4/52; **wythoute** 6/132

wiþdroȝe (sg.pt.) *to withdraw* 9/70

wiþsegge (sg.ps.) *to object, contradict* 9/8;
withseide (sg.pt.) 5/103

wiue; wo → **wife; who; woo**

wod (adj.) *mad, insane, raving* 8/129; **wode**
4/84 *10.6/55; **woode** 12/344

woddis, wodds → **wode**

wode → **wod**

wode 8/1, 55 *10.5/2; **woddis** 14/146; **wodds**
14/211

woȝe (inf.) *to woo, love* 9/72; **woweþ** (sg.ps.)
10.3/41; **wowes** (pl.ps.) 10.3/5; **wowyng** (sb.)
10.1/15

wok, woke → **wake**

woke (sb.) *week* 11/11; **wyke** 5/19

woken → **wake**

wol, wold, wolde, wolden, wole → **will** (2)

wolf (sb.) 4/16 *8/54, 59, 63, 65, 69, 75–76,
84, 86, 91, 95, 97, 100, 105, 113, 118,
120–122, 129, 139–141, 144 *13/279
*14/197, 211; **volf** 8/74; **volff** 14/14–15, 20,
25, 29, 32, 36, 50, 61, 67, 76, 83, 87, 107,
111, 127, 134, 138, 149, 153, 169, 185–186,
190, 192; **vuolf** 8/111

woll, wolle, wolleth, wollez → **will** (2)

Wolstan, Wolston → **Saints**

wolt, woltou, woltow → **will** (2)

wom → **who**

wombe (sb.) *body, belly, stomach* 4/20–22, 76
*7/57, 240 *13/514

wommon (sb.) *woman* 10.2/13; **wyman** 3/8;
wymman 10.5/25, 49, 53; **wymmon** 10.2/12
*10.3/25 *10.8/3; **wymmen** (pl.) 10.1/6
*10.3/10, 13, 37; **wimmen** 1/36 *8/4

won → **wanne**

won (sb.) *dwelling, abode* 6/44 *10.3/28;
wones (pl.) 7/18

wonand, wond → **wunen; winde**

wonde (inf., ps.) *to neglect, refrain* 6/275
*10.2/7

wonder (1) (sb.) *wonder, marvel; atrocity*
5/159, 183 *6/16, 254, 267 *10.6/44;
wunder 2/53 *9/35, 81; (pl.) 1/30, 49;
wonderes (pl.) 5/44; **wonderez** 6/29;
wondres 7/4

wonder (2) (adv.) *wonderfully, amazingly*
10.7/16 *11/89

wonderes, wonderez → **wonder** (1)

wondes → **wounde**

wondrede (sg.pt.) *to wonder* 5/150, 158

wondres; wone, woned, woneden →
wonder; wunen

wones → **won**

wonges (sb.pl.) *cheek* 10.1/11 *10.7/34

**wonne, wonnen, wonnes, wonnys, wont,
wonyes** → **winne; wunen**

wonyng (sb.) *dwelling* 13/62

woo (sb.) *woe, grief* 12/18, 266, 379; **wooe**
12/300; **wo** 7/10, 216 *8/1, 27, 34, 48, 51,
73, 82, 143 *9/127 *10.2/5 *10.6/30
*10.8/14, 28 *11/78 *13/424; **wa** 14/220;
waa 12/406

woode; wooe → **wod; woo**

woot → **wit** (2)

worche (inf.) *to work* 7/38; **worchyng** (psp.)
7/21; **ywroht** (ptp.) 10.3/32

word (sb.) 5/20 *7/221 *8/66 *11/24, 27
*13/291, 472 *14/21; **worde** 6/101; **wordes**
(pl.) 5/119 *6/99, 112 *7/70 *8/74 *9/27
*11/31

wore (sb.) *eddy* 10.1/15

world (sb.) 5/201 *7/4, 10, 21, 100, 104, 216
*10.1/13 *10.3/28 *10.5/59 *13/100; **worlde**
5/208 *8/75, 81–82; **worldes** (gsg.) 6/48
*8/81 *10.3/42; **werldes** 11/63

worly (adj.) *beautiful* 10.3/10

worse (adj., adv. comp.) 7/183, 186 *12/320;
werse 1/57 *12/200; **uuerse** 1/51; **werre**

12/334; ♦ col.: **the wers** 13/96; **the wors**
7/104; **þe wors** 8/101
worth, worþ, worþe, worþed → **wurðeð**
worth (adj.) 7/76 *14/56, 132; **worþ** 4/25, 37
worþilych (adj.) *honoured* 6/130
worthi; worthit → **worthy; wurðeð**
worthy (adj.) 12/132, 324, 357 *13/206;
   worthi 11/37; **wuyrþe** 5/120, 130, 172, 174,
   177; **worthyest** (sup.) 6/48; ♦ neg.: **vnwurþe**
   5/131
wot, wote, wotte → **wit** (2)
woþe (sb.) *danger* 6/275
wouȝ (sb.) *error* 5/100
wounde (sb.) *wound* 10.4/39 *10.7/4, 28
   *13/177; **wund** 9/41; **wunde** 2/55; **woundes**
   (pl.) 10.4/35 *10.6/8; **wounden** 10.7/30;
   wondes 10.6/48; **wundes** 9/82
wous (adj.) *eager* 8/6
wowes, woweþ, wowyng → **woȝe**
wox; woxe → **foxe; waxe**
wrake (sb.) *distress* 6/16
wrang → **wrong**
wrastle (inf.) *to wrestle* 13/152
wrathþe (sb.) *wrath* 5/114
wrecce (adj.) *wretched, poor* 1/49, 55;
   uurecce 1/33, 52
wreccehed (sb.) *misery* 1/57
wrecche (sb.) *wretch* 8/127; **wreche** 4/72
   *8/144
wrecchednesse (sb.) *misery* 13/121
wreche → **wrecche**
wreche (inf.) *to avenge* 9/12; **wroken** (ptp.)
   12/199
wreke (sb.) *revenge* 12/191
wrenche (sb.) *trick, wile* 8/42; **wrinkis** (pl.)
   14/148
wrengðe (sb.) *deformation* 2/17
wreþi (inf.) *to become angry* 4/99
wrighte (sb.) *workman* 13/70; **write** 12/230
wrinkis → **wrenche**
writ (sb.) *writ, document* 14/48; **holy writ** *the
   Holy Bible* 7/104; **hooly writ** 13/126
write → **wrighte**
writeth (sg.ps.) *to write* 13/93; **iwriten** (ptp.)
   8/102
wroggen (sb.pl.) *frog* 8/128
wroȝt, wroȝte, wroȝten → **werke**
wroht; wrohte → **wroth; werke**
wroken → **wreche**
wrong (adj., adv., sb.) 10.4/47; *twisted* 2/4, 14;
   wronge 10.8/6; **wrang** 12/264–265, 305
   *13/476
wroth (adj.) *wrath, angry* 6/106; **wroþ** 8/110;
   wrothþ 5/107; **wroht** 10.7/16; ♦ col.: **þe
   wrother** 7/117

wroþe (adv.) *fiercely* 8/146
wu; wua → **how; who**
wulde, wuldes, wule, wulle → **will** (2)
Wulston → **Saints**
wund, wunde → **wounde**
wunder → **wonder** (1)
wunderlice (adj.) *wonderful* 1/89
wundes → **wounde**
wunen (inf.) *to live, reside* 2/46–47; **wone**
   6/44; **wonne** 12/15, 168, 228, 239; **wuneð**
   (sg.ps.) 2/44; **wunieþ** 9/33; **woneþ** 10.2/13
   *10.5/56; **wonnes** (ps.) 12/379; **wonnys**
   12/235; **wonyes** 6/186; **wonand** (psp.) 11/36,
   38; **woned** (sg.pt.) 7/18; **woneden** (pl.pt.)
   8/131; **wond** (ptp.) 11/39; **woned** *wont* 8/53
   *10.5/52; **wont** 6/17 *11/70, 91
wurðeð (sg.ps.) *to become, grow* 2/12; **worþ**
   8/124; **worth** 14/220; **worþe** 8/48, 96;
   warth (sg.pt.) 1/5; **werþ** 8/33; **uuard** 1/2;
   wurðe (pl.pt.) 1/20; **wurþen** 1/4; **worþed**
   (sg.pt. impv. (weak)) 6/272; **worthit** 14/23, 27
wurche → **werke**
wurtscipe (sb.) *honour* 1/72
wuschen; wuste → **wesse; wite**
wuyrþe; wy → **worthy; why**
wyche; wyde → **which; wide**
wyf → **wife**
wyȝ (sb.) *man, knight* 6/171; **wyȝe** 6/39;
   wyȝes (gsg.) 6/101
wyȝtest (adj. sup.) *valiant* 6/48
wyht, wyhtes; wyke → **wight; woke**
wyke (sg.ps.) *to languish* 10.6/53
wyl → **will** (1, 2)
wyld (ptp.) *to beguile* 14/211
wylde → **wilde**
wyle (sb.) *trick* 13/271 *14/151
wyll, wylle → **will** (1, 2)
wylleþ → **will** (2)
wylly (adj.) *deceitful* 10.9/4
wylt → **will** (2)
wyman, wymman, wymmen, wymmon →
   wommon
wyn; wynde → **wine; wind**
wyne, wynes → **wine**
wynkyng (psp.) *to wink* 7/11
wynne → **winne**
wynne (sb.) *joy, bliss* 6/15 *10.6/59
wynners (sb.pl.) *workman* 7/141
wypinge (sb.) *weeping* 10.6/3
Wyrecestre, Wyricestre → **Wirecestre**
wys, wyse → **wiis; wise**
wyseste → **wiis**
wyste, wyt → **wit** (1, 2)

wyte (sb.) *blame* 14/137
wytene → wit (2)
wyter (adj.) *wise* 10.1/13
wyteþ (sg.ps.) *to blame* 10.8/6
wyth, wyþ, wyþ-oute, wythoute → with
wytnesse → witnes
wytt; wyttes → kinde; wit (1)
wyves → wife

X

xal, xall → shall

Y

Y → I
yaf → give
ybake (ptp.) *to bake* 13/536
ybete → bete (1)
yblessed → iblessed
yboht; ybounde → buy; bind
ybroht → bring
ybrokene → breke
y-by → be
ycast; ych → cast; I
ychabbe → have
ychose → cheosen
y-come, ycomen → come (2)
ycrammed (ptp.) *to cram* 7/42
ydele (adj.) *idle* 4/60
y-do → do
ydolatrie (sb.) *idolatry* 7/96
ydon → do
ydres (sb.) *tub, vat* 3/12–13
ydronke → drinke
ye → eye; ȝe
ye (adv.) *yes, yea* 13/322, 398, 492
yede → go
yeer (sb.) *year* 13/57, 113, 194–195; gær 1/5,
   68, 80; gære 1/1, 21; ȝeir 14/4; ȝer 5/28, 57,
   203, 207, 209; ȝere 5/205 *10.3/21, (pl.)
   11/39 *12/39, 354; ȝeres (pl.) 7/63; yeris
   13/93
yef; yefþes → if; gift
yelde (inf.) *to give, repay, requite, confess*
   4/51, 84; ȝelde (sg.ps.) 7/226; ȝolden (ptp.)
   6/240; i-ȝolden 5/144; yeldynge (sb.) 13/52
yeme (sb.) *heed* 4/41
yemer (adj.) *evil, bad* 3/32; yemere (pl.) 3/32
yendles; yeris → endles; yeer
yerne (inf.) *to hasten, run* 4/45; yernþ (sg.ps.)
   4/16
yes → eye

yesteneuen (adv.) *last night* 4/27
yet (adv.) 3/36 *13/68, 106, 112, 262, 273,
   277, 320, 345, 400, 427, 535; gæt 1/57; get
   1/23; ȝeot 5/77, 90, 98, 164; ȝet 2/14, 30–31,
   36 *6/84, 252 *8/77; ȝit 11/93, 115 *14/15,
   88, 120, 151, 195; ȝitt 12/136, 373; ȝut
   7/137, 242; ȝutt 9/50; ȝuyt 5/230
yeve → give
yexeth (sg.ps.) *to belch* 13/375
yf; y-faith → if; faith
yfalle → fall
y-fayth; yfel → faith; euel
yfostred (ptp.) *to educate, raise* 13/170
yglobbed (ptp.) *to gulp down* 7/198
ygrounde → grynde
ygrowen (ptp.) *to grow* 13/197
yȝe-lyddez (sb.pl.) *eyelid* 6/233
yȝen → eye
yȝyrned → ȝerne (2)
yhent → hente
yhere, y-herþ, y-hyerd → hear
ylaft; yleaue → leave; leue
ylefth → believe
ylent → lende
ylle → ill
ylong (adj.) *dependend* 10.4/10; long 10.2/4
ylost → leose
ylyk → like (1)
ymake, ymaked → make (2)
ymel → emell
Ynde (pn.) *India* 10.3/12
ynoȝe → enough
ynoȝliche (adv.) *enough* 4/58
ynoh → enough
ynorissed (ptp.) *to educate* 13/172
yomanrye (sb.) *free birth* 13/173
yon, yone → ȝone
yonge (adj.) *young* 13/7, 226; ȝong 5/3; ȝonge
   (pl.) 9/66; ȝoung 14/10; ȝynge 10.5/22
yoore → full (2)
youe, your, youre, yourseluen → ȝe (2)
youthe (sb.) *youth* 13/69
yow → ȝe (2)
ypayd; yplyht → pay; plighten
yreke (ptp.) *to rake over, cover* 13/106
yren → iren
Yrisse → Irisse
Yrlonde → Irlond
yronne → ryn
ys → be; he
Ysaias (prn.) *Isaiah* 12/50
ysene; ysent → see; send
yserued; yset → serve; sette

yshadwed (ptp.) *to shadow* 13/63
yshapen → **shappis**
yshorn (ptp.) *to shear, cut* 13/45
ysi → **see**
ysped → **spede**
yspred (ptp.) *to spread* 13/364
yswoʒe (ptp.) *to swoon* 9/110
ytoold; ythryueth → **tell; þryue**
yu → **ʒe** (2)
yueld → **feld** (2)
yuele, yvele → **euel**
ywedde → **wedden**
ywet (ptp.) *to wet* 13/379
ywroht → **worche**
ywynne → **winne**
yzed → **say**
y-zycþ → **see**

Z

Zabulon (pn.) 12/52
zayþ; ze → **say; se** (2)
zeche; zecheþ → **sak; seke**
zede; zelþ → **say; selleþ**
zeneʒeþ → **synne**
zenne, zennen, zennes → **sin**
Zephirus (prn.) 13/5
zeuende (ord.) *seventh* 4/1–2
zigge; zoþe → **say; for**
zuelʒ (sb.) *swallowing, eating* 4/3, 61, 64, 72
zuerie → **swere**
zuetnesse (sb.) *sweetness* 4/52–53
zuich, zuiche; zuo → **such; so**
zuych, zuyche → **such**
zuyn → **swyn**

8. Bibliography

Journals are abbreviated according to the *MLA International Bibliography*. Editions of the *Early English Text Society* (EETS) are abbreviated with "O.S." and "S.S." for "Original Series" and "Supplementary Series".

AERS, D. (1975), *Piers Plowman and Christian Allegory* (London).

AITKEN, A. J. (1977), "How to Pronounce Older Scots?", in: *Bards and Makars. Scottish Language and Literature: Medieval and Renaissance*, ed. A. J. Aitken, M. P. McDiarmid, D. S. Thomson, pp. 1–21 (Glasgow).

ALLEN, R., ED. (1984), *King Horn: An Edition Based on Cambridge University Library MS Gg.4.27 2* (New York).

ARENS, W. (1973), *Die anglonormannische und die englischen Fassungen des Hornstoffes: Ein historisch-genetischer Vergleich* (Frankfurt).

BÄHR, D. (1997), *Einführung ins Mittelenglische*, 4th ed. (Munich).

BÄHR, D. (2001), *Einführung in das Altenglische* (Munich).

BAKER, P. S. (2003), *Introduction to Old English* (Oxford).

BARBER, C. (2006) *Early modern English* (Edinburgh).

BARRON, W. R. J. (1987), *English Medieval Romance* (London).

BATELY, J. (1970), "King Alfred and the Old English Translation of Orosius", *Anglia* 88, 433–460.

BATELY, J., ED. (1980), *The Old English Orosius*, EETS S.S. 6 (London).

BAUGH, A. C. / CABLE, T. (1978), *A History of the English Language*, 3rd ed. (London).

BAYLESS, M. (2009), "The Text and the Body in Middle English Seduction Lyrics", *Neophilologus*, 93, 165–174.

BEADLE, R., ED. (1982), *The York Plays* (London).

BEADLE, R., ED. (2009), *The York Plays. A Critical Edition of the York Corpus Christi Play as Recorded in British Library Additional MS 35290*, EETS S.S. 23 (Oxford).

BENNETT, J. A. W. / SMITHERS, G. V., ED. (1968), *Early Middle English Verse and Prose*, 2nd rev. ed. (Oxford).

BENSON, L. D. (1965), *Art and Tradition in Sir Gawain and the Green Knight* (New Brunswick).

BENSON, L. D., ED. (1987), *The Riverside Chaucer*, 3rd ed. (Boston).

BERCOVITCH, S. (1966), "Clerical Satire in *The Vox and the Wolf*", *JEGP* 65, 287–294.

BERGNER, H. (1973), "*The Fox and the Wolf* und die Gattung des Tierepos in der mittelenglischen Literatur", *GRM* NF 23, 268–285.

BERGNER, H. (1983), "Die mittelenglische Lyrik", in: *Lyrik des Mittelalters II: Probleme und Interpretationen*, ed. H. Bergner, pp. 229–379 (Stuttgart).

BERNDT, R. (1960), *Einführung in das Studium des Mittelenglischen* (Halle).

BERNDT, R. (1982), *A History of the English Language* (Leipzig).

BETHURUM, D. (1932), "The Form of Ælfric's *Lives of the Saints*", *SP* 29, 515–533.

BETHURUM, D., ED. (1957), *The Homilies of Wulfstan* (Oxford).

BLAKE, N., ED. (1992), *The Cambridge History of the English Language. Vol. II: 1066–1476* (Cambridge).

BLOOMFIELD, M. W. (1963), *Piers Plowman as a Fourteenth Century Apocalypse* (New Brunswick).

BÖDDEKER, K., ED. (1878), *Altenglische Dichtungen des Ms. Harl. 2253* (Berlin).

BOROFF, M. (1962), *Sir Gawain and the Green Knight: A Stylistic and Metrical Study* (New Haven).

BREDEHOFT, T. A. (2005), *Early English Metre* (Toronto).

BROOK, G. L., ED. (1968), *The Harley Lyrics*, 4th ed. (Manchester).

BRUNNER, K. (1960–62), *Die englische Sprache*, 2 vols. (Tübingen).

BRUNNER, K. (1965), *Altenglische Grammatik*, 3rd ed. (Tübingen).

BRUNNER, K. (1967), *Abriß der mittelenglischen Grammatik*, 6th ed. (Tübingen).

BURROW, J. A. (1965), *A Reading of Sir Gawain and the Green Knight* (London).

BURROW, J. A. / TURVILLE-PETRE, T. (1996), *A Book of Middle English*, 2nd ed. (Oxford).

CAMPBELL, A. (1974), *Old English Grammar* (Oxford).

CLARK, C., ED. (1970), *The Peterborough Chronicle, 1070–1154*, 2nd ed. (Oxford).

CLARK, G. (1968), "The Battle of Maldon: A Heroic Poem", *Speculum* 43, 52–71.

COLLIER, R. J. (1978), *Poetry and Drama in the York Corpus Christi Play* (Hamden).

COOKE, T. D. (1978), *The Old French and Chaucerian Fabliaux: A Study of Their Comic Climax* (Columbia).

CRAWFORD, S. J., ED. (1922), *The Old English Version of the Heptateuch, Ælfric's Treatise on the Old and New Testament and His Preface to Genesis*, EETS O.S. 160 (London).

DAVENPORT, A. W. (1978), *The Art of the 'Gawain'-Poet* (London).

DAVIDSON, C. (1977), "From *Tristia* to *Gaudium*: Iconography and the York-Towneley *Harrowing of Hell*", *ABR* 28, 260–275.

DIEKSTRA, F. N. M. (1985), "The *Physiologus*, the Bestiaries and Medieval Animal Lore", *Neophil* 69, 142–155.

DOBBIE, E. V. K., ED. (1942), *The Anglo-Saxon Minor Poems*, The Anglo Saxon Poetic Records, 6 (New York and London).

DU BOULAY, F. R. H. (1991), *The England of* Piers Plowman. *William Langland and His Vision of the Fourteenth Century* (Cambridge).

DUCKETT, E. S. (1956), *Alfred the Great: The King and His England* (Chicago).

EINENKEL, E., ED. (1884), *The Life of St. Katherine*, EETS O.S. 80 (Oxford).

EKBLOM, R. (1960), "King Alfred, Ohthere and Wulfstan", *SN* 32, 3–13.

ELLIOTT, C., ED. (1974), *Robert Henryson, Poems*, 2nd ed. (Oxford).

FAISS, K. (1989), *Englische Sprachgeschichte* (Tübingen).

FICHTE, J. O. / KEMMLER, F., ED. (1989), *Geoffrey Chaucer, Die Canterbury-Erzählungen: Mittelenglisch und Deutsch*, 3 vols. (Munich).

FLOWER, R. / SMITH, H. ED. (1941), *The Parker Chronicle and Laws. A Facsimile*, EETS O.S. 208 (London).

FÖRSTER, M. (1955), "A New Version of the Apocalypse of Thomas in Old English", *Anglia* 83, 6–36.

FOX, D., ED. (1981), *The Poems of Robert Henryson* (Oxford).

FRANK, R. W. (1957), *Piers Plowman and the Scheme of Salvation* (New Haven).

FRESE, D. W. (1986), "Poetic Prowess in *Brunanburh* and *Maldon*: Winning, Losing, and Literary Outcome", in: *Modes of Interpretation in Old English Literature. Essays in Honour of Stanley B. Greenfield*, ed. P. R. Brown, G. R. Crampton and F. C. Robinson, pp. 83–99 (Toronto).

FRIES, U. (1985), *Einführung in die Sprache Chaucers. Phonologie, Metrik und Morphologie*, Anglistische Arbeitshefte, 20 (Tübingen).

GARMONSWAY, G. N., trans. (1954), *The Anglo-Saxon Chronicle*, 2nd ed. (London).

GEROULD, G. H. (1905), "The Hermit and the Saint", *PMLA* 20, 529–545.

GNEUSS, H. (1976), "*The Battle of Maldon* 89: Byrhtnoth's *ofermode* Once Again", *SP* 73, 117–137.

GÖRLACH, M. (1994), *Einführung ins Frühneuenglische* (Heidelberg).

[GOLLANCZ] (1923), *Pearl, Cleanness, Patience and Sir Gawain. Reproduced in Facimile from the Unique MS. Cotton Nero A.x in the British Museum. With an Introduction by I. Gollancz*, EETS O.S. 162 (London).

GOODRIDGE, J. F., trans. (1959), *Piers Plowman* (Harmondsworth).

GOOLDEN, P., ED. (1958), *The Old English Apollonius of Tyre* (London).

GOPEN, G. D., ED. (1987), *Robert Henryson, The Moral Fables of Aesop* (Notre Dame, Ind. – with translation).

GRAY, D. (1979), *Robert Henryson* (Leiden).

GREEN, R. L., ED. (1977), *The Early English Carols*, 2nd ed. (Oxford).

GRIFFITHS, L. (1985), *Personification in Piers Plowman* (Cambridge).

HALL, J., ED. (1920), *Early Middle English*, 2 vols. (Oxford).

HILL, D. M. (1957), "An Interpretation of *King Horn*", *Anglia* 75, 157–172.

HOGG, R. M., ED. (1992), *The Cambridge History of the English Language. Vol. I: The Beginnings to 1066* (Cambridge).

HOGG, R. M. (1992), *A Grammar of Old English. Vol. 1: Phonology* (Oxford).

HOGG, R. (2002), *An Introduction to Old English* (Oxford).

HOROBIN, S. / SMITH, J. (2002), *An Introduction to Middle English* (Oxford).

HORSTMANN, C., ED. (1887), *The Early South English Legendary or Lives of Saints*, EETS O.S. 87 (London).

HOWELL, R. B. (1991), *Old English Breaking and its Germanic Analogues*, Linguistische Arbeiten, 253 (Tübingen).

JANKOFSKY, K. P., ED. (1992), *The South English Legendary: A Critical Assessment* (Tübingen).

JOHNSON, A. S. (1968), "The Rhetoric of Brunanburh", *PQ* 47, 487–493.

JOHNSTON, A. J. (2001), *Clerks and Courtiers. Chaucer, Late Middle English Literature and the State Formation Process* (Heidelberg).

JONES, C. (1989), *A History of English Phonology* (London and New York).

JORDAN, R. (1968), *Handbuch der mittelenglischen Grammatik. Lautlehre*, 3rd ed. (Heidelberg).

JORDAN, R. (1974), *Handbook of Middle English Grammar: Phonology*, tr. and rev. by E. J. Crook, Janua Linguarum, Series Practica, 218 (The Hague, Paris).

KEMMLER, F. (2002), "Facts and Fictions – The Norman Conquest" in: *War and the Cultural Construction of Identities in Britain*, ed. B. Korte and R. Schneider, Internationale Forschungen zur Allgemeinen und Vergleichenden Literaturwissenschaft, 59, pp. 39–60 (Amsterdam, New York).

KELLNER, L. (1892; 1974), *Historical Outlines of English Syntax* (New York).

KER, N. R., ED. (1956), *The Pastoral Care. King Alfred's Translation of St. Gregory's Regula Pastoralis*, Early English Manuscripts in Facsimile, 6 (Copenhagen).

[KER] (1965), *Facsimile of British Museum MS. Harley 2253. With an Introduction by N. R. Ker*, EETS O.S. 255 (London).

KLAEBER, F. (1923), „Zu König Alfreds Vorrede zu seiner Übersetzung der *Cura Pastoralis*", *Anglia* 48, 53–65.

KOLVE, V. A. (1984), *Chaucer and the Imagery of Narrative* (London).

KUHN, S. M. (1973), "Was Ælfric a Poet?", *PQ* 52, 643–642.

LAING, M. (1993), *Catalogue of Sources for a Linguistic Atlas of Early Medieval English* (Cambridge).

LASS, R. (1994), *Old English. A Historical Linguistic Companion* (Cambridge).

LASS, R., ED. (1999), *The Cambridge History of the English Language. Vol. III: 1476–1776* (Cambridge).

LAWLER, T. (1973), "*Brunanburh*: Craft and Art", *Literary Studies: Essays in Memory of Francis A. Drumm*, ed. J. H. Dorenkamp, pp. 52–67 (Wetteren).

LAWLOR, J. (1962), *Piers Plowman: An Essay in Criticism* (London).

LEE, N. A. (1972), "The Unity of *The Dream of the Rood*", *Neophil* 54, 469–486.

LEHNERT, M. (1990), *Altenglisches Elementarbuch*, 10th ed. (Berlin).

LIGGINS, L. M. (1970), "The Authorship of the Old English *Orosius*", *Anglia* 88, 289–322.

LIPP, F. R. (1969), "Ælfric's Old English Prose Style", *SP* 66, 689–718.

LOYN, H. R., ED. (1971), *A Wulfstan Manuscript: Containing Institutes, Laws and Homilies. British Museum Cotton Nero A. I*, Early English Manuscripts in Facsimile, 17 (Copenhagen).

LUICK, K. (1964; 1914–1940), *Historische Grammatik der englischen Sprache.* Neudruck, ed. F. Wild und H. Koziol (Stuttgart).

LURIA, M. S. / HOFFMAN, R. L., ED. (1974), *Middle English Lyrics* (New York).

LUTZ, A. (1991), *Phonotaktisch gesteuerte Konsonantenveränderungen in der Geschichte des Englischen*, Linguistische Arbeiten, 272 (Tübingen).

MANN, J. (1973), *Chaucer and Medieval Estates Satire: The Literature of Social Classes and the General Prologue to* The Canterbury Tales (Cambridge).

MARKUS, M., ED. (1974), *Sir Gawain and the Green Knight – Sir Gawain und der Grüne Ritter* (Stuttgart).

MARKUS, M. (1990), *Mittelenglisches Studienbuch* (Tübingen).

MARSDEN, R., ED. (2004), *The Cambridge Old English Reader* (Cambridge).

MARSDEN, R., ED. (2008), *The Old English Heptateuch and Ælfric's Libellus de Veteri Testamento et Novo*, EETS O.S. 330 (Oxford).

MCINTOSH, A., SAMUELS, M. L., BENSKIN, M., ED. (1986), *A Linguistic Atlas of Late Medieval English*, 4 vols. (Edinburgh).

MCKNIGHT, G. H., ED. (1901), *King Horn, Floriz and Blauncheflur, The Assumption of Our Lady*, EETS O.S. 14 (London).

MCKNIGHT, G. H., ED. (1913), *Middle English Humorous Tales in Verse* (Boston and London).

MILLER, T., ED. (1890–98), *The Old English Version of Bede's Ecclesiastical History of the English People*, 4 vols., EETS O.S. 95, 96, 110, 111 (London – with translation).

MINKOVA, D. (1982), "The Environment for Open Syllable Lengthening in Middle English", *FLH* 3, 29–58.

MINKOVA, D. (1991), *The History of Final Vowels in English: The Sound of Muting*, Topics in English Linguistics, 4 (Berlin, New York).

MITCHELL, B. (1985), *Old English Syntax* (Oxford).

MITCHELL, B. (1995), *An Invitation to Old English and Anglo-Saxon England* (Oxford).

MITCHELL, B. / ROBINSON, F. C. (1992), *A Guide to Old English*, 5th ed. (Oxford).

MOESSNER, L. (2003), *Diachronic English Linguistics*, Narr Studienbücher (Tübingen).

MOESSNER, L. / SCHAEFER, U. (1987), *Proseminar Mittelenglisch*, 2nd ed. (Tübingen).

MOORE, A. K. (1951), *The Secular Lyric in Middle English* (Lexington).

MORRIS, R., ED. (1872), *An Old English Miscellany*, EETS O.S. 49 (London).

MORRIS, R., ED. (1965), *Dan Michael's Ayenbite of Inwyt, or Remorse of Conscience*, 2nd ed., ed. P. Gradon, EETS O.S. 23 (London).

MOSSÉ, F. (1969), *Handbuch des Mittelenglischen* (Munich).

NEEDHAM, G. I., ED. (1976), *Ælfric: Lives of Three English Saints*, 2nd ed. (Exeter).

NEVANLINNA, S., ED. (1972–84), *The Northern Homily Cycle*, 3 vols., Mémoires de la Société Néophilologique de Helsinki, 38, 41, 43 (Helsinki).

NICHOLS, A. (1971), "Ælfric and the Brief Style", *JEGP* 70, 1–12.

OBST, W. / SCHLEBURG, F. (1999), *Die Sprache Chaucers. Ein Lehrbuch des Mittelenglischen auf der Grundlage von »Troilus and Criseyde«* (Heidelberg).

OBST, W. / SCHLEBURG, F. (2004), *Lehrbuch des Altenglischen* (Heidelberg).

ORTON, P. (1980), "The Technique of Object-Personification in *The Dream of the Rood* and a Comparison with the Old English Riddles", *LeedsSE* 11, 1–18.

PANTIN, W. A. (1955), *The English Church in the Fourteenth Century* (Cambridge).

PATTERSON, L. (1991), *Chaucer and the Subject of History* (Madison).

PEARSALL, D., ED. (1978), *Piers Plowman by William Langland: An Edition of the C-text* (London).

PEARSALL, D. (1985), *The Canterbury Tales* (London).

PFANDER, H. G. (1936), "Some Medieval Manuals of Religious Instruction in England and Observations on Chaucer's *Parson's Tale*", *JEGP* 35, 243–258.

PILCH, H. (1970), *Altenglische Grammatik* (Munich).

PINSKER, H. E. (1969), *Historische englische Grammatik: Elemente der Laut-, Formen- und Wortbildungslehre*, 3rd ed. (Munich).

PINSKER, H. E. (1976), *Altenglisches Studienbuch* (Düsseldorf).

PLUMMER, C. / EARLE, J., ED. (1892–99), *Two of the Saxon Chronicles Parallel*, 2 vols. (Oxford).

POWELL, M. (1983), *Fabula Docet: Studies in the Background and Interpretation of Henryson's Moral Fables*, Odense University Studies in English, 6 (Odense).

PRATT, R. A., ED. (1974), *The Tales of Canterbury* (Boston).

PYLES, T., ALGEO, T. (2004), *The Origins and Development of the English Language*, 5th ed. (New York).

QUIRK, R. / WRENN, C. L. (1973), *An Old English Grammar* (London).

RAITH, J., ED. (1956), *Die alt- und mittelenglischen Apollonius-Bruchstücke* (Munich).

REISS, E. (1972), *The Art of the Middle English Lyric* (Athens).

ROBERTSON, D. W. / HUPPÉ, B. F. (1951), *Piers Plowman and the Scriptural Tradition* (Princeton).

ROBINSON, F. N., ED. (1957), *The Works of Geoffrey Chaucer*, 2nd ed., (London).

ROBSON, C. A. (1952), *Maurice of Sully and the Medieval Vernacular Homily* (Oxford).

ROMAINE, S., ED. (1998), *The Cambridge History of the English Language. Vol. IV: 1776–1997* (Cambridge).

SALTER, E. (1962), *Piers Plowman: An Introduction* (Oxford).

SAMUELS, M. L. (1963), "Some Applications of Middle English Dialectology", *ES* 44, 81–94.

SAMUELS, M. L. (1972), *Linguistic Evolution. With Special Reference to English*, Cambridge Studies in Linguistics, 5 (Cambridge).

SAMUELS, M. L. (1983a), "Chaucer's Spelling", in: *Middle English Studies Presented to Norman Davis in Honour of His Seventieth Birthday*, ed. D. Gray and E. G. Stanley, pp. 17–37 (Oxford).

SAMUELS, M. L. (1983b), "The Scribe of the Hengwrt and Ellesmere Manuscripts of *The Canterbury Tales*", *SAC* 5, 49–65.

SAMUELS, M. L. (1985), "Langland's Dialect", *MÆ* 54, 232–247.

SAMUELS, M. L. (1988), "Dialect and Grammar", in: *A Companion to* Piers Plowman, ed. J. A. Alford (Berkeley, Los Angeles, London).

SANDS, D. B., ED. (1966), *Middle English Verse Romances* (New York).

SANDVED, A. O. (1985), *Introduction to Chaucerian English* (Cambridge).

SCHIPPER, J., ED. (1899), *König Alfreds Übersetzung von Bedas Kirchengeschichte*, Bibliothek der angelsächsischen Prosa, 4 (Leipzig).

SCHIRMER, W. F. (1983), *Geschichte der englischen und amerikanischen Literatur. Von den Anfängen bis zur Gegenwart*, 6th rev. ed., ed. A. Esch, 2 vols. (Tübingen).

SCRAGG, D. G. (1974), *A History of English spelling* (Manchester).

SCRAGG, D. G. (1991), *The Battle of Maldon A.D. 991* (Oxford).

SHORES, D. L. (1971), *A Descriptive Syntax of the Peterborough Chronicle from 1122 to 1154* (The Hague).

SISAM, C., ED. (1976), *The Vercelli Book: A Late Tenth-century Manuscript Containing Prose and Verse*, Early English Manuscripts in Facsimile, 19 (Copenhagen).

SKEAT, W. W., ED. (1881–1900), *Ælfric's Lives of Saints*, 4 vols, EETS O.S. 76, 82, 94, 114 (London).

SKEAT, W. W., ED. (1886), *The Vision of William Concerning Piers the Plowman, in Three Parallel Texts*, 2 vols. (Oxford).

SMITH, L. T., ED. (1885), *York Plays* (Oxford).

SPEARING, A. C. (1970), *The Gawain-Poet: A Critical Study* (Cambridge).

STEMMLER, T., ED. (1970), *Medieval English Love-Lyrics* (Tübingen).

STRANG, B. M. H. (1970), *A History of English* (London).

SWANTON, M., ED. (1970), *The Dream of the Rood* (Manchester).

SWANTON, M., ED. AND TR. (1996), *The Anglo-Saxon Chronicle* (London).

SWEET, H., ED. (1871), *King Alfred's West-Saxon Version of Gregory's Pastoral Care*, 2 vols., EETS O.S. 45, 50 (London).

SWEET, H., ED. (1883), *King Alfred's Orosius*, EETS O.S. 79 (London).

SWEET, H. (1967), *Sweet's Anglo-Saxon Reader in Prose and Verse*, rev. ed., ed. D. Whitelock (Oxford).

THOMPSON, A. B. (2002), *Everyday Saints and the Art of Narrative in the South English Legendary* (Ashgate).

THORPE, B., ED. (1861), *The Anglo-Saxon Chronicle According to the Several Original Authorities*, 2 vols. (London).

TOLKIEN, J. R. R. / GORDON, E. V., ED. (1967), *Sir Gawain and the Green Knight*, 2nd ed., ed. Norman Davis (Oxford).

TOWERS, T. H. (1963), "Thematic Unity in the Story of Cynewulf and Cyneheard", *JEGP*, 62, 310–316.

TREHARNE, E., ED. (2004), *Old and Middle English c.890-c.1400. An Anthology*, 2nd ed. (Oxford).

[TSCHANN] (1996), *Facsimile of Oxford, Bodleian Library, MS Digby 86. With an Introd. by J. Tschann and M. B. Parkes*, EETS S.S. 16 (London).

TURVILLE-PETRE, J. (1976), "The Metre of *Sir Gawain and the Green Knight*", *ES* 57, 310–328.

VASTA, E. (1965), *The Spiritual Basis of Piers Plowman* (The Hague).

VON KREISLER, N. (1970), "Satire in *The Vox and the Wolf*", *JEGP* 69, 650–658.

WALDRON, R. A., ED. (1970), *Sir Gawain and the Green Knight* (Evanston).

WEIMANN, K. (1990), *Einführung ins Altenglische*, 2nd ed. (Heidelberg).

WENZEL, S. (1986), *Preachers, Poets, and the Early English Lyric* (Princeton).

WETHERBEE, W. (1989), *Geoffrey Chaucer: The Canterbury Tales* (Cambridge).

WHITE, B. (1954), "Medieval Animal Lore", *Anglia* 72, 21–30.

WHITELOCK, D. (1963), "The Old English Bede", *PBA* 48, 57–90.

WHITELOCK, D., ED. (1976), *Sermo Lupi ad Anglos* (Exeter).

WILCOX, J. (2000), "The Wolf on Shepherds: Wulfstan, Bishops, and the Context of the *Sermo Lupi ad Anglos*", in: *Old English Prose: Basic Readings* ed. P. E. Szarmach, pp. 395–418 (New York).

WILLIAMS, J. M. (1975), *Origins of the English Language* (New York).

WIRTJES, H., ED. (1991), *The Middle English* Physiologus, EETS O.S. 299 (Oxford).

WOLPERS, T. (1964), *Die englische Heiligenlegende des Mittelalters* (Tübingen).

WOOLF, R. (1958), "Doctrinal Influences on *The Dream of the Rood*", *MÆ* 27, 137–153.

WOOLF, R. (1970), "Christ as Hero in *The Dream of the Rood*", *NM* 71, 202–210.

WOOLF, R. (1972), *The English Mystery Plays* (London).

WRIGHT, D., trans. (1985), *Geoffrey Chaucer, The Canterbury Tales* (Oxford).

ZIEGLER, G. (1980), "Structural Repetition in *King Horn*", *NM* 81, 403–408.

narr VERLAG francke VERLAG attempto VERLAG

Paul Skandera / Peter Burleigh

A Manual of English Phonetics and Phonology

narr studienbücher
2., überarbeitete Auflage 2011
2011, X, 169 Seiten + CD
€[D] 19,90/SFr 28,90
ISBN 978-3-8233-6665-2

This is a fully integrated course book aimed at university students of English in the German-speaking region.
It presents a staged and clearly developed introduction to the theory of pronunciation combined with a wealth of transcription exercises and an accompanying CD. The book requires no prior knowledge of linguistics. From the outset, it explains key concepts in easy-to-understand language, highlights key terms in the text for easy review, and gives translations of many of the terms into German. Additionally, a glossary provides students with a handy quick reference. The transcription exercises guide students from exploratory tasks to basic transcription to the more demanding transcription of natural dialogue, and all exercises are supplied with annotated solutions.
The book is carefully divided into lessons and exercises which can be managed in 12 two-hour classes, leaving enough time for review and examination in a university term of 14 weeks or more.
In this second edition, the book has been thoroughly revised and adapted for better readability and increased consistency in the use of terminology.

Narr Francke Attempto Verlag GmbH+Co. KG · Dischingerweg 5 · D-72070 Tübingen
Tel. +49 (07071) 9797-0 · Fax +49 (07071) 97 97-11 · info@narr.de · **www.narr.de**

 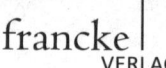

Helge Nowak

Helge Nowak

Literature in Britain and Ireland:
A History

UTB M
2010, XII, 628 Seiten, zahlreiche Abbildungen,
€[D] 24,90/SFr 44,00
ISBN 978-3-8252-3148-4

Literature in Britain and Ireland is a survey of literature on the British Isles since the time of the Anglo-Saxons. Despite this deliberately wide angle, the linguistic, regional and ethnic differentiations in each particular period are being emphasized. Because of its combination of traditional and innovative components of English Studies, this history of literature is useful as a study book accompanying courses as well as an incentive for discoveries while reading. The chapters are systematically structured to allow profiles along the history of genres. In addition to poetry, drama, short stories and the novel, different forms of non-fictional prose are being highlighted, too. Innovative tendencies in teaching English literature are taken into account beyond the consideration of popular and contemporary literature.

francke
VERLAG

Narr Francke Attempto Verlag GmbH + Co. KG
Postfach 2560 · D-72015 Tübingen · Fax (07071) 9797-11
Internet: www.francke.de · E-Mail: info@francke.de